THINKING MESOLITHIC

THINKING MESOLITHIC

by

Stefan Karol Kozłowski

Published by
Oxbow Books, Oxford, UK

© Oxbow Books and the individual author, 2009

ISBN 978-1-84217-335-0

This book is available direct from:

Oxbow Books, Oxford, UK
(Phone: 01865-241249; Fax: 01865-794449)

and

The David Brown Book Company
PO Box 511, Oakville, CT 06779, USA
(Phone: 860-945-9329; Fax: 860-945-9468)

or from our website

www.oxbowbooks.com

A CIP record of this book is available from the British Library

Library of Congress Cataloging-in-Publication Data

Kozlowski, Stefan Karol.
  Thinking / by Stefan Karol Kozlowski.
      p. cm.
  Includes bibliographical references.
  ISBN 978-1-84217-335-0
  1. Mesolithic period--Europe. 2. Europe--Antiquities. 3. Human ecology--Europe--History. 4.
Prehistoric peoples--Europe. 5. Industries, Prehistoric--Europe. 6. Excavations (Archaeology)--
Europe. 7. Europe--History, Local. I. Title.
  GN774.2.A1K69 2009
  936--dc22
                            2009035393

All cover images are taken from the figures inside the volume
On the front: deer and hunters: 12.2.3h, patterns 12.2.3c
On the spine: 12.2.3c
On back: Profile horse heads: 12.2.1c, front-on horse heads: m12.2.3d, site plans: 2.2.5b

Printed in Great Britain by
Short Run Press, Exeter

For most people the world ends on the threshold of their own home, the outskirts of their own village, the borders of the valley they live in at the farthest.

Ryszard Kapuściński, "Heban"

Contents

Preface

It all started fifty years ago when a young student at Warsaw University heard one of his professors lecturing on the small Mesolithic microliths which he considered as little more than arrowheads for hunting wild game, small because degenerate in form…

This view of the Mesolithic was quite common back then and few researchers thought otherwise. Among the few were Grahame Clark, Therkel Mathiassen and Hermann Schwabedissen (even their definition of the Mesolithic included Late Pleistocene phenomena). Something had to be done to escape the magic ring of the ubiquitous "Tardenoisian" ("discovered" even in the Crimea!) and the simplified and rather naïve view of the chiefly bone "Maglemosian". In other words, the time had come for professionals to take the stage.

This they did and in several countries all at once. Researchers active in the field since the 1960s have included S.H. Andersen (Fig. 0), S.K. Arora, O.N. Bader, B. Bagolini, H.G. Bandi, I. Barandarian, M. Barbaza, C. Barrière, J. Barta, C.J. Becker, P. Biagi, P. Binz, A. Bohmers, K. Bokelmann, C. Bonsall, V. Boroneant, E. Brinch-Petersen, A. Broglio, G.M. Burov, V. Chirica, G.A. Clark, G. Cremonesi, E. Cziesla, R. Daniel, M. Egloff, M. Escalon de Fonton, J. Fortea-Perez, R. Feustel, J.M. Fullola i Pericot, I. Gatsov, P.A. Gendel, A. Gob, B. Gramsch, N.N. Gurina, J. Hinout, L. Jaanits, R. Jacobi, T. Jacobson, M.A. Jochim, R. Kertesz, B. Klima, V.Y. Koen, L.V. Koltsov, J.K. Kozłowski, S.K. Kozłowski, V.P. Ksiendzov, M. Lanzinger, L. Larsson, I. Loze, V. M. Lozovski, V. Luho, V. Markevich, F. Martini, G.N. Matiushin, L.G. Matskevoi, H. Matiskainen, K. Narr, R.R. Newell, B. Nordquist, S.V. Oshibkina, T. Ostrauskas, A. Paunescu, C. Perlès, D.T. Price, I. Radovanović, R. Rimantiène, J. Roche, J.G. Rozoy, J. Roussot-Laroque, A.N. Sorokin, F. Spier, D. Srejović, V. Stanko, W. Taute, D.Y. Telegin, A. Thévenin, C. Tozzi, P. Vermeersch, S. Welinder, H. Więckowska, P. Woodman, A. Wouters, R. Wyss, I. Zagorska, F. Zagorskí, L.L. Zalizniak, M.G. Zhilin and many others. This generation (which was not all that homogeneous in age, Jean-Georges Rozoy being the most senior member!) approached the task of systematic research on the Mesolithic material mostly from their countries or regions of origin in an ambitious and relatively modern way. In the effect, various monograph studies began to be published, presenting several local cultural sequences and local or regional taxonomic units identified on the basis of homogeneous assemblages.

In this place the author wishes to thank all his colleagues for discussion, access to material, important information, criticism and words of support.

Researchers naturally differed in opinions on specific issues, depending on the school they represented and their way of thinking. All things considered, however, the body of professionally published evidence was greatly augmented over a rather short period of time. Exact dating was still an issue in many instances and mistakes were not all that rare, but knowledge of the Mesolithic had been given a great push forward. The "Mesolithic in Europe" conference held in Warsaw in May 1973 provided the first opportunity for interested researchers to meet. We got to know one another, exchanged opinions, struck up relations. Then we, the participants from Warsaw, established the Mesolithic Commission of the UISPP, attracted an army of students and inspired successive European-wide meetings (next were Potsdam '78, Edinburgh '85, Leuven '90, Grenoble '95, Nynneshamn '00 and Belfast '05), not to mention numerous regional conferences. Our present knowledge of the Mesolithic of Europe is considerable, even if there are still problems of behavior, taxonomy and paleohistory to consider.

The present author was an active member of this community of researchers (having met personally all of those mentioned here by the first name) in the organizational sense, as well as studying and writing. Over the years, his work has fruited in a sizable body of publications, often offering ideas on issues viewed in a supraregional scale. It seemed a good idea to bring out a collection of the more interesting papers in revised version and when approached on the subject, Oxbow Books enthusiastically agreed. The present book is thus a collection of fragments of the author's papers from different periods, as well as

ABOUT THIS BOOK

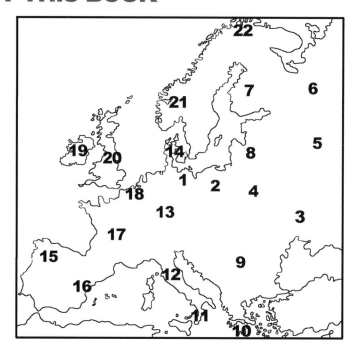

1 GRAMSCH FEUSTEL GEUPEL	SIRIAINEN MATISKAINEN	TOZZI S.KOZŁOWSKI	S.H.ANDERSEN NORDQVIST	GOB VERMEERSCH SPIER
2 S.KOZŁOWSKI	**8** JAANITS ZAGORSKA	**12** BROGLIO BAGOLINI	**15** ROCHE G.CLARK	**19** MOVIUS
3 TELEGIN ZALIZNIAK STANKO KOEN	RIMANTIENE OSTRAUSKAS INDREKO	BIAGI TOZZI S.KOZŁOWSKI	**16** PERICOT FORTEA	WOODMAN **20** J.G.D.CLARK
MATSKEVOI MARKEVICH	**9** KLIMA VALOCH	**13** BOKELMAN SCHWABEDISSEN	BARANDIARAN	JACOBI MELLARS
4 KSENDZOV OBUCHOWSKI	PAUNESCU CHIRICA BORONEANT	ARORA CZIESLA TAUTE	**17** DANIEL ESCALON DE FONTON ROZOY	WYMER BONSALL
5 KOLTSOV SOROKIN ZHILIN	SREJOVIC GATSOV KERTESZ J.KOZŁOWSKI	BANDI WYSS **14** MATHIASSEN	HINOUT THEVENIN BINZ BARBAZA	**21** J.G.D.CLARK BJØRN HAGEN BJERCK
6 BUROV OSHIBKINA	**10** PERLEZ **11** MARTINI	BECKER BRINCH-PETERSEN ALTHIN	**18** BOHMERS WOUTERS NEWELL	**22** BOE NUMMENDAL ODNER
7 LUHO		LARSSON	GENDEL	

THE MAIN AUTHORS CONSULTED

some new ones written specifically for this edition, all treating on the Mesolithic of Europe.

Taxo-chronological issues on a supraregional scale were of paramount importance in preparing this presentation, determining the division of the book into chapters by supra-regions of Europe: South, Southeast, West and Center, East, North, followed by the "Pre-Neolithic/Castelnovian". As noted already, the text is largely a re-edition of papers published earlier – hence the unavoidable repetitions – but revised, updated, often shortened and commented on, also with new material and ideas, and with changed figures. Thus, it is an entirely new quality, reflecting the author's present, not past, views and attitudes (except for the text "Warsaw '73"). In any case, seldom are older papers included whole; in most cases, a selection has been made and new parts of text added. Words of thanks are addressed to all the Publishers, Editors and Co-Authors who have kindly granted permission for these fragments of texts to be reproduced.

Naturally, for the exposition to be clear, the author has also found it essential to introduce fragments that bridge particular sections. After all, not all of his earlier works had covered issues in the same way, and indeed not all issues had been covered. Thus, each section devoted to a macro-region is preceded by a broader introduction, followed by "archival" texts. Summing up each chapter is a description of cultures, taxonomic units and historical processes occurring in specific regions.

In putting this "puzzle" of texts together, the author has felt compelled to introduce encyclopedic comments on certain issues. These texts appearing in chapters 1, 2 and 3 may prove of interest to some readers.

The book opens with a chapter on definitions, including remarks on the typology used and the change dynamics in time and space. Following the presentation of particular macro-regions (i.e. South, Southeast, West and Center, etc.) is a discussion of "Pre-Neolithic"/Castelnovian, and finally, a "historical" synthesis/conclusion. Each "archival" text is sourced at the end of the book, including co-authors, if there were any; a selected bibliography has been added at the end of the volume. Again, I am deeply grateful to my colleagues – Carlo Tozzi, Alberto Broglio, Giampaolo Dalmeri, Janusz K. Kozłowski, Ivana Radovanović, Jan Michał Burdukiewicz, Michel Dewez and René Desbrosse – for permission to republish our joint articles.

Already working on the text of this book, the author has benefited from the assistance of André Thevenin, Paolo Biagi, Carlo Franco, Carlo Tozzi, late Wiktor Obuchowski, Janusz K. Kozłowski, Iwona Zych, Magdalena Różycka, Andrzej Piotrowski, Regina Dziklińska, Olivier Aurenche and Camille Henry, as well as the Polish Foreign office (MSZ). Deep felt thanks to all of them! Needless to say, any mistakes remaining in the text are the author's responsibility alone.

The chronological system used in the book is based on radiocarbon datings, of which an excellent, if by now incomplete catalogue was once presented by André Gob. Where necessary, new dates have been considered. Since calibration of radiocarbon dating was introduced in the meantime, all dates in the text are given as calendar years, signaled by the abbreviation "cal. BC"; some ^{14}C dates on figures are in the "BP" convention.

The typological system for stone points and microliths (the types marked with double capital letters in the text) has been taken from my own "Atlas of the Mesolithic in Europe" (cf. 4.4 in this volume).

Letter codes have been used in the text and in some of the figures, following the system:

A – end-scrapers
B – side-scrapers
C – burins
D – truncated blades
E – retouched blades
F – perforators
G – combined tools
H – core tools
I – leaf-shaped points
J – tanged points
K – microliths
L – splinters
M – other

Object presentation in the plates follows the following principles:
– macroliths/points: scale 1:1
– microliths: usually actual size
– other products: different scales indicated in most cases, although not always

The source has been mentioned in each case, although rather frequently it was an original collection.

The figures are numbered identically as the corresponding parts of the text.

Finally, the list of references. The abundance (and repetitions!) of bibliographical items has necessitated a selection with preference for the more exhaustive monographs in book form and conference acts, especially those of the European Mesolithic Symposia. The "Bibliography" is located at the end of the volume. Omissions from the list should not be viewed as neglect, but are the effect of strict and naturally subjective selection criteria.

Last but not least, the author wishes to thank Clare Litt and Julie Blackmore for their good will and publishing expertise. Without their kind and wise assistance, this book would probably never have been produced!

Warsaw, Spring 2007

PART I

1

Definitions

1.1. The First Steps

Embarking in 1971 on the organization of the first
International Symposium on the Mesolithic in Europe,
the author had already published his study of the Polish
Mesolithic ("Prehistory of Polish Territories from the
9th to the 5th Millennium BC", Warsaw: PWN 1972
[in Polish]), as well as ten articles devoted to the Polish
Mesolithic (under the common title "The problems of the
Polish Mesolithic"). In the territorial sense, these works
exceeded the actual borders of Poland, extending from
the Elbe in the West to the Dnepr in the East and even
further afield. The reason lay not in the author's sphere
of interests alone. It arose from two extensive surveys of
available material, covering Moscow, St. Petersburg (then
Leningrad), Vilnius, Minsk, Potsdam, Schwerin, Stralsund,
Dresden, and Weimar (for the East German visit I remain
deeply indebted to Bernhard Gramsch) during which the
author had the opportunity to meet with specialists and
acquire inside knowledge of many Mesolithic collections,
regardless of their importance.

In Poland, this was a time of intensive archaeological
research on the Mesolithic and great opportunities for
the young and dynamic students of Stefan Krukowski,
attending a seminar chaired by Waldemar Chmielewski
at the Institute of the History of Material Culture of the
Polish Academy of Sciences in Warsaw. Poland's partial
opening to the West fruited in exchanges with scholars
not only from the Eastern bloc (Carl J. Becker, Hermann
Schwabedissen, P.V. Glob, Wolfgang Taute, Hans-Jürgen
Müller-Beck and others).

The time was ripe for an overview of the neglected
Mesolithic of Europe, starting with the definition (it was
then widely believed to be a terminal phase of Late Glacial
adaptations) and going on to fundamental description and
divisions, not to mention economy. It should be kept in
mind that not many specialists in the field were around.

At the time the author was young and ambitious, not
to say naïve, and he immediately tried to bite off more
than he could chew. His earliest texts presented here

are proof of this, where he treats on the definition of the
Mesolithic, on a continental system of cultural divisions
and extensive cartography. Following these are some texts
from later years, which are more balanced and – should I
say – less naïve?

1.2. Warsaw '73

*Introduction to the history of Europe in the Early
Holocene*

Archaeological literature notes these two basic definitions
of the Mesolithic:

A. The first comprises the prehistoric period between the
Paleolithic and the Neolithic (chronological order)
upon the assumption that the "Mesolithic" covers the
area of the Old World independently of ecological
zones and is characterized by cultures of "microlithic"
and "geometric" forms of tools.

B. The second definition, and I fully support it, restricts
the term "Mesolithic" both in area and environment
(Fig. 1.2a–b). The word "Mesolithic" is used here in
the meaning of an economic-developmental pattern. It
is synonymous with the hunting-fishing-gathering economy which had developed in the European Lowland (*sic*
SKK in 2006) with the already developed forestation
during the Early Holocene. For this reason then it should
be appropriate to take the term to mean the "Mesolithic
stage of cultural and economic development" which
had distinctly been determined by environment but not
necessarily circumscribed in time.

I am of the same opinion as regards the terms "Paleolithic"
and "Neolithic", which should correspond to the respective
stages of economic and cultural development. These
stages can be variously dated in particular areas, having
developed, for instance, parallel to the Neolithic cultures
in the Near East and the Epi-Paleolithic and Paleolithic
cultures respectively in the Balkans and Scandinavia.
Meanwhile some of those stages never took place in other

WARSAW'73

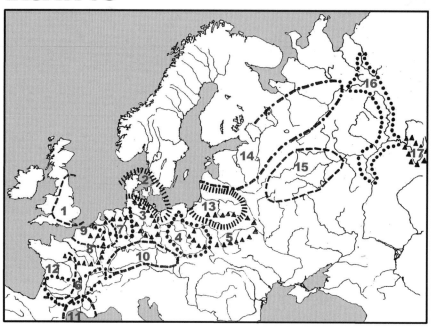

1	STAR CARR	10	BEURONIAN
2	MAGLEMOSE	11	CASTELNOVIAN
3	DUVENSEE	12	CUZOUL
4	KOMORNICA	13	NEMAN
5	JANISLAWICIAN	14	KUNDA
6	SAUVETERRIAN	15	UPPER VOLGA
7	BOBERG	16	KAMA
8	COINCY	17	YANGELKA
9	LOWER RHINE		

FIRST ATTEMPT, FIRST MISTAKES, MOSTLY CHRONOLOGICAL...
BUT NOT ONLY (E.G. 8 VIZ 10)

Fig. 1.2a

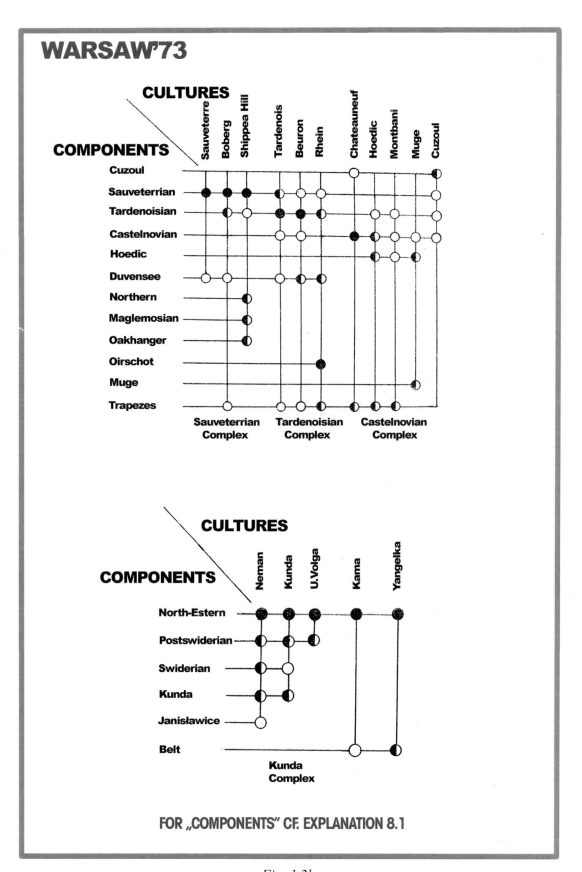

Fig. 1.2b

regions, e.g., there was no Neolithic stage in the Early and Middle Holocene forests of Canada and Siberia.

It seems that the Mesolithic stage resulted from the adaptation of Paleolithic tundra communities to the new ecological conditions, that is, to the forest which appeared in the European Lowland (and Western Europe – SKK in 2006) during the Early Holocene. Important environmental changes which took place at the turn of Late Glacial and Post Glacial forced the original inhabitants of the Lowland to emigrate or to adapt. Adaptation meant a switch to the only available kind of economy, i.e., Mesolithic type of economy. In contrast to the Mediterranean countries, the poor soil of the European Lowland did not create favorable conditions for a direct change from the Paleolithic to the Neolithic economy (*sic* SKK in 2006).

This is why still more emphasis should be laid on the striking ecological change which accounted for the formation of this basically local or regional stage which the Mesolithic in fact was. Similar changes took a long time to occur in North European territories inhabited in the Early Holocene by the Paleolithic communities of reindeer hunters: Hensbacka, Fosna, Komsa and Suomusjärvi. These tundra-to-forest changes occurred earlier south of the Carpathians. In these regions, the forest communities of Mediterranean type had developed since the Late Pleistocene and, with no big changes occurring, they survived into the Holocene (Epi-Gravettian).

Briefly speaking, the Mesolithic is a stage of "WAITING" or "QUARANTINE", which was realized in an environment where primitive agriculture could not develop.

Comment in 2006

The above text demonstrates the naiveté of the author's writing in 1973. The Mesolithic or whatever you call that which followed after the Latest Pleistocene in all of Europe and which lasted until the next great supra-regional change, which was the ceramization (cf.) and Neolithization, is not to be described with a single formula apart from a chronological one perhaps (cf. "The Mesolithic: What we know and what we believe") . But "waiting" and "quarantine" sound nice, don't they?

Observations of the conservative approach of Late Glacial/Early Holocene Balkan and Scandinavian communities remain true today (no important techno-typological evolution or change). The same can now be said of the Early Holocene groups in South Italy and Iberia. From this perspective, the European Lowland appears much more dynamic at the time, and so does the region between the Pyrenees and the Dynaric Alps. (cf. "Rhythms").

Thirty some years later, the author can say he has gained the wisdom to modify his definition of the Mesolithic from a "behavioral" to a chronological one. It hardly changes the fact that the Early and Middle Holocene were characterized by highly diversified adaptation models. At the beginning of the period, the region between the Pyrenees and the Ural mountains, north of the Alps and south of the North Sea and the Baltic was seething with activity. The southernmost (both in the East and West) and northern extremes of the

continent either continued placidly in the old traditions without any breeze of evolution to disturb the picture, or were only starting to be settled by pioneers streaming in from the south who introduced very few changes in their culture. For an explanation of the term "component" used in the figures, cf. "Les courants interculturelles".

1.3. Forli '96

Early postglacial adaptations in central Europe

Introduction

The objective of this paper is a concise presentation of selected aspects of communities of hunters, gatherers, and fishermen inhabiting Central Europe (area between the Rhine and Dnieper, and the Baltic and Adriatic) during the Early and Middle Holocene, i.e. from c. 9400/9000 cal. BC to 6300/5600 (Balkan Peninsula and Carpathian Basin) and 5500/3800 cal. BC (Central European Lowland). The earlier date marking the appearance in Central Europe of communities described as "Mesolithic" is similar throughout the area in question (cf. radiocarbon dates for Star Carr in England, Klosterlund in Denmark, Friesack, Duvensee and Jägerhaushöhle in Germany, Romagnano III in Italy, Padina in Serbia, Frankhthi in Greece, Chwalim I and Całowanie in Poland, Pulli in Estonia). Not so in the case of the final dates which differ considerably from region to region (c. 6900 cal. BC for the Balkan Peninsula – Frankhthi; 6350 for Odmut, Lepenski Vir and Vlasac in Serbia and Montenegro; c. 4900 for northern Italy – Romagnano III, Riparo Gaban; c. 5100/4350 for Switzerland and southern Germany, cf. Birsmatten-Basisgrotte, Jagerhaushöhle, Tschäpperfels; c. 5500/4900 for the southern part of the Central European Lowland, but c. 4350/3750 in its northern part, e.g. in Polish Pomerania or in Denmark).

I have begun with a definition of the phenomenon described as 'Mesolithic' and have proceeded to discuss the pertinent evidence, the environment which conditioned the formation and existence of this phenomenon, and the differentiation (zonation) of this environment. Further on, I have presented the principal features of the system of adaptation to the described environment, devoting separate attention to regional adaptation systems, particularly to the stylistic differences of flint artifacts, this differentiation being due only partly to limitations imposed by the various biotopes, and in some degree to stimulation by specific cultural traditions.

Definition

The cultural-economic formation of interest to us here, referred to as the 'Mesolithic', appears to be a peculiar type of adaptation (transformation) of regional Paleolithic communities to novel conditions of the Early Holocene.

The first half of the 10th millennium cal. BC was marked by considerable and relatively rapid environmental changes consisting of climate improvement and a resulting swift northward expansion of the forests. These now occupied not only the Balkan and Apennine peninsulas, as was the case in the 11th millennium, but spread all the way to southern and central Scandinavia and later even to the north of Russia. Such a serious modification of the biotope, bringing about the disappearance of open expanses of tundra and periglacial steppe inhabited mainly by reindeer, caused this animal to recede gradually northwards, giving way to forest fauna (red deer, roe deer, wild boar, aurochs, horse, elk, etc.). Such major "environmental innovations" had to elicit appropriate adaptive reactions from the inhabitants of Central Europe of the times. The response may have been either the northward migration of Paleolithic hunters in pursuit of a receding familiar biotope, or rapid on-the-spot adaptation to entirely new living conditions. Regardless of the option chosen by the inhabitants of Central Europe, the culture of the new age differed either slightly (south of the Alps and Carpathians) or substantially (the Lowland in the north) form that in evidence during the 11th millennium.

Admittedly, as before, the people in the North were hunters and gatherers, but now they exploited a completely new and richer environment (forest) with its non-migratory fauna and moreover, they evidently conquered new environments (rivers, lakes, marine coastland) together with their resources. It appears, particularly on the northern Plain, that well organized population groups became less mobile than in the Final Paleolithic, and that they occupied and maintained their own permanent territories, which corresponded to hunting ranges, often for many centuries. These territories boasted their own individual spatial organization (cf. "Territory"). Large, possibly permanent or semipermanent "base camps" appeared, surrounded by short-lived temporary "satellite" camps (cf. "Camp"). The settlement pattern does not seem to have altered much over the ages (cf. "Territory"), and local and imported stone raw material was supplied efficiently. Full adaptation occurred swiftly. The emergent model was that of a highly specialized, and hence conservative, hunting-gathering-fishing economy, guaranteeing considerable economic and settlement stability and avoiding change for centuries (cf. "Conservatism of Mesolithic cultures"). Naturally, the local adaptive models displayed differences, brought about mainly by the specific nature of ecological zones (e.g. particular importance of fishing in the lakeland areas) and the differentiated origins of newly formed cultures.

In order to meet the requirements of an adaptive process thus envisaged, man had to introduce and disseminate a number of technological and organizational innovations. The former will be enumerated below; the latter can only be guessed at.

In technology, large flint raw material concretions, not available everywhere, were abandoned in favor of commonly available small-sized nodules (cf. "Raw material"). This reduced, one may say, the Mesolithic world to local dimensions. The hunter pursuing relatively immobile forest fauna and using flint raw material within easy reach was no longer willing to embark on distant migrations; his was a small universe and he preferred to stay "at home".

Following on the changes in raw material economy was a severe reduction in core size and the dimensions of blanks produced from it (no longer blades but bladelets, cf.); this led in consequence to smaller tools and arrowheads. In textbooks this phenomenon has been described as "microlithization" (cf.), but we prefer the term "miniaturization", with a similar process in modern electronics coming to mind as a parallel. This situation must have naturally occasioned changes in the technology of production of particularly small flint arrowheads; the microburin (cf.) technique (already known from the Late Glacial) developed along with the blade and bladelet sectioning (cf.) technique, and finally, the pressure technique of core reduction. For obvious technological reasons, the shapes of arrowheads, and of other tools in fact, underwent increasing standardization, becoming more and more similar one to another (cf. "Geometrization" and "Koine"). Arrowheads of this kind were very effective in intense hunting of large, but also smaller forest animals. In other regions (in the north and east), the tanged arrowhead (cf.) was still in use at the same time.

Man is able to "make anything out of almost nothing": the smallest arrowheads (or at least single microliths) are under 0.4 cm in size (e.g. Romagnano III in Italy)!

In time, however, the mastering of the environment proceeded even further. In the 7th millennium cal. BC (cf. "Castelnovisation"), the demand for large concretions, giving bigger bladelets, reemerged and immediately prompted the appearance of veritable mines of the raw material and launched its long-range distribution (e.g. "chocolate" flint in Poland, obsidian from Melos in Greece, or the Wommerson quartzite in Belgium, to name but a few). Also in use was a range of organic raw materials, such as bone, antler and, most importantly, the wonderfully malleable and easily available wood (cf.).

Throughout the Mesolithic (cf. Chapter 2), timber and the other organic raw materials were of crucial significance in the subjugation of the water environment. The boat and the paddle make their appearance (Pesse, Star Carr, Duvensee, etc.) in the young lakeland (cf.) zones, but also in river environments (e.g. Noyen-sur-Somme in the Paris Basin), together with the tools for their making (axe/adze/chisel, cf., polished in the circum-Baltic countries and unpolished in the Center and West); numerous fishing implements also appeared, including nets, fishing hooks, bow-nets, and fishing spears (cf.). It seems that fishing, both inland and maritime, was a source of particular affluence for certain Mesolithic communities.

The abundant large-mammal forest fauna (cf. "Game") provided rich food resources and evidenced the considerable hunting skills of the bowmen and trappers (cf.) of the times. Small fauna and birds were also hunted (the latter with special arrows, cf., furnished with bolt heads), more for pelts or feathers than for meat.

The diet was augmented by gathering activities which locally achieved considerable importance. All that was edible or useful in the forest or next to a body of water was collected: nuts (*Coryllus*, *Trapa natans*), plant grains (among others, lentils in the South-West) and cereals and glans in the Near East, timber, mollusks (land and marine, as well as river species, cf. Chapter 3), resin, firewood, mushrooms and many other goods.

All this justifies the claim that the 'Mesolithic', being of course a direct continuation of Paleolithic adaptations, was nevertheless a highly specialized, stable, conservative, and self-sufficient adaptive system, emerging (in the north) or continuing (in the south) mainly in the rich forest environment of the early Post-Glacial period. This system, created by people who might be called the "last Indians of Europe", could have well survived for millennia were it not for the destructive advent of foreign newcomers bringing with them the illusory benefits of the Neolithic Revolution.

Evidence

The area which interests us here covers over two million square kilometers (or about 780 thousand square miles). We know some 3500 Mesolithic sites in Poland (status for 1989), which means that there is one site for every 89.4 square kilometers. The figure for Denmark is 197.7, and for Lithuania 822.8 square kilometers. Thus, the Central European Lowland may be considered to be well saturated with source material, although locally there are fairly extensive "white spots" (cf. "Where"). The situation is quite different south of the Carpathians, where we know of only a few dozen sites (cf. "Southeast").

The aforementioned material, although often recovered unmethodically, provides excellent information about the rules of terrain occupation (settlement pattern, cf.) and reveals the territorial range of various classes of artifacts, thereby enabling the presentation of the "cultural" or stylistic zonation, and the borders separating different zones.

Source material from methodical and well-documented excavations is not the most frequent, but it is naturally more valuable. Excavations of this kind provide chances for obtaining homogeneous material (both "culturally" and chronologically) in its more or less authentic distribution (*sic*), and opportunities for precise (?) radiocarbon dating and for reconstruction of the environment and economy (pollen, bones, etc.).

However, such splendid sites are rare, even in the region we are considering (e.g. Vedbaek Boldbaner in Denmark, and Friesack in Germany). In most cases, the features, even those explored methodically, and especially those on Late Glacial sands, lack stratigraphy, and so the often doubtful planigraphic analysis of artifacts distribution and typology must suffice to determine site homogeneity. We have in mind here the stylistic coherence of the inventory on the one hand, and its temporal coherence on the other. This temporal coherence is best established by radiocarbon dating, a method which, applied to sandy sites, often gives results that are not very univocal (200–300 year duration of large camps in Holland, cf. Raymond R. Newell in the Potsdam Symposium acts, and the continuing resettlement of one site over 1500 years, cf. Romuald Schild for the Całowanie site in Poland in the acts of the Edinburgh Symposium, for difficulties with dating of the Flanders site, cf. Pierre M. Vermeersch in the Leuven Symposium acts).

Incidentally, how do you establish the connection between charcoal from such sites and the archaeological material?

In all, there are more than 200 methodically explored sites in Central Europe.

Environmental zonation

Today, as in the past, the area of interest to us is strongly diversified ecologically. This diversification is so perceptible in the field that one may speak with full confidence of ecological zonation of Central Europe conditioned by terrain morphology (lowlands and uplands, plains and hilly country, big-mountain) and small barriers and passes or gates, various hydrographic systems and by differences in climate (oceanic and continental, Mediterranean and temperate) which, of course, produce diverse biotopes. One other element of zonal differentiation are lithic raw materials, marked by various dimensions and technological properties, and occurring (or missing!) in various concentrations throughout the area in question.

It appears that the ecological zonation in Central Europe was not without bearing on the form of postglacial adaptation models; in other words, it may have stimulated the "cultural", that is, stylistic differentiation of the local Mesolithic.

Territory

A paramount aspect of the adaptation of Central European Mesolithic communities is the manner of spatial organization and utilization of the areas occupied (cf. "Where"). We perceive here a model of exceptionally perfect adaptation of man to the surrounding environment which, if skillfully exploited, provides ample resources and offers considerable stability.

Settlement pattern (cf.) is an extremely important element of the adaptation process, and it can be discerned in concrete archaeological material. The network is not identical in all of the distinguished ecological zones. First of all, its density differs, as does the density of the hydrographic network in the various zones. In all instances, the settlement pattern is based on medium-sized and small rivers and/or lakes, avoiding the smallest rivers and streams (most probably because of the absence of fish there). The densest network is in the North European Lowlands with its well developed hydrographic system; it is perhaps less dense in the Central European Uplands, and sparsest in the Carpathian basin. It follows from this that population density also could have varied from zone to zone, being probably the greatest in the north (cf. Douglas T. Price's suggestions on population density in the acts of the Potsdam Symposium). A notable fact is that in all the zones we are dealing with chains of concentrations of sites lining water courses and separated by uninhabited areas, except of presence or absence of raw material. The only differences being in the size of these less irrigated and hence poorer, drier and cooler unoccupied interspace territories.

In Poland we have observed a number of small (20–40 kilometers) elongated site concentrations (sporadically larger at important hydrographic junctions), flanking rivers and lake troughs and shunning the drier, poorer and cooler base moraine or loess elevations. In wide valleys camps are set up in low-lying places on sandy terrace remnants or dunes, and in narrower valleys on the edges of low sandy terraces. Not so in the highlands and the intra Carpathian Lowland where not all of the sites lie squarely in valleys, sometimes occupying prominent positions several dozen meters above valley floors (with their backs to the river, so to say), and sometimes caves or rockshelters (similar situation is to be observed in Southern Germany, cf. studies by Michael Jochim).

Coming back to the Mesolithic settlement pattern in Poland, one should now ask what is it actually indicative of (discounting the natural connection with water and the penchant for fish).

It is for example conceivable that the individual small site concentrations are tokens of activity of the smallest social units occupying their own small territory corresponding to hunting range, separated from the nearest such territories by relatively settlement-free areas (cf. maps by Bernhard Gramsch for eastern Germany in the Warsaw Symposium acts).

Another possibility is that each such concentration is one in a series of successive occupations of the same microregion by a population group (or groups) migrating seasonally or periodically within a radius of, say, a few dozen kilometers, over a sufficiently long period of time. Such seasonal mobility is suggested for the European Mesolithic by many authors (Raymond R. Newell, Erik Brinch-Petersen, Douglas T. Price and Alberto Broglio) on the basis of the established differences in site dimensions, their equipment, and the observed results of economic activity (cf. "Seasonality").

This latter possibility, envisaging the limited mobility of population groups along rather short distances, might perhaps be correlated with Krzysztof Cyrek's observations of flint utilization in the Vistula basin during the Mesolithic. Cyrek distinguished nine "provinces" in this area, each different with regard to raw material structure, usually 100×100 or 100×200 kilometers in size (cf. "Mesolithic settlement pattern"). In each of the "provinces", a different local raw material dominated the Mesolithic assemblages, with the remaining raw materials, not necessarily of local origin, playing a secondary role.

The mentioned size of the "provinces", 100×100 to 100×200 kilometers, is smaller that the ranges of groupings of sites with identical style of flint artifacts (= cultures) distinguished in Central Europe. I refer to these groupings as "territorial or cultural groups", and they could be the smallest taxonomic units distinguished in the local Mesolithic. It is also known that the respective ranges of these "territorial-cultural groups" and the raw material "provinces" usually do not coincide. The boundaries of the "groups" are usually (although not always) based on prominent natural territorial barriers, such as front moraine ridges or mountain ranges and uplands, as well as on environmental zonation. The size of raw material "provinces" depends additionally on the localization of raw material deposits and on the hydrographic network, often being confined to the basin of one or two medium-sized rivers and separated from the neighboring ones by water divides (not very pronounced in the Lowland).

In any case, it may be surmised from the quoted information that in Poland (and Europe) of Mesolithic times, the maximum real distance of information flow did not exceed 100–200 kilometers ("raw-material province or territorial group"), this being additionally confirmed by maximum ranges of imports of attractive flint raw materials (e.g. "chocolate" flint in Poland, obsidian from Melos in Greece, or the Wommersom quartzite in northwestern Europe). And this extent appears to be the maximum size of the territorial unit in the period in question (cf. Michele Lanzinger on Trentino with smaller areas /= site concentrations, as well as Paolo Biagi, Carlo Tozzi and others for northern and central Italy with bigger areas (= territorial groups, cf. "South"); the latter are close to the values proposed by André Thévènin for the northwest of Europe (cf. "Territory").

In view of this, it must be assumed that the spatial organization of the Polish/Lowland/Central European Mesolithic rests on two absolute values (cf. "Settlement pattern" and "Raw material"):

a. site concentration, 20–40 kilometers in length, and
b. territorial-cultural group/raw material province, measuring 100–200 kilometers and embracing several site concentrations.

These two values seem to limit the maximal mobility of a population group of the period. It appears, however, that the upper limit is excessive and that it may be drastically reduced in view of the already mentioned discrepancy in the ranges of "territorial (stylistic) groups" and the raw material "provinces", which are usually smaller than the former (cf. also Bernhard Gramsch and Surendra K. Arora for Germany). Superimposing both phenomena, we can divide the area of Poland into smaller segments, with maximum distances amounting to about 100 kilometers. I regard this figure as a very probable value, intermediate between "site concentration" and "territorial group". If this were so, each such segment, remaining with several others within the range of one "territorial group", would be characterized by a distinct raw material structure.

Thus, in the Lowland, ranges of 100×100 (200?) kilometers could actually delimit the actual territories of given population groups, and their boundaries could coincide with the major water divides (possibly smaller territories in specific mountain conditions, cf. Michele Lanzinger for the Italian Dolomites). Consequently, the spatial and social organization of the Polish/Lowland/Central European (?) Mesolithic may have actually consisted of three levels:

a. site concentrations (20–40 kilometers long),
b. ca.100 kilometer territories (raw material "provinces"),
c. territorial groups, 100×100 and/or 100×200 kilometers in size.

Obviously, the second level, namely the c. 100-kilometer territory appears to be the most important from the organizational point of view. It is distinct in its own raw material structure and probably also in secondary stylistic features, apparently constituting a real organizational whole, with recurrent seasonal migrations (rather limited in fact) of related small population groups, repeatedly returning to the same settlement points (= site concentrations), and never stepping beyond a very local "country or parish horizon". Each such territory, or rather microregion (= site concentration) had its own local "history", its own boundaries (water divides), its own microenvironment, and so it ought to have been the domain of a concrete social unit, possibly a tribe or a part thereof (cf. works by Wiktor Stoczkowski and Peter A. Gendel).

If all this is true, it must be consistently assumed that each such population group was as a matter of course the owner of a given territory. This thesis is additionally confirmed by the presence in the Late Mesolithic of quite numerous cemeteries or concentrations of graves in 'base camps' (Vedbaek, Skateholm, Zvejnieki, Oleni Ostrov, Teviec, Hoëdic, Moita do Sebastiao, Vlasac, and other sites in the Iron Gates, cf. studies by Vasile Boroneant and Clive Bonsall), which evidently proves the considerable stability of settlement in this period.

Water, boat, and fish (cf. Chapter 2)
Speaking of characteristic features of the Mesolithic, we cannot fail to mention the specific importance of the water environment to the people of this time. The people of the Mesolithic were the first to really conquer this environment, thus securing for themselves a source of exceptionally abundant and easily obtainable protein. The connection of Mesolithic settlement with sufficiently large water courses and reservoirs was mentioned above. The fact that settlers avoided small water courses indicates that fish abundance must have motivated the choice of settlement niches, at least on the European Lowland.

The conquest of the considerably diversified water environment must have obviously differed from region to region. Here we will discuss the best researched exploitation of the great-valley and lakeland zones.

Firstly, there is effective water transport. The dugout boat (cf.) was invented (e.g. Pesse in Holland and Noyen in France) together with paddles to propel it (Star Carr, Duvensee, Tybrind Vig etc.). Man could traverse water expanses in any direction (also across the sea, 120 km (!) from Egaean Melos to Frankhthi in the Peloponnese), and fish in the best places, such as rivers, lakes and the sea itself. Naturally, turning tree trunks into boats forced Mesolithic man to develop suitable tools for felling trees and subsequent hollowing of the trunks. The flint or stone axe (cf.) or adze, a heavy chopping and hollowing implement, made its appearance (cf. fantastic handled examples from Hohen Viecheln and Lübeck in Germany, and Svaerdborg in Denmark). Its territorial range curiously coincided with the lakeland/Lowland marginal/great-valley zone, a fact which was hardly accidental according to Michał Kobusiewicz

(at the Warsaw Symposium). In the eastern Baltic (which is also lakeland) and in Scandinavia, polished axes-adzes were made of slate or other non-siliceous rock *in lieu* of the good flint not found there. Still, what was the tool used to fell trees in Spain, France and Italy at the time?

Once the boat became available, it could and was used for fishing, both active or passive. The former method required appropriate fishing spear points (cf.), mostly barbed, and these appeared in massive numbers in the lakeland and marginal valley zones. Some of them were probably arrowheads (cf.), while others were points of fishing spears (cf.), (single- or multi-point), fired from bows (cf.) or thrown by hand. The effectiveness of such fishing practices has been reported by Grahame Clark (e.g. fishing for pike, cf., "Pike from Kunda"). A fishing spear could be aimed with great precision, and this made it a very effective weapon. The bow (cf.) with the normal "land" arrow (cf.) could have also been used in seal hunting, for example.

Passive fishing had its own range of instruments, namely nets with floats (Antrea in Karelia, Friesack in eastern Germany), bow-nets and traps, and various types of bone hooks.

All this served fishing on a large scale (more in the lakeland than in the great-valleys region?), demonstrating the importance, indeed indispensability in some communities, of fish in the Mesolithic diet.

Bow and arrow (cf.)
The bow and arrow was the most universal and sophisticated piece of equipment used by the Mesolithic hunter. Although invented much earlier (at least in the Gravettian), its career as a hunting weapon peaked in those times. This long-range and very accurate weapon became very useful to the Mesolithic "trapper" (cf.) in hunting wary and not easily approachable forest fauna.

The few bow specimens recorded are large and straight, made from yew (Holmegaard IV in Denmark, Vis I in Russia) and often with narrowed grips. No particular differentiation (except for small specimens from Vis), either territorial, chronological or functional, is apparent. Not so in the case of arrows, which are obviously diverse (cf. "Atlas of the European Mesolithic"), in structure, shape and probably also function. Indeed, the morphological differences in arrowheads (cf. different tanged points, and very diversified microliths, cf.) provide possibly the most important grounds for a "cultural" or stylistic differentiation of the European Mesolithic. If we disregard the poorly known arrow shafts (wooden in Late Paleolithic German Stellmoor, cf. and Mesolithic Danish Holmegaard, Swedish Loshult and German Friesack, but made of bone in Russian Oleni Ostrov), we may divide arrowheads into bone, wooden (rarely preserved, e.g. Veretie I in northern Russia) and flint or stone (most widespread) examples.

Bone points (cf.) range from the simplest spindle-shaped (= *sagaies*) or triangularly sectioned types (no. 13 in G. Clark's classification), through various denticulated specimens, to specimens featuring slots with flint inserts. It is evident that they served as missiles (cf. barbed specimens found lodged in fish skeletons in Estonian Kunda and a harpoon in a Late Paleolithic elk skeleton from High Furlong in Great Britain), although it is not always possible to decide with certainty whether the specimens at hand are arrowheads or fishing spear points. In the area under consideration, bone points are known mainly from the lakeland and the marginal great-valleys zone, and this has prompted some archaeologists to regard them as markers of distinct, highly specialized "bone cultures" (cf. Chapter 2). However, their concentration in this zone was also due to geological conditions prevailing on the sites in the region, facilitating the preservation of organic materials. The actual territorial differentiation largely coincides with the territorial differentiation of some classes of flint or stone points and microliths (cf. "Points, *sagaies*…").

The rare bolt-headed wooden projectile points, known in fact from the entire European Lowland (Danish Holmegaard IV, German Friesack and Hohen Viecheln, Russian Vis I and Veretie I), are not significantly diverse morphologically. They may have been used to hunt small furry animals and birds.

The most numerous and very diverse group is that of the so called "microliths" (cf.) or "points", deciding about the different tradition of the assemblages. Their function as arrowheads or inserts of missile weapons (among others) is indisputable (finds of mounted points from Swedish Loshult and Karelian Oleni Ostrov; traces of resin on microliths from British Star Carr, conditions accompanying the finding of microliths in White Hill in Britain or on killing sites like Vig and Prejlerup in Denmark, cf.; microliths lodged in a human bone from Téviec; characteristic impact negatives seen on many specimens; microwear analyses by George Odell, etc.). Dmitriy Nuzhnyi recently studied the issue extensively (cf. his monograph).

We know for sure that both combined points, featuring more than one microlithic insert (e.g. White Hill in Britain, but mainly arrows with two or three microliths, such as those from Vig, Loshult, Friesack, Prejlerup, or the South and East – Baltic slotted bone points with unretouched inserts), as well as non-combined single-piece arrowheads (tanged points, like the Late Paleolithic hafted tangs from German Stellmoor (cf.), points from Oleni Ostrov (cf. "Quiver"), and trapezes (cf. "Hafting trapezes") were in use.

Combined multi-microlith arrowheads were concentrated in Central Europe and further west (cf. "Koine"), all the way to Spain and Great Britain, mainly in the earlier times (10/9th–7th millennium cal. BC, cf. "Rhythms"). In northeastern and eastern Europe, starting from northeastern Poland, and in Scandinavia (except for Scania), this period witnessed the domination of tanged points (cf.), i.e., non-combined implements. Admittedly, those from the North-East were accompanied by inserts of combined weapons which, however, at least in part, should be identified as daggers and knives rather than projectiles.

Whatever the approach, the Europe of those times appears to have been divided into the western and eastern parts, the dividing line running across eastern Poland (cf. "Mapping the Mesolithic"). It is interesting to note that the border between the eastern and western environmental zones of the European Lowland also runs across Poland (respectively units III and VIII, according to the "Regionalization of Europe").

"Cultural" differentiation (Chapters 6–11, Fig. 13a–b)
Environmental conditioning together with the fairly extensively shared hunting-gathering traditions finally led to the emergence of a peculiar stereotype of Mesolithic adaptation, expressed in the mass archaeological record by features like stone tool miniaturization, standardization (referred to as "geometrization" in the narrower sense, cf. "Koine"), and considerable specialization (the particularly well developed group of missile points, also those made of bone and wood).

However, the similarities are in fact confined to this rather functional level; below it we observe considerable differentiation in artifact morphology and technology, i.e., "style". Such stylistic differences are sometimes interpreted by "traditional" archaeology as "cultural", but cultural anthropology, for example, admits other interpretations as well (adaptational, functional).

The author's view is that the overlapping ecological and stylistic zonation is indicative of the adaptive character of Mesolithic culture which, being in some general sense homogeneous (mostly forest), splits into distinct regions with specific local types of environment exploitation, and hence with local styles, traditions and "cultures", often in accord with Europe's division into large territorial and environmental zones.

One cannot overlook here, of course, the other important element shaping local "cultural" variance, namely tradition in the genetic or heritage sense. It is tradition which stimulates and regulates the form of local cultures, preserving standards, so to say. Its powers are obviously limited, and it cannot completely isolate its "own" cultural environment from external influences and various outside "trends". Now and then, there appear in Europe certain interregional, and hence intercultural trends (cf. "Les courants interculturels"), causing unifying changes of various intensity over extensive areas of the continent (cf. "Pre-Neolithic"/Castelnovian). Such trends are exemplified by the spread throughout western and central Europe in the 8th millennium cal. BC of elements of Sauveterrian origin (cf. "Sauveterrization") or of trapezes which appeared almost everywhere in Europe around 7000 cal. BC.

1.4. Lille '00

E pluribus unum? Regards sur l'Europe mésolithique
Introduction
Il est depuis long temps communément admis que le Mésolithique constitue un phénomène assez homogène, sans grandes distinctions régionales. Cette thèse contestable résulte d'une tradition de la recherche plutôt locale et plutôt

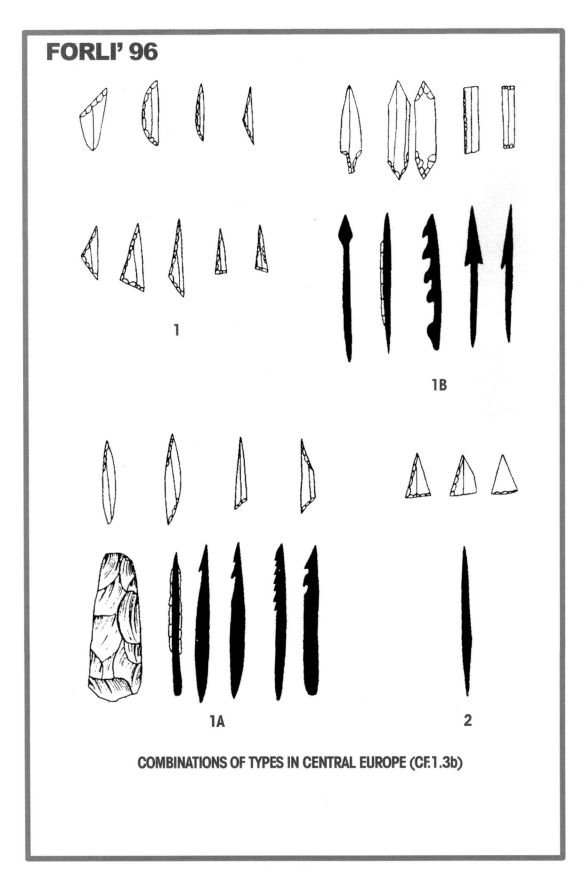

Fig. 1.3a

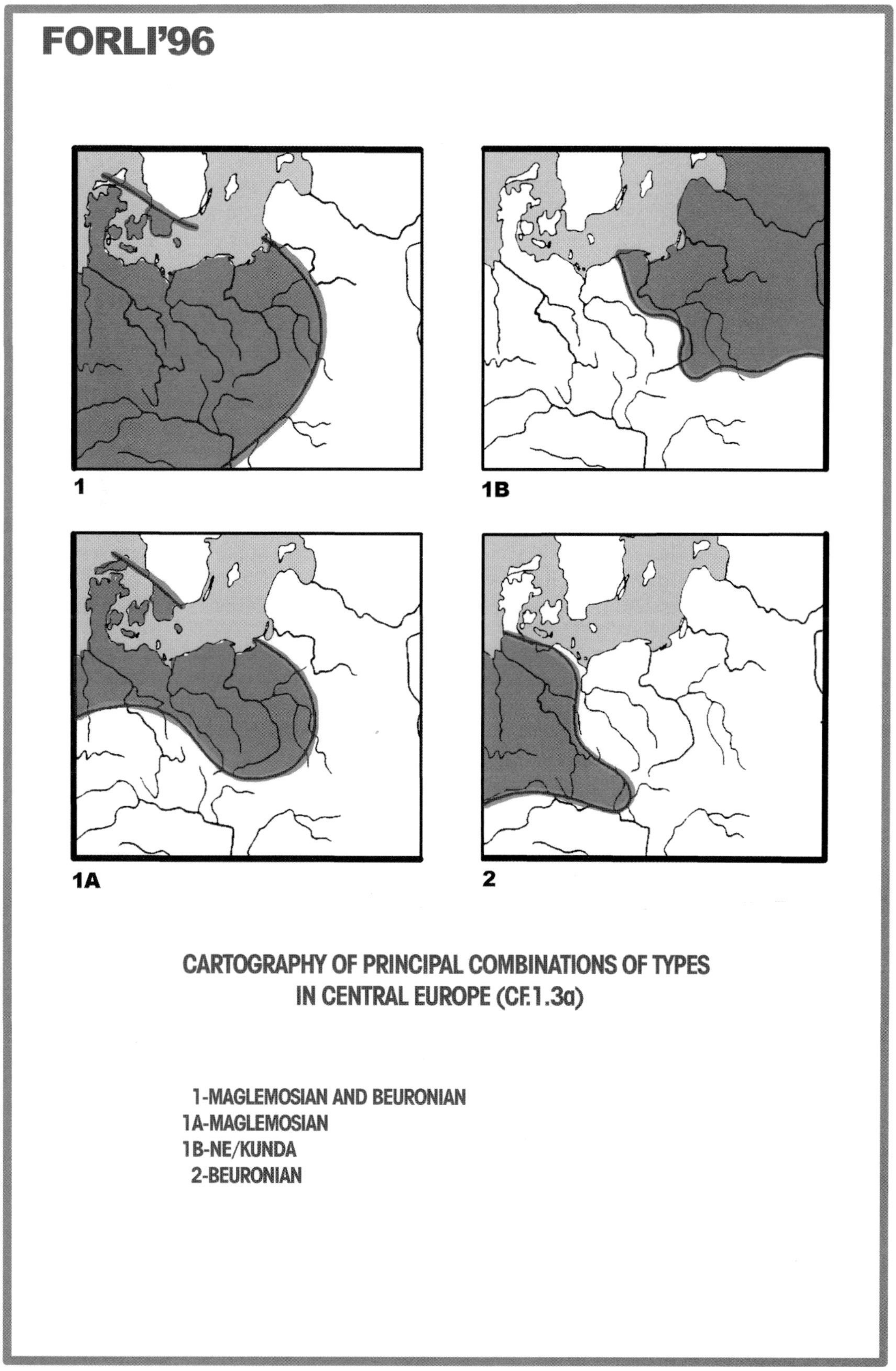
FORLI'96
1
1B
1A
2
CARTOGRAPHY OF PRINCIPAL COMBINATIONS OF TYPES
IN CENTRAL EUROPE (CF. 1.3a)
1-MAGLEMOSIAN AND BEURONIAN
1A-MAGLEMOSIAN
1B-NE/KUNDA
2-BEURONIAN

Fig. 1.3b

amateur. Cependant, même depuis que la recherche est aux mains de préhistoriens professionnels, la tendance est toujours de minimiser les différences locales à l'intérieur du Mésolithique européen, en le traitant comme un phénomène compact qui se développe partout au même rythme.

On distingue partout les mêmes étapes de développement (Mésolithique "ancien", "moyen" et "récent"), sans admettre que la culture d'un continent aussi vaste que l'Europe (env. 10,500,000 km^2) ne pouvait évoluée au même rythme pendant plusieurs millénaires (entre 10,400/10,000 et 3900 ans cal. AC localement), alors que ce n'était pas le cas avant ou après cette période, où l'on met depuis longtemps en avant des particularismes régionaux.

Le texte qui suit, présente un choix d'arguments pour et contre cette prétendue homogénéité du Mésolithique européen.

"UNUM"

La thèse sur l'unité/homogénéité du Mésolithique européen repose sur des arguments assez générales comme, par exemple:

- le caractère interglaciaire du climat, du milieu, et par conséquent, une économie quasi uniforme (chasse, cueillette, pêche) pratiquée à l'échelle du continent;
- un processus d'adaptation forcée des communautés humaines du Tardiglaciaire (surtout au nord) aux nouvelles conditions interglaciaires et à de nouveaux territoires parfois jamais occupés auparavant;
- un processus de spécialisation poussée de l'équipement dû à un milieu forestier: arcs, flèches à pointes multiples (mettant en œuvre les fameux microlithes et géométriques -cf.), sauf au Nord et à l'Est, où dominent des pointes pédonculées, (cf. "Tanged points"), sagaies et pointes barbelées, harpons (cf. "Points, *sagaies*...");
- une augmentation du rôle de la pêche, avec un matériel adéquat: canots (cf. "Boat"), pagaies, filets, nasses, hameçons, pointes barbelées (cf. "Fishing spear");
- une augmentation du rôle de la cueillette, due au développement d'une forêt riche et des riches milieux littoreaux, mais aussi à l'introduction du tamisage sur les chantiers de fouilles (ça concerne aussi des hipermicrolithes!);
- une organisation supposée du territoire tribal: propriété et organisation du territoire, frontières, saisonnalité avec des camps d'été et d'hiver;
- une hiérarchisation de l'habitat avec des agglomérations étendues de cabanes construites (camps -cf. de base) et petits arrangements avec une cabane (campements satellites);
- un approvisionnement en matières premières d'abord autarcique, puis parfois extra-régional.

Cet ensemble d'éléments est généralement considéré par les spécialistes et les non-spécialistes comme la définition même du Mésolithique. Le problème est que la quasi-totalité de ces éléments sont présents, au moins en partie ou régionalement, dès la période précédente, c'est-à-dire dès le Paléolithique tardif/final ou même avant. Cueillette-pêche, arcs, flèches à pointes multiples et singulières, sagaies, harpons, pointes barbelées, organisation du territoire, saisonnalité, diversification des campements, construction de cabanes, systèmes d'approvisionnement, sont déjà présents, soit de manière moins prononcée (mais le nombre de sites est aussi limité!), soit limités à certaines régions. La microlithisation, la géométrisation et la technique du microburin ont été inventées avant l'Holocène dans le Sud européen, où la forêt de type interglaciaire s'installe et existe au moins depuis le Tardiglaciaire.

On peut ainsi remettre en cause la définition économique, sociale ou stylistique admise jusqu'à présent, en mettent accent sur la diversité du Mésolithique européen plutôt que sur la prétendue unité.

"PLURIBUS"

Cette diversité se manifeste dans les traits suivants (Fig. 1.4a–f):

- environnements différents occupés: toundra, forêts de conifères, forêts de feuillus, bords de mer, steppe;
- paysages variés: plaines, collines, montagnes, plateaux;
- différence dans les gibiers chassés: renne au nord extrême de l'Europe, élan au nord et à l'est, faune forestière avec le cerf, le sanglier et le chevreuil dans les forêts de feuillus, aurochs dans la steppe et steppe-forêt, bouquetin dans les montagnes, phoque au bord de la mer;
- variété dans les ressources de la cueillette, par exemple les moules sur la Baltique et les noisettes dans la plaine du nord, contre les escargots et les lentilles au sud-ouest méditerranéen;
- les techniques, l'équipement, les proies de pêche et même sa richesse différentes en rivière, en lac ou en mer;
- technologies lithiques différentes: petits nucléus à double plan de frappe et percussion indirecte, remplacés par un nucléus à un plan de frappe au sud, au centre et à l'ouest (cf. "Blade/bladelet"), nucléus en forme de "crayon" et technique de pression à l'est;
- typologies variées: pointes de flèches pédonculées (cf. "Tanged points") prépondérantes à l'est et au extreme nord, nombreuses pièces à dos et microlithes géométriques (cf.) au sud, au centre et à l'ouest;
- les sagaies à l'ouest et au sud, les pointes barbelées à l'est et au centre (ces dernières plutôt pour la pêche, les premières pour la chasse !), les pointes à rainures armées de lamelles, à l'est et au centre (cf. "Points, *sagaies*...").

Ces différences semblent résulter de la diversité des cultures/traditions et des milieux présents sur le continent dès avant le Mésolithique. Sans nier, donc, une certaine homogénéité globale du Mésolithique, force est de constater une diversité régionale assez poussée qui apparaît bien sur la carte. Ce régionalisme n'est visible qu'au niveau macrogéographique, ce qui explique, qu'à d'autres échelles, il soit passé inaperçu.

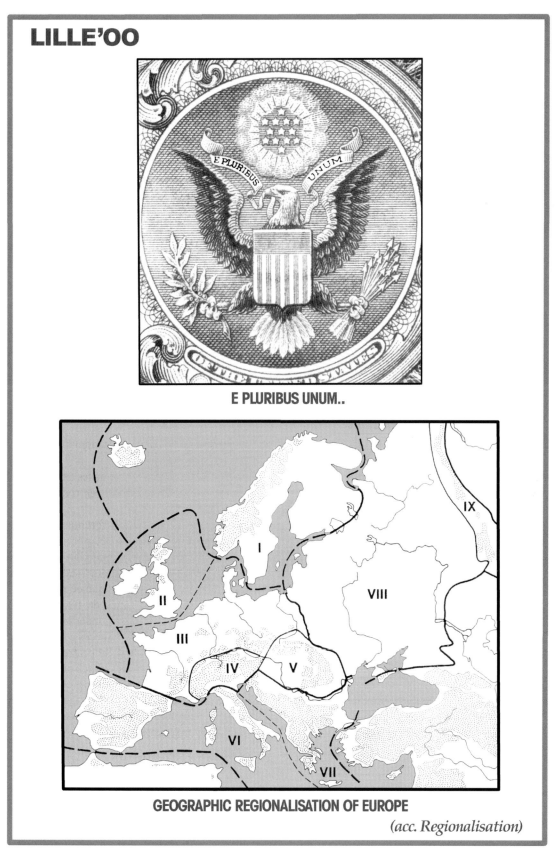

LILLE'OO

E PLURIBUS UNUM..

GEOGRAPHIC REGIONALISATION OF EUROPE

(acc. Regionalisation)

Fig. 1.4a

LILLE'00
E PLURIBUS UNUM ?

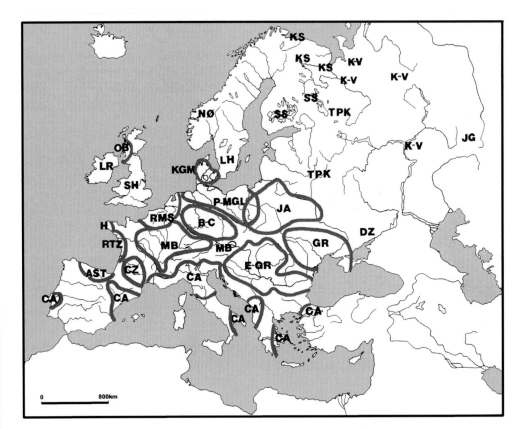

LATE MESOLITHIC (C.6500 CAL.BC)

CA	CASTELNOVIAN	KGM	KONGEMOSIAN
CZ	CUZOUL	JA	JANISLAWICIAN
RTZ	RETZIAN	E-GR	EPI-GRAVETTIAN
TV	TEVIECIAN	GR	GREBENIKIAN
MB	MONTBANI	DZ	DONETZ
RMS	RHENANIAN	TPK	KUNDA-BUTOVIAN
BC	BEURONIAN	KV	KAMA-VYCHEGDA
SH	SHIPPEA HILL	SS	SUOMUSJÄRVI
OB	OBANIAN	KS	KOMSA
LR	LARNIAN	NO-LH	MICROBLADELET
P-MGL	POST-MAGLEMOSIAN	JG	YANGELKA

Fig. 1.4b

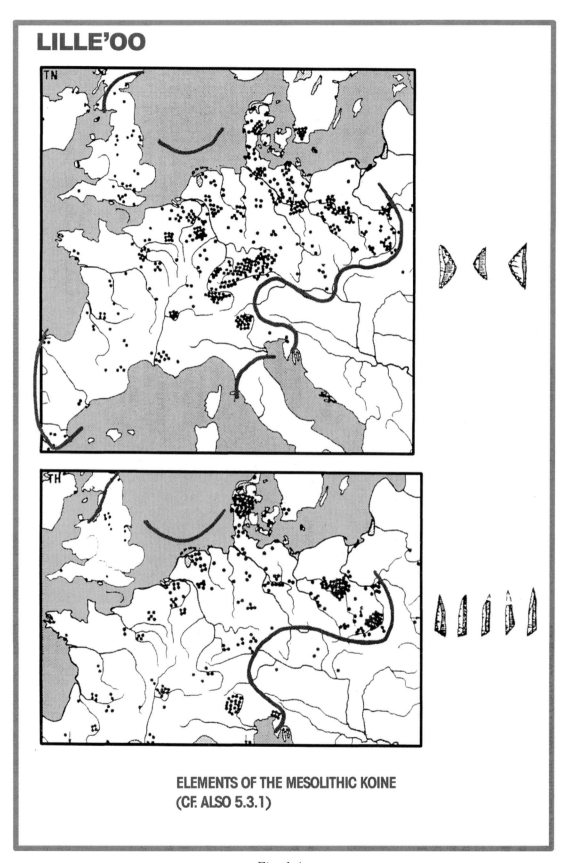

LILLE'OO

ELEMENTS OF THE MESOLITHIC KOINE
(CF. ALSO 5.3.1)

Fig. 1.4c

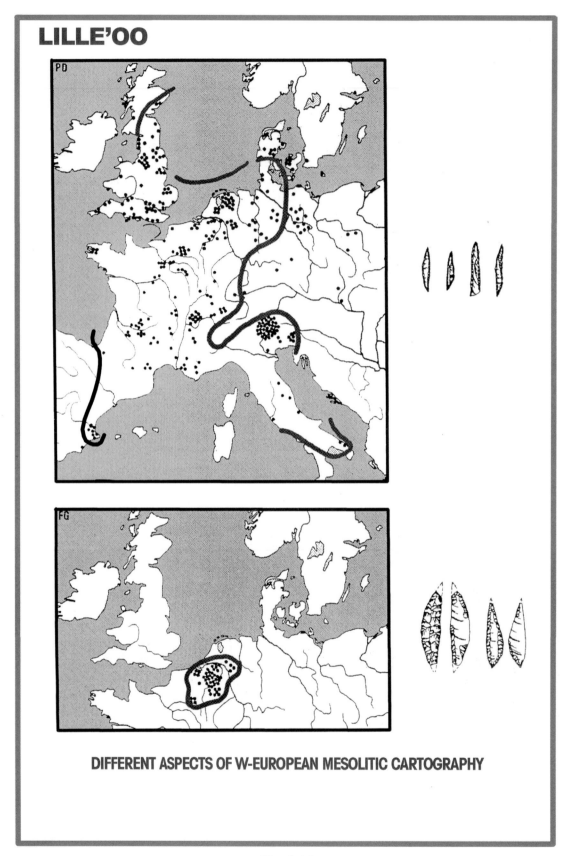

Fig. 1.4d

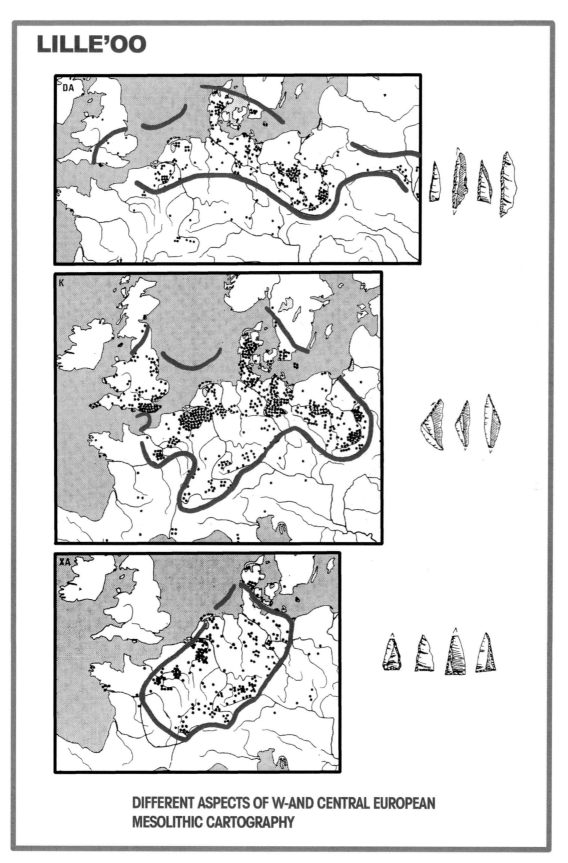

Fig. 1.4e

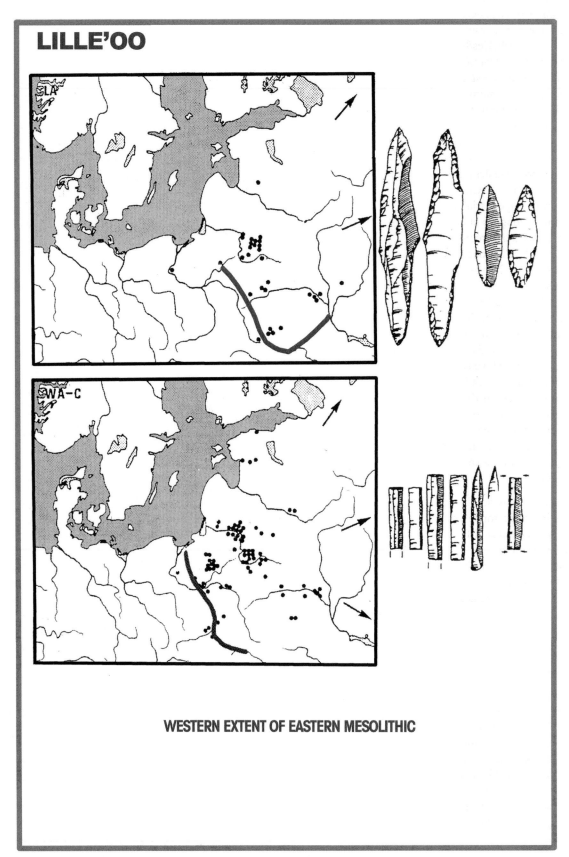

Fig. 1.4f

Les régions et les frontières

L'analyse de la répartition des différents types de pointes et de microlithes mésolithiques (cf. "Atlas of the Mesolithic in Europe") à l'échelle du continent révèle des régionalismes et fait apparaître des frontières (cf. "Mapping the Mesolithic"). On obtient le même résultat avec la répartition des sagaies et des pointes barbelées/harpons.

A. La première frontière coupe le continent en deux zones: nord et est d'un côté, ouest, centre et sud de l'autre. Le nord et l'est se caractérisent par des pointes pédonculées, l'ouest, le centre et le sud par des microlithes géométriques et des pièces à dos (cf. "Koine"). Ce dernier ensemble est relativement homogène, avec des tendances communes dans le développement des industries et des cultures régionales (cf. "Rhythms"). On y observe en effet une évolution en trois étapes: triangles courts et larges, suivis de triangles longues et étroits, puis de trapèzes.

B. Ces deux macrorégions, couvrant chacun une bonne moitié de l'Europe, montrent des subdivisions en territoires moins vastes (mésorégions) couvrant chacun une superficie comprise autour de 600,000/1,800,000 de km^2. Dans le sud et dans l'ouest, ce sont respectivement les complexes du Sauveterrien et du Beuronien. Au centre et au nord-ouest, il s'agit du Maglemosien au sens large, le nord et l'est se subdivisant à leur tour en deux: le complexe scandinave à pointes pédonculées (partie d'un "Tanged Points Complex") et le complexe nord-oriental, ou Kunda. À la périphérie de ces deux macrorégions, le sud-est de l'Europe ainsi que Iberie et le sud de l'Italie offre un Epigravettien marginal méditerranéen, tandis que la steppe ukrainienne donne un complexe caucaso-caspien dans sa variante pontique.

La caractérisation de chacune de ces entités à l'échelle mésorégionale se fonde en particulier sur la technologie et la typologie des différents outils, mais surtout les pointes/microlithes.

À une échelle plus fine, ces complexes mésorégionaux se subdivisent territorialement en "cultures"/entitées/taxons différenciées qui se caractérisent par des traits secondaires, comme des types rares ou régionaux (ex: feuilles de gui de la culture Rhein-Meuse-Schelde au nord-ouest du continent).

"E PLURIBUS" OU "UNUM"?

L'ensemble des faits constatés conduit à une conclusion nuancée: tout en reconnaissant une certaine unité méso-lithique au niveau économique et social (chasseurs, cueilleurs, pêcheurs, forestiers specialisés), il faut bien admettre l'existence de régionalismes stylistiques (parfois forts), traces probables d'une diversité héritée des traditions diversifiées du Tardiglaciaire, renforcées encore par le traditionalisme (cf. "Conservatism") typique des sociétés forestières et un isolationnisme poussé.

Comment in 2006

It belongs to the philosophy, if not ideology of researchers whether in their understanding of human history they will place more emphasis on its uniformity, meaning lack of differentiation, or on its variation, meaning how human populations and their respective cultural formations differed from one another.

In some circles, the predominant view is a global – one could even say, biological – approach that tends to eliminate differences ("we are all human beings!"). In other cases, the trend is to stand in defense of distinction, whether great or small. It is the opinion of the present author that both approaches, if applied in parallel mode with reason and restraint, can be of importance. The point is actually in the reason and restraint....

1.5. Stockholm'00

The Mesolithic: What we know and what we believe?

Twenty-seven years have passed since our first meeting in Warsaw in May 1973. Later we met in Potsdam (1978), Edinburgh (1985), Leuven (1990) and Grenoble (1995). It is perhaps a good opportunity here, in Nynäshamn, to consider our accomplishments and our failures, to take a look at what we really know and what we only believe we know about the Mesolithic. The Meso-cartoon shows some of our recent achievements and discoveries. The picture is somewhat pessimistic.

What is the Mesolithic?

There are those who would like to believe that the Mesolithic is characterized by some highly specific attributes (Fig. 1.5a–d), such as a uniform economic model based on individual hunting, gathering and fishing; which was adapted to specific interglacial (Early and Middle Holocene) forest conditions; also believed to be in opposition to the Late Glacial model (Paleolithic/tundra vs. Mesolithic/forest); with a developed social and territorial organization (ownership and probably defended borders of highly organized territories), settlement hierarchy and structuring (base vs. satellite camps), seasonal population movement (seasonal change of hunting niches and seasonal people's gatherings/festivals, common cemeteries); raw material procurement systems (well organized mines/extraction points, specialized work-shops, far reaching distribution); microlithisation and geometrization of backed and differently truncated points/ bladelets serving as arrowheads (for hunting small game, of course?). Indeed, there is a man who fails to recognize the existence of the Mesolithic in Russia because of the lack of geometrics there (!).

According to this restricted definition, the European Mesolithic (not including Scandinavia and the Russian Plain) seems to be, in the eyes of some authors, surprisingly uniform or practically uniform with regard to technology and typology (= "culture"), something that does not fit well with our experience concerning the preceding (Paleolithic) and following (Neolithic) periods. It is even believed (cf. below) that the evolution of the flint industry of this

Fig. 1.5a

Fig. 1.5b

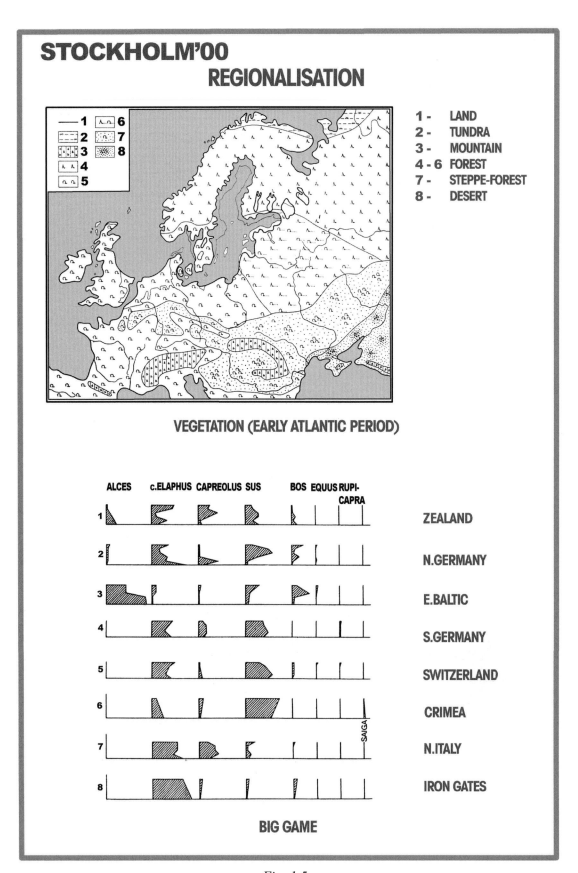

Fig. 1.5c

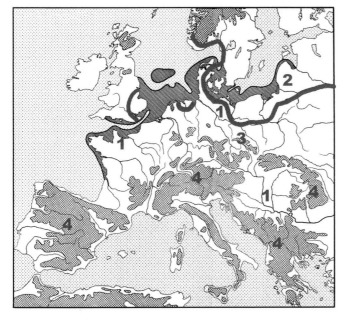

STOCKHOLM'00
REGIONALISATION

1 LOWLAND/PLAIN
2 FRESH PLAIN
LAKELAND

3 HIGHLAND/PLATEAUS
4 MOUNTAINS

RELIEF

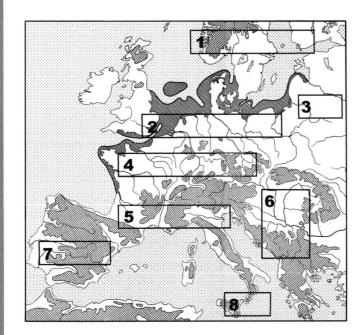

1 TANGED POINTS
2 MAGLEMOSIAN
3 KUNDA/NE
4 BEURONIAN
5 SAUVETERRIAN
6
7 EPI-GRAVETTIAN
8

CULTURAL TRADITIONS

Fig. 1.5d

practically uniform Mesolithic is unidirectional and follows the sequence: broad triangles – narrow triangles – trapezes (cf. "Rhythms").

There is, even now, a tendency to abandon traditional "cultural"/taxonomic subdivisions/names and to replace them with more neutral terms, like "Early" or "Late" Mesolithic. These chronological terms, when employed to describe contemporary phenomena from distant regions are totally misleading, if it is not taken into consideration that they describe completely different stylistic units/structures/worlds (e.g. Sauveterrian in Italy and Maglemosian in southern Scandinavia).

Consequently, existing (often local) definitions and characteristics of the Mesolithic are based on criteria that are frequently contradictory. They are as follows:

1. environmental (interglacial forest),
2. techno-stylistic (alleged uniformity featuring micro-lithism, geometrism, microburin technique and a common evolutionary rhythm),
3. economic (hunting-gathering-fishing),
4. social (highly organized, developed and specialized communities, featuring a social hierarchy, territorial systems, raw material procurement, seasonality),
5. chronological (Early and Middle Holocene).

Definitions of this kind consist of contradictions, while not covering phenomena that have been considered traditionally as Mesolithic (cf. below).

With regard to environment, there were never any forests directly north of the Black and Caspian seas in the Holocene (with the exception of the big river valleys), nor were there any forests in the northern extremes of the continent. By contrast, the entire southern part of Europe was wooded during the Late Glacial and had already in these times its own microliths and geometrics!

As for technology and typology, while there are no geometrics from Russia and the territories of the Eastern Baltic states, such elements are well known from the Late Magdalenian, Epi-Gravettian and Ahrensburgian, as well as from the Late Glacial industries of the Middle East, Northern Africa and even India(?). The same concerns microliths. In the eastern regions of Europe and in Scandinavia tanged points constituted substitutes for microliths/geometrics.

The evoked socio-territorial organization had in fact started at least during the Middle Paleolithic period (e.g. studies of J.-M. Geneste), and some of these accomplishments are well known from the animal world! (social hierarchization, territorial organization, primitive dwellings).

The only remaining feature in common is the chronology, which places the "Mesolithic" in a period after 10,400? cal. BC and before the local/regional neolithization and ceramization (cf.).

The incoherent description presented above is indeed a simple summary of various regional experiences and definitions, and it demonstrates clearly enough how much we need to apply the extra-regional approach in studies of the Mesolithic, and also how little success we have had in this approach.

The approach is still dependent on that of local priests and pastors, schoolteachers and retired army officers. Those first Mesolithic explorers and "experts" in many places and regions had only their local or parish experience or perspective, and were obviously incapable of achieving an extra-regional understanding of the problem.

Most of the evoked attributes are in fact either poorly documented or not exclusive or discriminating, some of them even banal. The former are mostly based on biological and ethnological/anthropological experience, and suggest nothing more than a naive picture of the hunting-gathering community on a developed, specialized level (Western cinema experience).

In turn, seasonality, raw material procurement, territory, settlement hierarchy, all appear real enough (documented), but are hardly exclusively Mesolithic in nature (cf. above). Indeed, even the geometrics, backed pieces, microliths and microburins on one hand, and the tanged points on the other, were invented and used before the Holocene (respectively by the Late Magdalenians, Epi-Gravettians and the Tanged Point Complex people, all of whom were Paleolithic/Pleistocene populations).

What we actually know?
Instead of the above described picture of an allegedly uniform European Mesolithic, we are suggesting a more professional and thorough but subtle description of the phenomenon, based on a study of extra-regional differences. These differences concern a variety of environmental attributes, as well as cultural traditions, which can be determined on stylistic and technological grounds. The Early/Middle Holocene European environment differed in many ways:

1. Morphology of terrain (plain/plateau/mountain barriers and passages),
2. Hydrography (sea/lake/river/stream/dry terrain),
3. Raw materials (outcrops for extraction/mining vs. surface sources; rock diversity, its presence or absence),
4. Climate (subarctic/cool/temperate/Mediterranean; dry/wet; oceanic/continental),
5. Flora (tundra/coniferous/mixed/deciduous forests/steppe/Mediterranean vegetation),
6. Mammals (reindeer, elk, mixed forest fauna, aurochs, ibex, seal, all occupying individual habitats),
7. Food to be gathered (nuts, lentil, glans, cereals, land and marine snails, regionally diversified).
8. As for manufacturing technologies, the stylistic, typological and technological differentiation that can be observed in the tools, among others, concerns both technology (shape and mode of core pre-formation, e.g. conical, bullet, subconical, discoidal, single- or double-platform etc.; chipping techniques, e.g. pressure vs. punch technique; size, e.g. big Castelnovian items vs. smaller Sauveterrian, also the size and shape of blades/bladelets: short and irregular at the beginning,

then much more regular, smaller and bigger; kinds of retouching: e.g. abrupt, semi-steep, flat; special techniques: e.g. microburin, pseudo-microburin, blade sectioning, etc.) and morphology (mostly shapes of alleged arrow- and spearheads, e.g. flint/stone tanged points, *feuilles de gui*, backed points/bladelets, various triangles, various microtruncations, micro-retouched bladelets, various trapezes, etc., also bone/antler barbed, slotted, spindle-shaped or biconical points, also *sagaies*, unpolished and polished axes/adzes/chisels, denticulated Montbani bladelets, irregular scrapers, etc.).

To judge by our historical experience, environmental differentiation of the kind evoked above could strongly condition human culture, imposing differentiation/zonation/regionalization/territorial separation. This is what we observe in the European Mesolithic.

As for style, typology and technology, Mesolithic Europe demonstrates an extra-regional differentiation and zonation that can be summarized in the following list of big, extra-regional taxonomic entities (techno-complexes): Scandinavian Tanged Points (far North), Maglemosian or Northern (West and Center), Western (West and South), North-Eastern (or Kunda), Epi-Gravettian, Caucaso-Caspian, Castelnovian. The extent and borders of these entities (and their regional components – cultures/groups) can be traced cartographically when mapping the territorial ranges of characteristic attributes (cf. "Atlas"). These maps indicate the existence of extra-regional, regional and even local territories and zones (cf. "Settlement pattern"), characterized by evident almost linear or banded borders, each with their own distinct tradition. This is what we expected. It also means that the European Mesolithic was not as uniform as supposed.

Conclusion

Summing up, here is what we know.

The Mesolithic is a Postglacial/Interglacial continuation (in the south) and/or adaptation (in the north) of Late Glacial specialized hunters for a more temperate climate and especially for a mostly forest environment which dominates almost the entire continent from the first half of the 11th millennium cal. BC. There is no shared attribute (except for the chronology) that could be safely used to define the entire Mesolithic formation.

The Mesolithic populations had highly specialized hunting-gathering-fishing structures that were not invented in the Holocene, but were inherited from or were the continuation of Late Glacial predecessors. This observation concerns not only material objects, but also the more intangible and hence only selectively known elements of social culture, like territorial organization, raw material procurement system, seasonality, settlement pattern and hierarchy of settlements, hunting strategies, etc. Last but not least and contrary to what has often been suggested, the Mesolithic is a highly differentiated phenomenon.

2

What and How?

The structure of this chapter is hardly consistent and not even very logical, because it is for the most part a collection of encyclopedic sketches that the Author felt might be of use to readers. These remarks are on matters that are more or less obvious, perhaps even banal at times, although not always recognized or fully comprehended. There is no taxonomy or paleohistory here, just a collection of important facts, some more or less significant impressions and descriptions of unique objects, finally a few interpretations…

My apologies to those who will not be interested by any of these texts, my gratitude to those who will read and benefit.

2.1. Stone

2.1.1. Flint and stone tools

Ambiguous in itself, the term "tool" is used in this book as a conventional reference to the concept of a "retouched tool". Originally, a "retouched tool" was considered as hafted (either individually or in series, forming what could be referred to in abstract and colloquial terms as a "tool" or "implement"). Such abstract hafted specimens are not really common in the Stone Age and what's more, similar "retouched tools" from different regions tended to be hafted differently (e.g. arrow armed with armatures from Loshult in Sweden -cf. and the sickle or knife from Columnata in North Africa). The following is a list (Fig. 2.1.1a–e) of presently known important combinations of retouched tool and handle:

- tubular bone/antler handle plus end-scraper, burin or burin spall (all from Pékarna in the Czech Republic), or unpolished adze (Hohen Viecheln in Germany, Svaerdborgmose in Denmark);
- bone/antler slotted dagger handle with retouched or unretouched inserts (eastern Mesolithic), flat slotted point armed with retouched or unretouched sectioned bladelets (East Baltic area, Upper Volga), plus slotted bone points (eastern Europe, southern Scandinavia) and Near Eastern "sickles";

- wooden or antler arrow shafts with either single-tanged points (Oleni Ostrov, Stellmoor) or trapezes (Tvaermose in Denmark and Petersfelsner Moor in Germany), or multiple armatures/microliths (Loshult);
- L-shaped antler handles of polished and unpolished (Lübeck in Germany) axes, adzes and picks;
- Arched antler handles for end-scraper and burin (Oleni Ostrov).

The list is naturally not exhaustive. Importantly, however, it shows that unretouched flints, including blades, bladelets and trimming blades, could have constituted the working part of a functional tool, pointing to one more possibility: that the flint/stone parts of tools could have been unretouched (!) or bore evidence of nothing but macrowear-use retouch (e.g. use-retouched inserts, cf. "Blades/bladelets", but also impact negatives on arrowheads), or even only microwear invisible to the naked eye.

Thus, unretouched or only use-retouched implements appear next to complete (meaning hafted) specimens and retouched ones (formed by retouch from the typological point of view).

To reiterate, the term "tool" is used in this volume to designate implements that have been "retouched" intentionally (burin blow, side/truncation/front-retouch and sectioning) or through use, and which are always morphologically specific, but not hafted as a rule.

2.1.2. Blade/bladelet

Blades and bladelets were the principal blanks used for the production of Mesolithic retouched and unretouched tools. They were obtained through different core reduction techniques (depending on the time and region), using a variety of flint cores. In northeastern Europe, for example, the pressure technique was used throughout the Mesolithic to produce virtually identical bladelets, very regular in shape, from "pencil-like" cores. In other regions, the technique evolved and debitage styles were differentiated in time and space (Fig. 2.1.2a–c).

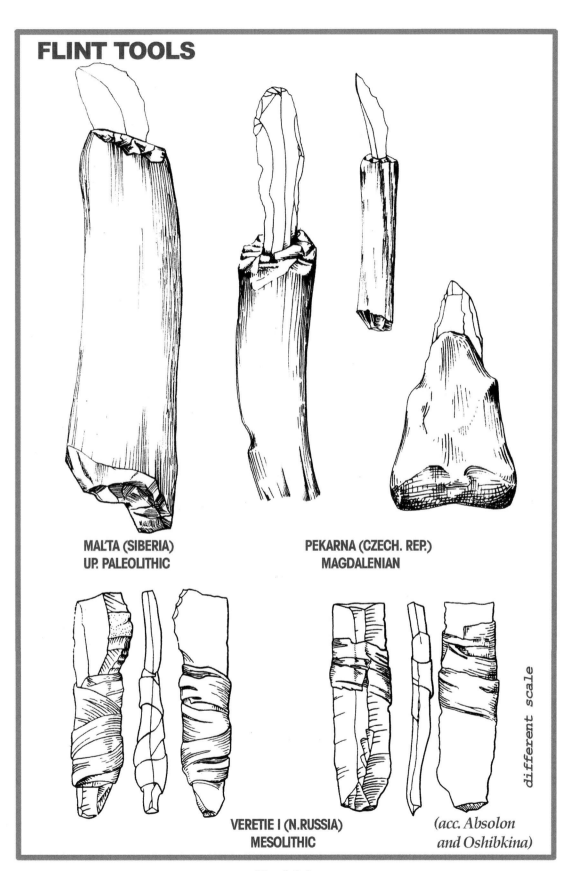

FLINT TOOLS

MAL'TA (SIBERIA)
UP. PALEOLITHIC

PEKARNA (CZECH. REP.)
MAGDALENIAN

VERETIE I (N.RUSSIA)
MESOLITHIC

*(acc. Absolon
and Oshibkina)*

different scale

Fig. 2.1.1a

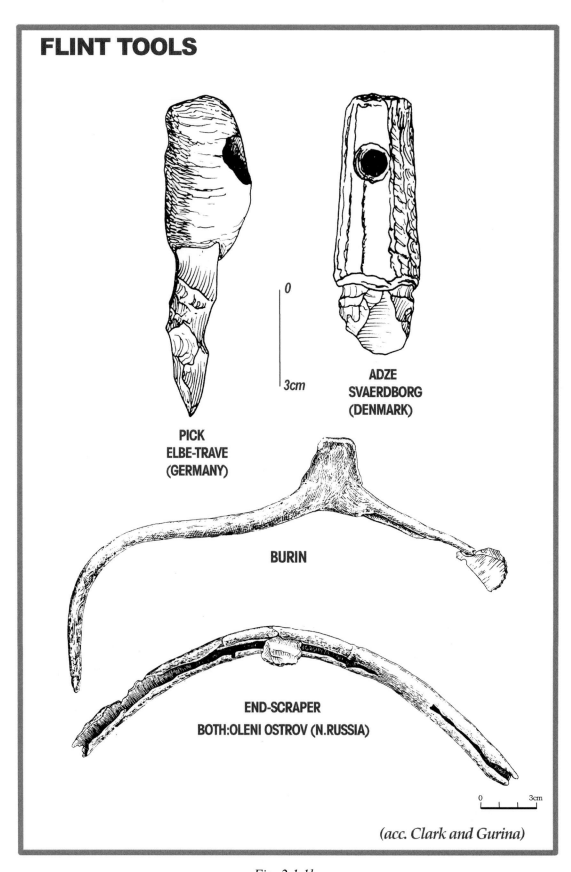

FLINT TOOLS

0

3cm

**ADZE
SVAERDBORG
(DENMARK)**

**PICK
ELBE-TRAVE
(GERMANY)**

BURIN

**END-SCRAPER
BOTH: OLENI OSTROV (N.RUSSIA)**

0   3cm

(acc. Clark and Gurina)

Fig. 2.1.1b

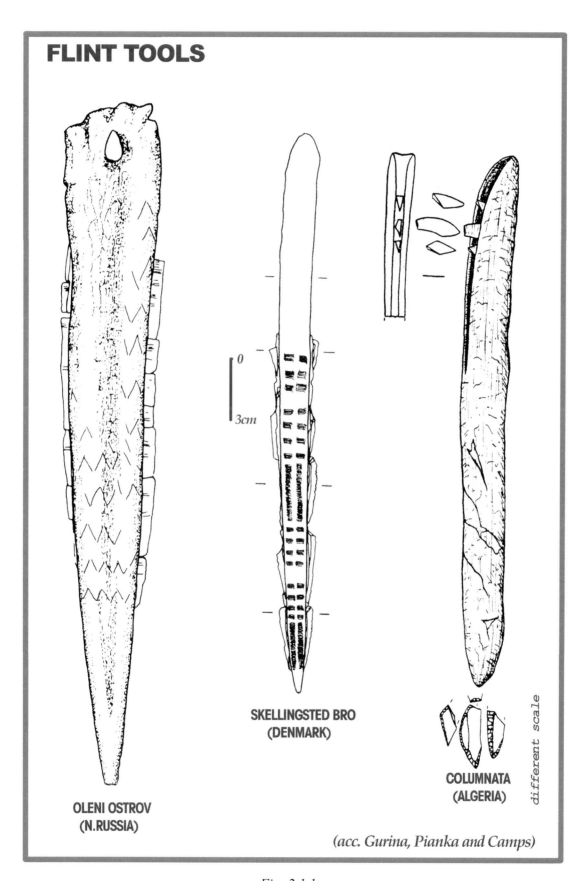

Fig. 2.1.1c

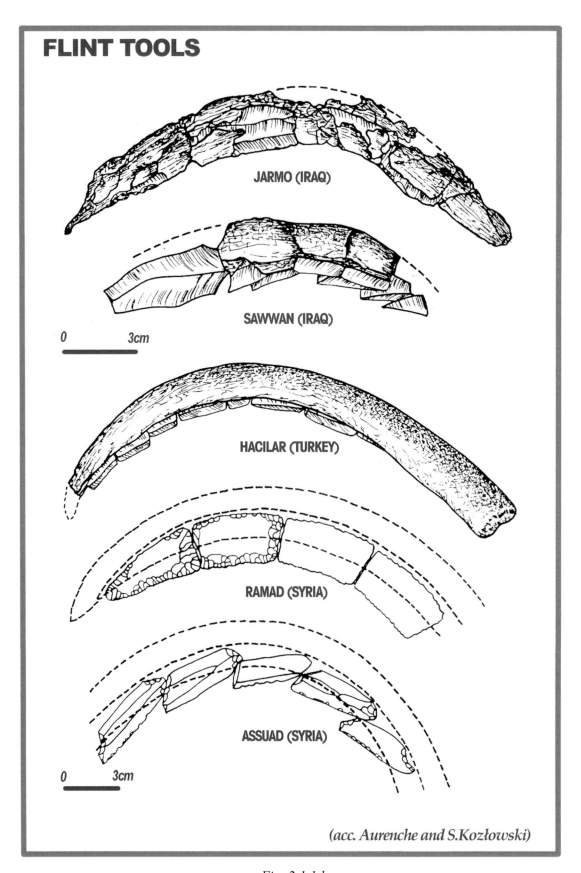

FLINT TOOLS

JARMO (IRAQ)

SAWWAN (IRAQ)

0   3cm

HACILAR (TURKEY)

RAMAD (SYRIA)

ASSUAD (SYRIA)

0   3cm

(acc. Aurenche and S.Kozłowski)

Fig. 2.1.1d

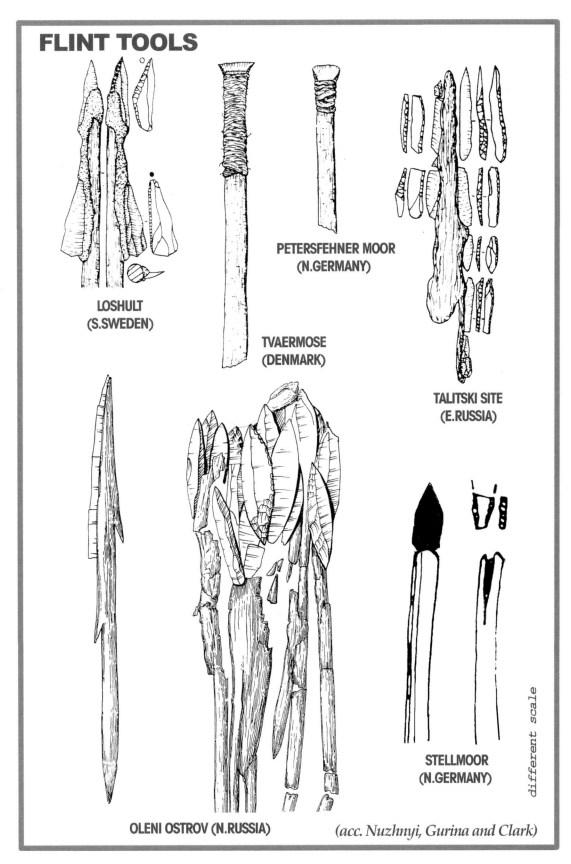

FLINT TOOLS

LOSHULT
(S.SWEDEN)

TVAERMOSE
(DENMARK)

PETERSFEHNER MOOR
(N.GERMANY)

TALITSKI SITE
(E.RUSSIA)

STELLMOOR
(N.GERMANY)

different scale

OLENI OSTROV (N.RUSSIA)

(acc. Nuzhnyi, Gurina and Clark)

Fig. 2.1.1e

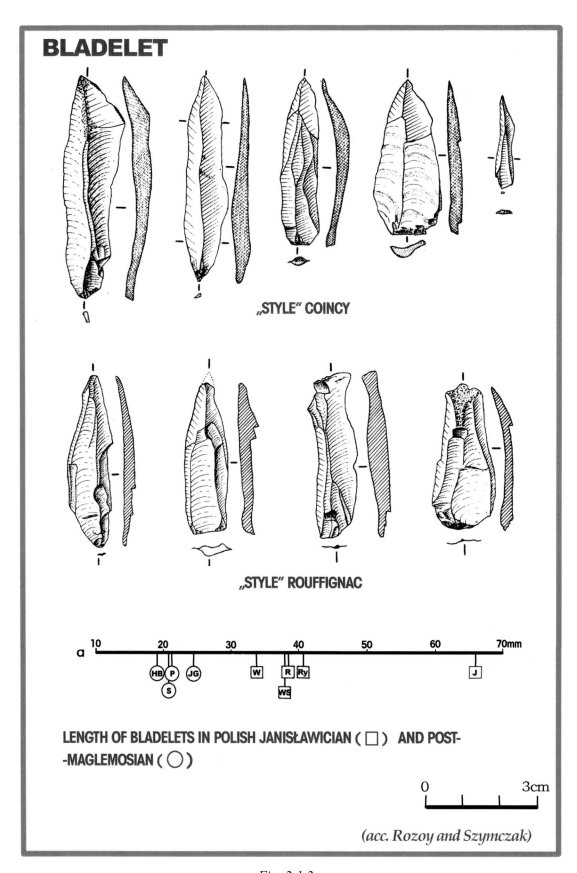

Fig. 2.1.2a

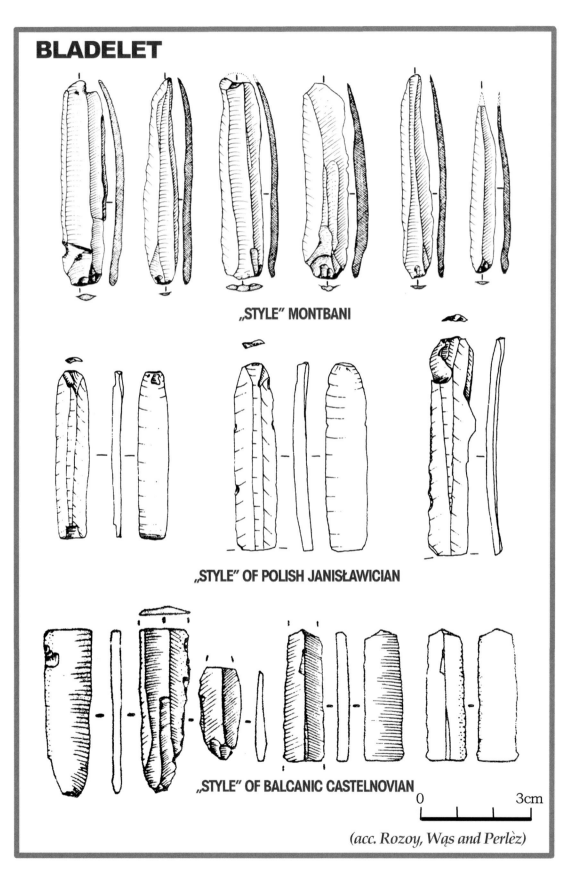

Fig. 2.1.2b

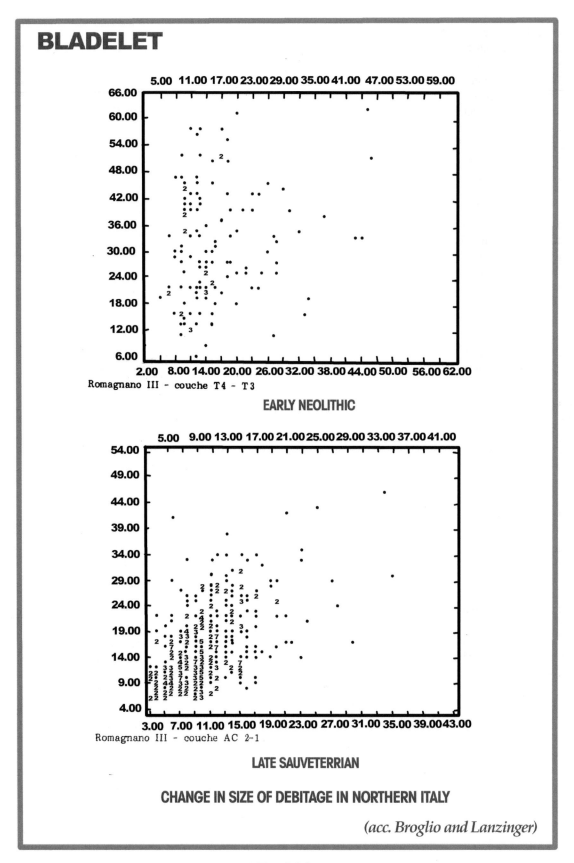

Fig. 2.1.2c

The biggest changes took place in the South-West-Central European "koine" (cf.). The change in core reduction technology and the resultant change of bladelet parameters followed the same "rhythms" (cf.) of evolution that can be observed for armatures and microliths. The period starts with discoidal or sub-discoidal small cores giving irregular, short and rather broad bladelets (the "Coincy style" of Jean-Georges Rozoy, cf. "Blade/bladelet"). Then came the 'revolution' of the Middle Mesolithic with conical/keeled cores being exploited by punch or pressure techniques; the latter technique, which was known earlier, but had not been used widely, now spread like wildfire. The end effect were British "narrow bladelets" and the Danish very regular bladelets known from the old collections from Svaedborg I, but also in miniature form from the Carl J. Beckers, collection from the same site, as well as the later western Swedish and western Norwegian "micro-bladelets", and ultimately the bladelets from Beuronian C in the west and the Post-Maglemosian industries in the north.

These new and very regular blanks (which are known also from the Sauveterrian) provided the inspiration for a new shape of elongated microliths. Scalene triangles with short base (TD, TI, TH, TE) appeared together in several variants. The sectioning technique seems to have developed at this time.

The next stage was the Late Mesolithic "Castelnovization" (cf.) of the continent, proceeding at various pace and intensity, covering not just the area of the "koine" (cf.), but reaching out to the Black Sea, the Balkans and the eastern frontiers of Central Europe. Big, pre-formed, mostly keeled cores were used to obtain, mostly by pressure technique, very big regular bladelets, which Jean-Georges Rozoy described as "Montbani-style debitage" (cf. "Blade/bladelet"). These blanks could be used as micro-retouched or use-retouched knives, but they were also reworked either by microburin or sectioning technique into blades with retouched truncation and foremost into trapezoid and rhomboidal arrowheads. The size of these trapezoids and rhomboidal pieces was determined by the standard and rather considerable width (7–10 mm) of the new bladelets.

Already at this stage in history, some of the raw material was mined and/or imported, violating the existing autarchic raw material system (cf. "Pre-Neolithic/Castelnovian"). In the further perspective of a ceramic Neolithic, the need for ever bigger and broader blades and bladelets would lead to the creation of an entire independent and artisanal (?) production and an open distribution system of products (= "market").

The evolution described here can be synchronized to a large extent with the "rhythms" (cf.) of stylistic change, although not completely, as regional anachronisms continue to be observed (e.g. East Germany and Poland).

2.1.3. Sectioning

Sectioning (Fig. 2.1.3a–b) is a technique for segmenting blades and bladelets by transversal breaking. The resulting rectangular medial parts of blades and bladelets were used for arming spearheads, as well as knives and sickles (cf. "Inserts"). Specimens of this kind are known mainly from the Mesolithic cultures of eastern Europe (Northeastern or Kunda complex with its slotted points and daggers), but also from southern Scandinavia (Scanian Maglemosian with its slotted points), and finally from the Proto-Neolithic cultures of the Near East (reaping knives). The presence of this technique was observed also in the Castelnovian (cf. "Pre-Neolithic") complex, although only single bone specimens with such inserts have actually been attributed to this unit. Sectioning, which was also used to make some of the trapezes (e.g. in the Balkans and Ukraine), was a rival technique for microburins technique.

2.1.4. Inserts

Inserts are usually the rectangular, medial parts of sectioned bladelets, shaped by micro-retouching or left unretouched, fitted into slots in bone points (circum-Baltic region and eastern Europe), daggers (Kunda, Oleni Ostrov), perhaps knives and sickles (the latter confirmed for the Near East: reaping knives from Natufian, Sawwan and Zawi Chemi sites). Retouched specimens of WA-C type (cf. "Atlas"), characteristic of eastern Europe and Siberia, are also included in this group (Fig. 2.1.4).

The technology was inherited from the Upper Paleolithic (cf. retouched inserts from the Talitski site in the Ural mountains in Russia and an unretouched mounted Magdalenian example from La Garenne in France).

2.1.5. Geometrization/microlithization

Retouch technique (the retouching usually abrupt) forming tool edges (most often microliths) with the aid of two or seldom three backs or truncations. The resultant form is a small or very small (even only 4–5 mm! Fig. 2.1.5) triangle, trapezoid, rectangle or segmental piece. Such geometrically shaped microliths had been presumed initially to be specifically Mesolithic products. Sieving of deposits on pre-Holocene sites has demonstrated, however, that microliths were present also in some late Upper Paleolithic industries (Epi-Magdalenian, Epi-Gravettian etc.). Formed often by microburin technique, but also by sectioning and pseudo-microburin technique, geometric microliths create the impression of a continental-wide uniformization of the European Mesolithic (cf. "Koine"). This could partly be due to the limited repertory of executable formal variants (cf. "Rhythms"). Even so, geometrics occurred only in a part of Europe (central, southern, southeastern and western) and moreover, there were relatively numerous specimens of a regional or even local importance, occurring beside the banal forms that could be differentiated regionally, by size, for example (cf. Beuronian vs. Sauveterrian), and testifying to a varied Mesolithic tradition (cf. "Atlas"). It was once thought with some naiveté that microliths represented degeneration or degradation; not so today, when we are inclined to consider them as an expression of progress and effective miniaturization.

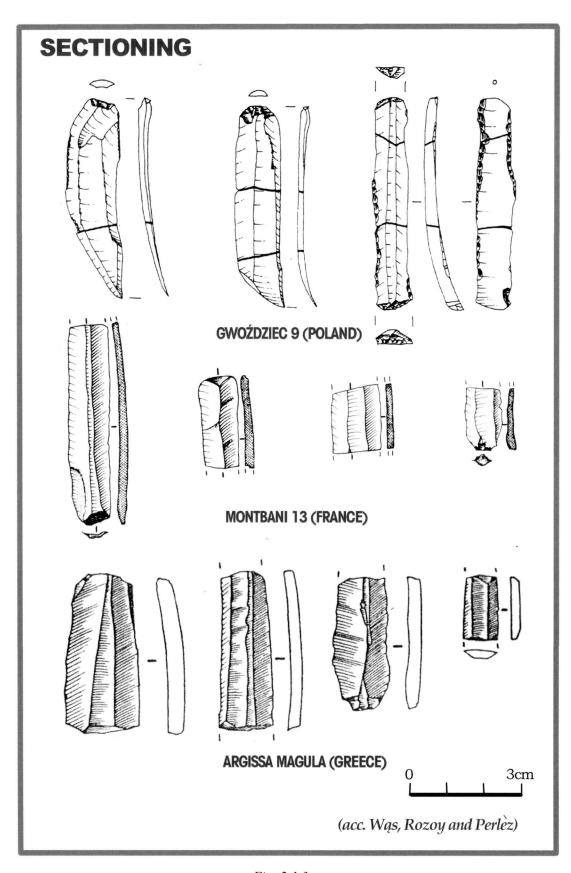

Fig. 2.1.3a

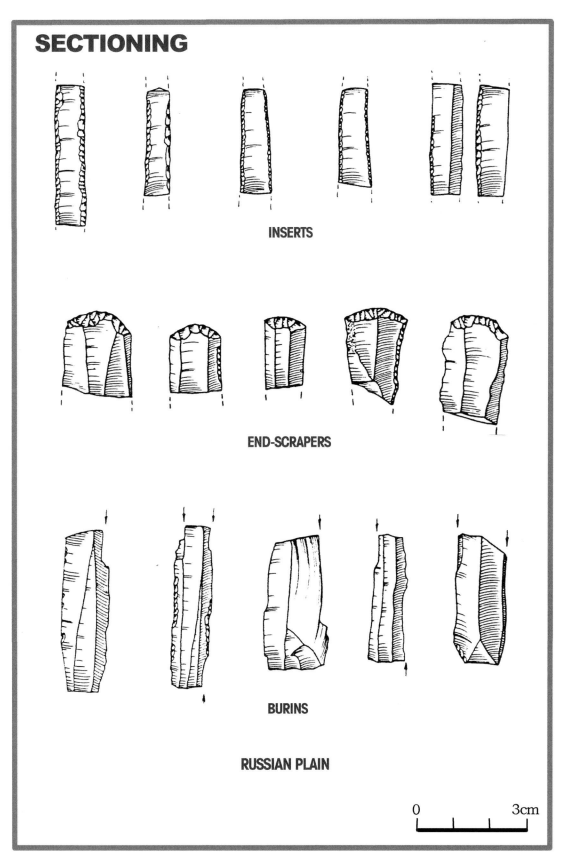

Fig. 2.1.3b

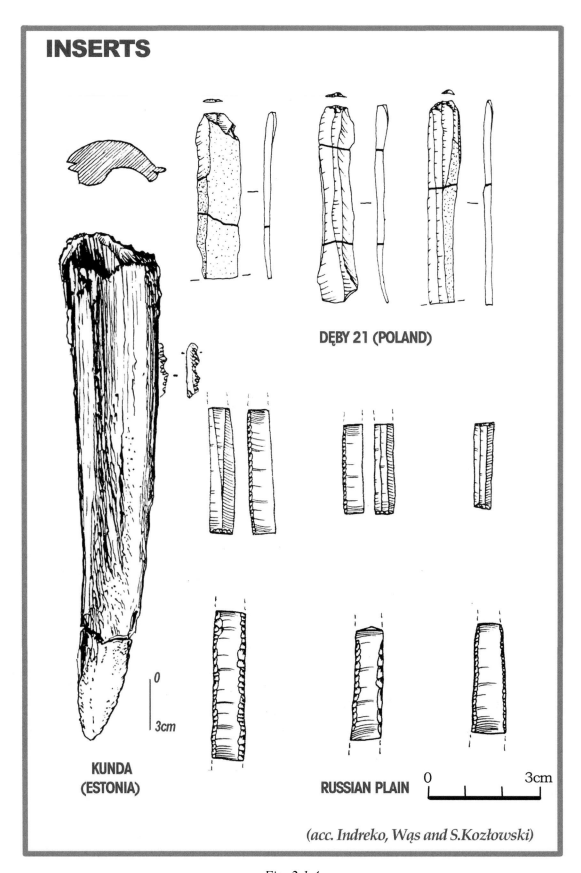

INSERTS

DĘBY 21 (POLAND)

KUNDA (ESTONIA)

RUSSIAN PLAIN

(acc. Indreko, Wąs and S.Kozłowski)

Fig. 2.1.4

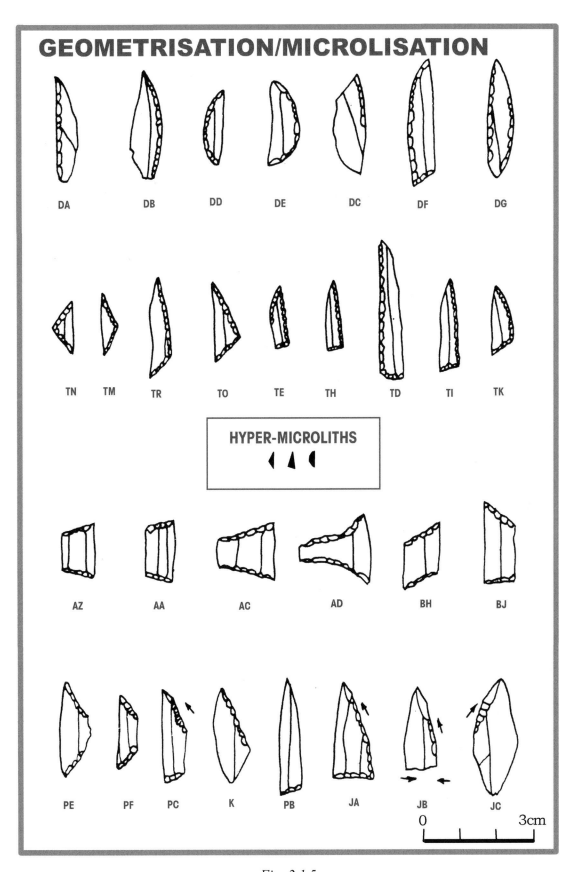

Fig. 2.1.5

2.1.6. Armatures

Armatures (Fig. 2.1.6) are small, mainly microlithic, but also hyper-microlithic (only 4 mm long!) and backed, mostly geometric (triangles, crescents and trapezes) specimens with back(s) and truncations, considered as inserts arming arrowheads, but also knives, sickles, daggers and spearheads, as proved by infrequent finds of mounted specimens from Europe, Africa and the Near East (cf. "Arrow"). Armatures were formed by microburin and pseudo-microburin techniques (cf.), but also by sectioning (cf.). Based on morphological characteristics, they are traditionally classified as points, backed blades/bladelets, crescents, triangles (isosceles and scalene), microtruncations, trapezes; moreover, specific groups like the Tardenois and Sauveterre points, *feuille de gui*, Janislawician points etc.

Despite semblances of uniformity (cf. "Atlas") resulting from metric (microlithization) and formal (geometrization) characteristics, armatures can vary by territory, enabling great cultural regions with evident borders to be established. In the south and west of Europe and in the center of the continent similar evolutionary trends (cf. "Koine") have been observed (naturally connected to arrowhead structural development) from rather broad forms to narrower ones (mainly triangles), later replaced with trapezes (cf. "Rhythms"). In northeastern Europe and the East-Baltic zone, the role of armatures was taken over by retouched and unretouched bladelets/inserts (cf. "Inserts") and tanged points (cf.).

The huge diversity of forms and their standarization (cf. "Atlas") suggests far-going specialization, especially prior to the appearance of trapezes. The impression is that they were closely adapted to complicated arrow construction, which surely changed over time, even though the actual process partly escapes our observation.

2.1.7. Trapezes

Flint and stone projectile points shaped as geometric trapezes with transversal-lateral unretouched tip and two, usually flaring, angled truncations. Considered as geometric microliths typical of the Late Mesolithic, they express a single, supra-regional or supra-cultural trend (cf. "Intercultural trends"). These blade/bladelet arrowheads are varied formally by region (symmetrical, asymmetrical, high, low) and execution technique (microburin vs. sectioning), this being the effect of local communities adapting in different and individual ways to a widespread trend (Fig. 2.1.7).

During the 7th millennium cal. BC, trapezes gradually replaced other microliths in emerging Castelnovian/Pre-Neolithic (cf.) groups. They also appeared in the interior of the continent, in the local, traditional cultures, where the process of replacing the old microliths lasted much longer and may have never been completed (cf. "Castelnovization" model B).

From the technical point of view, the entire process depended on a change of arrow construction. The composite projectiles of old times were replaced with single-point arrowheads, mounted transversally (finds of mounted products from Denmark, Schleswig-Holstein and Egypt, cf. "Hafting trapezes").

The replacement of non-trapezes with trapezes caused a diametrical change of the statistical composition of assemblages. Altered arrow construction evidently cut down the microliths index at least by half.

2.1.8. Microburins

Characteristic processing waste left over from the manufacture of microliths and initially believed to have been a tool in itself (hence the name). Proximal microburins were often a side product from the making of trapezes, while distal ones (of the Krukowski type, among others) from the forming of tips of fine sharp points and triangles. Pseudo-microburins are also known; they are actualy waste from the sectioning of backed bladelets. Believed once, erroneously, to be an indicator of Mesolithic industries, microburins are not known from the Mesolithic of northeastern Europe and most of Scandinavia, while they are present in the Late Pleistocene Mediterranean Epi-Gravettian, Hamburgian and Late Magdalenian. As far as Europe is concerned, microburins appeared in the Maglemosian, Beuronian, Sauveterrian and (West) Castelnovian complexes, as well as in the Epi-Gravettian of southern Europe.

2.1.9. Tanged (pedonculated) points

These typologically differentiated points (Lyngby, Ahrensburgian, Swiderian, Desnian, Kundian, *feuille de gui*, etc.) have a well-formed tang or base and a piercing tip. To judge by the evidence, which includes quivers from Oleni Ostrov (cf.), shafts from Stellmoor (cf.), impact negatives, not to mention Anders Fischer's brilliant experimental research, these points were mounted individually on arrow shafts. In the Holocene they are typical of Scandinavia (cf. "North") and a large part of eastern Europe (cf. "East"), and are known also locally in the West (Fig. 2.1.9a–b).

2.1.10. Axe/adze/chisel/pick

Heavy and massive stone tools (Fig. 2.1.10a–c), the presumed function of which was felling, cutting and chiseling (e.g. wood, logs for dugouts, flint in mines). They could have also been an object of status and prestige. It was most likely for these tools to be mounted on shafts made of antler (e.g. specimens on antler handles from Lübeck, Hohen Viecheln), but some of the axes/adzes could have had wooden shafts.

These tools were especially characteristic of central and northern Europe and were evidently differentiated both territorially and chronologically. Chipped specimens (both unifacial and bifacial) were spread throughout the European Plain from Britain to northern Poland (Maglemosian). Starting with Latvia and reaching up to Finland, Norway and Sweden, the predominant form were polished axes of all kinds (including trapezoid specimens of rectangular

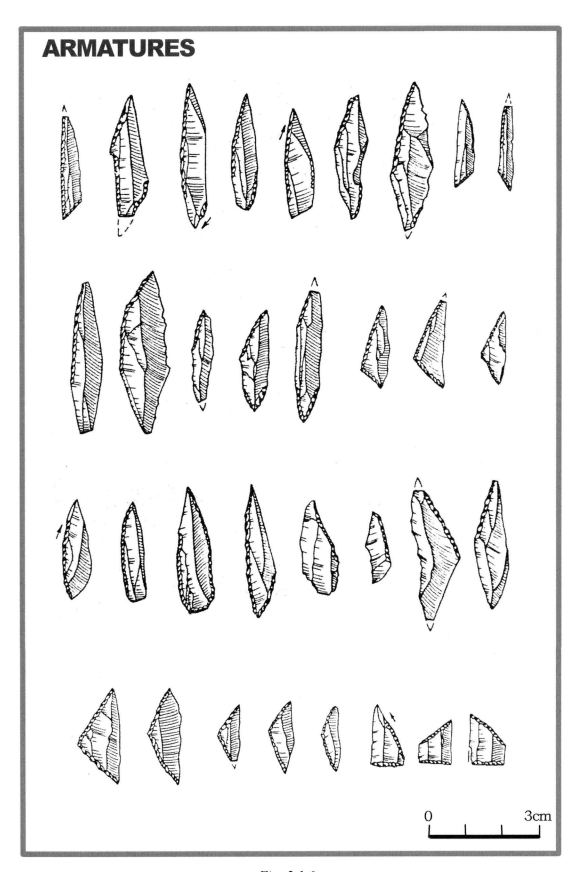

Fig. 2.1.6

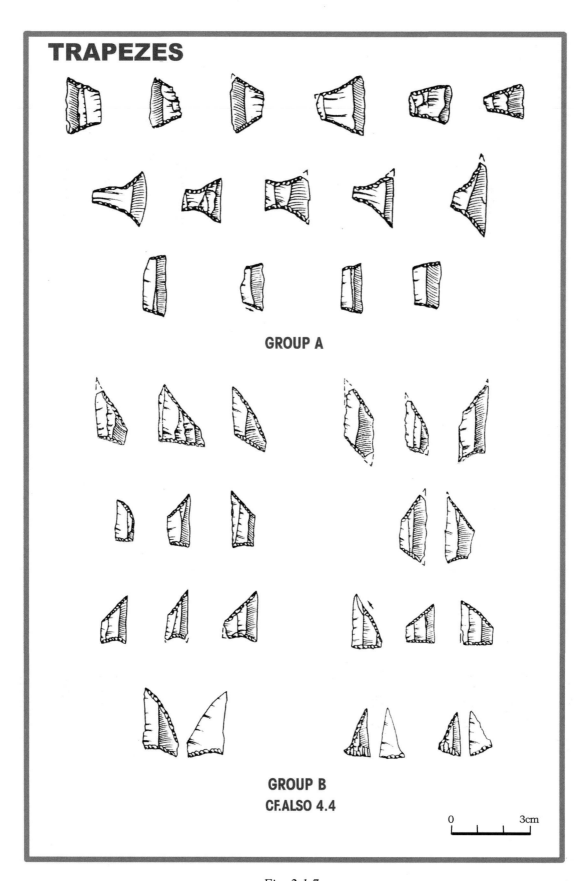

Fig. 2.1.7

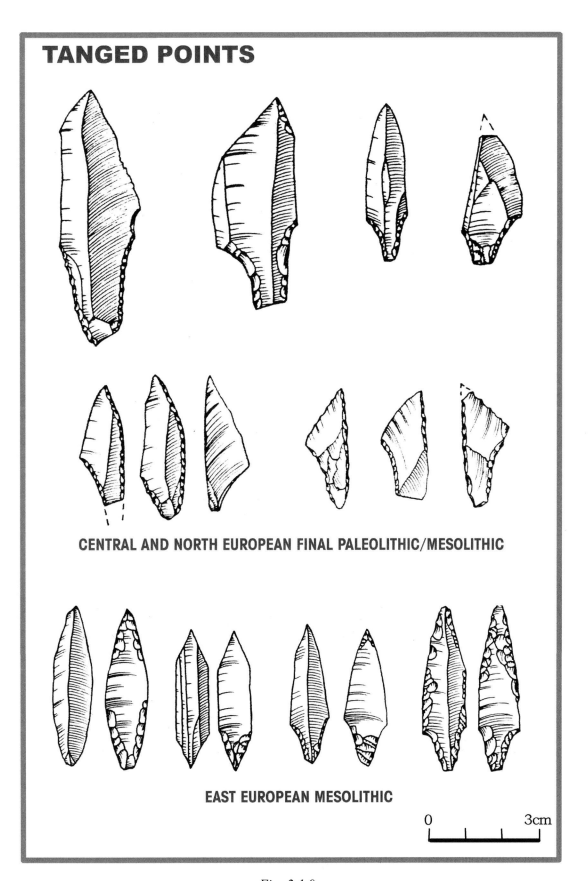

Fig. 2.1.9a

TANGED POINTS

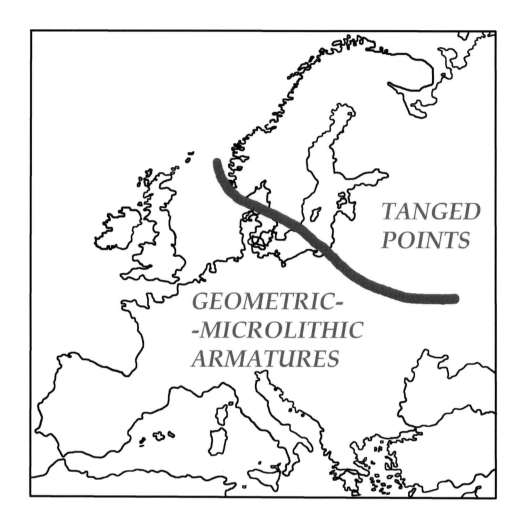

TANGED
POINTS

GEOMETRIC-
-MICROLITHIC
ARMATURES

MESOLITHIC TANGED POINTS
VIZ. GEOMETRICS/MICROLITHIC ARMATURES
FOR GEOMETRICS-MICROLITHIS
CF. 2.1.5, 2.1.6 AND 2.1.7
FOR TANGED POINTS
CF. 2.1.9a-9.1d AND 10.3a-10.3b

Fig. 2.1.9b

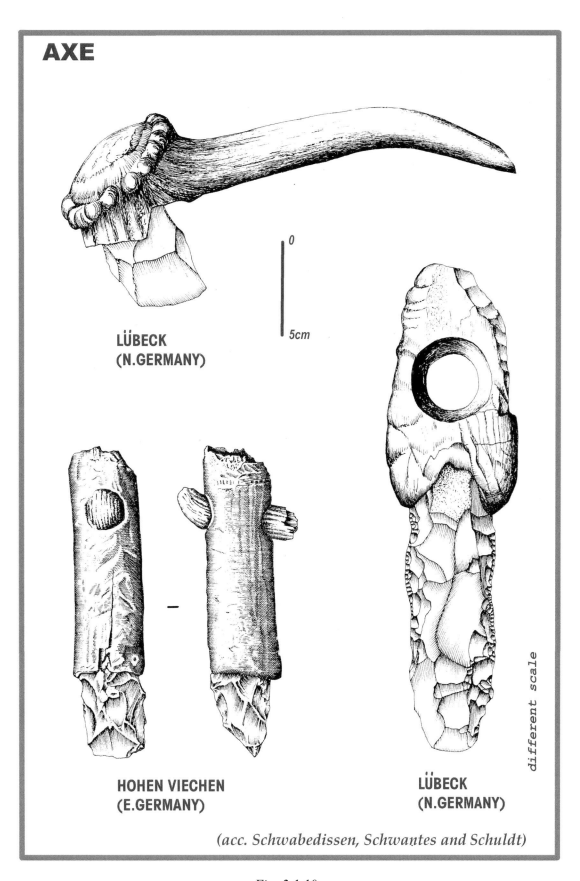

AXE

0

5cm

LÜBECK
(N.GERMANY)

HOHEN VIECHEN
(E.GERMANY)

LÜBECK
(N.GERMANY)

different scale

(acc. Schwabedissen, Schwantes and Schuldt)

Fig. 2.1.10a

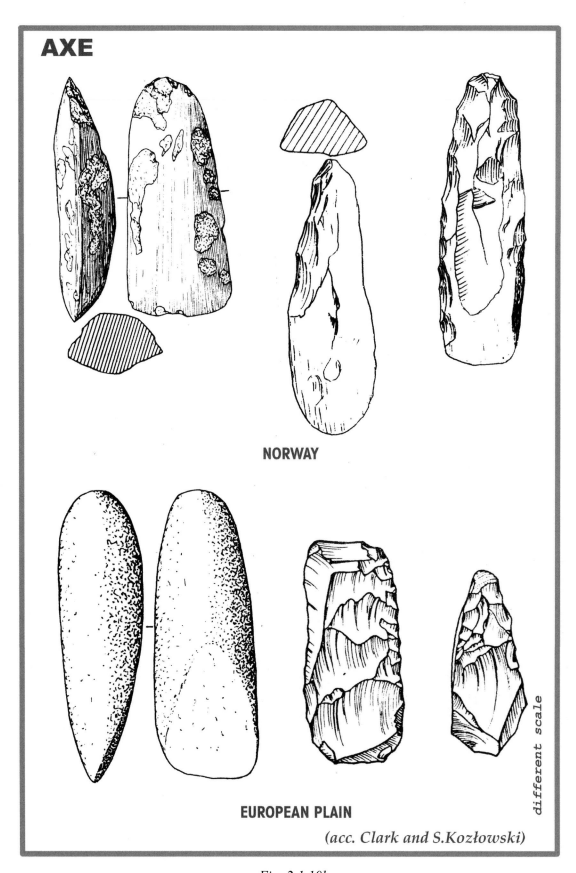

Fig. 2.1.10b

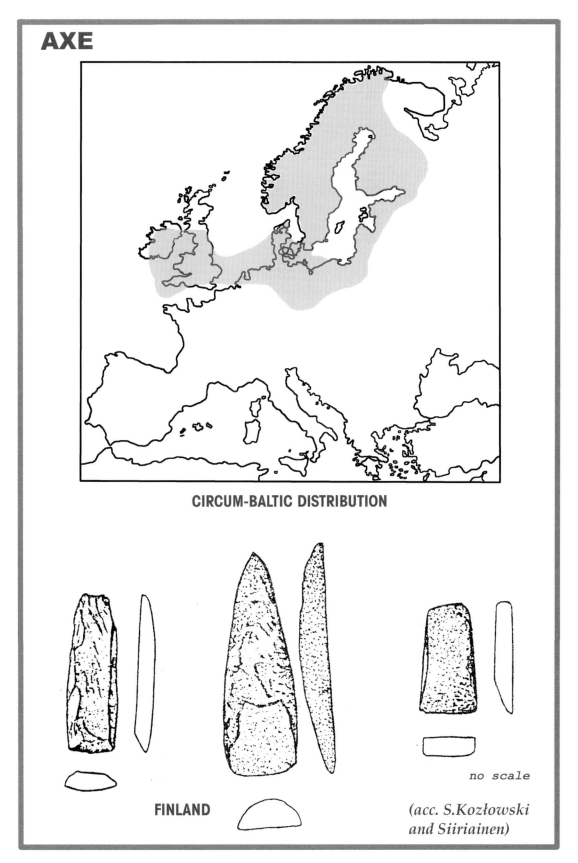

Fig. 2.1.10c

section) made of non-siliceous rock (Walzenbeil, Linhamn, Nøstvet and other types). Finds from Lübeck and Hohen Vieheln in Germany demonstrate that chipped specimens were used both as axes and as picks or adzes (mounted transversally in the latter case), possibly for hollowing dugouts (Michał Kobusiewicz). In turn, examination of outcrops of raw materials used in the production of axes from southern Sweden and southern Norway draw attention to the prestigious rather than practical role of these objects, which did not really travel far from their place of manufacture.

2.1.11. Irregular scrapers

Poorly studied because difficult to classify, this group of flake scraping tools (B in our statistics, Fig. 2.1.11) includes amorphous examples which are frequently omitted from publications. Also included here are side-scrapers recalling Middle Paleolithic types, denticulates, *raclettes* (similar to the pieces from the Badegoulian), Polish *skrobaczes* and use-retouched flakes. All of these, except for the last, are characterized by regular, intentionally prepared scraping edges (including those with ventral retouch) accompanying an overall irregular shape. Classifications of irregular scrapers have been proposed by Jean-Georges Rozoy, as well as by Alberto Broglio and Stefan K. Kozłowski.

2.2. Bone and antler

2.2.1. Bone/antler industries

Bone/antler industries are less known than the stone industries, being preserved only in specific geological conditions (peat bogs, cave sediments). From many areas they are simply unknown.

Bone and antler objects are best represented in the circum-Baltic and Upper Volga lakelands. They are differentiated in three separate ways:

- functionally (hunting vs. domestic, cf. "At home and abroad");
- territorially (a number of styles, such as Maglemosian, Atlantic-Mediterranean and east European, cf. below);
- chronologically (e.g. well investigated internal variability of the Maglemosian and eastern European industries over time, cf. Chapter 12).

The "domestic" elements of bone industries are morphologically dependent on the parts of the animal skeleton that the bone material came from, hence the interregional character and repeatability of many of the forms (awls, punches, chisels, unpierced "axes", etc).

A few of the forms had greater regional significance (e.g. perforated and decorated "Maglemosian" axes/adzes, and specific, Early Mesolithic perforated adzes made of elk antler, finally specific slotted daggers from the eastern European Plain and Finland).

2.2.2. Hunting and fishing gear (Fig. 2.2.2)

The part of the bone, antler and stone industries that was used "away from home" was highly specialized and strongly differentiated, territorially as well as chronologically (cf. "Atlas" and "Pointes, sagaies"). The reason for this was undoubtedly the specific function of these objects. Most of them were projectile points, seldom shafts of hunting gear (spears, harpoons, arrows). Indeed, some of these stone and bone points have been found fortuitously still mounted (cf. below) or in positions testifying to their effective application in hunting.

Microlith fragments have been found embedded in human and animal bones (Trou Magrite in Belgium, Ringkloster, Kongemose in Denmark, Téviec in France etc.):

- two harpoons found embedded among the bones of an elk found on the Allerød site of High Furlong in Britain;
- barbed point still embedded in the skeleton of a pike at the bottom of the fossil Kunda Lake in Estonia;
- two pairs of harpoons found in a position suggesting composite mounting (Star Carr in Britain);
- still shafted harpoons or preserving traces of mounting from Friesack in eastern Germany;
- two sets of stone arrowheads on antler shafts from Oleni Ostrov in Russian Karelia;
- tangs of flint arrowheads, shafted, from Stellmoor in Germany (Dryas 3);
- a few shafted Mesolithic microliths (Loshult, Friesack, Tvaermose, Oldenburg);
- skeletons of aurochs from Vig and Prejlerup in Denmark, preserving microliths/elements of composite arrows among the bones.

The multiple, if obvious, function of the majority of bone, antler and stone projectile points is thus presented in clear, albeit incomplete fashion. Single bone (but also wooden!) points were mounted as harpoons and spears, and the same role was served by two and even three points mounted together. Smaller points were mounted either singly or in sets of more than one as arrows, while barbed points were also mounted with stone arrowheads (e.g. Oleni Ostrov), *de facto* serving as shafts.

These projectiles may have had other functions or ways of application (e.g. blunt-headed arrows, cf., etc.), just as there is often no way of telling which were thrown by hand and which shot from a bow. The truth of the matter is that the only criterion, and one that is obviously unreliable, is the size: 'big' pieces considered as harpoons (for hunting) or spears (for fishing), 'small' ones as arrowheads. The uses of this criterion are obviously rather limited.

The harpoons/spears/points/arrows of the European Mesolithic are differentiated by raw material, type, age and territory. They are, in fact, one of the chief "cultural"/stylistic and chronological discriminants of the Mesolithic.

I should think that ethnological parallels could broaden considerably our understanding of the flung weapons of the Mesolithic.

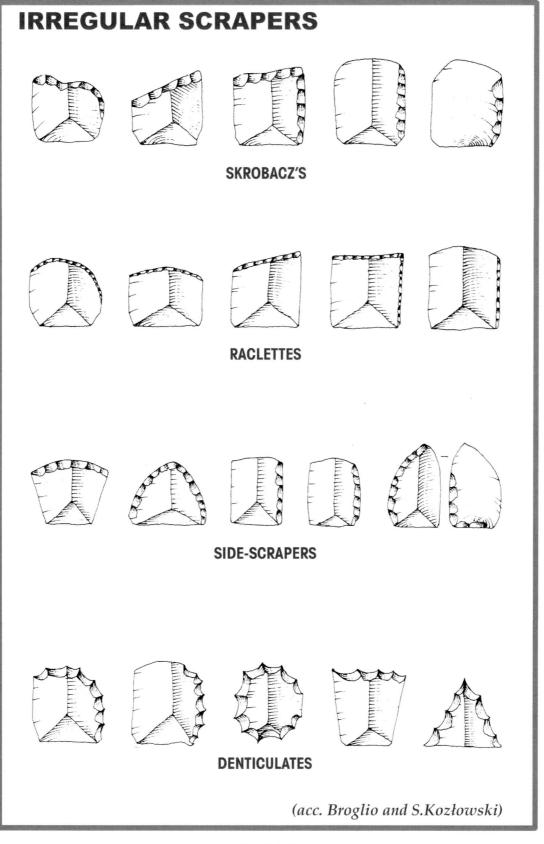

IRREGULAR SCRAPERS

SKROBACZ'S

RACLETTES

SIDE-SCRAPERS

DENTICULATES

(acc. Broglio and S.Kozłowski)

Fig. 2.1.11

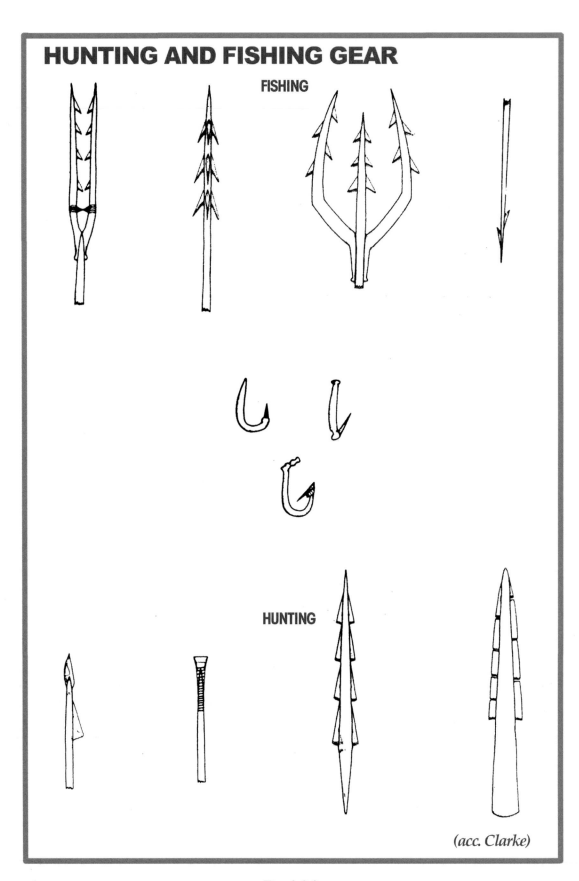

Fig. 2.2.2

2.2.3. Bone equipment of domestic use

Hunting weapons, however dominant (or more interesting to the researcher), had their counterparts in objects of bone and antler intended for domestic use. These have been preserved at several cave sites in the south and on bog sites in the north. Indeed, they are much more numerous on the latter kind of site (Fig. 2.2.3a–c).

This group of tools has often been avoided in studies so far, perhaps because so much depends on the original morphology of a piece of bone or antler, too often totally determining the shape of a tool.

Added to the difficulty is the function of these tools, the terminology used in their description being either neutral or functional (cf. symposia on the bone industry organized by Henriette Camps-Fabrer).

This is neither the place nor the occasion to discuss the issue, but a few synthesizing remarks of a general nature are in order. Foremost, the variety of the bone/antler industry is largely dependent on the hunted fauna (shape of raw material), although the role of tradition cannot be excluded. Secondly, particular industries are subject to local evolution (e.g. partial "atlantization" of the Maglemosian industry in the Late Mesolithic).

In general, it is possible to distinguish the following "home" Mesolithic traditions:

- Maglemosian
- East European
- Atlantic

The latter occurs in western and southern Europe and partly in the center of the continent (Switzerland, southern Germany); apart from the spindle-shaped *sagaies*/points described elsewhere (chapter 12) and the locally known flat harpoons, this industry features "wedges", massive unpierced "axes" of red-deer antler, pierced T-shaped axes also of red-deer antler, deer and doe spikes of unknown function, "knives-scrapers" made of boar tusks, chisels and daggers of the long tubular bones (of the auroch, for example). The tool kit is further augmented by simple bone awls and tubular handles of deer antler, and the pierced metatarsal bones of big mammals, which are in itself difficult to explain (handles, whistles?).

The Maglemosian industry, which is best known from southern Scandinavia and northern Germany, was characterized by a variety of barbed and slotted points (described for the first time by Grahame Clark), as well as the following:

- unpierced "axes" of deer antler
- adzes/axes of deer antler, pierced, with or without ornament (which is mostly geometrical, seldom anthropomorphic or zoomorphic); the shape was largely dependent on the antler shape (e.g. differences between earlier adzes made of elk antler and later ones of deer antler)
- chisels and daggers of long bones, mostly belonging to aurochs, and also slotted daggers with flint inserts
- fishing hooks

- pierced metatarsal bones of mammals (whistles?)
- "knives-scrapers" of boar tusks
- roe deer spikes
- T-shaped pierced axes of deer antler

Also found occasionally are bone mountings or handles for stone tools (both tubular and L-shaped), as well as bone awls.

Beside the harpoons and points (cf. classification by Grahame Clark in Chapter 12), the eastern European industry featured, among others, slotted daggers (as well as unslotted ones, referred to as "knives"), heavy unpierced antler "axes", simple awls and fishing hooks.

2.2.4. Slotted objects

Called *reinures* in French, these slots of various length are carved, either one or two (and seldom more), in wooden or bone shafts or mountings (Fig. 2.2.4). Bone products include:

- single- and double-slotted points, armed with retouched and unretouched inserts (for Mesolithic southern Scandinavia, the eastern European Plain, but also eastern European Upper Paleolithic)
- double- and single-slotted "daggers" armed with retouched and unretouched bladelets (Mesolithic of eastern Europe and southern Scandinavia)
- single-slotted reaping knives and "sickles" (Near East) with retouched and unretouched inserts (Natufian, Zagros region) and a knife/sickle(?) (Columnata in North Africa, armed with geometric microliths)

Short-slotted wooden shafts come from southern Scandinavia (Loshult, Vinkel, Holmegaard); they were armed with geometric microliths and served as arrows.

Earlier examples of slots with inserts come from the Magdalenian site of La Garenne and Pincevent in France and the East Gravettian site of Talitski in the Russian Ural. Slotted bone points are also known from Mezin in Ukraine, for example.

2.3. Wood (Fig. 2.3)

Ubiquitous and easily processed, wood must have been the most common raw material with multiple applications. This is confirmed by abundant ethnological data. Unfortunately, so little has been preserved to our times that the present remarks are handicapped by lack of sufficient data. Sensible generalizations are hardly possible with so few finds available, especially as these finds are limited chiefly to the northern regions, where they had the opportunity to be preserved in the peat bogs of the Early and Middle Holocene. In any case, the discoveries from Denmark, Sweden, northern Germany and Finland, as well as Russia and Latvia, indicate that the use of wood was widespread and varied.

A review of the finds reveals a number of wood-use categories. Hunting weapons consisted primarily of bows (cf.) made of yew (Holmegaard IV and Ringskloster

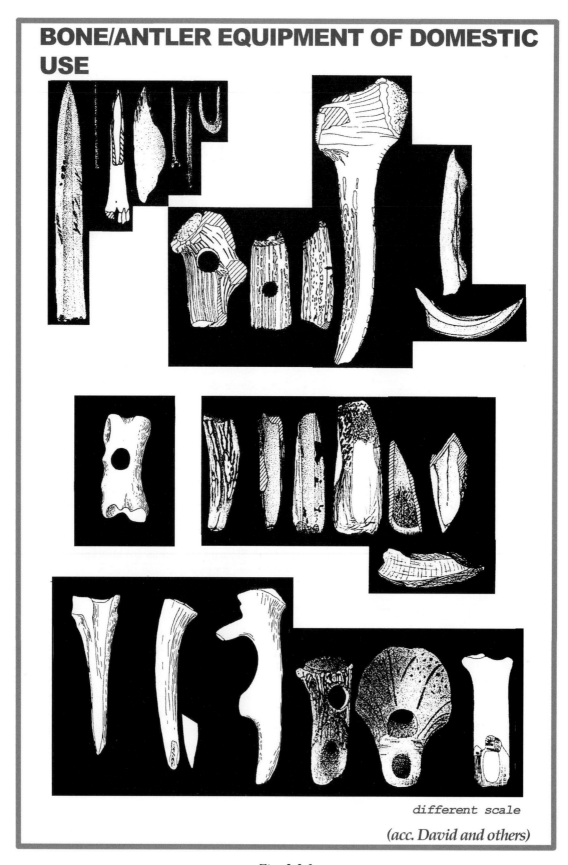

Fig. 2.2.3a

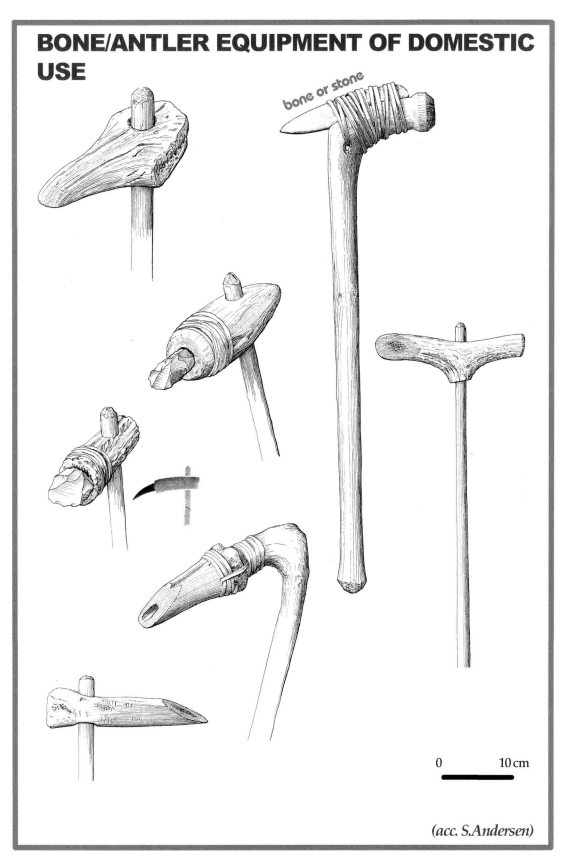

Fig. 2.2.3b

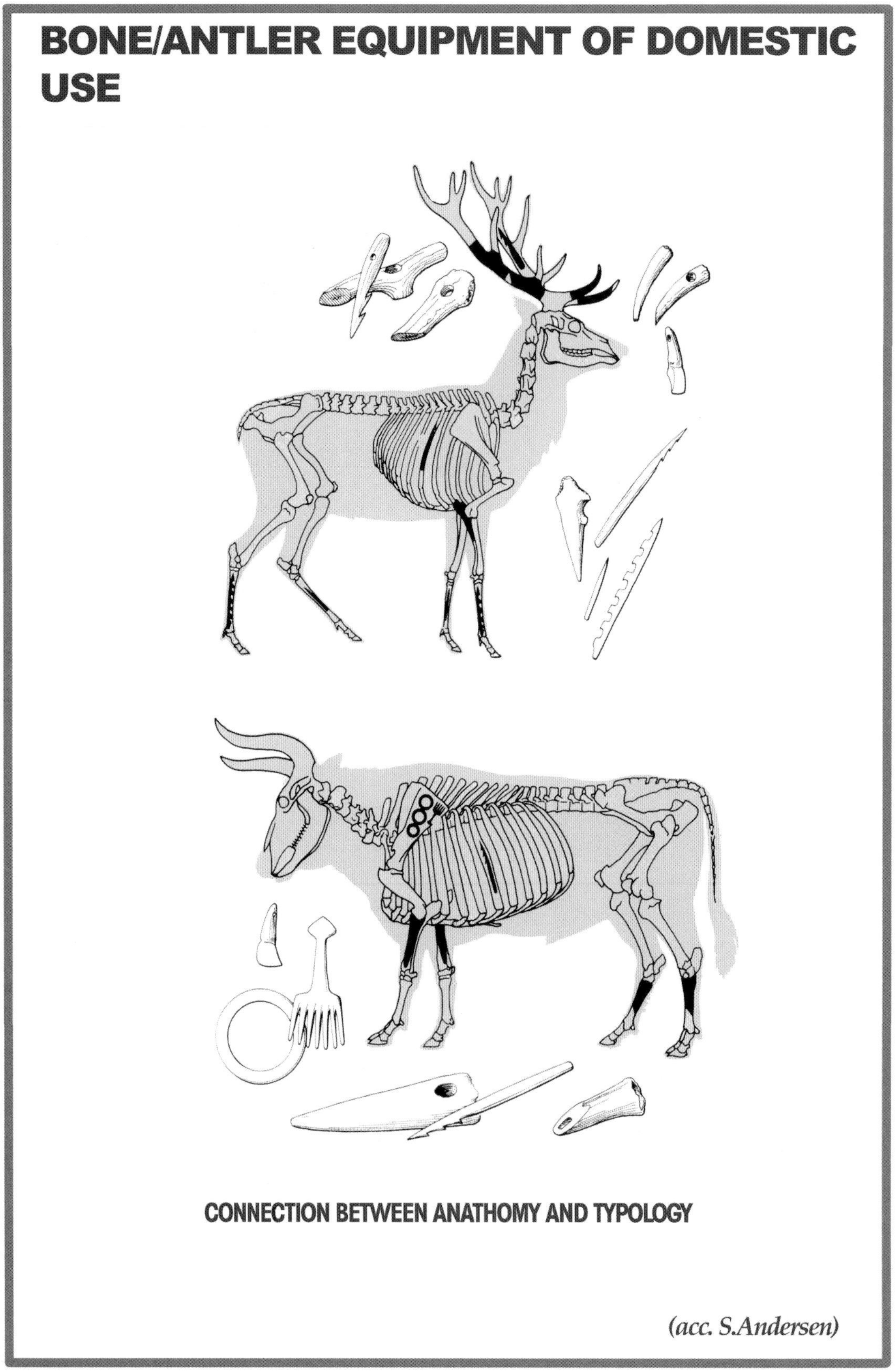

BONE/ANTLER EQUIPMENT OF DOMESTIC USE

CONNECTION BETWEEN ANATHOMY AND TYPOLOGY

(acc. S.Andersen)

Fig. 2.2.3c

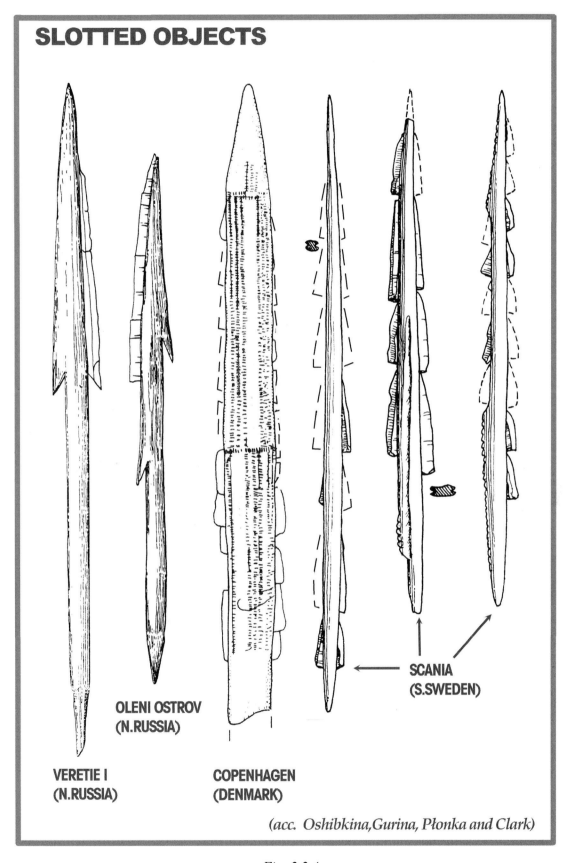

SLOTTED OBJECTS

VERETIE I
(N.RUSSIA)

OLENI OSTROV
(N.RUSSIA)

COPENHAGEN
(DENMARK)

SCANIA
(S.SWEDEN)

(acc. Oshibkina, Gurina, Płonka and Clark)

Fig. 2.2.4

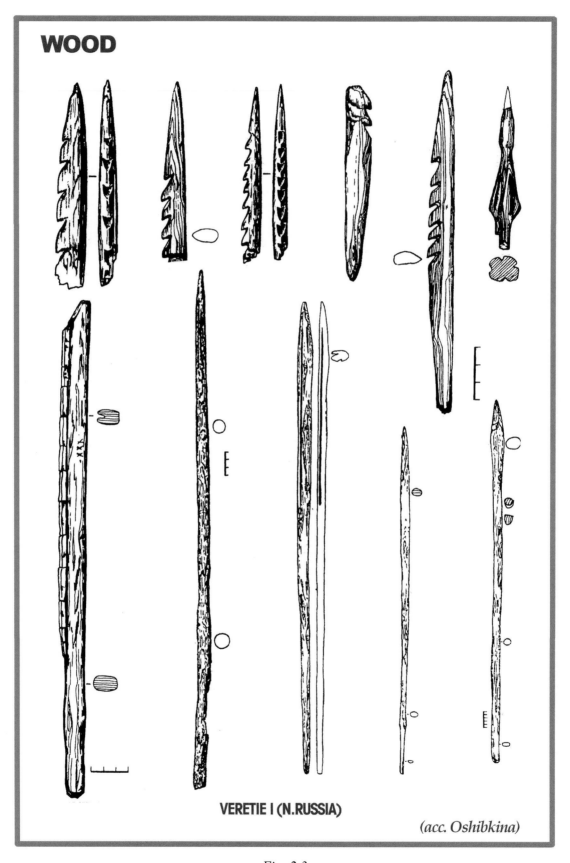

WOOD

VERETIE I (N.RUSSIA)

(acc. Oshibkina)

Fig. 2.3

in Denmark and Vis I in northern Russia), formally differentiated for that matter (Danish finds are characterized by a narrowed grip, while some examples from Russia are not, but they come in two sizes, big and small).

These bows were used with a variety of arrows (cf.) of differentiated construction, always however on shafts which were chiefly of wood (Holmegaard IV in Denmark, Stellmoor and Friesack in Germany, Loshult in Sweden, Tvaermose in Denmark, vicinity of Oldenburg in Germany). What differentiated the arrows was head style. Actually, arrows could be made entirely out of a single kind of material, like the blunt-headed arrows known from Danish Holmegaard IV, Hohen Viecheln in northern Germany, Vis I and Veretie I, both in northern Russia, which were differentiated, it is not clear whether accidentally or intentionally, by the shape of the heads.

Finally, wooden points have also been discovered (Veretie in northern Russia), identical in shape with some of the bone points (barbed – type 6, and biconical – type 16, following Grahame Clark's typology).

One should not forget the shafts of hurled weapons like harpoons and fishing spears. Fragments of shafts with still mounted bone harpoon points were uncovered at Friesack in northeastern Germany, as well as in Ulkestrup Lyng in Denmark.

Another special spear-head is the leister from Skjoldnaes. Other fields in which wood found multiple uses was water transport and fishing. Suffice it to mention the dugouts from Pesse in the Netherlands, Noyen-sur-Seine in France and Ringkloster in Denmark, and the paddles representing considerable typological variety (Star Carr in Britain, Duvensee and Rüde 2 in northern Germany, Tybrind Vig in Denmark). Added to this are passive fishing instruments like bow-nets/traps (several finds in Denmark, one in France and one in the Netherlands). Net bobbers were produced of bark (Hohen Vieheln in northern Germany, Antrea in Finland, etc.).

Overland transport made use of skis (Vis I in northern Russia) and sledges (Heinola in Finland).

Mesolithic huts were also made of wood, including wall structure (sticks of c. 2–3 cm in diameter used in Mszano in northern Poland), roof posts (many post-hole pits), beams and boards for floors (Ulkestrup Lyng in Denmark).

Domestic furnishings made of wood included clubs (Holmegaard IV in Denmark).

Finally, there is wood bark (*Betula*) used to prepare containers or recipients (Friesack in Germany, Vis I and Veretie I in northern Russia), and as handles for flint tools (blades coated with bark from Veretie).

Naturally, the limited character of this review is due to the rarity of wooden objects preserved from the Mesolithic. Nonetheless, what survives forms a picture typical of later traditional hunting forest communities, also those already described by ethnologists, suggesting that the European Mesolithic was largely "wooden" in nature, stone having dominated the archaeological record solely because of its obvious durability as material. Even so, it would be incorrect to assume that the wooden side of Mesolithic culture was the same everywhere in Europe. Some of the

surviving objects (bows, paddles and arrows with wooden heads, huts) are strongly suggestive of variety, which we are not equipped to describe.

2.3.1. Boats

Boats were an important means of transport for Mesolithic man, not only for the more far-flung expeditions (for example, from the Peloponnese to Melos island in search of obsidian or from Tuscany and Provence to Corsica and Sardinia), but also for everyday fishing, especially in the lake districts.

Nothing but dugouts have been discovered so far (Fig. 2.3.1a–c). These were produced from tree trunks (oak, for instance). Judging from ethnological data, the methods included part burning and part cutting and scooping out with relatively heavy stone tools, such as the unpolished flint axes and adzes (cf.) mounted transversally in tubular antler handles (Hohen Viecheln in eastern Germany) and the polished stone axes known from Scandinavia. Interestingly, the territorial range of these heavy tools, unpolished and polished, roughly corresponded to the region of young Würmian lakes, the biggest concentration of such inland water reservoirs rich in fish on the European continent. We have no idea what tools were used to make boats in regions lying further to the south (Noyen-sur-Seine in the Paris Basin).

Dugouts were a few meters long. Examples are known from southern Scandinavia (Ringkloster), the Netherlands (Pesse) and France (Noyen-sur-Seine). Paddles used with these boats have been found at Duvensee (Germany) and Star Carr (Great Britain), as well as at Tybrind Vig (Denmark-painted) and Rüde 2 (Germany).

2.3.2. Skis and sledges

Fragments of wooden runners from either skis or a sledge found in northeastern Europe remain unique in the archaeological record. Their evidently northern provenience is justified environmentally by the need to follow hunted game in large open spaces (Fig. 2.3.2).

Skis are known from Vis I and Veretie I, both sites in northern Russia. Two variants have been recorded, one with long pointed and upturned tips (Veretie type after Georgi Burov) and the other with transverse tips topped with carved elk or animal heads (Vis type). These finds are unique because of the raw material, but the custom of using skis was quite common among the early hunting communities of northern Europe, especially in the marginal forest zone bordering with the tundra. Hunting scenes preserved among the Zalavruga petroglyphs (North Russia) are excellent proof of this.

Sledge runners from the Mesolithic have been recorded in Finland (Heinola and Saarijärvi) and Russia (Vis I) and later specimens also exist. The Mesolithic runners are long (up to 2.5 m), boat-shaped, with structural holes on the sides. Wooden platforms must have been mounted on pairs of such runners, to be pulled by dog teams (dog as a species is known from Mesolithic Finland) or by reindeer.

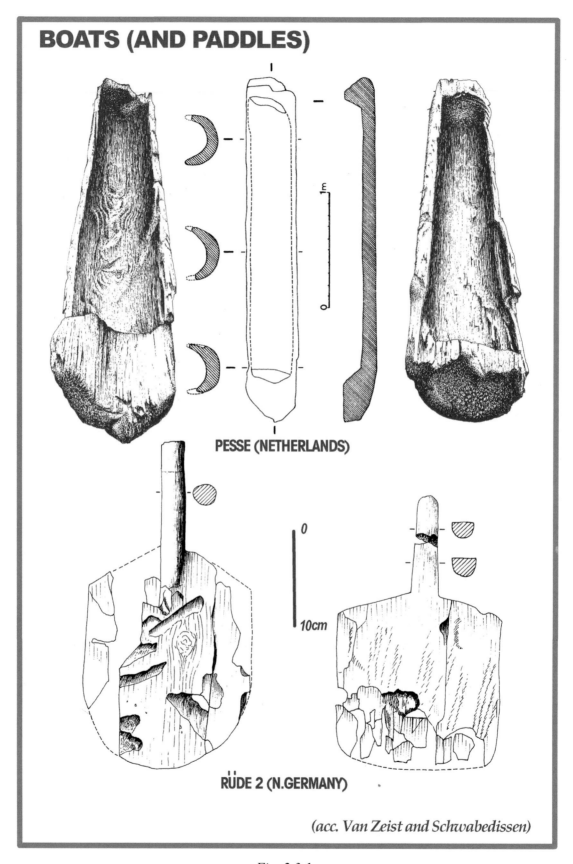

BOATS (AND PADDLES)

PESSE (NETHERLANDS)

RÜDE 2 (N.GERMANY)

(acc. Van Zeist and Schwabedissen)

Fig. 2.3.1a

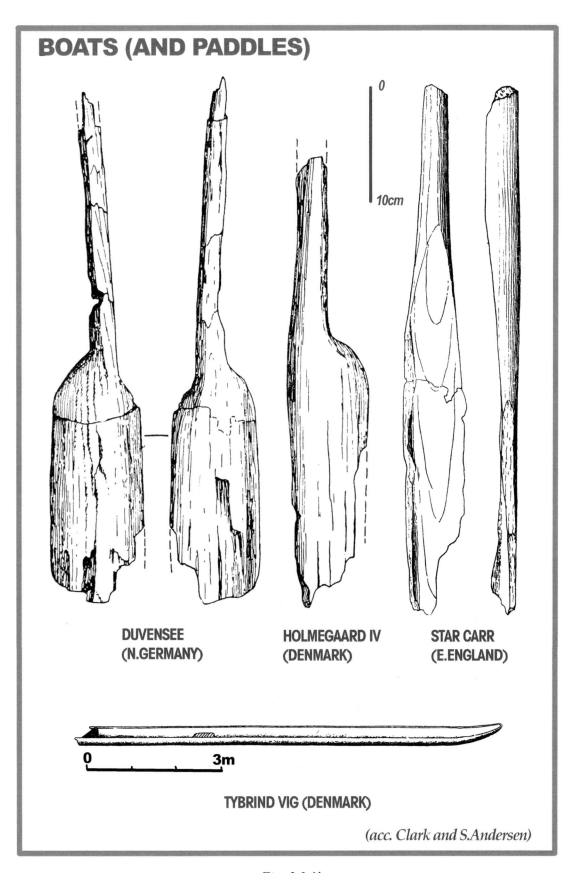

BOATS (AND PADDLES)

0

10cm

DUVENSEE
(N.GERMANY)

HOLMEGAARD IV
(DENMARK)

STAR CARR
(E.ENGLAND)

0   3m

TYBRIND VIG (DENMARK)

(acc. Clark and S.Andersen)

Fig. 2.3.1b

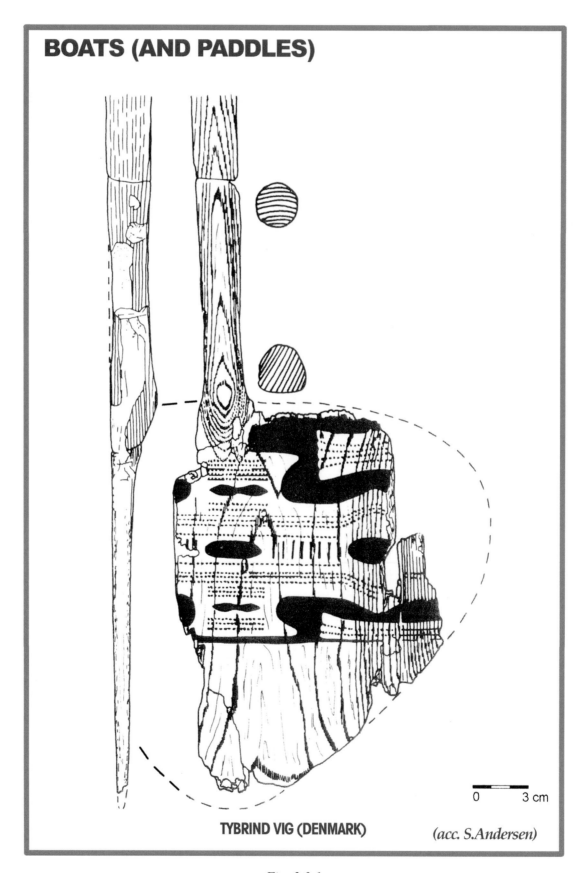

Fig. 2.3.1c

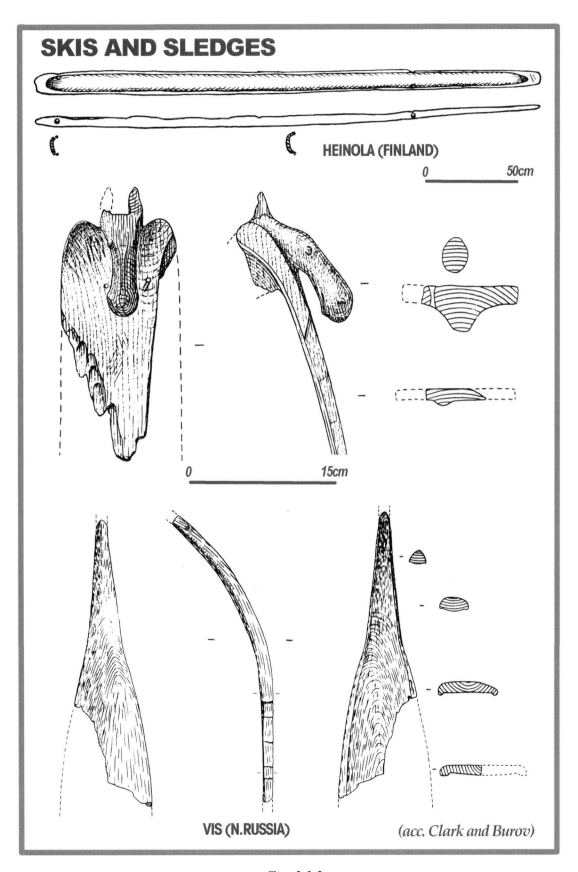

SKIS AND SLEDGES

HEINOLA (FINLAND)

0   50cm

0   15cm

VIS (N.RUSSIA)   *(acc. Clark and Burov)*

Fig. 2.3.2

2.4. Hunting gear

Mesolithic communities exploited big and small forest game. Some of the ways of catching fish and land and marine animals can also be called hunting (spearing fish and harpooning land-game, cf., for instance). Appropriate arms are required for the purpose. Passive forms of hunting (traps) have not been evidenced for the period, although they surely must have been in use.

The weapons used for the purpose were hurled, a form known practically since the appearance of man which had become highly specialized and regionally differentiated by the time the Mesolithic arrived.

A hunter could either hurl a weapon by hand (spear, harpoon) or fling it mechanically (bow and arrow). The first method seems better adapted either to a water environment (spear), or land hunting (harpoon) where distances are not big and the hunted animal is often of considerable size. The second method gives better results when hunting from a distance, permitting accuracy and piercing strength impossible to achieve when throwing by hand. The bow and arrow may have also been used to hunt smaller fish (e.g. pike, cf., hit by a barbed point, found at the bottom of the Kunda lake in Estonia) and animals gathering at a waterhole from a tree top or from overhanging branches.

The above remarks are based on ethnological studies and on some fortunate and exceptional archaeological discoveries in the form of almost complete spearheads, as well as arrowheads and spearheads embedded in animal skeletons (cf. below).

Nevertheless, the archaeological reality of Mesolithic finds is that most objects interpreted as hunting weapons are found outside any functional context. The record yields either alleged stone projectiles (or constituent parts) without shafts or much less frequent harpoons and spearheads made of organic materials. Bows are extremely rare. In many cases, it is simply impossible to distinguish functionally between arrowheads and spear- and harpoon-heads.

2.4.1. Bow

The bow is a quintessence of the Mesolithic. This main propulsor of various projectiles, chiefly highly variegated arrows (cf. "Arrows and arrowheads"), but also of fishing spears perhaps (cf.), assured a number of unique characteristics: speed, energy, accuracy, range, and last but not least, effectiveness (cf. "Aurochs from Prejlerup"). Known probably from the Upper Paleolithic (Gravettian, Magdalenian) and developed in the Terminal Paleolithic (among others, the Tanged Points Complex), it peaked in popularity in the Mesolithic.

The rare examples known from the period (Fig. 2.4.1a–b), made of yew wood, are big and simple, one-part weapons with thinned grips and pointed endings (Holmegaard IV in Denmark). Contrasting with them are big and small bows without grip (Vis I in northern Russia) and with broadened, cleaver-like endings (Vis, Veretie I). Finds are too few for this typological list to be considered as closed.

In rock art images from the Spanish Levant (Cueva de los Caballos), huge simple bows are represented. The art itself is believed to be from the Late Mesolithic or (and this seems much more likely) Early Neolithic, but the chronological attribution (6500/6000 cal. BC?) is hardly an obstacle to assuming that the rock painting depicted a reality known to the artist since at least the Late Mesolithic, if not earlier.

2.4.2. Arrows and arrowheads

The arrow is a projectile shot from a bow or another weapon which would have permitted good aim. Due to archaeological considerations (shafts are practically never found) arrowheads are frequently impossible to distinguish from spearheads, although logic would suggest that the former should be smaller as a rule.

The Mesolithic arrow had a wooden or bone shaft and an arrowhead(s) most commonly made of stone, but also occasionally of bone (Shigirskoe points in the East – Clark's type 16). It could also be carved from a single piece of wood (e.g. blunted specimens). Some could have also been barbed? (wooden specimen from Veretie I in Russia).

Judging from the very few preserved stone specimens mounted on wooden shafts (Fig. 2.4.2a–c), as well as stone arrowheads embedded in the bones of animals and humans (cf. monograph by Dymitro Y. Nuzhnyi), arrows can be generally divided into several groups. The first consists of arrows armed with stone arrowheads, further subdivided into composite and uncomposite examples. The latter are single points mounted at the top of the shaft. They form at least two internally differentiated groups: tanged points (cf., also experiments by Anders Fischer) and trapezes (Tvaermose in Denmark, vicinity of Oldenburg in northern Germany). The composite group, on the other hand, consists of a number of microliths mounted at the top of the shaft (Loshult in Sweden, cf., Friesack in Germany) or found in sets embedded in the skeletons of hunted animals (from three to 14 in a set) in Denmark (Vig and Prejlerup, cf. "Aurochs from Prejlerup").

The proposed classification is quite poor and surely does not exhaust all possibilities, but finds are so rare that little can be done in this respect. There exists other evidence for the function of Mesolithic tanged points (cf.) and microliths. It comes in the form of characteristic impact negatives of arrows entering an animal's body, as well as damage caused by removal from the body (broken pedoncules, as for example in Stellmoor, cf.), not to mention traces of resin on the microliths (Star Carr in Britain).

Neither should the tanged points mounted on bone shafts from Olenyi Ostrov (cf.) in Russian Karelia be neglected here.

A special form of arrow was the blunt wooden arrowhead forming a single piece with the shaft, found solely in the European Plain. Grahame Clark suggested, based on ethnographical data, that these projectiles served a very special purpose, namely, they were used to hunt birds and small fur mammals, where the objective was to protect precious feathers or fur.

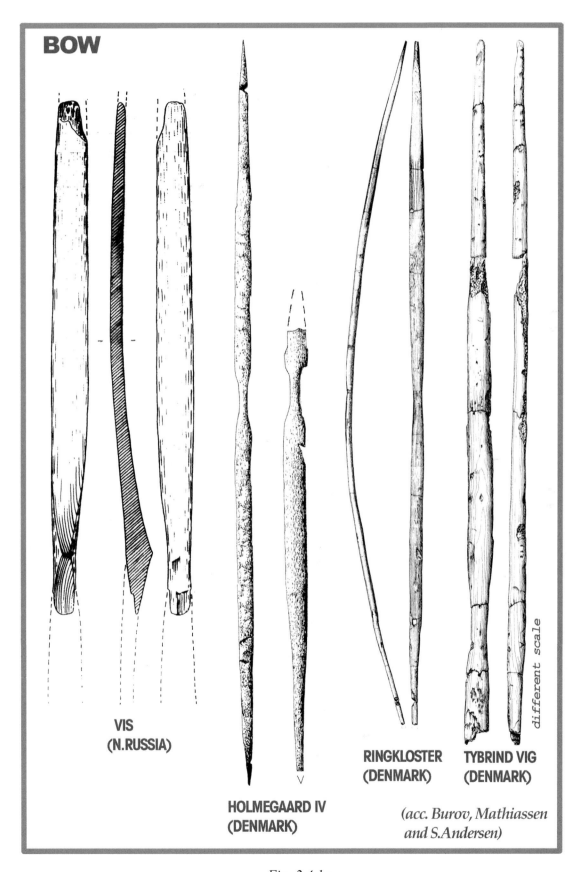

BOW

VIS
(N.RUSSIA)

HOLMEGAARD IV
(DENMARK)

RINGKLOSTER
(DENMARK)

TYBRIND VIG
(DENMARK)

different scale

*(acc. Burov, Mathiassen
and S.Andersen)*

Fig. 2.4.1a

BOW

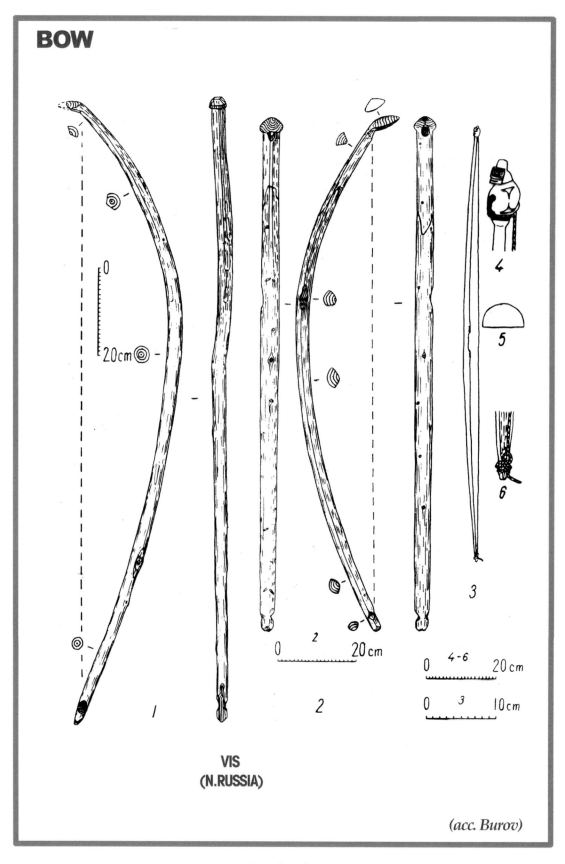

VIS
(N.RUSSIA)

(acc. Burov)

Fig. 2.4.1b

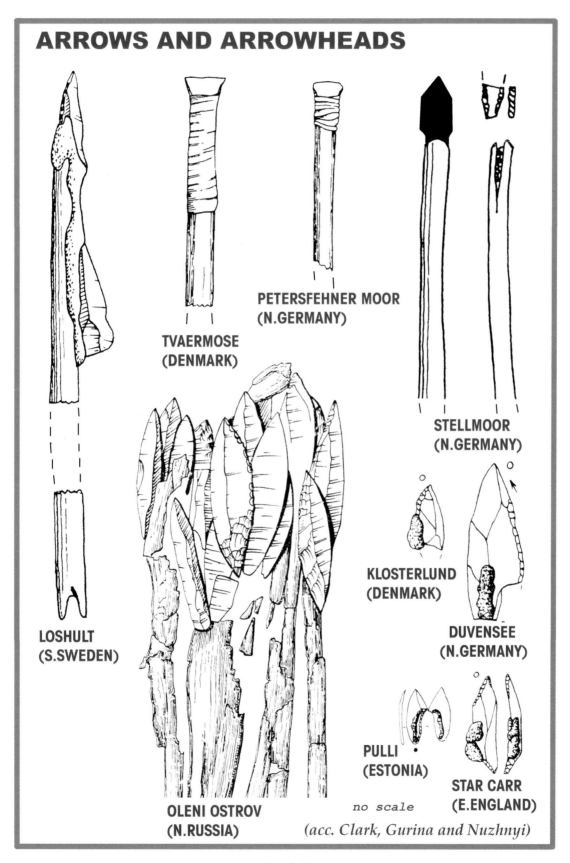

ARROWS AND ARROWHEADS

TVAERMOSE
(DENMARK)

PETERSFEHNER MOOR
(N.GERMANY)

STELLMOOR
(N.GERMANY)

LOSHULT
(S.SWEDEN)

KLOSTERLUND
(DENMARK)

DUVENSEE
(N.GERMANY)

PULLI
(ESTONIA)

STAR CARR
(E.ENGLAND)

OLENI OSTROV
(N.RUSSIA)

no scale

(acc. Clark, Gurina and Nuzhnyi)

Fig. 2.4.2a

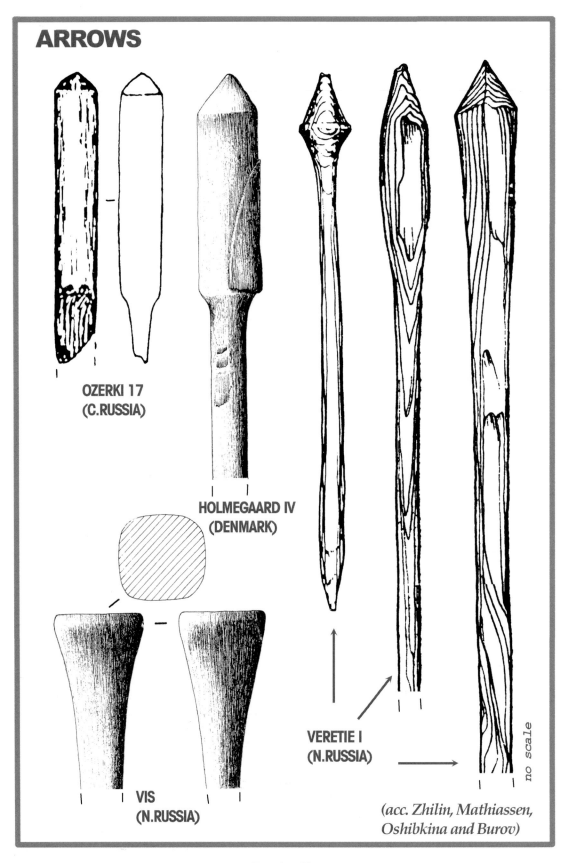

ARROWS

OZERKI 17
(C.RUSSIA)

HOLMEGAARD IV
(DENMARK)

VERETIE I
(N.RUSSIA)

VIS
(N.RUSSIA)

(acc. Zhilin, Mathiassen, Oshibkina and Burov)

no scale

Fig. 2.4.2b

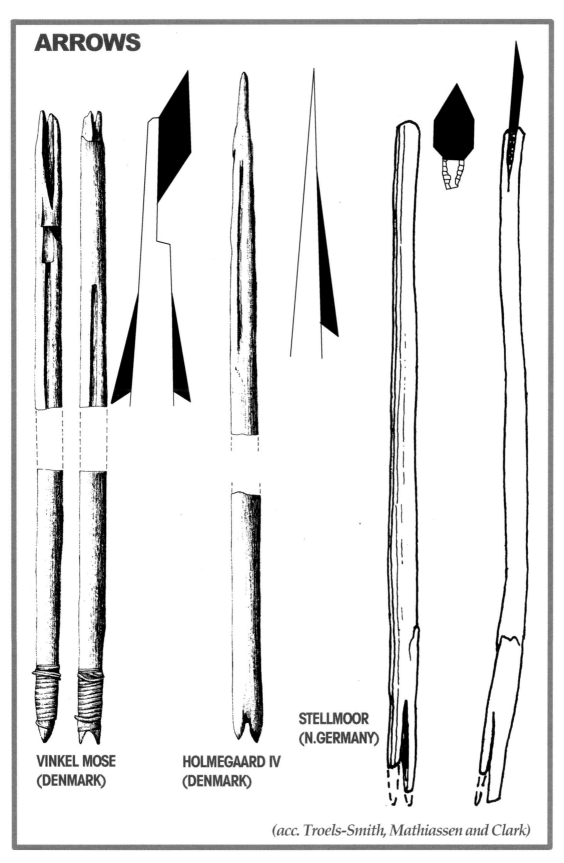

ARROWS

VINKEL MOSE
(DENMARK)

HOLMEGAARD IV
(DENMARK)

STELLMOOR
(N.GERMANY)

(acc. Troels-Smith, Mathiassen and Clark)

Fig. 2.4.2c

Two forms of heads of these weapons can be distinguished, one like a cylinder with rounded ends, the other like a reversed cone. The former type is known from Denmark and Germany, from the Maglemosian or to be more specific, from its Svaerdborg (Holmegaard IV) and Duvensee (Hohen Viecheln) groups, while the latter type from the Ertebøllian, as well as from northeastern Europe (in association with assemblages of the Kundian and related types, e.g. Vis I).

It seems that the morphological similarity of specimens from territorially distant units, such as the Danish-German and Russian finds, is due to the nature of the raw material and the simple form of the discussed projectile.

It should be pointed out that the East European Plain has yielded undoubted counterparts in bone for the presented kinds of arrows. These are the so-called Shigirskoe points, variant with long stem (type 16 in Grahame Clark's classification), known also as a matter of fact as a variant in wood (Veretie I).

2.4.3. Fishing spears and harpoons for hunting

Fishing spears appear to be a specific and highly local adaptive measure, designed to take full advantage of what the environment could offer. This invention, which is known from the central and northeastern regions, is exceptionally well represented in the lake districts circumventing the North and Baltic seas.

The pike (cf.) skeleton with harpoon still embedded in it, found at the bottom of the Kunda lake in Estonia, as well as the double-mounted harpoons from Star Carr (?) and various other later double mounted examples cited by Grahame Clark, not to mention fish hunted with harpoons (also cited by Clark) and grass-wrapped objects from Friesack in Germany and Veretie I in northern Russia indicate that different harpoons (mostly with small barbs) were in common use around the Baltic (cf. "Points, *sagaies*"); neither should one forget the totally wooden leister from Skjoldnaes (Denmark) .

Naturally, not all bone barbed points were fishing spears, as demonstrated by two harpoons used for hunting elk in Great Britain (cf. "Harpoons from High Furlong").

Spearheads and harpoons came either singly (Kunda, Friesack) or in pairs (Star Carr) (Fig. 2.4.3a–b).

Apart from the Würmian lake district, barbed fishing spears and hunting harpoons have also been recorded in the East European Lowland and on the Upper Volga, also in lakeland context. They are missing entirely – and presumably not accidentally – from the rest of the continent (with the exception of flat harpoons present on the northern slopes of the Alps).

2.4.4. Shafts from Stellmoor (Fig. 2.4.4)

The Ahrensburgian, that is, Final Paleolithic (Dryas 3) site of Stellmoor in northern Germany yielded a few wooden shafts (with notches at either end), some of them still armed with broken tangs of flint arrowheads or tanged points, indicating the function of the latter. The arrowheads were broken off presumably when the valuable wooden shafts were retrieved from the carcasses of hunted animals.

Add to this the information about two sets of arrows from Oleni Ostrov (Russian Karelia, cf.) and the pioneer experimental research on the function of Lyngby points conducted by Anders Fischer.

2.4.5. Arrow from Loshult (Fig. 2.4.5)

The unique discovery of two armatures (backed points) inserted into a one-sided slot at the top of a wooden shaft should be interpreted as a complete arrow; it also has a V-shaped notch. Apart from an unpublished find from Friesack in Germany (personal information from Bernhard Gramsch), this is the only example of non-trapezoid and geometric armatures mounted as an arrowhead on a shaft.

2.4.6. Hafting trapezes (Fig. 2.4.6)

Trapezes mounted transversally (the tip unretouched longer edge) of wooden hafts were discovered at Tvaermose, on Fünen island in Denmark, near Oldenburg in Schleswig-Holstein (Germany) and also in Egypt. Traces of wear (impact scars) on numerous unhafted Polish or Ukrainian examples confirm that symmetrical trapezes were mounted transversally as a rule.

2.4.7. Auroch from Prejlerup (Fig. 2.4.7)

This Danish find of an auroch, interpreted as an animal that was hit but not hunted down, has provided us with information on the mounting of arrowheads of the composite type. The animal had been hit a number of times, but the fourteen microliths that were found among the bones seem to represent less than fourteen hits. Thus, it was conceived that the microliths had been mounted in groups of three or four, bringing down the number of arrows to five or six. After all, a similar auroch from Vig in Denmark was hunted down with just three microliths!

2.4.8. Pike from Kunda lake (Fig. 2.4.8)

At the bottom of the fossil Kunda lake in Estonia, in a layer dated to the 8th millennium cal. BC, R. Indreko discovered a complete skeleton of pike fish, preserved in anatomical order and with a barbed point of Kunda type (type 6 in Grahame Clark's classification) still embedded in the back. The point must be what was left of a single fishing spear; similar barbed points mounted singly on shafts were excavated by Bernhard Gramsch in Friesack in eastern Germany (Pritzerbe type 8 in Clark's classification) and in Ulkestrup Lyng (Denmark – type 7). Grahame Clark noted examples of fish skeletons pierced with harpoons also from later North-European contexts.

2.4.9. Quivers and handles from Oleni Ostrov (Fig. 2.4.9)

Oleni Ostrov on Onega Lake in Russian Karelia is an

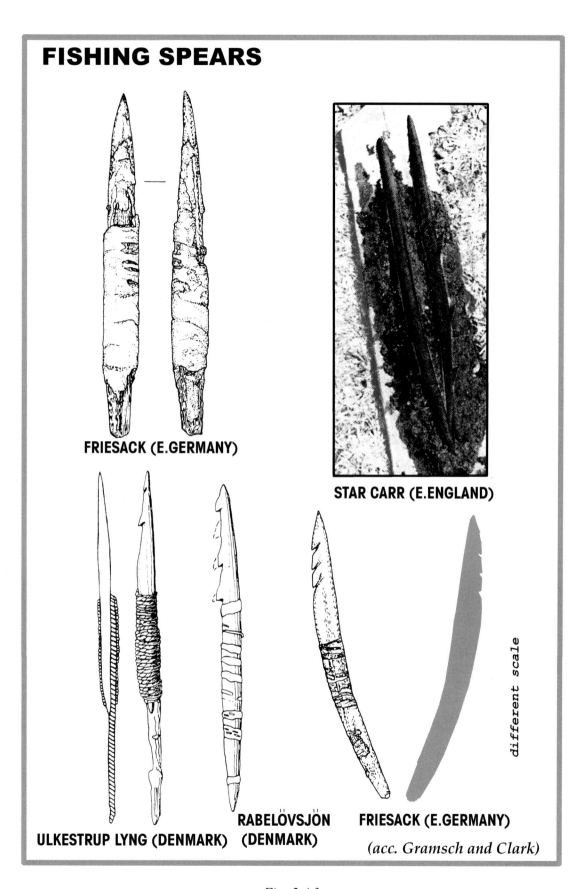

FISHING SPEARS

FRIESACK (E.GERMANY)

STAR CARR (E.ENGLAND)

ULKESTRUP LYNG (DENMARK)

RABELÖVSJÖN (DENMARK)

FRIESACK (E.GERMANY)

different scale

(acc. Gramsch and Clark)

Fig. 2.4.3a

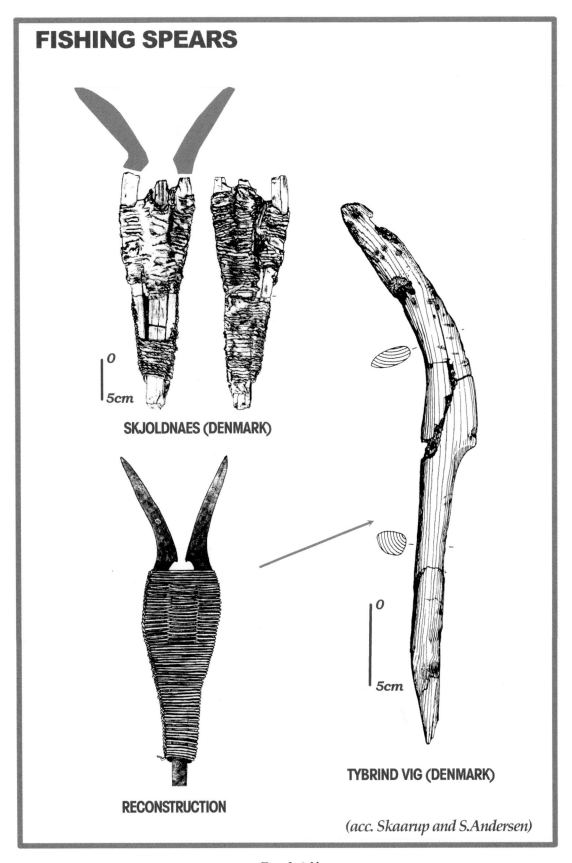

FISHING SPEARS

SKJOLDNAES (DENMARK)

RECONSTRUCTION

TYBRIND VIG (DENMARK)

(acc. Skaarup and S.Andersen)

Fig. 2.4.3b

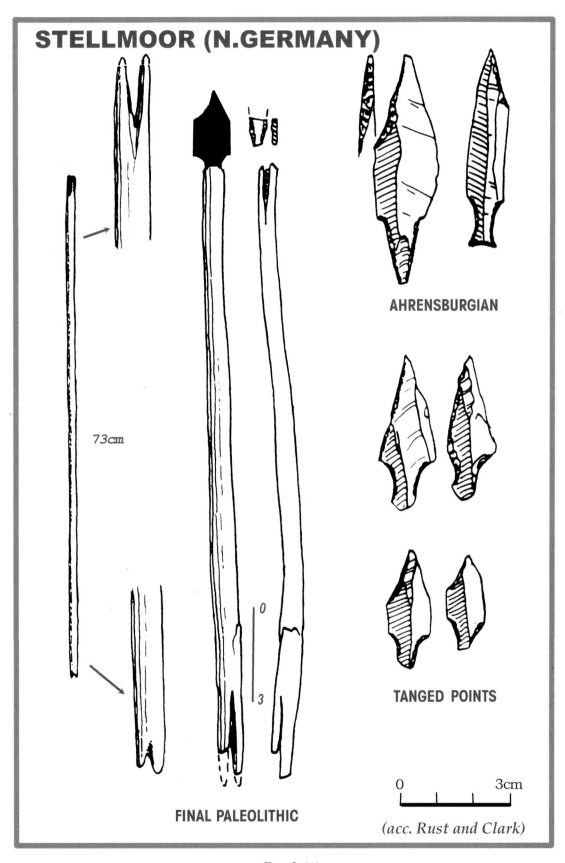

STELLMOOR (N.GERMANY)

73cm

0

3

AHRENSBURGIAN

TANGED POINTS

0   3cm

FINAL PALEOLITHIC

(acc. Rust and Clark)

Fig. 2.4.4

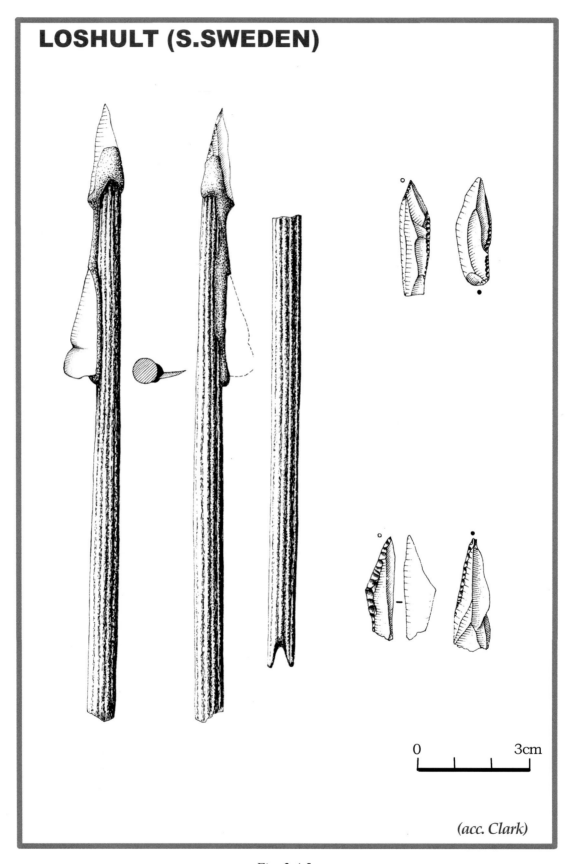

LOSHULT (S.SWEDEN)

0   3cm

(acc. Clark)

Fig. 2.4.5

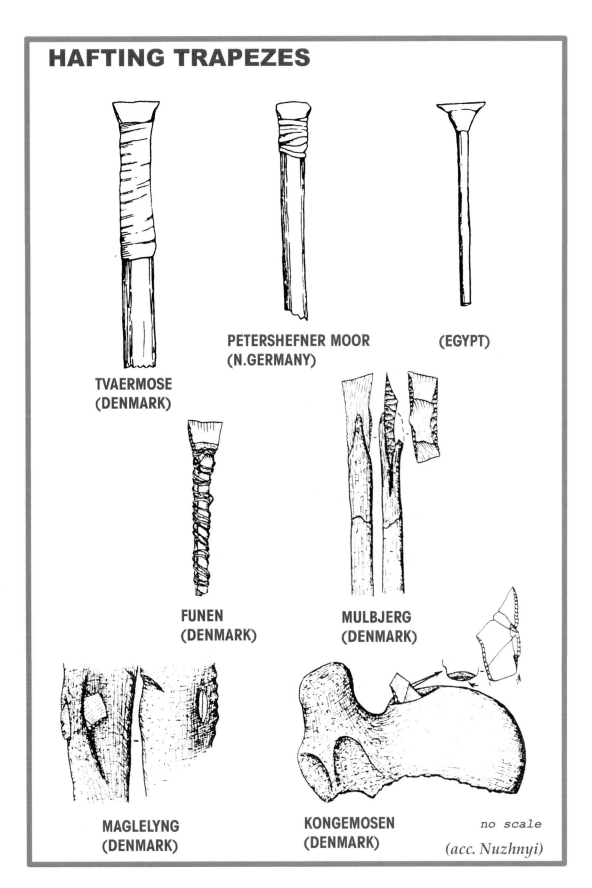

HAFTING TRAPEZES

TVAERMOSE
(DENMARK)

PETERSHEFNER MOOR
(N.GERMANY)

(EGYPT)

FUNEN
(DENMARK)

MULBJERG
(DENMARK)

MAGLELYNG
(DENMARK)

KONGEMOSEN
(DENMARK)

no scale

(acc. Nuzhnyi)

Fig. 2.4.6

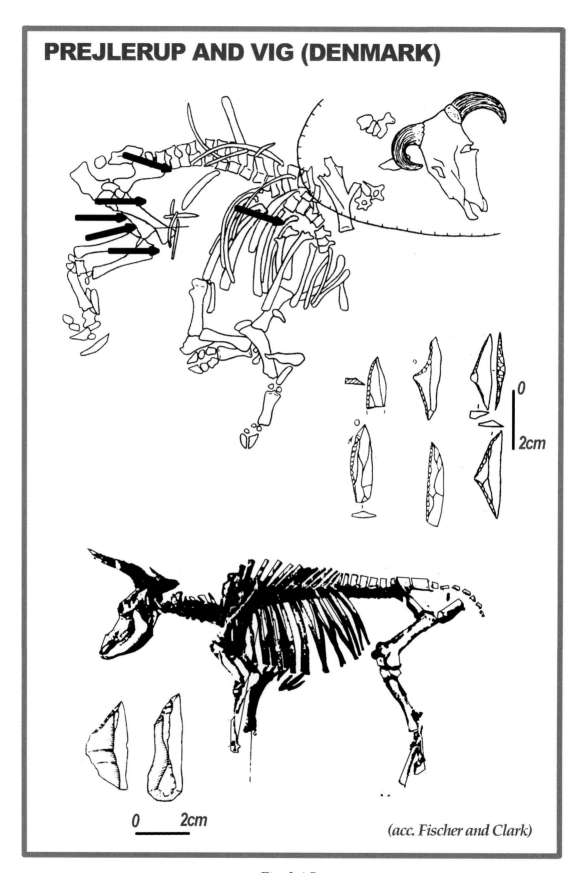

PREJLERUP AND VIG (DENMARK)

0

2cm

0   2cm

(acc. Fischer and Clark)

Fig. 2.4.7

PIKE FROM KUNDA (ESTONIA)

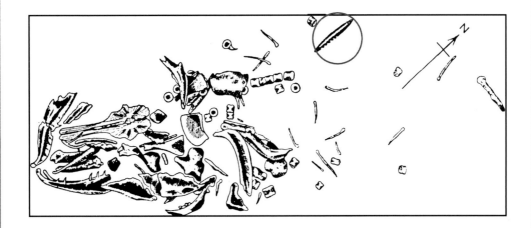

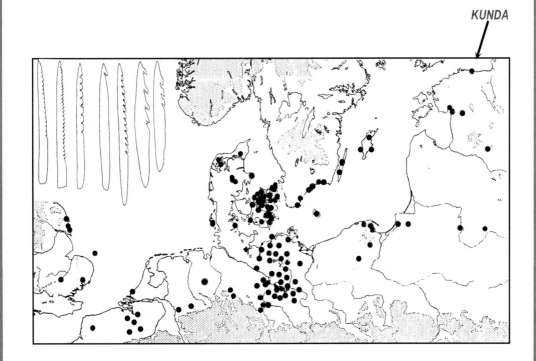

SPEARHEADS, FINETOOTHED IN EUROPE

(acc. Indreko, Clark, Gramsch, S.Kozłowski and Verhoven)

Fig. 2.4.8

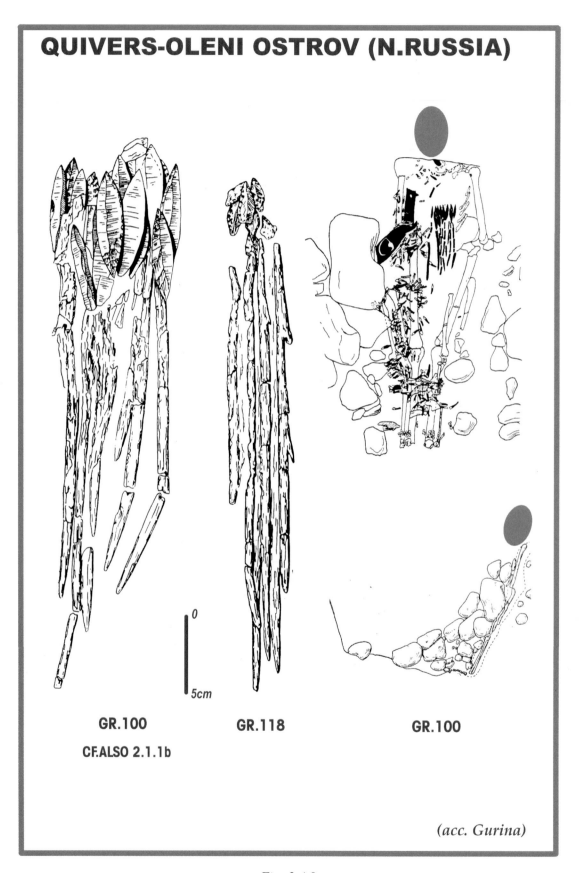

Fig. 2.4.9

island with a big Mesolithic cemetery of the classical Kunda culture (c. 180 richly furnished inhumations). Grave no. 100 yielded a set of bone barbed points or harpoons, armed with flint arrowheads, the tanged points being of willow-leaf shape. In another grave (no. 118), a dozen or more quartz pedonculated points were discovered in similar position. No stronger argument in favor of the functional interpretation of tanged points is needed!

Oleni Ostrov also yielded two hafted 'home' tools made of flint: an end-scraper and a burin.

2.4.10. Harpoons from High Furlong (Fig. 2.4.10)

Unique find from a peat bog, preserved together with the skeleton of hunted elk (including evidence of cuts on the bones). The points, which were made of antler (type 9 according to Clark), were discovered near one of the back legs of the animal. They were of the Paleolithic type and age (11th/12th millennium cal. BC) and their position in the excavation suggested that two harpoon heads may have been mounted on a single shaft somewhat like a trident but with two prongs, resembling much later Scandinavian finds cited by Grahame Clark, as well as a find of two pairs of harpoons from Star Carr (Britain).

Overall, at least some of the big-barbed harpoons of the Mesolithic, similarly as in Late Magdalenian, Hamburgian and Tanged Points times, were used for inland big-game hunting (A. Rust's suggestion with regard to the harpoon from Meiendorf piercing the shoulder-blade of a reindeer).

2.5. How?

2.5.1. Numbers and percentages

The 1950s brought a quantitative revolution in European prehistory with François Bordes acting as its Robespierre. Bordes was the first to attempt a description of the entire tool kit, using a specially constructed "language" or "list of types". He was also the first to observe the recurrence of some of the percentage indices, which led him to the correct conclusion that the quantitative element in the description of the world is as important as the qualitative one.

Other local lists followed in the wake of Bordes' list, usually adapted to a given macroregion, period and time (Denise de Sonneville-Bordes for the Upper Paleolithic, Jean-Georges Rozoy, Henri de Lumley and Max Escalon de Fonton, A. Bohmers, A. Wouters etc.), and everyone rested in the fond belief that here was an excellent tool for comparative studies of different assemblages (Fig. 2.5.1a–c).

Agreement was lacking, however, as to how to interpret the differences between assemblages. Initially, it was thought that the differences were primarily cultural (French researchers), other interpretations suggested a more functional approach (L. Binford). Today, it is assumed that quantitative differences between stone tool assemblages may be caused by any of three factors, namely:

- They can reflect a relatively constant internal set of proportions that are characteristic of a given cultural tradition (each having a specific ratio that is typical for assemblages attributed to it)
- They can be the result of the position of an assemblage in the evolutive sequence of a given cultural tradition (good examples from the Mesolithic of northern Italy, southern Germany, but also France and Denmark, cf. "Rhythms")
- They can reflect the function of a given site ("home" opposed to "hunting" site, "home" vs. "workshop/mine", etc.) and its place in the *chaine operatoire* of a given cultural tradition

The first two cases demand no special explanation and the statistical similarity between, as we believe, assemblages belonging to the same tradition or even to a specific stage in the development of a given tradition, is confirmed also and foremost by stylistic similarities.

The third case is more complicated, although obvious, considering that it is based on an assumption drawing from life experience that different kinds of activities generate different kinds of waste and tools despite being produced by representatives of a single cultural tradition (this was suggested by Stefan Krukowski in the 1930s!). Thus, sites will be differentiated by type and nature of work activities conducted on the spot: "domestic" sites will have knives, scrapers and burins, while "hunting" sites will yield numerous microliths (cf. "At home and abroad").

It may also be assumed that a higher percentage of flint concretions either entirely raw or left at an early stage of the processing will be found at mining sites (plus a few mining tools), but a neighboring workshop site will yield much more heavily exploited cores, abundant debitage and few "domestic" tools. In this case, however, the technological differentiation of product groups (cores, blades, flakes, tools) should be considered on equal basis with the tools percentage indicators.

Janusz K. Kozłowski has taken advantage of this differentiation to carry out a more advanced functional analysis on the simple assumption that each group of hunters and gatherers had similar needs, which they met in similar ways and consequently left similar traces of their activities. If we imagine the principal functional models obligatory in a hunting-gathering community ("home camp" vs. "hunting camp", "base" vs. "satellite" camp, long-lasting vs. briefly occupied camp, also "home" vs. "mine" and/or "workshop", etc.), we can also imagine the different technological and percentage structure representing in each case different assemblage models.

The "home base" sets are usually abundant, the proportions of the four technological groups (cores, flakes, blades, tools) analyzed by Janusz K. Kozłowski being as follows: few cores in advanced stages of exploitation, many blades, about the same number of flakes or less, average number of tools, including many home tools (scrapers, burins and retouched blades, also ones showing only use-wear).

The "hunting/satellite" assemblage would be character-

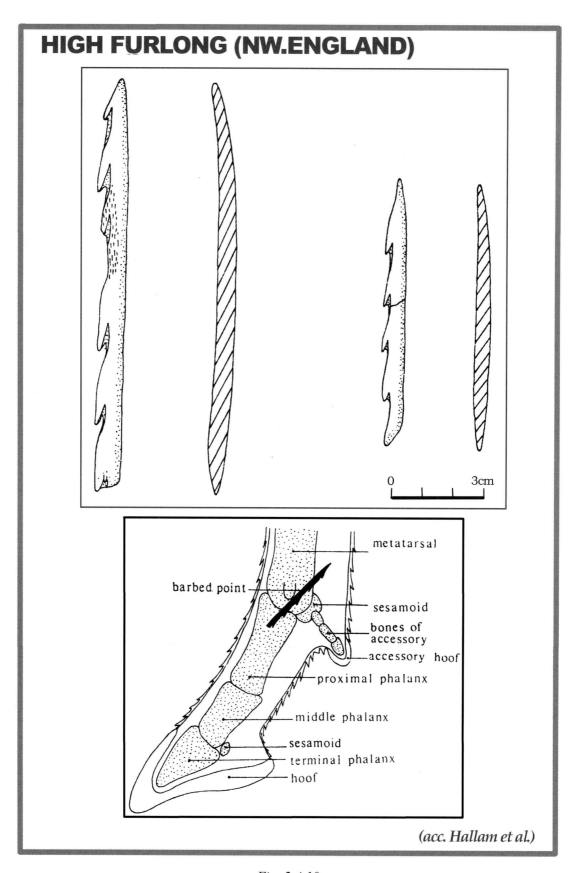

HIGH FURLONG (NW.ENGLAND)

0   3cm

metatarsal

barbed point

sesamoid

bones of
accessory

accessory hoof

proximal phalanx

middle phalanx

sesamoid

terminal phalanx

hoof

(acc. Hallam et al.)

Fig. 2.4.10

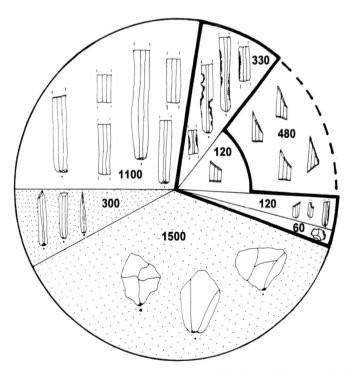

NUMBERS AND PERCENTAGES

BRECHT-MOORDENAARSVEN 2

BALEN-WEZEL STATION

HOLSBEEK-MARRANT

BELGIAN/FLANDRIAN LATE MESOLITHIC (MICROLITHS)

330

480

120

1100

300

120

60

1500

FRENCH LATE MESOLITHIC, TECHNOLOGICAL STRUCTURE

(acc. Vermeersch and Rozoy)

Fig. 2.5.1a

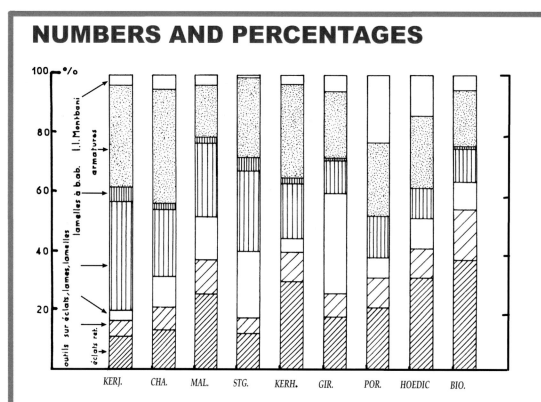

FRENCH LATE MESOLITHIC TOOLS INTERNAL STRUCTURE

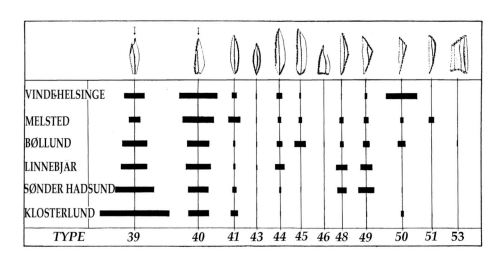

S.SCANDINAVIAN SERIATION OF MAGLEMOSIAN MICROLITHS

(acc. Rozoy and Brinch-Petersen)

Fig. 2.5.1b

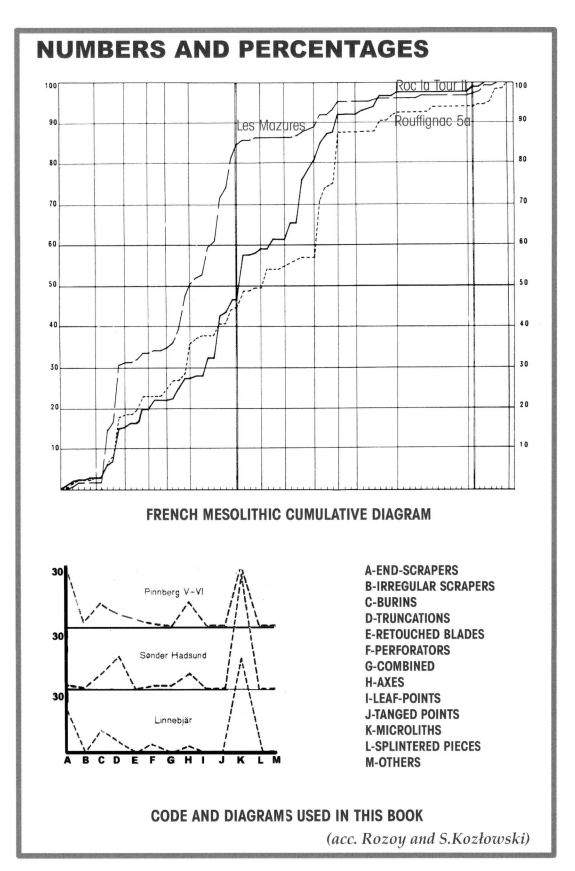

NUMBERS AND PERCENTAGES

Roc la Tour II

Les Mazures

Rouffignac 5a

FRENCH MESOLITHIC CUMULATIVE DIAGRAM

Pinnberg V–VI

Sønder Hadsund

Linnebjär

A B C D E F G H I J K L M

A-END-SCRAPERS
B-IRREGULAR SCRAPERS
C-BURINS
D-TRUNCATIONS
E-RETOUCHED BLADES
F-PERFORATORS
G-COMBINED
H-AXES
I-LEAF-POINTS
J-TANGED POINTS
K-MICROLITHS
L-SPLINTERED PIECES
M-OTHERS

CODE AND DIAGRAMS USED IN THIS BOOK

(acc. Rozoy and S.Kozłowski)

Fig. 2.b.1c

ized by a rather modest set: few tools (usually arrowheads), much less "home" tools, a few blades and flakes, almost no cores, if at all. The *chaine operatoire* is usually incomplete at such sites, unlike at "home/base" sites.

Dwellings may be connected with the former of the two, while they are extremely rare in association with the latter.

"Extracting point/mine" and "workshop" assemblages stand at the beginning of the *chaine operatoire*, contrary to "home" and "hunting" camps, which are placed at the very end. In the former, the prevailing objects represent early stages in flint processing (preformed cores, numerous cortical flakes, preliminary exploitation, eliminated useless concretions, trimming and cortical blades, unworked concretions). Selected blades are less numerous (because the best blades were taken from the workshop to be used), "home" tools are rare, while the 'mine' tools are quite abundant (thick denticulates, adzes).

The paradigm presented here (changing proportions of the technological groups) served Raymond R. Newell to develop the functional interpretations cited here ("home" vs. "hunting"). Janusz K. Kozłowski's hypothesis only broadened the interpretation. The issue becomes somewhat more complicated, however, if we take into consideration additional data, like arrow construction (composite vs. single-piece arrowheads) in particular Mesolithic cultures. It appears that arrows could be single-pointed (tanged points, trapezes) or multi-pointed (armatures). In other words, the number of these elements will differ in the analyzed assemblages not only because of their different function, but also different arrow construction.

2.5.2. "Stone" and "bone" cultures

Tools used by the Mesolithic hunter, gatherer and fisherman were dependent on a variety of factors, of which only some were dependent on man. Need was the first factor and it is addressed by man in every age appropriately to means and circumstances. In the Mesolithic, this meant basically seeking the right implement to fulfill the necessary functions or activities demanded by the hunting and gathering way of life. Consequently man used a variety of techniques and materials to produce various "domestic", "hunting" and "fishing" tools (cf. "At home and abroad") and to build the required structures, etc.

Considering the situation overall, the needs of all the developed communities of the time were more or less similar, hence the tool kit in various regions could not have been much differentiated from the functional point of view. At "home", one needed scrapers, knives/blades and burins (the latter not in every region); bows, arrows, spears and harpoons were used mostly outdoors for hunting, while fishing required dugouts, paddles, nets, traps, hooks, spears, etc.

Differences are expected to appear when technology and style are considered. These were stimulated by a number of factors, an important one being cultural tradition and skills inherited from previous generations and sometimes

modified over time. Raw materials were also a factor, different regions being rich (or poor) in different rocks which demanded different processing techniques and which determined (and even limited) the shape and size of the final products.

Limitations ensuing from dressing techniques heavily restricted the style of stone/flint objects; hence, it is only natural to expect similar or even identical solutions , especially in the case of simple forms, such as very short end-scrapers and backed bladelets and points, triangles etc. Even so, regional differences could and have been observed and mapped (cf. "Atlas"), determining territories characterized by a common style, clearly separated from other areas and other styles.

It should be reiterated that material was as much a factor determining the form of investigated Mesolithic products, as was tradition. For instance, Scandinavia with the exception of Scania, but adding the East Baltic states had little flint, but abundant sources of quartz and quartzite, as well as slate and other rocks (including magmatic). This had enormous influence on the morphology of Mesolithic chipped and polished stone products.

Wherever there was little good stone for chipping, the local communities invested in other materials, like bone and antler (and naturally wood), giving rise to what is called a "bone" culture. For these people, stone tools were marginal in their kit, which was made up chiefly of bone products (at Kunda-Lammasmägi in Estonia a few chipped-stone products accompanied hundreds of bone tools!). The sheer number of bone and antler products in the circum-Baltic area prompted Grahame Clark and R. Indreko to identify separate territories occupied by "bone" Maglemosian (in the west) and Kunda (in the east) cultures. However, in the light of newer research, the difference between "stone" and "bone" cultures seems to be purely ecological and the Mesolithic hunters' knowledge of style ("typological potential") was broader than required and included both the "bone" and "stone/flint" fields.

2.5.3. The last "Indians" of Europe?

Our ideas concerning the European Mesolithic were developed over a fairly long period of time, partly by our youthful reading (Karl May, James Fenimore Cooper, James Oliver Curwood) and partly by our predecessors in research, mostly local amateur scientists, priests and pastors, retired officers and teachers, who had no methodological tools to help them in understanding a very difficult set of sources. The present picture of the Mesolithic is a factor of these two trends, the Mesolithic hunters of Europe appearing in this literature as the "Last Indians" of Europe who hunted with microliths (geometric ones, naturally) small game (clearly!!! not big animals). The stereotype is so strong that anything said in opposition goes virtually unheard. Wiktor Stoczkowski's recent discussion of the issue is worth recommendatiom.

Despite little hope of success, I would like to deal with the stereotype in this book. Primarily, I want to distinguish between three aspects: firstly, what we actually know, meaning our knowledge on the matter; secondly, what we believe, meaning the ideas we have formulated or adopted; and thirdly, the current stereotypes.

Stereotypes

The most crucial of the incorrect ideas is that the Mesolithic is some kind of unity that shows little cultural/stylistic or economic differentiation, filling in the "hiatus" between the Paleolithic and Neolithic, perhaps subdivided into the "Tardenoisian" (= geometric microliths) and "Maglemosian" (= bone harpoons). Other important common suppositions could be that "microlithisation" and "geometrization" of arrowhead elements were typical of all the Mesolithic and that "geometric microliths" were used to hunt small game. Finally, that people in the Mesolithic had this mysterious predilection to put up their camps on sandy rises and as a last resort to occupy rock shelters.

What we actually know

Countering these stereotypes is actual knowledge, which can be summed up as follows:

1) The Mesolithic flint industries were highly differentiated in terms of style, technology and statistical structure, and the same can be said of the bone/antler industries. This is actually a standard in all of European prehistory and it draws from the regional differentiation of various traditions. In the light of this, it is surprising to note how some colleagues shy from using existing taxonomic names, preferring instead the dull descriptors like "Early" or "Late" Mesolithic.

2) These differentiated traditions are fairly well dated as a rule, especially by the radiocarbon method. They demonstrate a long-lasting resistance to change, which makes them conservative in consequence.

3) The Mesolithic population was highly specialized in hunting, fishing and gathering activities, exploiting successfully and with differentiated strategies many different biotopes, using appropriately adapted techniques and differentiated instruments.

4) The economy clearly followed a seasonal cycle adapted to given territories, people being organized most likely into efficient communities occupying individual well organized territories with specific boundaries, camps of different size, duration and function, as well as cemeteries. Several elements of the raw material procurement system are also known.

What we believe

At this point of the analysis, we enter the magic world of individual beliefs, even ideologies, I should say. In effect, we are forcibly enlightened by some scholars on the following issues:

- Details of the social organization (nuclear family, enlarged family, tribe)
- Details of territorial organization (borders; hierarchy and network of settlement units, i.e., base and satellite camps etc.; seasonal niches and activities – hunting and/or fishing; brief forays and long-range expeditions; number and density of the population; social organization, etc.)

As said elsewhere in this book, good direct premises are usually missing, as is proof, whether local or regional. Consequently, the proposed generalizations are of little use in the local perspective (although not the continental one, cf. *supra*).

2.5.4. The population of Mesolithic Europe

It is commonly accepted that Mesolithic Europe was weakly populated. Douglas J. Price estimated the population of the Great European Plain (western and central parts) at 27,000, assuming an average density of inhabitants per square kilometer. Jean-Georges Rozoy speaks of about 50,000. Neither number draws from any straightforward source information, for none is available; instead, ethnological data was used concerning specialized hunting people in the forest zone of North America, coupled with estimates of the maximum capacity (studies by A.L. Kroeber) of forest ecosystems exploited by modern hunters, fishermen and gatherers. There is also the enlightened belief that population size in Europe increased over time, paralleling the changing environment which reached an optimum in the Atlantic period, reflecting the Mesolithic communities allegedly better adaptative skills and perhaps a more sedentary life than before (e.g. semi-sedentary camps of Ertebølle culture in southern Scandinavia and the almost permanent village at Lepensky Vir in Serbia). The latter phenomenon could be connected with the cemeteries (Skateholm in Sweden, Oleni Ostrov and Popovo in Russia, Zvejnieki in Latvia, Moita do Sebastao in Portugal, Téviec in France, etc.) and the concentrations of graves inside camps (Vlasac in Serbia, Vedbaek-Boldbaner in Denmark) that appeared mostly in the Late Mesolithic.

Testifying indirectly to poor population density are the cemeteries which appear to have been used over even very extended periods (Oleni Ostrov in Russian Karelia, Zvejnieki in Latvia).

According to Wiktor Stoczkowski, the complex tribal systems of Mesolithic Europe could have counted from 800 to 1200 individuals each.

All estimates of this kind are burdened by a degree of uncertainty, as it is simply impossible to count all the base camps of Europe occupied at the same time, multiply them by the number of members of an average enlarged family and arrive at an appropriate figure. Knowledge of particular regions of the continent is uneven and too many gaps exist; moreover, some sites (like Całowanie in Poland, according to Romuald Schild) were quite obviously visited regularly for hundreds of years, while others were merely one-season or even one-day stops. Nor are we aware of all the settlement niches occupied at the time (cf. *supra*) and we have not identified all the settlement voids (cf. "There"). Not until all of these factors are considered can we speak of an actual population density for the Mesolithic communities of Europe.

2.5.5. Dwellings

Traces of Mesolithic dwellings are seldom discovered and well preserved features are rare indeed. Apart from the presumed lightness and hence impermanence of the possibly seasonal shelter-type construction, there are other factors to consider, such as the not very precise excavation methods of old. It was often the case that the deposits in Holocene cave sites and rock-shelters were dug with a pick-axe. Only recently has there been major improvement in this field (Fig. 2.5.5a–c).

Another factor with negative impact is the geological nature of thousands of sub-surface sandy sites in the European Plain. The sandy substratum has frequently undergone processes of deflation and the very nature of sandy layers and the trees with their roots growing there do not favor the preservation of even traces of sunken dwellings. In any case, most dwellings were simply not sunken at all, making it even more difficult to observe any traces whatsoever in the archaeological record. Many of the features initially recognized as remains of "dwellings" proved to be pits several centimeters deep, left by trees which were pulled up with their roots.

Following Raymond R. Newell's very convincing study, we know that Mesolithic dwellings were rarely sunk into the ground and most of the time they were simply built on the surface.

Traces of Mesolithic huts (most researchers agree on their hut-like form) are manifested either as negatives of the original construction (postholes, troughs cut around the feature, domestic and fire pits, more seldom whole features) or the more seldom encountered "positive" elements, like earth embankments, e.g. low walls. Walls without bonding, occasionally walls made of stones, wooden branches (well preserved in Mszano, Poland) or beams, stone fireplaces, anchor-stones etc.

Exceptionally, a floor will be found (Duvensee, Ulkestrup Lyng) or traces of burning, and very seldom indeed, a concentration of finds, most often stone artifacts (cf. studies of Ole Grøn), occasionally the outlines of a grey occupational/cultural layer or another coloring of the deposit altogether (e.g. due to hematite, like in Grzybowa Góra XIII/59 in Central Poland).

These elements or whichever ones that are present should form a coherent whole, meaning the outline of outer walls, tentative entrance, fireplace and concentration of artifacts (the latter not necessarily, as it used to be believed, inside the outlines of a feature, because it can also be found outside).

Assuming these conditions are met, we can speak of a dwelling having been found. In Europe, such known features have been recorded to be no more than 4–5 m in diameter (or length, if rectangular) with a surface area of c. 18–20 m². The plan can be round or oval, rectangular and trapezoid. There is virtually nothing to distinguish these huts from their Paleolithic predecessors, although structures made of mammoth bone no longer appear and neither are they as deeply sunk into the ground (except comparable PPNA structures), an improved climate having eliminated the need for this.

According to some researchers, such dwellings were intended for single nuclear families (ethnological parallels) and a number of these huts in one spot formed a "base camp" inhabited by a number of related nuclear families forming an enlarged family (cf. "Camp"). On the other hand, Ole Grøn believes that two Mesolithic families could have lived in one bigger hut, as is the case with the Eskimo peoples. The distribution of functionally different objects attributed respectively to men and women would stand in favor of his hypothesis.

Of the different types of European Mesolithic huts, the following basic forms can be discussed. In the north of Scandinavia, dwellings were rectangular with foundations often built of stone. The size was from 3 to 5 m. Fireplaces and postholes are in evidence. Another clearly distinguishable type occurring in different regions is a light structure of oval or round shape, the outlines of which are marked by a row or rows of postholes, sometimes connected with anchor-stones. Structures of this kind are from 4 to 5 m across. The next type is slightly sunk into the ground, with a tentative central post in the middle, round or oval, occasionally rectangular in plan. One should also mention very rare features furnished with wooden and bark floors. These could be rectangular or oval in plan. Not to be neglected are the simple oval huts outlined on the ground by a foundation trench dug around the feature (as at German Pinnberg, for example). Finally, there are oval features surrounded by low stone or clay foundation walls.

More stable settlement yields structures characterized by greater permanence, such as, for example, the Near Eastern type of house from the Early Holocene, which was round or oval, often sunk into the ground and furnished with a regular low wall made of tamped mud or cigar-shaped bricks of dried mud with chaff. These small features, usually 3–4 m across (exceptionally more!), had almost no inside furniture. The bigger ones were functionally subdivided (benches for sleeping, solid posts or even pillars supporting the roof, pits).

Added to this are the astounding trapezoid dwellings known from the Serbian-Romanian border or the long rectangular, somewhat sunken dwelling features from northern Russia.

2.5.6. Camp

Site inhabited by a human group for a shorter or longer period, but usually not permanently (hence not a village). Some researchers distinguish between a "base" camp, meaning a few huts inhabited by an enlarged family (Fig. 2.5.6) for one summer season and possibly occupied again repeatedly (or in extreme cases, one-hut smaller installations) and small "satellite" camps acting as short-lived shelters for individual fishing and hunting forays or a task group procuring raw material. This picture assumes the existence of more permanent structures, one or more, at the

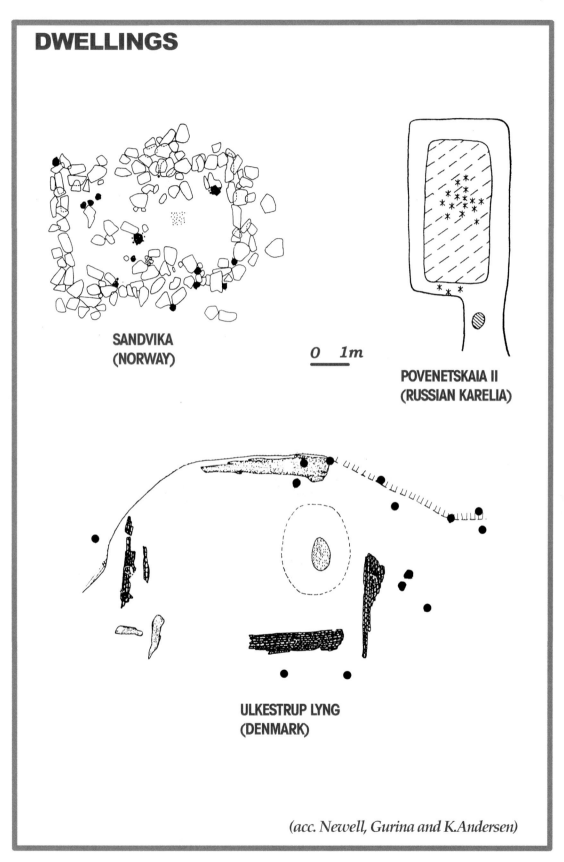

Fig. 2.5.5a

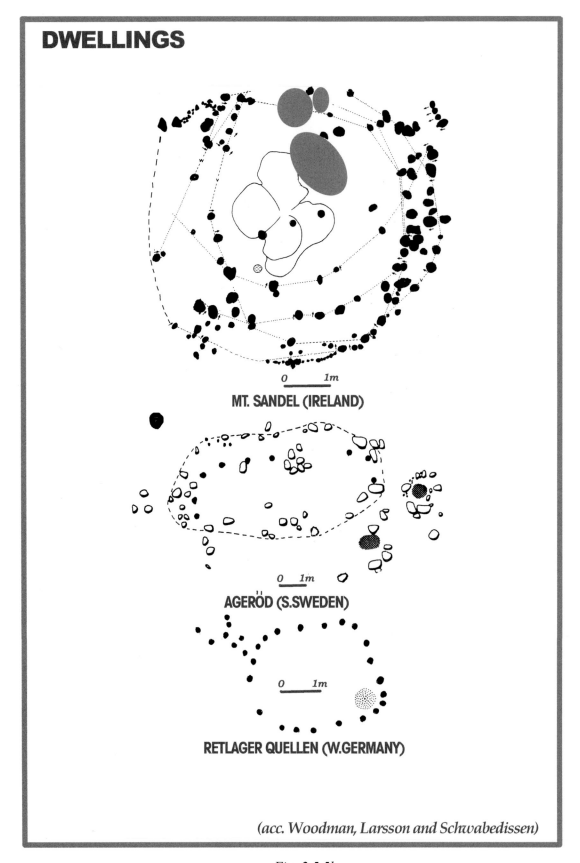

DWELLINGS

MT. SANDEL (IRELAND)

AGERÖD (S.SWEDEN)

RETLAGER QUELLEN (W.GERMANY)

(acc. Woodman, Larsson and Schwabedissen)

Fig. 2.5.5b

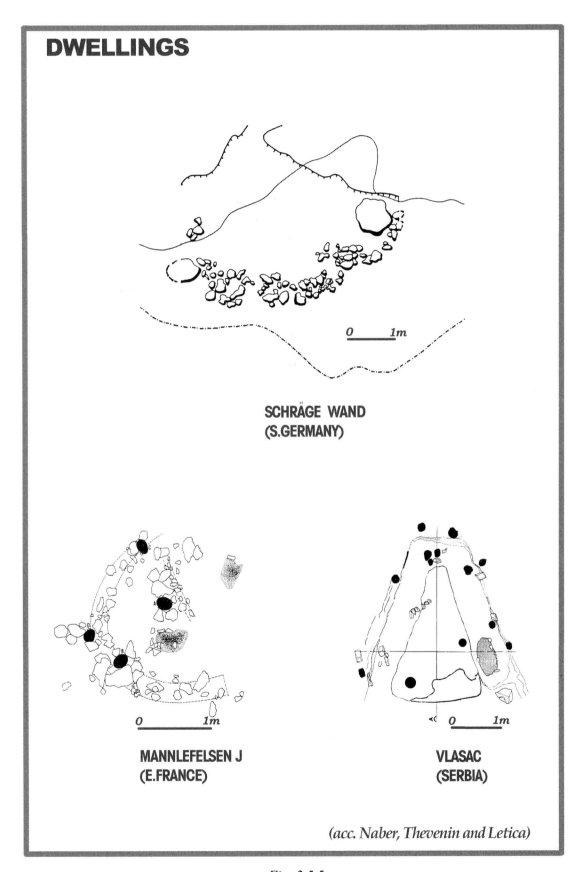

DWELLINGS

SCHRÄGE WAND
(S.GERMANY)

0 — 1m

MANNLEFELSEN J
(E.FRANCE)

0 — 1m

VLASAC
(SERBIA)

0 — 1m

(acc. Naber, Thevenin and Letica)

Fig. 2.5.5c

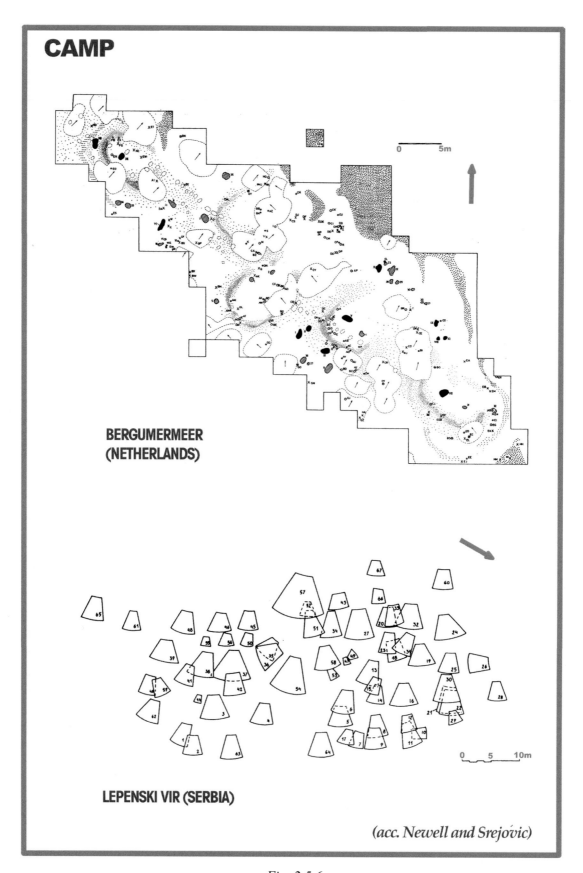

CAMP

BERGUMERMEER
(NETHERLANDS)

0   5m

LEPENSKI VIR (SERBIA)

0   5   10m

(acc. Newell and Srejovíc)

Fig. 2.5.6

base camps and less durable because short-lived shelters at the short-lasting satellite camps. It also assumes a structural differentiation of the assemblages found at the two kinds of sites (cf. "At home and abroad"), with "domestic" tools (scrapers, burins, knives) being more likely to be present in abundance in the base camps and hunting gear (armatures, points) occurring at the satellite camps. There is logic in this, but it all (except for the seasonality, which could be confirmed by archeozoology) draws from ethnological data rather than from archaeological facts. There is no way to test how long a base camp remained in use and no way to determine the actual contemporaneity of all the features and/or dwellings found in it and the related functional concentrations of objects. For the same reasons, we cannot tell whether a big camp is evidence for one or more likely several stays by a single human group or repeated penetration of a given place for a hundred years (cf. the well-dated site of Całowanie in Poland, which has an apparently homogeneous planigraphic arrangement that is a sum of many visits to the site occurring over a period of centuries! – information from Romuald Schild).

The richer the tool inventory at any given site, the more likely it is that it represents a similar case to the Całowanie site. Ethnological research has indicated that a statistical flint-knapper produced less than one flint piece, including waste, in a day's work.

On the other hand, one wonders about the Near Eastern PPNA villages and camps with their fairly solid dwellings or huts. Perhaps they were permanently inhabited. The camp with six huts from Bergumermeer in Friesland could also exemplify semi-permanent habitation, as also the camp/village at Lepenski Vir in Serbia.

2.5.7. At home and abroad

It is to be expected from experience that equipment is dependent on site function and should therefore be different in different functional situations. Without going into too much detail – for one thing, the available material is insufficient (e.g. issues of single occupation and homogeneity of assemblages) – it is easy to imagine the differentiation of equipment at sites that are functionally as different as a base and satellite camp (cf.).

The first is by definition a settlement inhabited for a longer period of time (even if abandoned on a seasonal basis) and this is archaeologically evidenced mainly by a large number of finds (assuming they are all from one period). As a rule, a settlement of this kind was inhabited by a bigger group of people, probably an enlarged family, who engaged in all kinds of "domestic" activities with the exception of food and raw-material procurement. These were usually carried out outside a base camp.

A satellite camp is organizationally subordinate to a base camp. It is an emanation (or seasonal split) of the base camp, but at the same time in total opposition to it (short-lasting, small collection of finds, small group of inhabitants). It is formed when a 'task force' from the base camp sets out to explore, specifically in search of

food and raw materials (but not an enlarged family when it splits seasonally?). It is obviously smaller, for it serves a smaller group of dwellers and it could not be either for the winter season but only short-lived, its "domestic" activities curtailed in favor of the needs of "exploration".

Considering the possible considerable specialization of Mesolithic tools (cf.), it is natural to anticipate that the different site functions will be appropriately reflected in the structure of flint/stone and bone/antler tool assemblages. Those from the "home base" should contain more "domestic" features: active debitage, numerous "home-tools", like end-scrapers, burins, knives, blades and tools production, use, destruction, repairs and functional zonation (kitchen activities, bone/antler work, filleting carcasses, leather-tanning, flint knapping, arrow shafts reuse through removal of destroyed fragments and mounting new arrowheads, etc.) with a lesser representation of "out-of-home" activities (elements of destroyed arrowheads, amorphous or accidental scrapers, heavily used knives in game filleting).

This knowledge of tool function comes from trace-ological and microwear studies, as well as experimental research. Otherwise we would have never known what a scraper was used for, what was the function of an unretouched blade and what purpose a burin served. By the same, we have acquired some general knowledge as to how microliths and points functioned in Mesolithic society. Consequently, the present author would like to recall Raymond R. Newell's definition of "satellite camp", according to which the proportions of various elements of the equipment should be different, with "domestic" tools indices at lower levels, and the zonation much less evident. Moreover, one should expect a series of *ad hoc* tools which would be less standard in appearance, that is, less regular and mass-produced, tools that a good flint-knapper would discard, if working at home. The categories expected to be dominant in a "satellite" short-lived camp should include hunting implements (microliths and points) or mining tools (axes/adzes), and more irregular scrapers (cf.) at the expense of typical ("correct") end-scrapers, burins and knives. But a winter-season long-lasting "home" camp will be a miniature copy of a summer base camp rather than a satellite one.

A similar differentiation into "base/home" and "satellite/hunting" sites should also be anticipated in the bone/antler industries (cf.).

2.5.8. Seasonality

Despite semblances of being independent from climate, human communities remain dependent, at least in part, on season change. Suffice it to mention mass tourist excursions in the summer and seasonal holiday celebrations and pilgrimages, not to say great sports events.

Ethnological studies as much as simple common sense prompt the thinking that things could not have been all that different in a distant prehistory when man's subsistence was based entirely on simple forms of exploitation of nature which vibrated cyclically with the changing seasons.

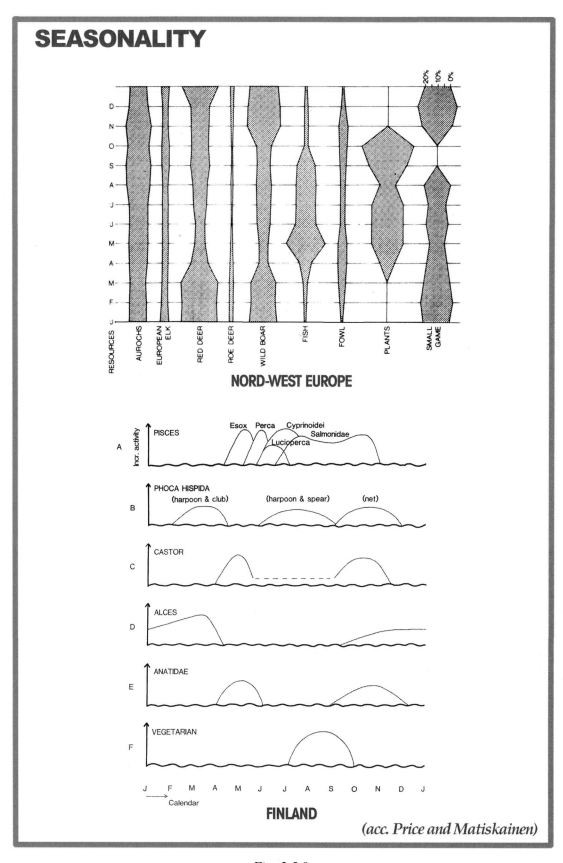

Fig. 2.5.8

Everything was grounded in the opposition of summer and winter, wealth and poverty, reality and dreaming, activity and hibernation. This was the principal rhythm of life, complemented by two transitional periods, spring and autumn; it was this rhythm that everything in the life of the Mesolithic hunters and gatherers had to be tuned to.

Firstly, there was the yearly vegetation cycle with its periods of flowering and bearing fruit (hazel, lentil, pistachio, wild cereals and legumes, edible acorns and full beehives), ending in autumn saturation and winter hibernation. The seasonal rhythm has as much effect on animals as it does on man. Herds of animals sought by the hunter, like reindeer, could travel even long distances; forest fauna are also on a limited move, the young are born and reared, animals put on fat and fur thickens seasonally, making them more attractive from the hunters' point of view, etc.

Mesolithic man must have known all this (Fig. 2.5.8) and acted opportunistically to take advantage of all of the Maker's gifts. This naturally imposed on him a variability of seasonal behavior – hunting first, followed by gathering, fishing at another time – as well as place of residence, forcing him to migrate between points separated on the map by several hundred kilometers in extreme cases (reindeer hunters), although commonly (forest game, cf.) the distance would not be more than a few dozen kilometers, all enclosed within the same territorial range.

This is entirely logical: an abundant and lazy life is no stimulus for revolutionary change – man remains a traditionalist.

Not long ago Douglas J. Price used data from North American forest aboriginal communities to reconstruct the annual calendar of such comfortable seasonal life carried on by the Mesolithic hunters and gatherers. They started the year with big-game hunting (mainly red deer and boar), followed by an intensive fishing season and concurrent plant gathering (an activity that peaked later in the year). Big-game hunting re-intesified at the end of the year.

The picture is coherent and it is difficult to avoid the impression that as a general model of Mesolithic seasonality it is fairly accurate, despite potential regional differentiation which could and should have individualized it (e.g. Heiki Matiskainen for Finland).

One should also consider Wiktor Stoczkowski's suggestion of mass summer gatherings of Mesolithic tribal communities, contrasted with winter dispersion into small groups.

But how can seasonality be translated into the archaeological record?

Well, it can, and the data can be quite direct, as well as indirect, confirming the phenomenon of Mesolithic seasonality.

Firstly, there are kitchen middens containing animal bones found on some sites (Star Carr in Britain, Svaerdborg II and Ulkestrup Lyng in Denmark, etc.). The condition of the remains (shed antlers, molar cementation indicating age of hunted animals at death, etc.) and even the very presence of individuals of migratory species is enough to determine at which period of the year a site was occupied. The evidence is quite clear; what is at issue is the extent to which such isolated examples can be generalized. In any case, Grahame Clark first suggested that the winter occupation of Star Carr could correspond to summer residence at the twin site of Deepcar in the Pennines. In Denmark, Erik Brinch-Petersen assigned the hut from Ulkestrup Lyng to the winter season and the Svaerdborg II site to the summer.

Despite the absence of archeozoological studies, the case of sites high up in the mountains, sometimes even at an altitude of 2500 m a.s.l. (Italian Dolomites, Apennines, Pyrenees, French and Swiss Alps, the mountains of Norway), seems quite clear. Comfortable life was possible here in the summer, while winters were more likely to be spent at lower altitudes.

To be honest, one should not expect a greater individualization of the general model anytime in the nearest future. Not only fortuitous discoveries are required for such work, but also intelligent researchers.

2.5.9. Forest trappers?

Finds, like those from Vig and Prejlerup (cf. "Auroch from Prejlerup") in Denmark throw some light on life in the Mesolithic. Whole skeletons of aurochs were found there, flint arrowheads, which had killed the animals, still embedded among the bones. Obviously, the animal from Prejlerup had been wounded, but had got away from the hunter or hunters and had bled to death in seclusion. Upon examining these finds, we can say more about human behavior in the Mesolithic.

It turns out that the microliths embedded in the carcass counted from three (at Vig) to 14, indicating the composite character of the projectiles and the use of several arrows at the same time (at Prejlerup). Heavy damage in the latter case (impact negatives and breaks) merely proves that microliths were used as arrows.

The impression is of high hunting effectiveness with big animals (weighing up to even 800 kg, like aurochs!) being brought down with just a few small flint pieces (at Prejlerup the projectiles seem to be grouped in threes). This suggest individual hunting, perhaps as trappers do, when a single man can hunt down even a big animal, although obviously he cannot transport the whole carcass by himself. Such a hunting strategy based on the bow (cf.) as a long-range and accurate weapon seems best suited to a forest environment. A similar example is provided by a Final Paleolithic elk skeleton discovered in High Furlong in Britain (cf. certain parts of the skeleton are missing, suggesting the hunter carried away the tastiest bits). The animal had been hit by a double-pointed harpoon, presumably by an individual hunter tracking it.

3

Where?

The selected aspects of the Early Holocene natural environment on the European continent presented at the beginning of this chapter, both geographical and economic, determined to a large extent the continent's history in the Mesolithic, including cultural differentiation (cf. "*E pluribus unum?*"), as well as migrations and proliferation of ideas.

The next chapter consists of a few casual remarks on the organization of Mesolithic settlement (cf. "There").

3.1. The screen (Fig. 3.1)

3.1.1. The relief

The relief of Europe is so richly differentiated that it must have stimulated in a significant way the life of Mesolithic communities. First of all, there is the issue of communication, secondly, the impact of ground topography on the hydrographic network and indirectly on settlement by the same.

In terms of communication tracts, Europe can easily be divided into two kinds of landscape: the southern (but also Scandinavian!) mountains and uplands and the northern plains (Fig. 3.1.1). The former imposes limitations on communication because of the barriers constituted by mountain ranges and high uplands, not to mention that it is hardly encouraging as a place for permanent settlement (biomass!).

As for the southern landscape, it is composed of many relatively isolated microworlds restricted to the basins of the great rivers (Seine, Garonne, Rhône, Upper Danube, Po, Arno, middle Danube, Adige, Ebro, etc) or stretches of seashore (Dalmatia, Provence, Spanish Levant, Norwegian coast). It is a matter of course that each of these separate isolated areas (even if connected with neighbors through gates and passes) should develop culturally according to its own cycle and should be characterized therefore by a sequence of specific, local industries more or less different from those existing in the neighboring regions. The limited hydrographic network and dry, elevated plateaus of the

south (compared to the north) could affect the range of settlement and its potential.

The Lowland is of entirely different character. With no serious land barriers to overcome, the communication potential was practically unhindered, although here also there are less elevated uplands (front moraines, for example), acting more as separators than as connectors. The richly developed hydrography of the lowland is an added connecting advantage. Consequently, land under settlement is much more extensive in this region (confirmed by the number of identified sites) and the lack of more serious barriers is a deterrent to the formation of topographically isolated settlement units. The range of particular taxonomic units is thus much greater than in the south.

Another important conclusion is that settlement capacity in the lowland was naturally greater; consequently, the plains could support bigger populations. A sizable number of sites discovered in the region appears to testify to this theory.

3.1.2. The mountains

In view of their morphology and altitude, mountains could not be exploited by Mesolithic communities the year round. Firstly, mountains are a natural territorial barrier, dividing peoples and cultures. While technically passable (through the lower passes and gates), they constitute a psychological barrier that was difficult to overcome, presumably due to the Mesolithic people's fairly "parochial" perspective.

Mesolithic Europe was divided into two huge provinces, one in the north and the other in the south, divided by the Alps, Carpathians and the less imposing Czech Mountains (Fig. 3.1.2). The Alps effectively separated the Sauveterrian of Italy and France from the Beuronian of Germany, Switzerland and Austria, while the Carpathians (together with the Czech Mountains, the eastern slopes of the Alps and the Dynaric Alps) enclosed the Carpathian Basin with its local, Epi-Gravettian Mesolithic. The Slovenian Ljubliana Gate through the Dynaric Alps permitted northward passage for the Sauveterrian, but was clearly

SCREEN

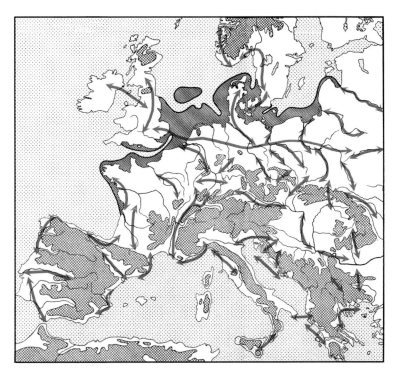

THE MAIN ROADS CONNECTING PEOPLE ALONG RIVER VALLEYS, THROUGH GATES, CORRIDORS AND LOWER PASSES

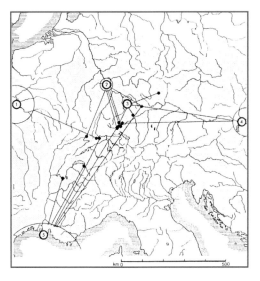

EXEMPLE OF IMPORTED FOSSIL ORNAMENTS

(acc. Cziesla)

Fig. 3.1

RELIEF

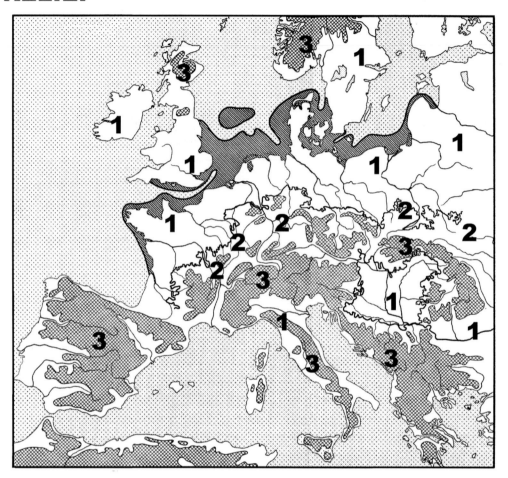

1 -PLAIN/LOWLAND
2 -PLATEAU/UPLAND
3 -MOUNTAINS

MOUNTAINS OFTEN SEPARATED PEOPLE,BEING STRONG CULTURAL BORDERS
-BUT ALSO LESS PRONOUCED MORPHOLOGICAL DIFFERENCES,
E.G. 200M CONTOUR LINE IN CENTRAL EUROPE COULD SEPARATE THE PEOPLE
(CF.4.5.6c)

Fig. 3.1.1

MOUNTAINS

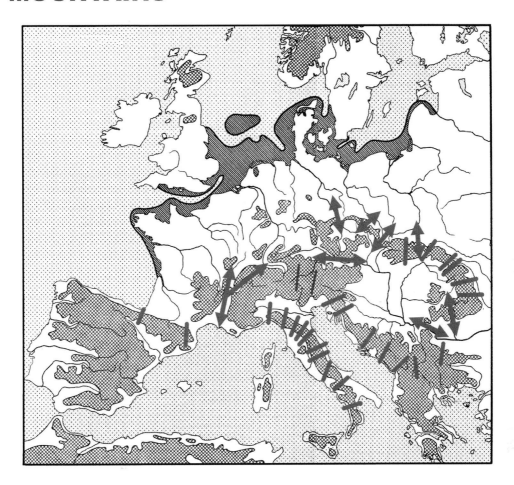

— PASSES BELOW 1050m A.S.L.

— PASSES BETWEEN 1050 AND 1500m A.S.L

← → GATES

LOWER PASSES COULD FACILITATE THE TRANSMONTANE
COMMUNICATION BUT MUCH MORE EFFECTIVE ARE THE GATES

Fig. 3.1.2

difficult to penetrate for these communities. Later, the Castelnovian-like industry did not penetrate easily to the north. Existing north-south Alpine passes were practically not functional at this time (only one Sauveterrian site, Ullafelsen, is known from the Tyrol in Austria) and the same seems to be true of the Carpathian and Sudeten section in the east, despite the passes there being at lower altitudes (one Janislawician site in Transcarpathian Ukraine). The passes from Czech lands into Poland through the Sudeten Mountains (the Kłodzko Basin), even not very elevated, appear to have been difficult to navigate for the Beuronians (one site near Kłodzko, in Poland).

The third great mountain barrier in Europe were the Pyrenees. The only way through was actually to go around them via the sea coasts. Consequently, the Iberian Peninsula was effectively protected from any Mesolithic "novelties", the Iberian Epi-Azilian/Epi-Gravettian of the Early Holocene being excellent proof of this isolation. Sauveterrian "trends", but not the classic Sauveterrian, reached the Spanish Levant apparently down the eastern sea coast.

On the other hand, the Italian Apennines are penetrable for the Mesolithic hunters, although undoubtedly they veritably isolated the Epi-Gravettian Mesolithic of the Mezzogiorno from Sauveterrian Tuscany and Pianura del Po.

Apart from being great continental divides, mountains have always regionalized Europe: the *Sierra* of Spain and Portugal divided Iberia into three coastal regions – Cantabria, the Levant and the Atlantic coast; France with the Mesolithic of the southwest and south separated one from the other and also from the north by the Central Massif; former Yugoslavia with the Mesolithic of the Iron Gates and the basin of the river Sava separated by the Dinaric Alps from that of the Dalmatian coast; Scandinavia with the coastal culture of Fosna/Komsa separated from the central Swedish Mesolithic, etc.

To sum up, the strongly accentuated topography of certain regions of Europe with their plateaus and mountains, but also their lower passes and gates, has tended to separate population groups, thus stimulating the development of different independent traditions and being conducive to the development of different local histories.

Nonetheless, some of the mountains were visited seasonally, in the summer, most often to hunt, less often for other purposes (raw materials). Such excursions, even up to altitudes of 1700–2500 m a.s.l., have been recorded in the Swiss and French Alps (Chartreuse, Vercors) and the Italian Dolomites (Colbricon), as well as the Central Alps. The same can be said of the Apennines and the Central Massif in France (Longetray), the Pyrenees (Margineda), the mountains of Monte Negro (Crvena Stjena, Odmut) and Scandinavia (southern Norway) and finally the southern Ural (Yangelka).

In his studies, François Djindjan has presented consistently and not without reason his theory on the importance of mountain chains and existing passes and gates for the earlier prehistory of Europe. Therefore, the present author is very careful to consider morphology when discussing particular regions of Europe.

3.1.3. The sea

The sea is a great divide because it is difficult to cross, but the challenge can be and is undertaken successfully, as evidenced by Early and Middle Holocene finds in Cyprus (Shillurokambos), the Aegean (Melos), Corsica and Sardinia, not to mention coastal islands (cf.), such as Téviec and Hoëdic in Brittany, the coastal islands of western Sweden and western and northern Norway, Scottish Jura, Italian Sicily and in the Late Mesolithic Bornholm, Britain and Ireland, as well as the Isle of Man.

The Mesolithic people were not sea travelers by nature (Fig. 3.1.3). What we are dealing with are individual acts rather than established connections, singular expeditions mounted to obtain goods like obsidian brought from Cappadocia to Cyprus and from Melos to Frankhthi.

Perhaps in the south of the continent (around the Mediterranean) marine contacts were easier than in the north, where the English Channel proved a very effective barrier for millennia between Britain and the Continent.

The coast also constitutes a rich and highly specific biotope with seals, cetaceans and countless mollusks (cf.). Specific littoral cultural adaptations often repeated themselves in such regions (Asturian, Larnian, Obanian, Kongemosian, Ertebøllian, etc).

Unlike the inland units, many of these biotopes occupied small but protein-rich (game, fish, seal, mollusks) territories, determined in this by the specific morphology of the narrow coastal zone, for example.

3.1.4. The maritime coast

The maritime coast, especially the warmer littoral to the south, is a very rich biotope abounding in land game, as well as seafood (mollusks, fish, cetaceans, seals etc.). This could have led to the emergence of highly specialized coastal communities (Asturian, Larnian, Obanian, Ertebøllian etc.) concentrated on intensive exploitation of rich but very narrow coastal zones (which in the south of Europe was additionally determined by ground relief, that is, mountains steeply falling straight into the sea as in Provence, southern Italy and Dalmatia). The material culture of these zones differed from their inland counterparts (including numerous choppers, denticulates and picks).

3.1.5. Shell middens

Features in the form of, among others, banks of consumption refuse (Fig. 3.1.5), especially shells of marine mollusks located in the coastal zones, were usually associated with camp sites. They are known from the Ertebøllian in southern Scandinavia (*Kjøkkenmödding*), the Obanian of Scotland, Larnian of Ireland, Castelnovian of the mouth of the Tag in Portugal (*concheiros*) and the Capsian of the Maghreb (*escargotières*), as well as the

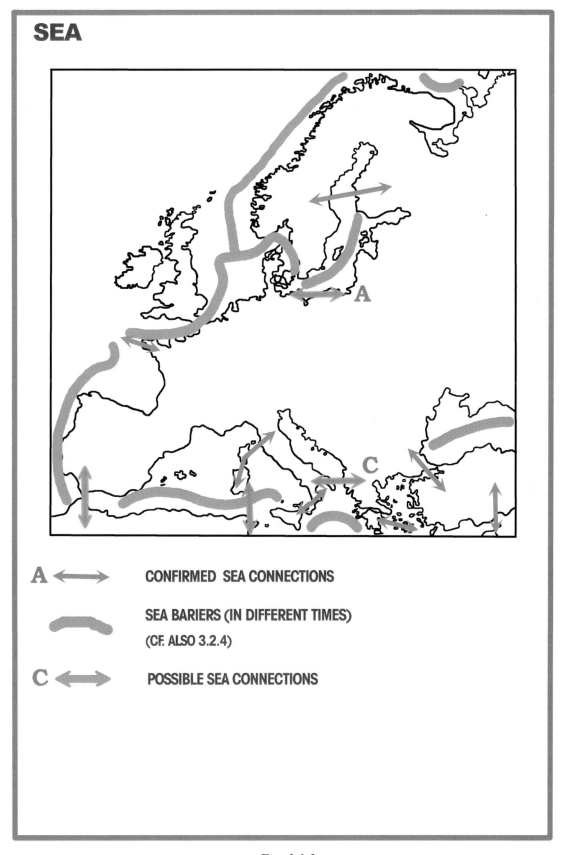

Fig. 3.1.3

SHELL MIDDENS

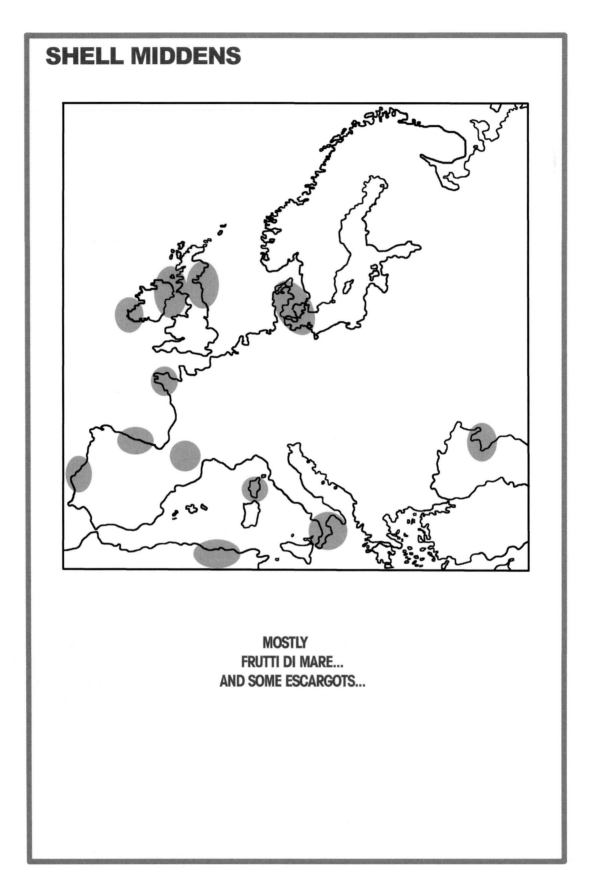

MOSTLY
FRUTTI DI MARE...
AND SOME ESCARGOTS...

Fig. 3.1.4/3.1.5

Téviècian of Brittany and Normandy (Ty-Nancien). Added to this are naturally the dumps of *escargot* shells from Sauveterrian sites in southwestern France, or Crimean finds (Murzak-Koba).

3.1.6. Islands

Mesolithic man was not afraid of the sea and overcame this barrier by simply sailing across it in boats (cf.), unless the water divide was too wide – in the south – or too dangerous, as in the north. Practically from the beginning of the age, Mesolithic peoples were settling islands and the phenomenon intensified just before the end of the period (Fig. 3.1.6). Nonetheless, not all settlement existing on modern islands can be considered insular. The Danish islands, including Bornholm, Great Britain, Ireland and the Isle of Man (all in the Early/Middle Period) were part of the continent before they became islands and as such were already settled in Mesolithic times. The islands I am referring to are those which were islands already for Mesolithic man, inviting on one hand and challenging on the other – a mysterious isolated place not easy to get to. These "original" islands (the islands mentioned above as "secondary" for the Late Mesolithic peoples, turned finally into "original" ones) are all around the continent and were populated sooner or later by Mesolithic man, especially if they were within sight (a distance of up to 20–30 km) and the sea was sufficiently calm.

Motives for settling such islands included searching for adventure as much as for new territories to colonize or for raw materials (the case of the Estonian islands in the Baltic, Jura in Scotland, also Corsica, Sardinia and Sicily, the islands of the Aegean (Melos and Cyprus).

This "pioneer" approach is contrasted with the case of the Danish Isles which previously had constituted a "dry" bridge between Jutland and Mecklemburg on one side and Scania on the other. The gradual appearance of the Danish Straits (about the middle of the 8th millennium cal. BC) did not break off the contacts and people crossed the original rivers (today straits) by boat. The original unity of southern Scandinavia was maintained (Kongemosian and Ertebøllian). The situation appears to be similar in the case of the Ahre/Åland islands on the Baltic between Finland and central Sweden (bridge between Suomusjärvi culture and the Mesolithic of central Sweden) and the Scottish Orcades (coastal and insular Obanian where the islands "cooperated" with the nearby mainland in a single economic system). A similar role was played by the coastal islands off western Sweden and Norway. Neither was the Messina Strait between Italy and Sicily considered a barrier and this already in the Upper Paleolithic.

In special instances, the islands functioned as intentionally chosen "places of seclusion", as in the case of, for example, the Oleni Island/Ostrov on Onega Lake in Russian Karelia, which features a large Mesolithic cemetery that functioned for a long time, necessitating the location of camp sites outside of the island and the lake. A similar situation may have existed on the Hoëdic and Téviec islands of the Brittany coast with their sepulchral installations. In these cases, it was perhaps not a challenge for explorers and pioneers, but a place of seclusion and eternal rest....

Finally, an example of the exploratory ambitions of man not being put into life despite proximity of the shores (c. 35 km). Great Britain became Europe's biggest island around 7500/7300 cal. BC and it is then that its "splendid isolation" began. Contacts with the continent, which had been so lively before, clearly stopped. None of the trapezes so common on the continent (from ca. 7000/6500 cal. BC) nor the *feuilles de gui* characteristic of the northwest of continental Europe ever crossed the Channel.

The contrast with the Mediterranean is surprising. There, even a few dozen kilometers were not a problem (Shillurocambos on Cyprus connected with the coast of Anatolia, obsidian outcrops on Melos connected with Frankhthi in the Peloponnese, contacts of the French and Italian coasts with Corsica and Sardinia). In the north, these few kilometers (some 150 km in the case of Melos, but only 35 km in the case of the Channel!) constituted an impassable barrier, probably because of bad weather. The Ormuz strait on the Adriatic, much wider but located much further south, was not as impassable.

Overseas contacts to the south pose a mystery. Gabriel Camps provided evidence of contacts between Europe and North Africa for a period shortly after the Mesolithic (obsidian from Lipari – 360 km, but through Sicily), and I find it difficult to believe that these contacts did not reach back into the Mesolithic age (Montbani trapezes and lamelles in the Castelnovian on one hand and the *Capsien Supérieur* of the Maghred on the other). Malta must have played some role in these contacts.

3.1.7. The changing shape of a continent

The geological history of Europe in the Late and Post-Glacial period had enormous impact on the Mesolithic of the continent. The prime mover in this case was the rapid deglaciation of the north. The gradual melting of the Pleistocene glacier was completed in the 7th millennium cal. BC, and it triggered at least three different processes that had direct influence on the later shape of the continent and consequently on its history in the Mesolithic.

Firstly, the permanent freeing of water from the continental ice sheet, occurring in Asia and North America as much as in Europe, constantly increased the volume of the World ocean which resulted in rising levels (maximum reached in the Atlantic (Late Mesolithic) period), causing the flooding of lower-lying lands (Fig. 3.1.7): Dogger Bank Shelf (harpoons fished out from the sea bottom), the area between the British Isles and Ireland, the Danish Straits (submerged Ertebøllian sites), the west Baltic land bridge, and finally, the Atlantic and Mediterranean coasts of Europe and the Near East (submerged PPNB site of Atlit Yam in Israel). The outcome was on one hand migrations of animals and people, and on the other, the inaccessibility of sites for research, especially supposed sunk coastal sites

ISLANDS

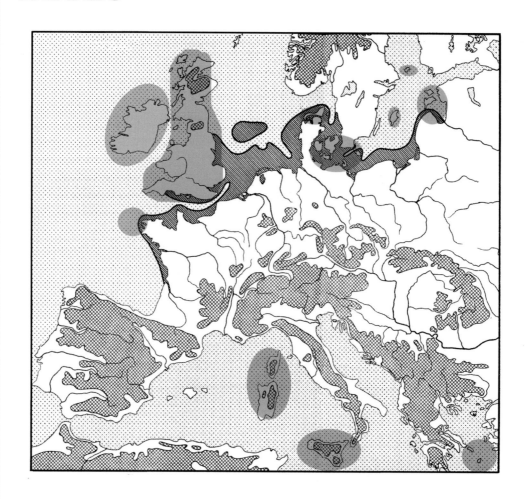

 **CONFIRMED INSULAR MESOLITHIC PRESENCE**

**IRELAND, BRITAIN AND DANISH ISLANDS BECAME
ISLANDS ONLY IN MIDDLE/LATE MESOLITHIC**

Fig. 3.1.6

CHANGING SHAPE OF CONTINENT

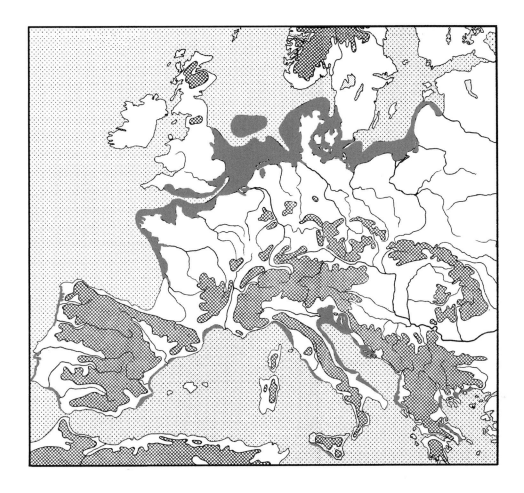

MAXIMAL EXTENTION OF HOLOCENE LAND-BRIDGES
(Africa not concerned)

**NORD SEA (BALTIC) LAND BRIDGE PLAYED A CRUCIAL ROLE
IN EUROPE'S EARLY/MIDDLE HOLOCENE HISTORY**

(acc. Pirazzoli)

Fig. 3.1.7

in the Mediterranean. The specific topography of the latter coastline (mountains descending straight into the sea) has deprived us irretrievably of many Mesolithic sites (among others, the Dalmatian coast?).

Added to this is the planet's return to its previous roundness in parts freed from the great pressure of the continental ice sheet. This resulted in the depression in Northwestern Europe and the simultaneous rising of the Scandinavian plate (parallel to the rising of sea level). The first part of this mechanism, resulted in the fairly rapid flooding of the northern parts of lowland Europe, the second in the appearance of modern Finland and the rising altitude of many old sites in western Norway.

The end outcome of these processes (e.g. successive stages in the development of the Baltic Sea: Yoldia, Ancylus, Littorna) is the disappearance of traditional bridges and ecumenes and the appearance of new ones. Europe was divided then, the Britain becoming separated from Ireland on one side and the Continent on the other (the English Channel) and Denmark was separated from Britain, Germany, Sweden and Poland. These processes should be kept in mind when considering the Mesolithic history of Europe.

3.1.8. Inland

"Inland" means most of the continent, apparently opposed to the lakelands (cf. "Lakes") and coasts in many respects. Water resources constitute the first difference, being obviously more extensive in the Vistulian/Würmian lakelands and heavily limited to streams and rivers in the inland. Such biotopes are never as rich as the great lake water reservoirs. The lesser importance of the water biotope was surely compensated for by the land/forest biotopes (Fig. 3.1.8a–b), hence big-game hunting as a standard. Fishing in the Inland was rather for pleasure? (cf., e.g., finds from Montclus in France). Actually, even here there were some bigger water reservoirs, like oxbow lakes (e.g. Noyen in the Paris Basin with its boat, the Upper Volga shallow lakes – Ozerki and Zamostie sites, or the Alpine Lakes, e.g. Colbricon and Wauwillermoos).

An entirely different world with other things to offer and another lifestyle. Settlement was concentrated along the small and medium river valleys (cf. "Settlement Patern"), on riverine terraces and dunes (in the Plain) and plateaus (southern circum-Alpine and other similar uplands and eastern European steppe plateaus, e.g. the Dniester valley in Ukraine and Moldova), mostly as open camps and rock shelters, the latter chiefly in the south (in limestone rocks).

There was little reason to venture outside the river valleys where the vegetation was not as rich and the climate was drier and cooler in winter compared to the valleys. Consequently, the less inviting and more exposed rises (e.g. ground moraines) were actually empty of settlement and could have constituted borders of varying importance. Sites were visited repeatedly (by the same human group?) over dozens and even hundreds of years (cf. Całowanie

in Poland, excavated by Romuald Schild), forming large concentrations of objects (similarly as on lakeside sites in Danish Zealand, e.g. Øgaarde) which reflect not so much extensive base camps as the sum of frequent or repeated stays in a single place over extended periods of time.

The settlement voids backing the river valleys (or the lake microregions) were emphasized by strongly differentiated ground topography, especially in the southern uplands (e.g. limestone plateaus and ridges in Swabish southern Germany). It has also been noted in several regions of Europe that sites tended to be concentrated in groups reaching 20–40 km across, apparently separated by equally large and empty areas (cf. "There").

The Inland appears to have been divided by the said water divides (dry areas, uplands, but also front moraines), as much as by the mountain barriers that were also often important cultural boundaries.

The Inland features described above, differentiating it partly from the lakelands, appear to be reflected in the available archaeological record of the Mesolithic cultures in continental Europe. First of all, flint objects are in the absolute majority, greatly overshadowing the number of bone objects, which are known from a few lakeside sites (e.g. the site of Schötz on the Wauwillermoos lake in Switzerland, excavated by René Wyss), but chiefly from rock shelters. There is never the incomprehensible extravagance in the number of bone objects so well known from sites in the lakelands. One gets the wrong impression of there being two different cultures or traditions: bone ("Maglemosian" and stone Tardenoisian) (cf. "Stone and bone cultures"). The fact is that these were two different worlds! The number of microliths found on sites, especially hunting sites, in the Inland is considerable as a rule, while on sites from the lakelands the proportions can vary substantially; Maglemosian microliths are more numerous than the local bone points, but in some places of eastern Europe the situation is reversed.

Apart from the banal standard, stimulated in terms of form by the initial shape of the blanks or bone of specific animals ("knife-scraper" from boar tusk, daggers, awls, axes/adzes of antler, etc. cf. "Bone/antler industries"), one observes differences in the field of specialized hunting and fishing gear (arrow- and spearheads, cf.). The lakeland region, demonstrates greater morphological complexity of its products, including barbs, tangs, slots with inserted flint microliths/bladelets. The Inland is characterized by the simple spindle-shaped *sagaies* inherited in unchanged form from the Upper Paleolithic. Where there was no need, no appropriately adapted product was developed. As simple as that.

3.2. The resources

3.2.1. Forest

The forest is Mesolithic man's element. It created Mesolithic man, determined him and gave him the means to live. The first regional signs of a new Mesolithic formation

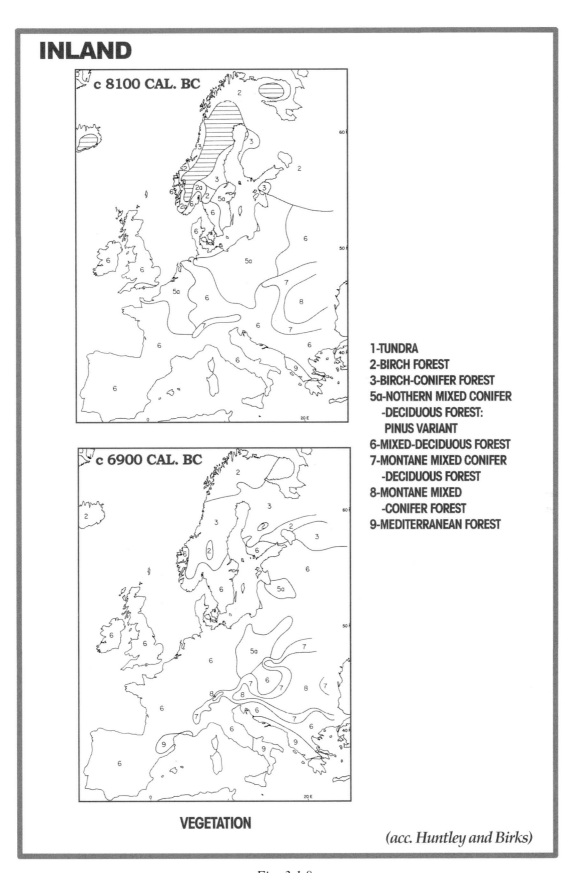

INLAND

c 8100 CAL. BC

1-TUNDRA
2-BIRCH FOREST
3-BIRCH-CONIFER FOREST
5a-NOTHERN MIXED CONIFER
  -DECIDUOUS FOREST:
  PINUS VARIANT
6-MIXED-DECIDUOUS FOREST
7-MONTANE MIXED CONIFER
  -DECIDUOUS FOREST
8-MONTANE MIXED
  -CONIFER FOREST
9-MEDITERRANEAN FOREST

c 6900 CAL. BC

VEGETATION

(acc. Huntley and Birks)

Fig. 3.1.8a

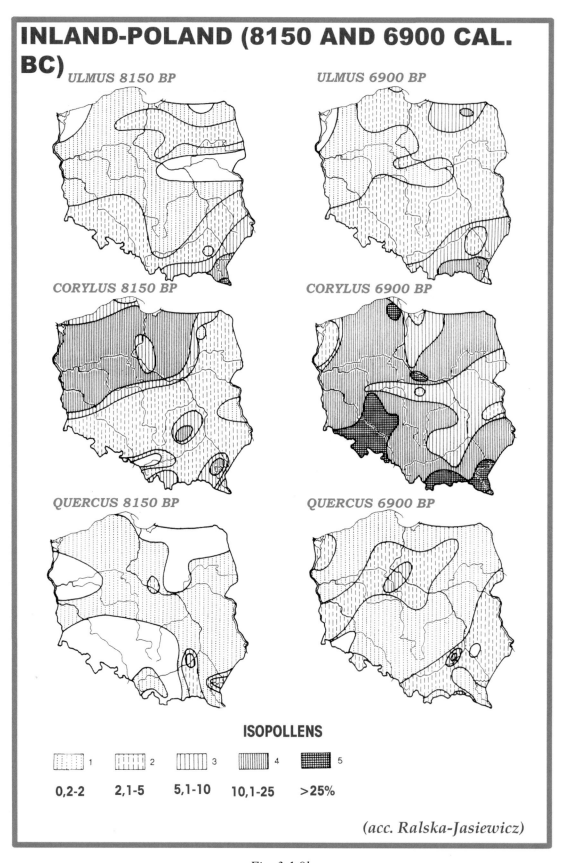

Fig. 3.1.8b

characterized by microlithization and geometrization of armatures can be observed in the forest biotopes of the terminal Upper Paleolithic of southern Europe. Although the essence of the matter escapes us, we can safely assume that to be a Mesolithic man in those times meant to live in the vast forests that covered almost all of the continent from the end of the 11th millennium cal. BC (= the very beginning of the Holocene).

The biotope in Europe had not been equally rich in protein mass for at least twelve thousand years. A.L. Kroeber estimates the capacity of the forests (Fig. 3.2.1) at much more than the tundra on one hand and of the steppe-forest on the other, so the forest is absolutely the richest biotope of the times.

The abundance of green mass available in the forests stimulated growth of the animal population. Of greatest economic importance were the big mammals, like elk, deer, roe, auroch, boar, horse, etc. Added to this were numerous smaller forest and water mammals (beaver, otter, badger, fox, etc.), as well as birds. The forest was also a rich biotope for gatherers. It supplied honey and undergrowth plants, and was an obvious source of fuel and building material.

It must have been paradise on earth, especially north of the Alps, following after the hardships of the Pleistocene tundra environment. Specific adaptive models were triggered, considering the specificity and habits of dominant animal species, seasonally migrating (but on short distances) within their own ranges. Hunting concerned a number of coexistent species and occurred mostly in specific autumn/winter seasons and in specific parts of the animals' own territory. It appears to have been rather individual hunting (?) with the use of accurate long-range weapons like the bow (skeletons of shot aurochs from Vig and Prejlerup, cf., in Denmark).

The impression is of high specialization and adaptation to the environment. The apparent cost of this abundant life without stress was a resistance to novelties and a closing to the world (cf. "Conservatism of the Mesolithic"). Mesolithic cultures and peoples were strongly conservative, living in considerable mutual isolation.

The story of forests in Europe in the early and middle Holocene, reconstructed on the basis of palynological studies, started at the end of the Pleistocene and in the early Holocene with the spreading of forest formations from southern refuges toward the north. During the climatic optimum in the Holocene (7000–4000 cal. BC), forests reached to the northern extremes of Scandinavia and Russia where they bordered with a tundra environment. In the earliest period (Preboreal), the forest line in the north ran across Scandinavia at about the middle. Steppe formations (earlier) and forest-steppes (Atlantic period) developed along the northern Black Sea coasts and in the Carpathian Basin.

Throughout the early and middle Holocene, the European forest featured a zonation that developed from south to north, starting with deciduous forest, followed further to the north by a mixed model and finally coniferous forest. These zones shifted gradually toward the north, in the wake of optimized climatic zones. The forest was also differentiated along an East-West line with deciduous forest dominating in the west, especially in the Atlantic optimum (influence of the Gulf Stream), and simultaneously mixed formations in the east. Local differentiation was richer in fact, being dependent, among others, on the soils. Over time, the forest became denser and the species variability was based on the sequence: birch-pine-oak, which sequence parallels forest density as a mark of climatic evolution in the Holocene.

Variability over time and the zonality of European forest are reasons for a similar regionalization of the forest fauna (cf. "Game") and this in turn was one of the factors determining the varied cultural behavior of human communities observed on the European continent.

3.2.2. Steppe

In the Early and Middle Holocene, this habitat (which is unique in Europe), extended north of the Black and Caspian seas and in the Hungarian Plain. The ground is flat or slightly undulating, but not obviously low, characterized by a rather continental climate and vegetation of two kinds: the deciduous or mixed forests that grew in the deep valleys of the few big and medium-size rivers (Danube, Tisa, Prut, Dniester, Dniepr, Boh, Severski Donetz, Don) and the grasses growing in the vast, poorly watered plateaus or plains between them. Thus, it was a forest-steppe or park steppe habitat, with a biomass less rich than in the case of the forest. Game included the big forest mammals (deer, roe, boar in the river valleys) and the auroch which was especially numerous in the Hungarian Plain. Saiga antelope may have lived in the grassy regions of Crimea and Ukraine (Fig. 3.2.2).

Settlement is specific in this habitat, for it is limited to plateaus and the big and medium-size river valleys; the small rivers and streams were much less frequent than on the European Plain and in the uplands of southern Europe. The soil was a rich chernozyem and loess. The ubiquitous plateau erosion and abundant valley accumulation on the Hungarian Plain in the Early Neolithic and later has apparently covered up much of the Mesolithic settlement there.

The Mesolithic cultures of the Black Sea littoral refer, among others, to the Caucasian groups, hence they can be considered as a bridge to the Middle East.

3.2.3. Lake and river

The post-Würmian lakelands (Fig. 3.2.3a–b) covering originally a sizable part of northern Europe (about a fourth or third of the continent), but also the Alpine region, constituted a highly specific environment for activity by Mesolithic man. The region stretched from East Anglia through Friesland, northern Germany, southern Scandinavia, Polish Pomerania and Masuria to Lithuania, Latvia, Estonia, Finland and, finally, northern and central Russia. Even today, there are still thousands of shallow

FOREST AND STEPPE

EAST-
-EUROPEAN
FOREST..

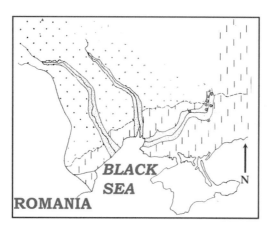

AND THE
UKRAINIAN
STEPPE

(acc. Dolukhanov)

Fig. 3.2.1/3.2.2

LAKE AND RIVER

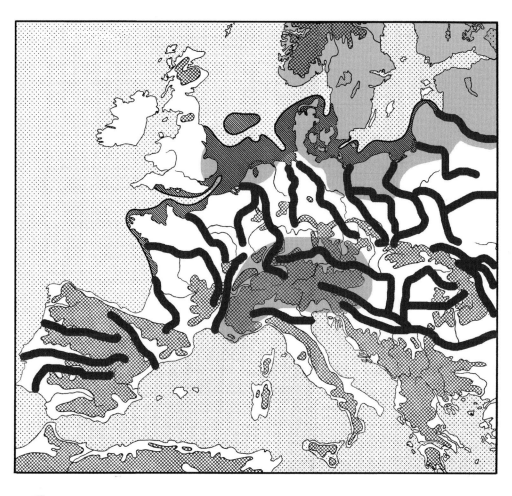

LAKELAND (CF. 2.1.10c AND 2.3.1)

BIG RIVERS MAINLY SERVED AS CONNECTION AXES BUT THE SETTLEMENT WAS ORGANIZED MOSTLY ALONG MEDIUM SIZE RIVERS (CF. 4.2)

Fig. 3.2.3a

LAKE AND RIVER

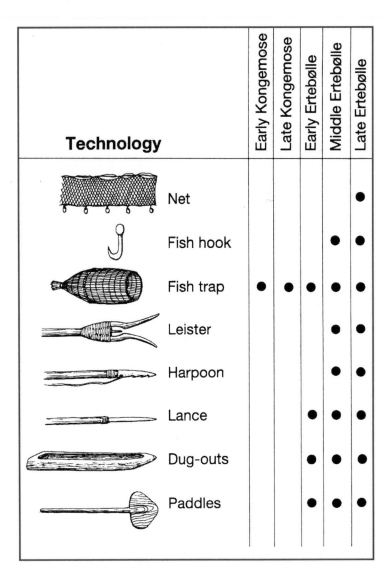

Technology	Early Kongemose	Late Kongemose	Early Ertebølle	Middle Ertebølle	Late Ertebølle
Net					●
Fish hook				●	●
Fish trap	●	●	●	●	●
Leister				●	●
Harpoon				●	●
Lance			●	●	●
Dug-outs			●	●	●
Paddles			●	●	●

FISHING EQUIPMENT IN S.SCANDYNAVIA

(acc. S.Andersen)

Fig. 3.2.3b

lakes with calm, but not totally standing water, despite many being silted up naturally or eliminated in effect of land melioration. Such "fossil"' and shallow lakes include the classics of Mesolithic studies: Star Carr in Britain, Bergumermeer in the Netherlands, Duvensee, Hohen Viecheln and Friesack in Germany, Maglemose, Svaerdborgmose and Aamose in Denmark, Agerödmose in southern Sweden, Lubana in Latvia, Kunda in Estonia, Ozerki and Zamostie on the Upper Volga, Vis and Veretie in northern Russia, and also Wauwillermoos lake in Switzerland and Colbricon in Italy (both in the Alps).

On the banks of the lakes or on lake islands, numerous Mesolithic sites are to be found, often of long duration (?) or rather inhabited repeatedly. The exceptional preserving properties of peat bogs connected with such lakes have protected down to our times objects made of organic materials, both animal and plant, as well as those made by man (even wooden ones!).

Finds from lakeside sites have strongly colored our ideas of the Mesolithic in Europe, although it is doubtful to what degree this casus was truly typical of the whole Mesolithic.

Shallow postglacial lakes with rather low terraced banks, often connected by a network of small rivers, streams and channels, constituted ideal fishing biotopes, especially rich in biomass. The case of British Star Carr and Danish Ulkestrup Lyng seem to show that settlement was seasonal in these lakesides, the remaining part of the year being spent on hunting in other regions.

The intensity of this fishing is surprising. At Kunda-Lammasmägi (Estonia), 450 finely barbed spearheads (contrasted with a mere dozen chipped stone tools) were found, and at Star Carr the number of spearheads reached over 120. Perhaps instead of citing numbers, one should emphasize the recurrence of visits by fishermen to these places.

The lakeside environment imposed appropriate adaptive behavior to take full advantage of its riches. Firstly, it was necessary to ensure proper water transport and secondly, proper fishing gear. The first need was filled by dugouts/ boats (cf.), among others, the famous discovery from Pesse in the Netherlands, but also from near Paris (Noyen), the latter from outside the lakeside region (!). These vessels were put in motion with wooden paddles (Star Carr, Duvensee, Rüde, Tybrind Vig, etc.). Finds are few but meaningful; in any case, it would be difficult to imagine control of these occasionally fairly large water reservoirs without boats and paddles of some kind. Flint and stone axes, mounted as axes (Lübeck) or adzes (Hohen Viecheln) were most surely used to make dugouts, the other technique being burning the inside. The polished stone axes (cf.) and chisels from the circum-Baltic area may have served a similar purpose.

Fishing methods and equipment varied (nets, traps, hooks, spears), but they represented an overall division into passive forms (hook, net, trap) and active ones (spear, cf.). The former were most likely to be used also outside the lake environment, while the latter seem to be strongly linked with lake fishing, as suggested by discoveries made at Star Carr, Kunda-Lammasmägi, Ozerki, Zamostie, Friesack and Øgaarde. A few finds (Star Carr, Kunda) inform of the use of harpoons/barbed points, straightforward single-pointed or two- or three-pronged as tridents(?). The abundance of bone harpoons and points persuade as to the intensity of fishing (and/or hunting?) activities. Finally, strong interregional stylistic differences can be observed, dividing the original lakeland into two zones: the eastern-"Kunda" (cf.) and western "Maglemosian" (cf.)

Again, we are faced with the issue of having to decide whether Mesolithic Europe was in its entirety like the lakeside cultures. Was Grahame Clark correct in 1936 when he assumed a division into the "Maglemosian" (lakelands) and the "Tardenoisian" (inland)? Were there separate "bone cultures" (cf.) in the lakelands and "stone cultures" inland? Contemporary ethnological experience suggests that Europe of the lakelands had to differ from inland Europe and cannot be considered as fully representative of the Mesolithic on the continent in its entirety. Clark could indeed have been partly right to consider separate traditions for the "bone" and "stone" cultures or regions (e.g. lakelands with different barbed points, inland with single *sagaies* points). The example of the Alpine lakeland suggests that it was not true every time.

3.2.4. Game

The principal food resource of most Mesolithic communities living in the Inland were big land mammals from the forest biotopes of Europe. These animals were descended from the Late Pleistocene fauna minus a number of the great mammal species which disappeared shortly before, leaving room for the slightly smaller species, like reindeer, elk, auroch, deer, roe, boar, horse, etc., sufficiently big, however, to engender the lively interest of the hunters of the time. These species have been known in Europe since a long time ago, preferring different environments, the reindeer and elk more to the north where it was colder, the forest fauna more to the south and west in a warmer climate (Fig. 3.2.4a–c).

The end of the Pleistocene and the beginning of the Holocene witnessed the northward expansion of forest habitats, corresponding to the northward drift of forest fauna species which quickly occupied considerable stretches of the continent, pushing the reindeer and elk gradually further and further to the north.

The northward shift of the Early and Middle Holocene biotope resulted in at least two noteworthy phenomena (based on excavated osteological faunal remains):

- zonality of big game on the continental scale, with the tundra in the north being inhabited by reindeer, the dark coniferous forest by elk and seasonally by reindeer, and the mixed and deciduous forest by deer, roe and boar;
- local fauna variability over time, corresponding to the changes of climate in the Holocene (e.g. gradual disappearance of elk from central Europe during the

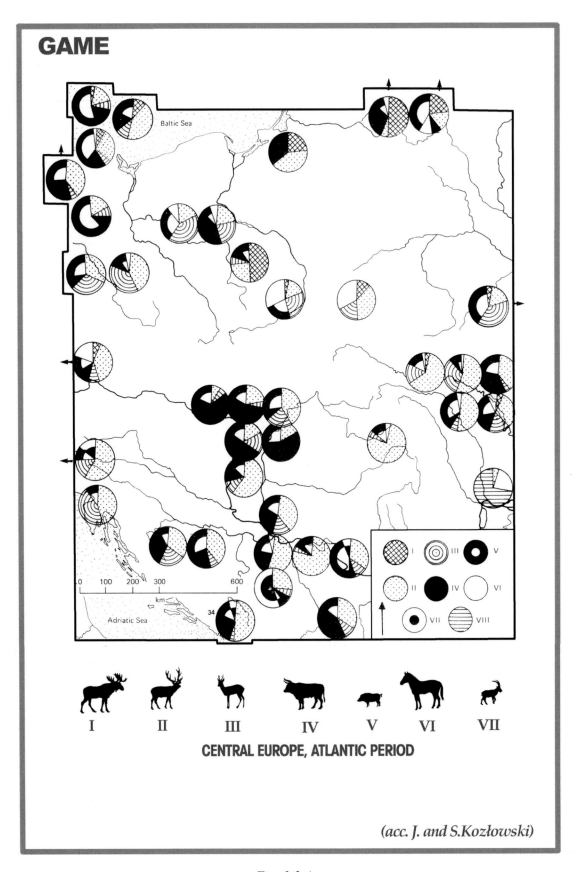

GAME

Baltic Sea

0 100 200 300 600
km

Adriatic Sea

34

I   II   III   V

II   IV   VI

VII   VIII

I   II   III   IV   V   VI   VII

CENTRAL EUROPE, ATLANTIC PERIOD

(acc. J. and S.Kozłowski)

Fig. 3.2.4a

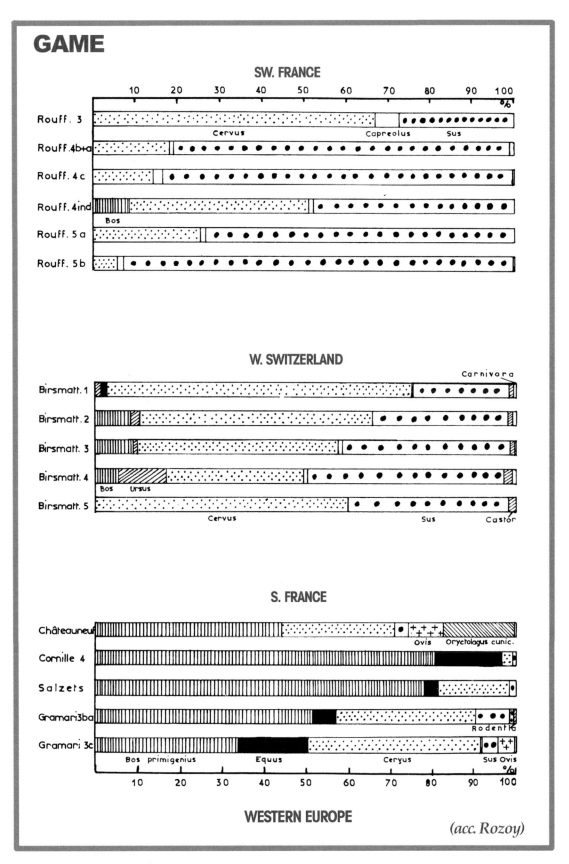

Fig. 3.2.4b

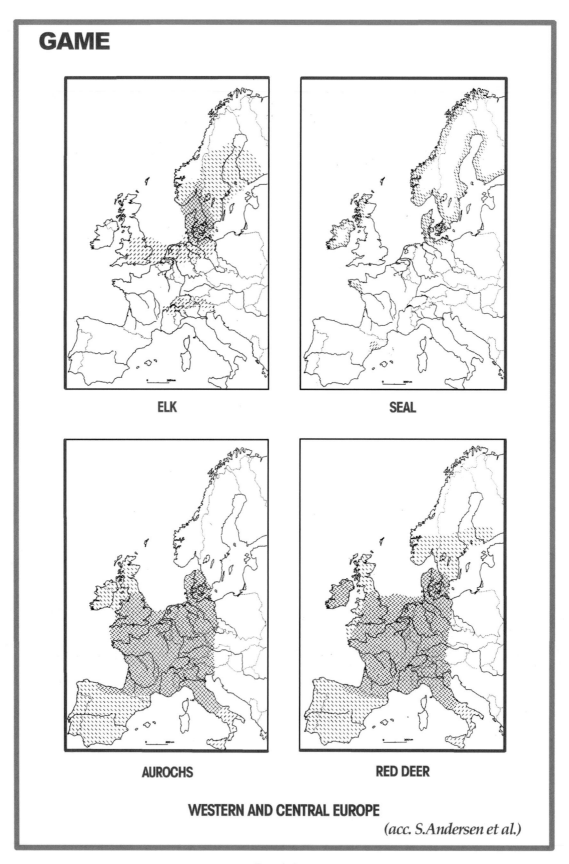

Fig. 3.2.4c

Boreal phase and the appearance a little later at the same time of deer and roe in the East Baltic area and even southern Scandinavia in the Atlantic period).

Mesolithic hunters also aimed for the small forest and water animals and birds. Such remains are frequently found on Mesolithic sites (cf. for example, Erik Brinch-Petersen's extensive lists for southern Scandinavia or maps edited and published by Raymond R. Newell, as well as by the author). The consumption value of these animals was low, but they were useful for their fur, musk, feathers, as well as bones for tool production. Apparently their role in Mesolithic culture has yet to be studied in detail.

The hunters' lifestyle depended on which animals were hunted. Greater mobility in the case of reindeer, lesser for forest fauna, herd size, specific habits of different species, skittishness of animals, etc., necessitated different adaptive models, organization of the hunt, even gear and hunting strategies (cf. "At home and abroad").

M.R. Jarman's today forgotten theory about the Mesolithic hunters' alleged deer control is interesting to consider. Similar ideas were once expressed regarding prehistoric reindeer control in the ex-Soviet Union. After all, it is believed that similar behavior in the Near East led to animal domestication. In Europe, it never did.

3.2.5. Mollusks

Mollusks were consumed by some Mesolithic communities and their shells were used as ornaments. Shell middens (southern Scandinavia, Atlantic coast, Maghreb, southwestern European Inland) are proof of local littoral land and marine species being part of consumption, as are specific tools like, for example, the Asturian pick, made perhaps to open mollusk shells. The shells were also treated as ornaments (and "traded"?) and this has led Raymond R. Newell to suggest that the regional differentiation of such ornaments could have reflected the linguistic differentiation of Mesolithic Europe(!).

3.2.6. Economic potential of Mesolithic Europe

Climate and climate-related flora and fauna were one of the stimulators of Mesolithic life. Added to this were elements of hydrography, considering that water reservoirs and the river valleys were usually among the richest biotopes.

North Scandinavia and the northeastern provinces seem to have been handicapped the worst by a climate that was the most severe and of a continental character. Snow must have taken longer to melt and the vegetation period was undoubtedly shorter; the flora here was also evidently less abundant in biomass than in the other provinces. Thus, apart from the circum-Baltic lakelands, the north and northeast were in some sense handicapped and this may be reflected in less intense settlement in these regions (partly settled in the Late Mesolithic, e.g. north Russia?). It is worth noting that the neolithization (and ceramicization, cf.) of these areas was also seriously retarded.

The more humid and temperate climate of the remaining provinces of Europe offered larger quantities of biomass and thus supported the subsequent development of settlement.

The Atlantic zone with its rich mixed and deciduous forests appears to have dominated somewhat over the central European one covered mostly by pine forests. The Mediterranean zone was also rich, while the economic potential of the biomass in the Pontic steppe was limited by the rather impaired hydrographic system (big dry spaces between big rivers).

As for the faunal count in particular provinces, there are no grounds for determining what the animal population was, although it seems that game was not lacking anywhere. The fauna, especially the big mammal species, was differentiated regionally and variable over time (cf. "Game").

An added attraction in the circum-Baltic region were the numerous lakes rich in fish, while in the western Baltic and Atlantic-Mediterranean zones edible mollusks, both the land and the marine varieties, appeared in quantity.

Also, the harvest of the gatherers was regionally differentiated and attractive (hazelnut in the north and lentil in the southwest), augmented in the Near East with cereals, beans and glans.

3.2.7. Raw material

Stone raw material was used for manufacturing hard and very basic tools (more often by chipping technique than by polishing). The physical nature of rocks have made them a mass find on archaeological sites. The variety of rock used for the purpose was considerable. "Stone" can be said to be of different geological age, different macroscopic appearance (aesthetic feelings not excluded) and technical properties (e.g. knapping quality, size), also outcrop accessibility (whether on the surface or sub-surface, if available at all). These differences have bearing on what the rock was used for.

First of all, it should be said that Europe can be divided into two great macro-zones as far as raw material is concerned. The northern zone includes Scandinavia (without Scania), Karelia and the East Baltic states (without Lithuania), the southern the remaining part of the continent without the Czech lands, Sardinia and Corsica and rather poor Balcanic region. There is no flint or any other rock good for knapping in the northern zone, which offers instead quartzite and quartz, as well as both hard and soft magmatic and sedimentary rocks (including shale/slate, for example). The second, huge zone is characterized by a variety of rock that is easily knapped (flint, radiolarite, chert, obsidian, etc.) in the weaker surface version (so-called Baltic erratic flint), which is weathered (usually small concretions, easily cracking), and the better sub-surface variety (bigger nodules or tablets, without cracking, either from primary deposits or found in river alluvial deposits, and mined in both cases).

This differentiation demands the application of a variety

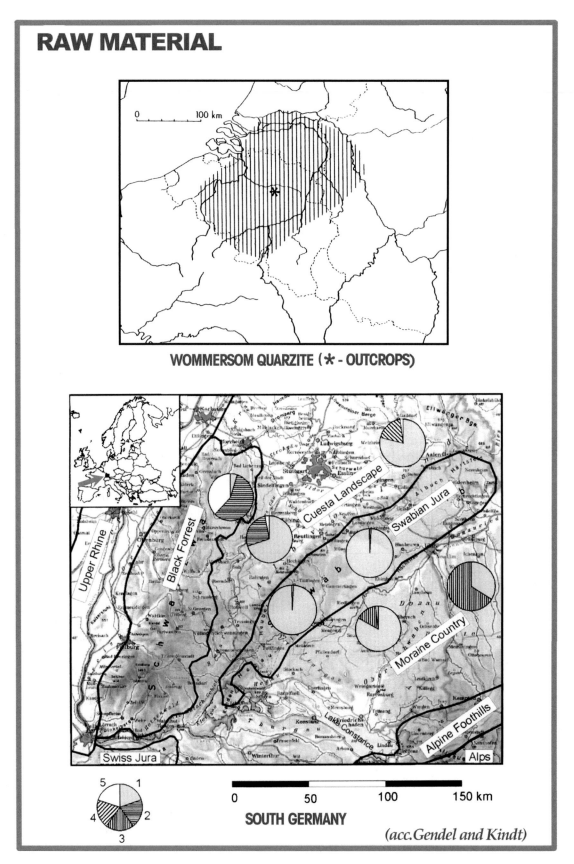

Fig. 3.2.7a

RAW MATERIAL

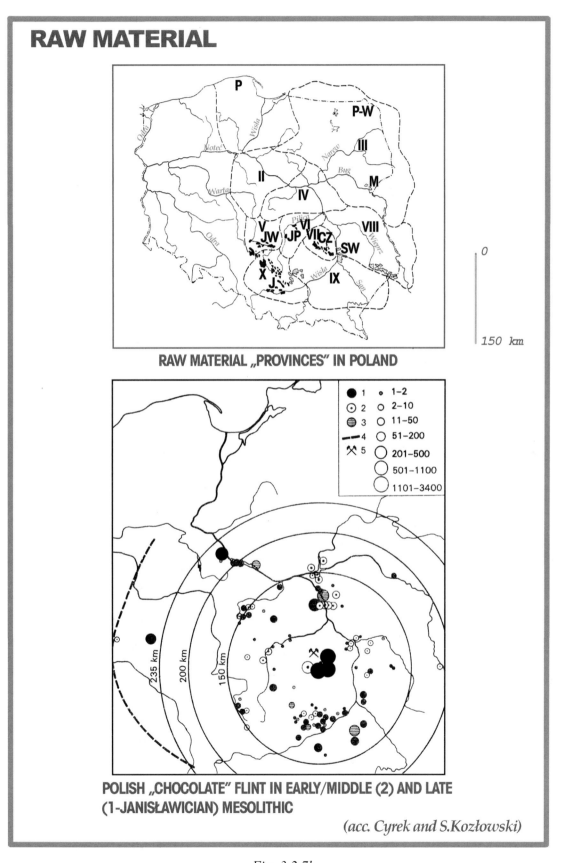

RAW MATERIAL „PROVINCES" IN POLAND

POLISH „CHOCOLATE" FLINT IN EARLY/MIDDLE (2) AND LATE
(1-JANISŁAWICIAN) MESOLITHIC

(acc. Cyrek and S.Kozłowski)

Fig. 3.2.7b

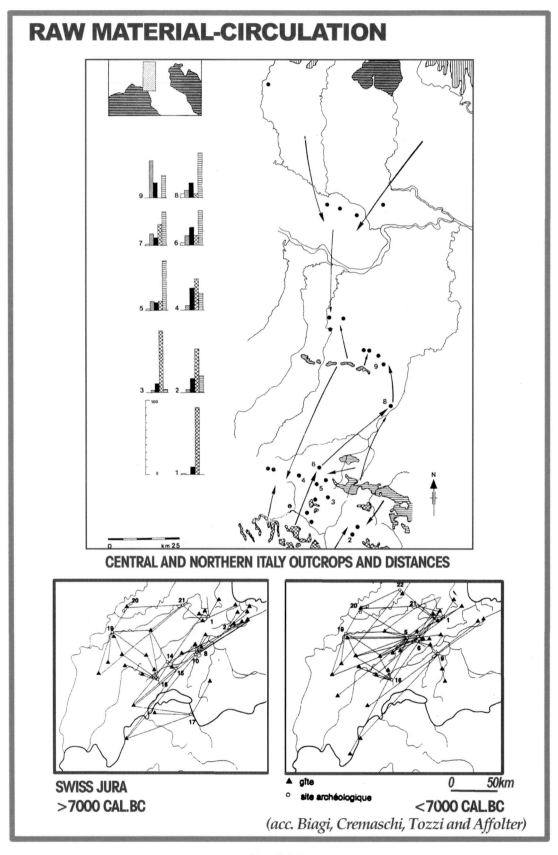

Fig. 3.2.7c

of techniques, shaping in effect significantly the style and morphology of objects that fill the archaeological record.

After all, the manner in which a cultural tradition was "realized" could be subject to change, due to the deterioration of raw material (for example, the forced shift from blade cores to flake cores). Even in the face of such outside factors, there was a strong push toward preserving the "tradition of the fathers" (meaning the traditional techniques, shapes and sizes of tools) regardless of how this was achieved. Another way out of the difficulties, when appropriate raw material was lacking, was to enlarge the *instrumentarium* to include products made (or rather finished) with a different technique, not chipping, but polishing (the axes and chisels of Scandinavia). It should be kept in mind that similar products are not unknown in the "flint" Mesolithic of the European Plain, but there they were made of easily knapped rock that required no further processing, such as polishing. Yet another solution is to consider the so-called "bone cultures" (cf. "Stone and bone cultures") as representing a situation in which most of the *instrumentarium* was made of organic materials in view of the simple fact that no rock suitable for chipping and polishing was to be found in the vicinity (e.g. Mesolithic of Latvia and Estonia, but also the absence of stone raw material and in consequence of Mesolithic occupation in the Italian Western Alps).

Most of the continent, however, had access to good quality rock that permitted easy manufacture of blades/bladelets and flakes, and easy further processing into well recognized typologically tools. These rocks are strongly differentiated genetically and macroscopically, also in terms of size and inner consistency (resistance to cracking) which is dependent on the amount of weathering to which a given concretion is subjected.

In the Early and Middle Mesolithic (and even later in the interior of the continent), local raw materials sufficed to fill the needs of local communities, which were thus autarchic formations in terms of raw material. Research by Krzysztof Cyrek for the basin of the Vistula, Mauro Cremasci and Michele Lanzinger for northern Italy, Michael Jochim for southern Germany, Peter A. Gendel for northwestern Europe, Cathèrine Perlèz for Greece, Janusz K. Kozłowski

and the author for the area of the Iron Gates on the Serbian-Romanian border, as well as for Montenegro, has demonstrated that raw material came from different outcrops outside the site, but located no further than 40–50 km away. It was not important then whether the material came from the surface or sub-surface, because the tool size was always small. For the basin of the Vistula, as well as for the Italian Dolomites, it proved possible to distinguish territories demonstrating unified raw material economy which could perhaps be interpreted as corresponding to tribal territory (cf. "Settlement pattern").

At the close of the Middle Mesolithic (mostly c. 7000 cal. BC), blanks of greater size and regularity than previously used became the object of desire over some parts of Europe (cf. "Castelnovization"). Such products could be obtained only from suitably big and pre-formed cores which needed to be made from good-quality material that was not weathered and did not crack subsequently. This kind of raw material was best mined straight from a deposit, whether primary, as in the case of the Astartian/Kimmerian bedrock in the piedmont of the Holy Cross Mountains in Poland, or secondary but not subject to weathering erosion (especially river alluvial deposits); evidence of Mesolithic flint mining has been noted in Poland, cf. "chocolate" flint outcrops in Tomaszów II, and the discovery of more sites should be anticipated. Mines and points of extraction were usually or could be accompanied by workshops producing "for export" either pre-formed cores or else ready blades and bladelets.

Exports could have traveled wider than before, reaching a hundred and more kilometers (Wommersom, Melos, "chocolate" flint in Poland, obsidian in the Near East; in the latter cases, raw material could have travel even a few hundred kilometers!). The export of some less knappable rocks or products in Scandinavia covered from a few dozen (in the case of axes) to a few hundred (the Olonetz slate) kilometers.

It is not clear whether the producers and exporters were at the same time the future users of these raw materials or whether there existed specialist task forces engaged for the job. In the Near East, the latter concept is imaginable from about 8000 cal. BC.

4

There!

It must be temperament, I guess. Right from the start the author felt no inclination for local studies that delved deeply into very minute issues of a single 'parish', so to speak. He had always looked across political borders, perhaps because even in his lifetime he had seen the Polish boundaries changing dramatically. His enthusiasm for geography had always stirred his interest in maps and what happened on them. Finally, he had dreamed of following in the footsteps of Grahame Clarke and Hermann Schwabedissen in defining Mesolithic territory based on numerous, apparently hopelessly mixed but rich museum collections of surface material. Recognizing the importance of homogeneous assemblages, the author was still hard put to reject the enormous quantities of mass surface material from all over Europe. Was it really worthless, he wondered until he came up with the idea for a mapping of the Mesolithic (cf. "Atlas").

The following chapter is devoted to this mapping project, presenting the actual enterprise, followed by excerpts from the already completed "Atlas" (a series of maps with remarks on terrain barriers impacting the cultural differentiation of Europe), a few studies of selected types of microliths, complete with the author's synthesis, a paper prepared for and presented at the "Meso 2005" symposium in Belfast in 2005 (cf. "Mapping").

4.1. Pyrénées, Alpes et Carpates: barrières culturelles pour les derniers chasseurs-prédateurs

(co-author – R. Desbrosse)

Introduction

Les chaînes de montagne (Fig. 4.1) ont, le plus souvent, constituées, même de nos jours, des obstacles aux contacts humains en isolant des cultures, des ethnies, des états. L'histoire nous montre que les rois de France, par exemple, ont longtemps rêvé d'une nation bien protégée par les barrières naturelles que constituent les Pyrénées, les

Alpes et le Rhin. De même, les Habsbourg, leurs rivaux séculaires, ont toujours cherché la protection naturelle de l'arc carpatique au nord et à l'est et, au sud celle des Alpes dinariques. L'exemple napoléonien annexant le canton de Genève et l'occupation de la Bosnie par les Autrichiens en 1878 sont d'autres exemples de cette politique générale.

Dans l'Europe préhistorique, ces barrières montagneuses ont pu jouer un rôle encore plus prononcé à cause, entre autres, de péjorations climatiques et de structures sociales moins évoluées.

Au cours des améliorations climatiques, la moyenne montagne devient franchissable tandis qu'au Tardiglaciaire des altitudes de quelques centaines de mètres (p. ex. Les Carpates Blanches) ont empêché les Magdaléniens de l'actuelle Pologne méridionale et de Moravie de coloniser la Slovaquie.

Les grandes vallées de fleuves et les bandes côtières ont, le plus souvent, servi d'axes naturels pour les contacts entre les groupes humains précités. Ainsi, le Danube nous fait connaître la diffusion de l'Aurignacien vers l'Europe atlantique et l'expansion, à partir du Jura souabe, du Magdalénien vers l'Europe centre-orientale.

Pour les bandes côtières, encore plus larges aux temps glaciaires et au Holocène ancien, nous citerons la côte atlantique, le Levant espagnol, la côte dalmate, la Ligurie, les deux extrémités de la chaîne pyrénéenne, mais aussi les terres actuellement innondés entre la Grande Bretagne, le Danemark et la Pologne.

Il est plus exceptionnel de citer les rares cas d'échanges transcarpatiques (les passages : Orava, Spisz, Poprad, Dukla, Uzhok, Yablonitse, Priscop, Bicaz) de matières premières au cours du Paléolithique supérieur ou celui de contacts sauveterriens entre les Dolomites italiennes et le Tyrol autrichien par Brenner (environ 1300 m d'altitude, site de Ullafelsen fouillé par Dieter Schäfer).

Dans ce court article, nous prétendons illustrer cette théorie par des exemples choisis dans les cultures du Postglaciaire ancien.

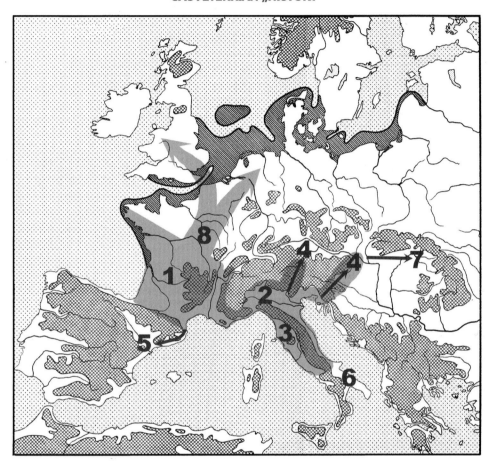

PYRENEES, ALPES...

SAUVETERRIAN „HISTORY"

1-CLASSICAL TERRITORY

2-3-ITALIAN GROUPS

4-PUSH TO CENTRAL EUROPE

5-7-INFUENCES (FILADOR,MARISA,TISZA SITES)

8-"SAUVETERRIANISATION" OF THE NORD

Fig. 4.1

Le Mésolithique

Alpes et Carpates influencent les différences technologiques, stylistiques et culturelles du Mésolithique ancien (11e/10e cal. millénaires AC) et nous permettent de distinguer quatre grandes provinces européennes:

- Le Maglemosien, ou Mésolithique nordique, occupe la Grande Plaine nord-européenne, le sud de la Scandinavie et l'est de l'Angleterre, ainsi que Pologne. Il se heurte au sud à l'arc carpatique, les Sudètes et les plateaux sud-allémaniques.

- L'Épigravettien postglaciaire nous montre une culture immuable depuis le Paléolithique supérieur dans le bassin carpatique (Hongrie, Slovaquie, Roumanie, Bulgarie, Bosnie, Serbie, Croatie, Slovénie, Montenegro et Grèce) et sur la mer Adriatique, qui joue alors le rôle de cul-de-sac tandis que cette même culture évoluait vers le Sauveterrien d'Italie et de France méridionale. Une ou deux dizaines de sites assez bien datés se répartissent entre l'arc carpatique, la côte dalmate et les Alpes. Quelques-uns montrent des particularités internes : Frankhthi (Grèce), Dekilitach (Bulgarie), Ćrvena Stijena (Monténégro), Padina, Lepenski Vir et Vlasac (Serbie), Breg (Slovénie), Pecs, Jasztelek, Jaszbereny (Hongrie), Cuina Turcului, Cremenea et Gìlma (Roumanie), Barca et Dolna Streda (Slovaquie).

- Le Beuronien (ou faciès Coincy du Tardenoisien français selon Raoul Daniel) s'étend du Bassin Parisien à la Moravie et la Basse Silésie polonaises, à travers l'Allemagne méridionale, la Suisse, l'Autriche et la Czechie, sans jamais franchir vers le sud la barrière alpine ni à l'est, les Carpates Blanches. En France, la meilleure documentation nous est fournie par les sites de Rochedàne (Doubs), Oberlarg (Haut Rhin) – fouilles André Thévenin, Piscop (Val d'Oise), Montbani 2, Coincy 2 (Aisne), Chaintreauville, la grotte du Troglodite à Nemours (Seine-et-Marne) – fouilles René Parent et Raoul Daniel. Citons aussi Birsmatten-Basisgrotte en Suisse – fouilles Hans-Georg Bandi, Jägerhaushöhle et Zigeunerfels de Wolfgang Taute, Schrägewand, Ensdorf, Falkensteinhöhle et Mücheln-Möckerling en Allemagne, Limberg-Mühlberg en Autriche, Tašovice en Bohême, Smolín et Přibice en Moravie fouilles de Karel Valoch.

- Le Sauveterrien couvre une aire plus large que les cultures précédentes puisqu'on de connaît du Pyrenées (Barma Margineda), à la Slovénie (Pod Crmuklio) en passant par la moitié sud de la France: Rouffignac (Dordogne) – fouilles Claude Barrière, Le Martinet (Lot-et-Garonne), Montclus (Gard) – fouilles Max Escalon de Fonton, Culoz et Abri Gay (Ain), les sites d'altitude du Vercors (bien connus grâces aux fouilles exemplaires de Pierre Bintz à Charmate, Coufin et Grande Rivoire), Abeurador, Fontbregoua et La Tourasse dans le sud-ouest de la France (fouilles entre autres de Michel Barbaza). Le site breton de la Pointe Bertheaume fait figure d'exception géographique. Le

Bassin Parisien (Grotte Chateaubriand) de Jacques Hinout, le Jura suisse (Ogens de Michel Egloff) et le Valais (Vionnaz) en Suisse ont aussi été colonisés. Dans la moitié nord de l'Italie, il faut citer Isola Santa de Carlo Tozzi, Romagnano III, Vatte di Zambana, Pradestel, Plan de Freia d'Alberto Broglio et Colbricon et Gaban de Bernardino Bagolini, ainsi qu'une unique incursion tyrolienne en Autriche (Ullafelsen de Dieter Schäfer). La Slovaquie donne enfin le site de Sered', fouillé par Juraj Barta.

Il semble que les Sauveterriens aient été les rares Mésolithiques à fréquenter la haute chaîne alpine (autour de 2500 m – Pyrenées, Alpes) et parfois, peut-être, à la franchir au cours d'activités estivales.

Durant le Mésolithique ancien et moyen, les massifs montagneus paraissent avoir favorisé les cloisonnements culturels et développé les particularismes régionaux.

Conclusions

Dans cette étude trop rapide, nous avons essayé de montrer que les barrières montagneuses d'Europe ont été franchies par les Mésolithiques des 11ᵉ–8ᵉ millénaires cal. A.C. seulement, à de très rares exceptions. Les chaînes élevées ont joué un rôle essentiel dans la création des zones culturelles continentales et ont favorisé les particularismes régionaux des grandes provinces de faible ou moyenne altitude. On regrettera toujours l'insuffisance des recherches sous-marines (trop onéreuses) qui nous prive d'une masse importante de renseignements sur le peuplement préhistorique de l'Europe littorale.

4.2. Mesolithic settlement pattern

Contrary to the thinking of some amateur archaeologists, the European Mesolithic is not a monolith. Indeed, it can well be divided into smaller fragments, on the grounds of style (cf. characteristics of technocomplexes and cultures in separate chapters), as well as settlement patterns (Fig. 4.2a–e). The latter differentiation is of interest at this point and we shall see that sensible determinations are hardly easy to make in this respect.

Historical experience and ethnological data demonstrate two facts. Firstly, hunting-gathering communities are characterized by a rather constant model of social organization regardless of geographical latitude (cf. L. Binford's works), from nuclear family through enlarged family to bigger structures, and they maintain a numerical equilibrium. Secondly, each group or entity in this hierarchy corresponds to a certain territory which has a specific internal organization (ownership, borders, areas of seasonal penetration, special function areas) and comparable surface area. According to Wiktor Skoczkowski, who studied human groups and territory size in traditional North American forest communities, comparing them with the territories of European Mesolithic cultures, particular organizational units tend to present the following parameters:

- nuclear family: 5–6 persons

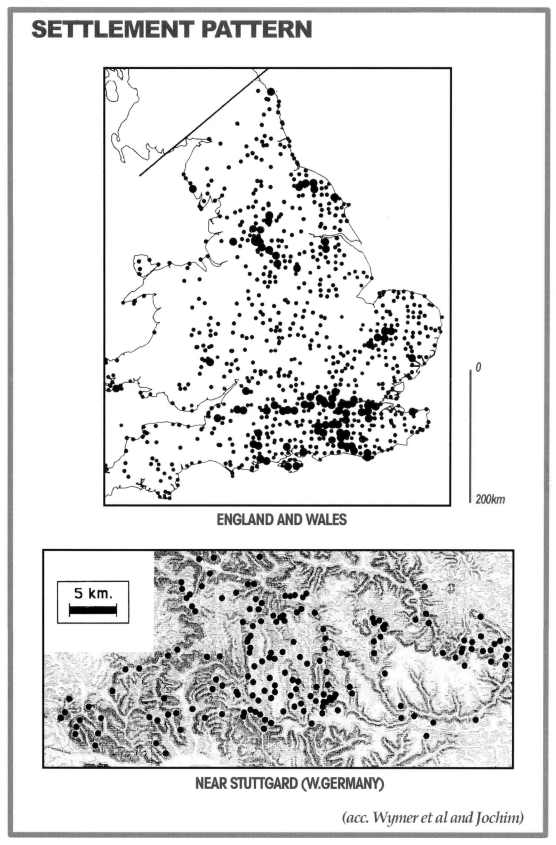

SETTLEMENT PATTERN

ENGLAND AND WALES

0

200km

5 km.

NEAR STUTTGARD (W.GERMANY)

(acc. Wymer et al and Jochim)

Fig. 4.2a

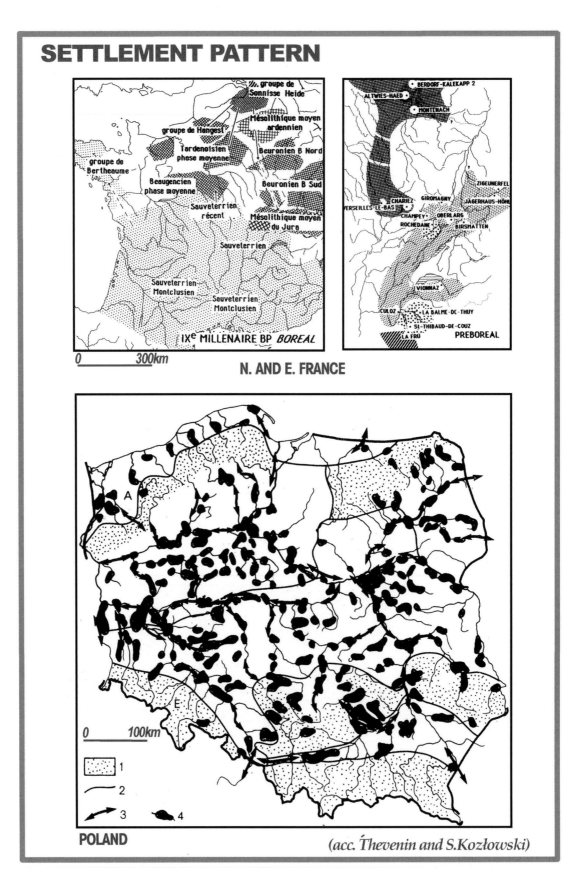

Fig. 4.2b

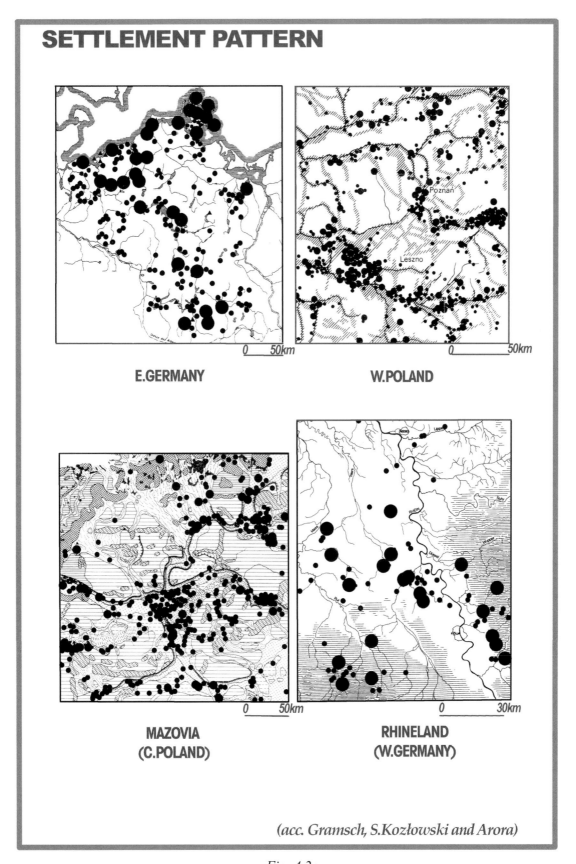

(acc. Gramsch, S.Kozłowski and Arora)

Fig. 4.2c

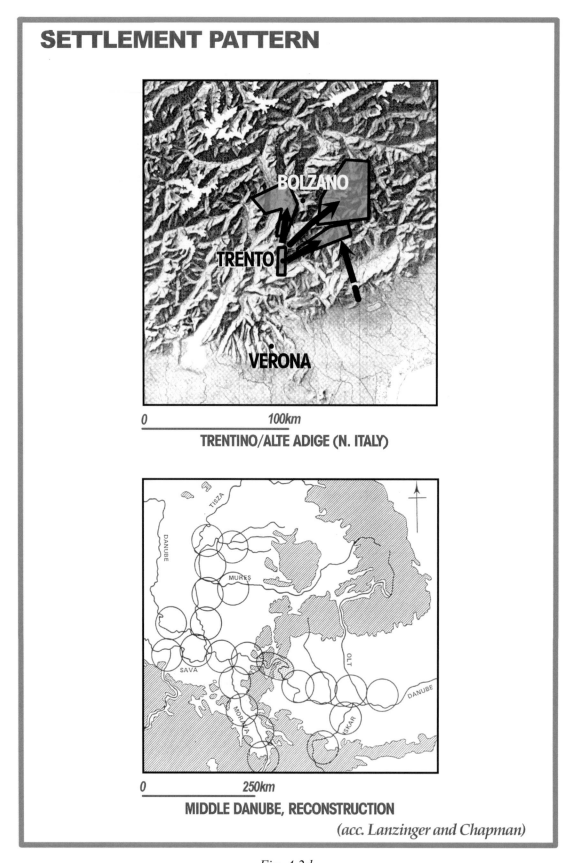

Fig. 4.2d

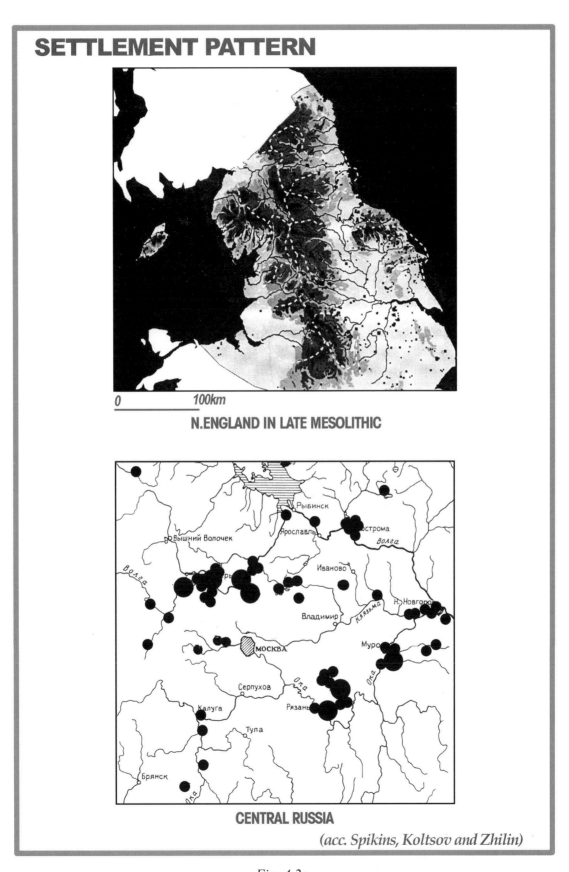

Fig. 4.2e

- local group: up to 25 (maximum 75) persons
- regional group: 50–200 (maximum 300) persons
- tribe: 800–1200 persons

It is likely that the below-described different degrees of grouping of Mesolithic European sites reflect to some extent the above divisions.

Skoczkowski suggested that the units of cultural division described as "cultures" (40,000–300,000 sq.km) in the present volume reflected in fact Mesolithic tribes, because the areas they occupied roughly corresponded to the size of territories occupied and exploited by specific North American aboriginal tribes.

In turn, researchers working on the Mesolithic who have concentrated their studies on larger sections of the continent (regions), are apt to note a variety of territorial divisions of a higher degree, that is, foremost, different degrees of stylistic and perhaps social differentiation (Hermann Schwabedissen, Stefan K. Kozłowski, Jean-Georges Rozoy, André Thevenin, John Wymer and co-authors, Raymond R. Newell, Bernhard Gramsch, etc.). They have also observed the existence of empty areas between particular groups of sites, concentrations featuring a similar style (Michael A. Jochim, Bernhard Gramsch, André Thevenin, Erwin Cziesla, Surendra K. Arora), which at least theoretically are entitled to minor stylistic differentiation and separate evolution. In the light of the above territorial considerations, these concentrations should range from 30 to 40 km in diameter.

Another important source of information on territorial division is the analysis of raw-material economy on particular sites and territories. Polish experience in this field (research by Krzysztof Cyrek for the Vistula basin) has shown that autarchic economies lead in the Early and Middle Mesolithic to the emergence of several local systems of raw material supply. Applied in areas reduced to several dozen kilometers in diameter, they can, on occasion, last for extended periods of time. Similar distances have been proposed for southern Germany by Michael Jochim, for northwestern Europe by Jean-Georges Rozoy (quartzite from Wommersom), for Italy by Carlo Tozzi, Paolo Biagi and Michele Lanzinger. The present author once arrived at the conclusion that Mesolithic territories with uniform raw material structure in Poland ranged in size from 100 to 200 km.

Thus, in every case the mapping method based on the material is the sole source of data for distinguishing separate territories, whatever these would be, naturally assuming the following reservations. Firstly, any cartographic analysis must be based on all the avaibale, including mixed material. Secondly, the entire area under investigation needs to be studied with equal attention in order to be certain that the concentration of sites and the presence of empty spaces reflect the actual state of settlement in a given region. Depending on the assumptions made, different researchers tend to separate out territories of very different size, attributing them in fairly arbitrary fashion to particular units of the social organization. While avoiding the same, the present author cannot but confirm the existence of an undoubted hierarchy in the territorial structure of the European Mesolithic.

Successive structures lower than a "culture" in the hierarchy are referred to most often as "cultural groups", identified based on technological and typological distinctions within the framework of particular "cultures". They consist of smaller territorial units, the average size of which reaches from 30 to 40 km (research by Michele Lanzinger for the Italian Dolomites, data from Surendra K. Arora for the Rhineland, determinations of Stefan K. Kozłowski for the Polish Plain, propositions of André Thévenin for northwestern Europe, and H. Schilling for Denmark). These, too, are naturally organized along water courses, separated one from the other by dry and empty spaces.

The biggest unit to be distinguished on the grounds of stylistic criteria is a "Technocomplex" and its constituent "cultures" (respectively 1,000,000–2,000,000 and 150,000–300,000 km^2 in area). "Cultures" are frequently distinguished from neighbors on the grounds of merely secondary techno-stylistic criteria, often (but not always) being surrounded by topographical barriers without settlement, such as mountains, plateaus, front moraine chains, water divides, dry lands, or separated by the hydrographic system (river catchment, areas around large lakes, fiords) and ultimately a local raw material economy or e.g. lack of raw-material outcrops.

A typical area of the kind finds parallels in ethnological examples (Stoczkowski), in which case a population number between 800 and 1200 will be derived from the model. Assuming the validity of this observation, one can assume that such areas characterized the European Mesolithic: each followed a separate line of development, and each, in keeping with the principles of isolationism, separated itself from other similar groups. Thus, inhabitants could be said to have their own, not too extensive "parish" perspective.

4.3. Une cartographie des éléments typologiques mésolithiques en Europe

En 1936 le Professeur Grahame Clark publia un ouvrage consacré au Mésolithique d'Europe du Nord. Cette publication constitua la base d'une étude moderne du Mésolithique et, depuis, les recherches s'intensifièrent et se développèrent dans ce domaine. Cette étude moderne du Mésolithique visait essentiellement à:

1. Préciser la notion du terme "Mésolithique".
2. Developper l'étude des structures économiques et sociales des populations mésolithiques.
3. Etudier les problèmes des divisions chronologiques et culturelles.
4. Proposer des systèmes typologiques.
5. Réaliser des monographies régionales recouvrant à peu près l'Europe entière.

Cependant on peut reconnaître certaines lacunes à ces monographies réalisées depuis l'ouvrage de Clark: le fait qu'elles soient limitées territorialement rend difficile les comparaisons avec les monographies consacrées à des régions voisines. On peut également regretter que bien souvent l'étude d'une entité taxonomique culturelle ne s'etend pas à son extension réelle, mais à des limites artificielles imposés par les frontières politiques. Il en résulte qu'une même entité mésolithique possède plusieurs dénominations (p. ex. Coincy en France, Beuronien en Allemagne, Sauveterroide Horizont en Suisse, etc.).

Ce problème touche également la répartition géographique des types particuliers.

En égard à ceci, il nous paraît évident que, afin de rendre les comparaisons possibles entre les phénomènes régionaux et de progresser vers une plus large synthèse du Mésolithique, nous devons tenter d'unifier notre point de vue et notre connaissance des données récoltées jusqu'à présent (Fig. 4.3). Dans ce but, nous avons décidés de composer un "Atlas" (cf.) comprenant les cartes présentant des principaux types mésolithiques (éléments discriminants).

L'intérêt de cette recherche

L'atlas sera un informateur international sur le Mésolithique européen et pour sa réalisation nous avons poursuivi plus particulièrement les buts suivants:

1⁰ Dans une première étape du travail:

a) L'unification des méthodes de description du matériel (typologie), ce qui nous a permis de démontrer les similitudes et dissimilitudes réelles entre les principaux phénomènes et eléments regionaux du Mésolithique européen.

b) L'aboutissement à une réelle comparativité des matériaux archéologiques régionaux en les examinant dans une large quasi-complète perspective spatiale.

c) La suppression (ou la redefinition) d'ambiguïté de certains termes utilisés dans la littérature (Maglemosien, Tardenoisien, etc.).

d) Présentations cartographiques et unification de la nomenclature taxonomique, la répartition réelle de certains éléments typologiques (p. ex. les types d'outils et leurs variantes) complétées par une documentation sous forme de catalogue.

2⁰ Dans une seconde étape du travail, dépendant entièrement de la première, nous aborderons les points suivants:

a) Présentation de l'évolution de certains types d'outils (origine, développement territorial et chronologique, déclin, place et signification dans chaque faciès culturel).

b) Reconstruction de l'évolution de chaque entité culturelle en particulier (dont les composantes sont les éléments analysés dans le point "a"). Seront donc inclues dans cet historique, non seulement les composantes typiques et permanentes de chaque entité culturelle, mais également celles qui n'apparaissent que dans certaines phases chronologiques ou groupes régionaux de cette entité. Il sera possible, par conséquent, de définir l'aire de répartition des entités culturelles, même à partir de matériaux mélangés, non-homogènes.

c) A plus longue échéance, nous pourrons envisager un texte sur la paléohistoire de l'Europe dans l'Holocène inférieur.

Ce plan n'a jamais été entièrement réalisé (remarque en 2006).

Les limites

Notre atlas est limité chronologiquement à la période s'étendant de l'env. 10,000/9500 au 6ᵉ/5ᵉ millénaire cal. BC.

Nous excluons du cadre géographique le Nord et le Sud-Est de l'Europe, ainsi que la Plaine Russe, à cause du nombre trop restreint des trouvailles.

La richesse des sources mésolithiques dont nous disposons (surtout entre la Grande Bretagne, la France du Nord et la Lithuanie-Bielorussie) est telle qu'il nous a fallu sélectionner les éléments les plus caractéristiques, c'est-à-dire les armatures et pointes qui, par leur abondance numérique et surtout leur richesse typologique, permettent d'établir les divisions culturelles et chronologiques.

La composition de l'atlas (voir dans ce volume)

1⁰ La première partie comprend, outre l'introduction, les définitions des types d'outils qui figurerent sur les cartes. L'auteur y mentionne également les systèmes typologiques locaux/régionaux ainsi que les comparaisons éventuellement possibles entre ces systèmes (J.G.D. Clark, H. Schwabedissen, C. Barrière, GEEM, J.G. Rozoy, A. Bohmers et A. Wouters, T. Mathiassen etc.).

Dans la même partie l'auteur présente plusieur cartes de la distribution des types d'outils sans distinction chronologique. Chaque carte sera complétée d'un commentaire (ça n'avait jamais été réalisé completement – remarque en 2006) reprenant les informations que nous avons pu recueillir sur chaque type. Ces commentaires comprendront entre autres nos remarques sur l'exactitude du résultat obtenu. Ils traiteront en outre des subdivisions régionales et de la situation des éléments étudiés dans le schéma culturel et chronologique du Mésolithique (voir les études sur pointes K, PE, PB, PC etc. dans ce volume).

Il est indispensable que notre "Atlas" soit complété d'un répertoire de nos sources d'information, à savoir:

a) d'une liste des sites mésolithiques étudiés et d'un index de référence aux cartes

b) d'une liste bibliographique

c) d'une liste des collections étudiées

2⁰ La deuxième partie de l'atlas, qui ne pourra être réalisée qu'à plus longue échéance (voir remarques sur la deuxième étape des travaux), contiendra entre autres la liste des outillages homogènes, des dates absolues, l'historique des types et structures typologiques, ainsi que les cartes synthétiques et les cartes de l'évolutions chronologique et spatiale de certains types. En effet nul, sauf les "cartes synthetiques", n'était realisé dans ce projet (remarque 2006, cf. ausssi "Mapping the Mesolithic").

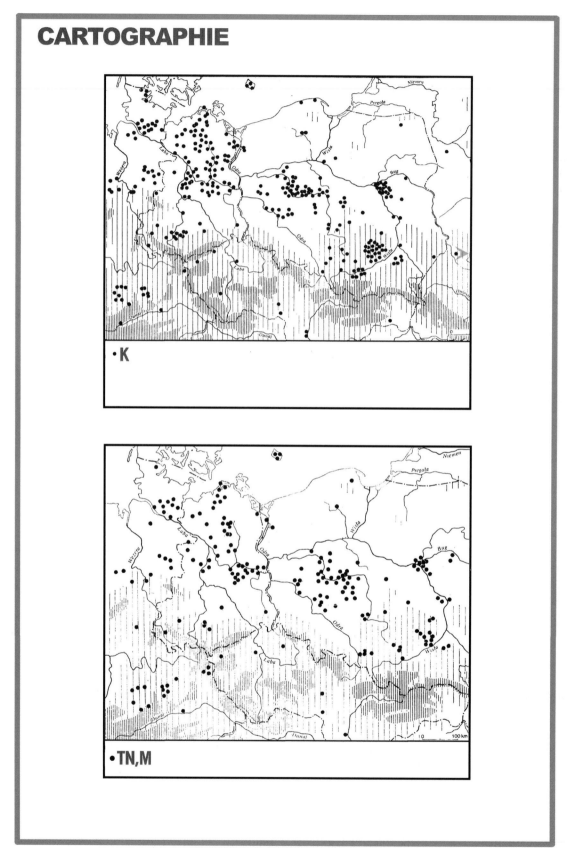

Fig. 4.3

Les sources

Il est évident que les résultats que nous obtiendrons dépendent non seulement de la méthode utilisée, mais également de l'état des sources. A ce propos nous avons bénéficié de conditions privilégiées, puisque nous avons eu l'occasion d'étudier les matériaux originaux de presque tous les pays européens. Nous avons également pu constituer une abondante bibliographie complétée de travaux inédits que certains de nos collègues ont bien voulu nous communiquer (Raymond R. Newell, Søren H. Andersen, Jean-Georges Rozoy, Bernhard Gramsch, Wolfgang Taute). Ces travaux ont un caractère complémentaire pour la bibliographie du sujet, utilisée dans notre atlas.

Il n'en est pas moins vrai que les sources étant parfois incomplètes, il subsiste encore des grandes lacunes sur les cartes qui ne reflètent donc pas exactement la situation réelle, mais plutot l'etat de recherche.

D'autre part, signalons que la majeure partie des matériaux dont nous disposons, provient des récoltes de surface, souvent mélangés. Nous les acceptons même mélangés; tels matériaux ont toujour un valeur pour l'étude cartographique.

Outre l'inégalité de l'état des recherches dans chaque région, nous regrettons également que certaines collections demeurent inaccessibles et que le nombre de sites publiés varie d'une région à l'autre. Les progrès de notre travail dépendront donc du nombre des sites connus pour chaque région ainsi que de la régularité de leur répartition. Si nous disposons d'un site pour 1000 km², nous obtiendrons une proportion assez satisfaisante (pour la Pologne + 300 sites, pour la Belgique ± 30, tandis que pour la France ± 550 sites, dans ce dernier cas, jamais malheureusement atteinte!).

Certains pays ont livré un nombre de sites suffisant (Belgique, Grand Bretagne, Allemagne, Pays-Bas, Danemarque, Suède, Pologne, Italie, etc.) mais dans d'autres pays (Portugal, Espagne) ce nombre est trop restreint et risque malheureusement de fausser les résultats.

Comment in 2006

The "Atlas" or at least the first part of this projected idea was put into life in 1990 (cf. extensive fragments in this volume).

4.4. *Atlas of the European Mesolithic*

Introduction

The idea of preparing the present "Atlas" emerged during the author's work on a book entitled "The Prehistory of Polish Territories from the 9th to the 5th Millenium BC" (PWN, Warsaw 1972), which included many maps showing the ranges of chosen Mesolithic types in Central Europe, mainly for the purposes of "cultural" taxonomy. It appeared then that the applied method of cartographic analysis not only enabled the presentation of spatial aspects

of particular taxonomic units but also led to interesting conclusions in the field of palaeohistory (cf. "Mapping the Mesolithic"). It was clear, too that many of the typological elements utilised in the spatial analysis reached beyond the territory of Central Europe. Also many fragments of the Early/Middle Holocene history of Central Europe could not be undestood without a wide and multidimensional spatial analysis.

Consequently, following the works of Hermann Schwabedissen and of Wolfgang Taute, the author has made an attempt to collate cartographically chosen elements of the European Mesolithic in the belief that such cartograms may be an adequate basis for future historical synthesis.

Specifically:

1. By showing the spatial ranges (Fig. 4.4a–y) of the phenomena the "Atlas" should make researchers of the Mesolithic aware of what is universal and what is local. Hence, it should show them, for the first time in this field of prehistory, the basic Mesolithic sources in a carefully weighed perspective. Such a perspective has seldom occurred so far, the field being predominated by local studies, which did not take into consideration the importance of space, concentrating the whole effort on vertical analyses. Therefore, it is not difficult to guess that such results could not lead to a wide synthesis.

2. The above statements about the right perspective of research and about differentiating between local elements and those of a wider range lead to the formulation of the next aim of this work: to make more objective the existing "cultural" divisions, which are too often determined by the present political boundaries and lack of knowledge of materials from a nearer and farther neighbourhood.

3. The third aim of the "Atlas" is to present materials for the reconstruction of the "history" of particular classes of artefacts (cf. texts following the "Atlas"), whole sets of classes and, finally, "sets of sets" (= cultures). All this in preparation for a larger synthesis. It is thus necessary to eliminate banal, otherwise irrelevant classes of artefacts, created convergently, while leaving those that are homogeneous and of intercultural significance (= elements of "intercultural trends", cf.) or else of more or less regional or perhaps local importance.

A future aim will also be the investigation of spatio-temporal variations of the particular classes, whole components and, as a result, "cultures". The author hopes that the above remarks as well as acquaintance with the published maps will give the reader an idea of the importance of the factor of space in studies of the Mesolithic, persuading him in effect of the need for this publication.

The author reported the introductory assumptions of the "Atlas" at the 20th Session of the French Prehistoric Congress, July 1974, in Mantigues (cf. above). Detailed interpretations of some of the cartograms (classes K, PB, PC, PD, PE, DF, RA, RB, RC) were published elsewhere (cf. also this volume). They were utilized for

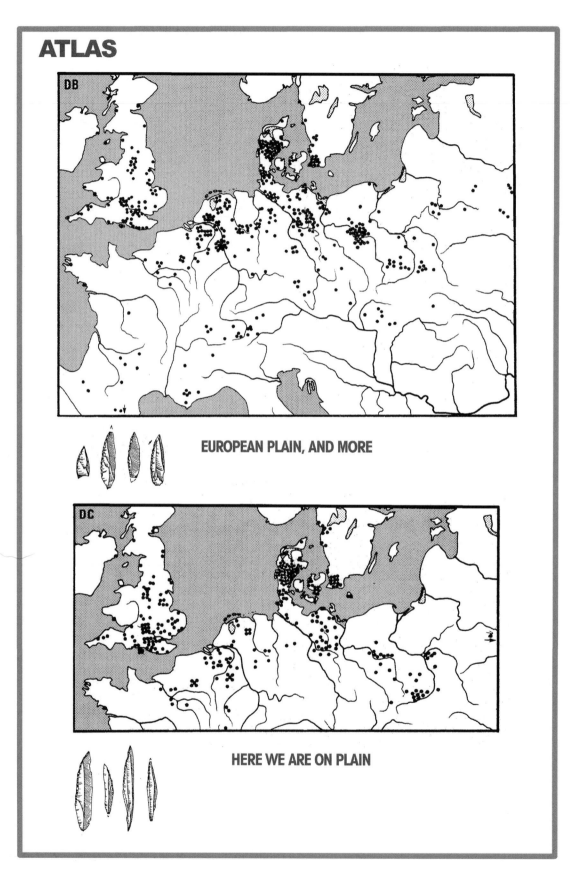

Fig. 4.4a

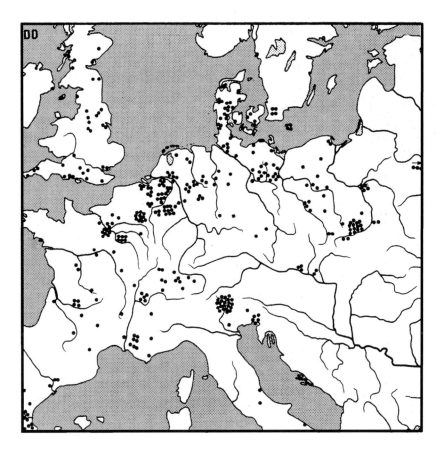

ATLAS

NARROW SEGMENTS, EVERYWHERE AND EVERYTIME

Fig. 4.4b

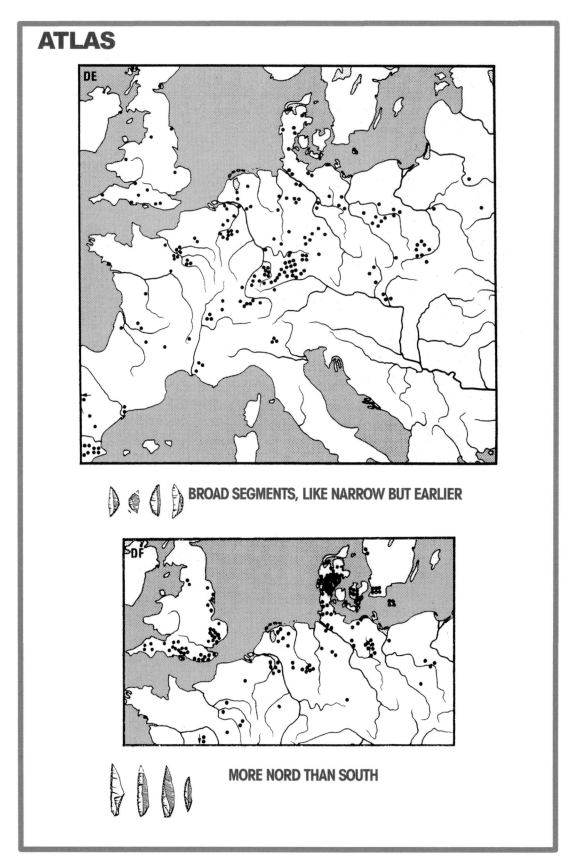

Fig. 4.4c

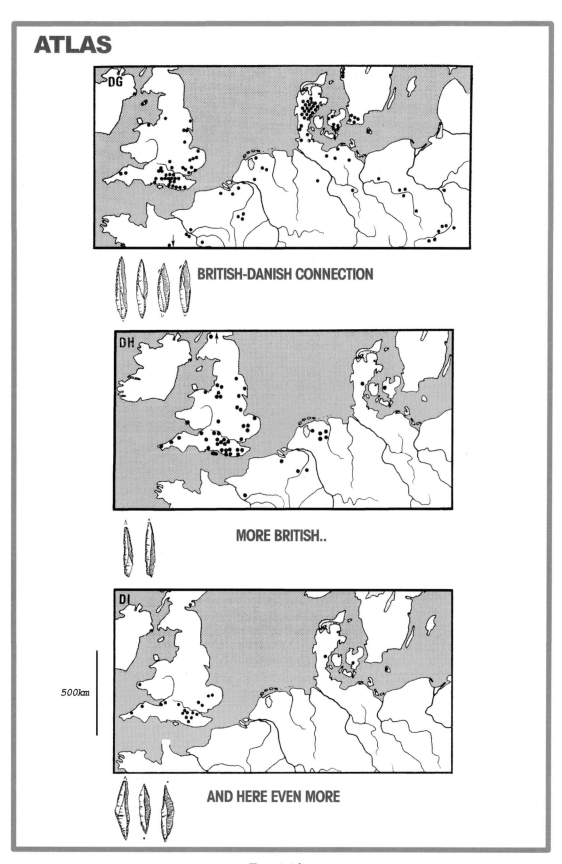

Fig. 4.4d

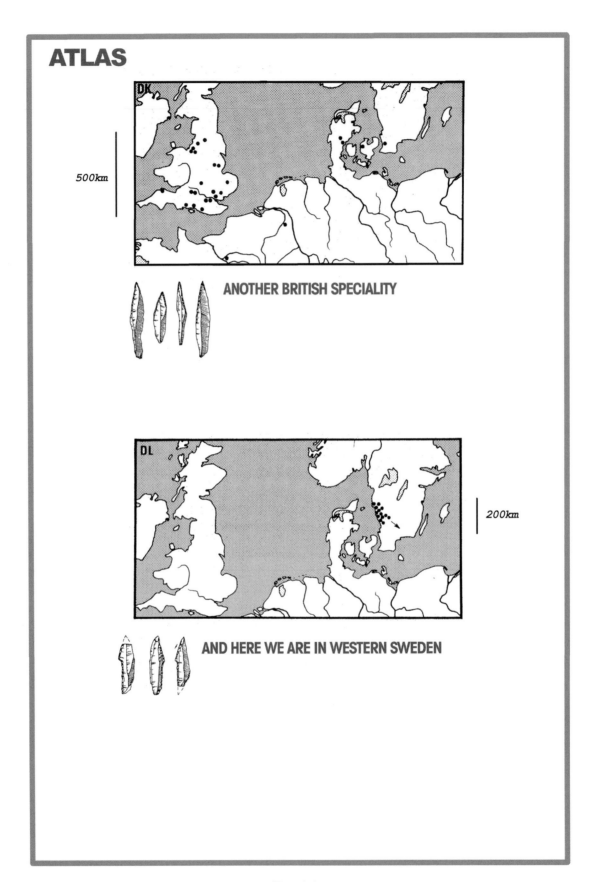

Fig. 4.4e

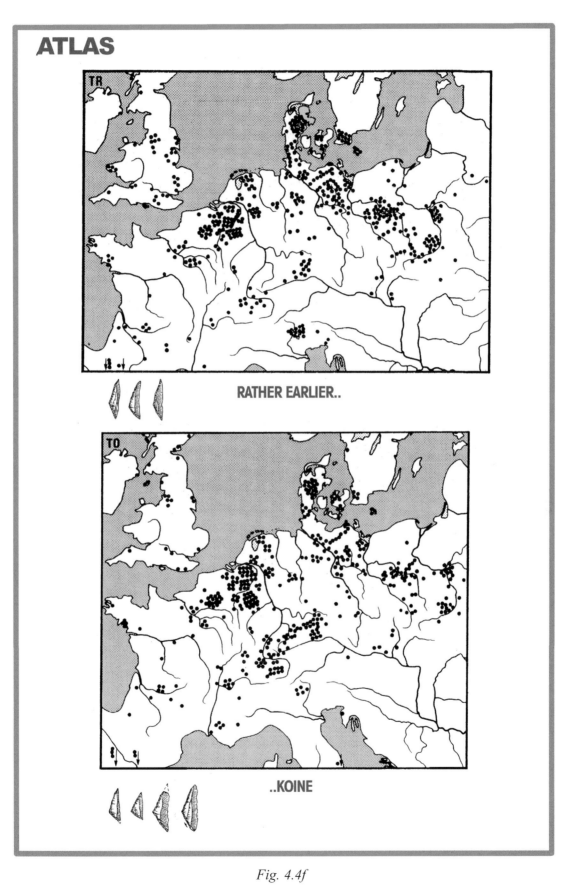

Fig. 4.4f

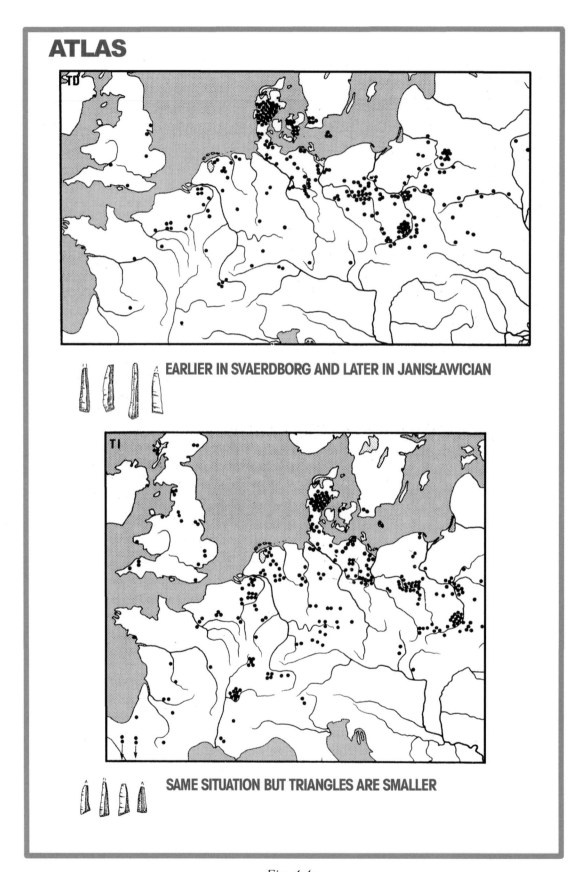

Fig. 4.4g

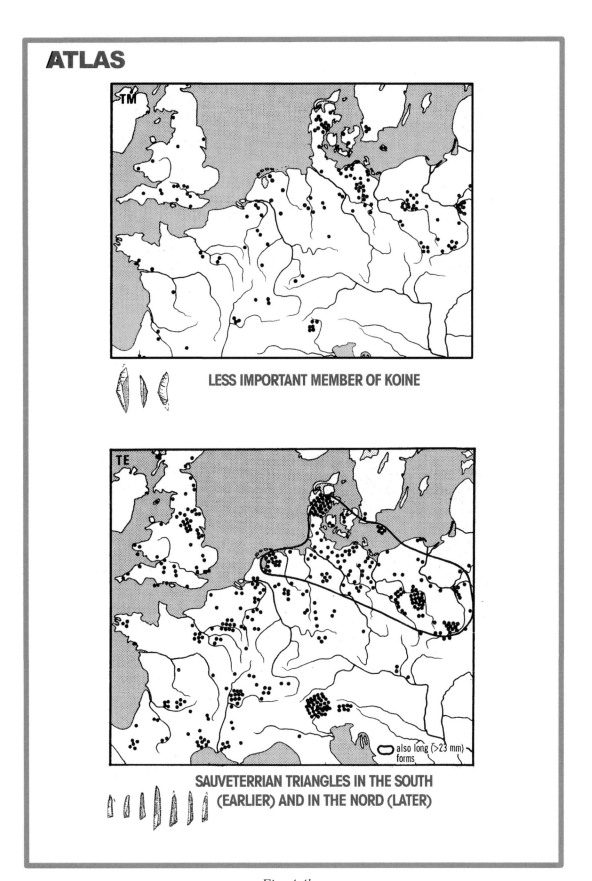

Fig. 4.4h

ATLAS

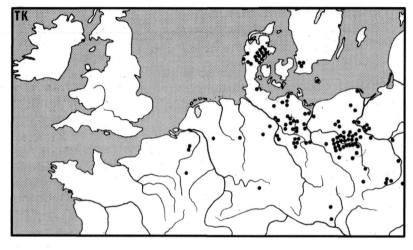

SCANDINAVIAN-POLISH CONNECTION

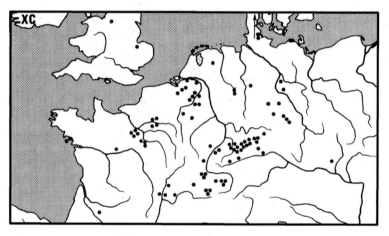

**HERE SOME FRENCH-BELGIAN--GERMAN-
-SWISS TARDENOIS POINTS**

Fig. 4.4i

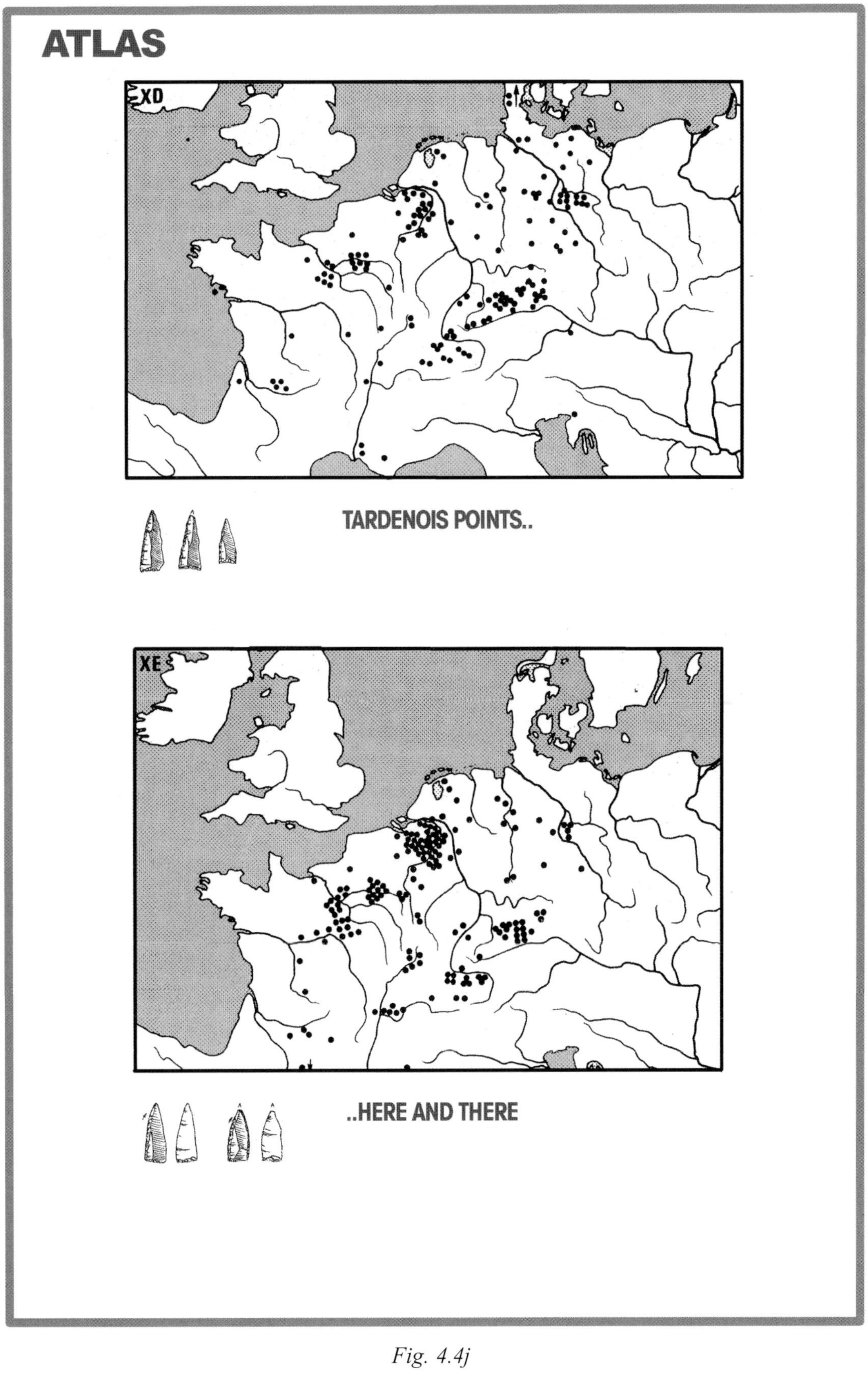

Fig. 4.4j

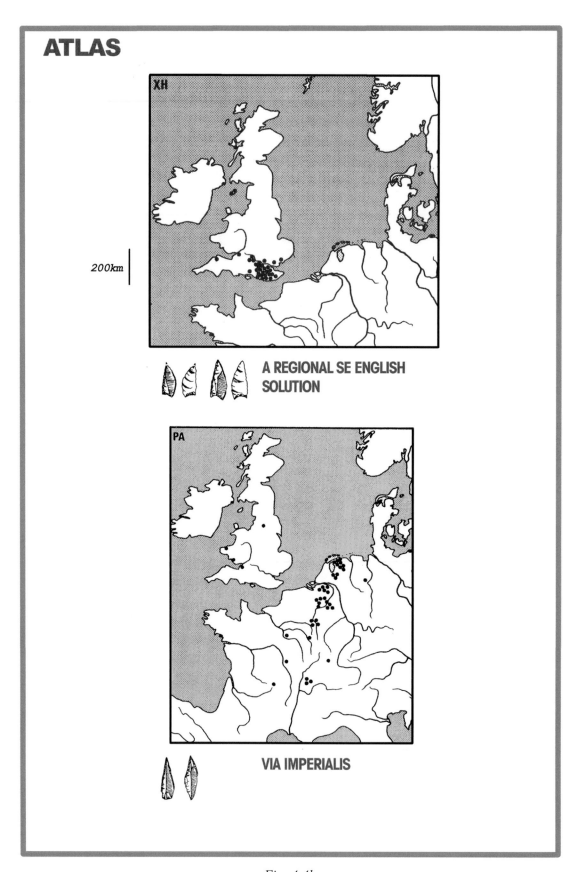

Fig. 4.4k

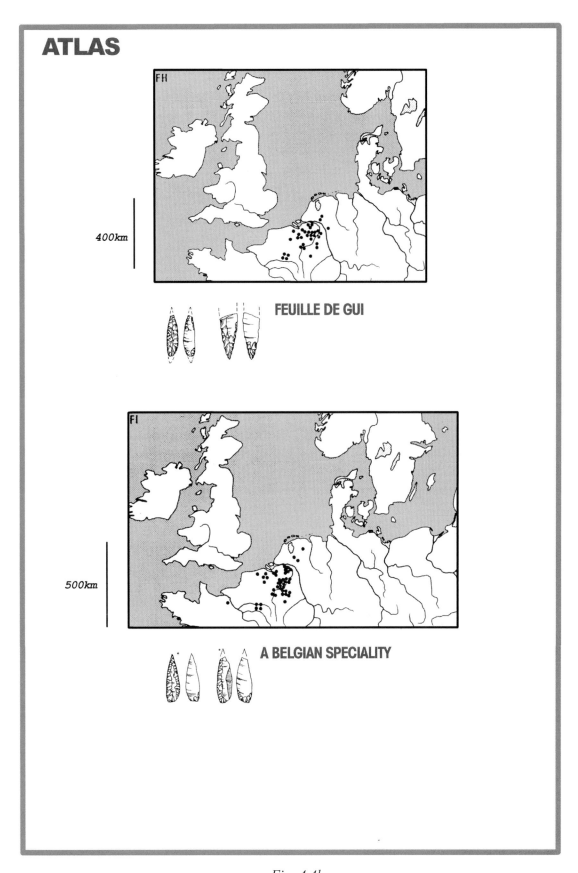

Fig. 4.4l

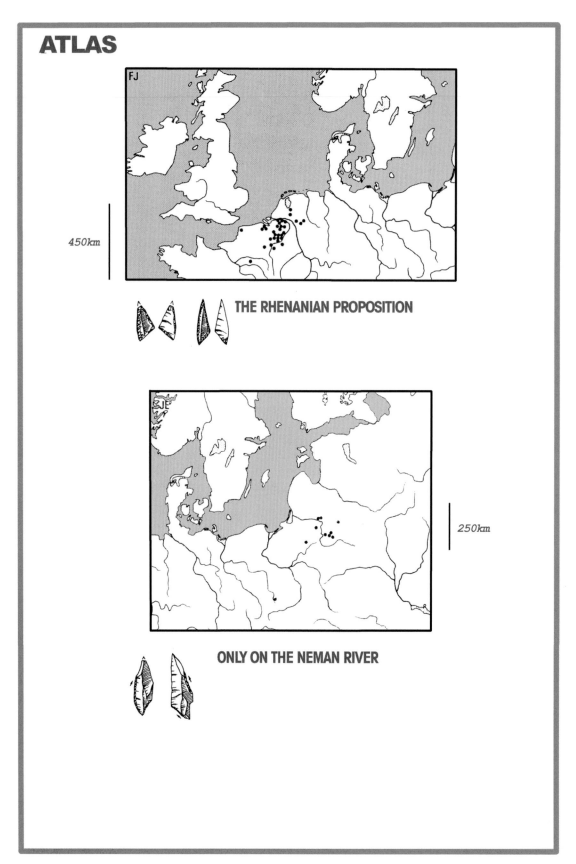

Fig. 4.4m

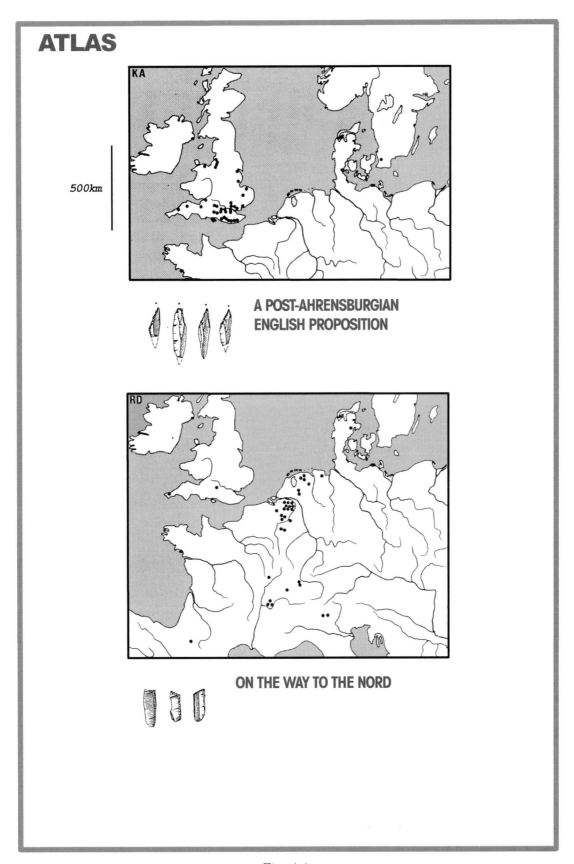

Fig. 4.4n

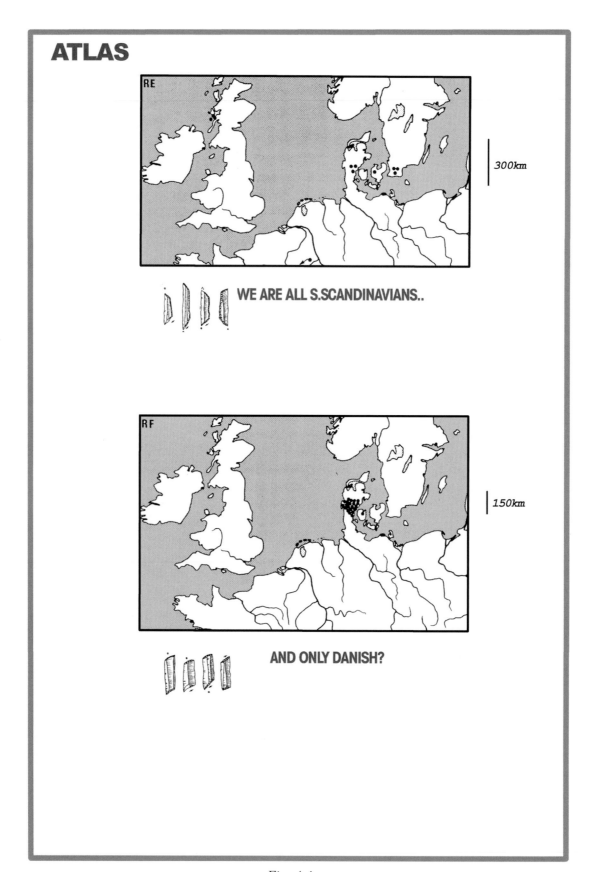

Fig. 4.4o

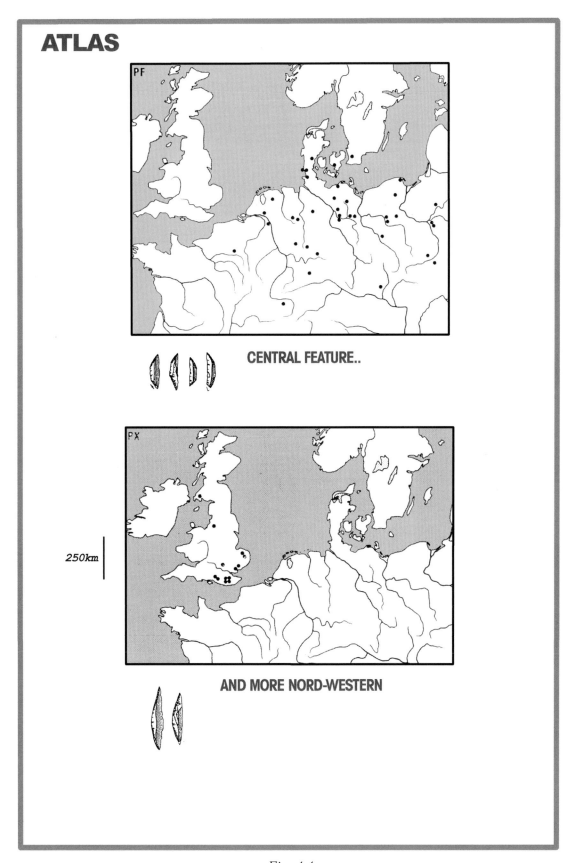

Fig. 4.4p

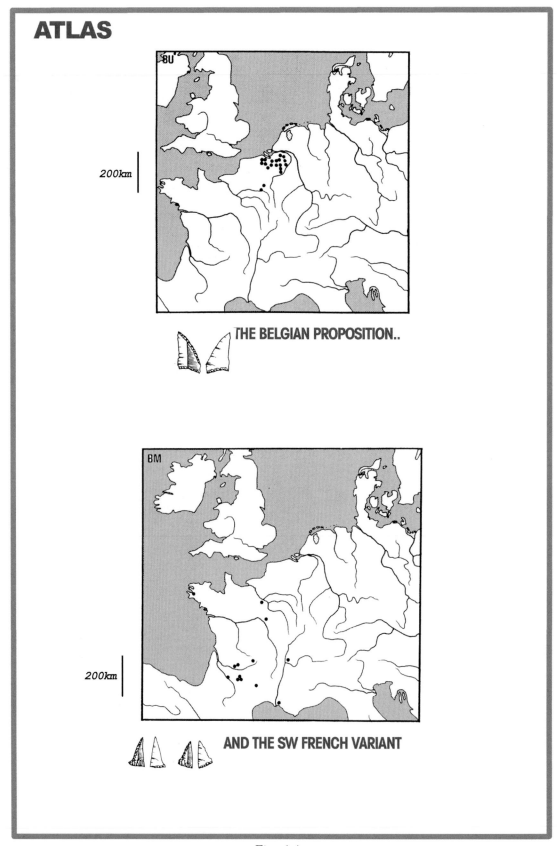

Fig. 4.4q

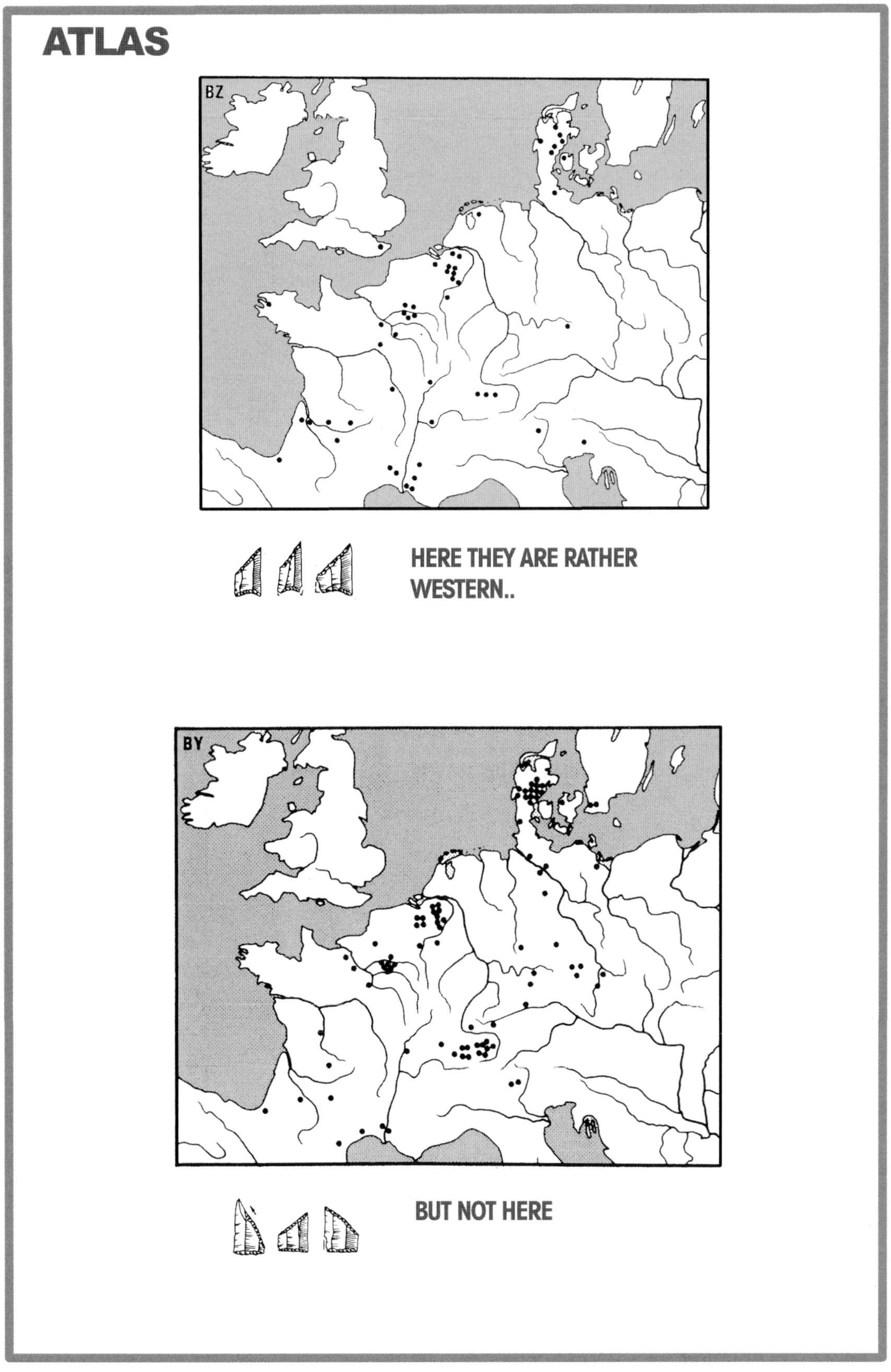

Fig. 4.4r

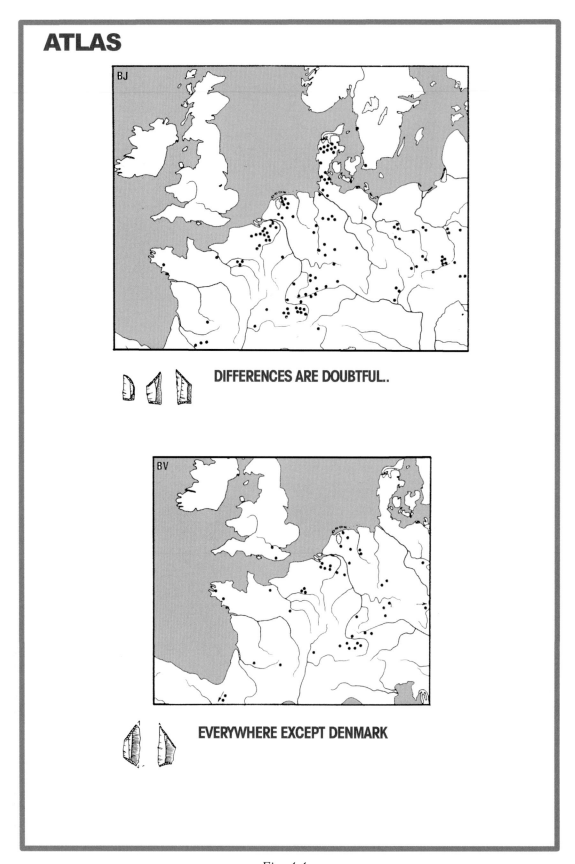

Fig. 4.4s

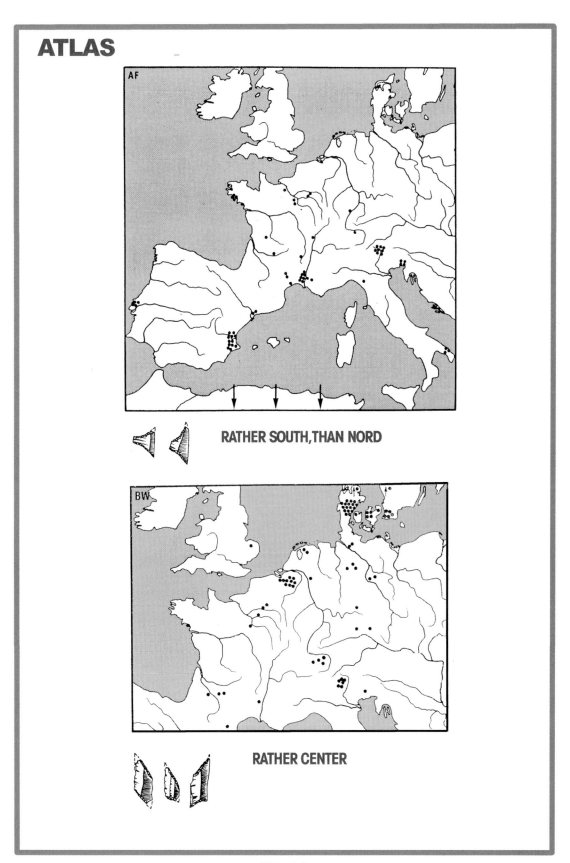

Fig. 4.4t

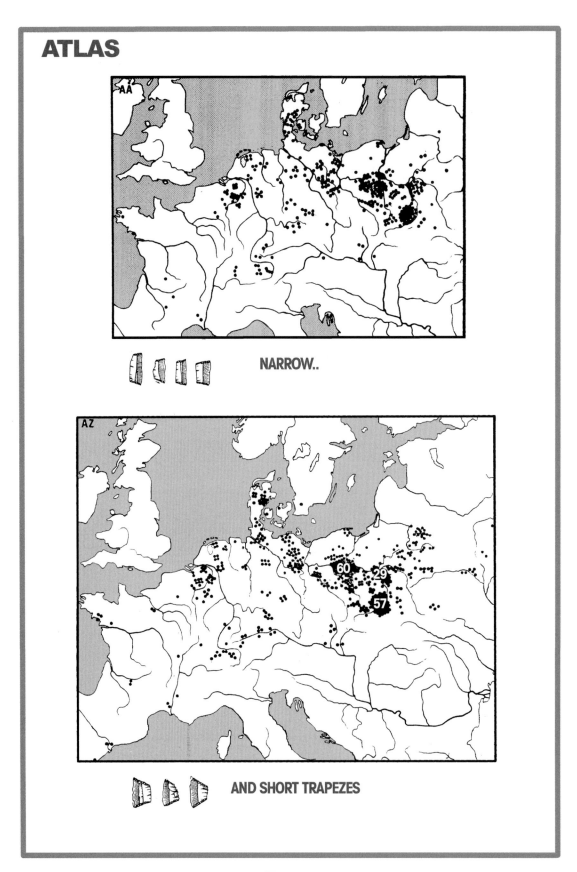

Fig. 4.4u

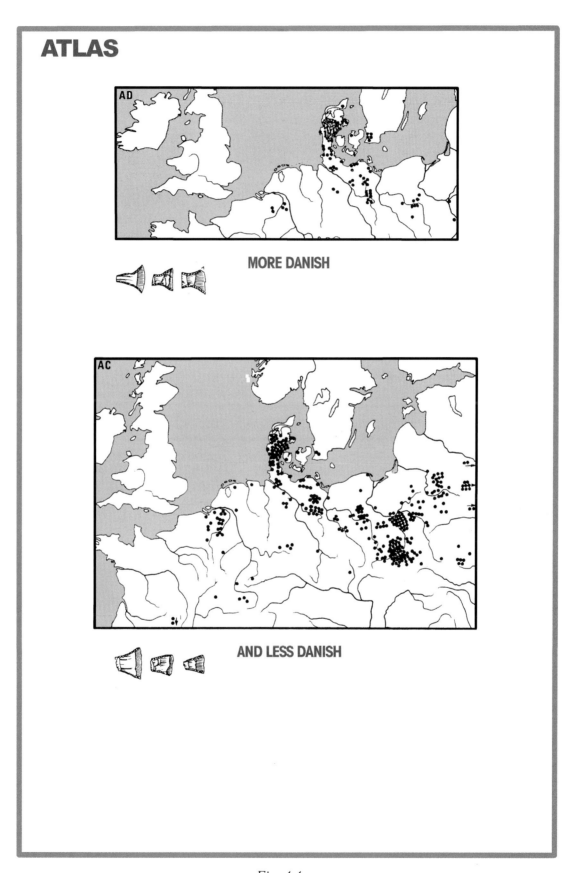

Fig. 4.4v

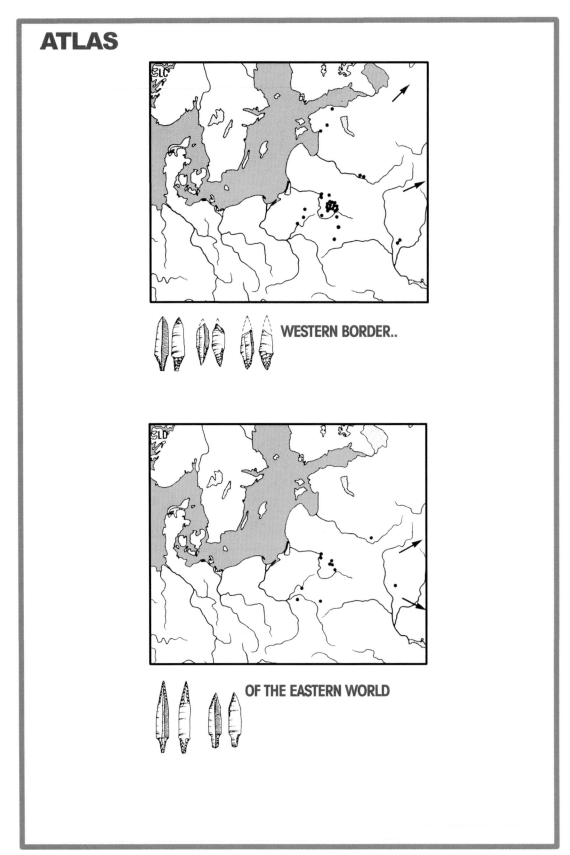

Fig. 4.4w

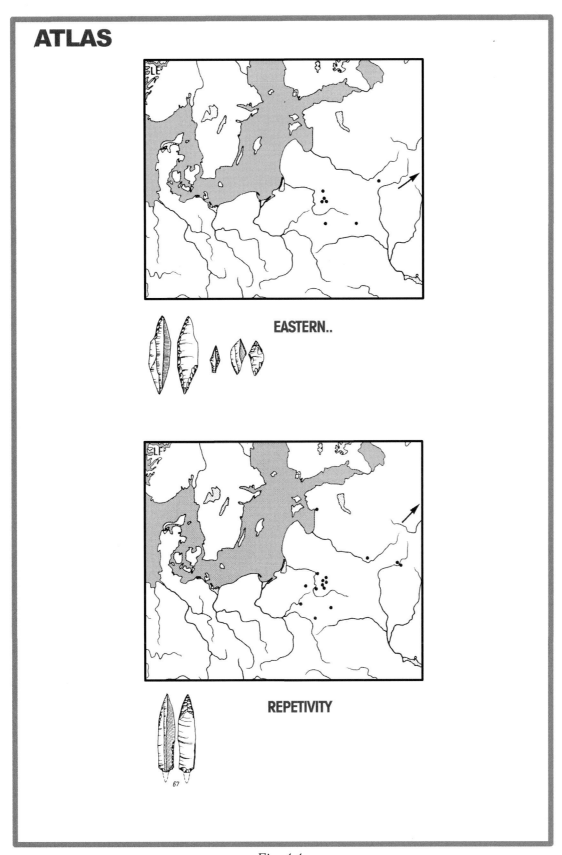

Fig. 4.4x

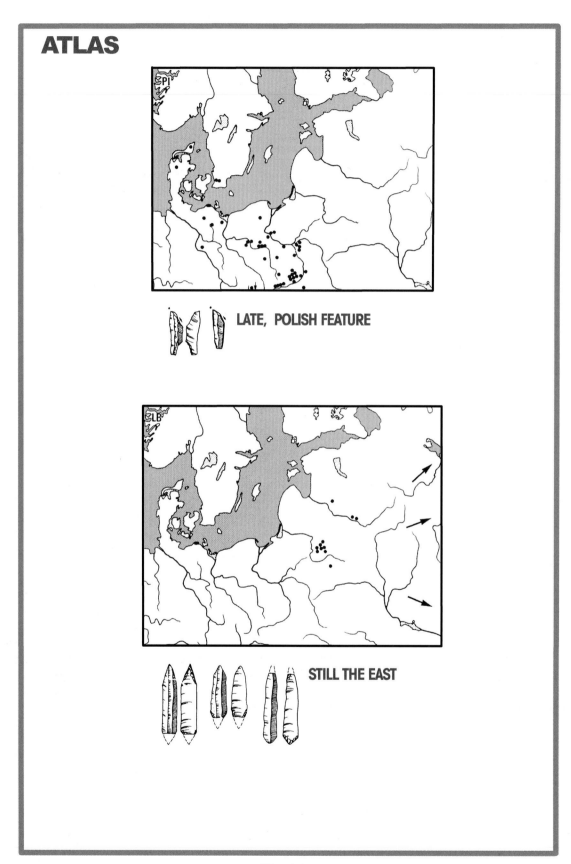

Fig. 4.4y

palaeohistorical interpretations and for determining the taxonomy. The work presents the next phase of the author's studies and leads, similarly as the previous ones, towards a future paleohistorical synthesis.

The Balkan territories which have not been extensively explored yet were purposefully omitted from the "Atlas". Also considerable areas of easternmost Europe were omitted, for there are more "blanks" in these areas than concentrations of Mesolithic sites (more numerous material is to be found only in the upper part of the Volga river basin, in the southern Ural Mountains and in the Crimea). Whenever the range of some classes of artefacts was continued in areas not included in the cartograms, this fact was marked by arrows.

Scandinavia has also been omitted, except for its southern part.

Typology (Cf. also the maps of types PB, PC, PE, K, RA, RB, RC in this chapter, as well as JA–C in chapter 11).

The all-European system of classification of chosen Mesolithic elements suggested below is based on over a dozen more or less local systems. Despite all its deficiencies, it is the only acceptable solution at the present moment, permitting a possibly homogeneous and objective classification of materials from distant territories.

The author has isolated in European material a number of groups of artefacts with similar primary features (D, T, R, A, B, X, L, W) and has subdivided them into a number of classes differing with respect to secondary features (e.g. the shape of base in group X, metrical differences in group T or proportions and place of retouch in group A).

It is clear, then, that the criteria for the detailed division were individualized. Some of the suggested detailed divisions were very well confirmed in spatial differentiations (cf. e.g., maps AD and AF, DF and DE, XH and XD, etc.), others were found insufficiently detailed or simply of more interregional character (e.g., for classes TN, TE and DB, in case of additional divisions based on metrical criteria, we could expect to obtain relevant internal territorial verification, e.g. hypermicrolithic specimens in the South and only microliths in the north). Thus further studies of a more detailed nature seem to be in order in some cases. Our typological scheme, restricted to some elements typical of the Mesolithic (microliths and tanged points), omits on purpose classes of artefacts which are not well represented in the material. This concerns in particular southwestern Europe, e.g. isosceles triangles of Muge type, segments with Helwan retouch, etc.

Each of the classes of artefacts distinguished above (except K) was marked by a two-letter symbol (e.g. DB, AZ), in which the first letter denotes belonging to a defined group of types. The reader will find below the characteristics of each of the groups as well as descriptive and graphic characteristics of the particular classes of artefacts related to the more important European typological

systems. Each of the distinguished classes is presented in this Atlas cartographically.

Comment in 2006

This system of letter markings for typological identification has been applied consistently throughout this volume.

Maps

The main part of the "Atlas" is comprised of several dozens of point maps presenting maximal ranges of types of artefacts included in this work. It is worth noting that areas containing the largest amounts of material, i.e., most reliable, are the West and Central European Lowlands mainly. The amounts of material in many uplands and plateaus are often insufficient for interpretation.

An attempt was made to place next to one another maps presenting typologically related classes of artefacts for the sake of introductory comparisons and to check the typological system. Such confrontations were in many cases very instructive, for it was found that some morphological differences of relevance to us were not really relevant, at least from the spatial point of view (cf. group F) and others (e.g. the differentiation into DD and DE) are important but, in order to notice and appreciate them, analyses on a continental scale have to be applied (cf. also remarks on the typology and maps of types PB, PC, PE, K, RA, RB, RC in this chapter, as well as JA–C in chapter 11).

Comment in 2006

In preparing this volume, the author has undertaken to complete some of the presented maps (cf. "Mapping the Mesolithic") with new material from regions in southern France and Italy, not as strongly represented in the original work. As it turned out, this did not change the original picture, hence I have refrained from updating all of the maps.

The detailed cartographical presentations published here are only "first generation" maps showing all of the currently known material of a defined class of artefacts in its maximal territorial range, disregarding temporal stratification. Thus the maps are, at least in some cases, sums of several different temporal and spatial ranges.

Further detailed studies could undoubtedly allow the creation of "second generation" maps, divided in time, for which, on the basis of the above mentioned map of all European sites, the degree of reliability may be defined, explaining among others the meaning of the "blanks" (illusory and actual) dividing particular groups of sites (the question of range homogeneity). These maps, in which, among others, graphical differentiation would be introduced depending on the amounts of artefacts of a given class in an inventory, could eliminate the impression of universal typological convergence of the European Mesolithic (cf. "Koine") suggested by the first generation maps. The analysis should eliminate accidental convergences and emphasize relevant ones.

"Third generation" maps should be synthetic presentations of the ranges of particular taxonomic units. Maps of this type are not new for some territories (e.g. Hermann Schwabedissen for northwestern Germany, Stefan K. Kozłowski for Poland), but in 1973 such incomplete maps were prepared for the whole continent (cf. "Warsaw '73"). Now they are much more complete and accurate!

Comment in 2006

The original version of the "Atlas" contained a site gazetteer with bibliographic references as well as a list of sites separately for each particular map.

Typological scheme

D – Backed pieces

Characteristics

Shape: "Knife-like" or crescent.

Blank: Bladelets and flakes.

Retouched edge: Backed edge, including at least half the length of a specimen, parallel or oblique to the axe of the tool.

Unretouched edge: Opposite to the back, parallel or oblique to the axe of the tool, natural edge of the blank.

Base: Sometimes retouched.

Division and synonyms

DA – Więckowska, Marczak: Stawinoga backed point.

DB – Taute: 17; Schwabedissen: Lanzettspitze.

DD – Clark: D 2a; Mathiassen II: 81; Brinch Petersen: 41; Mathiassen I: A 12; GEEM: segment + segment asymmetrique; Naber: 45c.

DE – Bokelmann: 3; GEEM: segment large; Naber: 45d.

DC – Clark: A 2a, c; Mathiassen II: 76; Mathiassen I: A2; Kozłowski: Maglemosian point.

DF – Clark: C 1b, d; Bokelmann: 6; Mathiassen I; B4; Brinch Petersen: 45, 46; Kozłowski: backed point with obliquely retouched base; Gramsch: Lanzettspitze.

DG – Clark: C 1a, c; Mathiassen I: A 7; Kozłowski: rhomboidal backed point.

DH – Clark: B 2, 4; Newell: B – point.

DI – no description in the literature

DE – Clark: A 2b, d.

DL – no description in the literature

Details of differentiation

DD – length : width > 3 : 1.

DB – length : width < 3 : 1.

T – Triangles

Characteristics

Shape: Triangle.

Blank: Bladelets.

Retouched edges: Two convergent truncations/backs, forming the blunted/backed shorter edges.

Unretouched edges: With few exceptions, the third (longest) unretouched.

Division and synonyms

TN – Clark: D 1a; Bokelmann: 10, 11; Mathiassen II: 85; Taute: 31–33; GEEM: triangle isocèle; Naber: 39b–d, 40a–c; Schwabedissen: gleichschenkeliges Dreieck.

TM – GEEM: triangle isocèle allongé.

TE – Clark: D 1b II, IV; Mathiassen II: 84; GEEM: triangle de Montclus; Schwabedissen: Svaerdborg Spitze.

TR – Clark: D 5; Bokelmann: 12; Bohmers, Wouters: triangular blunted back blade; Arora: 4.1.1.3c; GEEM: triangle scalene allongé.

TO – Bokelmann: 8; Brinch Petersen: 49; Taute; 34; Arora:4.1.1.3b; GEEM: triangle scalène; Naber: 42d; Schwabedissen: breites ungleichschenkeliges Dreieck.

TH – Arora: 4.1.1.3d II; Kozłowski: Pieńki triangle.

TD – TI – Arora: 4.1.1.3d I; GEEM: triangle scalène allongé à petit coté court; Kozłowski: Janisławice triangle.

TK – Kozłowski: Chojnice triangle.

Details of differentiation

TN – length : width < 3 : 1.

TM – length : width > 3 : 1.

TR – angle between retouched edges > 120^0.

TO – length : width < 3 : 1.

TH – length < 25 mm, width < 5 mm.

TI – length < 25 mm, width > 5 mm.

TD – length > 25 mm, width > 6 mm.

X – West European points with transversal base

Characteristics

Shape: Triangular, symmetric on the longitudinal axis.

Blank: Broad irregular bladelets.

Retouched edges: One edge oblique and backed, base transversal to the axe of the tool.

Unretouched edge: Second edge (natural edge of the blank) symmetrical to the back.

The whole group is called in the European literature as follows: C-points, Tardenoisian points (Bohmers, Wouters), Mikrospitzen mit dorsale und Basisretusohe (Taute); pointes à base transversale (GEEM); pointes à base retouchée (Rozoy); Dreieckspitzen (Arora).

Division and synonyms

XA – Taute: 19; Newell: C-point aI.

XC – Taute: 18; Newell: C-point aII.

XD – Naber: 37; Taute: 20; Newell: C-point a III.

XE – Naber: 36; Taute: 21–26; Arora: 4.1.1.4a, c; Newell: C-point b.

XH – Clark: F 1a, Horsham point.

The author has not included in this classification the similar, but smaller and narrower points occurring in the Sauveterrian of southern France.

Points with convergent backs

Characteristics

Shape: Borer-like.

Retouched edges: Two equal backs converging on one or both ends of the tool.

Unretouched edges: Possibly one end of the specimen (the natural edge).

Division und synonyms

PD – Bokelmann: 5; Bohmers, Wouters: Sauveterre + needle-shaped point; Brinch Petersen: 43; GEEM: pointe de Sauverterre; Gramsch: nadelförmige Spitze.

PA – GEEM: pointe à deux bord abbatus; Newell: lancette point; Schwabedissen: Kremser Spitze.

A – Symmetrical Trapezes

Characteristics

Shape: Symmetrical trapeze.

Blank: Broad regular bladelets.

Retouched edges: Two symmetrically located, slightly convergent truncations across the bladelet.

Unretouched edges: Two natural edges of the bladelets.

The whole group is called in the European literature as follows: Trapeze (Schwabedissen, GEEM) and Querschneiden (Schwabedissen) as well as *tvaerpile* (Danish authors).

Division and synonyms

AA – Clark: D 8b; GEEM: trapeze symétrique long; Kozłowski: narrow trapeze.

AZ – Mathiassen II: 93; Taute: 10; Arora: 4.1.1.5, Viereck b; GEEM: trapèze symétrique court.

AC – Clark: D 8a; Mathiassen II: 99; Mathiassen I: E 2, 3, 7, 8; Bohmers, Wouters: narrow trapezes; Taute: 1; Kozłowski: broad trapeze; Naber: 47; Gramsch: lange Pfeilschneide.

AD – Mathiassen II: 100, 103; Mathiassen I: E 5, 6.

AF – GEEM: trapèzes symétriques à troncatures concaves; Tixier: trapèze à deux côtés concaves.

Details of differentiation

AA – length : width > 1.7 : 1.

AZ – length : width 1.65 : 1–1,05 : 1.

AC – length : width < 1 : 1.

B – Asymmetrical Trapezes

Characteristics

Shape: Asymmetrical trapeze or rhomb.

Blank: Broad regular bladelets.

Retouched edges: Two asymmetrically located convergent (rarely almost parallel) truncations across the bladelet.

Unretouched edges: Natural edges of the bladelet.

Division and synonyms

BH and BW – Newell: broad trapeze, rhombic; GEEM: trapèze à base décallées; Mathiassen II: 94–96; Mathiassen I: D 7–10; Bohmers, Wouters: trapezoids with one basal obtuse angle; Taute: 2; Arora; 4.1.1.5. Viereckspitze.

BJ – Clark: C 2a, c; Mathiassen II: 92; Mathiassen I: D 6; Bohmers, Wouters: trapezoids with one or two basal right angles; Taute: 12, 13; GEEM: trapèzes asymétriques à grande troncature longue.

BV – GEEM: trapèzes-rectangles à grande troncature longue.

BZ + BY – GEEM: trapèzes-rectangles à grande troncature courte.

BU – Newell: broad trapeze, derived.

BM – GEEM: trapèze de Martinet.

Details of differentiation

BH – Length : width < 2 : 1.

BW – Length : width > 2 : 1.

BJ – Length : width < 2 : 1.

BZ – Length : width > 2 : 1.

Truncated Bladelets

Bitruncated specimens

Characteristics

Shape: Narrow trapeze, most frequently symmetrical.

Blank: Bladelets.

Retouched edges: Two convergent, symmetrical and oblique and very oblique truncations.

Unretouched edges: Natural.

Division and synonyms

PE – Bokelmann: 15; Taute: 38; Arora: 4.1.1.5 Viereck a

PF – no description in the literature

PX – no description in the literature

PC – Mathiassen I: C 14; Kozłowski: Nowy Młyn Point.

Single-truncation specimens

Characteristics

Shape: Subtriangular.

Blank: Bladelets.

Retouched edge: On a truncation, transversal and oblique proximal.

Unretouched edges: Natural.

Division and synonyms

PB – Mathiassen II: 82; Mathiassen I: B 1; Kozłowski: point with retouched base.

K – Clark: A 1a, c; Bokelmann: 1; Naber: 32; Mathiassen I: D 1–4; Bohmers, Wouters: points type B; Taute: 8, 14; Arora: 4.1.1.1a; GEEM: points à troncature oblique 3 + lamelle tronquée; Gramsch: Spitze mit Schrägretuschierung + mit partieller Kantenretuschierung.

KA – Clark: A 1b, d.

Note: the basic criterion for division of truncated bladelets in this work was the number of truncations (1 or 2), though, e.g. the style of blanks (narrow or broad) may be a very important criterion here. Similar to K-points, but distal pieces, known mostly from the sub-Alpine region, were omitted.

R – Rectangular Microliths

Characteristics

Shape: Narrow quadrangular form.

Blank: Small bladelets.

Retouched edges: Always one edge of the blade (back), which is most often continued by two truncations (in the case of RD, the butt of the blank).

Unretouched edges: Natural edge (exceptionally retouch on it).

Note: Additionally I have included in this group the RF microlith, which is devoid of back.

Division and synonyms

RA – Mathiassen I: C 12; Kozłowski: rectangle; Newell: rectangular backed blade.

RD – Naber: 50; Arora: 4.1.1.

RB – Clark: D 7b, c; Mathiassen II: 89; Mathiassen I: C 16; Kozłowski: rhomboid.

RC – Clark: D 6a, b; Mathiassen I: C 20; Kozłowski: trapezoid.

RE – no description in the literature

RF – Clark: D 7a; Mathiassen I: C 15; Mathiassen II: 88.

F – Northwest European Micro-leaf-points and Microliths with flat retouch – Mistelblatspitzen (Narr)

Characteristics

Shape: Leaf or triangle.

Blank: Bladelets.

Retouch: Semi-abrupt, flat, abundant on dorsal face where it was made on most of the edges of the specimen. On ventral face exclusively flat, often restricted to the ends of the specimen.

Division and synonyms

FG – Rozoy: feuille de gui; Bohmers, Wouters: double points; Arora: 4.1.1.7 oberflächig Ret. a.

FH – Bohmers, Wouters: leaf-shaped points.

FI – Rozoy: pointe à base arrondie + pointe à base viaise.

FJ – Bohmers, Wouters: triangles with surface retouch; Arora: 4.1.1.7 oberflächig Ret. c; Newell: surface retouched triangles.

J – Central European Microliths with Microburin scar on tip

(Janisławice points after Kozłowski)

Shape: Most often triangular.

Blank: Broad, regular bladelets.

Retouched edges: Semi-abrupt truncation or back; tip with flat microburin scar; retouch or bearing retouch of transversal base.

Unretouched edge: Natural.

Division

JA – retouched base.

JB – broken base.

JC – natural base.

JE – oblique, retouched base

Points PI – Pieńki points (Kozłowski)

Similar to JC, but on smaller and narrower blanks and longer.

Note: Some microliths from the Castelnovian sites of Southwest Europe omitted in the present atlas should be included in this group; the same concerns some microliths from southern Ukraine.

East European micro-retouched Bladelets

Characteristics

Shape: Rectangle (most frequently).

Blank: Regular delicate bladelets, struck by pressure technique.

Retouched edges: Delicate semi-abrupt (dorsal, ventral or alternate) retouch of edge/edges of the blank, infrequently of the transversal base (sometimes both) or the sharp tip.

Unretouched edges: Natural edge of the blank and/or intentionally broken, transversal base/bases.

Division and synonyms

WA – retouch of one edge

WB – retouch of both edges

WC – borer-like tip

Koltsov: *vkladishi*

Schild: Borki bladelets

Kozłowski: microretouched inserts

L – East European small leaf and tanged points, post-Swiderian tanged points

Characteristics

Shape: Willow leaf, or with tang/pedoncule.

Blank: Broad, regular bladelets.

Retouch: One of the tips of the specimen formed into a tang or pointed base with semi-abrupt retouch on dorsal face and/or flat + semi-abrupt retouch on the ventral one. The opposite tip sometimes similarly formed.

Unretouched edges: Most frequently the natural edge of the blank.

Division and synonyms
LA – willow-leaf shaped.
LB – leaf-shaped, geometric
LC – broad, triangular head and pointed tang
LD – narrow, pointed tang
LE – rhomboid.
LF – very short tang

Soviet authors: Post-Swiderian tanged points
Koltsov: *nakonechniki strel*
Kozłowski: Kunda tanged points

Comment in 2006

A number of microlith types (PB, PC, PE, K, RA, RB, RC, cf. "Stories") is presented in detail in this volume, hence their absence from the version of the "Atlas" included here. Others have been shown and discussed in the text on "Mapping the Mesolithic" and have therefore also been partly omitted from the presentation at this point. Many of the remaining ones have been commented on briefly (cf. titles of individual maps), which is a novelty compared to the previous version of the "Atlas". On the other hand, some of the concrete maps have been generalized (cf. "Janislawician") and in a few cases several maps believed to be too detailed have been merged.

4.5. The "stories" of some Microliths

The examples presented below of "monographs" of selected types of microliths concern chiefly the region north of the Alps, especially the European Lowland, which belonged to the Mesolithic *koine* (cf.) of central and western Europe. The sole exception are rectangles RA, which contrary to the author's original opinions, are also present in southern Europe.

4.5.1. K-points

Introduction

Among many works dealing with the European Mesolithic, very few have provided data concerning the territorial range of particular cultural phenomena and conclusions resulting from their analysis. When reaching the stage of cartographic conceptions, however, only synthetic maps were produced, based indeed on authentic facts (archaeological materials), but often not fully verifiable, and hardly comprehensible to readers. This was the result of, on one hand, monographs omitting descriptions and composition of many poorer inventories, and on the other, lack of analytic, earliest (that is, "first generation") maps in these monographs, maps which lead to synthetic cartographic conceptions. By this I mean maps, which could have furnished data on the territorial range of single types of artefacts, or even their particular subtypes or variants, provided with appropriate analytical comments preceding a final, synthetic conclusion.

Some of Grahame Clark's, K. J. Narr's, Hermann

Schwabedissen's and finally Stefan K. Kozlowski's maps are an exception here. Similar exceptional conceptions for the Final Palaeolithic have been published by Wolfgang Taute. The quoted Mesolithic cartographic elaborations are, however, not complete – Clark was far from making use of all existing sources, while Schwabedissen and the author of this paper limited the range of their territorial conceptions.

My deep conviction is that for many reasons, the preparation and publication of full cartographic presentations, showing the range of important typological elements, occurring in the European Mesolithic, is indispensable. One of the arguments in favor is the need to provide information on the territorial extent of phenomena observed so far and analysed only in a local or regional range.

Definition

The name "K-points" (Fig. 4.5.1a–b) (abbreviation for "Komornica point") is derived from the site Komornica VI, district of Nowy Dwór Mazowiecki (Poland), and was first proposed by Hanna Więckowska and Maria Marczak in 1969.

For more details, cf. "Typology" in the text of the "Atlas" above.

K-points in European typological systems

K-points are known to specialists in all of the countries of their appearance; it often happens, however, that they are joined into one type with specimens which, in my opinion, should be classed in other types. To make the proposed definition clear we present it in comparison with other definitions of type. Exact synonyms of the discussed type of points, known from various typological systems, have been given first, followed by the names of types, the range of which is not exactly in accordance with the proposed definition. Each of the latter is provided with an appropriate comment.

Synonyms (cf. "Atlas"):

1. *Pointe à troncature très oblique.*
2. Simple obliquely blunted microlith.
3. A1a + A1c Microliths.
4. *Pointe à base naturelle.*
5. Trekanter B6+B8.

Partial synonyms (cf. "Atlas):

1. B-points. Next to the more numerous K-points, also microtruncated points with distal truncation (or bulb on base) are classed in this type; they are particularly characteristic of the French/German Beuronian and occur far less frequently on the European Lowland, where K-points are very numerous.
2. *Einfache retuschierte Spitze* + *Feingerätige Spitze.* Their range is identical or very close to B-points.
3. *Spitze Typ* II B2. Their range is principally in agreement with the definition of B-points.
4. *Pointe à troncature très oblique.* Besides the most numerous K-points, French colleagues (GEEM,

K-POINTS

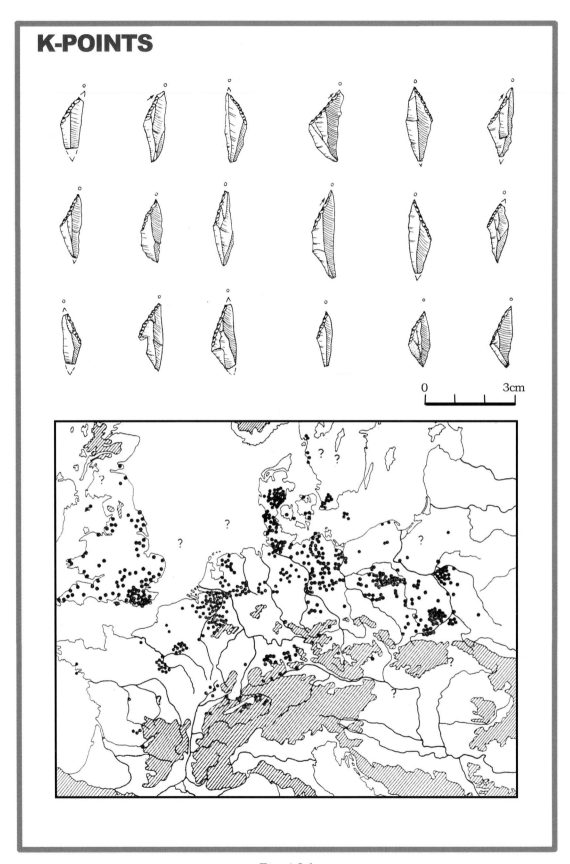

0   3cm

Fig. 4.5.1a

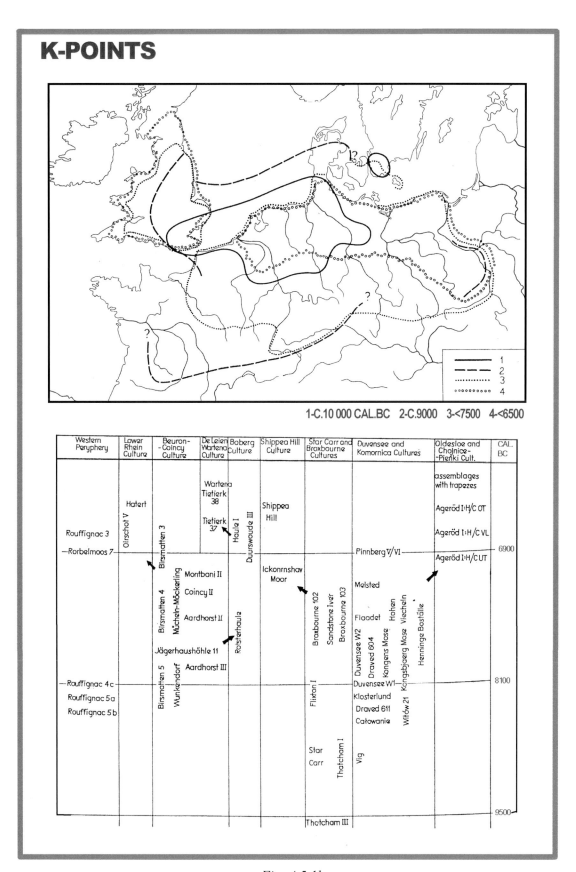

Fig. 4.5.1b

Jean-Georges Rozoy) have classed: short lanceolate points, a part of A. Bohmers and A. Wouters A-points, obliquely backed Maglemosian points (DC of Stefan K. Kozłowski), finally small truncated points with bulb on the base. The three last metioned types, if considered in a European perspective, should not be taken together with K-points, for they certainly have different cultural and geographic connotations. Maglemosian backed points (DC) occur most frequently in England and south Scandinavia (Broxbourne, Shippea Hill and Svaerdborg cultures). Short lanceolate points and small truncated points with bulb on the base are known from the rather southern Beuronian (broadly taken northern forehills of the Alps).

5. *Pointe à dos abattu partiel*. Maglemosian (Kozłowski's DC) backed points have been classed in this type, not attaining, however, the wide territorial extent of K-points.

Territorial range

The general map presents a territorial range of all Mesolithic inventories containing K-points known to the author. It indicates that the specimens of interest here have been found over a vast territory and were a rather popular type in the European Mesolithic, making up the *Koine* (cf.). Nonetheless, it has been proved that their range is closely limited, for they fail to occur in eastern, southern and southwestern Europe.

Two important issues should be emphasized at this point:

1. The map presents the range of the phenomenon in a temporal "flattening"; consequently, it is not unlikely that the range of K-points in different periods of the Early Holocene could differ theoretically.
2. The obtained cartographic result is not only dependent on prehistorical facts. It also depends on the state of field research and accessible materials from certain areas and collections.

Wishing to present the most objective picture, we need to provide it with appropriate comments. We shall further attempt a chronological and cultural "delamination" of the map, concentrating for the moment on a discussion of the widest range of the phenomenon considered.

WESTERN EXTENT. Presently I have knowledge of a considerable series of inventories with K-points, mostly from the Paris Basin and the Haute-Saône department, while single specimens reach to the western borders of the Central Massif and the Atlantic coast. I believe that the southwestern limit of the range of K-points reaches the Loire River in France, perhaps extending slightly beyond the river valley to the south, and reaching the Atlantic Ocean in the west. In Great Britain, K-points reach as far as the western coasts, and pass into Northern Ireland.

NORTHERN EXTENT. K-points are known from scarcely a few Scottish sites, reaching out furthest to the northern coast of the British Isles. Finally, it should be considered

as very probable (as confirmed by cartographic data from Great Britain, Belgium, Holland and Denmark, and paleogeographical and paleohistorical data testifying to their presence on the now submerged Dogger Bank Shelf). In Denmark, the type discussed reached nearly to the northern edge of Jutland; it is not clear, however, whether the known Swedish northern range corresponds to the actual situation in prehistoric times. It is in fact somewhat larger, particularly to the east, but also along the western coast of Sweden and Norway (microbladelet, Late Mesolithic culture).

The northeastern frontier follows further the ancient coast of Ancylus Lake, through Bornholm (which was once a peninsula) up to Polish Pomerania.

EASTERN EXTENT. A relatively advanced state of research in Poland permits the assumption that what is shown on the map corresponds in outline to prehistoric reality, although, for instance, K-points may have reached east beyond the mouth of the Vistula.

SOUTHERN EXTENT. K-points, as shown on the map, do not extend very much beyond the mighty Carpathians and Alps. It is to be remarked, however, that few data is available from the direct forehills of both mountain chains (e.g. hardly more than a dozen Mesolithic sites from the Czech Republic and Slovakia, and even poorer Mesolithic material from Hungary and Austria); the north Italian Sauveterranian has yielded some K-points (Romagnano III).

Finally, it ought to be stated that K-points are a spatially limited phenomenon; moreover, in their known territorial range, isolated clusters of sites are difficult to distinguish, which can be proof that they can be of common origin and can represent a single homogeneous phenomenon.

Should the conjecture of common genetic bonds linking all European K-points be confirmed by other sound proof, the fact may indeed assume capital importance for research concerning mutual relations of Mesolithic human groups, inhabiting the area north of the Alps and the Carpathians, between England, northern France, southern Scandinavia and Poland (cf. "*Koine*"). In order to have full proof, it would be necessary to reconstruct the history of K-points in Europe, analyzing the problem of their chronological position in various territories, their role in various cultural units, finally territorial alterations that they underwent in the Early and Middle Holocene. Such an attempt will be presented further on.

Chronology and the problem of local evolutive continuity

K-points appeared in the European Lowland in the Late Pleistocene and lasted locally in this area into the 6th–5th millennia cal. BC. K-points are dated by the radiocarbon method and pollen analysis, only exceptionally by typological analysis (some Oldesloe and Chojnice-Pieńki assemblages are dated by the presence of trapezes), to the early 7th millennium cal. BC and later.

We note the existence of certain unbroken local sequences, mostly in Great Britain (Star Carr, Broxbourne and Shippea

Hill cultures, all displaying K-points), Central European Lowland (Duvensee and Komornica, later respectively Oldesloe, and Chojnice-Pieńki, all with K-points), finally on the northern foreland of the Alps, down to the northwestern European Lowland (Beuronian and later Boberg, as well as Rhenanian cultures, all also with K-points).

As it is simultaneously possible to prove the close kindredship of Duvensee, Komornica and Star Carr cultures (cf. "Komornicien"), and there exists proof of relations, although perhaps more distant, of the Beuronian and the three entities mentioned above (e.g. PE points), it should be supposed that some kind of community (the western-central European Mesolithic *koine,* cf.) may have existed between the said cultures with K-points as one of their characteristics, from the earliest Holocene (from at least the first half of the 10th millennium cal. BC). It may be yet more proof of the genetic bonds linking all K-points.

The role of K-points in particular Mesolithic cultures

As shown above, there is serious data (absolute datings and typological bonds) for the assumption that in at least three regions (Great Britain and the northwestern Plain, the forehills of the Alps, and the central European Plain) a local evolution of Mesolithic cultures occurred from the beginning of the first half of the 10th millennium to the 7th–6th millennia cal. BC (cf. "Rhythms"). As said above, the first rudiments of evolution in all the mentioned regions were certainly common (*koine*), which does not, however, imply that the role of K-points in the said related cultures (Star Carr, Duvensee, Komornica and Beuronian) was everywhere the same. The table is meant to explain the role of obliquely blunted points (K-points and connected types) in particular cultures. It shows that Star Carr and Duvensee cultures, typologically closest and nearest to the eastern (Komornica) and southern (Beuronian) cultures, display a far higher index of K-points. It is not excluded that genetic causes brought about that difference – Star Carr and Duvensee cultures occurred in true Ahrensburgian territory, where K-points were present already in Dryas III. Recent research discerns more and more clearly the presence in the region of (Epi-) Ahrensburgian (definition of André Gob) elements also in the earliest Holocene phase (Pinnberg in northern Germany, Zonhoven in Belgium, Öbacken in Sweden, Aabenraa and Bare Mose in Denmark), moreover the earliest assemblages of Star Carr type (e.g. Star Carr and Thatcham III) and Duvensee (e.g. Klosterlund) contain tanged points. Considering all these facts together, the theory of direct genetic bonds (local or nearly local development) of Star Carr and Duvensee cultures with Ahrensburgian may be accepted.

On the contrary, neither the northern forehills of the Alps nor the land lying east of the Oder (where the Ahrenburgian was absent), should have known very early K-points, so it can be supposed that the latter were an allochtonic element there in the 10th millennium cal. BC, adopted probably from an alien *milieu,* i.e., from the west (?).

One more practical conclusion can be drawn from the above. The role of K-points in particular Mesolithic cultures should be studied separately, following two distinct lines of development:

1. The history of K-points in the native British-South Scandinavian-Mecklemburgian-Brandenburgian area,
2. the "history" of K-points in territories of secondary/ allochtonic development or appearance.

Ad. 1. The native area demonstrates a generally similar evolutive tendency – the amount of K-points gradually decreases over time in favor of other types of armatures. This can be proved on the example of the Star Carr → Broxbourne and Duvensee → Oldesloe sequences. It should be noted, however, that the youngest culture in the British sequence, i.e., Shippea Hill/Narrow Blades Industry, displays a growth of the K-points index (*sic!*, push for the Dogger Bank landbridge?).

Ad 2. Areas where K-points were secondary do not show an equally marked change of index. For example,in the Beuronian → RMS/Rhenanian sequence in the Northwest, evolutional changes concern other type groups (triangles, flat retouched points); furthermore, the Polish sequence Komornica → Chojnice-Pieńki shows alterations in the group of backed points and triangles. It may be assumed from the above that RMS/Rhenanian and Chojnice-Pieńki cultures of the Late Mesolithic developed from local backgrounds under influence from outside, which, however, did not come from a *milieu* knowing K-points (for the Chojnice-Pieńki it may have been the Svaerdborgian, for RMS the South Montbanian?).

Finally, it should be said that the sporadic presence of K-points in other *milieus* (Sauveterrian, Montbanian, Tévièc, Hoëdic) is probably evidence of unstable neighbourly contacts (Sauveterrian) or partly genetic bonds (Montbanian) with cultures having K-points uninterruptedly in their inventories.

It cannot be excluded that not all K-points are the result of common evolution. Considering their fairly simple construction, they might be the effect of a certain convergence in development (e.g. classic upland Beuronian).

Changes in the territorial range of K-points

As said above, the general mapping of K-point distribution should and can be "delaminated" to form a number of maps presenting the situation in smaller time divisions. Such an operation, in conjunction with already presented statements, may provide noteworthy data for researchers working on paleohistorical reconstructions. For it may appear that in certain areas K-points functioned within local cultures from the beginning of the Holocene up to the 7th and 6th millennia cal BC, while in others they occurred for longer or shorter periods, then disappeared not to return. This kind of changes, correlated moreover with different values of the K-points index (depending on the history and perhaps also on the origins), provide material for reconsideration.

Several phases, differing by their territorial range, can be distinguished in the "history" of K-points:

1. In their Ahrensburgian/Epi-Ahrensburgian period (11th/9th millennium cal. BC), K-points occurred mostly in the European Lowland, between the mouth of the river Meuse and southeastern England (Thatcham III), down to the foot of the Jutland peninsula and Brandenburg, reaching even to west Sweden in a northeastern direction (Tosskärr A).

2. In the mid 9th millennium cal. BC, we know K-points from a far vaster area: to the east they reach the middle Vistula course (Całowanie III–VII–1, Witów 21), to the south they touch the Alps (Wunkendorf-Schrägewand, Birsmatten-Basisgrotte 5), to the southwest they come near to the Central Massive (Rouffignac 4c–5b), to the northwest their range reaches eastern England (Star Carr, Flixton I), they certainly occur in southern Scandinavia (Vig, Klosterlund) and of course also on the Dogger Bank Shelf. A tendency for excentric radiating development of the the K-points range is now obvious.

3. The middle of the 8th millennium cal. BC, particularly its second half, brought rather serious changes in the range of the phenomenon: K-points occurring even in northern England and Scotland, were reduced in range in southern Scandinavia to the western part of today's Baltic Sea and the southern part of the North Sea, and the land bridges there. Southwestwards, the range of K-points receded to the Paris Basin. The changes of their northern range were of complex origin: in the place of the local southern Scandinavian variation of Duvensee culture (of the Klosterlund-Sønder-Hadsund–Melsted type) there appeared (after the Bøllund-type Maglemosian) a culture almost deprived of K-points, i.e., Svaerdborgian (Vinde Helsinge-Svaerdborg I type). So sudden a decline of K-points indicates a strong outside influence being exerted on the local Duvensee/Klosterlund tradition, most probably from the south (cf. "Les courants interculturels").

   The northern range of K-points was reduced also due to environmental reasons – the Dogger Bank Shelf and the West Baltic land bridge were gradually disappearing under sea. The inhabitants of these areas moved back gradually, consequently and logically to the south, west and north (and K-points appear in Limhamn/Nøstvet culture from 7000 cal. BC).

4. In the 7th millennium cal. BC, the range of K-points decreased first of all in the south and southwest: the new South Montbanian did not (except for transitional assemblages) principally take over K-points from its predecessor, the Beuronian or Rhenanian (the Nord Montbanian).

Final remarks

The author has purposely avoided drawing concrete conclusions from the presented analysis. Instead, he is inclined to several remarks of a more general nature.

The outlined cartographic conceptions open a broad research perspective, allowing to understand matters that had remained in the darkness until now. It would seem that paleohistorical data – obtained from the maps – is valuable material, for it supports a potential reconstruction of the history of our continent in the Early and Middle Holocene. The important thing is a conscious view of the range of certain phenomena, and also their changeability in time and space and within the frame of specific cultures. Should it prove possible to reconstruct the "record" of particular elements composing the European Mesolithic, we might be able perhaps to attempt a palaeohistorical reconstruction of the whole continent.

4.5.2. PE-points

Typological characteristics
(for typology, cf. "Atlas of the Mesolithic in Europe").

Range
The map shows the distribution of mostly Mesolithic sites with PE-points known to the author. It is easy to see that the discussed microliths are chiefly a lowland phenomenon limited by the Vistula on the east, and reaching as far as the Atlantic Ocean in the west. Their northern range is roughly that of the Lowland frontiers (including the ex-land bridges of Dogger Bank and the West Baltic), and in the south they reach the Alps, extending to the central European Highlands. The map shows the phenomenon in a certain temporal flattening.

Notwithstanding the fact that the map is a specific sum of chronologically differentiated, perhaps unequal(?) territorial ranges, it is by no means a good presentation of prehistoric reality. Therefore, the range presented should and ought to be reconstructed for the areas that are blank.

The map shows that PE-points were infrequent and that they were distributed unequally over the area of their occurrence. The following remarks are also in order:

1. PE-points persisted longer in the west than in the east.
2. In the west, they might have had a higher average percentage in assemblages than in the east.
3. In the west, they could have been a steady element, while in the east they had all the features of a peripheral phenomenon subject to fluctuation.

In order to close the discussion of territorial range, it should be said that the Dogger Bank Shelf, as well as the submerged West Baltic land bridge, ought to be recognized as part at the territory occupied by PE-points as early as the 10th/9th millennium cal. BC.

Summing up the above considerations, we can say that PE-points covered the Lowland from Britain to the Vistula and the northern Alpine foreland. It seems that gaps observed inside this range are partly the consequence

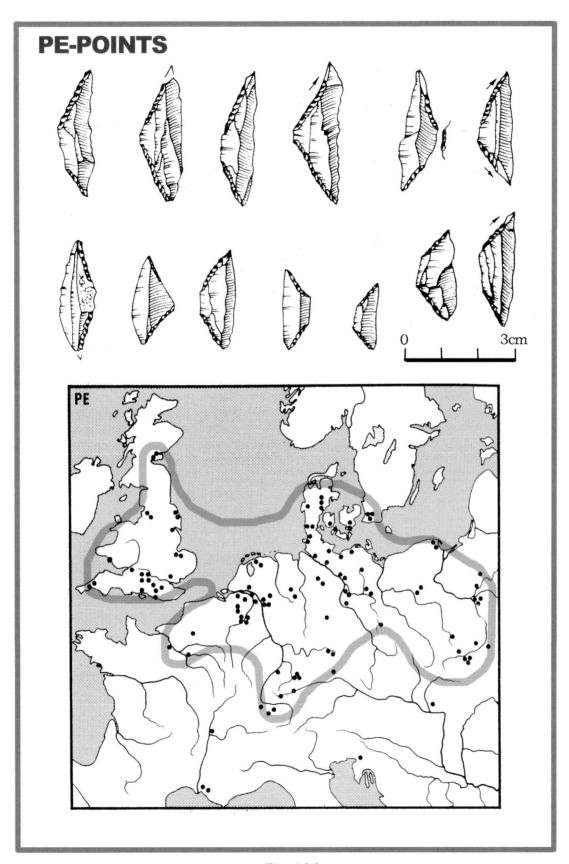

Fig. 4.5.2

of insufficient research. Should this be true (cf. remarks on chronology), we can assume that in one period at least (the earliest Holocene) all European PE-points derived from the same tradition (constituting a base for the future Mesolithic *koine*, cf.) and would therefore provide evidence of actual genetic bonds linking contemporary users. In short, observed similarities between PE-points of the earliest Holocene are not accidental.

Chronology

Since few assemblages with PE-points have radiocarbon dates, they are insufficient to form opinions concerning the dating of the phenomenon discussed. Fortunately, there exist a few convenient typological indicators in the Lowland (with the uplands the matter is less clear), in tolerably established temporal horizons. The following type groups will be useful in our analysis:

1. The last Ahrensburgian and Lyngby points (9th millennium cal. BC)
2. Sauveterroid elements (Sauveterrian points – PD, scalene triangles with short base – TH and retouched on three edges – TE, rectangles – RA, rhomboids – RB and trapezoids – RC, narrow blade technology after c. 7800–7700 cal. BC or later)
3. Points with retouched base – PB and Nowy Młyn points – PC (after c. 7500 cal. BC in Scandinavia, and farther south from c. 7000 cal. BC)
4. Microliths with surface retouch – F, asymmetrical – B and symmetrical – A trapezes (from c. 7000 cal. BC or a little earlier)

Ad. 1: In several cases (Deimern 45, Hohler Stein, Stelmoor, Hörpel 7 I in Germany and Remouchamps-Grotte in Belgium) PE–points were accompanied by Ahrensburgian points, while in the English site of Thatcham III and also in the somewhat later Star Carr we see the last tanged points of Lyngby type occurring together with PE-points. This observation can be supplemented by ^{14}C dates for Remouchamps (c. 10,500 cal. BC) and Thatcham III (c. 10,500 and 9600 cal. BC). The quoted data proves that PE-points appeared at the turn of the 11th and 10th millennium cal. BC and were in that period territorially limited to the northwestern part of Europe.

Ad. 2: In the 9th and the first half of the 8th millennium cal. BC, the range of PE-points seems to have reached its maximum. This is confirmed by ^{14}C dates (Star Carr and Morton A in Britain, Jägerhaushöhle, Duvensee 2, Friesack and Hohen Viecheln in Germany, Klosterlund, Kongens Mose and Flaadet in Denmark, and Całowanie in Poland), as well as by pollen dates (Flixton I in Great Britain). Moreover, we find confirmation of this in typological data – PE-points occur in rather numerous undated, "middle phase" assemblages (cf. "Rhythms"), which appear only towards 7500 cal. BC with Sauveterroid elements, rectangles – RA, rhomboids – RB and trapezoids – RC), i.e., in the British Deepcar, German Schinderkule and Swedish Linnebjär.

Ad. 3. The latest observable stage of PE-point existence is the 7th millennium cal. BC. In this period, the discussed microliths are known from Great Britain (e.g. Shippea Hill), Holland (de Leien and Bergumermeer), and southern Sweden (Ageröd I: H/C-HT). In this last region, they occur only at the beginning of the 7th millennium cal. BC. So far, there has been no confirmation of the presence of late PE-points in Poland and eastern Germany. They seem to have disappeared from there earlier. However, they are known from western Germany at least in the beginning of the 7th millennium (Klein Vollbüttel with trapezes).

In conclusion, we may suggest a three-stage evolution of PE-points, which, deriving from the Latest Paleolithic of northwestern Europe, spread (?) east in the Early Holocene, and died out gradually, surviving only in the Late Mesolithic of its native region.

In this situation, the said type could be included in the central-western European *koine* (cf.).

Taxonomy

PE-points are connected with quite a number of European taxonomic units.

They were initially connected with the western fraction of Ahrensburgian and Star Carr culture. Two conclusions seem to result from the above:

1. The relationship (genetic?) of Ahrensburgian (through Epi-Ahrensburgian, cf.) and Star Carr cultures (Grahame Clark's "Proto-Maglemosian") is very probable. It is confirmed not only by the presence of PE-points in both units, but also by the territorial contiguity of both cultures (thanks to Dogger Bank Shelf), their mutual chronological interrelation and the presence of numerous identical types (tanged points, broad isosceles triangles – TM, micro truncations – K, very short end-scrapers, burins).
2. It is not possible to determine the degree of that relationship today. We do not know whether we are dealing with local evolution, or whether the British unit derives from the continental one.

    In their further evolution, PE-points are steadily linked with their native region in Great Britain, first in Star Carr, and later in its direct successors (Broxbourne and Shippea Hill cultures).
4. Further to the east, between the Meuse and Oder rivers, PE-points are characteristic of Duvensee culture. Their presence in its assemblages, and in those of local Ahrensburgian which preceded Duvensee, seems to speak in favor of the local origins of the North German Mesolithic, particularly between the Meuse and the Elbe, and perhaps also in Denmark (passing through the Epi/Post-Ahrensburgian of Bare Mose-Pinnberg), in an area where PE-points had been known already in the younger Dryas period.
5. East of the Oder river, PE-points are characteristic mostly of early Komornician in the 10th/9th millennium cal. BC. They do not exist in the Swiderian, which preceded the local Mesolithic.

Both mentioned entities (Duvensee and Komornica) are strongly related and together with Star Carr they form what is called the Duvensee Culture Group (cf. "West and Center"), comprising in the early Holocene all of the territory from Britain through northern Germany to Poland and southern Scandinavia.

Thus, in the Lowland, PE-points are obviously connected with a complex of interlinked cultures: Ahrensburgian, Epi-Ahresnburgian, Star Carr, Duvensee (also the Melsted variant in Bornholm) and less Komornica, constituting a permanent characteristic present there from the end of the Pleistocene.

Were this so indeed, we would have the right to presume that the lack of PE-points in assemblages of the 10th and the beginning of the 9th millenium cal. BC between the Elbe and the Vistula, and their appearance only from the second half of the 9th millennium cal. BC, indicates a western source of cultural influence (shift?) coming most probably from the Duvensee environment. Consequently, the eastern element of the Duvensee Culture Group, that is, the Komornician, should be seen as taking example from trends coming from beyond the Oder.

PE-points from Early Beuronian assemblages (in the south, i.e. Jägerhaushöle – lower layer, and Wunkendorf) merit special attention. Specimens known from the south seem to be rather short-lived there and embrace only early phases of the local Mesolithic (= Beuronian A).

It is finally worthwhile to recall that PE-points are linked with yet another culture of the northern type, i.e., Post-Maglemosian De Leien-Wartena in Holland. It may be useful to remember that Raymond R. Newell derives it from the inundated Dogger Bank Shelf, which was part of the area where PE-points originated. Therefore, their very late occurrence in Friesland (7th millennium cal. BC) is not surprising in a region where they previously existed, in the neighbouring British Shippea Hill culture.

Conclusions

In summing up the present outline, it may be said that a chronological-and-spatial analysis of PE-points permits the following paleohistorical conclusions:

1. From the 11th/10th millennium cal. BC, PE-points appear in related Ahrensburgian, Epi-Ahrensburgian and Star Carr cultures, lasting uninterruptedly in northwestern Europe up to the 7th millenium cal. BC. Therefore, in this region, they are living proof of the endurance of a strong local tradition.
2. Perhaps in the 10th millennium, their range increases in the east (Vistula basin) and north (Scotland, southern Scandinavia). Both directions could express the territorial spread of PE-points in the Duvensee Culture Group (= Early Maglemosian), the first local representative of the Maglemosian Technocomplex in new territories (?).
3. The duration of PE-points is shorter in the east than in the west; they vanish probably much before the end

of the 8th millennium cal. BC, when old units, such as Duvensee and later its cousin Komornica, undergo deep changes, and finally disappear.
4. In the European Lowland, PE-points are evidence of always one and the same tradition which developed between Britain and the Vistula basin from the 10th/9th to the 6th millennium cal. BC. This tradition brought about a great unity of cultures known as the Maglemosian/Northern Technocomplex (cf.), one of the characteristic features of which was the occurrence of PE-points, chiefly in its early phases.
5. In the foothills of the Alps, PE-points are known only from the Early Mesolithic.

4.5.3. Les Pointes PB et PC
(co-author – J. M. Burdukiewicz)

Introduction

Dans cet article nous nous occuperons des pointes à base retouchée (PB) et des pointes dites de Nowy Młyn (PC, cf. typologie dans l'"Atlas") qui apparaissent dans certaines industries du Maglemosien (au sens large), dans sa phase moyenne et récente.

Les deux types semblent liées par de forts liens génétiques et typologiques. S'il en est réellement ainsi, on peut formuler deux thèses expliquant ce phénomène, qui s'excluent réciproquement, à savoir:

1) les pointes à base retouchée (PB) ainsi que les pointes de Nowy Młyn (PC) auraient apparu simultanément, étant synchroniques sur tout le territoire entre les Pays Bas et la Pologne, englobant l'Allemagne du nord, le Danemarque et la Suède meridionale;
2) leur apparition sur l'étendue du Maglemosien aurait un caractère diachronique.

Selon que nous admettrons l'une ou l'autre de ces deux thèses, les conclusions paléohistoriques seront elles-aussi différentes. Dans le cas de la thèse première, nous pourrons adopter le thèse de Grahame Clark et Erik Brinch-Petersen sur l'évolution, en principe synchronique, de tous les éléments/provinces du Maglemosian, sans grande différenciation régionale; par contre, l'admission de la thèse seconde nous fera reconnaître implicitement les développements locaux, fortement individualisés, du Maglemosien et ainsi que le voulaient Hermann Schwabedissen, Bernhard Gramsch, Raymond R. Newell et Stefan K. Kozłowski, l'asynchronisme des variétés régionales et parfois typologiquement similaires du Maglemosien. Les arguments en faveur de la thèse seconde semblent prédominer et nous essaierons plus loin de le prouver.

Le présent article comprend:

L'analyse spatiale et chronologique des points PB et PC, et des conclusions paléohistoriques. Pour la description detaillée des deux types le lecteur est renvoyé à la typologie préparée pour l'"Atlas du Mesolithique" dans ce volume.

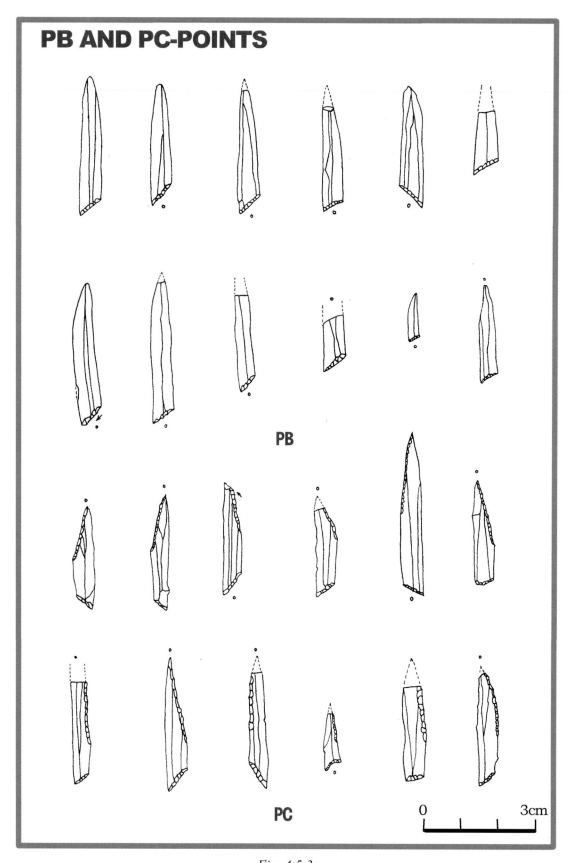

Fig. 4.5.3a

PB AND PC-POINTS

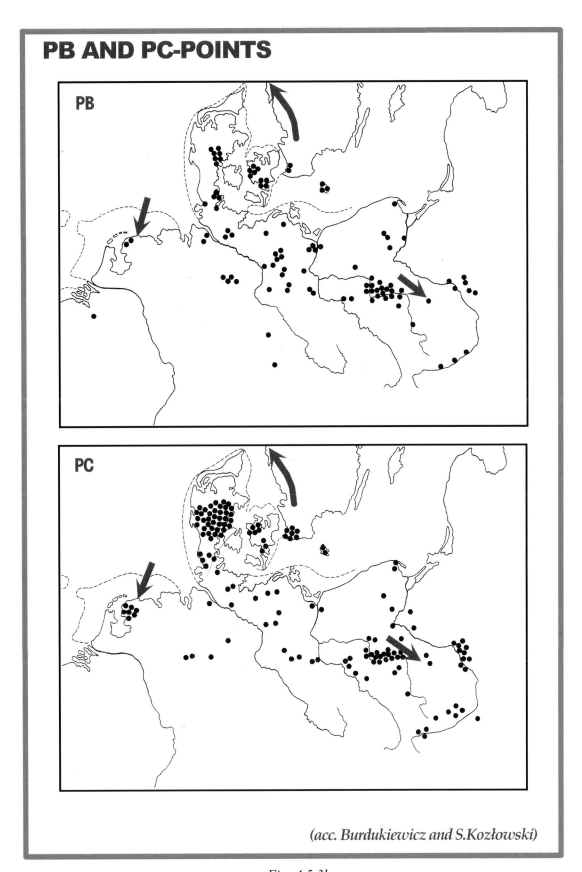

(acc. Burdukiewicz and S.Kozłowski)

Fig. 4.5.3b

Chorologie

1. Les pointes PB et PC apparaissent dans la zone septentrionale de l'Europe centrale, sur le territoire délimité à l'ouest – par le Rhin, et à l'est – par la Vistule.

   Au nord, elles sont presentes sur le territoire du Danemark et de la Suède méridionale (Scanie), ainsi que sur le littoral norvegien (surtout PB), alors qu'au sud leur portée territoriale maximale ne dépasse pas les limites de la Plaine.

2. a) Les pointes PB se trouvent groupées principalement sur le territoire du Danemark et de la Pologne (sur le cours moyen de la Warta et de la Vistule); à l'ouest, on observe une les sites au nord des Pays Bas, dans le Friesland. Sur le reste du territoire apparaissent des trouvailles dispersées;

   b) Les sites à pointes PC sont répartis plus régulièrement sur toute l'étendue indiquée au pt. "a" (à l'exception de la Norvège ?), bien que, dans ce cas également, ils soient plus nombreux sur la Warta moyenne et moins nombreux à l'ouest de la basse Elbe en Allemagne.

   Tout en relevant certaines différences locales quant à la répartition de ces deux catégories de pointes, nous pouvons néanmoins souligner la concordance générale de leur répartition géographique et leur co-apparition fréquente dans les mêmes outillages.

3. Les sites présentés sur les cartes peuvent dater d'une période de temps relativement étendue (cf. plus loin): par conséquent, les cartes nous montrent une situation en quelque sorte «applatie» dans le temps. Aussi, peuvent-ils être considérés comme représentant les sommes de différentes répartitions du même phénomène datant de périodes diverses (p.ex. les différentes phases de développement territorial d'un élément typologique).

L'analyse chronologique effectuée à chaque fois peut éventuellement faciliter la division d'une carte sommaire en plusieurs horizons chronologiques. Evidemment, la réserve ci-dessus formulée n'exclue pas l'existence de phénomènes de longue durée, lesquels dû à leur caractère invariable, peuvent être indiqués sur les cartes collectives d'une manière relativement adéquate.

Chronologie

Les deux classes de microlithes examinés ici apparaissent dans certains sites scandinaves et hollandais datés; on les connaît également par les outillages polonais et allemands datés par ^{14}C, mais aussi par la méthode typologique. Les données relatives à la chronologie des pointes PB et PC sur toute l'étendue où elles apparaissent, se présentent comme suit:

1. Sites datés par la méthode ^{14}C (cal. BC):

   PB : Haule I – env. 7000 et 6550, De Leien – 6250 et 6050, Siegerswoude – 7050, Wartena – 6500, Ulkestrup Øst II – 7250, 7150 et 7100, Bare Mosse II – 7850, 7750, 7600 et 7450, Ageröd I:D – 7000, Ageröd I.B – 7050, Ageröd I:H/C VL – 6950, Ageröd I:H/C ÖT – 6800, Ageröd I:H/C UT – 7000, Parleza Mała (Pologne) – 5610 et 5280;

   PC : De Leien – env. 6250 et 6050, Wartena – 6500, Ulkestrup Øst II – 7250, 7150 et 7100, Ageröd I:D – 7000, Ageröd I:B – 7050, Ageröd I:H/C VL – 6950, Ageröd LH/C ÖT – 6800, Jastrzębia Góra (Pologne) – 5755.

2. Sites datés par la méthode de l'analyse pollinique:

   PB : Ulkestrup Øst II – env. 6300–6100, A.C, Mullerup S. – 7500, Øgaarde – 7400–6800, Holmegaard I – 7500–7250, Sværdborg I – 7500–6900, Lundby I – 8100–7400, Bare Mosse II – 7300–7100, Ageröd I: B – 6950–6700, Ageröd I:D – 6950–6650, Ageröd I: H/C UT – 7700–7200, Ageröd I:H/C VL – 7200–6950, Ageröd I:H/C 0T – 6950–56500;

   PC : Øgaarde – env. 7400–6800, Mullerup S. – 7500, Ulkestrup Øst II – 6300–6100, Sværdborg I – 7500–6900, Ageröd I:B – 6950–6700, Ageröd LD – 6950–6650, Ageröd LH/C VL – 7200–6950, Ageröd LH/C OT – 6950–6500 A.C.

3. Sites contemporains des sites scandinaves provenant du territoire où apparaissent les pointes PB et PC mais dépourvus de ces pointes (cultures Boberg et du Rhein-Meuse-Schelde):

   Beerzel Belten II: env. 7530, Drouvener Zand I – 6925, Duursvoude I – 6750, Duursvoude III – 6760 et 6750, Een II – 6850 et 6775, Rotsterhaule – 7415, Ermelo – 7260, Hatert – 6720, Nijnsel II – 6835, Oirschot VI – 7080.

4. Sites à pointes PB et PC datés typologiquement : les trapèzes apparaissent dans les cultures mésolithiques de la Plaine Européenne vers l'an 7000 cal. BC. Cette thèse est appuyée par de nombreuses dates ^{14}C assemblées par André Gob.

   Les trapèzes accompagnent presque toujours les pointes PB et PC dans les outillages allemands (p.ex. Rüde 2), hollandais (p.ex. De Leien) et polonais (p.ex. Swornigacie I); par contre, en Scandinavie méridionale, seuls les sites à pointes PB et PC les plus récents (à partir de 7000 cal. BC) contiennent des trapèzes.

5. De l'analyse des datations mentionnées, il ressort que:

   a) en Scandinavie méridionale, les pointes PC n'apparaissent pas avant l'an 7500 cal. BC environ (aparition de la technique de lamelle étroite), et les pointes PB à la même époque. Ces deux catégories disparaissent d'ici vers l'an 6800 cal. BC. L'information coincide bien avec le schéma évolutif pour cette région proposé par Erik Brinch-Petersen. Il convient de reveler l'absence totale des pointes PB et PC en Grande Bretagne laquelle, jusque vers 7550 cal. BC était encore reliée au Continent.

   b) si l'on admet la thèse avancée au pt 4 ainsi que les datations ^{14}C pour la Hollande et typologiques pour la Pologne, on est tenu à reconnaître implicitement que les pointes PB et PC ont apparu sur les Plaines Allemande et Polonaise principalement beaucoup après l'an 7500 cal. BC et sans doute vers 7000 (à l'exception de la Kuiavie et la Poméranie occidentale polonaise, ou un Svaerdborgien à été trouvé par Lucyna Domańska et Zbigniew Bagniewski), et y ont subsisté pendant les 7e–5e (nord) et 7e (sud) millénaires cal. BC (pour date la plus récente, voir Dąbki en Poméranie polonaise, avec la céramique du type Ertebøllien – information de Jacek Kabaciński).

Les arguments ci-dessus nous portent à admettre le caractère diachronique des pointes PB et PC dans le technocomplexe nordique/Maglemosien. Ceci témoigne, à son tour, d'un rythme divers de son histoire, réfutant la conception traditionnelle du Maglemosien en tant que monolithe qui poursuit un modèle evolutif unique sur toute l'étendue de son territoire.

Il est aussi clair, que les rares pointes PB (et PC?), connues du littoral norvegien, doivent être datées après 7000 ans cal. A.C. (dans la "Microblade tradition").

Conclusions

Tout en admettant pour fortement vraisemblable notre thèse détaillée, nous nous devons de souligner qu'elle est conforme à la conception générale du formation de la phase moyenne et tardive (= Post – Maglemosian) du Technocomplexe Nordique/Maglemosien formulée par Hermann Schwabedissen. L'auteur allemand admet une forte affinité des industries du type Svaerdborg (Mésolithique moyen local) et Oldesloe (Mésolithique recent local), mais il relève en même temps des différences notables dans leur chronologie et chorologie. Des observations similaires ont été faites par Raymond R. Newell pour la Hollande (parenté des industries non-contemporaines du type De Leien recent avec celle de Svaerdborg plus ancien), Bernhard Gramsch pour la Allemagne orientale (industries du type Kobrow/Jühnsdorf vs. Svaerdborg) et Stefan K. Kozłowski pour la Pologne (industries du type Chojnice-Pieńki et Svaerdborg). Tous les auteurs cités s'accordent pour affirmer que l'apparition tardive de certains éléments du type post-Svaerdborgien sur les territoires plus méridioneaux de la Plaine peut s'expliquer le plus plausiblement par des migrations forcées de Svaerdborgiens vers le sud, lesquels, se heurtant là au substrat local, ont contribué à la naissance de groupes locaux nouveaux, de tradition maglemosienne tardive ou post-maglemosienne.

Les causes de ces présumées migrations résident dans la sphère écologique; dans la seconde moitié du 8e millénaire cal. BC a eu lieu un rétrécissement notable du continent qui s'étendait initialement entre la Jutlande et la Grande Bretagne, et entre la Scanie et la Poméranie polonaise. Paralellement, le littoral ouest-suédois et norvegien est occupé par la culture Nøstvet-Linhult (ou Microbladelet Tradition), depuis c. 7000 ans cal. A.C. Le phenomène est sans doute lié au Svaerdborgien. Dans ces circonstances, les populations habitant les terrains progressivement submergés, ont dû, au fur et à mesure s'en retirer. Des terrains similaires à ceux initialement habités par les Svaerdborgiens se trouvaient, à la limite des 8e et 7e millénaires, dans le Friesland, le Schleswig-Holstein, le Mecklembourg, le Brandenbourg, la Poméranie polonaise et la Grande Pologne. C'est – comme l'indique p.ex. Raymond R. Newell – la région des lacs de la plaine, rappelant les territoires d'origine du Svaerdborgien.

Il ne faut pas oublier toutefois que les territoires d'origine du Svaerdborgien englobent non seulement le shelf Dogger Bank, la Jutlande, la Zélande, la Scanie et le nord du Mecklembourg, mais également la Poméranie occidentale polonaise (découvertes recentes). Aussi, en occident, où la submersion presque totale de son territoire natal a forcé la population Svaerdborg à s'établir sur des terrains tout à fait nouveaux, les choses se sont-elles déroulées diversement sans doute de ce qui advint à l'est, où il lui a suffi parfois d'étendre son propre territoire vers le sud, sans qu'elle dût abandonner totalement ses terrains d'origine (une partie du territoire a été sauvée). On peut donc présumer que ce processus s'est développé (p.ex. à l'est) de deux manières, à savoir: par la continuation des traditions locales du type Svaerdborg (en Jutlande, Scanie, Zelande, Mecklembourg et la Poméranie) et par la création de variétés locales nouvelles du type Post-Maglemosien (Chojnice-Pieńki, Oldesloe et Jühnsdorf, mais aussi "Microbladelet Tradition" au nord), sur des terrains extérieurs au territoire d'origine Svaerdborgien. A l'ouest, nous n'avons affaire qu'à cette seconde alternative, et notamment la formation de la variété locale nouvelle du type De Leien-Wartena, à l'exterieur du territoire natal.

La thèse relative au déplacement de la population Svaerdborg vers le sud et vers le nord n'exclue pas la possibilité qu'une partie de cette population a subsisté sur les terrains non-submergés en Danemark et en Suède méridionale, ainsi qu'au Mecklembourg et en Poméranie, comme montre l'industrie très microlithique trouvée à Svaerdborg I par Carl J. Becker, ou l'industrie post-maglemosienne de la Scanie.

4.5.4. Rectangles, Rhomboids and Trapezoids in the Northern and Western European Mesolithic

Introduction

This essay deals with the three Mesolithic types of armatures characteristic of northern and western Europe and resembling each other in many respects. These are rectangles (RA), rhomboids (RB) and trapezoids (RC). The chronological and spatial analysis of these microliths may provide important data valid for future synthesis.

Typological characteristics (Fig. 2.5.4a–c)

Common features

1. Blanks: Regular bladelets,
2. Shape: Elongated quadrangle with two parallel (or nearly parallel) longer sides,
3. Retouch: Semiabrupt, high, on (at least) three sides, two of which are the shorter ones.

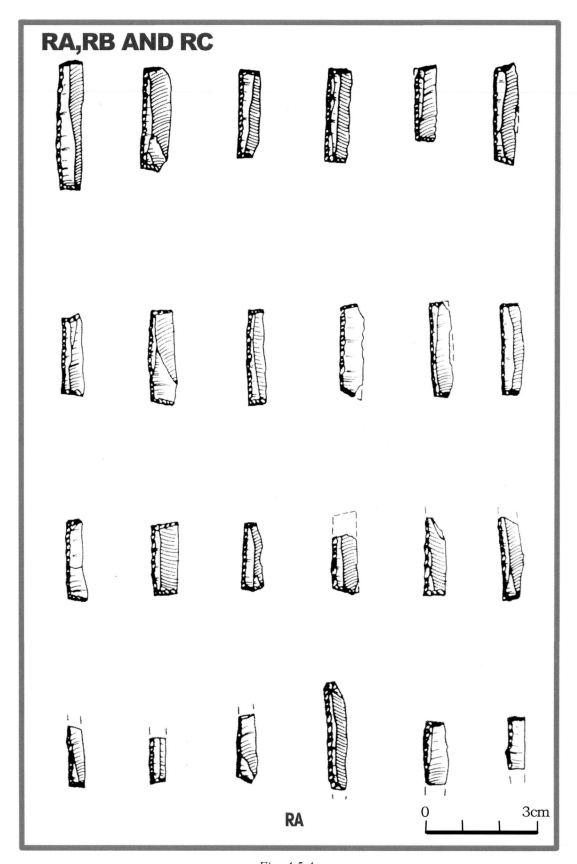

Fig. 4.5.4a

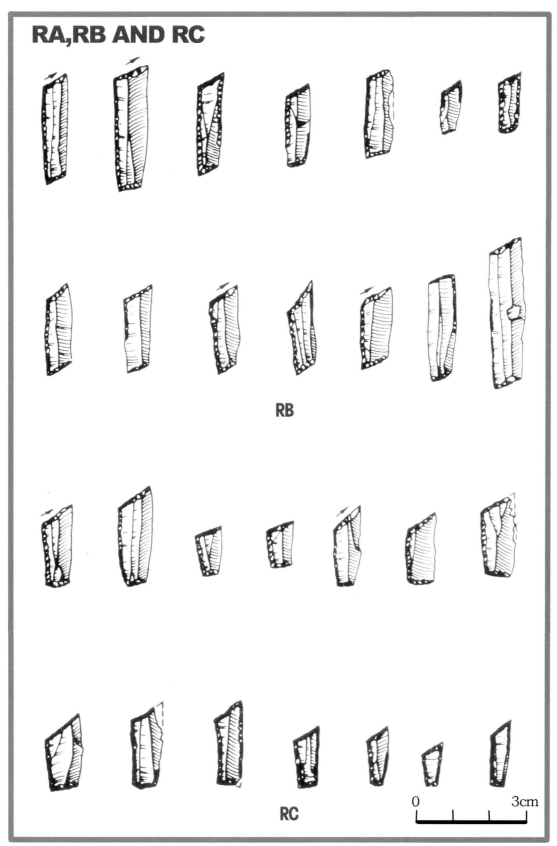

Fig. 4.5.4b

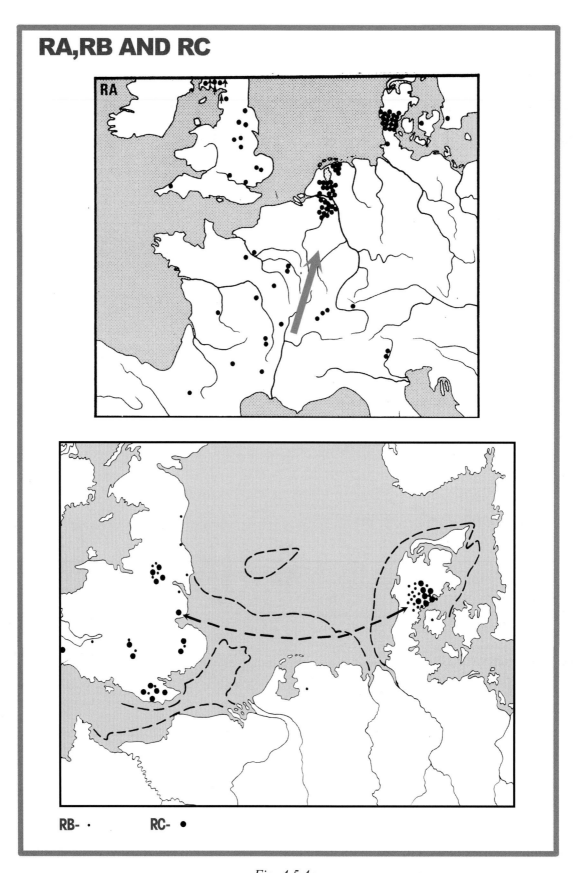

Fig. 4.5.4c

Differences

1. Rectangles RA: Transverse, parallel truncations; these armatures are sometimes called "smalle trapezer 2 + 12" (T. Mathiassen) or "microlithic blunted back blades with retouched end" (A. Bohmers, A. Wouters).
2. Rhomboids RB: Oblique, parallel truncations; they are called sometimes "rhomboids" (Grahame Clark) and "smalle trapezer 16" (Mathiassen) in the available publications.
3. Trapezoids RC: Oblique and transverse truncation; they may also be referred to as "smalle trapezer 20" (Mathiassen); Clark calls them "sub-triangular points".

Cf. also the typology discussed in the "Atlas" in this volume.

Spatial analysis

1. Rectangles RA occur mainly in four regions: in Jutland, in the basins of the Lower Rhine and the Meuse rivers, in southeastern England as well as along the Rhône, Loire, (west of the) Rhine and Seine rivers in France. These concentrations of sites are almost certainly the elements of a spatial structure of considerable size which comprised the southern part of the Jutland-British landbridge existing in northwestern Europe up to the second half of the 8th millenium cal. BC. This idea is supported not only by the cartographic and palaeogeographical data, but also by radiocarbon dates (cf. further remarks on chronology).
2. The ranges of rhomboids RB and trapezoids RC are identical and their chronology agrees. This indicates that the typological difference between them is of no practical value. It should be stressed, however, that the common range of RB and RC differs considerably from the range of RA. The former are located further to the north; they can be found in all of Britain and Jutland, but are almost absent in the Rhine-Meuse region. Also in this case, many factors indicate that the similarities between the Jutland pieces and the British ones are not accidental (cf. also "Local and foreign..."). It may therefore be concluded that we are dealing with a remnant of a greater territory that comprised primarily the central and southern parts of Great Britain, central Jutland and the northern edge of the Dogger Bank Shelf. This allows us to date the RB–RC phenomenon to well before the end of the 8th millenium cal. BC, that is, to a period when the Shelf was still inhabited.

Chronology

Chronological frames of the three classes of armatures in question may be defined on the basis of not very numerous (especially for Denmark) ^{14}C dates. They are as follows:

1. Rectangles RA: a series of the earliest dates, in the north, refers to the middle of the 8th millenium cal. BC (Coincy II 7240; Rotsterhaule 7415; Hulshorst – earlier date 7840; Stallerupholm c. 7350 cal. BC). In the Netherlands and Great Britain, but not in Denmark, evidence for the occurrence of rectangles is also to be found in the 7th/8th millenium cal. BC (Oirschot V 7080; Duurswoude III 6750; Nijnsel I 6685 and 6360; Shippea Hill 7350 cal. BC). In Great Britain, separated from the Continent from the second half of the 8th millenium cal. BC, rectangles survived up to the 5th millenium (Wawcott I?). The South offers early datings, e.g. from Romagnano III (cf.) in Trentino in North Italy (cf.), and much older appearances in the Late Magdalenian and Late Epi-Gravettian of the region (cf. also "Mapping the Mesolithic").
2. Rhomboids RB and trapezoids RC are dated on four sites only, all of them in Great Britain (Ickornshaw Moor 7150; Shippea Hill 7350; Lominot IV 4660 and Wawcott I 4310 cal. BC). The first date does not differ much from the early dates for the rectangles RA in the north.
3. The aforementioned dates support the conclusion that at least at the beginning the RA microliths in the north were generally contemporary with RB + RC armatures; all of them have a similarly early origin throughout the territory of their northern occurrence (RB+RC in Jutland as well? – thay occur there without trapezes), dating back to the middle of the 8th millenium cal. BC, and they appear to have survived in the local Mesolithic cultures throughout the 7th millenium cal. BC and even longer in Great Britain.
4. The presumable, common date of introduction for all the classes (RA, RB, RC) in the area stretching from England to the Netherlands and Denmark seems to be of particular importance here. The date refers to the final period of existence of the land connection between the Continent and Great Britain, which was broken just after 7500 cal. BC. This date is simultaneously the latest date for the emergence of the armatures of interest in the territories of the Low Countries, Scandinavia and Great Britain.
5. In conclusion, the introduction of rectangles, rhomboids and trapezoids in the Mesolithic cultures of northwestern and northern Europe may be said to date back to the middle of the 8th millennium cal. BC, i.e., the time in which this region was subjected to influence from the south (cf. "Sauveterrisation" and "Local and foreign elements in the British Mesolithic") and to strong stylistic and technological (narrow bladelet!) changes in the local flint inventories. These changes may account for the creation of two new types RB and RC.

Taxonomic links

Microliths RA, RB and RC overlap (partly or entirely), as regards both their territorial and chronological range, with some cultural units being distinguished in northern and southern Europe.

1. Rectangles RA: On the Lower Rhine and the Meuse rivers, rectangles RA are connected mainly with assemblages of Boberg Culture ("Boberg Stufe" of Hermann Schwabedissen); evidence is provided, among others, by the assemblages of Rotsterhaule, Duurswoude III or Havelte (all at the Biologisch-Archaeologisch Instituut in Groningen, Holland). Moreover, some assemblages of the Rhein-Meuse-Schelde/Rhenanian culture contain rectangles (e.g. Oirschot V in the collections of the BAI, Groningen); rectangles are present also in the assemblages of the Beuronian (e.g. Rocher d'Auffargis I from the Paris Basin). In the territory of southeastern England, these rectangles are known from the assemblages of Shippea Hill culture/Narrow Blade Industry and the evidence is provided by, for example, the assemblages of Shippea Hill or Wawcott I (the former at Cambridge University). Finally, from Jutland come the rectangles connected with local assemblages of Svaerdborg/Gudenaa cultures(?); this is confirmed by the Stallerupholm assemblage and others, not yet published (all at the Institute of Archaeology in Moesgaard, Denmark).

   In the south, the RA rectangles are present, even earlier, in the Sauveterrian (Culoz, La Tourasse, both in France, Romagnano III in Italy), and Epi-Gravettian (cf. "South").

   It may be concluded from all the presented facts that rectangles have an intercultural value and belong to the *koine* (cf.): Epi-Magdalenian, Epi-Gravettian, Sauveterrian, Boberg, RMS, Beuronian, Shippea Hill and Svaerdborg. It is also possible that they were the result of a spectacular "push" from the south in the 8th millennium cal. BC.

2. Rhomboids RB and trapezoids RC are found in Great Britain in assemblages of Shippea Hill culture, e.g. Shippea Hill and Farnham (Cambridge University); in Jutland they are probably connected with the Svaerdborgian, though this connection has not been sufficiently proven by homogeneous assemblages (most of the pieces are derived from surface collections in the Gudenaa river basin).

Remarks on the origin of the "cultural" differentiation in the Middle Mesolithic of Northwestern Europe.

The phenomena described above constitute only a part of complex structures and processes characteristic of the Middle (second half of the 8th millennium cal. BC) Mesolithic in this part of Europe. Among the typological components which made up the Mesolithic assemblages of the region in question, one can distinguish on one hand local and foreign components, and on the other hand, components with a more universal (intercultural) as compared to a regional range.

The classes of the Mesolithic tools discussed here cannot be treated as purely local phenomena, but neither do they possess the extremely intercultural (except RA) character of some other classes of armatures (e.g. Sauveterrian points – PD, long scalene triangles retouched on three edges – TE, asymmetric trapezes, etc., cf. "Les courants interculturels").

It seems that microliths RB and RC, undisputably of intercultural nature (cf. above), delimited in northwestern Europe a definite but not very large territory sometime in the middle of the 8th millenium cal. BC (?). Such territories became characteristic as a result of the greater changes occurring in northwestern Europe during the Middle Mesolithic. These territories, the average area of which accounted for some hundred thousand square kilometers in the 8th/7th millenia cal. BC, were characterized by several spreading "fashions", such as, among others, the microliths RB + RC, Sauveterrian points PD, points with surface retouch – F in the north, Martinet trapezes in southwestern France (Jean-Georges Rozoy's information), or Nowy Młyn – PC points in the Baltic region (cf. "PB and PC points").

Nonetheless, the range of such "fashions", as of most other fashions, is not very stable and rather accidental(?). First of all, fashions do not respect old boundaries and divisions, their range is not limited either by environment or local tradition. Thus, they spread their "coat" over a native, differentiated substratum irregularly, even missing some territories.

The RA case, on the other hand, has a much wider range, starting from the Mediterranean, and this range could result from a "push" coming from the south to the north (cf. "Mapping the Mesolithic").

Territorial expansion (e.g. spread of RA from the Sauveterrian south, cf. André Thévenin's important ideas on the issue), as well as the creation of cultural phenomenon, "fashions" included, in a certain habitat are determined by far-reaching factors. These are easy to present theoretically, but it is far more difficult to support them with real evidence. We shall not discuss the reasons now – it is still too early for that. We shall attempt to present the phenomenon in a wider framework, because it seems to constitute part of a great trend that can be distinguished in the history of northwestern Europe somewhere around 7700/7500 cal. BC.

At the beginning of the 8th millenium cal. BC, certain cultural entities created in the 10th/9th millenium cal. BC were still present in northwestern Europe:

1. The wide, north forehills of the Alps were occupied by the Beuronian (Coincy I and Piscop in France, Aardhorst-Vessem in the Netherlands, Jägerhaushöhle and Ensdorf in Germany, Birsmatten-Basisgrotte in Switzerland).

2. The Lowland of northwestern Europe was occupied by Early Maglemosian cultures: Star Carr, Duvensee (Klosterlund, Sønder-Hadsund in Denmark, Duvensee in Germany and Ter Horst in the Netherlands) and Broxbourne (Broxbourne 102, Abinger Common and Kelling Heath sites in Great Britain).

   Considerable changes started in northwestern Europe around 7700–7500 cal. BC:

3. The "Sauveterrian component" (among others, Sauveterrian points PD and PA, scalene triangles with short base TH, TE, rectangles RA) was spreading from the south to the Netherlands, England and Denmark; its presence is marked, among others, by Sauveterrian points and long and narrow triangles found in the Beuronian C, Boberg and Shippea Hill cultures. The latter was in the process of formation at the time, as claimed by Roger Jacobi.

4. More or less at the same time scalene triangles with short base appeared in the Mesolithic of southern Scandinavia, as described by Eric Brinch-Petersen; the formation of the Svaerdborgian (= Maglemosian 3) was completed.

5. In the cultures mentioned in points 3 and 4 above, rectangles RA, rhomboids RB and trapezoids RC appeared as well; they were differentiated territorially, RA coming from the south, RB and RC being local.

6. In 7700–7500 cal. BC, narrow-blade technology became popular in northwestern Europe. It probably came together with the Sauveterrian phenomenon from the south and gave rise to all the narrow microliths (TH, TE, TI, TD, PB, PC, RA, etc.).

As a result of these changes, old "cultural" structures either disappeared or changed, and new ones came into existence. These new structures were represented by the assemblages that may be treated technologically and typologically as a sum of, firstly, elements constituting the old, local base and, secondly, new components (cf. points 3–6), that in part at least came from the outside.

The new elements did not concern the entire new area in the same extent. There is, for example, a complete lack of Sauveterrian PD points in southern Scandinavia, or rectangles in the north of England. It should also be added that the old – "receiving" – *milieus* had been differentiated long before that time. Thus, this summing up of old, differentiated structures and new differentiated "fashions" and influences may have resulted in the end in nothing more but a very strong "cultural" differentiation of the area starting from the second half of the 8th millenium cal. BC.

4.5.5. Some general remarks after mapping the K, PE, PB, PC, RA, RB and RC microliths

The above presentations of mapping for selected types of microliths lead to the following conclusions:

1. Ranges do not match (macroregions and regions) and they can overlap (K and PE, PB and PC, RB and RC), but not necessarily. Each time, these ranges end in some linear border which is repeated (like the eastern border of the K, PE, PB and PC ranges).

2. Ranges can last for a long time (K, PE, RB, RC) or else change dynamically (RA, PB, PC).

4.5.6. Mapping the Mesolithic

Introduction

Studies of the European Mesolithic have always been very much locally-oriented, hardly ever exceeding the regional overview at best. Long-term research experience has demonstrated, however, that particular taxonomic variants of the phenomenon have a supraregional aspect as well. Thus, it is of paramount importance for an understanding of the spread of the European Mesolithic to consider it from a point of view surmounting modern political boundaries, abandoning the local or regional description that has lain so heavily on studies in the past. The following are a few remarks illustrating the opportunities given by this new approach for a tentative mapping of the European Mesolithic with all its diversification and cultural territories.

"One" Mesolithic and the vertical approach (Fig. 4.5.6a–f)

The paleontological-geological paradigma about evolution's universality, applied to the Paleolithic by 19th-century French researchers (influenced by the ideas of Charles Darwin), was later uncritically extended to the Mesolithic by various French amateurs who trusted in its universality. These enthusiasts – teachers, physicians and retired army officers – used it to describe particular surface collections from the Paris Basin and were quickly followed in this by a host of parish priests, pastors and schoolteachers from virtually everywhere in northern Europe, eagerly taking the easy path to serious science.

It soon became apparent that non-French Mesolithic material was more or less "similar" to the French finds (in terms of the presence of microliths and geometrics). In the effect, these finds were quickly and unquestionably recognized as "Azilian" and "Tardenoisian" to everyone's complete satisfaction…

The European Mesolithic did not come to be differentiated (except for separating "bone" Maglemosian from "flint" Tardenosian), local researchers having neither knowledge nor the broader perspective necessary to abolish the conviction about the uniform development of the Paleo-Mesolithic world. Once trained professionals like Gustav Schwantes, Therkel Mathiassen, Grahame Clark, Carl J. Becker and Hermann Schwabedissen took over, they either concentrated on local studies, or took a broader look. The former (e.g. Schwantes, Mathiassen and Becker) limited themselves to specific regions, building local evolutionary sequences that often failed to compare with similar models prepared for neighboring areas. The result was that local evolution(s) was/were well studied and known, while the supraregional perspective lagged behind. In recent decades, this approach has brought some important studies: Erik Brinch-Petersen's for southern Scandinavia, Alberto Broglio's for part of North Italy and Jean-Georges Rozoy's for France or to be more precise, for a dozen regions ("cultures") of this country, Belgium and Switzerland.

In the 1960s, these local studies, which led to the reconstruction of local evolutionary sequences, started

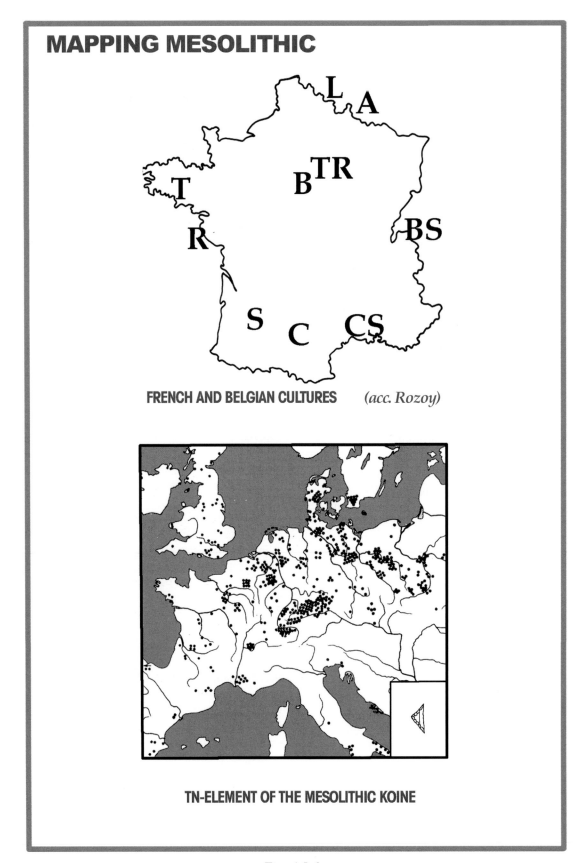

MAPPING MESOLITHIC

FRENCH AND BELGIAN CULTURES   *(acc. Rozoy)*

TN-ELEMENT OF THE MESOLITHIC KOINE

Fig. 4.5.6a

MAPPING MESOLITHIC

BORDERS

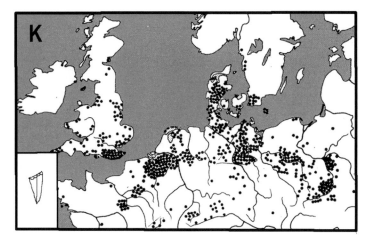

WEST

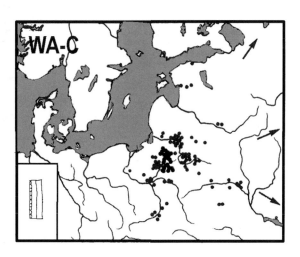

VIZ. EAST

Fig. 4.5.6b

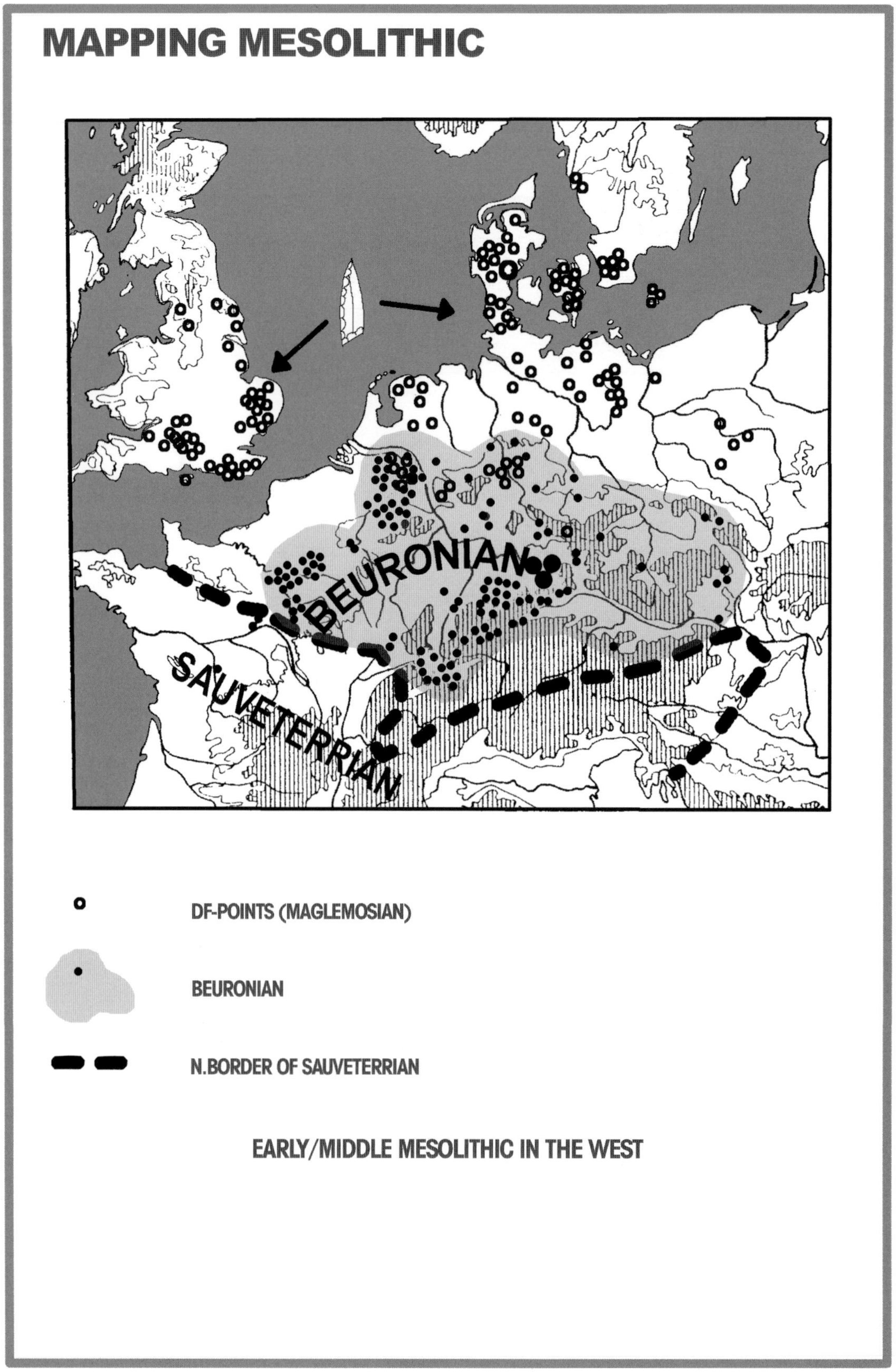
MAPPING MESOLITHIC
BEURONIAN
SAUVETERRIAN
DF-POINTS (MAGLEMOSIAN)
BEURONIAN
N.BORDER OF SAUVETERRIAN
EARLY/MIDDLE MESOLITHIC IN THE WEST

Fig. 4.5.6c

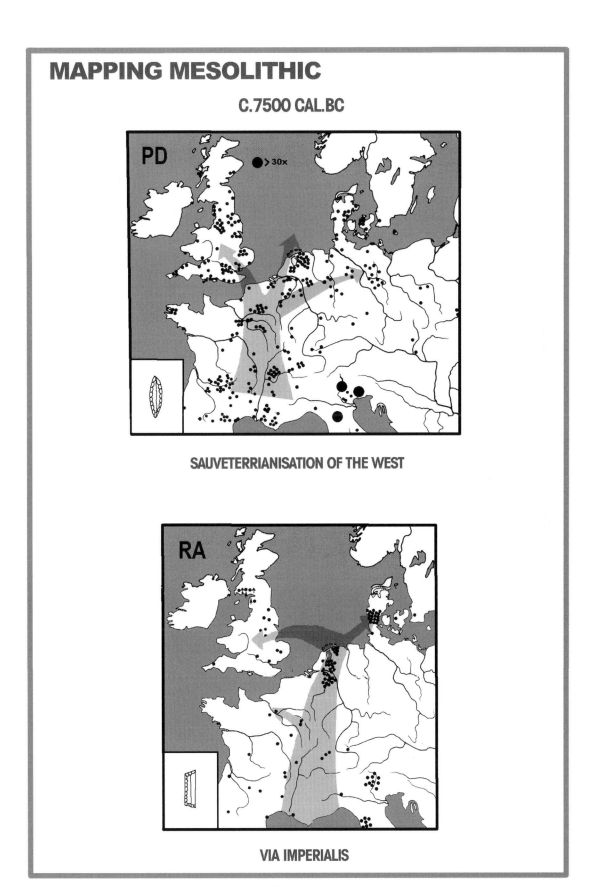

Fig. 4.5.6d

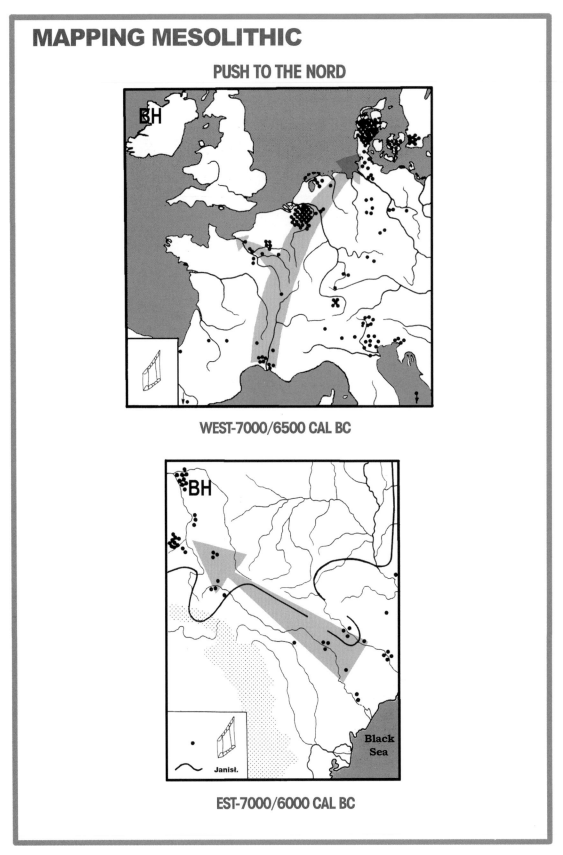

Fig. 4.5.6e

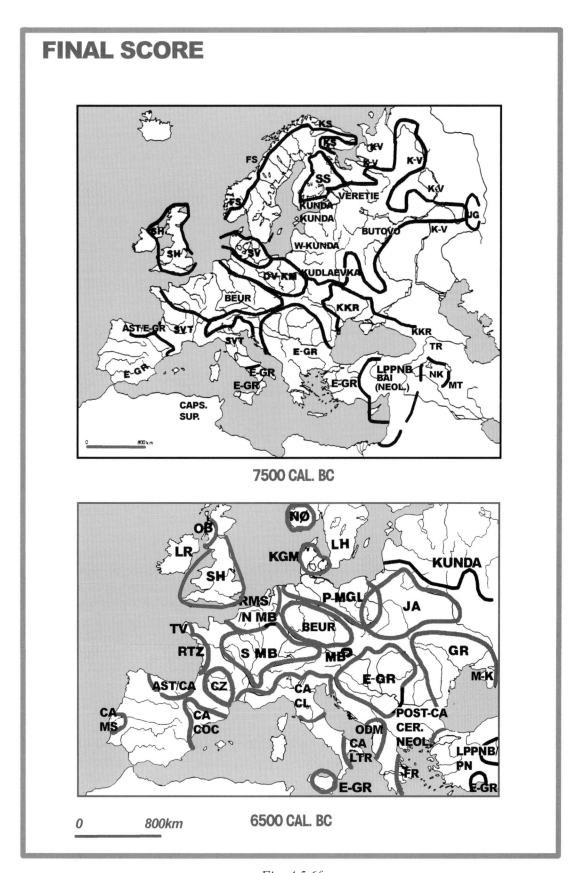

Fig. 4.5.6f

being supplemented with regional and even supraregional surveys, coupled on occasion with tentative mapping (Grahame Clark and Roger Jacobi for Great Britain, Peter Woodman for Ireland, Raymond R. Newell, André Gob and Pierre Vermeersch for the Benelux countries, Hermann Schwabedissen, Surendra K. Arora, Bernhard Gramsch, Erwin Cziesla and Wolfgang Taute for Germany, René Wyss for Switzerland, Alberto Broglio, Paolo Biagi, Carlo Tozzi and Fabio Martini for Italy, Jean-Georges Rozoy and André Thévenin for France, Josep Fullola i Pericot for Spain, Vasile Chirica for Romania, Georgi M. Burov, Lev V. Koltsov, Mikhail Zhylin and Svetlana V. Oshibkina for Russia, Heikki Matiskainen for Finland, Rimute Rimantiène and Thomas Ostrauskas for Lithuania, Ilge Zagorska for Latvia, Dmitryi Telegin, Volodymyr Stanko and Leonid L. Zalizniak for Ukraine, Janusz K. Kozłowski and Stefan K. Kozłowski for the Balkans, Stefan K. Kozłowski for Central Europe. Upon consideration, this appeared sufficient for undertaking a mapping of the Mesolithic in Europe.

The horizontal approach

The first large-area mapping projects are dated back to the turn of the 1940s. These were either regional studies (Hermann Schwabedissen for northwestern Germany in 1942) or supraregional ones (Schwabedissen in 1964 and Wolfgang Taute in 1968 for the Final Paleolithic, referred to until recently as the "Mesolithic", and Grahame Clark in 1936 for the Mesolithic/Late Paleolithic). By the same, a horizontal analysis of the Final Paleolithic/Mesolithic material proved not only possible, but also successful in the supraregional scale, determining territories and borders that quite often exceeded state boundaries. From this point onward, the small-time pastors and educators were out of their depth.

The present author was one of the first to overstep modern state boundaries in his studies of the Mesolithic (1972).

At the root of territorial differentiation

The stage on which the Mesolithic plays itself out is of considerable size, stretching c. 5300 km from east to west and c. 4000 from north to south. These distances are in themselves sufficient to indicate that no cultural uniformity could have been achieved over such a large area. There was no way that small hunting and fishing communities could have communicated and thus exchanged cultural information over such distances, separated as they were from one another by a wild "no man's" land (and by huge distances) that must have figured large in scary stories told by the shamans.

This enormous territory was further differentiated morphologically (mountains, uplands and lowlands), cut across in different directions by watercourses and communicated through mountain passes, gates and river valleys (cf. "Settlement pattern"). It appears therefore that the barriers between particular regions and their inhabitants

were substantial and the passages between them in better or worse condition. Not only mountains (Alps, Pyrenees, Carpathians, Dynaric Alps, Appenines etc), but also seas (Baltic, Adriatic and the English Channel) were an onerous topographical barrier.

The third factor differentiating the region was climatic zonation, which naturally determined the flora and fauna. The break-up was generally (although not always) latitudinal, from the tundra in the north to Mediterranean vegetation in the south, from the reindeer in the north, through elk, roe deer and boar further south, and aurochs and red deer still further south.

Hydrology was yet another differentiating factor. A network of small and medium-size rivers in some regions was contrasted with the big rivers with a less number of tributaries in others or with lakelands still elsewhere.

Finally, there was the cultural factor, the Mesolithic in Europe not having developed everywhere from the same roots. In the south, it originated mainly from the Epi-Gravettian, in the north from the Epi-Magdalenian, Ahrenburgian, Swiderian and Desnian, in the Pontic region from the Caucasian Paleolithic industries to name just the most important of the predecessors. Moreover, the same roots need not have resulted in exactly the same cultural developments, meaning that the Early Holocene culture is often not an exact reflection of what preceded it in the previous period.

Once these factors are considered, the strong territorial differentiation of the European Mesolithic stops being surprising. It could hardly be otherwise!

The first results

The results to start with were predictable: the Mesolithic was differentiated territorially and it was possible to distinguish areas of specific size with concrete, identifiable borders, characterized by specific types of assemblages. The Mesolithic proved no different from other periods with a cultural and territorial division in place. It turned out that particular characteristics could be charted (cf. "Atlas of the Mesolithic") and that a "trans (political) border" description of European Mesolithic cultures could be proposed (Kozłowski 1975) covering broad expanses of the territory.

Europe turned out to be culturally and stylistically differentiated across the continent with particular taxonomic units not only occupying well defined territories (of a transborder nature as a rule), but also having their own traceable external borders. It also proved possible, especially between the Atlantic and the Vistula, to isolate types characteristic of the different cultural traditions, as well as contemporaneous types of an intercultural and interregional nature, which evolved at their own pace (various triangles, trapezes, cf. "Rhythms"). Some of these types were found to be of a supraregional character (cf. "*Koine*"), others were no more than regional or just local.

Ultimately, a confrontation of homogeneous, stratified

and dated assemblages with the mapping argument of abundant surface collections (especially when territories or border lines proved to be superimposed, being documented by more than one type) led to the tracing of "cultural" maps of Mesolithic Europe, and even allowed some "historical" events occurring in the European Mesolithic to be identified (cf. below).

Intraregional characteristics and interterritorial and cultural trends

A fresh look at the classification of available European Mesolithic material, meaning the microliths and points, unbiased by any ideas and opinions voiced hitherto, gives a new overall division into several dozen classes or types (cf. "Atlas"), which can all be dated better or worse and which, moreover, can be mapped.

The mapping exercise demonstrates forthwith that, contrary to the opinions of some researchers, each of the classes or types are limited territorially, meaning that the boundaries of their occurrence can be traced (opposition between "filled" and "empty"). It also shows that each class or type had its own shorter or longer history, which reflected either boring stabilization (range remains unchanged) or interesting dynamics (changing ranges). The former case is excellent for mapping "cultures" in the sense of long-lasting traditions in Mesolithic Europe and the latter illustrates the dynamics of change during the period.

This vitality is especially well visible in the area between the Atlantic, Mediterranean and Baltic. The industries present here appear undividable, all of them being characterized by a large number of similar types of armatures (backed pieces, triangles, trapezes). These triangular, crescent-like and trapezoid geometric microliths had "always" been called "Tardenoisian", and their interpretation had left scholars hopeless. Now, we can suppose that they can be interpreted as a South, West and Central European common *koine* (cf.), quite evidently associated with regionally differentiated specific types. The *koine* itself evolved in separation from or parallel to the local traditions, following its own, western-central-northern evolution. This development can be described as follows (cf. also "Rhythms"):

- 10th–9th millennium cal. BC: domination of broad microliths/points (backed – D, single – K and double truncations – PE, isosceles – TM and scalene – TO, TR triangles, crescents – DD, DE);
- 8th millennium cal. BC: appearance and finally local or regional (?) domination of narrow scalene triangles with short base – TH, TI, TD and retouch of the third edge – TE in the second half/at the end of the millennium; number of broad microliths diminishes.
- 7th millennium cal. BC: domination of trapezes – A, B and rhombs – BH.

The changing trend is more or less common across a large territory (interregionally), but their individual application differs. For example, triangles in the south are clearly smaller than in the north, and the trapezes from the two regions are also internally differentiated. Anyhow, the great potful, so to speak, of "Tardenoisian culture" now appears to contain distinctively discriminating local characteristics (e.g. Tardenois points, Sauveterrian points, *feuilles de gui*, unpolished axes, lanceolates, etc.) alongside intercultural and interregional "trends" (cf. "Les courants interculturels"), which extended over the entire territory from the Atlantic to the Baltic and which evolved more or less similarly over the entire area (cf. "Rhythms").

The poor local pastor could not have conceived of this idea, for the phenomenon can be understood only when considered on a continental scale.

The following are a few suggested mapping reconstructions for different areas of Europe and/or different periods of the Mesolithic, presented in illustration of my point.

The main borders

East vs. West

The first is the border located somewhere between the Vistula and Bug rivers in Poland, dividing in the 10th–8th millennium cal. BC two geographical and cultural zones of the European Mesolithic, the Maglemosian and the Kunda. The border ran from the mouth of the Vistula on the Baltic Sea in a generally southeastern direction to Volhynia in Ukraine. In the material sense, the "Maglemosian" is documented by geometrics, among other things, and especially small proximal truncations (K), isosceles (TN) and different scalene triangles (TO, TR, TH, TE), as well as some trapezes (A) along with unpolished axes and adzes. The Kunda technocomplex, on the other hand, is characterized, among others, by a few variants of Kunda "post-Swiderian" tanged points (L) and a few varieties of microretouched inserts (WA–C). There is naturally some overlapping of the western and eastern ranges and individual types (e.g. "Maglemosian" backed points – D) can penetrate (in this case into the east) the major cultural border described here.

On both sides of the Alps

The Alps have always been a dividing border between the Mediterranean ("Imperial") and the northern zone ("Barbaricum"). They were hardly ever easy to cross and the few regular transalpine roads did not allow even the German Holy Roman Emperors to hold Italy. The same was true in the 10th–8th millennium cal. BC. The uplands of Belgium, southern Germany, Switzerland, Austria, Czech Republic, southwestern Poland, but also the plains of the Paris Basin and the Netherlands were occupied by the Beuronian unit, while the areas of France south of the Loire, westernmost Switzerland, almost all of Italy, western Slovenia and southern Slovakia all the way to Tyrol in Austria were the home of the Mediterranean Sauveterrian.

In the 8th millennium cal. BC, Sauveterrian influence spread toward the north (cf. below). This is expressed in the Beuronian C by the appearance of such elements, like scalene triangles with short bases (TH, TE) and Sauveterrian points (PD) (cf. "Les courants interculturels").

In this case, the Sauveterrian-Beuronian border north of the Loire is curious to say the least, being determined not by any territorial barrier. On the other hand, we observe the overcoming of the high Alpine barrier (3500 m a.s.l.) across the Italian-Austrian border in the Tyrol (i.e., Ullafelsen, a Sauveterrian site in the Austrian Tyrol).

Between the North (plain) and South (upland)

In Central Europe the north, i.e. Maglemosian, is separated from the south, i.e. Beuronian, by the 200 m a.s.l. ground contour interval, which is an arbitrary division between the lowlands and the uplands.

Ignoring typologically similar elements constituting the *koine* (cf.) in these two territories (i.e. mainly different triangles and backed pieces), we are left with some characteristic differentiating elements typical of the 10th–8th millennium cal. BC. In the north, these distinctive elements include primarily slender backed D points (also those with retouched oblique base – DF), small proximal truncations (K) and unpolished axes and adzes. In the south, there are the broad backed points, small distal truncations and variants of "Tardenoisian" points (with transversal base –X).

The two regions are further divided by the plant cover and the fauna: deciduous forests in the uplands and pine and birch in the lowlands, elk and prevailing roe deer in the north vs. the predominance of red deer in the south.

Raw material borders

It is a known fact that except for Scania, the Scandinavian peninsula with Finland, Karelia and Estonia offers almost no flint raw material. The local Mesolithic was based therefore on material that was difficult to knap, like quartzite, or almost impossible to knap hard rock, like quartz. It also made use of other kinds of rock, like slate, working them with polishing techniques (axes, daggers, maceheads). Consequently, the character of the local Mesolithic culture appears to have been determined at least in part by the technical properties of the available raw material, which in extreme cases (like quartz) actually excludes any proper typologization.

This factor should also be taken into account by archaeologists studying territorial borders (cf. maps by Lars Larsson in the volume of the Mesolithic conference of Stockholm/Nynäshamn'00).

The issue of borders in the east

The Mesolithic of the Eastern European Lowland causes particular trouble as far as cultural divisions are concerned for two key reasons. Firstly, the Russian Plain is not as well researched as other regions, and secondly, because the core of the chipped industries of the area shows considerable techno-typological uniformity across the region.

Recognizing the territorial-typological aspects of the western borders of the Eastern Mesolithic does not appear to be a problem now (i.e. Kudlaevka culture and the Lithuanian/western variant of Kunda, cf.). What presents definitely more difficulty is the interior of Russia with its Butovo culture on the upper Volga and the classical Kunda culture extending along the Baltic shores all the way to Karelia. The lithics of the two regions are so similar that any potential division will have to be based on the bone industries. Bone artifacts from the upper Volga are partly different from those found on the Baltic Sea, but since there is a dearth of bone finds from the territories in between, it is difficult to say where the actual border ran (perhaps on the Valdai Mounts?).

Contact routes

Push to the North

The present author has already in his time, following Grahame Clark's earlier suggestion, recognized as probable an organic connection between the British Late Mesolithic (= Shippea Hill culture or Narrow Blades Industry) and the southern European Sauveterrian. This naturally assumes a northward proliferation of Sauveterrian elements (e.g. Sauveterrian points – PD and small scalene triangles with short base – TH, occasionally with retouch of the third edge – TE). The idea sprang from analyses of mapping and chronology, which revealed that the said elements south of the Loire river were present already in the 10th–8th millennium cal. BC, while north of it they did not appear until the 8th (second half) millennium cal. BC and reached Britain and Ireland in the same period.

This phenomenon of the "Sauveterrianization" (cf.) of northwestern Europe (cf. "Les courants interculturels"), as the present author called it then, concerned the Beuronian (phase C according to Wolfgang Taute), the Boberg but also a part of the "Maglemosian" (appearance of Svaerdborg industry in southern Scandinavia). In Britain, it was a younger variant of the Maglemosian, the so-called Broxbourne industry, that became "sauveterrized".

'Via imperialis'

The route from the Mediterranean to the North Sea via the valleys of the Rhône, Saone and Rhine turned out to be of special importance for the evolution of the early and middle Western and Northern Mesolithic (not only in this period, but also in Classical Antiquity and even more so in the Middle Ages). André Thevenin concurs with the present Author in this opinion. This trail between the Sauveterrian and Beuronian territories appears to be marked in the 8th millennium cal. BC by rectangular RA microliths (cf.), occurring at least from the lower Rhône Valley, where it squeezes through between the Central Massif and the Alps, all the way to northwestern Europe, reaching the Paris Basin, Britain and southern Scandinavia.

Sauveterrian elements most likely spread along the same route. In the 8th millennium cal. BC, Sauveterrian points, for example, are found in western Beuronian C contexts, extending not only into the Netherlands, but also down the valley of the Seine all the way to the Paris Basin and across the still inexistent Channel into Britain (cf. "Push to the North").

This route through the valleys of the Rhône and Rhine may have been traveled again in the 7th millennium cal. BC by rhomboids of the BH type, occurring in Western Europe from Provence and Trentino (Castelnovian) to the basin of the upper Rhine and Seine (Montbanian) and in southern Scandinavia (Kongemosian). Assuming all the sites mentioned here constituted links in the same chain (they differ in France and Belgium into left- and right-hand variants as far as orientation of the truncation is concerned, as Peter A. Gendel emphasizes), we would be dealing with a "Castelnovization" (cf.) of Europe that spread from the south (around 7000 cal. BC) and proceeded in a northerly direction (into Denmark in c. 6500 cal. BC), among others along the Rhône and Rhine valleys.

The Tartar route
Mapping routes marked by BH rhombs in the eastern part of Central Europe leads to the following conclusions. The armatures form a band 300 km wide, running southeast-northwest, from the Black Sea in the south to the eastern reaches of the Vistula basin in the north, east of the Eastern Carpathians, along the rivers Prut, Dniestr, Boh, San, Bug and Vistula (cf. "Pontic elements"). These rhombs appeared, contrary to Western Europe, only from the second half of the 6th millennium cal. BC (?). They are encountered in the south in the Grebeniki, Bug-Dniestr (ceramic culture) and early Tripolye cultures, and in the north only locally in the late Janislawician (cf.) (= Polish Late Mesolithic) and perhaps also the Funnel Beaker Culture(?). Evidently the BH rhombs were not limited to a single cultural setting and they seem to have come from the south, being obviously later in the north.

The same route from the Ponticum to the Balticum would be traveled heavily down the ages – by Armenian merchants from Kaffa, Crimean Tartars, Ottoman Turks, Poles and Cossacks setting out for the Black Sea....

Comment in 2006
Territorial proliferation in prehistory is always a matter of individual determination. It suffices the present author to signal the existence of the phenomenon without undertaking at this point to interpret the mechanism.

In a few special cases, however, this mechanism of proliferation is to be reconstructed. One such example is the settlement of the previously uninhabited North of the continent (Fosna, Komsa, Suomusjarvi in Scandinavia), another the Mesolithic settlement in the far north of Russia, the third similar phenomenon observed earlier in Britain.

A similar real and multidirectional movement of human groups can be documented in the case of the gradually submerged Dogger Bank Shelf and the Western Baltic bridge.

5

When?

5.1. Chronology

Time in the Mesolithic used to be marked off according to typological indicators. These have now been replaced with radiocarbon datings, a useful catalogue of which, updated to 1989, was published by André Gob. Naturally, more dates have become available in the meantime, especially from the ex-Soviet Union, filling out our knowledge of Mesolithic chronology. Even so, we continue to have few, none or often wrong dates from sandy sites which are exceptionally numerous on the European Plain. Available dates are controversial (cf. dates published by Pierre Veermeersch for Flanders and Zbigniew Bagniewski for the southwest of the Polish Lowland).

Thus, it cannot go without comment that not all radiocarbon dates for the European Mesolithic are acceptable and for a number of reasons at that. First of all, subsurface sand sites, which dominate in the European Plain, are burdened with the need to prove a connection or contemporaneity between the dated charcoal and archaeological material. With absolutely no stratigraphy observable on these terrace or dune sites, we can never be sure whether the datings actually refer to human settlement (which may be represented on these sites by successive periods of occupation from very different ages – a typical case on Polish sites) or natural phenomena perhaps, like spontaneous forest conflagrations on a huge scale, for example.

Secondly, isolated dates, which are frequent on sandy sites, are of little significance statistically, considering that, based on the example of peat and cave sites (as well as Near Eastern Neolithic villages), it takes a series of radiocarbon dates from each stratigraphic unit which are then subjected to statistical analysis to form an opinion concerning the actual chronology of a given assemblage.

Radiocarbon dates are supported occasionally, although more seldom today, by dates obtained with the much less precise palynological method (e.g. Roger Jacobi for Britain and Erik Brinch-Petersen for Denmark), which was still used for dating in the early years of the second half of the 20th century.

On bog and cave sites located more to the south, early palynological dates were supplemented (but not always), before radiocarbon dates became common, by stratigraphical analyses (e.g. Birsmatten-Basisgrotte, excavated by Hans-Georg Bandi), developing on this basis relative chronologies and establishing (same as with the pollen method) local cultural sequences. Once radiocarbon dating was introduced, it was enough to obtain dates for already established stages of local sequences (cf. "Rhythms").

At present, full sequences demonstrating local stylistic variability have been developed for most of Europe, but they are not available in some areas (Portugal, most of Spain, among others).

The benefit of local sequences is obvious. If local technological and stylistic variability is established, it becomes a fairly reliable technical and typological indicator of date, useful for typological dating of materials from smaller or bigger areas not dated by other methods.

Finally, the AMS method for dating individual artefacts, for Mesolithic Britain, introduced by Clive Bonsall deserves mention here.

Considering the matter of Mesolithic chronology overall (Fig. 5.1), it may be said that our understanding of the issue is fairly developed and rather uncontroversial. Indeed, we now refer to dates in the Mesolithic not in terms of BP or bc, but as calendar years (=cal. BC).

5.2. Conservative character of Mesolithic cultures

It is commonly accepted that contemporary and sub-contemporary hunting-gathering cultures/communities are characterized by considerable conservatism, meaning a resistance to external influence and weak variability over time. All known cultures/communities of the European Mesolithic were hunting-gathering groups, occasionally and regionally with a leaning toward more intensive fishing. Thus, they appear to be predestined to conservatism. This is confirmed by the poor variability / changability of the flint and bone industries during the time: they can go unchanged

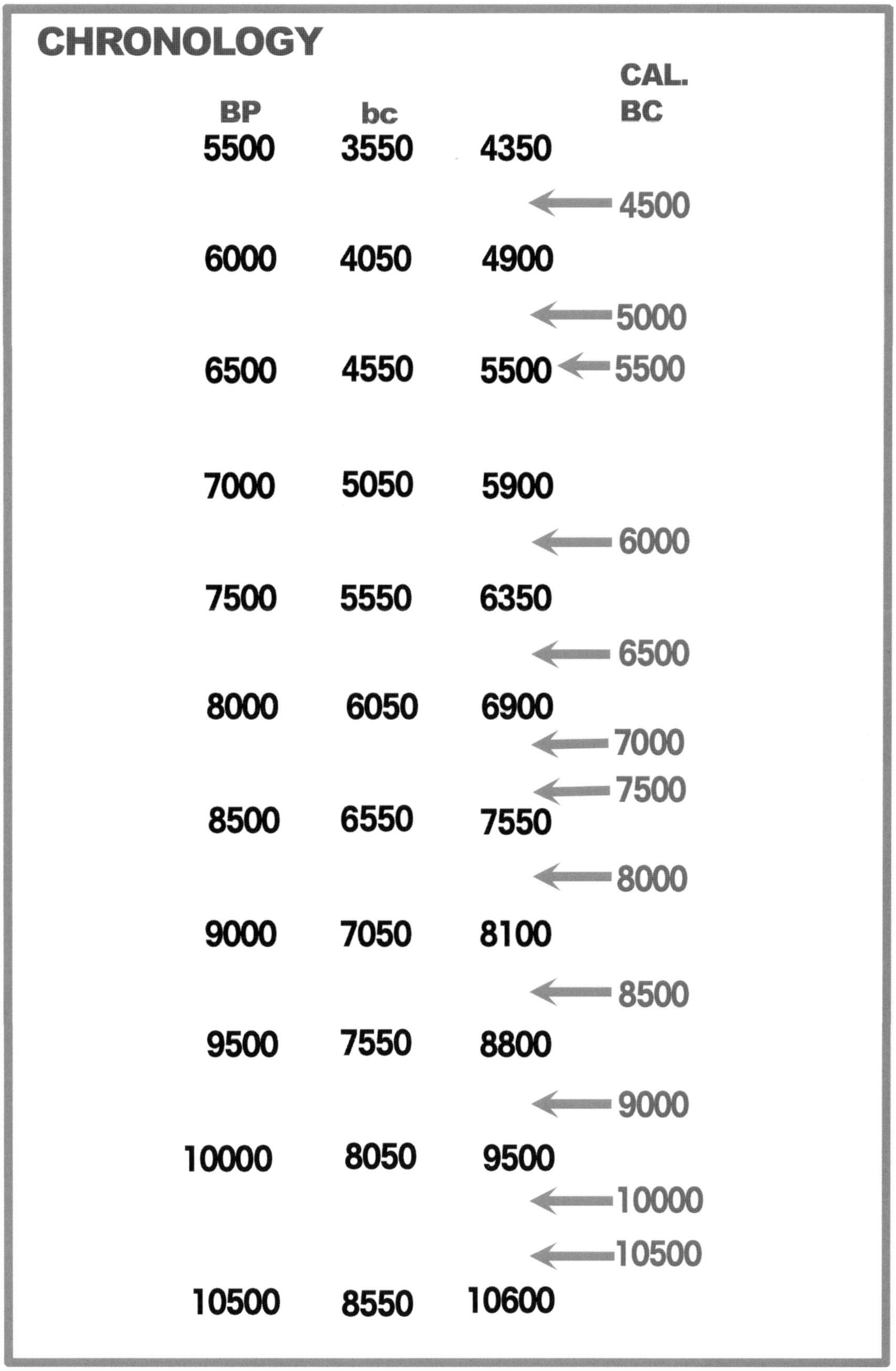

CHRONOLOGY

BP	bc	CAL. BC	
5500	3550	4350	
			← 4500
6000	4050	4900	
			← 5000
6500	4550	5500	← 5500
7000	5050	5900	
			← 6000
7500	5550	6350	
			← 6500
8000	6050	6900	
			← 7000
			← 7500
8500	6550	7550	
			← 8000
9000	7050	8100	
			← 8500
9500	7550	8800	
			← 9000
10000	8050	9500	
			← 10000
			← 10500
10500	8550	10600	

Fig. 5.1

or almost unchanged for millennia (cf. "Rhythms"). The Butovian culture of central Russia seems to be an extreme case, its flint industry remaining virtually unchanged (or only slightly modified) for about 6000 calendar years. Also, the somewhat less long-lasting cultures of central and western Europe are characterized by considerable morpho-technical stability, despite some slow internal evolution (cf. "Rhythms").

This hardly departs from the standards for the Upper Paleolithic, where variability in time is not a frequent phenomenon and when it occurs, it is usually forced by some dramatic change in the biotope. Such changes were observed, among others, on both sides of the Alps at the end of the Pleistocene and the beginning of the Holocene (the resulting appearance of Mesolithic cultures of the region), although nothing much was happening in the Balkans at the same time. Another more substantial change is the late appearance of cultures of the Castelnovian (Pre-Neolithic) kind (cf. "Castelnovization").

5.3. West, center and south

5.3.1. Koine

A veritable community or *koine* (Fig. 5.3.1), characterized by considerable interregional convergence, existed in the Early and Middle Mesolithic (cf.) from Catalonia, the Pyrenees and Ireland in the west to the Vistula and Bohemia in the east and even further east in the Late Mesolithic (cf. "Castelnovization"). This included the miniaturization and geometrization of elements of arrowheads and the formal repetition of shapes (backed pieces, triangles, crescents, trapezes, etc., cf. "Atlas of the Mesolithic") although these similarities (cf. "Atlas" and "Rhythms") did not eliminate a strong regionalization of Mesolithic culture. Interregional structural similarities have also been observed, expressed more or less in a similar evolution pattern (although local exceptions occurred as well, cf. "Rhythms").

Simple convergence of development of plain and uncomplicated tools, like combinations of backs and truncations, hardly suffices as an explanation. The phenomenon appears to have at least in part genetic roots and may be the effect of intensive intercultural and interregional proliferation of inventions, starting from the Late Pleistocene in a part of the vast expanse of the continent under discussion (mostly the South, cf. "Azilianization", "Sauveterrization", and "Castelnovization").

5.3.2. Rhythms

Change in whatever form is perhaps the most characteristic trait of the European Mesolithic, regardless of how regionally it is considered. Technology was impacted (cf. "Blades/bladelets") and morphology of chipped products, encompassing selected groups of objects or entire industries. Evolution was either cosmetic in nature, like in the case of the microliths in the Italian Sauveterrian (cf. "South"), or abrupt, in which case researchers have to adapt their

taxonomic descriptions (e.g. transition from Sauveterrian and Beuronian to the Pre-Neolithic/Castelnovian-like industries): respectively Classical Castelnovian and Montbanian. In any case, this evolution concerned *de facto* a change in arrow construction (Fig. 5.3.2a–h).

It would be going too far, naturally, to suggest one evolutionary rhythm encompassing the entire continent. Each region had its own specificity and rate of change. The most dynamic in this respect were the macroregions of the South, West and Center (cf.), which shared a certain common evolutionary trend, even in the face of distinct regionalisms (Sauveterrian, Beuronian, Maglemosian). The similarities between the three regions go beyond the presence of geometric microliths (backed points, scalenes, isosceles, crescents, rectangles, microtruncations, trapezes), covering also the evolution (changes) of these stone products or at least the proportions between them.

Our reconstruction of this evolution is based on stratigraphic data from Southern Europe (Jägerhaushöhle in Germany, Romagnano III in Italy, Birsmatten-Basisgrotte in Switzerland, Rouffignac and Montclus in France, and other stratified sites, cf. "Chronology") combined with André Gob's catalogue of C_{14} dates and numerous local or regional cultural sequences (reconstructed by Erik Brinsch-Petersen for Denmark, Hermann Schwabedissen, Bernhard Gramsch, Surendra K. Arora, Erwin Cziesla and Wolfgang Taute for Germany, Raymond R. Newell, André Gob and Pierre Vermeersch for the Benelux countries, Roger Jacobi for Britain, Max Escalon de Fronton, Jean-Georges Rozoy, André Thévenin and Michel Barbaza for France, Alberto Broglio, Paolo Biagi and Carlo Tozzi for Italy). The starting point were the broad and short microliths on irregular, short bladelets (10th–8th millennia cal. BC): single and double truncations (K and PE), isosceles (TM, TN), short scalenes (TO, TR). In the next phase (from c. 7500 cal. BC) scalene triangles with short base (TH, TI, TO, TE) appear or dominate, made on a new type of narrow bladelet; at the same time, some of the old types disappeared (together with old-fashioned "Coincy style" bladelets) completely or at least lose importance. Finally, the last phase (from c. 7000–6500 years cal. BC) is characterized by the introduction of trapezes (A and B) and in many instances a new Castelnovian technology with broad, very regular bladelets, which more or less quickly pushes out the "old" microliths made on microbladelets (cf. "Pre-Neolithic/Castelnovian"). Importantly, exactly the same changes of core technology and blanks were taking place in different cultural environments, but without leading to total cultural unification.

The *koine* did not include Iberia with the exception of Catalonia, where its elements could be observed in the Filador-Cocina sequence, and the Italian Mezzogiorno, as well as the Epi-Gravettian Balkans (assuming the phenomenon of the local trapezes appearing in both regions is disregarded).

The Late Mesolithic trapezes, which crown developments in the region from the Atlantic to the Black Sea mostly between c. ≥ 7000 and c. 6000 years cal. BC

KOINE

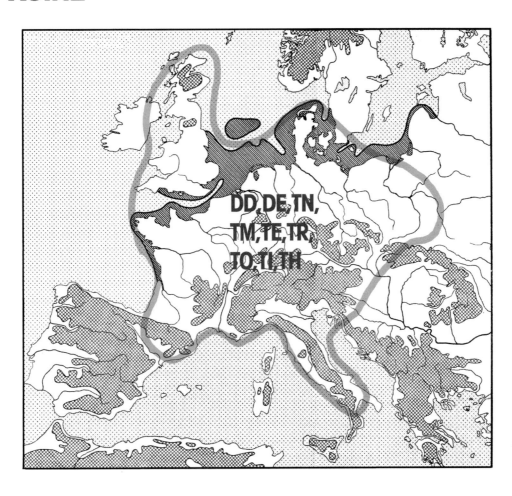

DD, DE, TN, TM, TE, TR, TO, TI, TH

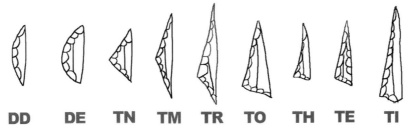

| DD | DE | TN | TM | TR | TO | TH | TE | TI |

**SIMILARITIES IN EVOLUTION
DIFFERENT ROOTS**

(CF. 5.3.2)

Fig. 5.3.1

RHYTHMS

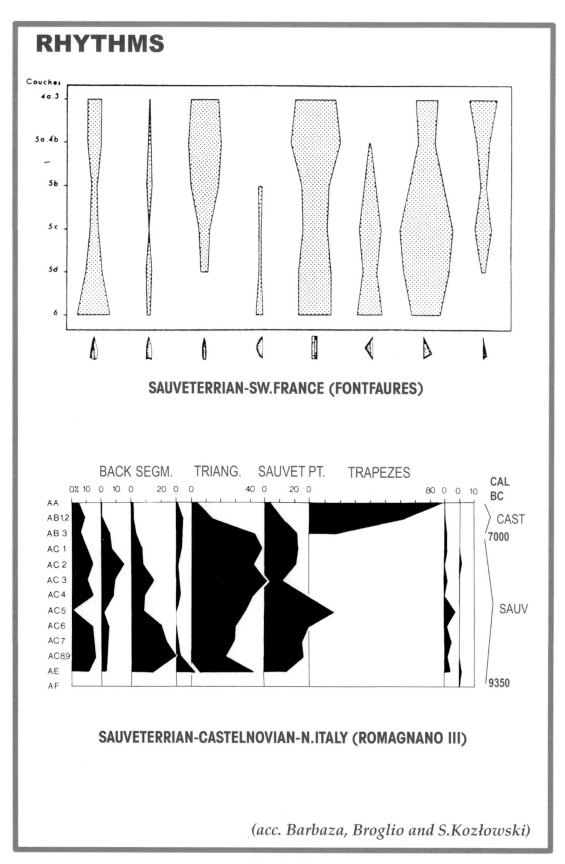

Fig. 5.3.2a

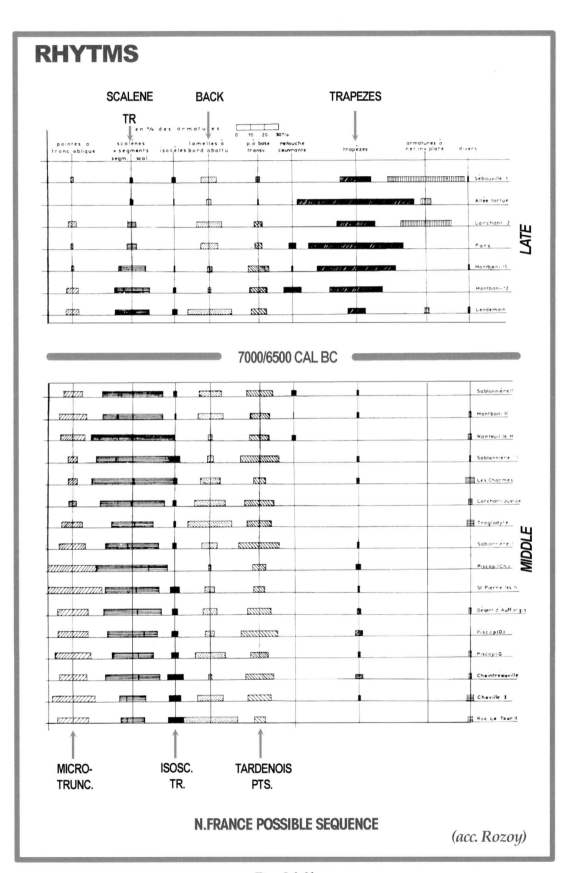

Fig. 5.3.2b

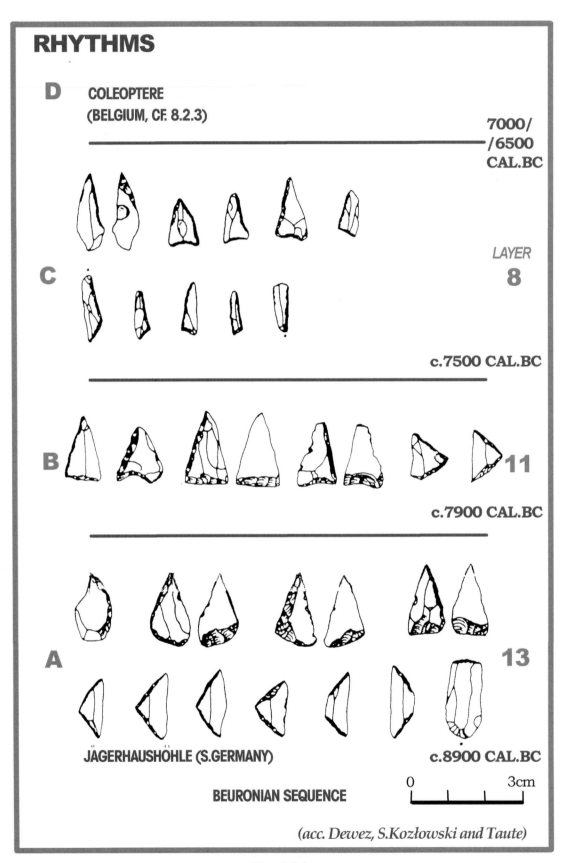

Fig. 5.3.2c

RHYTHMS

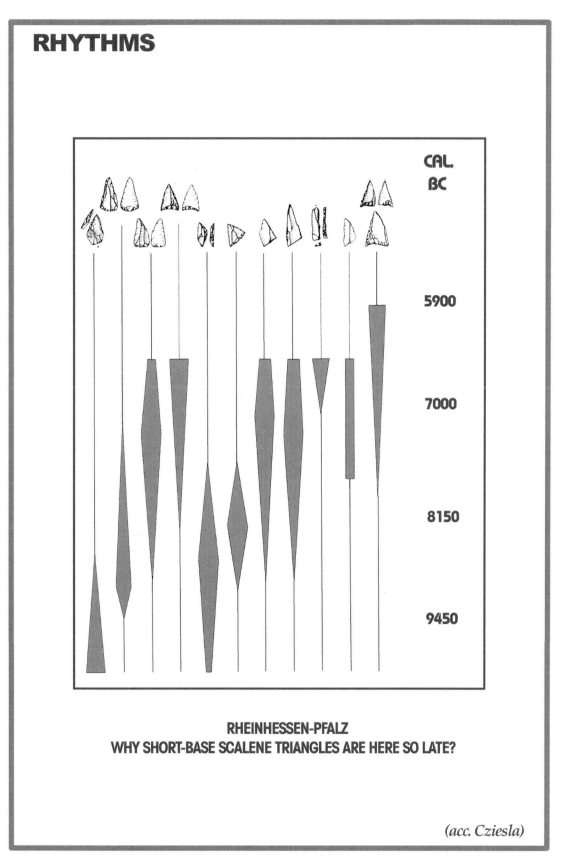

RHEINHESSEN-PFALZ
WHY SHORT-BASE SCALENE TRIANGLES ARE HERE SO LATE?

(acc. Cziesla)

Fig. 5.3.2d

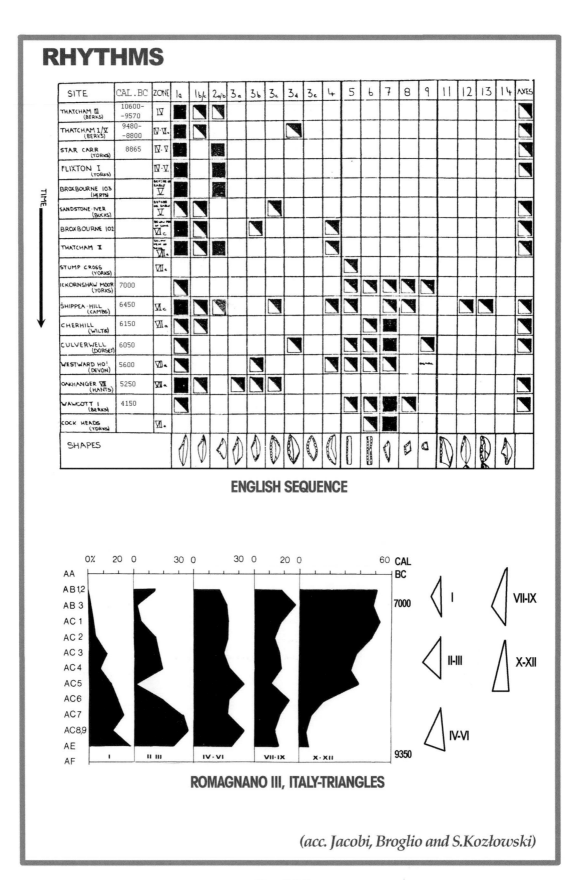

Fig. 5.3.2e

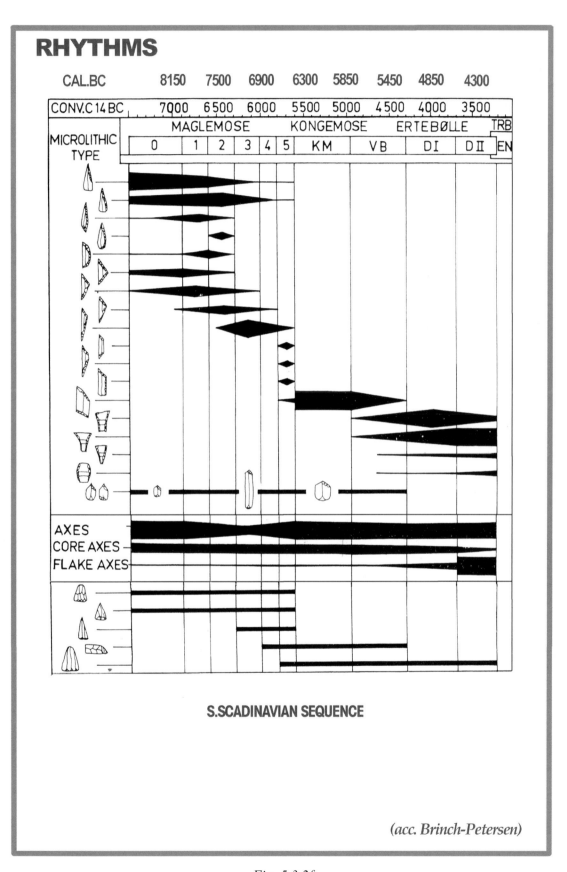

Fig. 5.3.2f

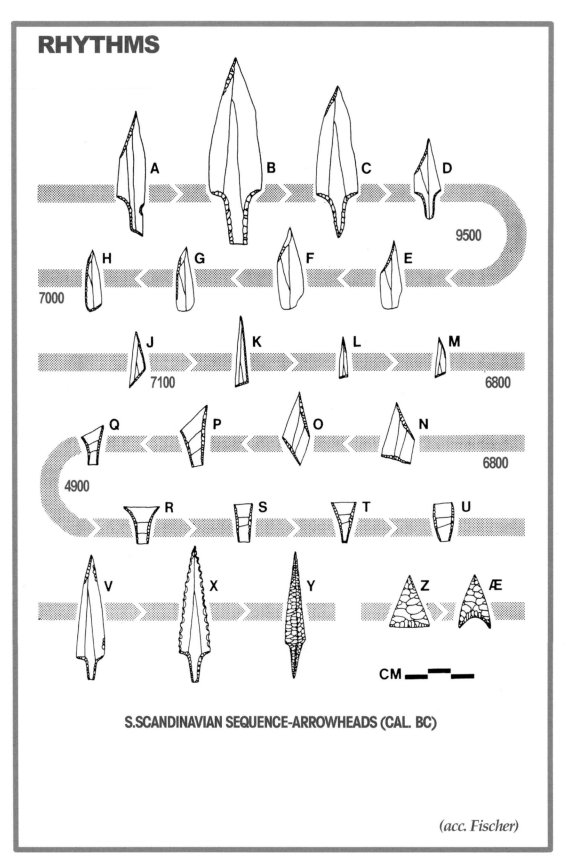

Fig. 5.3.2g

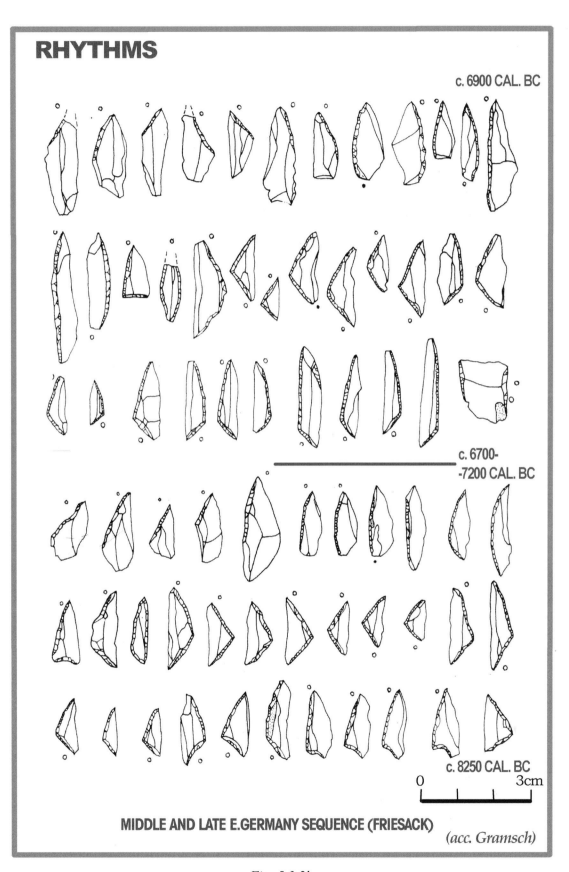

RHYTHMS

c. 6900 CAL. BC

c. 6700-
-7200 CAL. BC

c. 8250 CAL. BC

0   3cm

MIDDLE AND LATE E.GERMANY SEQUENCE (FRIESACK)

(acc. Gramsch)

Fig. 5.3.2h

(cf. "Les courants interculturelles"), extend beyond the territorial range of the *koine* described above. They appeared quite abruptly either together with the new Castelnovian technology, pushing out old elements (= model A of Castelnovization, cf.), or else as an addition to traditional local assemblages, mainly in the inland regions (= model B). The described change of core technology, blanks (irregular, short bladelet – microbladelet – broad regular bladelet) and microliths (among others, broad triangles – narrow triangles – trapezes) in the *koine* (cf.) area is strongly linked with (and determines) the evolution of arrowheads (cf.) and is determined by their construction.

PONTIC STEPPE: Before the said trapezes, these regions were populated by cultures/communities that do not fit in the European "rhythms" of development. They tend to be closer to cultural phenomena known from the Caucasus, Anatolia and the Near East.

NORTH AND EAST: Evolution of the chipped industries in the north (Scandinavia) and northeast (East European Plain) followed a completely different pattern. From the start, there were no geometrics there (consequently, no composite elements of arrowheads) but one-piece arrowheads that were less susceptible to change. Indeed, evolution in these regions is minimal (clearly early points with short tangs in Russia and on the east Baltic – type LF in the "Atlas", cf., minor modifications of Ahrensburgian points in the North) and it is distinctly slower. The only bigger change in the North is the result of migration from the south (microbladelet industries arriving c. 7000 cal. BC).

On the other hand, it should be kept in mind that some modification of the bone and antler industries (harpoons and spears) was observed in the circum-Baltic countries around the 9th millennium cal. BC, while in Finland, for example, Heikki Matiskainen demonstrated the gradual appearance of successive inventions which, however, do not modify in any major way the local chipped industry.

5.3.3. ...and no rhythm – problems of uneven development

Similar stages of stylistic change observed on the microliths group in the huge territory of Central and Western Europe from the Pyrenees to the Vistula, presented above (cf. "Rhythms"), cannot conceal a certain lack of general rhythm noted regionally, especially in Central Europe/"*Mittel-Europa*" and in the foothills of the Alps. These problems are particularly noticeable in the eastern Maglemosian (in the broad sense), the "older" regional variants abounding in isosceles triangles (Duvensee in Germany and Komornician in Poland) lasting in the east much longer than a similar model of industry in the north (Erik Brinch-Petersen's Early Maglemosian) and west (Grahame Clark's Proto-Maglemosian). In the former case, the "older" Maglemosian was replaced in southern Scandinavia with an industry of the Svaerborg "sauveterrized" (cf.) type, and in the latter case by a Broxboube industry (8th millennium cal. BC – Mother Groundys Parlor – uppes layer). In the east, no

such important and complete changes have been recorded (the region is too far?), although scalene triangles with short base and trapezes did appear in the local environment, but only at the end of the 8th millennium BC in Poland and in the early 7th millennium cal. BC in the territory of the Czech Republic (Eastern Beuronian).

Another alleged asynchronization is visible in the unequal proliferation of the Castelnovian elements (cf. "Les cournants interculturels…" and "Castelnovization"); it seems to be late by about 500 (?) years in the north, yet it is preceded by single trapezes occurring in local assemblages, like Scania (cf. studies by Lars Larsson). It is also very possible that it is even older than 7000 cal. BC in the southeast (Frankhthi). In Russia and Finland any rhythm is detectable (Fig. 5.3.3a–b).

5.3.4. Early-Middle-Late Mesolithic

The trend has been present in Mesolithic studies for some time now, gradually dropping "cultural" descriptors in favor of a chronological periodization (Early – Middle – Late – Fig. 5.3.4). Despite his moderate enthusiasm for this approach, the author has deemed it useful, although with reserve, to adopt these terms when writing on chronology in the current presentation defined as follows:

- Early Mesolithic – from 10,400 to 7500 cal. BC
- Middle Mesolithic – from 7500 to 7000 cal. BC
- Late Mesolithic – from 7000 cal. BC

5.4. The main evolutive trends in the European Mesolithic

5.4.1. Azilianization

The Late Pleistocene phenomenon (from the Bølling oscillation with a culmination in the Allerød and Dryas 3) constituted by the proliferation in the different industries of the time (Magdalenian, Hamburgian, Epi-Gravettian, Creswellian, later Azilian, Federmesser and Tanged Points cultures) of very short and short (including circular and subcircular) flake and more seldom sectioned blade end-scrapers (Fig. 5.4.1). It may have been caused by a general shift to small-size raw material nodules which were more commonly available at the time than large pieces (especially in the Plain). This shift may have been necessitated by more difficult access to outcrops of good, meaning big-size raw material because of developing vegetation. In the European Plain virtually all local sources of flint and stone are of small size (mostly erratic "Baltic" cretaceous flint).

The process resulted in serious stylistic and cultural modifications, leading to the appearance of new taxonomic entities (Azilian, Romanellian, Federmesser, Ahrensburgian, Swiderian, etc.) or a new opening for already existing ones (Epi-Gravettian). The phenomenon appears to have spread from the south to the north, covering vast stretches of Europe up to Dogger Bank and the Baltic. As an intercultural trend, it strongly influenced the later

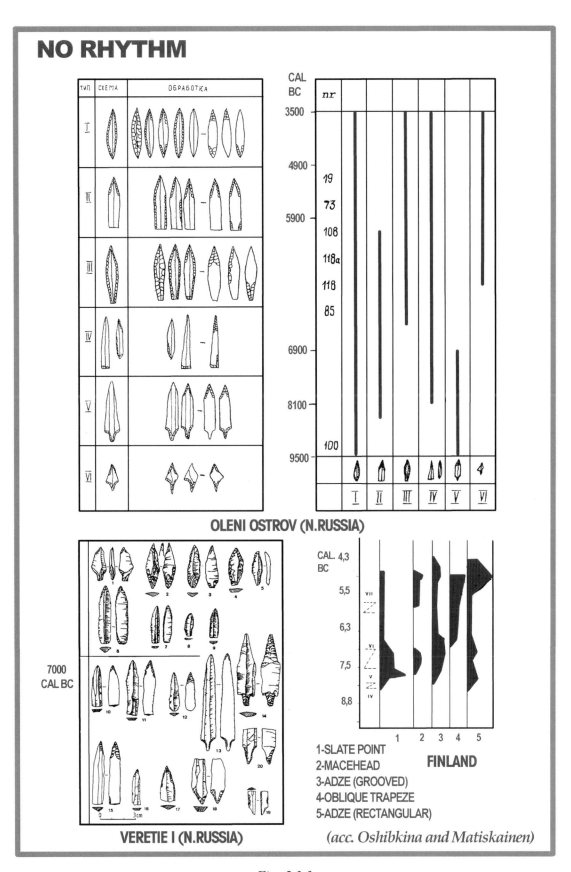

Fig. 5.3.3a

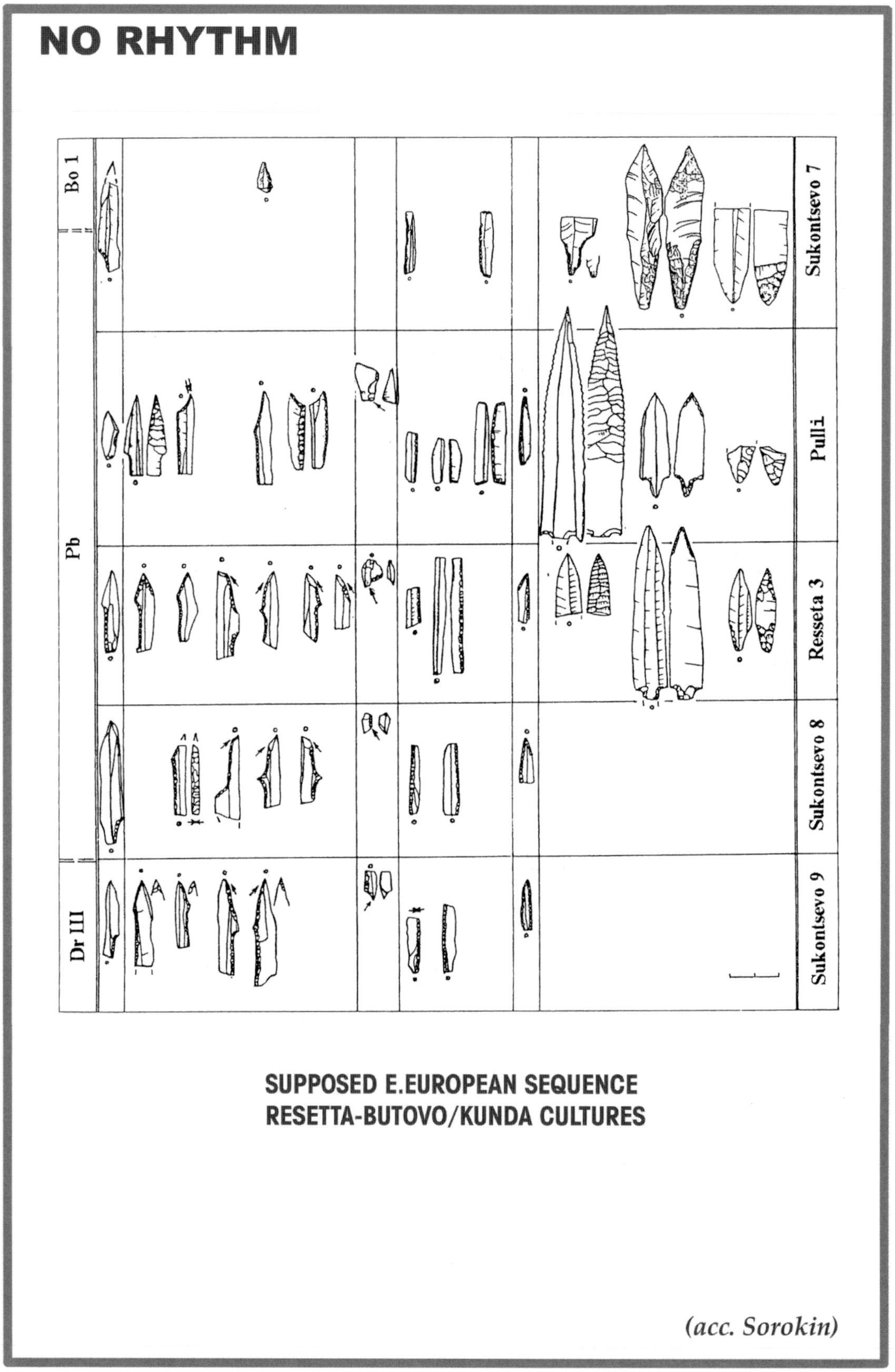
NO RHYTHM
Bo 1
Pb
Dr III
Sukontsevo 7
Pulli
Resseta 3
Sukontsevo 8
Sukontsevo 9
SUPPOSED E.EUROPEAN SEQUENCE
RESETTA-BUTOVO/KUNDA CULTURES
(acc. Sorokin)

Fig. 5.3.3b

EARLY-MIDDLE-LATE

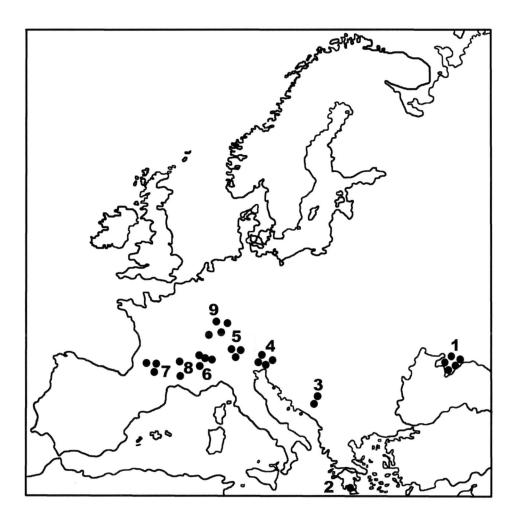

MIDDLE-LATE MESOLITHIC STRATIFIED SITES

1	FAT'MA KOBA, MURZAK-KOBA, SHAN-KOBA, ALIMOVSKI
2	FRANKHTI
3	CRVENA STIJENA, MEDENA STIJENA
4	BENUSSI, AZURRA, TARTARUGA, MALA TRIGLAVCA
5	GABAN, ROMAGNANO III, PRADESTEL
6	GRANDE RIVOIR, CHARMATE, COUFIN, MELLENDRUZ
7	CUZOUL, MARTINET, ROUFFIGNAC
8	MONTCLUS, LONGETRAY
9	BIRSMATTEN, FALKENSTEIN, INZIGKOFEN, JAGERHÄUS

Fig. 5.3.4

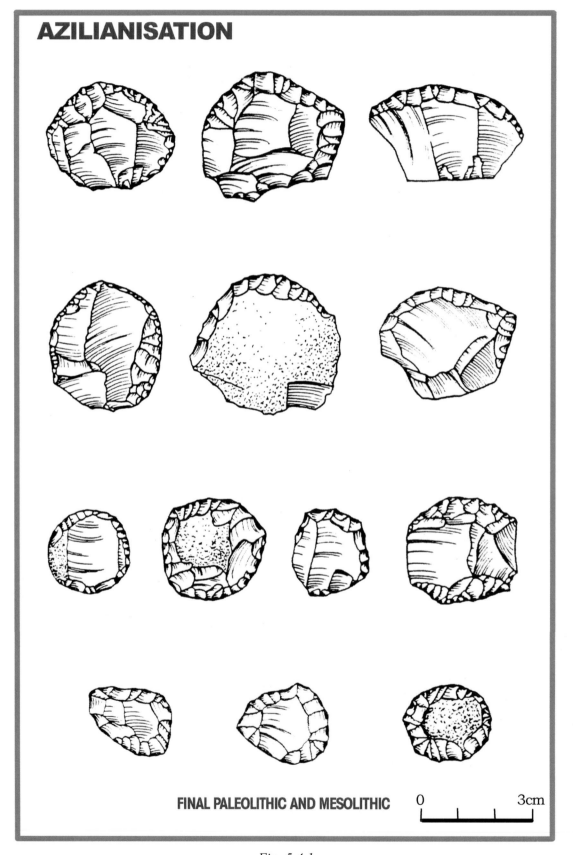

AZILIANISATION

FINAL PALEOLITHIC AND MESOLITHIC

0   3cm

Fig. 5.4.1

typological picture of the Mesolithic in western and central Europe, initiating the processes of miniaturization or microlithization of flint tools and determining the average typological characteristic of most of the European cultures of the Early Holocene (standard including small, very short, mostly flake end-scrapers and backed bladelets/points, plus other regionally differentiated elements).

5.4.2. Sauveterrization

This term describes the appearance in the second half or, as far as the eastern regions are concerned, in the end of the 8th and beginning of the 7th millennium cal. BC of a series of industries or cultures in western, northwestern and partly central Europe (Late Beuronian, Shippea Hill and Svaerdborg cultures in the west and later and weaker Duvensee, Komornician and Eastern Beuronian C in the east). The phenomenon is characterized by slender triangles with short bases (TH, TD, TI), often with retouch of the third edge (TE), resembling the earlier Sauveterrian specimens from southern Europe (Fig. 5.4.2). Moreover, the typical Sauveterrian points (PD) appear at this time in western Europe (Beuronian C, Boberg, Shippea Hill). These novelties may have resulted from a refining of core-reduction strategies and the introduction of narrow bladelets, but it is still difficult to avoid the impression that the technology is linked directly with the Sauveterrian South (cf.) and indicates a northward proliferation of elements of the southern model (cf. "Les courants culturels" and "Rhythms").

A broader definition of the term could also be assumed with the South becoming completely sauveterrianized, while the North experiencing only partial sauveterrianization at a later date and not in full form.

The marginal zones (Iberia, cf., with Filador, Mezzogiorno with Marisa, cf., and the Balkans with the Hungarian sites of Jasztelek and Jaszbereny, cf. "Outlying areas") were characterized by a specific form of "incomplete sauveterrianization".

5.4.3. Trend with trapezes

Virtually simultaneously, that is, about 7000–6500 cal. BC (but in Greece and Crimea (?) earlier), the Mesolithic cultures occupying most of the European continent witnessed the appearance of blade trapezes, which either pushed out quickly the traditional microliths (= model A of "Castelnovization", cf.) or else complemented the existing repertory (= model B). The phenomenon appears to be entirely consistent and the proliferation seems to be moving from south to north (cf. "Castelnovization", "Les courants").

This trapeze trend (Fig. 5.4.3) is in most cases an important chronological indicator as it appears in most of the region generally around 7000/6500 cal. BC.

5.4.4. Castelnovization

Castelnovization was an important technical and technological change taking its name from the Castelnovian culture in southern Europe (cf.) and occurring in territories around the Mediterranean, in the Pontic area and on the Atlantic coasts in the local cultures of the Middle Mesolithic. Initiated most likely at the end of the 8th millennium (?) in the south of Europe (Frankhthi, Crimea?), it did not take long (between ca. 7000 and 6500 cal. BC) to spread throughout territories lying roughly north of the Mediterranean Sea and in western Europe (but not Britain), perhaps arriving in the extreme west and north around 6500 cal. BC. It led to considerable, but not complete, formal uniformization of a number of local flint industries (Fig. 5.4.4a–b).

A new type of core appeared; it was used to produce larger than ever and more regular blades and bladelets which were essential in turn for the manufacture of tools of clearly larger size and more regular shape. The core was big in itself and it was preformed, the raw material being always of good quality and often procured by regular mining (Tomaszów in Poland, Wommersom in Belgium, Melos in Greece) and transported over long distances (Melos to Frankhthi – > 100 km, Tomaszów to Barycz Valley – 280 km).

Another new type was a blade/bladelet used simply as a knife (among others, *lamelle etranglée type Montbani*). This blade also served as a blank to make end-scrapers and truncations, but foremost trapezes and rhombs, often although not always (also sectioning) formed by the microburin technique (proximal microburins). Relatively quickly these trapezes replaced the old types of microliths.

Apparently, the new techniques and new types of tools are correlated with the appearance of cemeteries or numerous graves in settlements (Moita do Sebastiao in Portugal, Hoëdic and Téviec in France, Skateholm in Sweden), possibly testifying to a more sedentary lifestyle of the human communities undergoing castelnovization. Whatever the case may be, it is from these "castelnovized" cultures that the early local ceramic and finally Neolithic cultures sprang (cf. "Ceramization").

Consequently, I should think that the process of castelnovization can well be referred to as "Pre-neolithization" (cf.), even keeping in mind the strong differentiation that remained in force (cf. chapter on the Castelnovian complex) and the fact that not all units became Neolithic at an early point, although for the most part they adopted ceramics.

To sum up, a few remarks on the processes of proliferation. There seems to be no doubt that the phenomenon spread from south to north regardless of whether it was the eastern or western part of the continent. It seems to have followed in the west sea coastlines and moved up big river valleys (Rhône, Rhine), but it does not seem to have been connected with any major population shifts.

The phenomenon was described in-depth in a chapter devoted to the Castelnovian complex (cf.). I referred to it there as Model A, more extreme than Model B, which had only limited impact on the traditional cultures of the North.

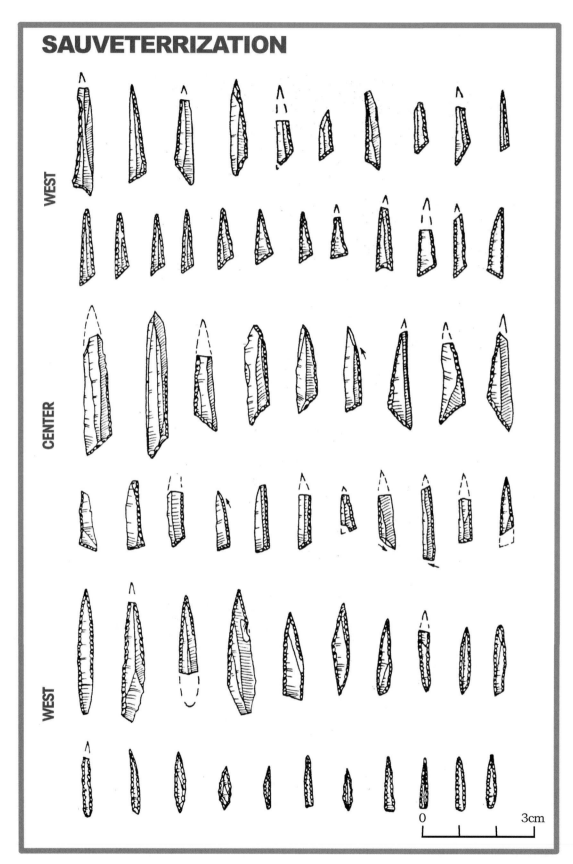

Fig. 5.4.2

TREND WITH TRAPEZES

ASYMMETRIC TRAPEZES

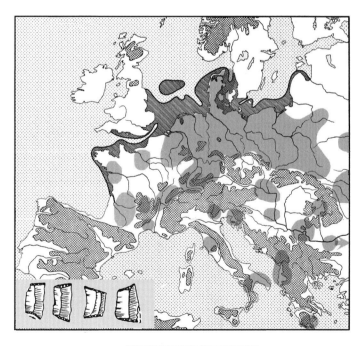

SYMMETRIC TRAPEZES

Fig. 5.4.3

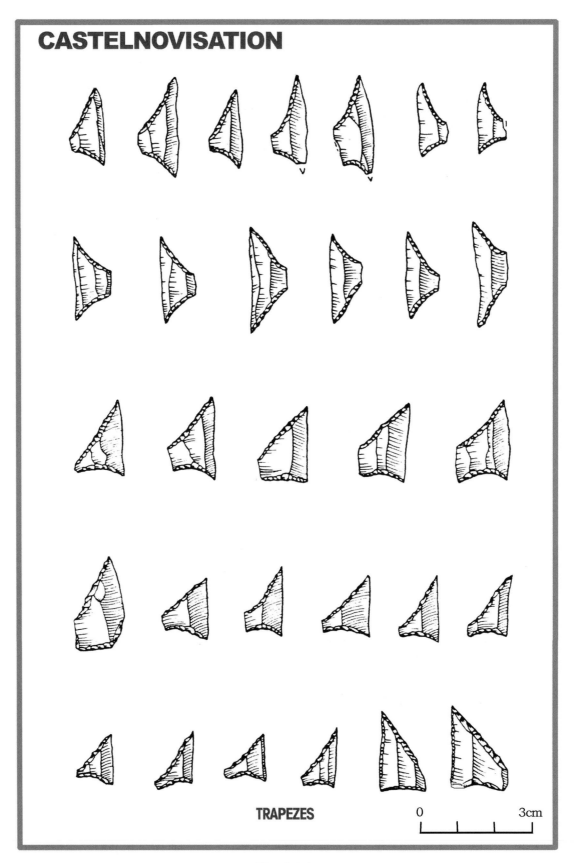

Fig. 5.4.4a

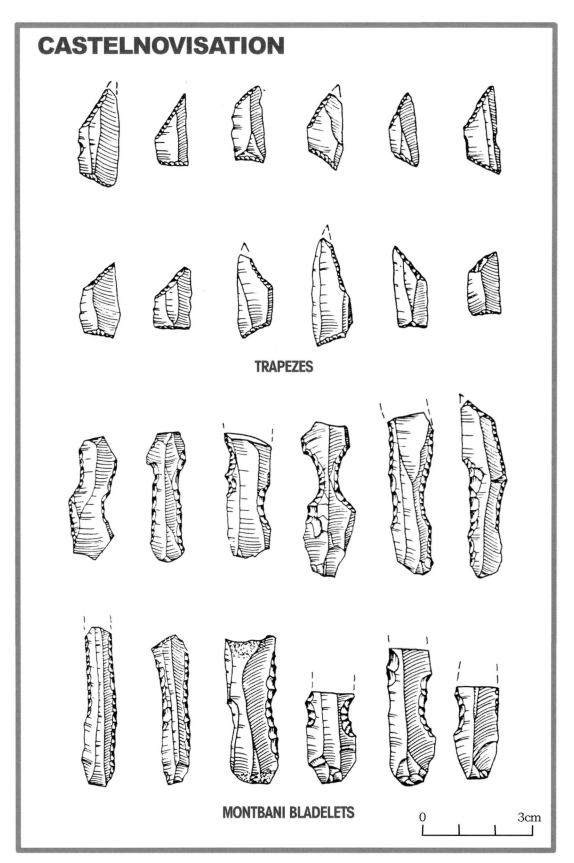

Fig. 5.4.4b

The Castelnovization should in fact be divided into two distinct phenomena: the Western and the Eastern (cf. "Pre-Neolithic").

5.4.5. Ceramization of the Mesolithic

The last stage of the European Mesolithic is its ceramization, a technical phenomenon that preceded or paralleled Neolithization understood as an economic event. On the whole, the phenomenon can be described as Mesolithic "aborigines" absorbing usually or frequently (although not always) the idea of pottery from their contemporary Neolithic neighbors (?). This first pottery is usually technically quite poor, often making the reconstruction of whole pots quite difficult. It frequently has a pointed base and is occasionally decorated with strongly differentiated ornaments ("impresso", pit, comb, shell impressions – "cardial"). Plain ceramics are also encountered.

The earliest pottery (Fig. 5.4.5a–e) to appear in the local Mesolithic/Early Neolithic (?) environment in the early and mid 7th millennium cal. BC originated from the Castelnovian complex (Italy, Balkans, Ukraine) or its local/regional successors (Spain, Portugal, France), excluding the central Balkan-Danubian "corridor", which was occupied by the earliest ceramic cultures of the 'true' Neolithic (white-painted Starčevo/Criš/Körös, Danubian). This may give a not fully justified impression of a certain marginality and possibly derivative nature of the said phenomenon (western and eastern peripheries of the "mainstream"; the fully Neolithic character of many French and Iberian early ceramic cultures is doubtful).

In the south of the continent, Mesolithic pottery of the "impresso" type appeared in mature South-Italian Castelnovian (Latronico) and Slovenian Castelnovian (Mala Triglavca – Vlaska ceramics) or Post-Castelnovian in Dalmatia (Smilćić), Italian Dolomites (Gaban), the Po Plain (Vho, Fagnigiola). Further to the west, it will be the southern French and Iberian "cardial" type ceramics and its regional variants, accompanied by Post-Castelnovian-type industries (e.g. pottery of the Rocadour type, following the Cuzoul/Pre-Rocadourian group in southwestern France), or else local variants of very strongly locally evolved Post-Castelnovian with the even more local Muge and Cocina II (aceramic) and III/IV (ceramic) or "ceramica impressa ligure" variants deriving from them (including various aberrational forms, usually trapezoid or triangular microliths, often with flat retouching, so competently listed for France by André Thévenin).

The same is true of Central Europe where ceramization did not put in an appearance before the Post- Castelnovian (in this case, Erteböllian, which is not described in this

volume) and the Post-Maglemosian, too, as far as the northern extremes of Poland are concerned (Dąbki in Pomerania with Erteböllian-type ceramics).

The southeast of the continent was ceramized in the (Post-?) Castelnovian style ("impresso" ware from the early ceramic level of Ćrvena Stijena, Starčevo and impresso types, both in the upper layers at Odmut in Montenegro). It does not mean that the Castelnovian style was characteristic exclusively of Late Mesolithic cultures. It had its counterparts (in the form of second standard/broader bladelets) also in the early ceramic Neolithic of the Balkans (Mehtelek in Hungary, Donja Branjevina in Serbia, Turkish Thrace), albeit in context with elements of a certain macrolithization of bladelets.

The east of Europe partly repeats this pattern. What is observed foremost is the ceramicization of Castelnovian-type cultures: Grebeniki culture, known as the ceramic Bug-Dniester culture, in Moldova and western Ukraine, once incorrectly suspected of being already Neolithic in nature, and Janislawician or maybe even Post-Janislawician further to the north and much later in time, which takes on (at least according to Mikhail Cherniavski from Minsk, but the evidence is not unanimous) pottery of the Dubičiai-Pripiat'-Neman type. The present author is of the opinion, albeit he has not found decisive arguments for his views, that also in Poland the mature Janislawician was ceramicized in similar fashion, sometime in the 5th millennium cal. BC (Łykowe site, excavated by Krzysztof Cyrek).

The phenomenon is thus quite common and apparently not necessarily connected with economic transformation, although it is naturally correlated regionally, mostly with the Neolithic "corridor" in the Balkans and along the Danube.

In the same way but further to the north, ceramization occurred successively in the Dnieper and Donetz region, Upper Volga (Butovian with pottery), eastern Baltic (Post-Kundian with Narva-type ceramics) and Finland (Suomusjärvi and ceramics of Sperrings type).

In conclusion, it may be assumed that the numerous Late Mesolithic cultures (and their later but still not Neolithic mutations) adopted the idea of pottery quite universally from perhaps the Neolithic (?) peoples and were later (or sometimes parallely) neolithized in effect, too.

The process of ceramization can be dated, depending on the region, relatively earlier in the south (7th millennium cal. BC) than in the north (6th/5th millennium cal. BC). Finally, it should be emphasized that Mesolithic ceramic styles do not necessarily coincide totally with the Late Mesolithic cultures/territories (e.g. Erteböllian ceramics going together with Post-Maglemosian industries in Polish Pomerania).

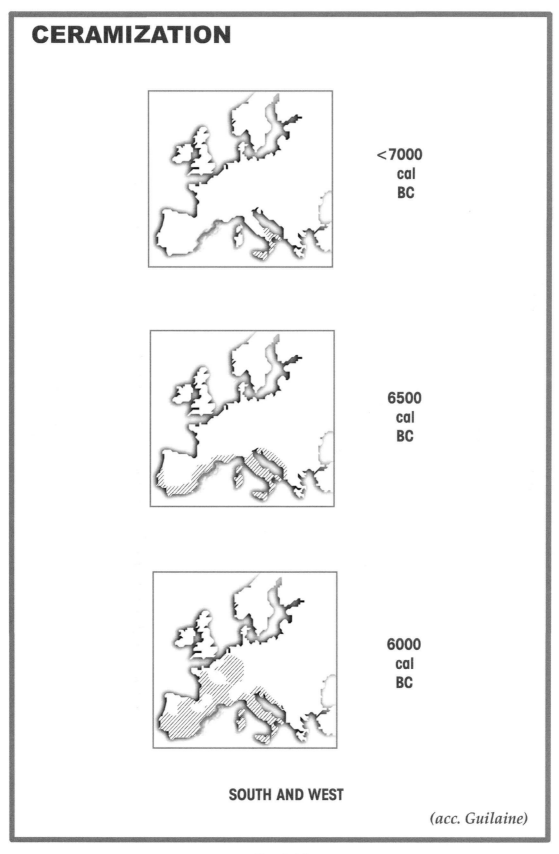

Fig. 5.4.5a

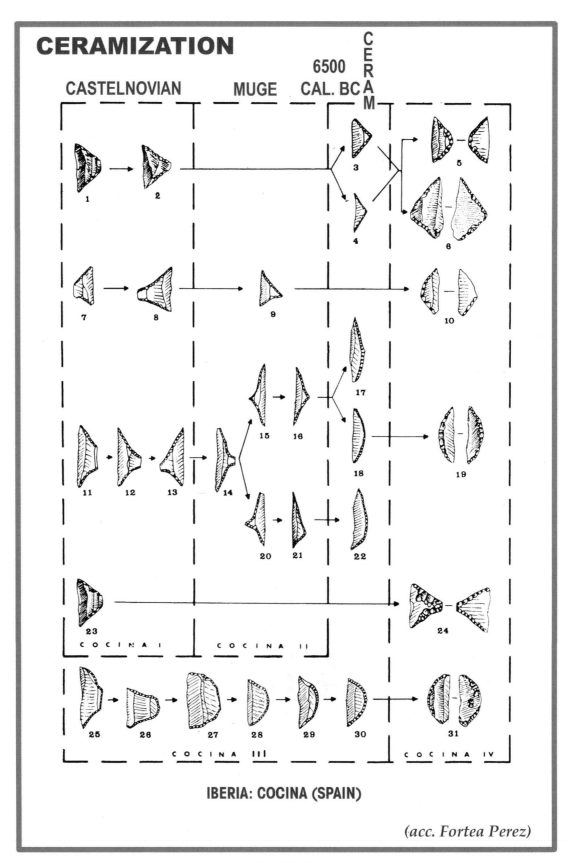

Fig. 5.4.5b

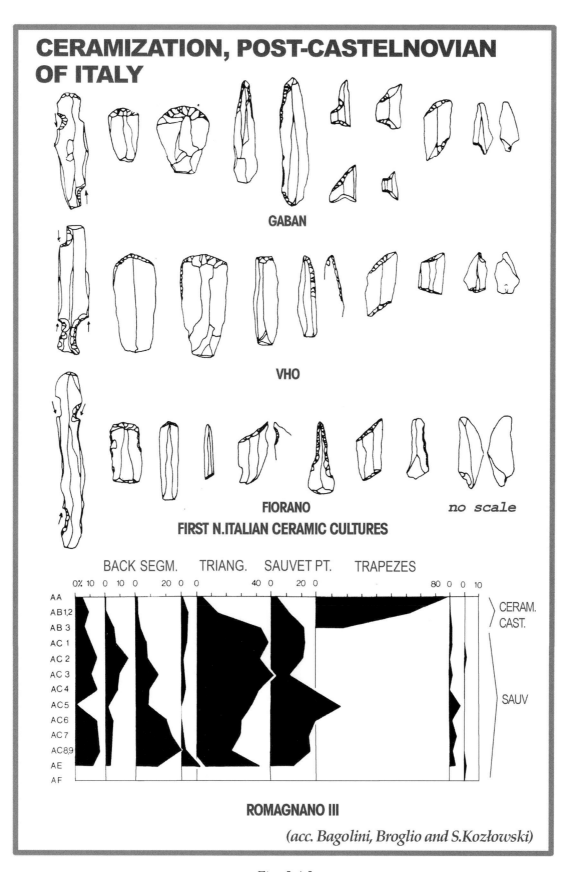

Fig. 5.4.5c

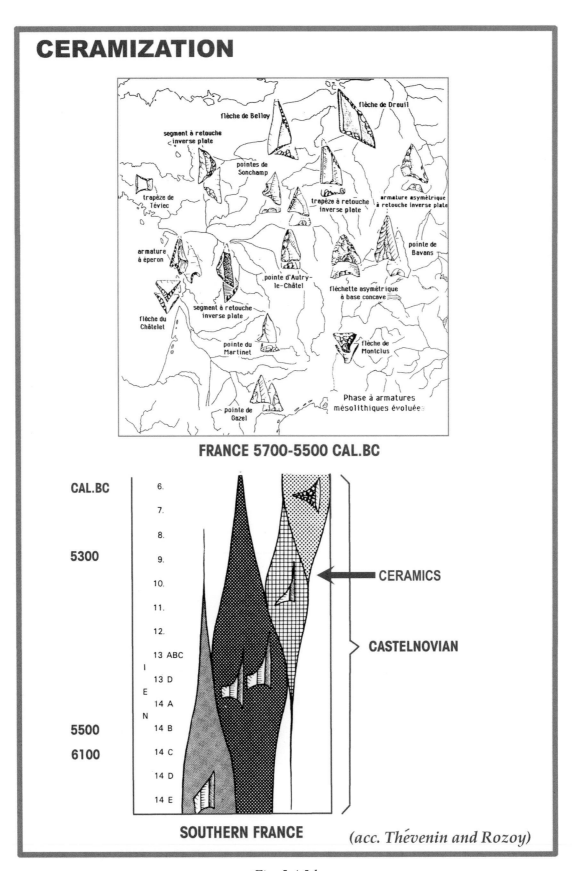

Fig. 5.4.5d

CERAMIZATION

EAST AND CENTER

1-SPERRINGS

2-ERTEBØLLE

3-NARVA

4-UPPER VOLGA

5-PRIPIAT'-DUBIČIAI

6-BUG-DNIESTER

7-CRIŠ-KÖRÖS

8-STARČEVO

Fig. 5.4.5e

PART II

REGIONS

This part of the book presents the main natural regions (Fig. 6) of Mesolithic Europe: South, South-East, West, Center, East and North in the environmental, cultural and historical dimensions. In view of the merging and crossing that took place depending on the period, two regions, West and Central, were described in conjunction.

Ending the presentation in this part is a chapter on supraregional range, which describes the Late Mesolithic/ Pre-Neolithic (Castelnovian) phenomenon.

Stylistic/"cultural" differentiation of the European Mesolithic

The European Mesolithic was strongly differentiated (Fig. 6.1) from the cultural/stylistic point of view. It can be divided into a number of technocomplexes, each of which can be further subdivided into smaller units, groups of cultures and cultures. In our case, the intermediary step in this classification has often been avoided.

Each of the key cultural divisions of Mesolithic Europe, meaning the technocomplexes, is different from its equivalent neighbors in a number of important characteristics. These include own technology and style of the flint and bone industries, a marked territory with own cultural "history" taking place in a fairly homogeneous environment with evolutionary trends shared by the whole unit.

The following technocomplexes can be distinguished: Tanged Points, Northern or Maglemosian, Western (term used interchangeably with Tardenoisian and Sauveterrian), Northeastern or Kunda, Epi-Gravettian, Caucaso-Caspian and Pre-Neolithic/Castelnovian. Added to this list are some, usually peripheral units. The technocomplex characteristics presented in this book (cf. "South", "Southeast", "West and Center", "East" and "North", "Castelnovian") cover in each case the following information: territory, chronology, inner division (vertical and horizontal), history of research, description of original environment and economy, settlement and basic data on the typical stone and bone/antler industries, including statistics and typology.

Following the description of units of higher rank (presentation of common features) are characteristics of cultures and of groups of cultures.

These characteristics are not all equally detailed, since they are based on current knowledge and the state of research is not the same in different parts of Europe. The source material also varies in abundance and the cultural division schemes can be very different as well (French visions of "*colonne stratigraphique/evolutive*" versus understanding of cultures in the aspect of their territorial extent and differentiation, borders etc.). The latter option has been adopted for the presentation in this book.

The above mentioned extremely rich nomenclature with regard to cultural divisions is the fruit of different research attitudes, as well as regional (cf. "Rhythms"), not to say local approaches. To overstep the limitations set by this ill-understood regionalism one needs to forget about modern political boundaries (the same units being called differently on the opposite sides of a border) and treat source data on a more or less equal footing that will assure in the end effect a fairly objective demarcation of territories characterized by the same "culture" or style, not "chopped up" by yet another modern state boundary (cf. "Territories").

Obviously, not all of the old nomenclature could be adopted in this situation. One such "absentee" is Tardenoisian, as it no longer retains sense in this new approach. Drawing on the achievements of regional studies, the author has presented his own view of Mesolithic Europe, a view for which he alone is responsible, which he has considered again and again, checking his conclusions on material coming from several thousand sites in different parts of the continent, analyzed in his "Atlas" (cf.) of the Mesolithic, among others.

Critics will raise the point – and they will be right – that the author has failed to include undoubtedly important details, but every time the answer will be that the author does not wish to compete with the expert knowledge of researchers studying local/regional aspects. They are all, each and every one, invited to present their view of the European Mesolithic to enrich our common knowledge. Even so, the present author is persuaded that he has managed in this book a fairly coherent presentation of the cultural divisions of the continent, quite so for the first time in the history of Mesolithic research. Hence, he is hopeful that he will be excused the errors in the discourse, which for whatever reason he has been unable to avoid.

REGIONS AND CULTURES

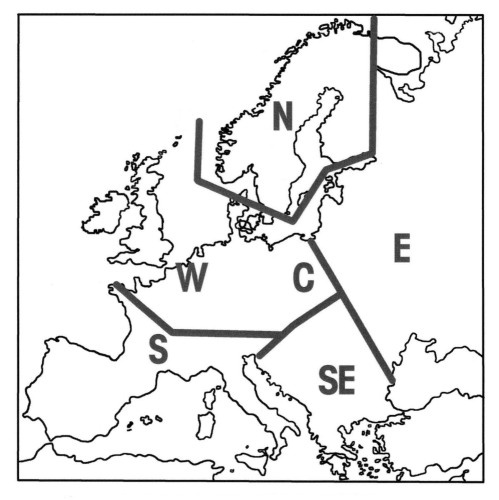

THE MAIN REGIONS OF THE MESOLITHIC EUROPE
AS DESCRIBED IN CHAPTERS 6 -10

Fig. 6

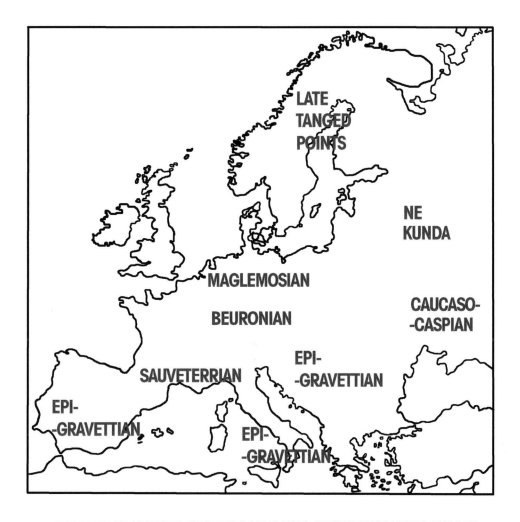

THE MAIN TRADITIONS/TECHNOCOMPLEXES OF THE MESOLITHIC EUROPE

Fig. 6.1

6

South

The region includes Portugal, Spain, France south of the Loire, Italy and western Slovenia. It is characterized by a multitude of multi-layer sites (Barma Margineda, Fontfaurés, Grande Rivoire, Botiqueria, Cocina, Filador, Le Martinet, Cuzol-de-Gramat, Montclus, Chateauneaf-lez-Martigues, La Tourasse, Edera, Benussi, Mala Triglarca, etc.), revealing the macroregional sequence of Epi-Gravettian/Sauveterrian/Castelnovian/Cardial-Impresso and the regional sequences: Romagnano III and Gaban for northern Italy, Isola Santa for central Italy, Montclus and Chateauneuf for Provence, Romanelli and Marisa for Mezzogiorno, Filador and Cocina for the Spanish Levant, etc. Moreover, these sites reveal regional and macroregional evolutionary trends (cf. "Rhythms").

Quite numerous radiocarbon dates have provided a fairly certain chronology.

Geography

The "South" is characterized by considerable morphological differentiation, resulting in a specific "closing" of particular regions, usually not too well communicating with one another and creating smaller *oikumene* in the macroregion. The barriers are as follows: mountains of central Spain, Pyrenees, Central Massif, Apennines, Alps and Dynaric Alps. The connections between regions, like the basin of the Tag, Cantabrian coast, Spanish Levant, Aquitania, Provence, Pianura Padana with the Adige valley in the Dolomites, Tuscany and Puglia/southern Italy, are often made difficult, even if not entirely blocked (through, among others, the valleys of the Rhône and Po, coastal plains/belts now flooded for the most part, various mountain passes below 1000 m).

The external borders with the north (Alps) and east (Dynaric Alps) are naturally determining. What is surprising, however, is the Loire river border which is hardly spectacular in the morphological sense, but which effectively cuts France into two: the Sauveterrian in the south and the Beuronian in the north.

Overall, there is every reason in the region for strong regionalism to be present in the Sauveterrian, for example. The same is true of various conservatist attitudes, ill-disposed to change under the impact of weak outside influence (e.g. the Spanish Levant with Filador and southern Italy with Marisa, cf., which were never completely sauvetarrized). Strong regionalism was especially evident in the Late (Castelnovian, cf.) Mesolithic technocomplex.

Regionalisms are further emphasized by differentiated fauna.

Cultures

Sauveterranian was the dominating culture in the region ever since the beginning of the Holocene. The southern peripheries (Mezzogiorno, Iberian Peninsula) were Epi-Gravettian until c. 7000 cal. BC, later undergoing complete castelnovization (cf.).

Sauveterrian (Fig. 6a–b)

This culture which prevailed in the south took its name from the French site of Le Martinet in Sauveterre-la-Lemance. Other important sites include Abri-des-Layes 2, Montclus, Culoz, Fieux, Rouffignac, Saint-Laurent-Medoc, Roc Allan, Fontfaurés, Grande Rivoire, Sermoyer, Gramari, all in France, Ogens and Vionnaz in Switzerland, Romagnano III, Vatte di Zambana, Benussi, Colbricon, Pradestel and Isola Santa in Italy, Mačanke Vršky in Slovakia and Pod Črmukljo in Slovenia.

The culture existed from the turn of the 10th millennium cal. BC until the end of the 8th, being differentiated regionally (cf. below) and evolving intensively according to the "Rhythms" (cf.) in the microliths group (cf. below text on Romagnano III).

It was characterized by a typical set of small and very small, delicate microliths, including scalene triangles (TO, TR, TH), also with the three-edge retouched variant (TE), Sauveterrian points (PD), isosceles (TN), crescents (DD), rectangles (RA) and, finally, small fine backed points. For details, also on non-microliths, see the texts on Romagnano

SAUVETERRIAN

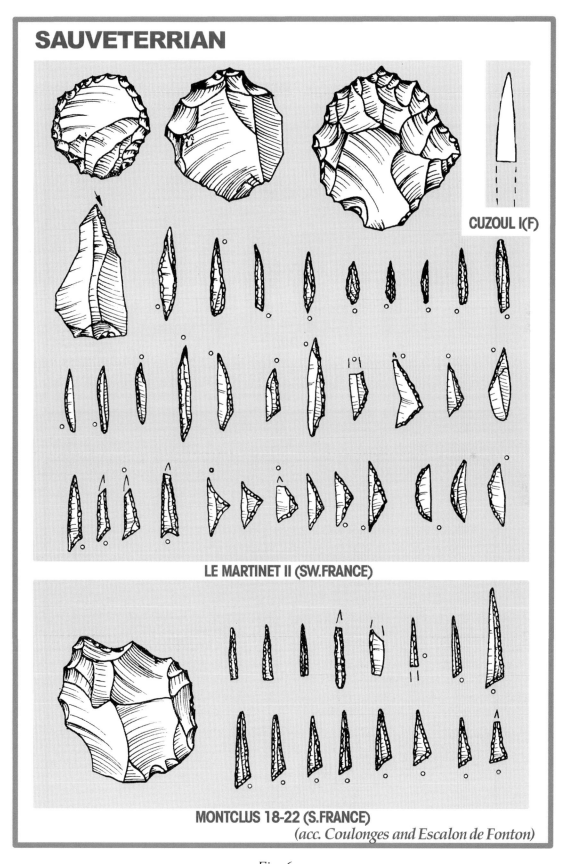

CUZOUL I(F)

LE MARTINET II (SW.FRANCE)

MONTCLUS 18-22 (S.FRANCE)

(acc. Coulonges and Escalon de Fonton)

Fig. 6a

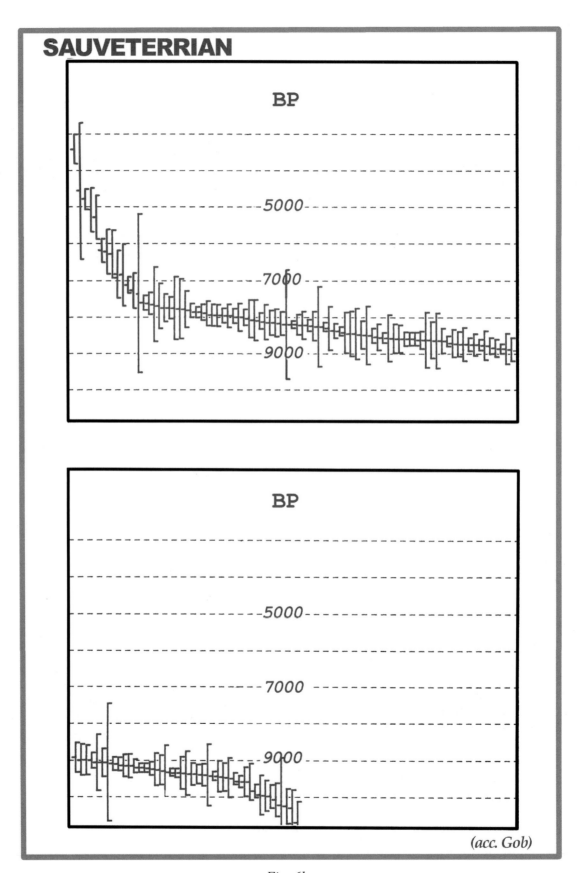

Fig. 6b

Groups of tools	min–max %	average %
A. End-scrapers	7.4–8.1	7.8
B. Retouched flakes	3.2–20.8	9.6
C. Burins	0–9.3	4.7
D. Truncations	3.4–14.2	8.3
E. Retouched blades	0–13.9	7.1
F. Perforators	1.1–1.6	1.3
K. Microliths	42.9–72.6	60.6

III, Gaban and Isola Santa sites in this volume. General statistics of the French assemblages have been presented in the table above:

Statistics for Italy are available in texts on Romagnano III, Gaban and Isola Santa in this volume.

Origins

Researchers today (Antonio Guerreschi, Alberto Broglio, André Thévenin) agree that the Sauveterrian is the outcome of the evolution of southern French-Italian Epi-Gravettian, which underwent a technological mutation at the turn of the Pleistocene and Holocene, going from a prismatic core to a discoidal one and increasing significantly the share of frequently geometric microliths.

Thévenin assumes, plausibly, that the Sauveterrian appeared in France first in the south and expanded northward, along the valley of the Rhône, among others.

Territorial differentiation

Upon analysis, the extensive Italian material indicates clear regionalization of the local Mesolithic, in the Sauveterrian as well as the Castelnovian. The north (Liguria, Piemont, Lombardy, Regio-Emilia, Trentino, Dolomites, Veneto, Friuli and the Carsto Triestino) is marked especially by the constant presence of tectiform scrapers (on blades and flakes), as well as massive burins (the question only is whether they were present everywhere in the region) and big backed knives (Rouffignac type after Jean-Georges Rozoy) especially in Trentino.

Central Italy (mainly Tuscany) has yielded no tectiform end-scrapers, while the big backed knives are extremely rare (only one specimen at Isola Santa). The same concerns scalene triangles with short base – TH and three retouched edges TE (Montclus type).

Further to the south, starting at Naples and including Sicily, the classic Sauveterrian does not appear at all, while the "mesolithico indiferenziato" (term of Fabio Martini), which is typical of that region, appears to be an incompletely sauveterrianized version of the local final Epi-Gravettian/ Romanellian (e.g. Grotta Marisa, but also Grotta La Mura). The Catalonian Filador and Hungarian Janszbereny and Jasztelek (cf. "Outlying areas"), which are marginal with regard to the Sauveterrian, also appears "not fully sauvetterrized" (cf. "Pyrenees, Alps…").

The overwhelming impression is that these regionalisms were produced by land morphology (as well as diversified origins), the Apennines separating the north from the center of the peninsula and the center from the south. It seems equally evident that the south of Italy was not completely sauveterrianized simply because the main centers of this phenomenon were in the north. That is why also Tuscany appears "somewhat less" sauveterrianized (Rouffignac knives, Montclus triangles) than the north of the country (?).

In this situation, France separated from Italy by the Western Alps should have its own variant(s) of the Sauveterrian, an idea borne out by the presence of narrow symmetric points with retouched base in the assemblages there, as well as the smaller percentage (something worth rechecking!) or even absence (?) of tectiform end-scrapers. One should also expect some differences between the Aquitanian-Pyrenean and the Rhône-Provençal Sauveterrian.

In the Late Mesolithic ("Pre-Neolithic/Castelnovian", cf.), the differentiation of the South as a macroregion is even more strongly revealed in the continuing differences in the group of scrapers and burins (cf. above), but also in the increasingly developed and very "baroque" trapezes. It is possible to distinguish a number of local units (Muge, Cocina, Cuzoul, Retzian, Téviecian, Provençal Castelnovian, northern Italian Castelnovian, etc.) as part of the Castelnovian *sensu largo* (cf. "Pre-Neolithic/ Castelnovian").

6.1. Italy

The texts presented in this section are devoted to the Mesolithic in Italy and were prepared in association with Italian colleagues Alberto Broglio, Diampaolo Dalmeri, Carlo Tozzi and Renata Griffoni-Cremonesi. Firstly, they discuss the typology and evolution of the Italian Mesolithic, the latter following overall the general evolutionary line of the western and central-European Mesolithic *koine* (cf. also "Rhythms"). Secondly, these texts point to a clear regionalization of the Italian Mesolithic, at least in its early and middle phases (cf. above).

Northern Italian cultural sequence

As said above, northern Italy from Liguria to Carso Triestino was characterized by a similar or perhaps even identical rhythm of cultural change, that is, final Epi-Gravettian turning into North-Italian Sauveterrian and the latter into North-Italian Castlenovian, and then into North-Italian early ceramic/Post-Castelnovian "Neolithic" cultures. This sequence is best observed in the Trentino-Alto Adige region, especially on the stratified sites of Romagnano III and Riparo Gaban. Presented below are extensive excerpts from the publications of the first, already classical site. After that come selected fragments from the publication of the Isola Santa site in Tuscany (central Italy) and Marisa in Puglia (southern Italy); a text on Gaban is in Chapter 11.

6.2. The Trentino Sequence (Fig. 6.2a–q)
(co-author – A. Broglio)

Tipologia ed evoluzione delle industrie mesolitiche di Romagnano III

Premessa

I giacimenti preistorici di Loc di Romagnano si trovano all'apice del conoide del Rio Bondone, lungo il fianco destro della Valle dell'Adige, una decina di km a sud di Trento. Nella località fu aperta nel 1968 una cava che mise in luce alcuni giacimenti preistorici, uno dei quali (Romagnano III) si rivelò particolarmente importante sia per l'ampiezza della serie, comprendente depositi mesolitici, neolitici etc., sia per la presenza di un'importante sequenza mesolitica. Nel 1971–73 furono scavati i depositi mesolitici (A. Broglio).

La serie mesolitica, fu suddivisa in vari strati e tagli, tutti datati radiometricamente. Nell'analisi delle industrie sono state mantenute le seguenti suddivisioni.

Nello scavo le suddivisioni tra le unità AA, AB, AC1–3, AC4–9, AE e AF sono stati individuate con criteri stratigrafici; le suddivisioni ulteriori sono artificiali:

a) Tagli AA1 e AA2 con industria castelnoviana associata a ceramica, datati assieme c. 5530 cal. BC.

b) Tagli AB1 e AB2 con industria castelnoviana, datati assieme c. 6450, 6700 e 6900 cal. BC.

c) Taglio AB3, con ogni probabilità rimaneggiato e contenente un'industria castelnoviana mescolata ad un'industria sauveterriana, datato c. 7190 cal. BC.

d) Taglio AC1, datato c. 7250 cal. BC, con industria sauveterriana.

e) Taglio AC2, datato c. 7600 cal. BC, con industria sauveterriana.

f) Taglio AC3, datato c. 7650 cal. BC, con industria sauveterriana.

g) Taglio AC4, datato c. 7900 cal. BC, con industria sauveterriana.

h) Taglio AC5, datato assieme al taglio sottostante AC6 c. 8300 cal. BC., con industria sauveterriana.

i) Taglio AC6, con industria sauveterriana.

l) Taglio AC7, datato c. 8300 cal. BC, con industria sauveterriana.

m) Tagli AC8–AC9, datati assieme c. 8450 cal. BC (due datazioni coincidenti), con industria sauveterriana.

n) AD: deposito alluvionale, sterile.

o) Tagli AE1, AE2, AE3, AE4 e AE5, datati assieme c. 8700, 8800 e 8900 cal. BC, con industria sauveterriana antica.

p) Taglio AF, datato c. 9400 BC, con industria sauveterriana antica.

In questa nota intendiamo esporre i criteri seguiti nella classificazione delle industrie, la loro tipologia, e la loro evoluzione nella serie mesolitica, dall'orizzonte sauveterriano più antico (tagli AF e AE) fino alla comparsa della ceramica (tagli AA).

Tipologia degli strumenti e delle armature microlitiche

Premessa

La classificazione dei manufatti ritoccati della collezione di Romagnano III è stata condotta secondo criteri derivati dall'esame diretto dei pezzi, alla luce delle nostre precedenti esperienze di studio di industrie mesolitiche; perciò abbiamo dovuto scostarci dalle liste tipologiche proposte da altri Autori.

Tipologia degli strumenti

Gli strumenti comprendono i seguenti gruppi: A – Grattatoi; B – Schegge ritoccate; C – Bulini; D – Lame troncate; E – Lame ritoccate; F – Becchi e Perforatori; G – Compositi; L – Pezzi Scagliati; M – Diversi ; N – Coltelli a dorso; O – Punte. Alla categoria M sono stati attribuiti i frammenti non determinabili di strumenti.

[Note that some of the letter markings of typological groups in the original text (A, B, C…) have been changed adapting them to the ones used in the present volume (Fig. 2.1.5); for the purposes of clarity letter markings have also been introduced for the microliths.]

A – *Grattatoi*. Nei grattatoi almeno una estremità è stata ritoccata, conferendole una forma regolare, più o meno arcuata. Sono stati suddivisi in base ai seguenti criteri:

I Classe: Grattatoi frontali su lama sottile, a lati paralleli, prevalentemente a sezione trapezoidale, a fronte generalmente poco arcuata. Negli esemplari integri l'indice di allungamento si aggira attor.

II Classe: Grattatoi frontali su lama spessa, generalmente di 1° ordine, talora con cortice.

III Classe: Grattatoi frontali su lama stretta o di larghezza media (mai molto larga), generalmente poco spessa. Fronte arcuata e obliqua. Angolo del ritocco della fronte compreso tra 45° e 80°.

IV Classe: Grattatoi ogivali su lama stretta.

V Classe: Grattatoi tettiformi su lama.

VI Classe: Grattatoi a spalla su lama.

VII Classe: Grattatoi frontali su scheggia massiccia allungata ($1 < ia < 1.5$).

VIII Classe: Grattatoi a fronte arcuata, qualche volta obliqua, su supporto massiccio. Lati ad andamento di solito irregolare; fronte a ritocco erto (60°–90°).

IX Classe: Grattatoi frontali su scheggia allungata (ia >1) con lati convergenti verso la base.

X Classe: Grattatoi frontali corti su scheggia (ia <2); fronte a ritocco erto (> 60°).

XI Classe: Grattatoi frontali molto corti su scheggia (ia < 1); fronte a ritocco erto (> 60°).

XII Classe: Grattatoi frontali doppi, corti e molto corti, su lama o scheggia. Fronte raramente obliqua.

XIII Classe: Grattatoi frontali circolari.

XIV Classe: Grattatoi frontali su margine laterale di scheggia.

XV Classe: Grattatoi frontali su scheggia massiccia o su placchetta.

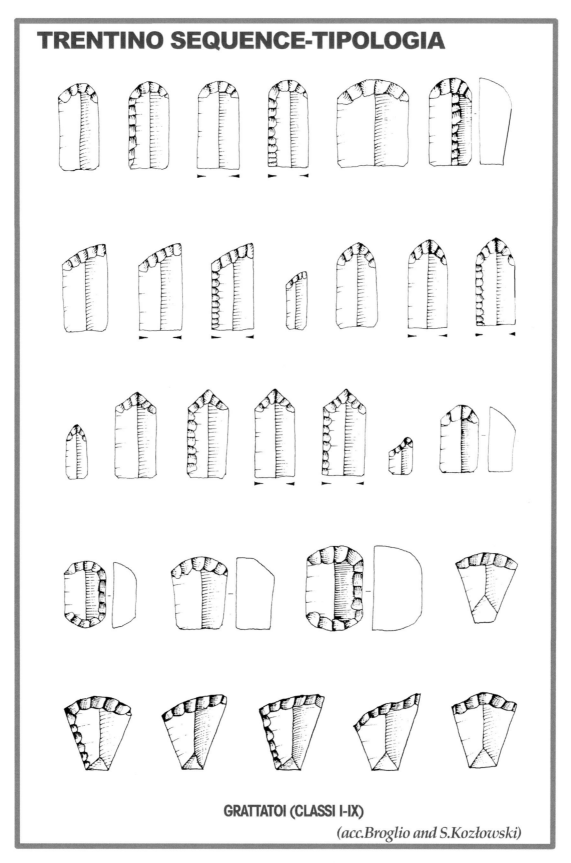

GRATTATOI (CLASSI I-IX)

(acc.Broglio and S.Kozłowski)

Fig. 6.2a

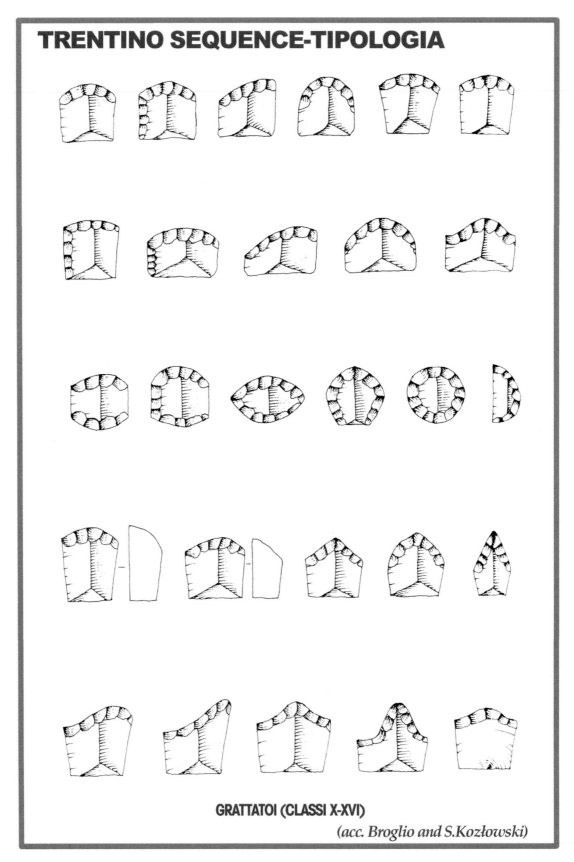

TRENTINO SEQUENCE-TIPOLOGIA

GRATTATOI (CLASSI X-XVI)

(acc. Broglio and S.Kozłowski)

Fig. 6.2b

TRENTINO SEQUENCE-TIPOLOGIA

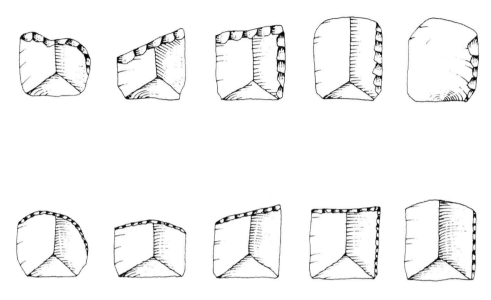

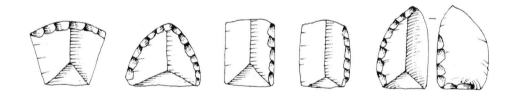

SCHEGGE RITOCATTE

(SKROBACZ, RACLETTES, RASCHIATOI, DENTICOLATI)

(acc. Broglio and S.Kozłowski)

Fig. 6.2c

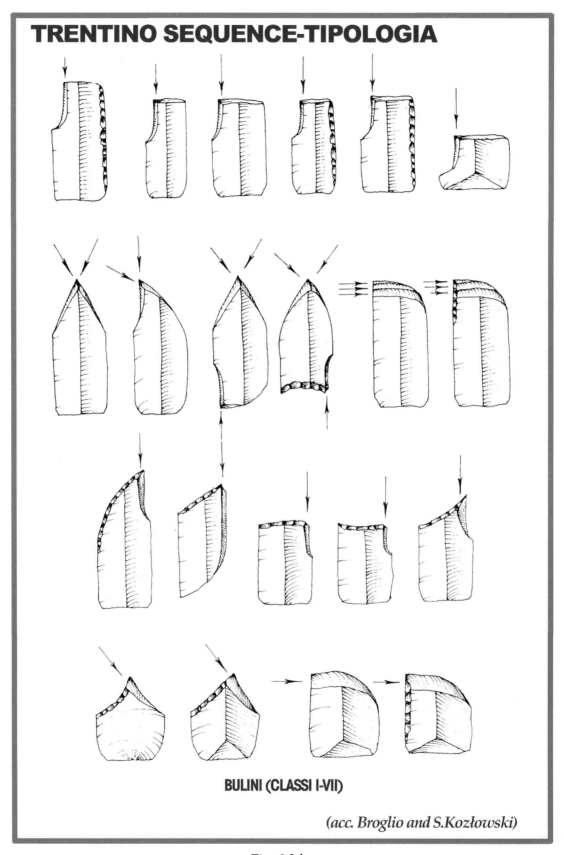

Fig. 6.2d

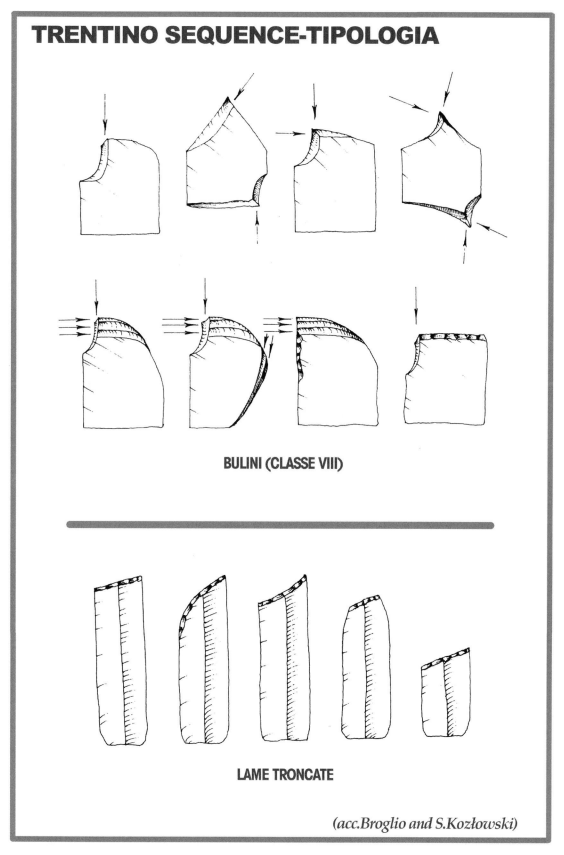

TRENTINO SEQUENCE-TIPOLOGIA

BULINI (CLASSE VIII)

LAME TRONCATE

(acc.Broglio and S.Kozłowski)

Fig. 6.2e

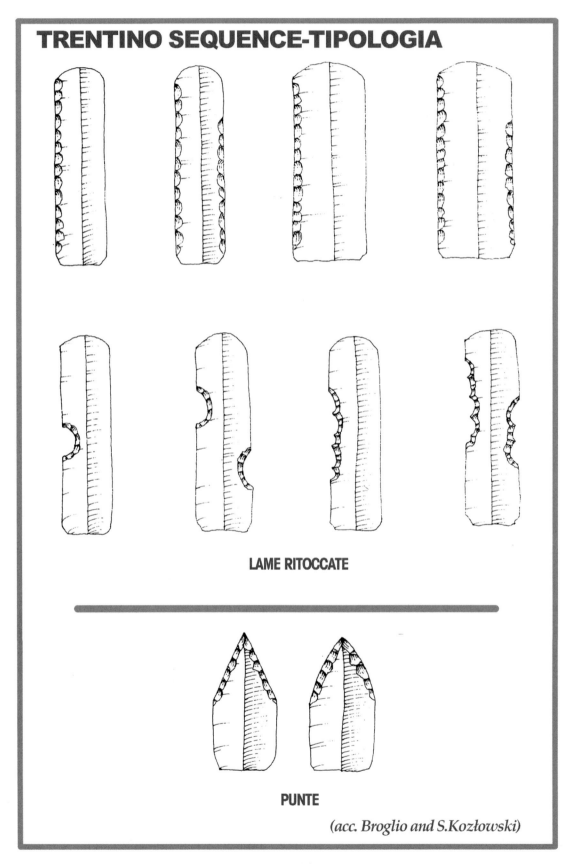

TRENTINO SEQUENCE-TIPOLOGIA

LAME RITOCCATE

PUNTE

(acc. Broglio and S.Kozłowski)

Fig. 6.2f

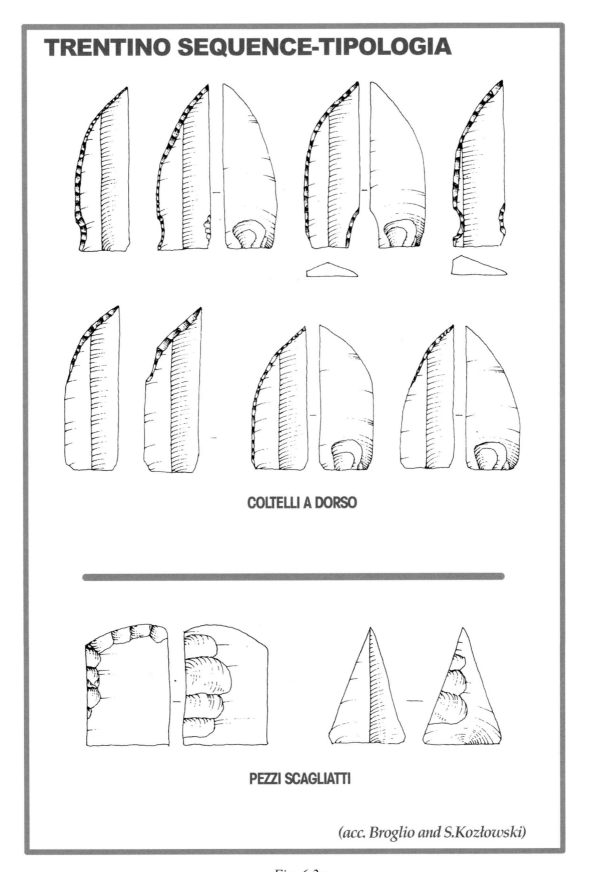

Fig. 6.2g

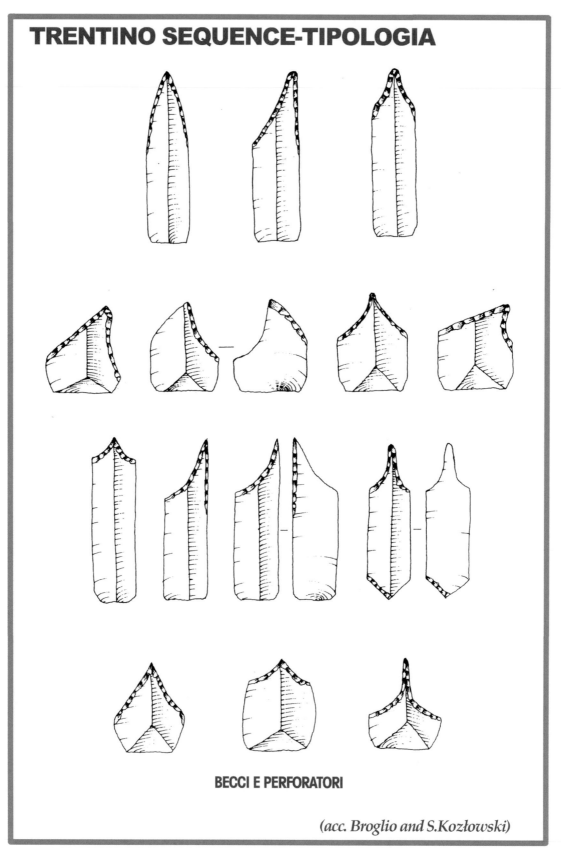

TRENTINO SEQUENCE-TIPOLOGIA

BECCI E PERFORATORI

(acc. Broglio and S.Kozłowski)

Fig. 6.2h

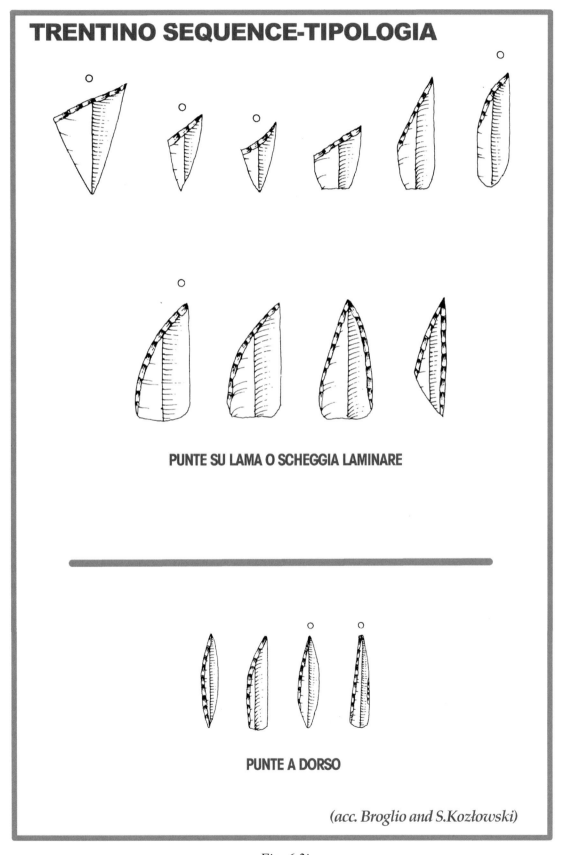

Fig. 6.2i

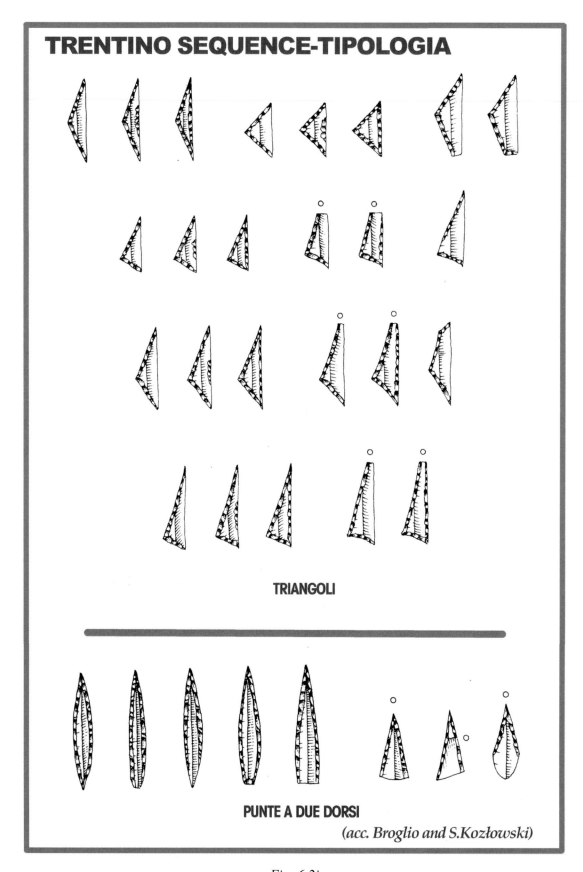

Fig. 6.2j

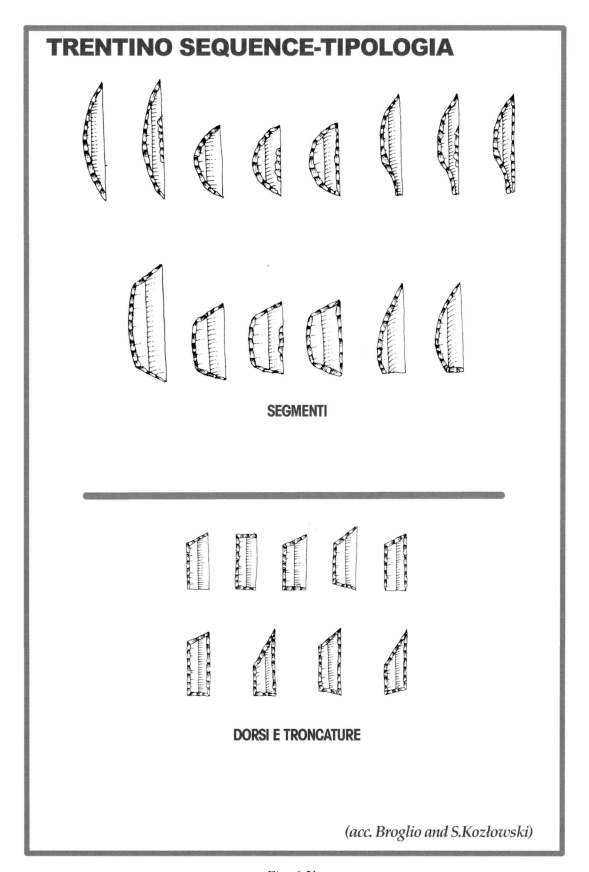

TRENTINO SEQUENCE-TIPOLOGIA

SEGMENTI

DORSI E TRONCATURE

(acc. Broglio and S.Kozłowski)

Fig. 6.2k

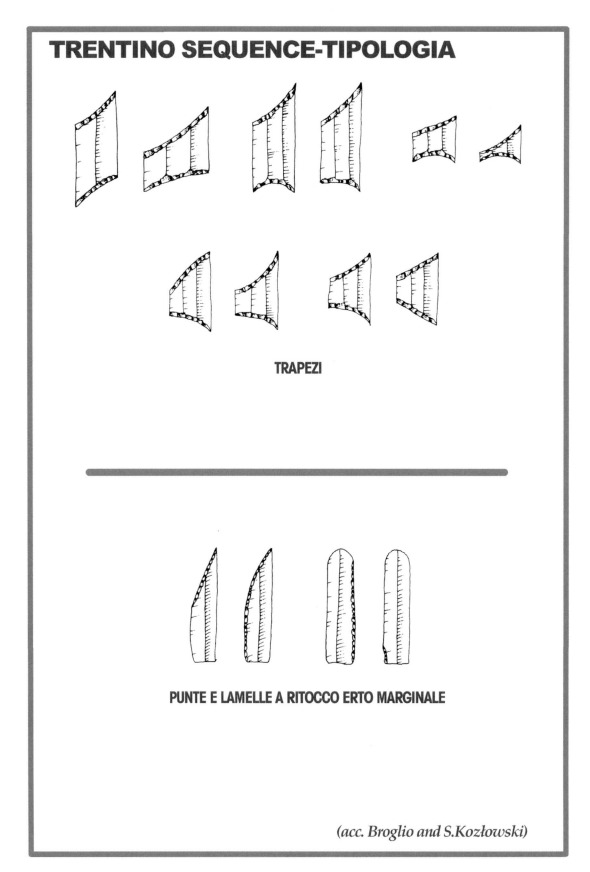

Fig. 6.21

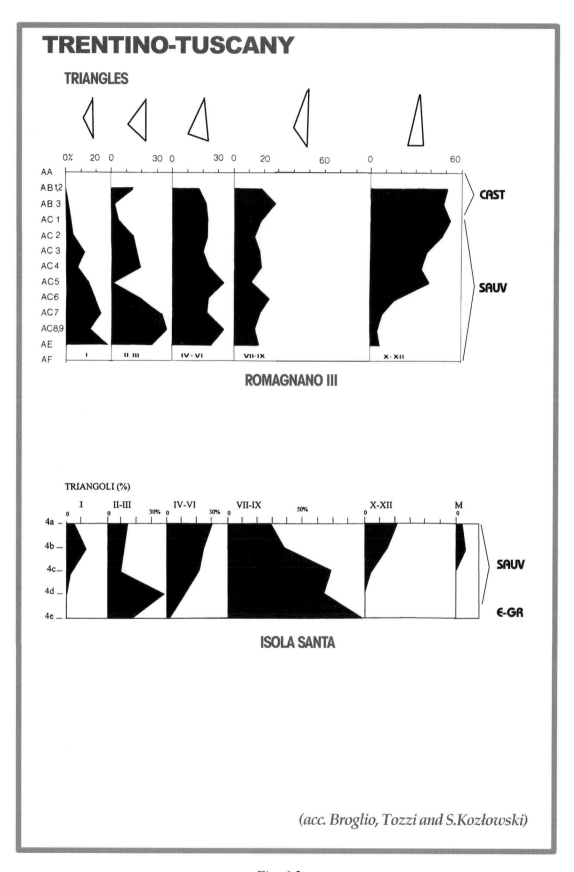

Fig. 6.2m

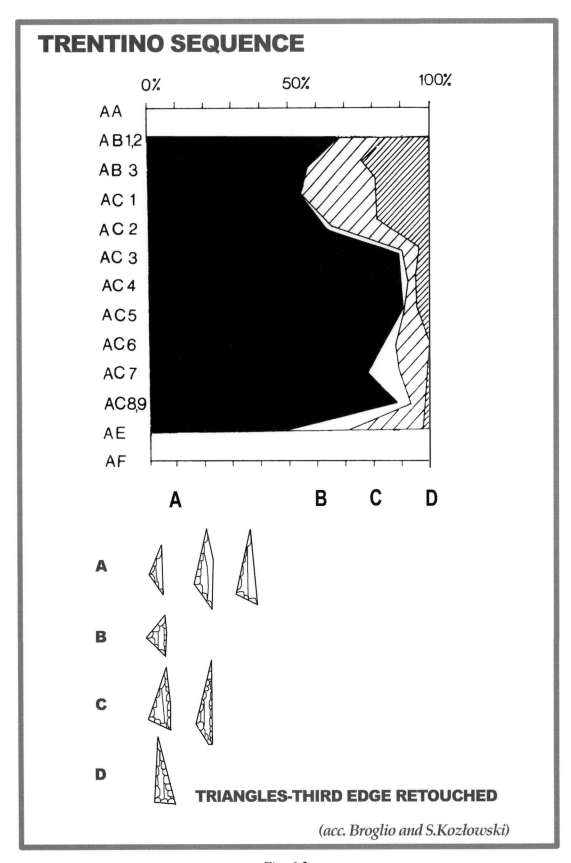

Fig. 6.2n

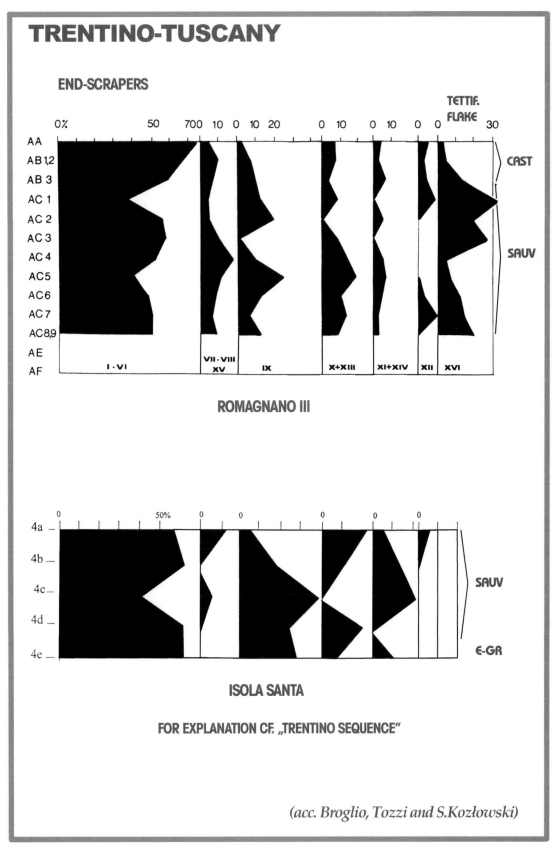

Fig. 6.2p

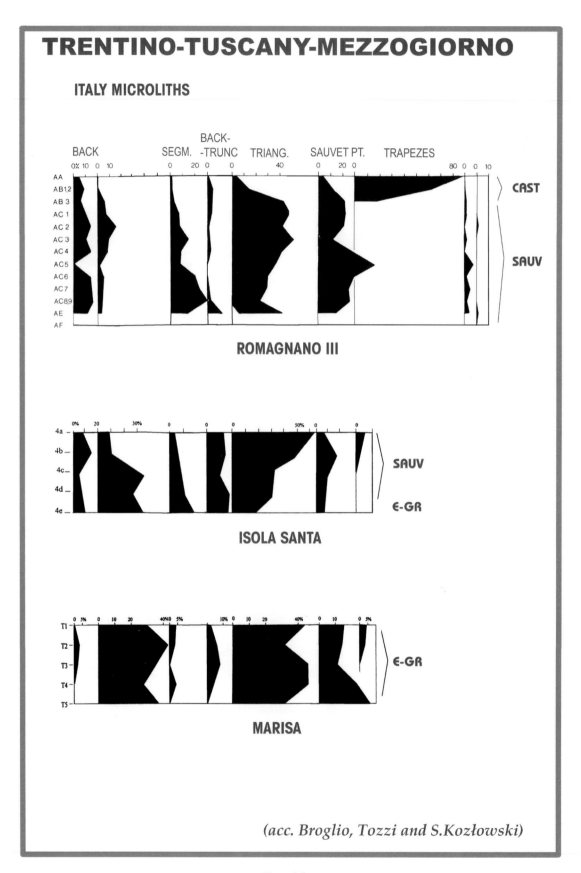

Fig. 6.2q

XVI Classe: Grattatoi tettiformi, ogivali, a spalla e a muso su scheggia. Ritocco generalmente semierto (45° ÷ 60°).

XVII: frammenti di grattatoi su scheggia.

B – Schegge ritoccate. È un gruppo eterogeneo, al quale sono state attribuite differenti categorie di strumenti, su scheggia o su placchetta. Anche se localizzato in tratti differenti, il ritocco è omogeneo.

I Classe: Grattatoi irregulari/*Skrobacz*. Schegge di forma irregolare, che presentano un ritocco regolare, simile a quello dei grattatoi, laterale, trasversale o latero-trasversale.

II Classe: Raclettes. Schegge a ritocco erto marginale, formato da piccoli stacchi simili tra loro e ben allineati.

III Classe: Raschiatoi. Schegge a ritocco semplice.

IV Classe: Denticolati. Schegge spesse o placchete che presentano un ritocco erto o semierto denticolato.

V Classe: Schegge a ritocchi o pseudoritocchi.

VI Classe: Frammenti indeterminabili di schegge ritoccate.

C: Bulini. Nell'attribuzione a questo gruppo tipologico ci si è attenuti ai criteri tradizionali. Nella classificazione sono stati seguiti i seguenti criteri:

a – natura del supporto (lama, scheggia, placchetta o scheggia spessa);

b – tipo di *biseau* (ad uno stacco su superficie naturale; ad uno stacco su frattura; a due stacchi; carenoide; a stacco laterale su ritocco trasversale; a stacco trasversale su ritocco laterale);

c – localizzazione del *biseau* rispetto all'asse del supporto;

d – dimensioni e rapporti dimensionali.

I Classe: Bulini su lama o su scheggia, ad uno stacco.

II Classe: Bulini su lama o su scheggia, su frattura. La frattura è generalmente normale all'asse del supporto, raramente obliqua. Lo stacco è sempre laterale, raramente multiplo. Prevalgono i tipi su lama, che sono stati suddivisi in relazione alla larghezza della lama (limite tra lama larga e lama stretta co 12 mm) e alla presenza di ritocchi laterali semplici (non di preparazione del bulino).

III Classe: Bulini su lama spessa, d'aspetto massiccio, con indice di allungamento relativamente elevato, a due stacchi (b. diedri). In molti casi il *biseau* è poligonale.

IV Classe: Bulini *à biseau* carenoide, su lame massicce, abbastanza lunghe, a stacchi piani.

V Classe: Bulini su ritocco trasversale a stacco laterale, su lama.

VI Classe: Bulini su ritocco, su scheggia. *Biseau* sull'asse del supporto.

VII Classe: Bulini a stacco trasversale, su scheggia.

VIII Classe: Bulini corti e massicci. Sono ricavati da placchette o da schegge corte e spesse. Indici di allungamento e di carenaggio bassi. Sono frequenti *biseaux* a stacchi multipli e tipi multipli.

D – Lame troncate. A questo gruppo sono stati attribuiti solo strumenti su supporto laminare (lame e lamelle).

Alcuni frammenti provenienti dal deposito con industria castelnoviana potrebbero in realtà essere frammenti di trapezi.

E – Lame ritoccate.

I Classe: Lame e lamelle a ritocco semierto, solitamente discontinuo, con tendenza al ritocco denticolato, frequentemente diretto, talora misto.

II Classe: Lame ad incavi o a ritocco denticolato.

I frammenti sono stati attribuiti ai tipi completi più prossimi.

F – Becchi e perforatori. A questo gruppo sono stati attribuiti gli strumenti che presentano una estremità isolata mediante ritocco, formante un becco o una punta.

I Classe: Becchi su lama o lamella.

II Classe: Becchi su scheggia.

III Classe: Perforatori su lama o lamella.

IV Classe: Perforatori su scheggia.

G – Compositi. Grattatoi – Bulini.

Grattatoi – Troncature.

L – Pezzi scagliati. Sono pezzi ricavati da schegge o da placchette, elaborati mediante ritocco scagliato.

Questi pezzi presentano forti affinità con alcuni tipi di nuclei.

M – Diversi.

Frammenti di strumenti indeterminabili.

N – Coltelli a dorso curvo. A questo gruppo sono stati attribuiti strumenti ricavati da lame o da schegge laminari, mediante ritocco erto profondo o marginale, di dimensioni costantemente ben differenziate rispetto a quelle di forme analoghe microlitiche.

I Classe: Coltelli a dorso profondo totale.

II Classe: Coltelli a dorso profondo parziale.

III Classe: Coltelli a dorso marginale.

O – Punte. A questo gruppo sono stati attribuiti gli strumenti a forma di punta, ricavati da lame o da schegge lunghe mediante ritocco semierto bilaterale e parziale.

Tipologia delle armature microlitiche (K)

Le armature microlitiche comprendono i seguenti gruppi: 1 – Punte su lama o scheggia laminare; 2 – Punte a dorso; 3 – Segmenti; 4 – Dorsi e troncature; 5 – Triangoli; 6 – Punte a due dorsi; 7 – Trapezi; 8 – Dorsi marginali; 9 – Diversi. Alla categoria 10. sono stati attribuiti i frammenti non determinabili di armature.

1 – Punte su lama o scheggia laminare. A questo gruppo sono state riferite le armature su lama o scheggia laminare relativamente larghe (larghezza > 15 mm), raramente a bordi paralleli, che presentano una estremità a punta, ottenuta mediante troncatura o dorso. Di solito la troncatura o il dorso hanno eliminato la parte (prossimale o distale) più larga del supporto.

I Classe: Punte-troncatura (DA, DB and K in the typology used in this volume).

II Classe: Punte a dorso.

2 – Punte a dorso. Punte di dimensioni lamellari o microlamellari ottenute mediante un dorso.

3 – Segmenti. Microliti formati da un dorso curvo opposto ad un margine rettilineo.

I Classe: Segmenti (DD and DE in the typology used in this volume).

II Classe: Segmenti a dorso sinusoidale.

III Classe: Segmenti trapezoidali.

IV Classe: Segmenti a base ottusa.

4 – Dorsi e troncature (R in the typology used in this volume). A questo gruppo sono stati attribuiti i microliti che presentano: un dorso; un bordo opposto al dorso ritoccato o non ritoccato; una o due troncature.

I Classe: microliti ad un dorso e ad una troncatura.

II Classe: microliti ad un dorso e a due troncature.

III Classe: microliti a due dorsi e una troncatura.

IV Classe: microliti a due dorsi e due troncature.

V: Frammenti.

5 – Triangoli (T in the typology used in this volume). A questo gruppo sono stati attribuiti i microliti che hanno una sagoma triangolare, coi due lati più corti ritoccati, opposti ad un terzo lato, ritoccato o no. Sono stati suddivisi secondo i seguenti criteri:

a – simmetria o assimmetria dei due lati corti (triangoli isosceli e triangoli scaleni);

b – rapporti dimensionali (lunghi e corti);

c – morfologia del margine opposto ai due lati ritoccati (naturale, a ritocco parziale marginale, a ritocco totale erto);

d – morfologia della punta, cioè dell'estremità formata dai due lati più lunghi (acuta, normale ottusa, troncata);

I Classe: Triangoli isosceli allungati (con indice di allungamento > 2.5) (=TM).

II Classe: Triangoli isosceli corti (con indice di lungamento < 2.5) (=TN).

III Classe: Triangoli isosceli con estremità ottusa (=TN).

IV Classe: Triangoli scaleni corti (con indice di lungamento < 2.5) (=TO).

V Classe: Triangoli scaleni corti con estremità ottusa (=TO).

VI: Frammenti e forme aberranti di triangoli scaleni corti (=TO).

VII Classe: Triangoli scaleni lunghi a base lunga. Indice di allungamento > 2.5. Angolo formato tra i due lati ritoccati ~ 120° (=TR).

VIII Classe: Triangoli scaleni lunghi a base lunga con estremità ottusa.

IX Classe: Frammenti di triangoli scaleni lunghi a base lunga.

X Classe: Triangoli scaleni lunghi a base corta (=TH). Indice di allungamento > 2.5. Angolo formato tra i due lati ritoccati compreso tra 90° e 110°.

XI Classe: Triangoli scaleni lunghi a base corta, con estremità ottusa (=TH).

XII: Frammenti di triangoli scaleni lunghi a base corta.

6 – Punte a due dorsi (PD and PA in the typology used in this volume). Punte microlitiche formate da due dorsi tendenzialmente equivalenti, con andamento simmetrico. Il dorso è ottenuto con ritocco erto generalmente diretto e profondo, talora bipolare su un bordo, raramente marginale. (In quest'ultimo caso il dorso è parziale).

I Classe: Punte allungate (indice di allungamento > 3) a due dorsi leggermente convessi.

II Classe: punte corte (indice di allungamento < 3), a due dorsi subrettilinei.

7 – Trapezi (=A and B in the typology used in this volume). Sono ricavati da lame mediante due troncature. I supporti sono costituiti da lame di forma regolare, a bordi paralleli, di sezione trapezoidale o triangolare. Le troncature oblique sono state ottenute con la tecnica del microbulino; talora il *piquant-trièdre* è stato successivamente ritoccato in tutto o in parte. Le troncature normali sono state spesso ottenute con un solo colpo, su lama già troncata normalmente (con troncatura concava). Come la tecnica del microbulino è documentata da microbulini provenienti da lamelle, così questa tecnica di troncatura sommaria è documentata da caratteristici residui di lavorazione. Gli AA si sono posti il problema se questi non derivino da fratture casuali della base dei trapezi, ed hanno scartato questa spiegazione in quanto la forma dei residui (presenza di un tallone; morfologia della superficie di distacco) suggerisce l'intenzionalità del colpo. Sono stati adottati i seguenti criteri di classificazione:

a – orientazione delle troncature (oblique subparallele; una obliqua, l'altra normale; oblique convergenti);

b – andamento delle troncature (rettilinea, concava, convessa);

c – rapporti dimensionali (forme allungate e forme corte).

I trapezi assimmetrici presentano quasi sempre l'estremità più appuntita (punta), orientata verso l'alto, sul lato destro.

I Classe: Trapezi assimmetrici a basi *decalées*, o romboidi (= BH, BW).

II Classe: Trapezi assimmetrici lunghi (= BJ, BV) (indice di allungamento > 2) a base normale.

III Classe: Trapezi assimmetrici corti (= BZ) (indice di allungamento < 2) a base normale.

IV Classe: Trapezi assimmetrici a base obliqua concava.

V Classe: Trapezi simmetrici (= AF).

VI Classe: frammenti di trapezi e trapezi in corso di fabbricazione.

8 – Punte e lamelle a ritocco erto marginale. A questo gruppo sono state riferite le armature ottenute mediante ritocco erto marginale, di solito molto fine, regolare, su supporto lamellare o microlamellare. Sono stati adottati i seguenti criteri di classificazione:

a – presenza di un'estremità puntuta od ottusa;

b – estensione del ritocco (totale o parziale);

c – andamento del ritocco (rettilineo o convesso).

I Classe: Punte a ritocco erto marginale.

II Classe: Lamelle a ritocco erto marginale.

III Classe: frammenti.

9 – Microliti diversi a ritocco erto.

10 – Frammenti di armature.

Struttura interna dei gruppi tipologici della categoria degli strumenti

A. – Grattatoi. In tutta la serie la frequenza dei grattatoi rispetto all'insieme degli strumenti oscilla attorno al 40%. L'analisi delle strutture interne del gruppo mette in evidenza i seguenti fenomeni.

Nella sequenza sauveterriana il rapporto tra grattatoi su supporto laminare e grattatoi su scheggia o su placchetta è stabile attorno a 1 (indice dei g. su lama: 50.0–56.5) con l'eccezione delle industrie di AC5 e di AC1, nelle quali dominano dei grattatoi su scheggia e su placchetta (indice dei g. su lama: AC5 38.7; AC1 37.5). Nella sequenza castelnoviana l'indice dei grattatoi su lama aumenta considerevolmente (73.2–75.6).

Nella sequenza sauveterriana il rapporto tra grattatoi frontali su supporto laminare e grattatoi frontali su scheggia o su placchetta e stabile attorno a 1; nella sequenza castelnoviana i grattatoi frontali su supporto laminare aumentano considerevolmente (60% in AB1.2; 71 % in AA).

Tra le classi dei grattatoi su scheggia o su placchetta (classi VII–XVI) non pare possibile individuare tendenze evolutive. Non si può tuttavia sostenere l'esistenza di una certa stabilità interna a causa dei seguenti fenomeni:

– un picco di forme poco corte (classe IX) e corte (classi X–XIII), con corrispondente diminuzione dei grattatoi convergenti su scheggia (classe XVI) in AC5;

– l'assenza di grattatoi poco corti (classe IX), in AC3;

– l'aumento dei grattatoi convergenti su scheggia (classe XVI) nella parte superiore della sequenza sauveterriana (AC3–AC1).

L'indice dei grattatoi convergenti (classi IV, V, VI e XVI) da un valore relativamente elevato in AC8–9 (38.9) scende al minimo in corrispondenza di AC5 (12.9) e quindi risale, presentando due picchi in AC3 (52.2) e in AC1 (54.2). Scende quindi nella sequenza castelnoviana (26.8 in AB1–2; 24.4 in AA).

Dal punto di vista stratigrafico, pur facendo molte riserve su questa osservazione (in quanto si basa su numeri troppo piccoli di pezzi), si nota che la classe XI è presente da AC6 ad AA, la classe XIV da AC8–9 ad AC4, il tipo 8 da AC7 ad AC3.

La presenza di numerosi tipi in tutta la serie suggerisce una continuità di tradizione culturale.

B. – Schegge ritoccate. L'indice di questo gruppo è stabile in tutta la sequenza sauveterriana (36.3–23.3) e diminuisce nelle industrie castelnoviane (10.2–9%).

Grattatoi irregulare/*skrobacz*, raclettes e raschiatoi sono presenti pressochè uniformemente in tutta la serie, mentre le schegge a ritocco denticolato (classe IV) sono presenti solo tra AC8–9 e AC3; pertanto esse paiono caratteristiche della fase media della sequenza sauveterriana.

C. – Bulini. L'indice dei bulini è stabile nelle parti inferiore e media della sequenza sauveterriana (18.7–10.7), con l'eccezione di AC5 (2.7) e subisce quindi una flessione (6.1–4.9).

Tra i bulini su frattura (II classe), osserviamo che i bulini su supporto laminare largo (tipi 3 e 5) si collocano nella sequenza sauveterriana, mentre i pochi esemplari su supporto laminare stretto si trovano prevalentemente nella sequenza castelnoviana. I bulini su frattura su scheggia corta sono presenti solo nella parte media della sequenza sauveterriana (AC8–9–AC6).

I bulini diedri (III classe), *à biseau* carenoide (IV lasse), su ritocco (V classe) e a stacco trasversale (VI classe) sono presenti soltanto nella sequenza sauveterriana (III: AE–AC2; IV: C7–AC1; V: AC8–9 – AC3; VI: AC8–9 – AC2).

I bulini corti su supporto massiccio (VIII classe) sono presenti in tutta la serie, in particolare coi tipi *à biseau* carenoide (28, 29, 30 e 33).

L'insieme di queste osservazioni suggerisce una continuità tipologica in tutta la serie.

D. – Lame troncate. Sono presenti in tutta la serie, con indice oscillante entro un breve intervallo (3.6–12.6).

E. – Lame ritoccate. Sono presenti con indice stabile in tutta la sequenza sauveterriana (4.5–11.0); hanno un brusco aumento nella sequenza castelnoviana (28.0 in AB1–2; 34.4 in AA). Questo aumento è determinato da lame e lamelle ad incavi e a ritocco denticolato (II classe), presenti sporadicamente nella sequenza sauveterriana (AC4, AC2), e largamente dominanti nella sequenza castelnoviana (63.6–69.0 %).

F. – Becchi e Perforatori. Sono presenti in tutta la serie (con l'eccezione delle industrie di AC4 e di AC2) con indici bassi (0.9–5.1).

L. – Pezzi scagliati. Sono presenti con pochi esemplari soprattutto all'apice della sequenza sauveterriana (1.8–1.5 %).

N. – Coltelli a dorso. Sono presenti in tutta la sequenza sauveterriana (con l'eccezione di AC1) con indici bassi (1.9–6.8).

O. – Punte. I rari esemplari sono presenti alla fine della sequenza sauveterriana (1.5 % in AC1) e nella sequenza castelnoviana (1.7–0.8 %).

Struttura interna dei gruppi tipologici della categoria delle armature microlitiche

1 – Punte su scheggia laminare o su lama. L'indice di questo gruppo è stabile nella sequenza sauveterriana (16.5–10.0) con l'eccezione di AC5, dove questa categoria di armature non è rappresentata; diminuisce nella sequenza castelnoviana (7.6–4.6).

Nella serie pare documentata una tendenza all'aumento delle punte-troncatura (I classe) a carico delle punte a dorso (II classe).

2 – Punte a dorso. L'indice delle punte a dorso presenta un progressivo aumento nella sequenza sauveterriana (da 2.9 in AE a 14.0 in AC2) e quindi diminuisce nella sequenza castelnoviana (0.7 in AB1–2; 0 in AA).

3 – Segmenti. L'indice dei segmenti inizia con il valore di 11.4% nell'industria dello strato AE, raggiunge i valori

massimi nalla parte medio-inferiore della sequenza sauveterriana, con l'apice (27.8%) in AC8–9, e quindi diminuisce progressivamente fino ai valori minimi, raggiunti nella sequenza castelnoviana (1.4–1.3%). È evidente una flessione dell'indice in corrispondenza di AC5–AC4.

I tipi lunghi sono presenti in tutta la serie, e tendono ad aumentare verso l'alto.

I tipi corti, regolari e simmetrici, sono presenti esclusivamente nella parte inferiore-media della sequenza sauveterriana (AE–AC3).

I pochi esemplari a dorso sinusoidale sono pure presenti nella parte inferiore-media della sequenza sauveterriana (AE–AC3); quelli a margine opposto ritoccato si trovano soltanto in AE–AC6.

I segmenti trapezoidali senza ritocco sul margine opposto (tipi 9 e 10) si collocano nella parte medio-alta della sequenza sauveterriana (AC5–AC1).

Il segmento trapezoidale con tutti i margini ritoccati è presente, al contrario, solo nella parte medio-bassa della stessa sequenza (AE–AC7).

I rari segmenti ad estremità ottusa sono presenti solo alla base della sequenza sauveterriana (AE e AC8–9).

4 – Dorsi e Troncature. Il loro indice è massimo alla base della sequenza sauveterriana (12.4); quindi diminuisce bruscamente mantenendo una certa stabilità (4.2–1.3). Queste armature mancano del tutto nelle industrie degli strati AC6, AC5 e AA.

II classe: microliti a un dorso e due troncature sono presenti solo nella parte inferiore-media della sequenza sauveterriana (AE–AC4).

5 – Triangoli. Nella sequenza sauveterriana l'indice dei triangoli varia tra 49.2 e 22.1; diminuisce nella sequenza castelnoviana (12.5 in AB1–2; 2.6 in AA). All'interno della sequenza sauveterriana raggiunge i valori massimi alla base (AE: 41.9) e nella parte medio-alta (AC4: 41.5; AC3: 49.2; AC2: 40.7; AC1: 47.7), mentre ha una flessione nella parte medio-bassa, con un minimo in AC8–9 (22.1).

I tipi principali sono rappresentati in tutta la sequenza sauveterriana: in questo senso non vi sono tipi che si possono considerare indicatori stratigrafici (cf. « Rhythms » in this volume). Tuttavia alcuni tipi sono frequenti soltanto in fasi ben determinate.

Suddividendo i triangoli in quattro grandi categorie, cioè in triangoli isosceli (classi I, II e III), triangoli scaleni corti (classi IV, V e VI), triangoli scaleni lunghi a base lunga (classi VII, VIII e IX) e triangoli scaleni lunghi a base corta (classi X, XI e XII) si può osservare che in tutta la sequenza sauveterriana e all'inizio della sequenza castelnoviana (AB1–2) gli indici dei triangoli scaleni corti e dei triangoli scaleni lunghi a base lunga sono stabili. L'indice complessivo delle classi IV, V e VI oscilla tra 33.3 e 20.0; l'indice delle classi VII, VIII e IX oscilla tra 22.6 e 12.8, con una flessione in AC5 (11.1). L'indice dei triangoli isosceli (classi I, II e III) da valori elevati nella parte

medio-inferiore della sequenza (56.4–51.3) diminuisce progressivamente (18.0 in AC2, 8.1 in AC1); questo processo riguarda sia i tipi lunghi (I classe) sia i tipi corti (II classe). L'indice dei triangoli scaleni lunghi a base corta da valori bassi nella parte medio-inferiore della sequenza (6.8–2.2) aumenta sino a raggiungere, all'apice, valori elevati (45.9 in AC2, 51.6 in AC1). In questo processo spicca l'assetto anomalo dell'industria dello strato AC5.

L'indice complessivo dei triangoli a tre lati ritoccati è elevato alla base e all'apice della sequenza sauveterriana (AE: 54.5; AC2: 37.7; AC1: 43.5); nella parte media oscilla tra 10.3 e 21.8. Tra i triangoli isosceli i tipi a tre lati ritoccati sono frequenti soltanto alla base della sequenza (AE: 43.5%); il loro indice scende poi bruscamente, fino ad azzerarsi all'apice. Tra i triangoli scaleni corti i tipi a tre lati ritoccati sono frequenti alla base (!?) e all'apice della sequenza (AE: 63.6; AC2: 64.3; AC1: 78.6%); nella parte media oscillano tra il 33.3 e lo 0%. I triangoli scaleni lunghi a base lunga a tre lati ritoccati sono relativamente frequenti soltanto alla base della sequenza (AE: 71.4%) il loro indice quindi oscilla tra 12.5 e 36.4. Infine i triangoli scaleni lunghi a base corta, presenti sporadicamente alla base della sequenza, aumentano nella parte medio-alta fino a raggiungere indici elevati al suo apice (AC2: 42.9; AC1: 37.5).

6 – Punte a due dorsi. L'indice complessivo di questo gruppo varia nella sequenza sauveterriana tra 12.0 e 30.0, con valori più elevati nella parte media della sequenza e un picco in AC5 (AC6: 30.0; AC5: 47.0; AC4: 27.8). Diminuisce nella sequenza castelnoviana (11.8–3.3).

Vi sono due fasi nelle quali si sviluppano i tipi larghi relativamente corti della II classe: una fase più antica alla base della sequenza sauveterriana, l'altra, più recente, all'apice della stessa sequenza e all'inizio della sequenza castelnoviana (indice delle punte a due dorsi corte in AE: 43.7; AC8: 21.7; AC7: 10.2; AC6: 9.4; AC5: 8.3; AC4: 10.6; AC3: 13.6; AC2: 54.8; AC1: 31.0; AB1–2: 41.2). Corrispondentemente nella fase media della sequenza sauveterriana si affermano le punte a due dorsi lunghe della I classe, il cui indice, tra AC7 e AC3, oscilla attorno a 90.

7 – Trapezi. Sono presenti esclusivamente nella sequenza castelnoviana, con indice largamente dominante (AB1–2: 61.1; AA: 88.2).

Considerando le due industrie degli strati AB1–2 e AA come tappe di un processo evolutivo, si osserva:
– la diminuzione dei romboidi (38.7–25.5%), e tra essi delle forme corte (tipo 2); si affermano all'interno della classe le forme lunghe;
– l'aumento dei trapezi lunghi (18.7–25.5%) e tra essi di quelli a base leggermente obliqua (tipo 5);
– l'aumento dei trapezi corti (8.0–15.5%), soprattutto di quelli molto corti a base normale concava (tipo 8);
– la stabilità dei trapezi assimmetrici a base obliqua concava (14.7–12.7%), all'interno dei quali dimin-

uiscono quelli a troncatura (punta) convessa ed aumentano quelli a troncatura (punta) concava;
- l'aumento dei trapezi simmetrici (37.3–43.6%), determinato dal tipo a troncature concave.
8 – Punte e lamelle a ritocco erto marginale. Questo gruppo, documentato nella sequenza sauveterriana (7.8–0.6%), è rappresentato soprattutto da frammenti.

Evoluzione tipologica e strutturale della sequenza

a) Fase sauveterriana antica. A Romagnano III l'industria dello strato AE comprende un piccolo numero di strumenti (31) e un discreto numero di armature (105), esclusi i frammenti.

I grattatoi sono rappresentati da tipi su supporto laminare, lunghi a fronte obliqua, da tipi su scheggia corti, frontali e ogivali. Tra le schegge ritoccate è presente qualche grattatoi irregolare/skrobacz. I bulini sono diedri e su frattura. Sono presenti qualche troncatura, qualche lama ritoccata e un coltello a dorso. L'insieme si inquadra bene nella sequenza sauveterriana.

Tra le armature dominano i triangoli (41.9%) su punte su scheggia laminare o su lama (10.5), segmenti (11.4), dorsi e troncature (12.4) e punte a due dorsi (15.2). Tra i triangoli prevalgono i tipi isosceli, e tra essi una larga parte presenta tre lati ritoccati. Va sottolineato l'indice relativamente elevato (rispetto all'altra parte della sequenza sauveterriana) dei dorsi e troncature.

b) Fase sauveterriana media. È la fase meglio rappresentata in tutta la serie di Romagnano III.

Tra gli strumenti prevalgono i grattatoi (30.8–42.7%) su schegge ritoccate (23.3–32.7) e bulini (10.7–18.7). Gli indici degli altri gruppi "varia" no entro i seguenti intervalli: lame troncate 4.4–12.6; lame ritoccate 4.7–11.0; becchi e perforatori 0–3.7; coltelli a dorso 1.9–4.4; pezzi scagliati 0–0.9. Non vi sono punte. La struttura di questa categoria resta quindi abbastanza stabile.

Nel gruppo dei grattatoi le classi dei grattatoi su supporto laminare (I–VI) costituiscono circa la metà dei pezzi (47.6–56.5%); tra essi sono presenti tipi a fronte obliqua e convergenti. Tra i grattatoi su scheggia sono presenti tipi corti e molto corti, a ventaglio; i semicircolari o subcircolari sono rari, i circolari rarissimi. È caratteristica la classe dei grattatoi su scheggia ogivali, a spalla e a muso.

Nel gruppo delle schegge ritoccate le classi più caratteristiche sono rappresentate da skrobacz e da denticolati. Tra i bulini sono caratteristici i tipi a supporto massiccio. Nei gruppi delle lame troncate e dei becchi non si incontrano forme microlamellari, che si incontrano in altre industrie.

Sono infine presenti dei coltelli a dorso curvo su supporto laminare, ad incavi nella parte basale, che si distinguono nella maggior parte dei casi dal coltello di Rouffignac descritto per Claude Barrière, per la presenza dell'assottigliamento dell'area bulbare.

Nella categoria dei microliti si osserva: la tendenza alla diminuzione dei segmenti D (27.8–14.8%) e all'aumento dei triangoli T (22.1–49.2%); la relativa stabilità di punte a due dorsi PD (26.1–30.0 – 27.8–12.0%), punte su scheggia laminare o su lama (16.5–10.4%) e punte a dorso (2.8–9.8%). Dorsi e troncature si riducono a qualche esemplare (2.3–1.6%).

Tra le punte su scheggia laminare o su lama si nota la tendenza alla diminuzione dei tipi a dorso, e un corrispondente aumento dei tipi su troncatura. Tra i segmenti diminuiscono le forme corte e larghe, a favore di forme lunghe e strette. Tra i triangoli diminuiscono le forme isosceli (TN, TM), rimpiazzate da forme scalene soprattutto lunghe e a base corta (TH, TE); diminuiscono fortemente i tipi isosceli a tre lati ritoccati. Tra le punte a due dorsi dominano i tipi lunghi PD (55–90%).

c) Fase sauveterriana recente. È rappresentata dalle due industrie di AC2 e AC1.

La struttura degli strumenti comuni non varia rispetto alla fase media. Tra i grattatoi diminuiscono i tipi su supporto laminare, mentre aumentano i tipi su scheggia ogivali, a spalla e a muso. Tra le schegge (B) ritoccate scompaiono quelle a ritocco denticolato. Tra le lame ritoccate (E) compaiono tipi ad incavi e denticolati.

Tra le armature si prolungano le tendenze evolutive della fase media: nel gruppo delle punte su scheggia laminare o su lama si affermano maggiormente i tipi a troncatura; nel gruppo dei segmenti i tipi corti sono rimpiazzati dai tipi lunghi; tra i triangoli dominano gli scaleni.

Le modificazioni più importanti, che caratterizzano questa fase, sono costituite dall'affermarsi dei triangoli scaleni lunghi a base corta, con tre lati ritoccati cf. Montclus (TE), che rappresentano circa, il 20% di tutti i triangoli e dalla diminuzione delle punte a due dorsi lunghe, alla quale corrisponde l'affermarsi dei tipi corti dello stesso gruppo.

d) Il problema dell'industria dello strato AC5 di Romagnano III. Nella sequenza sauveterriana di Romagnano III la fase media si presenta come un processo evolutivo uniforme, che si raccorda con la struttura della fase antica e che si prolunga nella fase recente. Tuttavia in questo processo uniforme si osserva un fenomeno anomalo, che è costituito dall'industria dello strato AC5. Essa rientra indubbiamente nel quadro tipologico del Sauveterriano, e più precisamente nella fase media già descritta; ma si distingue nettamente, all'interno della sequenza, per i seguenti caratteri anomali:

- inversione del rapporto strumenti/armature;
- tra le armature: assenza di punte su scheggia laminare o su lama; basso indice di segmenti laminare o su lama; basso indice di segmenti (7.8%); elevato indice di punte a due dorsi (47.0%);
- dimensioni delle armature generalmente un po' più grandi;
- tra i grattatoi: assenza di tettiformi e di ogivali su lama (classi IV e V); indice elevato di tipi su scheggia a ventaglio, e indice basso di tipi su scheggia tettiformi, ogivali, a spalla e a muso;
- tra i triangoli: assenza di tipi isosceli corti.

Queste osservazioni potrebbero suggerire l'appartenenza

dell'industria dello strato AC5 ad una sequenza sauveterriana parallela a quella svilupatasi nella conca di Trento questa ipotesi di lavoro è però priva di altri riscontri.

e) Le fasi castelnoviane. Nella serie di Romagnano III sono rappresentate soltanto una fase antica e una fase recente, nella quale compare già la ceramica.

In esse la struttura degli strumenti comuni continua, in un certo, senso, quella sauveterriana, differenziandosi dall'ultimo termine di questa per l'elevato indice di grattatoi A (37.2–40.2%), per la diminuzione delle schegge ritoccate B (10.2–9.0%) e dei bulini C (5.9–4.9%), per l'aumento delle lame troncate D (9.3–8.2%) e per il forte aumento delle lame ritoccate E (28.0–34.4%).

All'interno del gruppo dei grattatoi i tipi su supporto laminare dominano largamente i tipi su scheggia (65.9–73.8%). Il forte aumento delle lame ritoccate è determinato essenzialmente da lame a incavi e denticolate.

Tra le armature si osserva una forte diminuzione dei gruppi caratteristici del Sauveterriano (segmenti: 1.4–1.3%; triangoli: 12.5–2.6%; punte a due dorsi: 11.8–3.3%; dorsi e troncature: 4.2–0%; punte su scheggia laminare o su lama: 7.6–4.6%) che tuttavia persistono. Compaiono ed hanno subito grande sviluppo i trapezi – gruppo 7 (61.1–88.2%).

Conclusioni

ATTRIBUZIONE CULTURALE. I dati analitici mettono in evidenza nella serie mesolitica di Romagnano III due complessi industriali, uno più antico rappresentato dalle industrie degli strati AF–AC1, l'altro più recente rappresentato dalle industrie degli strati AB 1–2 e AA. Il contenuto archeologico del taglio AB3 rappresenta con grande probabilità il risultato di una commistione meccanica tra il termine superiore del complesso più antico e il termine inferiore del complesso più recente.

Il complesso inferiore presenta un'associazione di tipi sulla cui base è comunemente definito il Sauveterriano, inteso in senso stretto: schegge a ritocco denticolato (classe IV del gruppo B), coltelli a dorso curvo cfr. Rouffignac (gruppo N), piccoli segmenti (gruppo 3), vari tipi di picoli triangoli (gruppo 5), vari tipi di punte a due dorsi = punte de Sauveterre (gruppo 6). Il complesso superiore presenta un'associazione di tipi caratteristica del Castelnoviano, e cioè: lame e lamelle di forma regolare, a sezione trapezoidale o triangolare, a incavi o a ritocco denticolato (classe II del gruppo E = *lamelle Montbani*) e vari tipi di trapezi (gruppo 7). La sequenza Sauveterriano-Castelnoviano è nota in vari giacimenti mesolitici europei: in Italia nei ripari Gaban e di Pradestel, nella conca di Trento, e in varie grotte del Carso Triestino (Grotta Azzurra, Grotta Benussi, Grotta della Tartaruga) e Slovenia (Mala Triglavca); in Francia nella Baume de Montclus. Analoghe serie francesi presentano alla base il Sauveterriano, seguito da industrie a trapezi che rientrano nel cultura di Cuzoul, cf. Pré-Rocadourien (Le Martinet, Rouffignac), (cf. "Pre-Neolithic base..." in this volume).

Nonostante la brusca modificazione, che marca il passaggio tra i due complessi (modificazioni che si riscontrano all'inizio del VII millennio cal. BC in quasi tutte le differenti aree culturali d'Europa meridionale), nella sequenza della Valle dell'Adige si osserva la persistenza di una tradizione locale per oltre 3000 anni. Questa continuità è evidente soprattutto negli strumenti; in tutta la serie di Romagnano si osserva la presistenza di grattatoi su lama tettiformi e ogivali, e di grattatoi su scheggia a ventaglio, corti, molto corti, ogivali, a spalla e a muso; di grattatoi irregulari/*skrobacz*, *raclettes*, raschiatoi; di bulini su supporto massiccio; di punte su scheggia laminare o su lama. Nelle industrie castelnoviane sono inoltre presenti, anche se rari, microliti caratteristici della fase sauveterriana più recente.

Periodizzazione della sequenza mesolitica della Conca di Trento

Per meglio comprendere i fenomeni evolutivi della sequenza mesolitica atesina è necessario tener presenti anche i risultati dello studio delle industrie mesolitiche degli altri siti della Conca di Trento (Vàtte di Zambana, Pradestel, Gaban, cf.) soprattutto per gli intervalli cronologici non rappresentati nella serie di Romagnano III (cioè per i termini più recenti della sequenza sauveterriana, documentati a Vatte di Zambana 10–7, e per i termini intermedi della sequenza castelnoviana, documentati a Pradestel e al Riparo Gaban) e nei casi di serie stratigrafiche meglio scandite (come in generale nel giacimento di Pradestel).

Per esigenze di chiarezza espositiva faremo riferimento, nel descrivere i fenomeni evolutivi, alle seguenti fasi nelle quali è stata suddivisa la sequenza, precisando che non vi sono, tra una fase e l'altra, brusche interruzioni, ma che si tratta di stadi di un processo continuo.

a) Fase sauveterriana antica (Romagnano III AF–AE; probabilmente Pradestel M). Quattro datazioni assolute comprese tra c. 9400 e 8900 anni cal. BC, si riferiscono agli strati AF e AE di Romagnano III.

b) Fase sauveterriana media (Romagnano III AC8–9, AC7, AC6, AC4, AC3; Pradestel L14÷L1). Numerose le datazioni assolute. Il termine inferiore è datato a Romagnano III (strato AC8–9) c. 8400 cal. BC, cioè tra 8450 e 8300 anni cal. BC, a Pradestel (strato L8) c. 8500 cal. BC. Il termine superiore è datato a Romagnano III (strato AC3) c. 7640 e 7550 cal. BC. Le datazioni degli strati della serie di Romagnano compresi entro i due termini (AC7, AC5–6, AC4) sono in accordo con la successione stratigrafica.

c) Fase sauveterriana recente (Romagnano III AC2, AC1; Pradestel H2–H1). Vi si riferiscono tre datazioni assolute: Romagnano III AC2, c. 7610 cal. BC e AC1, c. 7300 cal. BC; Pradestel H, 7350 cal. BC

d) Fase sauveterriana finale (Vatte di Zambana 10 e 7; Pradestel F; non è rappresentata nella serie di Romagnano III). Sei datazioni assolute, comprese tra c. 7050 e 6850 cal. BC, si riferiscono agli strati 10 e 7 di Vatte.

e) Fase castelnoviana antica (Romagnano III AB1–2; probabilmente Pradestel E). Tre datazioni radiometriche, comprese tra c. 6900 e 6450 cal. BC, si riferiscono allo strato AB1–2 di Romagnano III.

f) Fase castelnoviana media (Pradestel D; non rappresentata nella serie di Romagnano III). Una datazione radiometrica, c. 5900 cal. BC, si riferisce allo strato D di Pradestel.

g) Fase castelnoviana recente (Romagnano III AA; probabilmente Pradestel A). In questa fase, che per le caratteristiche dell'industria litica rientra senza dubbio nella sequenza castelnoviana, compaiono i primi frammenti di ceramica: essa può pertanto essere considerata una fase di transizione al Neolitico Antico (tipo Gaban). Una datazione radiometrica attribuisce allo strato AA di Romagnano III un'età di c. 5500 cal. BC.

In conclusione si possono fissare sette fasi, la maggior parte delle quali è rappresentata nella serie di Romagnano III. Complessivamente la sequenza ha una durata superiore a 3000 anni, e i suoi stadi evolutivi così sì collocano cronologicamente:

a – fase sauveterriana antica: circa 9300–8650 cal. BC;
b – fase sauveterriana media: circa 8650–7600 cal. BC;
c – fase sauveterriana recente: circa 7600–7200 cal. BC;
d – fase sauveterriana finale: circa 7200–6800 cal. BC;
e – fase castelnoviana antica: inizia attorno al 6800 cal. BC;
f – fase castelnoviana media: attorno al 6000 cal. BC;
g – fase castelnoviana recente: attorno a 5500 cal. BC

Comment in 2006

The sequence from Romagnano III, partly repeated and supplemented in the upper part by the results from Riparo Gaban (cf. in this volume), turns out to be typologically representative (especially through the tectiform scrapers and big backed knives) for the entire region of North Italy starting from Carsto Triestino (and western Slovenia) and ending in Liguria and perhaps also French Provence (Max Escalon de Fronton cites tectiform examples in his publications).

On the other hand, the observed variability, especially in the microliths group, reflects the evolutionary trend known from a vaster territory (cf. "Koine" and "Rhythms").

It should also be recalled that in similarity to Iberia (cf.), the local Castelovian of Conca di Trento was ultimately ceramized (Romagnano III, layer AA with Gaban type pottery), although the evolution here was not as deep as that observed in the west (cf. "Ceramization"), meaning also in southern France. It was much the same, however, virtually all over Italy.

6.3. Central Italy (Tuscany)

As stated earlier, Tuscany presents a local variant of the Sauveterrian, even though the overall evolutionary sequence is much like what it was in the north. The oldest known Sauveterrian comes from successive layers of the Isola Santa site, explored in 1976–1977 by Carlo Tozzi. An analysis of this is presented here below, demonstrating the differences between the North Italian and Central Italian Sauveterrian (cf. earlier remarks on regional differentiation). A statistical analysis places Isola Santa in the middle phase of this culture.

Isola Santa
(co-author – C. Tozzi and M. Dini)
Il sito e la sequenza stratigrafica (Fig. 3.3a–b)
Il giacimento è situato sul fianco sinistro della valle della Turrite Secca (Alpi Apuane), frazione del Comune di Careggine in Provincia di Lucca, alla quota di 510 metri. Gli scavi di salvataggio (Carlo Tozzi) si svolsero nel 1976 e 1977.

Lo scavo fu condotto seguendo la stratigrafia e la litologia naturale, suddividendo le singole unità lito-stratigrafiche in tagli artificiali di circa 5–8 cm di spessore; il terreno fu setacciato in acqua con setacci a maglia di 2 mm.

Osservazioni sulla stratigrafia culturale

Tutta la collezione è sauveterriana, con l'eccezione di alcuni pezzi del taglio 4e e del taglio 4d, e si suddivide nei vari sottoinsiemi provenienti dai tagli 4d–4a.

In primo luogo sembra che la continuità e l'omogeneità litologica uniscano da un lato i tagli 4a, 4b e 4c, dall'altro uniscano i tagli 4d e 4e. In secondo luogo non vi sono strati sterili o quasi sterili, che potrebbero separare i livelli ricchi di materiali. Se a ciò aggiungiamo l'informazione che i sedimenti del sito di Isola Santa sono stati riforniti con continuità dai sedimenti di pendìo (colluvi), ci si potrà rendere conto del limitato significato della serie archeologica legata a ogni singolo taglio, considerando che i tagli sono stati stabiliti in modo almeno in parte arbitrario.

Di conseguenza le industrie legate a questi tagli non rappresentano delle occupazioni ben individualizzate, ma risultano da innumerevoli o multiple frequentazioni del sito nel corso di un lungo periodo di tempo; possiamo immaginare dei va e vieni stagionali con una sedimentazione permanente sia geologica di pendìo sia del materiale archeologico.

Le datazioni radiometriche

Due serie di datazioni sono state effettuate sui carboni: una presso il Laboratorio di Firenze, l'altra, più ampia, presso il Laboratorio di Geocronologia dell'Università di Roma.

Le date ottenute dal Laboratorio di Roma sono sette, così suddivise tra i vari tagli:

taglio 4a R–1525a: 7380±90 BP
taglio 4a R–1525: 7460±130 BP
taglio 4b R–1526: 8840±120 BP
taglio 4c R–1527: 8590±90 BP
taglio 4d R–1528: 8780±110BP
taglio 4e R–1529: 9220±90 BP
taglio 5a R–1524: 10720±120 BP

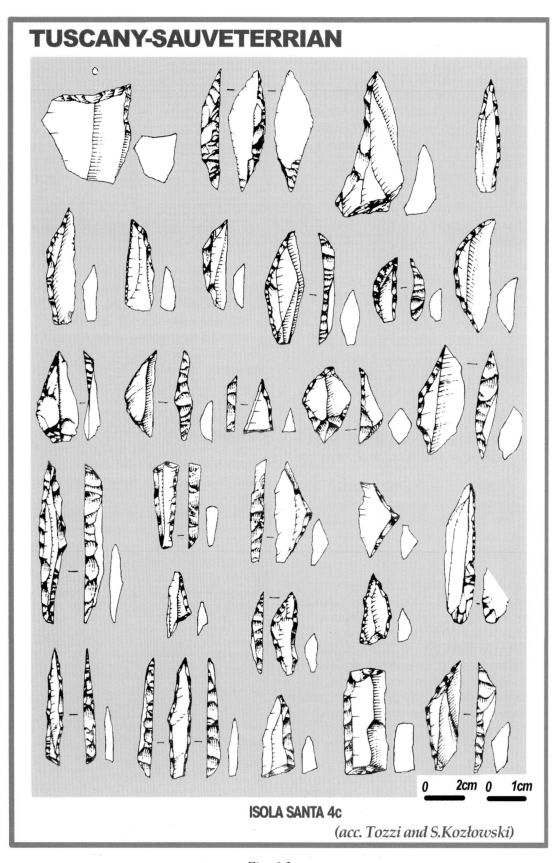

TUSCANY-SAUVETERRIAN

ISOLA SANTA 4c

(acc. Tozzi and S.Kozłowski)

Fig. 6.3a

TUSCANY-SAUVETERRIAN

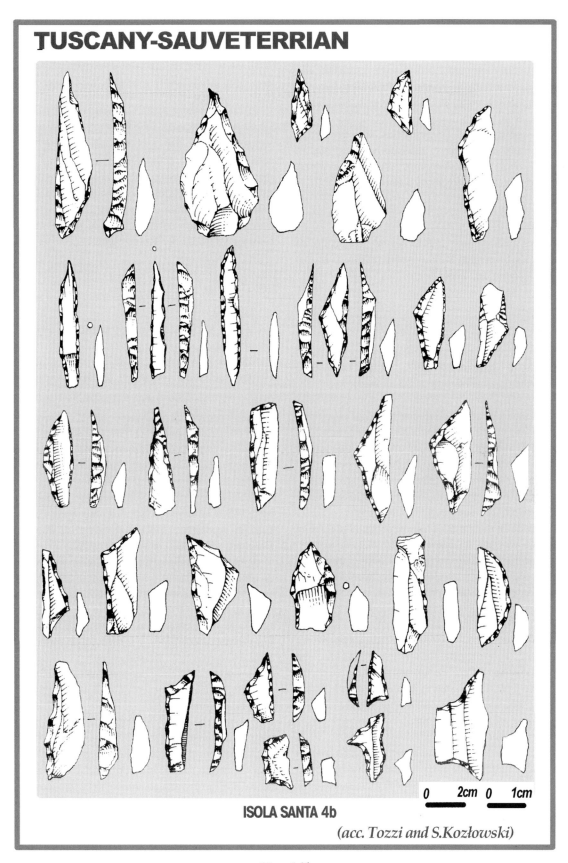

0 2cm 0 1cm

ISOLA SANTA 4b

(acc. Tozzi and S.Kozłowski)

Fig. 6.3b

Gli strumenti

La descrizione e la classificazione tipologica della litica di Isola Santa si appoggia sulla lista proposta nel 1983 per Romagano III da Alberto Broglio e Stefan K. Kozłowski (cf. "Trentino sequence"). La lista è in principio molto dettagliata, ma per questa pubblicazione è stata un po' semplificata perché gli studi fatti sulle collezioni sauveterriane hanno permesso di razionalizzarla ulteriormente. Il sistema utilizzato in questo articolo può essere facilmente assimilato al sistema di Georges Laplace, da tempo assai utilizzato in Italia. La sola difficoltà che interessa questa "traduzione" riguarda la classe dei "Dorsi e troncature", che è stata divisa secondo le nostre idee in "Triangoli" (i pezzi con due bordi convergenti) e in "Dorsi e Troncature" classici, cioè i pezzi a bordi paralleli.

Comment in 2006

In a few cases the letter markings of typological groups of the original were changed to suit model proposed in this volume (cf. "About this book").

Gli strumenti comuni

Gruppi tipologici e struttura interna

La struttura interna degli strumenti comuni a livello di gruppi tipologici sembra assai stabile, anche se si osserva una lenta evoluzione nel tempo di alcuni indici.

Dominano i Grattatoi (A), le Schegge Ritoccate (B) e le Lame Ritoccate (E) e ciascuno di questi gruppi raggiunge un indice di circa il 20–30%. Seguono le Troncature – D, che superano il 10% e i Bulini – C (2–6%). Gli altri gruppi (Perforatori – F; Coltelli a Dorso – N; Punte – O e Scagliati – L) sono debolmente rappresentati o del tutto assenti.

In questa statistica non sono stati contati rari strumenti di tipo epigravettiano: due nel 4d e due nel 4e.

Questa struttura differisce considerevolmente da quella tipica del Sauveterriano dell'Italia settentrionale (cf. above); a Romagnano III i grattatoi sono più numerosi, mentre le schegge ritoccate sono rappresentate più debolmente. Si nota pure a Isola Santa il tasso più elevato di lame ritoccate, che sono il 20–30%, a Romagnano III sono il 5–12%, ma al Gaban salgono al 19–29%.

Queste differenze non sembrano tali da differenziare regionalmente la tradizione sauveterriana italiana, ma indicano piuttosto le differenze funzionali che esistono tra il sito toscano e trentino. E ben evidente che a Isola Santa si producono più spesso strumenti *ad hoc* (vedi i ritocchi di utilizzazione più numerosi), mentre nei siti del nord i gruppi vivevano più stabilmente.

Se questa osservazione è giusta, può darsi che l'aumento del numero dei grattatoi e la diminuzione del numero delle schegge ritoccate nella parte superiore dello strato 4 di Isola Santa indichi una certa stabilizzazione dell'abitato alla fine della sequenza da porre in relazione a un cambiamento di funzione del sito (più residenziale e meno campo di caccia?).

A. Grattatoi. L'indice dei grattatoi oscilla tra il 20 e il 30% degli strumenti ritoccati. Le forme molto allungate e allungate su lama (gruppo I) sono dominanti ad eccezione del taglio 4c e oscillano intorno al 60–65% dei grattatoi, inclusi i frammenti. Al secondo posto troviamo i grattatoi allungati su scheggia (gruppo IX), che diminuiscono di numero dal 25–30% nel taglio 4c al 6–7% nel taglio 4a. Vi sono inoltre delle forme corte e circolari (gruppi X e XII), come pure dei grattatoi estremamente corti (gruppo XI). Tutte queste forme sono fatte su schegge e hanno degli indici poco stabili.

La struttura descritta qui sopra non sembra essere molto differente da quella della conca di Trento e alcune differenze tra le due serie possono essere spiegate con la scarsità numerica della serie di Isola Santa. Si possono tuttavia scorgere alcune differenze regionali nelle serie sauveterriane italiane riscontrabili in alcune classi di grattatoi, ben rappresentate al nord, ma assenti o quasi in Toscana. Si tratta soprattutto delle forme seguenti della tipologia stabilita per Romagnano III:

– classe III : grattatoi molto allungati su lama a fronte obliqua,
– classe IV : grattatoi molto allungati su lama a fronte ogivale,
– classe V : grattatoi molto allungati su lama a fronte tettiforme,
– classe XVI : grattatoi corti e allungati su scheggia a fronte ogivale, tettiforme, a *épaulement* e a muso.

Questa mancanza di forme "nordiche" segna sicuramente una differenza che possiamo dire "culturale"/stilistico tra la conca di Trento e la Toscana durante il Mesolitico medio. La presenza di grattatoi su lama fratturata (gruppo I) può spiegarsi sia a causa dell'intensa utilizzazione, sia per frattura volontaria (piu probabile).

B. Schegge ritoccate. Si trovano in tutti i tagli con indici tra il 26 e il 32% e sono rappresentate a Isola Santa da tutti i gruppi tipologici (I–VI) individuati al nord (*skrobacz*, raclettes, denticolati, schegge ritoccate).

C. Bulini. Oscillano tra il 2 e il 6% e sono rappresentati da quasi tutti i gruppi tipologici conosciuti al nord (bulini semplici a un pan, su frattura, diedri e trasversali), salvo quelli del gruppo V, bulini d'angolo allungati su troncatura. L'assenza di questi ultimi può essere dovuta anche a un fattore statistico, quale l'insufficiente numerosità della serie.

D. Troncature. Sono poco numerose (11–17%), allungate e larghe, con troncature poco oblique; sono molto simili a quelle del nord.

E. Lame ritoccate. Oscillano tra il 20 e il 32% e il loro indice diminuisce nel tempo. La maggior parte di esse ha un ritocco più d'utilizzazione che di fattura intenzionale e vi si trovano tutte le classi principali conosciute al nord (uno o due bordi ritoccati, con incavi e denticolati, le ultime due nella variante unilateral). Vi si possono aggiungere le lame a ritocco parziale e non continuo, che possono essere il risultato di una "stabilità" meno accentuata dell'abitato sul sito toscano.

F – O. Altri gruppi tipologici. Gli altri gruppi tipologici

degli strumenti comuni sono poco rappresentati a Isola Santa. Questo fenomeno riguarda i Perforatori (F), le Punte (O) e gli Scagliati (L), che tuttavia rientrano bene nello standard tipologico conosciuto al nord.

L'unico esemplare (frammento mediano) di Coltello a dorso (gruppo N) proviene dal taglio 4d e non rientra bene nello standard tipologico conosciuto al nord, dove si trovano piuttosto le forme a dorso curvo; tuttavia essendo unico e frammentario non è molto convincente.

Le Armature (K)

Gruppi tipologici e struttura interna

1. A differenza degli strumenti comuni le armature hanno una struttura almeno in alcuni casi particolari molto dinamica e si evolvono nel tempo. A Isola Santa l'evoluzione dei gruppi tipologici si realizza in due settori: le Punte a dorso (2) diminuiscono dal 36 all'8%, seguendo la stratigrafia; i Triangoli (5) aumentano dal 14 al 60% alla fine della sequenza. Si può osservare che l'evoluzione riguarda i due gruppi di microliti meglio rappresentati. Gli altri gruppi (Punte su Scheggia Laminare – 1, Dorsi e Troncature – 4, Punte a Due Dorsi – 6) hanno degli indici sia assai stabili (circa il 6–12%), sia in leggera diminuzione nel tempo (ad esempio i Segmenti – 3).

La struttura interna sopra descritta differisce da quella delle industrie del nord (il tasso di alcuni indici – 2, 4, 6 – che differisce costantemente da quelli di Romagnano III), mentre gli altri indici (1, 3, 5) sono simili nelle due regioni e alcuni essi pongono le serie di Isola Santa a livello del Sauveterriano medio e recente, ad esempio gli indici di 3 e 5 a Romagnano III.

2. Punte a dorso su lamella. Il loro indice diminuisce dal 36 all'8% e tutti i tipi conosciuti al nord sono presenti a Isola Santa.

3. Segmenti. Sono molto meno numerosi nei tagli superiori (3–4%) rispetto a quelli inferiori (18%). Come al nord, le forme allungate e corte regolari (gruppo I) dominano le altre forme note a Romagnano III; le forme a dorso sinuoso, gruppo II, sono rare e le forme quasi trapezoidali sono pressoché assenti, gruppo III. Questa assenza si può spiegare con la scarsità numerica della serie di Isola Santa (tra 12 e 29 esemplari nel sito toscano; tra 4 e 49 pezzi nel sito trentino).

4. Dorsi e troncature. Si sottolineano le differenze tra le definizioni di Georges Laplace e quelle di Alberto Broglio e Stefan K. Kozłowski; qui saranno utilizzate le seconde e cioè che un Dorso e Troncatura deve avere i due lati paralleli o sub paralleli. A Isola Santa oscillano intorno al 10–17% e vi sono rappresentate tutte le clasi note al nord.

5. Triangoli. È il gruppo che evolve più rapidamente nel Sauveterriano, ma anche in tutto il Mesolitico dell'Europa occidentale e centrale (cf. "Koine" and "Rhythms").

A Isola Santa costatiamo soprattutto l'aumento nel tempo dell'indice dei triangoli all'interno del gruppo delle "armature", che passa dal 14 al 61%, e ciò ripete l'evoluzione conosciuta al nord. Inoltre nell'insieme delle armature si osservano gli stessi cambiamenti sia

al nord – sostituzione dei triangoli isosceli corte (= TN) da parte degli scaleni lunghi a base corta (= TH, TE), con stabilità dei triangoli scaleni corti (= TO) e scaleni a base lunga (= TR) – che in Toscana, dove si constata una evoluzione un po' diversa da quella sopradescritta. Anche se generalmente i triangoli isosceli diminuiscono con il tempo, i triangoli scaleni corti e gli scaleni a base lunga non conservano la stessa stabilità osservata al nord. I primi infatti aumentano, mentre i secondi nello stesso intervallo di tempo diminuiscono. Le cause sono di origine non statistica, poiché le serie conosciute variano da 53 a 128 esemplari, e inoltre i triangoli scaleni a base corta a Isola Santa sono meno numerosi che nel nord, anche nel Sauveterriano medio o recente: a Romagnano III il tasso dei triangoli di Montclus (= TE) è più elevato rispetto a Isola Santa anche nel Sauveterriano antico (3–5%) e raggiunge nella fase recente del Sauveterriano l'indice di circa il 50%.

6. Punte a due dorsi (Sauveterre = PD e PA). Sono stabili per tutta la sequenza (5–12%), con la dominanza qui come al nord dei tipi allungati.

7. Trapezi. Presenti nei due tagli superiori non sono di tipo castelnoviano; tuttavia anche nel Sauveterriano recente di Montclus in Francia (strati 15 e 16) i trapezi non sono di tipo castelnoviano.

Conclusioni

1) L'industria dello strato 4 è tipicamente sauveterriana, sono stati esclusi solo alcuni strumenti di stile epigravettiano che si trovano nel livello 4e e che derivano probabilmente dal rimaneggiamento del sottostante strato 5.

2) Le date dei livelli 4e–4b oscillano tra 8200 e 7500 cal. BC e corrispondono dal punto di vista cronologico al Sauveterriano medio della conca di Trento; la tipologia delle armature ben si accorda con questa attribuzione cronologica. Le date troppo recenti (?) del livello 4a (mediamente circa 6400 anni cal. BC) indicano l'esistenza di un inquinamento della parte superiore dello strato. La struttura delle armature del livello 4a non differisce sensibilmente da quella del 4b, a parte la presenza di pochi trapezi, che confermano l'intrusione (?) di materiali più recenti avvenuta in seguito ad apporti colluviali, come indicano i dati di sedimentologia. Se supponiamo che l'evoluzione dei triangoli sia un buon indicatore cronologico, lo strato 4 di Isola Santa corrisponde al Sauveterriano medio della conca di Trento. A Romagnano la curva dei triangoli sale dal Sauveterriano antico fino a circa 7800 cal. BC (da AC8–9 a AC3) e successivamente la curva discende negli strati AC2–AC1. Questa discesa è ancor più visibile negli strati 30 e 29 del Riparo Gaban (cf.). In questo contesto il livello 4a di Isola Santa si pone nella fase di maggior sviluppo dei triangoli e cioè intorno alla data di circa 7600–7500 cal. BC. Questa osservazione è confermata dall'aumento regolare dei triangoli a base corta osservato a Romagnano, al Riparo Gaban e a Isola Santa (classi X–XII) a partire dal Sauveterriano medio verso il Sauveterriano recente.

3) A livello tipologico la serie di Isola Santa differisce dai complessi del Trentino per la scarsità dei grattatoi a fronte ogivale, a spalla e tettiformi, che variano tra 0 e 3%; questo gruppo di grattatoi raggiunge invece a Romagnano un indice ristretto compreso tra il 25 e il 55% e al Gaban è il 18%. Inoltre mancano practicamente del tutto a Isola Santa i coltelli a dorso (gruppo N) e i segmenti trapezoidali (classe III), che comunque non sono numerosi neanche al nord. A livello di percentuale gli indici delle classi 2 (Punte a Dorso) e 4 (Dorsi e Troncature) differiscono considerevolmente dagli indici dei siti della Valle dell'Adige. Si costata inoltre una differenza nell'evoluzione di alcuni indici dei triangoli: gli scaleni corti a base corta (cl. IV–VI) aumentano nel tempo, mentre gli scaleni a base lunga (cl. VII–IX) diminuiscono. A Romagnano i due gruppi sono piuttosto stabili in tutta la sequenza del Sauveterriano medio.

4) Dal punto di vista tipometrico l'industria di Isola Santa ha delle di mensioni molto piccole, assai più ridotte rispetto a quelle dei siti della valle dell'Adige. In particolare per quanto riguarda i grattatoi, ma anche le armature sono in media più piccole rispetto a quelle dei siti veneti e trentini.

5) Le osservazioni precedenti implicano l'esistenza di una regionalizzazione del Sauveterriano italiano, che comprende da un lato le industrie della valle dell'Adige – Pianura Padana, dall'altro le industrie della fascia e pedemontana della Toscana settentrionale e del Carso Triestino-Slovenia.

6) Centro e sud dell'Italia. L'industria di Isola Santa differisce ancora più fortemente dal Mesolitico sauveterroide meridionale, come ad esempio quello della Grotta della Serratura nel Cilento, e soprattutto da quello del Salento – Grotta Marisa (cf.), Grotta delle Mura, Torre Testa – dove persistono gli elementi di tipo epigravettiano/romanelliano (punte e lamelle a dorso, grattatoi minuscoli circolari e subcircolari corti), coesistendo con gli ipermicroliti geometrici e non geometrici. Questa industria si pone a cavallo tra antico e nuovo e sembra dimostrare che la "sauveterrizzazione" (cf. "Pyrenees, Alps...") dell'Epigravettiano italiano non era uguale e uniforme in tutte le regioni del paese: il nord e il centro si "sauveterrizzano" rapidamente e profondamente, formando tuttavia tre industrie differenti (nordico, toscano e carstino), che sono il probabile risultato della regionalizzazione della base epigravettiana, precedenta mentre il cambiamento al sud non è stato mai così profondo. Forse ciò può essere avvenuto per la distanza tra un sud isolato a causa della morfologia della Penisola e il nucleo delle innovazioni posto più a nord, vedasi ad esempio la presenza del Sauveterriano in tutta la metà meridionale della Francia. Il fenomeno della resistenza dell'Epigravettiano alla "sauveterrizzazione" è ben noto anche nei Balcani e Espania (cf. 6.3, 6.4 in this chapter). E questa idea ha dei precedenti anche nella letteratura italiana.

7) Se ammettiamo che il Mesolitico antico e medio italiano sia una mutazione più o meno profonda dell'Epigravettiano finale italiano, dobbiamo porci il problema della linea di demarcazione che separa le due identità. Si tratta naturalmente di una definizione fondata su una base tecno-tipologica, che si può applicare a una cultura "vivente" solo in modo assai teorico. Già nell'Epigravettiano finale, per esempio a Piancavallo, compaiono degli elementi detti "sauveterriani", come il microlitismo, la geometrizzazione, la tecnica del microbulino e il nucleo discoide stesso, che divengono dominanti dopo l'inizio dell'Olocene nelle industrie del nord e del centro Italia, in quello che definiamo il Sauveterriano. La situazione appare più confusa al sud, dove gli elementi detti "mesolitici" sono noti anche nelle industrie del Tardiglaciale (Grotta delle Mura, stato 3; Grotta della Serratura, strati 8AB), ma in cui gli elementi "antichi" si conservano in numero considerevole nelle industrie dell'Olocene antico e medio (strato 2 della Grotta delle Mura e strati 6–7 della Grotta della Serratura). È allora difficile, se non impossibile, parlare di un Sauveterriano al sud, ma sembra piuttosto trattarsi di un Epigravettiano parzialmente "sauveterrizzato".

8) La regionalizzazione del Mesolitico antico e medio in Italia sembra trovare, almeno in parte la sua continuazione nel Mesolitico recente, durante il quale il Castelnoviano italiano sembra seguire le suddivisioni regionali osservate nel Sauveterriano. Una analisi più approfondita del problema del regionalismo mesolitico in Italia sembra essere possibile e necessaria.

6.4. *The south of Italy*

According to Fabio Martini and Carlo Tozzi, the south of Italy from Lazio (?) and Campania to Sicily features a regional microlithic-geometric industry ("Mesolitico indifferanziato") or industries of Epi-Gravettian provenience (Romanelli C, B and A, Grotta Serratura, Grotta Madonna L?) or Romanellian to be more precise. It has been studied most fully for Grotta Marisa in Puglia (cf. below) and in its Holocene phase it was characterized by many technological and typological Sauveterrian characteristics (cf. "Sauveterrization") with the exception solely of inner proportions which are not at all Sauveterrian. Also featured here are small round scrapers of Romanellian type (characteristically on cortical flakes). Existing datings (one for Marisa and some for the similar industry from Grotta delle Mura(?), Uzzo, and Continenza) suggest that these industries continued until at least the end of the 8th millennium cal. BC. Their origins could thus be found in sites like Romanelli C–A, Aqua Fitusa or Grotta Madonna L (all 15th–11th millennia cal. BC) etc., all from the Mezzogiorno or central Italy and all yielding geometrics/microliths (isosceles – TM, crescents – DD, rectangles – RA, double backs – PD) and Romanellian small, circular end-scrapers.

It would be good to know whether the differences in the quantity of microliths from La Mura and Marisa and from other sites in the south were the effect of cultural differences or methods of explorations (sieving not being done everywhere), or finally state of publication of the latter.

Marisa
(co-authors C. Tozzi, R. Grifoni Cremonesi and M. Dini)

La grotta e gli scavi

Grotta Marisa si apre a circa 12 metri s.l.m. nei banchi della "Calcarenite del Salento". Gli scavi furono svolti da Giuliano Cremonesi nel 1978 e 1979. Il deposito mesolitico è stato setacciato a secco e il materiale archeologico è stato localizzato per tagli. Il sedimento contenente il materiale in posto ha uno spessore di circa 25–30 cm e dal punto di vista litologico è uniforme ed omogeneo. Nel corso dello scavo il deposito è stato suddiviso in 5 tagli artificiali, quasi orizzontali e di spessore compreso tra 4 e 7 cm, salvo il taglio 5 di 10 cm (Fig. 6.4, 6.4a).

Comment in 2006

In the present version of the text letter markings of typological groups (A, B, C...) and types (TM, TG, PD ...) have been changed to suit the model adopted in this volume (cf. "About this book", "Atlas").

Osservazioni sulla stratigrafia culturale

Tutta la collezione è molto omogenea dal punto di vista statistico e tipologico: l'industria non evolve nel corso della sequenza (vedi i microliti) e i tipi principali più caratteristici si ripetono nei vari tagli: grattatoi ipermicrolitici corti e molto corti su schegge corticate, bulini non-massici sottili su lama, schegge ritoccate, troncature, lame ritoccate e, soprattutto, alcune classi di microliti come le punte a dorso massicce e a ritocco ventrale (*gravettes*), le lame a dorso e troncatura massicce, i triangoli scaleni corti (= TO) e i triangoli isosceli corti (= TM), entrambi ipermicrolitici, le punte di Sauveterre (= PD, PA) e le punte a dorso microlitiche.

Le differenze tra i vari tagli si riassumono in una diminuzione molto lieve dell'indice delle punte di Sauveterre e nella comparsa di alcuni trapezi nella parte superiore della sequenza, comparsa che può essere anche interpretata come una introduzione secondaria e posteriore alla occupazione mesolitica.

Tenuto conto di questa mancanza d'evoluzione interna e della scarsità numerica del complesso, abbiamo descritto gli strumenti comuni senza alcuna distinzione stratigrafica, mentre le armature sono state analizzate taglio per taglio senza tuttavia aver ottenuto alcun risultato significativo.

Gli strumenti comuni

Sono presenti nella sequenza in numero di 520 e comprendono i grattatoi (A), le schegge ritoccate (B), i bulini (C), le troncature (D), le lame ritoccate (E) e le *pièces écaillées* (L).

Tenuto conto dell'assenza di evoluzione nel tempo, sia quantitativa che tipologica, presentiamo i livelli complessivamente senza tener conto della loro suddivisione nei vari tagli.

L'insieme è dominato dai grattatoi e dalle schegge ritoccate, i cui indici sono a livello del 31–32% ciascuno, seguiti dalle lame ritoccate e dalle *pièces écaillées* (16% e 13% rispettivamente); gli altri indici sono inferiori al 3%.

Questa struttura differisce nettamente da quelle conosciute in Sauveterriano al nord e al centro italiano (cf. texts on Romagnano III, Gaban and Isola Santa in this volume), dove sia i bulini (a Romagnano), sia le troncature e le lame ritoccate (Isola Santa) sono più numerose. Grotta Marisa si distingue anche per l'indice elevato delle *pièces écaillées* e per le dimensioni molto ridotte di tutti gli strumenti comuni.

A. Grattatoi. Sono in totale 166 e il loro indice raggiunge il 31,9% degli strumenti comuni. Sono piuttosto corti (circa il 60%) e molto corti (circa il 30%); sono ricavati soprattutto da schegge (circa il 70%), ma anche da lame corte o accorciate (circa il 20%). I grattatoi piccoli e microlitici (di stile romanelliano) su specifici supporti corticati sono numerosi.

Tipologicamente i grattatoi sono dominati da esemplari a fronte arcuata (circa il 70%) seguiti dai grattatoi a ventaglio (circa il 15%) e, molto meno numerosi, dai grattatoi molto corti doppi, semplici, ogivali e dai grattatoi circolari e carenoidi. Tutti questi tipi si ripetono per tutta la sequenza.

In generale i grattatoi della Grotta Marisa rientrano molto bene nello stile dei grattatoi della Grotta Romanelli, salvo le dimensioni più ridotte, e differiscono notevolmente da quelli dell'Italia del nord (ad esempio mancanza delle forme allungate oblique e dei numerosi tettiformi) e del centro per l'assenza dei gruppi VII, VIII e XIV (cf. typology of Romagnano III in this volume), per l'indice più basso delle forme allungate, per la forte differenza degli indici dei gruppi IX e X–XIII. Dobbiamo segnalare tuttavia che abbiamo considerato i grattatoi a fronte arcuata e su lama rotta, cioè in effetti le forme "corte", come appartenenti tutti alle classi I–VI, come è stato fatto per Romagnano, Gaban e Isola Santa, ma non è certo se si tratti sempre di forme accorciate intenzionalmente oppure se si tratti di strumenti rotti.

B. Schegge ritoccate. Sono in numero di 163, cioè il 31% dei manufatti ritoccati; questa frequenza è identica a quella delle industrie del nord e del centro. Come per le lame ritoccate, vi sono dei problemi per la classificazione di alcune schegge a ritocco sommario. Questi manufatti probabilmente non sono stati realmente ritoccati, ma si tratta piuttosto di ritocchi accidentali (post-deposizionali e/o d'utilizzazione) non legati a fattori culturali.

La nostra analisi ci porta tuttavia a constatare che la tipologia del gruppo delle schegge ritoccate della Grotta Marisa non differisce molto da quella del nord e del centro e vi troviamo degli grattatoi irregolari/ *skrobacz* (11), delle *raclettes* (19), dei raschiatoi (12), delle schegge ritoccate (91) e dei denticolati (10), tutte forme ben note nel Sauveterriano italiano, ma presenti anche nell'Epigravettiano holoceno balcanico (vedi Vlasac in Serbia e Frankhthi in Grecia, cf. "Southeast" in this volume).

SOUTH/MEZZAGIORNO-SAUVETERRIZED EPI-GRAVETTIAN

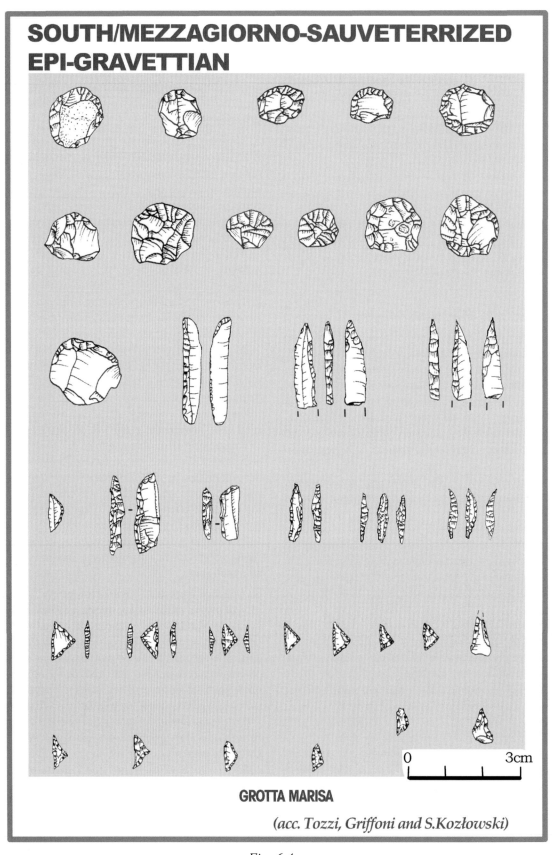

0   3cm

GROTTA MARISA

(acc. Tozzi, Griffoni and S.Kozłowski)

Fig. 6.4a

C. Bulini. Sono poco numerosi, in totale 11 pezzi corrispondenti al 2,1% degli strumenti comuni; questa percentuale si avvicina agli indici noti nel centro, ma è più bassa di quella del nord-Italia. Vi sono inoltre 5 stacchi di bulino. Nella Grotta Marisa abbiamo dei bulini piuttosto allungati e su lama, con la parte attiva assai sottile; si tratta di bulini d'angolo su troncatura e di bulini diedri. Mancano nella collezione di Grotta Marisa i pezzi corti e massicci, come pure i bulini trasversali e su frattura, che sono ben noti nelle industrie del nord e del centro. I pezzi tipici della Grotta Marisa trovano qualche analogia a Romagnano (gruppi III e V) e a Isola Santa (gruppi V e VI).

D. Troncature. Sono assai scarse (solo il 2.6% degli strumenti comuni) e sono sempre meno numerose che al nord e al centro, ma hanno la tipologia nota del Sauveterriano italiano con esemplari allungati su lama/lamella (11), con troncatura normale, obliqua e con esemplari microlitici su lamella (1).

E. Lame ritoccate. Sono assai numerose e arrivano al 15.7% degli strumenti comuni; sono quindi più frequenti rispetto al nord e un po' meno frequenti rispetto al centro. In realtà l'indice delle lame ritoccate, comprendente anche i ritocchi d'uso, riflette solo differenze funzionali e non stilistiche rispetto ai siti di confronto (?).

Dominano gli esemplari a ritocchi continui unilaterali (28) e a ritocchi discontinui (53) e nei livelli superiori compare un pezzo a ritocco denticolato di stile castelnoviano (lamella Montbani), che dal punto di vista tecnico deve essere legata alla presenza dei trapezi.

F. Becchi e perforatori. Sono molto poco numerosi (10– pari all' 1.9% degli strumenti comuni) come del resto si verifica al nord e al centro. Sono piccoli, piuttosto corti, comparabili alla classe II di Romagnano III; sono assenti dalla nostra collezione i pezzi su lama e i perforatori, sia con la punta a ritocco alterno sia quelli a punta ben evidenziata.

L. *Pièces écaillées* / pezzi scagliati. Sono assai numerose (68) e raggiungono il 13% degli strumenti comuni, mentre al nord e al centro questo indice è molto meno elevato. L'importanza numerica di questi manufatti è comparabile a quella della cultura di Lepenski Vir in Slovenia, cf. (Breg, scavi Mihai Budja) e in Serbia (Vlasac, cf. in this volume). A Grotta Marisa si trovano delle vere *pièces écaillées* bifacciali e bipolari su placchette rettangolari e subrettangolari, accompagnate da strumenti comuni, soprattutto grattatoi, che mostrano i negativi di scagliature secondarie.

N. Coltelli a dorso. Non sono presenti a Grotta Marisa, ma sono presenti a Isola Santa con un solo esemplare e caratterizzano il Sauveterriano del nord e del Francia.

O. Punte. Sono assai rare (5 punte pari all' 1,1% degli strumenti comuni) come al nord e al centro. Sono su lama e assai allungati e sono simili tipologicamente agli esemplari noti nell'Epigravettiano e nel Sauveterriano italiano.

Osservazioni sulla tipologia degli strumenti comuni

Il gruppo degli strumenti comuni della Grotta Marisa si distingue notevolmente dai manufatti dello stesso tipo presenti nel Sauveterriano contemporaneo italiano per i seguenti caratteri:

- per la struttura originale, caratterizzata da poche troncature e da numerose *pièces écaillées*;
- per l'assenza di una qualsiasi evoluzione interna;
- per le differenze tipologiche all'interno dei grattatoi, in cui si registra la mancanza totale del gruppo XIII e dei grattatoi allungati obliqui conosciuti al nord, come pure dei grattatoi circolari e semicircolari del tipo presente nell'Italia centrale; si trovano però a Grotta Marisa dei grattatoi molto piccoli di tipo "romanelliano", fatti su schegge ricavate da ciottoli frequentemente corticate; è questa una caratteristica regionale;
- i bulini della grotta Marisa differiscono dagli standard del nord e del centro per l'assenza di forme massicce (gruppi VII e VIII) e di bulini trasversali (gruppo IV) e su frattura;
- i coltelli a dorso sono assenti a Grotta Marisa, ma sono molto rari anche a Isola Santa.

Le armature microlitiche

Sono presenti in tutta la sequenza in numero di 202 e sono meno numerose degli strumenti comuni. Vi sono rappresentati tutti i principali gruppi tipologici del Mesolitico italiano (punte su schegge laminari, punte a dorso e a doppio dorso (= PD), segmenti (= DD), dorsi e troncature (= R), triangoli (= T), trapezi), ma sembrano essere ancor più microlitici degli equivalenti toscani e trentini.

Struttura interna delle armature

Diversamente dal procedimento utilizzato per gli strumenti comuni, le armature sono state suddivise per taglio dal 1 al 5 e successivamente sono state inserite nei gruppi tipologici da 1 a 7 ed è stato costruito un diagramma analogo a quello utilizzato per i siti mesolitici del nord (cf.) e del centro Italia per mostrare la variazione di frequenza nei vari tagli. Anche se il numero di armature per gruppo e per taglio non è elevato (tra 16 e 52 pezzi), si può tuttavia stimare che i principali indici tipologici non subiscono una evoluzione nel tempo, salvo forse il gruppo 6, cioè le punte di Sauveterre (= PD). Le piccole variazioni che si osservano non sono unidirezionali e probabilmente risultano dagli errori statistici dovuti al numero limitato di pezzi.

Questa stagnazione contrasta con la situazione ben nota nelle contemporanee (?) (cf. comment on the chronology at the end of this text) sequenze del nord e della Toscana, dove alcuni indici evolvono fortemente.

Le armature microlitiche della Grotta Marisa sono dominate dalle punte e dalle lamelle a dorso (gruppo 2) comprese tra il 27 e il 43% e dai triangoli (gruppo 5) compresi tra il 31 e il 46%. Al terzo posto si trovano le punte a dorso bilaterale (punte di Sauveterre, gruppo 6), che diminuiscono lungo la sequenza dal 30 al 15% dei microliti. Gli altri gruppi (1, 3 e 4) sono sempre presenti, ma debolmente rappresentati (3–8%). I trapezi (7) si trovano in piccola quantità solo alla fine della sequenza.

Questa struttura dell'industria non corrisponde molto a quella degli altri siti italiani contemporanei. E' quindi assai originale e contrasta con le strutture sauveterriane del nord e del centro Italia, caratterizzate sì da numerosi triangoli (= T) e punte a dorso bilaterale (= PD), ma anche dall'indice debole delle punte/lamelle a dorso.

Anche se l'industria della Grotta Marisa non rientra bene nel quadro del Sauveterriano in base alla struttura numerica dei microliti, alcuni dei quali conservano caratteristiche epigravettiane, non si può escludere che essa si ponga, almeno parzialmente, nel ritmo evolutivo generale del Mesolitico italiano. Se è questo il caso, si potrebbe forse porre la sequenza della Grotta Marisa, con la sua tendenza al cambiamento del valore dell'indice delle punte a dorso bilaterale, nel Sauveterriano recente alla fine del VIII millennio cal. BC, e ciò potrebbe coincidere con la presenza di qualche raro triangolo a base corta (= TH, TE) nei tagli 1 e 3.

1. Punte su schegge laminari. Sono molto scarse (solo 2 esemplari, pari in media all'1% dei microliti). Sono presenti le due forme principali : dorsi (II – 1 pezzo) e microtroncature (I – 1 pezzo). Gli stessi tipi sono presenti al centro e al nord in quantità assai più elevate, intorno al 10%.

2. Punte e lamelle a dorso. Sono molto numerose (66 pezzi) e il loro indice arriva complessivamente al 32.7% di tutte le armature, oscillando tra il 27 e il 42% a seconda dei tagli. Questa situazione non corrisponde a quella nota al nord e al centro, dove le punte a dorso sono assai meno numerose e oscillano tra il 5 e il 10%, ad eccezione dei livello inferiore di Isola Santa. Nella Grotta Marisa gli esemplari in stratigrafia sono meno numerosi dei triangoli (66 a 84), ma se consideriamo anche i pezzi fuori strato, che tuttavia non abbiamo incluso nei conteggi, le punte a dorso sono 5 volte più numerose dei triangoli (56 a 11). L'indice delle punte a dorso non mostra alcune evoluzione nella sequenza. Parallelamente alle forme microlitiche, di misure analoghe a quelle del Sauveterriano dell'Italia centrale e settentrionale, si trovano in tutta la sequenza degli esemplari non microlitici, assai massicci e su supporto laminare, che rientrano bene nella variabilità stilistica delle punte a dorso dell'Epigravettiano italiano. Questi dorsi sono delle "*gravettes*" tipiche e possono essere suddivisi in lamelle a dorso, fratturate e non, e in punte a dorso rettilineo, raramente arcuato. Queste *gravettes* hanno ritocchi complementari piatti, ventrali sia sulla parte prossimale che sulla parte distale, talora del bordo opposto al dorso.

La presenza di *gravettes* richiama la situazione presente nei livelli inferiori di Isola Santa, dove abbiamo segnalato la presenza di alcuni pezzi di stile epigravettiano, che abbiamo tolto, forse imprudentemente, dall'insieme sauveterriano. E' possibile che due gruppi così differenti tipologicamente e tecnicamente possano coesistere negli stessi strati lungo tutta la sequenza?

Le punte e le lamelle a dorso microlitiche del gruppo 2 sono più numerose delle *gravettes* e contengono tutte le forme note del nord e del centro; le lamelle prevalgono leggermente sulle punte.

3. Segmenti. Sono poco numerosi (4 esemplari, pari complessivamente solo all'1.9% dei microliti), mentre nel nord e nel centro sono più rappresentati (3%–20%).

Sono di piccole dimensioni, piuttosto allungati e sono presenti in tutta la sequenza; dal taglio 4 proviene un esemplare ipermicrolitico, molto corto. Al nord e al centro i pezzi allungati (gruppo I) dominano sulle altre forme.

4. Dorsi e troncature. Sono poco numerosi (8 esemplari), pari al 4% di tutte le armature con una oscillazione nei vari tagli tra lo 0 e 1.8%. La situazione è simile a quella del nord e del centro Italia.

Le forme microlitiche (tagli 1 e 3) sono accompagnate anche da esemplari non microlitici (2 nel triangoli 4), di tipo epigravettiano.

5. Triangoli. E' il gruppo più importante (84 esemplari, pari al 41.6% delle armature microlitiche); gli indici oscillano nei vari tagli tra il 31 e il 46%, senza mostrare alcuna tendenza evolutiva.

All'interno dei triangoli si possono individuare due gruppi principali, entrambi in versione microlitica e ipermicrolitica: quest'ultima arriva al 23% di tutti i triangoli. Gli esemplari corti isosceli (classi II e III = TM) sono 47, pari al 56% dei triangoli e sono più numerosi dei triangoli scaleni larghi e corti (classi IV–VI), che sono 27 (32 %). I triangoli isosceli hanno spesso il terzo lato ritoccato. Gli altri tipi di triangoli sono rari, come ad esempio 3 scaleni a base corta (classi X–XII = TH, TE), ivi compreso un triangolo tipo Montclus.

Le proporzioni tra i due gruppi principali di triangoli oscillano senza mostrare una tendenza evolutiva. Gli isosceli sono però sempre più numerosi.

Le differenze con il nord e il centro sono varie e profonde e tutta la ricchezza tipologica del Sauveterriano italiano in questo campo si perde nella Grotta Marisa a causa principalmente della mancanza o della scarsità dei gruppi I e VII–XII. La struttura quantitativa dei triangoli della Grotta Marisa, dominata dai gruppi II–VI, è totalmente diversa da quella sauveterriana delle altre regioni.

6. Punte a dorso bilaterale (Punte di Sauveterre). Sono numerose (35 esemplari, pari al 17.3% di tutti i microliti) e il loro indice evolve dalla base alla sommità della sequenza dal 31 all' 11%: è questo il solo caso in cui sia stato possibile individuare un cambiamento orientato. Al contrario questa tendenza evolutiva non è percepibile a Isola Santa e al nord la diminuzione numerica delle punte di Sauveterre è percepibile solo alla fine della sequenza sauveterriana.

I due gruppi principali, quello delle punte allungate (PA) e quello delle punte lunghe (PD) sono presenti in tutta la sequenza, ma il primo diventa più numeroso nella parte alta, il secondo prevale nei tagli 5, 4 e 3.

7. Trapezi. Sono presenti solo nei due tagli superiori 1 e 2 e sono poco numerosi, in totale 3 esemplari, pari allo 1.5% di tutte le armature; uno appartiene alla variante simmetrica e due a quella asimmetrica.

Rientrano nello standard castelnoviano noto al nord e al centro (vedi Passo della Comunella), ma anche al sud (Latronico) (cf. "Pre-Neolithic/Castelnovian"). La loro presenza nei tagli superiori, assai disturbati e rimaneggiati, può essere sia primaria che secondaria. Tuttavia a Grotta Marisa la tecnologia castelnoviana, di solito associata a questo tipo di trapezi, è poco attestata: si tratta di una sola lama Montani e di una lama ritoccata.

Osservazioni sulle armature

Le armature della Grotta Marisa sembrano essere allo stesso tempo caratteristiche e originali, poiché non seguono gli standard italiani contemporanei. Differiscono infatti dal Sauveterriano del nord e del centro per le seguenti caratteristiche:

– la struttura quantitativa dei vari gruppi tipologici è differente: indice elevato dei triangoli e delle punte/lamelle a dorso e bassi indici delle punte su supporto laminare, delle punte a doppio dorso e dei segmenti;
– stabilità degli indici in tutta la sequenza, salvo la lenta evoluzione delle punte a dorso bilaterale;
– differenze tipologiche per la presenza di lamelle a dorso, di *gravettes* e di dorsi e troncatura di grandi dimensioni, per l'assenza quasi totale di triangoli scaleni a base corta, incluso il tipo Montclus (= TE), e dei triangoli scaleni a base lunga e angolo aperto;
– differenze dimensionali dovute alla robustezza delle *gravettes* e dei dorsi e troncature, parallelamente all'esistenza dì forme microlitiche e ipermicrolitiche.

In conclusione, ci appare difficile considerare come tipicamente sauveterriane le armature della Grotta Marisa, perché la maggior parte di esse, per le caratteristiche tipologiche e tipometriche, ha un significato interculturale, e quindi soltanto all'interno di una struttura quantitativa caratteristica del Sauveterriano potrebbero essere considerate come appartenenti a questa cultura.

Conclusioni

L'industria litica della Grotta Marisa è molto omogenea e non presenta sensibili cambiamenti nel tempo. I manufatti si presentano con caratteri tipologici, tecnologici e strutturali stabili e di diversa importanza diagnostica. In alcuni casi si tratta di elementi che sono la continuazione di caratteri culturali già presenti regionalmente nell'Epigravettiano finale; in altri si tratta di elementi che non erano presenti in questo ambiente, ma che compaiono nell'Olocene antico in un ambiente culturale noto come "Sauveterriano".

A Grotta Marisa la tecnologia del débitage è totalmente di tipo sauveterriano e si basa sui piccoli nuclei discoidi e prismatici. Le lame sono di tipo sauveterriano e non si trovano tracce della tecnologia epigravettiana.

Gli strumenti comuni differiscono invece da quelli del Sauveterriano per l'indice più basso delle troncature e per l'indice elevato dei pezzi scagliati, la cui presenza sembra caratterizzare l'Epigravettiano finale dell'Italia meridionale

(Grotta Romanelli, Grotta delle Mura, Grotta Continenza, Tuppo dei Sassi). Tipologicamente gli strumenti comuni della Grotta Marisa differiscono da quelli del Sauveterriano per il microlitismo meno accentuato e per la mancanza di alcuni tipi come i grattatoi tettiformi su lama e quelli a fronte obliqua. Mancano i bulini massicci e su scheggia, i coltelli a dorso e i perforatori. Al contrario alcuni tipi di strumenti, quali i molto piccoli grattatoi corti e i circolari, i bulini su lama e le punte avvicinano la nostra industria all'Epigravettiano finale di tipo romanelliano (cfr. Grotta Romanelli, Grotta delle Mura, le Cipolliane, Grotta del Cavallo). Inoltre la struttura quantitativa dei microliti differisce da quella sauveterriana soprattutto per l'indice elevato delle punte a dorso. La struttura dell'industria della Grotta Marisa non rientra pertanto in alcun punto della sequenza classica del Sauveterriano.

Contrariamente a quello che conosciamo per il Sauveterriano, nella sequenza della grotta Marisa la struttura delle armature microlitiche non subisce cambiamenti [but how long did it last? – comment 2006] e mostra parecchie differenze con quella sauveterriana: nel gruppo delle punte a dorso si nota la presenza di *microgravettes* e di lamelle a dorso di dimensioni e di tipo epigravettiano, come pure i pezzi a dorso e troncatura larghi. Altri tipi sono microlitici e possono essere considerati sia come lo sviluppo locale di tipi già conosciuto nell'Epigravettiano (punte a dorso, segmenti, dorsi e troncature, triangoli corti, punte a doppio dorso), sia come il risultato di un'influenza esterna sauveterriana (triangoli corti a tre lati ritoccati, triangoli lunghi a base corta e punta a due dorsi a base larga).

Questa differenza tra il Sauveterriano del nord e l'industria di Grotta Marisa è sottolineata anche dalla tipometria dei manufatti ritoccati, che sono nel sito pugliese molto più larghi. Allo stato attuale delle nostre conoscenze si osserva che nel periodo di transizione tra Pleistocene e Olocene antico si è verificato nella Francia meridionale e nell'Italia settentrionale, compresa la Toscana e Carsto Triestimo, un cambiamento radicale dell'Epigravettiano verso il Sauveterriano (microlitizzazione totale, scomparsa delle *microgravettes* epigravettiane, comparsa di nuovi tipi di armature); al contrario in Italia meridionale l'evoluzione non è stata così profonda (persistenza di qualche punta a dorso, di dorsi e troncatura e di lamelle a dorso di dimensioni tradizionali) e l'acquisizione dei caratteri sauveterriani è incompleta. Nel Sauveterriano si può quindi riconoscere un'area nucleare dai Pirenei, alle Alpi, alla Toscana, mentre nelle regioni circostanti (Catalogna, Balcani, Italia meridionale) il processo di sauveterrizzazione dell'Epigravettiano locale è meno accentuato o non si verifica affatto, come, ad esempio, nei Balcani. Come già sostenuto da alcuni autori (Fabio Martini, Arturo Palma di Cesnola), nell'Italia meridionale la tradizione epigravettiana sembra essersi mantenuta più fortemente e più a lungo, e può aver dato origine a linee evolutive differenziate, una verso i complessi mesolitici a denticolati (Grotta della Madonna, Grotta della Serratura, Riparo Blanc, Ortucchio), l'altra in senso più sauveterroide, con numerose armature come a Grotta Marisa, Grotta delle

Mura e forse alla Grotta della Serratura, strati 6–7, ed alla Grotta Continenza, tagli 25–27.

La cronologia

Il Romanelliano e l'industria della grotta Marisa appartengono alla stessa linea evolutiva ì cui aspetti terminali sono riconoscibili fino al Neolitico antico della Puglia (cf. Torre Sabea e Terragne). La nostra industria rappresenta un momento successivo al Romanelliano e più antico del Castelnoviano meridionale (cfr. Latronico, Tuppo dei Sassi) e del Neolitico. Probabilmente è posteriore all'Epiromanelliano della Grotta del Cavallo e delle Cipolliane, di cui non si hanno datazioni, descritto da Palma di Cesnola. Se il ritmo di sviluppo delle industrie del sud è analogo a quello delle industrie dell'Italia settentrionale, possiamo supporre che lo sviluppo delle armature ipermicrolitìche si sia verificato in Puglia intorno delli 8800 anni cal. BC, parallelamente all'affermazione del Sauveterriano. Di conseguenza l'industria della Grotta Marisa, pur non rientrando nel Sauveterriano in senso stretto, è probabilmente contemporanea a una delle fasi di questa cultura. Nella Grotta Marisa il solo indice che mostra una tendenza evolutiva è quello delle punte di Sauveterre, che diminuiscono dal basso verso l'alto. Lo stesso fenomeno è chiaramente percepibile nel nord a Romagnano III e al Riparo Gaban, dove la fase recente/finale del Sauveterriano è datata ai due secoli finali del VIII millennio cal. BC. Una data comparabile è quella della parte superiore dello strato 2 della Grotta delle Mura (8240±120; 8290±50 B.P.), che contiene una industria molto simile a quella della Grotta Marisa.

Comment in 2006

A recent AMS date (LTL1222A) for Grotta Marisa is 8120 ± 45 BP, that is, c. 7200–7000 cal. BC, confirming the above remarks on the chronology (information from Carlo Tozzi).

6.5. Eastern and northeastern outlying areas (Fig. 6.5/6)

In the north, the Sauveterrian reaches surprisingly, presumably through the Brenner Pass (1375 m a.s.l.), into the Austrian Tyrol (explorations by Dieter Schäfer in Ullafelsen), western Slovakia (Sered', excavated by Juraj Barta) and, on the way, Pod Črmukljo in southern Slovenia (Mitja Brodar excavations). The Castelnovian elements/complexes of the Italian type are known from e.g. Mala Triglavca in Slovenia, as well as from Breg (Mark Frelih's excavations) from the vicinity of Ljubljana.

One could wonder about the Sauveterrian-like complexes from two northeastern Hungarian sites on the upper Tisa river excavated by Robert Kertesz (Jasztelek and Jaszbereny) (cf. "The Southeast"). They seem, to this author, to be incompletely sauveterrianized (meaning

miniaturization and geometrics) local Epi-Gravettian (in similarity to the Holocene southern Italian complexes like Marisa and della Mura (cf. above) and those from the Spanish Levant (e.g. Filador, cf. "Iberia").

6.6. Iberia

Poorly and unequally studied (the interior being virtually unknown), the Mediterranean coast presents a regional sequence, which is poorly dated (Fig. 6.6a–b):

– backed points (Epi-Azilian – Epi-Gravettian industries until the end of the 8th millennium cal. BC (?);
– Castelnovian-style industries with trapezes (from c. 7000–6500 cal. BC) of the Cocina and Moita do Sebastiao type;
– both phases/industries are divided in Catalonia by the Filador industry with isoscele triangles (8th millennium cal. BC).

Backed points are an evident continuation of a Final Paleolithic tradition of the Malleates type containing apparently no or only a few geometrics (?). A lasting tradition with backed points can be observed in Cantabria, in a local industry called Asturian (8th–7th millennium cal. BC) characterized by, among others, the macrolithic picks, but also Epi-Gravettian elements. Broadly understood Castelnovian followed (cf. below). Similar elements can be observed in the Portuguese littoral (Early Mesolithic backed points from the central-western Portuguese littoral and the macroliths from the south of the country, finally local Castelnovian of Moita do Sebastiao type and later the Muge culture, both from the Tag estuary).

In turn, P. Arias has signalled the presence of backed points also in the weakly explored Spanish interior in the 8th millennium cal. BC.

Castelnovian-style regional traditions (Cocina and Botiqueira in the east and Moita do Sebastiao in the west, but also Kobeaga V in "Asturian" Cantabria (!)) evolved from the 7th millennium cal. BC into the Muge type industry – Amoreira, Arruda among others with the Helwan retouch on segments – Betey type – and very original isosceles and at the end with cardial ware). Indeed, some are considered Neolithic from this period on. The so-called Levantine art (Chapter 12) apears to be linked to this period.

Note: Some of the assemblages of the Iberian Final Paleolithic have some non-trapezoid geometrics (rectangles, crescents, triangles) found despite the older inadequate methods of exploration. They are also present in Castelnovisation type assemblages. Whether investigations will confirm the presence of geometrics in Early Holocene assemblages, only time can tell.

Thus, the Iberian evolutionary sequence seems to be like that of southern Italy and the Balkans. In all of these areas no evident change can be seen at the end of the Pleistocene and beginning of the Holocene. Castelnovian and a real change with ceramization follows afterwards.

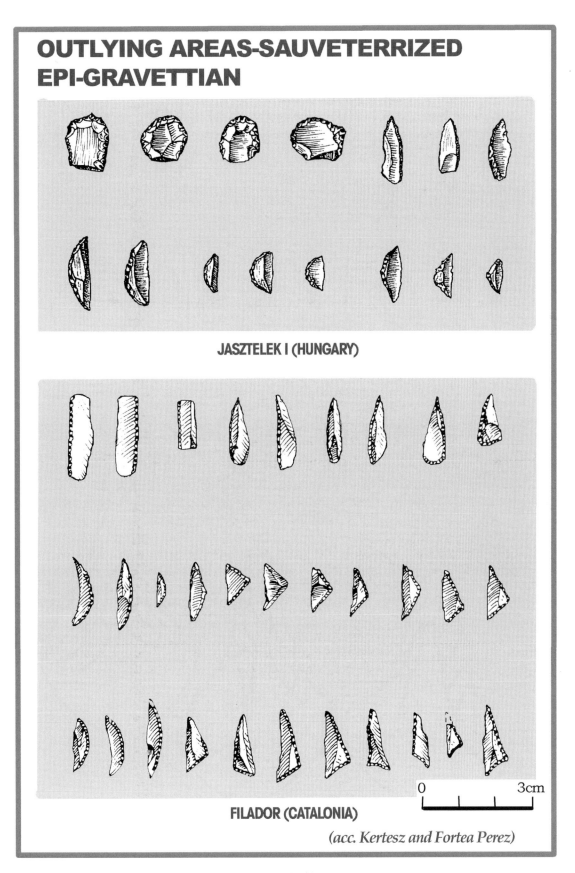

OUTLYING AREAS-SAUVETERRIZED EPI-GRAVETTIAN

JASZTELEK I (HUNGARY)

FILADOR (CATALONIA)

0   3cm

(acc. Kertesz and Fortea Perez)

Fig. 6.5/6

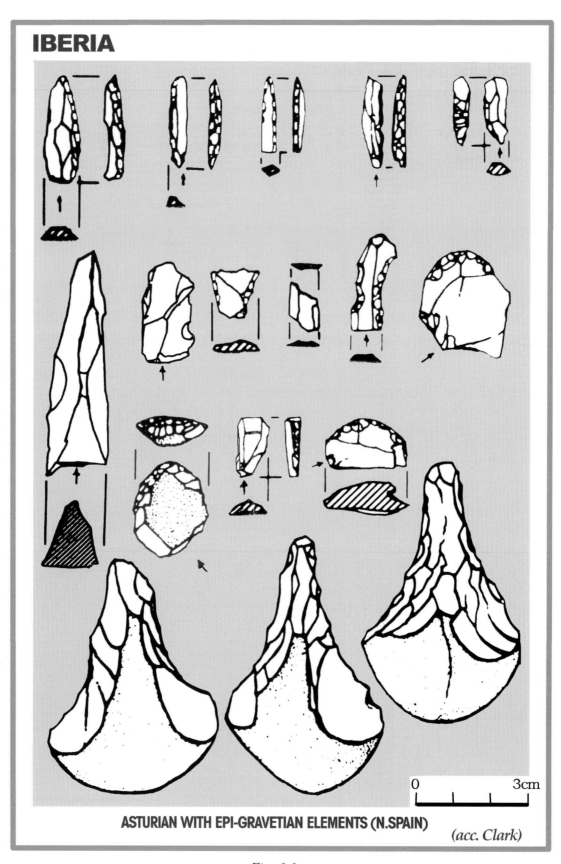

Fig. 6.6a

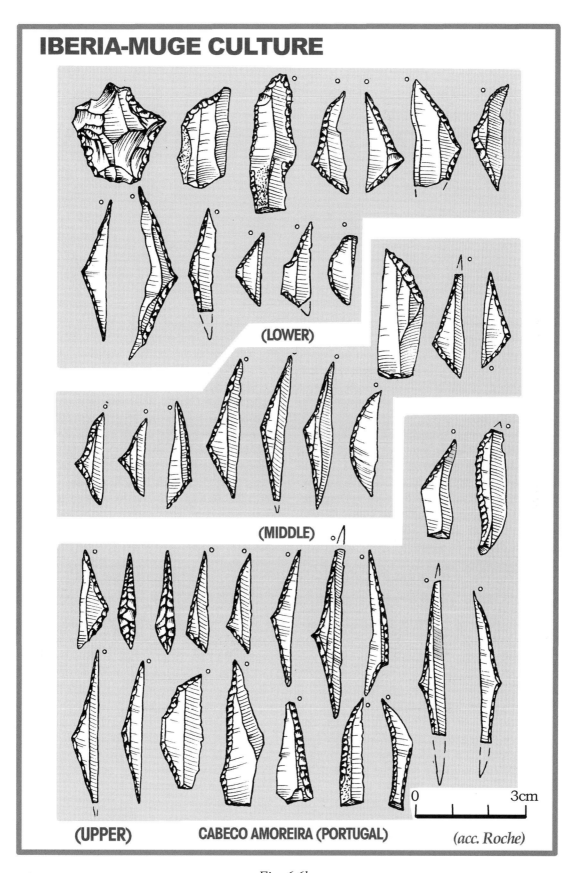

IBERIA-MUGE CULTURE

(LOWER)

(MIDDLE)

(UPPER) CABECO AMOREIRA (PORTUGAL) (*acc. Roche*)

0 3cm

Fig. 6.6b

7

The Southeast

The southeast of Europe is strongly differentiated morphologically and divided by mountainous barriers like the Dynaric Alps, Carpathians, Rhodopes, Balkans, Epirus etc. It is also isolated from the rest of Europe by a series of major mountainous barriers like the Western and Eastern Carpathians, Alps, bodies of water like the Black, Aegean and Adriatic seas. Hence, the specifically conservative development of this region, meaning a long-lasting Epi-Gravettian tradition. A poorly developed river network (except for the basin of the Danube) was also not conducive to long-distance contacts.

Few sites are known and even fewer have been excavated, dated and published; hence, local studies have naturally tended toward the spectacular Neolithic cultures. Despite this, knowledge of the Balkan Mesolithic has increased over the years with the appearance of publications by Dragoslav Srejović, Vasile Boroneanţ, A. Paunescu, Robert Kertesz, Juraj Barta, Ivan Gatsov, Ivana Radovanović and finally, Catherine Perlèz. Studies in a broader perspective have been produced by Ivan Gatsov, Janusz K. Kozłowski and Stefan K. Kozłowski. The present text is yet another significant contribution. Combining stratigraphic and chronological data from Greece (Frankhthi), Montenegro (Ćrvena Stijena, Medena Stijena, Odmut), the Serbian/Rumanian borderlands (Cuina Turcului, Padina, Vlasac etc.), Slovenia (Mala Triglavca, Viktorjev Spodmol, Breg) and finally Italy (Carso di Trieste, Trentino), it reconstructs with considerable likelihood the local cultural sequence(s). These sequences are statistically and technologically conservative to the core in almost all of the Balkans, meaning that the regional Epi-Gravettian tradition continues in virtually unchanged form throughout the region for a very long time (similarly as in the south of Italy (cf.) separated from this region by the not very wide strait of Otranto). Only the western fringes of the Balkans reveal some more specialized forms of the Mesolithic (Sauveterrian in Slovenia and southwestern Slovakia, with sets of diversified microliths/geometrics from the upper Tisa river in Hungary, cf. "Eastern and northeastern outlying areas").

The sequence is dated on the grounds of material from the Frankhthi Cave published by Catherine Perlèz. From the 13th millennium BP, it demonstrates typological/technological stability (lanceolates/backed points D, big scalenes TO-TR rectangles ?) and small isosceles (TN), segments (DD) and true rectangles (RA), plus small, mostly round end-scrapers. Very similar material came from undated layers at Ćrvena Stijena and Medena Stijena, both in Montenegro.

The picture is not full, for we lack good data (number of sites!) for Croatia, Romania, Hungary and Slovakia. The reasons for this are mostly geological (?), that is, later accumulation of sediments of alluvial or erosional origins, but perhaps and simply lack of raw material (?). Hence, we can be practically sure that not all the important variants of the Balkan Mesolithic have come to light so far, a fact further confirmed by isolated Sauveterrian finds from Slovakia, para-Sauveterrian from north Hungary and quasi Epi-Gravettian from Czech Šakvice (cf. "Eco/cultural … zonation"). Many of these finds are not dated, unfortunately, but the youngest of them should be at least from the Early/Middle Holocene, just as in the region of the Iron Gates in Serbian Padina (= industry of the Medena Stijena/Ćrvena Stijena type).

Thus, we have a uniform Epi-Gravettian tradition of the terminal Upper Paleolithic lasting in unchanged or almost unchanged form in all of this area from Serbia to Greece straight into the Holocene (perhaps only denticulated flakes from Frankhthi differentiate the complex from others found in the interior). The question is whether this situation can be referred to the region lying further north where small collections of rather Epi-Gravettian style can be found (undated in Barca in Slovakia, for example, and dated by trapezes to 7000 cal. BC and later in the inventory from Gîlma in Romania). The surface provenience of these collections is naturally a problem, as well as their limited number and size. For instance, we do not know whether the absence of geometrics, already known from the south, in the face of other obviously Epi-Gravettian characteristics, results from the size of the collection, the method of excavation, or reflects a separate taxonomic variant. Whatever the case, the Epi-Gravettian tradition in unchanged form appears to last well into the 8th millennium cal. BC, while from c. 7000 cal. BC evolution in the south went a different way (Castelnovian) than in the north (latest Epi-Gravettian) and in a number of different directions at that.

And so, along the Adriatic coast and inland radical changes can be observed in this period, going in the direction of forming differentiated Castelnovian-type industries (model A of castelnovization, cf. "Pre-Neolithic/ Castelnovian" in this volume); starting from the west, these are such Castelnovian-style industries as: northeastern Italian Castelnovian in Slovenia (Mala Triglavca), Odmut group (Montenegro, Albania, Greek Thessaly), Frankhthi Group (Peloponnese), southern Montbanian (Austria) and in the Czech Republic (Mikulčice).

North of the Dynaric Alps, in the basin of the Sava River (Breg, Michai Budja's collection), all the way to the Iron Gates (Vlasac), local Epi-Gravettian changes are to be observed in the Lepensky Vir culture (model B of castelnovization, cf.). Further to the north (Hungary, Western Slovakia?, Transylvania, Bulgaria) there appear to exist the above-discussed Epi-Gravettian industries with trapezes (Gîlma), perhaps without geomterics (?). One actually wonders whether these northern assemblages should not be simply attributed to the Lepensky Vir culture as well.

7.1. Eco-cultural/stylistic zonation of the Mesolithic in Central and Southeastern Europe

Basic concepts, chronological limits (Fig. 7.1a–j)

Chronologically, my study is confined to the period from the beginning of the Holocene to the disappearance of Mesolithic industries. This temporal ramification is only conventional, although for several reasons.

- It has become an accepted conclusion in the literature of the subject that the transition from the Paleolithic to the Mesolithic (economic and hence also stylistic changes) coincided with a radical ecological change which took place at the turn of the Pleistocene and Holocene, around 10,400/9500 years cal. BC. In fact, this is far from the truth since the oldest Early Mesolithic industries in Central Europe must be dated to a much later time, namely to around 9500 years cal. BC (Romagnano III in Italy, Całowanie and Chwalim in Poland, Pulli in Estonia, Thatcham in England, etc.). The cultural/stylistic change was thus not synchronous with the environmental one.
- The cultural/stylistic change takes place in most of Central Europe, its outward manifestation being a far-reaching evolution of style and technology, however with some exceptions to the rule, many of which are to be found in the inner-Carpathian and Balkan region of our area of interest. What we see there is a preservation (in a large part of the Carpathian basin and in the Balkans) of Epi-Gravettian type industries

which are evidently a continuation of local tradition, dating to the final stages of the Pleistocene, but also to the Early Holocene. It is often difficult or indeed impossible (based on archaeological analysis) to distinguish between Pleistocene and Early Holocene assemblages. Given the lack of radiocarbon dates, this creates a methodological problem; hence the division of assemblages into the "Paleolithic" and "Mesolithic" (if this is important at all) is often illusory. Hence the proposition to refer to assemblages of this type as "Epipalaeolithic", besides underlining the classificatory and methodological difficulties, also stresses the absence of pronounced change (in economy as well as environment) in this region at the junction of the Pleistocene and Holocene. In contrast to the "Epipalaeolithic", the "Mesolithic" industries/cultures are products of fundamental stylistic/technological/ economic changes taking place at the very beginning of the Early Holocene, partly inside or near the Carpathians (western and northern territories, e.g. in the Czech Republic, too).

- The end limit in this study is also conventional. Although we do know that it cannot be set at the time of the emergence of the first Neolithic cultures in the region in question. Both culture types seem to coexist, and a number of facts from areas north of the Carpathians indeed confirm this situation. It is also truth, that some industries of Mesolithic type go together with ceramics (Lepenski Vir, Odmut, Mehtelek).

Zonation, state of research

The observed area (between the Adriatic and Baltic) is geographically considerably diversified, and it was similar in the Late Pleistocene and Early Holocene. Now I will try to describe it, using, among others, the most comprehensive of the available data, namely for the Atlantic period (7th–6th millennia cal. BC).

A. To the north, we find the North-European Lowland, a relatively flat area with clayey-sandy soils and well developed river network, lakes and rivers overgrown with deciduous forests of the maritime type. The dominant wild fauna species is red deer, accompanied in the north by elk and throughout the territory by roe deer, aurochs, bison and wild boar. Abundant and often excellent-quality flint is to be found in the region. The settlement network is well developed: In Poland alone we know of more than 3,500 Mesolithic sites, and the situation in northern Germany and Denmark is not much different. We can thus assume that taxonomic problems in this area have been well dealt with. There is still a lack of sufficient number of datings, and moreover, we know exceptionally little about the economy in those times (especially in Poland).

B. The south is divided into several geomorphological, floral and faunal complexes:

- Bohemian basin, including Moravia
- Pannonian Lowland

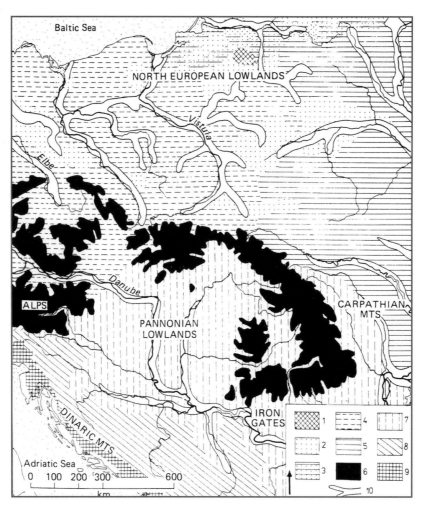

SOUTH-EASTERN EUROPE-ZONATION

VEGETATION

1-TAIGA
2-MIXED CONIFEROUS
3-MIXED DECIDEOUS
4-DECIDEOUS MARITIME
5-DECIDEOUS CONTINENTAL
6-MOUNTAIN
7-STEPPE-FOREST
8-OAK,MOUNTAIN
9-MEDITERRANEAN DECIDEOUS

(acc. J. and S.Kozłowski)

Fig. 7.1a

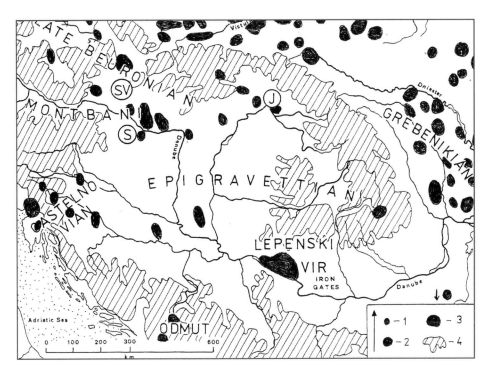

SOUTH-EASTERN EUROPE-ZONATION

LATE MESOLITHIC
SETTLEMENT PATTERN

1-3-SITES AND SITES CONCENTRATIONS
4-MOUNTAINS
S-SAUVETERRIAN
SV-ŠAKVICE
J-JANISŁAWICIAN
S-SAUVETERRIAN

(CF. ALSO CHAPTERS 6.2, 7.2 and 11 AS WEL AS 7.2)

(acc. J. and S.Kozłowski)

Fig. 7.1b

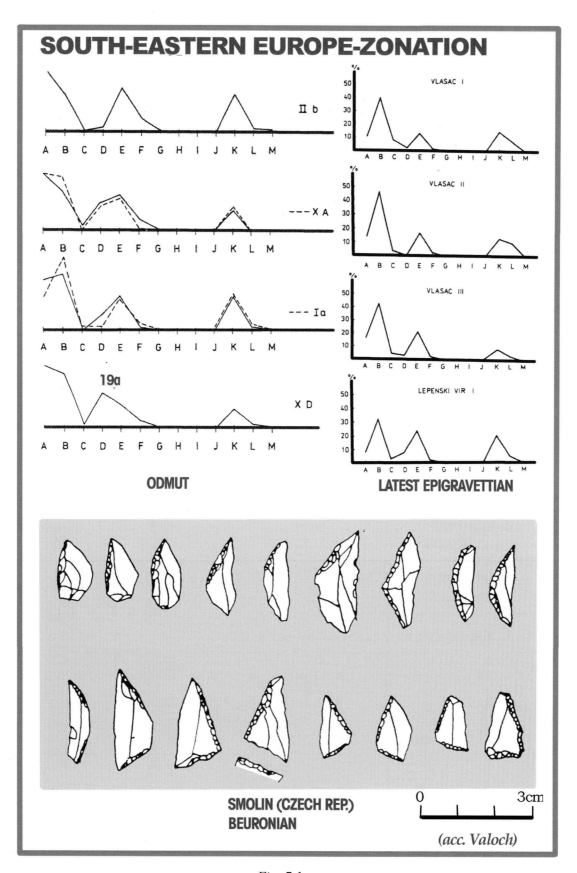

Fig. 7.1c

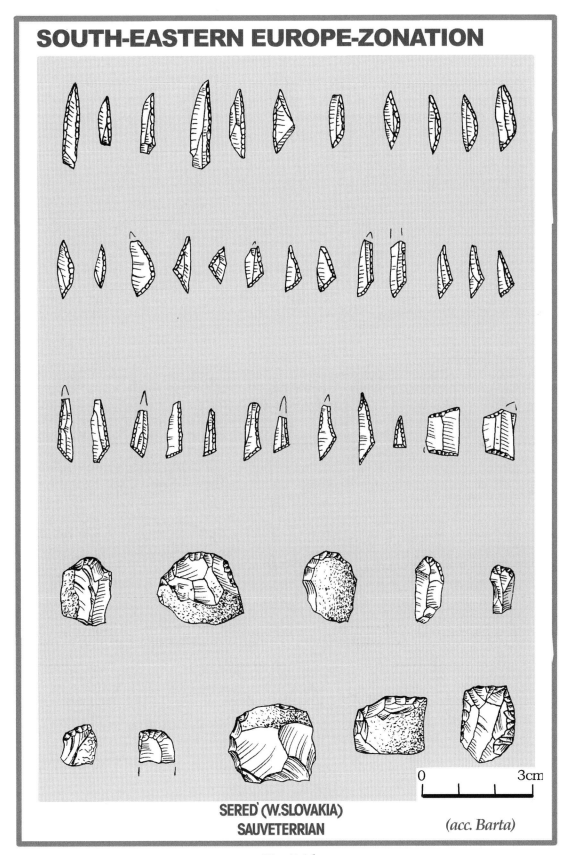

SOUTH-EASTERN EUROPE-ZONATION

SERED' (W.SLOVAKIA)
SAUVETERRIAN

(acc. Barta)

Fig. 7.1d

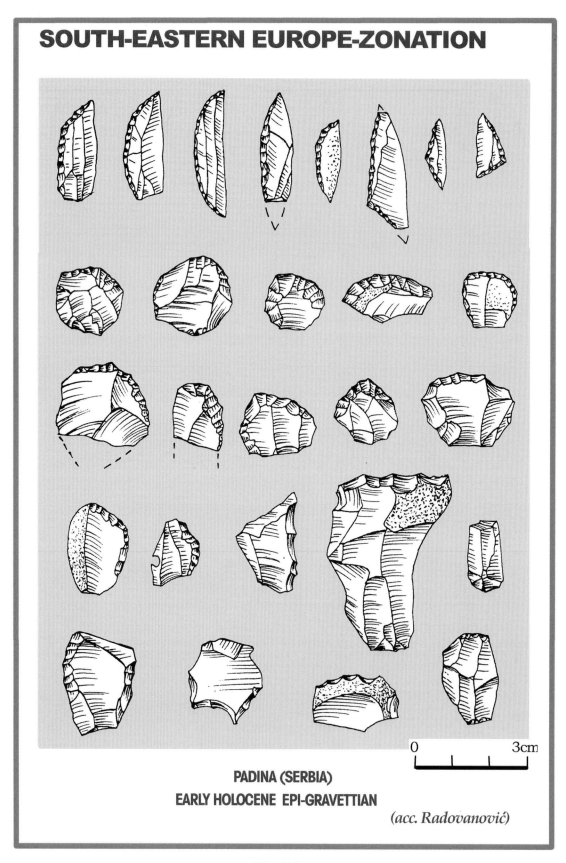

SOUTH-EASTERN EUROPE-ZONATION

0   3cm

PADINA (SERBIA)
EARLY HOLOCENE EPI-GRAVETTIAN

(acc. Radovanović)

Fig. 7.1e

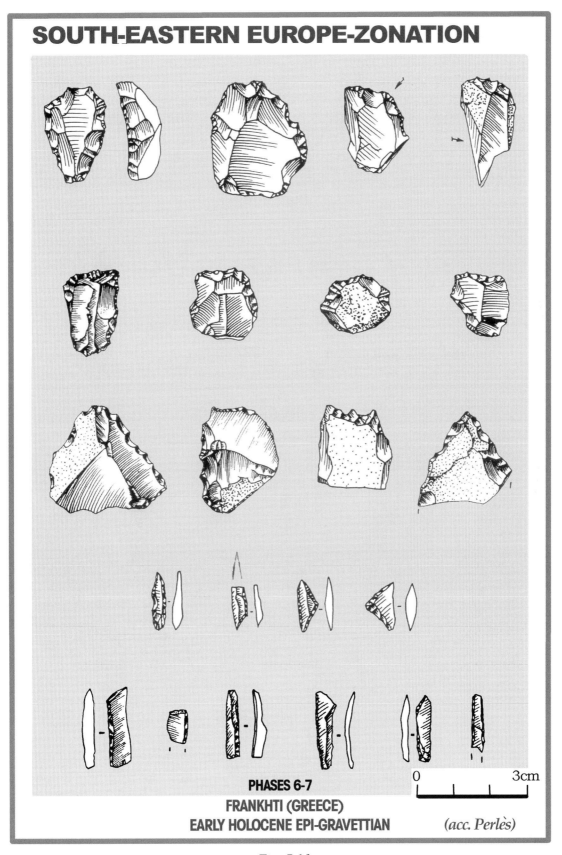

SOUTH-EASTERN EUROPE-ZONATION

PHASES 6-7
FRANKHTI (GREECE)
EARLY HOLOCENE EPI-GRAVETTIAN

(acc. Perlès)

0   3cm

Fig. 7.1f

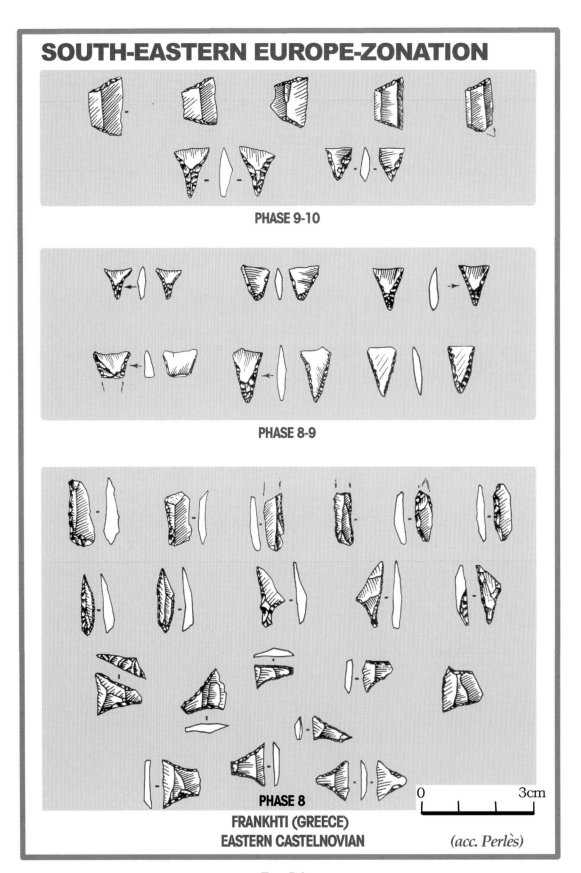

Fig. 7.1g

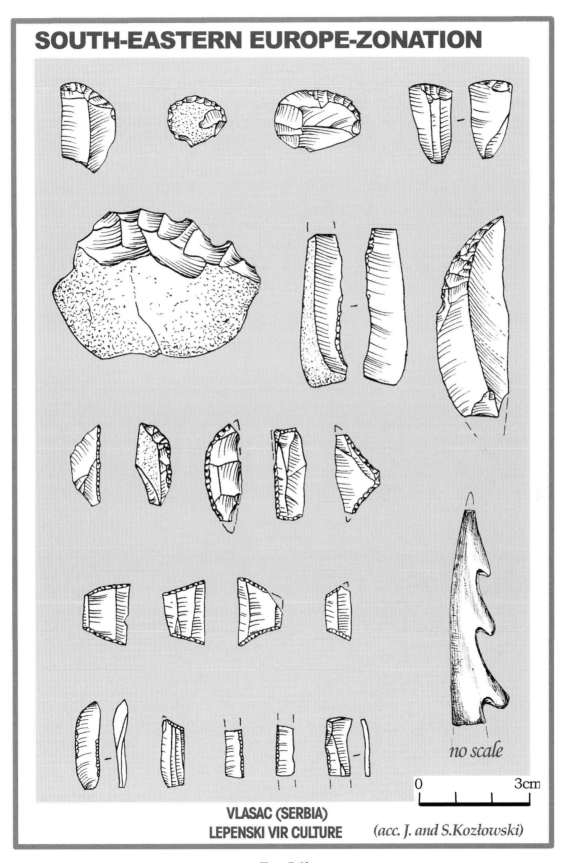

Fig. 7.1h

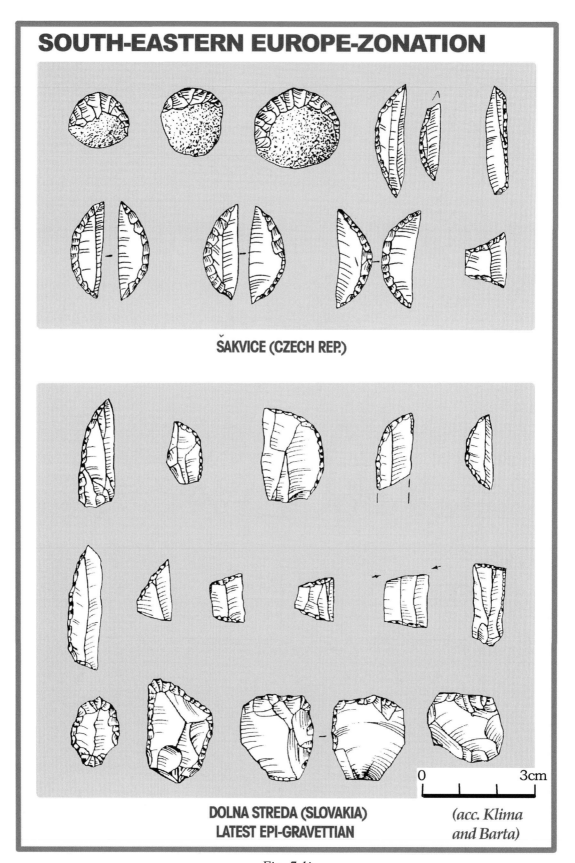

Fig. 7.1i

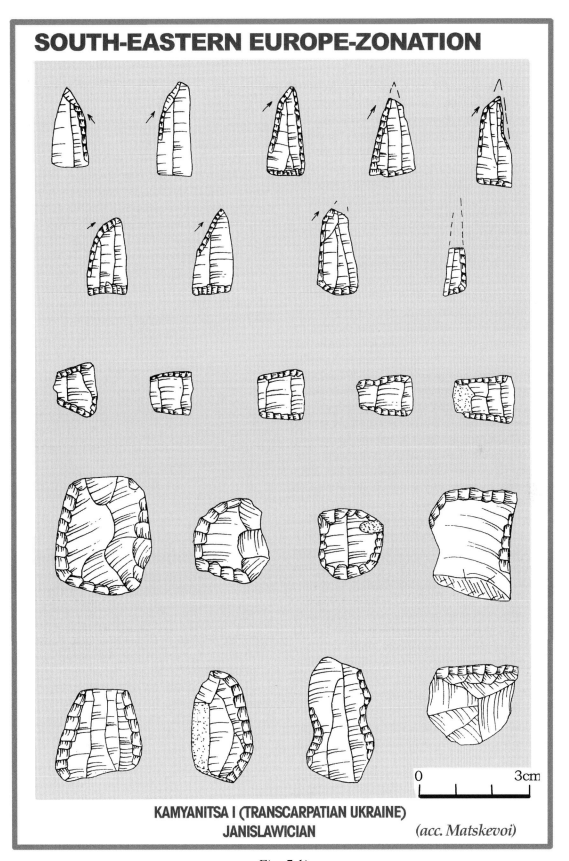

SOUTH-EASTERN EUROPE-ZONATION

0 3cm

KAMYANITSA I (TRANSCARPATIAN UKRAINE)
JANISLAWICIAN   *(acc. Matskevoi)*

Fig. 7.1j

- Dynaric Alps and Balkans
- Dalmatian coast

The vegetation cover and fauna in the Bohemian basin and Moravia were similar to those in the North European Lowland, which lies beyond the fairly serious barrier formed by the Sudeten range which, however, is not impenetrable – it can be and was crossed easily via the Kłodzko or Moravian Gates, for example. The known settlement network here is very sparse, the local raw materials are of poor quality or wholly absent, and ^{14}C dates are very rare. The area is opened to Franconia and Bavaria in Germany via the passes and gates in the Czech Rudava Mountains, as well as to Lower Austria and the Pannonian Lowland via the Danube valley. It also opens into the Polish Silesia (through the Moravian Gate). The local taxonomy is only partly established (mostly eastern Beuronian, cf. "Ost-Beuronian").

The Pannonian Lowland differs from the previous two units in a number of features and is separated from them by considerable barriers: the western Carpathians in Poland, Beskidy Mountains in the north, the westernmost White Carpathians, the eastern and southern Carpathians in the east, the Dynaric Alps in the south, and the Alps in the west. This flat and poorly irrigated area was covered by steppe-forest, inhabited in the 7th/6th millennium cal. BC mainly by aurochs, accompanied by red deer (cf. "Game"), wild boar and roe deer. Further east in Transylvania, most probably in a forest environment, the dominant animal, like in the forests of the North European Lowland, was red deer. The known settlement network is extremely sparse, the number of sites minimal (why?), and the taxonomic-chronological scheme most probably incomplete. The rare raw materials, of moderately good quality, have been studied only fragmentarily and there are almost no radiocarbon dates available.

The Dynaric Alps together with the river valleys cutting across them (including the Iron Gates) were overgrown with oak forests inhabited mainly by red deer, aurochs and roe deer; mountain areas are locally dominated by ibex (Odmut in Montenegro). The entire settlement network is hardly studied (cf. studies of John Chapman) and, given the ground relief, was most probably poorly developed. One must mention here the well explored concentration of sites in the Iron Gates (mostly excavations of Vasile Boroneanț and Dragoslav Srejović) for which we have several excavated sites, a description of raw materials and a series of ^{14}C dates (recently updated and reinterpreted by Clive Bonsall). The area is characterized by multilayer open sites, caves and rock shelters. Sites of the Slovenian Ljubljana plain should also be mentioned (cf. "Slovenian Mesolithic").

The Dalmatian coast together with Istria and the vicinity of Trieste is a specific zone, formed by a narrow strip of land (slightly broader in the Early Holocene) "pushed" against the sea by the Dynaric Alps, with communication routes oriented NW-SE rather than towards the continent interior (cf. the later spread of *impresso* ceramics – "Ceramization"). It is overgrown with Mediterranean-type deciduous forest inhabited mainly by red deer together with aurochs in the east and roe deer in the west. The settlement network is still unexplored, as well as the raw materials; almost no ^{14}C dates are available. The taxonomic system is known only locally (vicinity of Trieste, southwestern Slovenia and the Croatian Istria, then Montenegro), and we have multilayer cave sites here.

The above characteristic of the principal environmental zones of Central Europe warrants the following generalizations. There is a sharp contrast between the north (Lowland) and south (Pannonia, Dynaric Alps and Dalmatia) with regard to the flora and fauna, as well as climate, geomorphology and hydrology. This contrast has been reflected in history, culture and geography, for example in the border between the Roman Empire and Barbaricum, the present-day border between the wine and the beer/vodka consumption zones, the division into great physiographical units (III – pre-Alpine Western Europe vs. V – Carpathians together with its valleys, and VII – the Eastern Mediterranean subregion) (cf. "Regionalization", La Haye 1971), and has been stimulated in the past and still is today by the vast terrain barriers (Carpathians, Sudeten Mountains, Bohemian Massif, Alps, Dynaric Alps, Balkans, etc.) offering few convenient passages. How often have the mountain barriers formed long-lasting political and cultural barriers in the region! (cf. modern political, cultural and religious conflicts and divisions).

The described situation encourages the suggestion that the Mesolithic/Epipaleolithic of the North and South underwent independent cultural development, smaller territorial units in the south differing from one another in occupied and exploited environments, and separated by prominent barriers.

We thus have a sketchy taxonomy, shored up by data from the better researched neighboring territories.

Early/Middle – Late Mesolithic

In addition to local stylistic differences dividing Central Europe into meso-regions characterized by specific local industries, we can point to many shared features bringing together diverse contemporaneous industries, as well as to those distinguishing older and younger taxons. Generally speaking, we can put the chronological divide at about 7000–6500 years cal. BC, i.e., the accepted transition point from the Middle to the Late Mesolithic.

The Early/Middle Mesolithic is represented in Central Europe by the following cultures/industries:
1. Northeastern (= Kunda) Technocomplex:
   Western Kunda (northeastern Poland, Lithuania and Latvia);
   Kudlaewka (NE Poland, Belarus and N Ukraine);
2. Northern (= Maglemosian) Technocomplex:
   Duvensee in German Lowlands,
   Komornica in Polish Lowlands,
3. Western Technocomplex:
   Beuronian in Germany, Austria, the Czech Republic,

and SW Poland; Sauveterrian in France, western Switzerland, Italy, Slovenia and southwestern Slovakia;
4. Late Epi-Gravettian in Greece, North Slovenia, Croatia (?), Slovakia, Hungary, Serbia, Montenegro, Romania, Bulgaria, western and southern Turkey.

All of the above taxonomic units have a number of shared features but of course, they differ as regards detailed solutions. Their common features (except for Kunda) are:

- autarkic system of raw material acquisition, with several local varieties of rock and one principal raw material occupying a dominant position;
- a poorly specialized core formation technique (hence the autarkic raw material system) with irregular bladelets as blanks;
- diversified/typologically elaborate group of microliths/points, often including backed pieces (straight and curved back), crescents, small retouched truncations, isoscele and scalene triangles; in most cases, especially in the north and west, these are short and broad specimens while in the south and west smaller and narrower forms predominate;
- circular/sub-circular very short flake end-scrapers or specimens on shortened blades; short flake burins.

The individual features of the various cultures/industries/territories are discussed further on. The Late Mesolithic cf. "Pre-Neolithic/Castelnovian" in central Europe is represented by:

1. Northern (= Maglemosian) Technocomplex: Post-Maglemosian in Holland, Denmark, southern Sweden, Norway, northern Germany and Poland (cf. "West and Center");
2. Janislawician in Poland, Belarus, Ukraine and Lithuania, as well as Trans-Carpathian Ukraine (cf. "Pre-Neolithic/Castelnovian");
3. Castelnovian Technocomplex: Italian Castelnovian in north Italy and southwestern Slovenia; S. Montbanian in southern Germany, Austria and Moravia (?); Odmut group in Montenegro, Thessaly and Albania (?); Frankhthi group in the Peloponnese.
4. Latest Epi-Gravettian (including the Lepensky Vir culture) in Romania, Bulgaria, Hungary, Slovakia and former Yugoslavia.

The shared features of the Late Mesolithic/Epipalaeolithic industries include:

- greater openness to imported raw materials (at least in part of the area);
- greater regularity and bigger size of bladelets, now often produced from pre-formed cores representing specially selected and often imported raw materials;
- the emergence and gradual attaining of a dominant position of trapezes in the microliths group.

However, not every Late Mesolithic culture evolved equally far. They can be divided into more traditional ones, undergoing only the changes mentioned above (cf. "Pre-Neolithic/Castelnovian" – model B), while retaining many features of the earlier period (Post-Maglemosian in the north and Latest Epi-Gravettian in part of the southeast, represented either by the Gîlma type in the north or Lepensky Vir type in the south), and those which transformed completely, leading to the emergence of industries I refer to as Pre-Neolithic or Castelnovian, (Janislawician in the north, Italian Castelnovian, southern Montbanian, Odmut and Frankhthi in the south, cf. model A in "Pre-Neolithic"). The latter industries lost nearly all the features of their predecessors, introduced a standardized bladelet (often obtained by pressure technique) and the characteristic *lame à ètranglements* (or *lamelle Montbani*) mostly in the West. These industries continued in the south in the form of the local Early Neolithic and/or Early Ceramic (Gaban in Italy, Smilčić in Dalmatia, Upper Odmut in Montenegro, Frankhthi and Argissa Magula in Greece, Kriš/Körös in Hungary, etc.), often armed by broader bladelets.

Early Mesolithic

Beuronian (Fig. 7.1c)
This Early Mesolithic taxonomic unit, confined mainly to Western Europe (cf. "West and Center" in this volume) occurring in an East-West belt extending from Belgium, the Netherlands and the Paris Basin (Coincy Facies of local Tardenoisian, as Jean-Georges Rozoy called it) to Moravia, Lower Silesia and Lower Austria, through Switzerland and southern Germany, is teritorially differentiated. Its status in Hungary (Pécs ?) remains unclear, as the mentioned site is poor enough to be either Beuronian or Epi-Gravettian. Its geographical position suggest the latter possibility, although the wide Danube valley cutting across Austria and Pannonia was most probably conducive to contacts between human groups and the regions.

The Beuronian is dated from the 10th/9th millennia cal. BC, and locally up to the beginning/first half of the 7th.

The most characteristic Beuronian tool group is composed of microliths, distinct in the short/broad shape, considerable breadth and fairly large dimensions of the pieces, but mostly in the morphological variety of specimens. In addition to the characteristic Tardenois (or C) points (X), we have here broad-backed points, segments (DD, DE), broad isosceles (TN) and scalene (TR, TO) triangles, as well as a few proximal micro-truncations (K), as well as distal ones. All these armatures are accompanied by short and very short, also circular and semicircular end-scrapers and, in the younger assemblages (7th millennium cal. BC) also by trapezes (cf. "West and Center").

Sauveterrian (Fig. 7.1d)

Taxonomic unit typical of the Early Mesolithic in the western Mediterranean area (cf. "South") occurring throughout southern France and Italy (northern and central areas), known from western Switzerland (Vionnaz) and the vicinity of Trieste (Benussi) as well as from Slovenia (cf. text in this volume) and exceptionally from the Austrian Tyrol; in our region it is well represented by the Mačanske Vršky site near Sered' in Slovakia (excavations by Juraj Barta).

In its classical area in the West, the Sauveterrian existed from the second half of the 10th millennium until about 7000 years cal. BC, when it quickly changed into Castelnovian-type industries. In the discussed area, it is present in its classical but rather late form, which can be safely dated to the 8th millennium cal. BC (Slovenian-Italian border region). The Slovakian site of Sered' has trapezes and is perhaps to be dated to the turn of the 8th and 7th millennia cal. BC.

The most characteristic feature of the Sauveterrian is the group of very small, fine and in most cases narrow microliths, strongly diversified morphologically (cf. "Trentino sequence"), the most notable of which are Sauveterrian points (PD) occurring alongside isosceles (TN) and scalene (TO, TR, TH, TE) triangles, backed points, segments (DD) and micro-truncations.

Among the remaining tools are small circular and sub-circular, very short end-scrapers, accompanied by more elongated specimens and retouched flakes/irregular scrapers. The Slovakian site has also several splintered pieces, which are more of Balkanic (= Lepensky Vir) style.

The Epi-Gravettian of the Balkans (Fig. 7.1e–i)

Research and dating by Cathérine Perlèz of Pleistocene and Early Holocene industries from Frankhthi (Greece) contributed to the understanding that some of the Balkan assemblages considered so far as Pleistocene and undated could indeed have originated from the Holocene. Thus, possibly Early Holocene industries/cultures of the chief Balkan regions can be reconstructed as follows. Firstly, it is to be assumed that some of the complexes (upper or uppermost) from Medena Stijena (5?) and Črvena Stijena (VIII?) from Montenegro could have been, like complexes form phases 6/7 and 8 from Frankhthi, of Early Holocene date, a fact confirmed by very Early Holocene Serbian Padina A in the Iron Gates. Secondly, it has been proved (sequences at Frankhthi, Medena Stijena, Črvena Stijena, Cuina Turcului – this last a Dryas III site from Romania) that no stylistic or typological differences can be found between the Final Pleistocene and Early Holocene industries in the region. This is sufficient to fill out the Early Holocene map of the Balkans with Epi-Gravettian of the Padina type with small circular or subcircular end-scrapers, backed lanceolates (DB), *lamelles à dos*, scalene (TO, TR) and isoscele (TN) triangles and crescents (DD–DE). Doubts, described in the introduction to this section, remain concerning the attribution and potential distinction of scarce northern material, e.g. Slovakian Barca I, excavated by

Laszlo Banesz, as well as the distinctivity of denticulated Early Holocene retouched flakes of the Frankhthi industry (cultural or rather functional feature?, there are also few regular end-scrapers in these layers!).

The Frankhthi (Epi-Gravettian-Castelnovian) sequence (Fig. 7.1f–g)

Excavated by Thomas W. Jacobsen, this Peloponnesian cave provided not the first (this we had from e.g. Črvena Stijena excavations by Alojz Benac, followed by Medena Stijena), but well documented instead and dated Balkan sequence for the period in question.

Cathérine Perlèz's model publication has confirmed earlier assumptions of a rhythm of cultural/stylistic change in the Balkans in the terminal Pleistocene and Early Holocene other than in the west and north.

The story began in the 13th millennium cal. BC when the local Epi-Gravettian started to include small geometrics (crescents, and isosceles TN and big scalenes/backed truncation). Accompanying them already at this time were fine coin-like end-scrapers, as well as the earlier known lanceolates (phase 4). From this point onwards, through phases 5 (12th millennium cal. BC), 6 (11th millennium cal. BC), 6/7 (8th millennium cal. BC), 7 (9th–8th millennium cal. BC), through 8 (c. 7500 cal. BC) the same, above-described forms lasted unchanged. From the Early Holocene, they are accompanied by irregular scrapers and retouched flakes which push out regular end-scrapers, as well as starting from phase 8 (8th millennium cal. BC) trapezes (AZ) and various related trapezoid microliths. This is accompanied from phase 8 (very early!) by a progressive castelnovization of the lithic technology.

In the end effect, two stages of a local sequence can be distinguished at Frankhthi: Epi-Gravettian (continuing since the terminal Pleistocene) and Castelnovian *sensu largo* (from c. 7500/7000 cal. BC).

This pattern is repeated in undated sequences in Serbia and Montenegro (cf. above), although with insignificant differences (variants: the Frankhthi type of Castelnovian in the south and the Odmut in the north, cf. in this volume, chapter 11).

Jaszbereny – Jasztelek industry (Fig. 6.5/6)

In a surprising spot far to the north, on the upper Tisa river in northern Hungary, Robert Kertesz discovered a microlithic and geometric industry carbon-dated to the 8th millennium cal. BC. It features fine and small circular and sub-circular end-scrapers, beside the Epi-Gravettian lanceolates, crescents (DD, DE), isosceles (TN), and very rarely Sauveterrian points (PD); the size of these Epi-Gravettian tools is very small here and their sauveterrization (cf.) great, although absolutely not sufficient to speak of the Tisa Sauveterrian (cf. "Eastern and northern outlying areas").

Late Mesolithic

South Montbanian (?)

Taxonomic unit, typical for the Late Mesolithic at the northern foothills of the Alps, developing from the south Beuronian C (and Rhenanian into North Montbani) in the area extending from Belgium and Central France all the way to Austria and Moravia (since the beginning/middle of the 7th millennium cal. BC), displaying a territorial diversity. Its synonyms are: the *Montbani facies* in France (Jean-Georges Rozoy), the *Hirschhornharpunen Horizont* in Switzerland (René Wyss) and the *Spät-Mesolithikum* in southern Germany (Wolfgang Taute).

In our area, it is represented by sites such as Koblach and Gartkorn in Austria and Mikulčice (?) in the south of the Czech Republic. The characteristic features of the unit are based also on finds from outside the region considered here.

The cores are rather big, preformed, exploited with the pressure technique, most probably at least in part made from mined raw materials (morainic outcrops are known from German Bavaria, personal information from Wolfgang Taute). The bladelets are large, very regular, often sectioned; the microburin technique is known.

Among the retouched tools are numerous prominent trapezes (mostly of B group, cf. "Atlas"), in most cases high and asymmetrical, as well as *lames à ètranglements*, also termed *lamelles Montbani*. The remaining tools are very short end-scrapers and small numbers (in the initial period) of scalene triangles (TO, TR) and Tardenois points (X), reminiscent of the Beuronian tradition.

The chipped industries are accompanied by flat, single- and double-barbed harpoons made from deer antlers.

Classical Northeastern Italian Castelnovian (cf. Slovenia)

Territorially diversified taxonomic unit dominant in the Late Mesolithic (since 7000 cal. BC to the appearance of ceramics) of the western part of the Mediterranean Sea basin (cf. "Pre-Neolithic" in this volume), occurring in southern France (Chateauneuf-lez-Mantignes), Italy (Romagnano III, typical of the nord - Italian variant, cf. "Trentino sequence" in this volume), and in our area in the vicinity of Trieste and in Slovenia (Pod Ćrmukljo, Mala Triglavca, cf. "Slovenian Mesolithic"). It is always an evolutionary successor of the Sauveterrian, here in its regional variation. The cores, core technology, bladelets, as well as microburins are similar to those known from Montbani. As regards retouched tools, the flake and blade end-scrapers (also tectiform pieces) are accompanied by the *lamelles Montbani*, short symmetric and asymmetric trapezes with a *piquant trièdre*, as well as rare scalenes (TH, TE, perhaps from Late Sauveterrian layers?).

The single flat harpoon from Spehovka (Slovenia) may be Castelnovian, but may also display an affinity to the Montbanian tradition, given that similar specimens are known from Austria, Liechtenstein, southern Germany and Switzerland, among other places; only a few such specimens were discovered in a very late Castelnovian context.

On the other hand, flat harpoons are known from a tradition close to the Castelnovian (Odmut, cf. in this volume) in Montenegro, as well as from the Latest Epi-Gravettian (Lepensky Vir culture = Vlasac in Serbia, cf.).

Castelnovian continuation is apparent in the local Early Neolithic/Early Ceramic (Smilćić in Croatia, Ćrvena Stijena in Montenegro, upper Gaban in Italy, Mehtelek in Hungary, Donja Branjevina in Serbia).

Odmut Industry (cf.)

This is known from the Odmut (cf.) in Montenegro (as well as from Ćrvena Stijena IV in the same country, Argissa Magula in Thessaly – Greece, and from Albania). Odmut is a multilayer and well dated site, from 7000 to about 5700 cal. BC (ceramic layers). The industry is very similar to the Castelnovian (*sensu largo*) and differing from it only with regard to the morphology of trapezes which are symmetric and short, and were not formed by the microburin technique; also tectiform end-scrapers are absent. Perhaps the industry from Argissa Magula belonging in this group was already Neolithic.

Frankhthi

The cradle of Castelnovian are phases 8 and 7 from the Frankhthi cave in the Peloponnese, distinguished by some backed points and very simple (A) and very high, specific trapezes with ventral retouch, as well as denticulates and end-scrapers. The first domestic sheep in Europe is perhaps associated with these phases. The industry of phase 8 is one of the oldest Castelnovian assemblages in Europe (before 7000 cal. BC).

Janislawician (cf.) (Fig. 7.1j)

The site of this Late Mesolithic (para-Castelnovian) and obviously "Polish" unit was recently discovered (surprisingly because of the Carpathian barrier!) on the upper Tisza in Trans-Carpathian Ukraine by Leonid Matskevoî (Kamyanitsa I).

Latest Epi-Gravettian

It is a direct continuation of the earlier development of the Epi-Gravettian (cf. above) with only minor modifications.

The development stage of this phenomenon of interest to us here falls in the period of the 7th/6th millennia cal. BC. I refer to these industries as the latest Epi-Gravettian. The lower chronological limit for the appearance of trapezes, c. 7000/6500 cal. BC, is of course purely conventional. The latest Epi-Gravettian sites are known mainly from the Carpathian Basin (Hurbanovo and Dolna Streda in Slovakia; Šakvice in Moravia; Szödliget and Pécs in Hungary) but also from the mountainous fringes of the area (Gîlma in Romania; Breg in Slovenia; Lepenski Vir and Vlasac, Schela Cladovei in the Iron Gates region etc.) and even from territories outside our region (Dekilitazh in Bulgaria).

It seems that the latest Epi-Gravettian phenomenon is diversified and should be treated as a higher-order unit, i.e., technocomplex. At least three cultural/chronological variants can be distinguished during the middle Holocene:

- typical "simple" Late/Latest Epi-Gravettian;
- Lepensky Vir culture;
- Šakvice-type assemblages;

Latest Epi-Gravettian (undifferentiated)

The Latest Epi-Gravettian flint industry itself, in the area from Slovenia to Slovakia and Bulgaria, is not complex, based on small cores producing rather irregular and short bladelets. The tool set always features very short, circular and sub-circular flake end-scrapers, *raclette*-type denticulated flakes, infrequent short burins and retouched bladelets. The characteristics of the unit are based on the microliths which always (?) include arched backed points (DB) and segments (DD, DE), as well as backed pieces with straight backs; finally, we have the rare but constantly present isosceles (TN) and/or scalene triangles (TR, TO), and the even rarer but characteristic back + truncation(s) combinations (RA). The assemblages include simple trapezes (AZ).

Lepensky Vir Culture

This culture is best known from the Iron Gates region (cf. "Vlasac") and the Ljubljana Plain (?), and it is a local variety of the Latest Epi-Gravettian, distinct from the unit just described by the presence of numerous splintered pieces and micro-retouched bladelets similar to Dufour-type bladelets or inserts WA–C (cf. "Atlas"). A different possibility is the joining of the two units described above (based on the assumption that the former are poorer than the latter for statistical reasons alone). At the end (Lepensky Vir), the industry could have been joined by ceramics.

Assemblage from Šakvice (Fig. 7.1i)

This assemblage from the Moravian locality in the Czech Republic (published by Bohuslav Klíma) is a unique find. The small collection contains fairly evident Latest Epi-Gravettian elements in the form of wide and slender segments accompanied by a back + truncation (RA) and a trapeze (AZ), as well as by very short and subcircular flake end-scrapers. What is truly astonishing are large segments featuring Helwan-type (= bifacially formed back) retouch (!!!), so far entirely unknown in Europe (except for the western fringes of the continent: the "Betey-type" segments and triangles discovered along the Atlantic coast in French Gironde and in Iberia) and typical of the Near Eastern Early Natufian. These relics are so unique that they cannot but generate a number of doubts.

7.2. Slovenian Mesolithic

During a visit to Ljubljana, the present author had the opportunity to study the more important Mesolithic material of the country. At Michai Budja's request, he prepared a text that is published here with some minor revisions (Fig. 7.2a–g).

Sites of the Adriatic Strip

Pod Črmukljo

This rockshelter beneath a cliff was explored (with all of the sediment subjected to sieving) in 1965 by Mitja Brodar who excavated a total of some 14 square meters. Unfortunately, no attention was paid to microstratigraphy although the sediment was up to 45 cm thick, but an attempt was made to determine the planigraphy of uncovered material (information provided by Boris Kavur). The final publication does not distinguish assemblages, and material that appears not to be homogeneous, in the taxonomical sense ("Mesolithic" material and ceramics) and perhaps also in the planigraphic one.

Thanks to the kind permission of Prof. Mitja Brodar, I had the opportunity to study the entire collection, which is kept in the Institute of Archaeology of the Slovenian Academy of Sciences in Ljubljana.

My examinations, focusing mainly on technology and morphology, resulted in the following observations. Firstly, the collection features:

- discoidal cores,
- small end-scrapers on flakes (circular/subcircular and short),
- small end-scrapers on blades (long and short),
- small retouched truncations with straight or arched truncation.

Secondly, there are also small points in the form of:

- elongated backed pieces with straight back,
- backed pieces with arched back,
- scalene triangles with short base (TH, TE),
- points with double back (Sauveterrian – PD).

Thirdly, there occur:

- pre-formed single-platform cores for regular bladelets,
- regular bladelets, also sectioned or notched specimens (Montbani bladelets),
- trapezes formed with the microburin technique (asymmetric and symmetric specimens with *piquant trièdre*) accompanied by numerous broad microburins.

Fourthly, we have:

- narrow symmetric trapezes, which were not shaped with the microburin technique.

The above grouping of various technological and morphological elements makes possible the following suppositions. The first of the elements is typical of Early- and Middle-Holocene industries of the region (Sauveterrian, Castelnovian, Latest Epi-Gravettian) and identical with the first element in Mala Triglavca cave described below. The second element is evidently Sauveterrian or rather Late-Sauveterrian (cf. "Trentino sequence"). The third element, best represented on the site, is of course Castelnovian. The second and third elements, if combined into one assemblage, have good parallels in very Early-Castelnovian sites in northern Italy (e.g. Romagnano III, AB and AA, Plan de

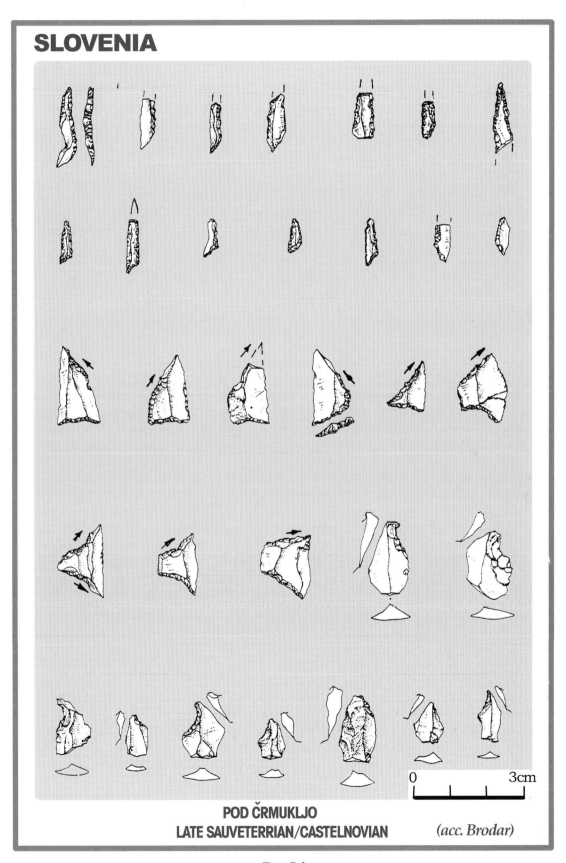

SLOVENIA

POD ČRMUKLJO
LATE SAUVETERRIAN/CASTELNOVIAN   *(acc. Brodar)*

0   3cm

Fig. 7.2a

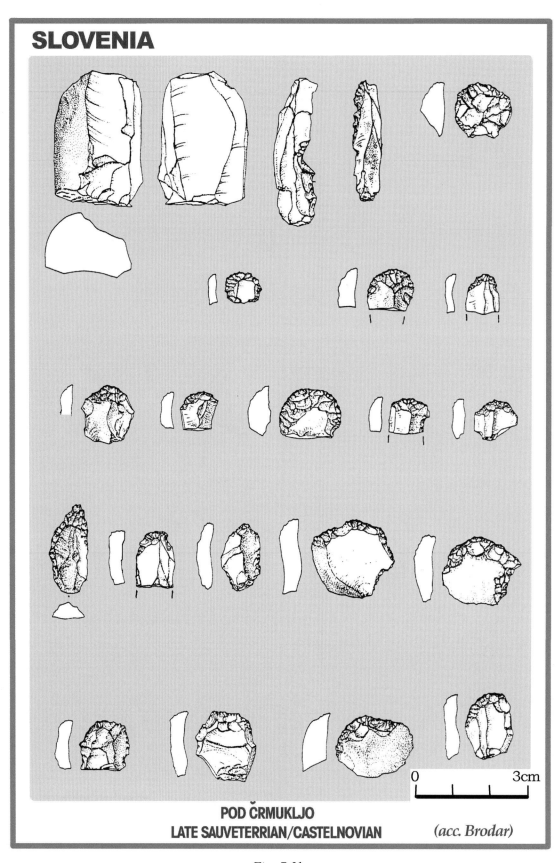

SLOVENIA

0   3cm

POD ČRMUKLJO
LATE SAUVETERRIAN/CASTELNOVIAN   *(acc. Brodar)*

Fig. 7.2b

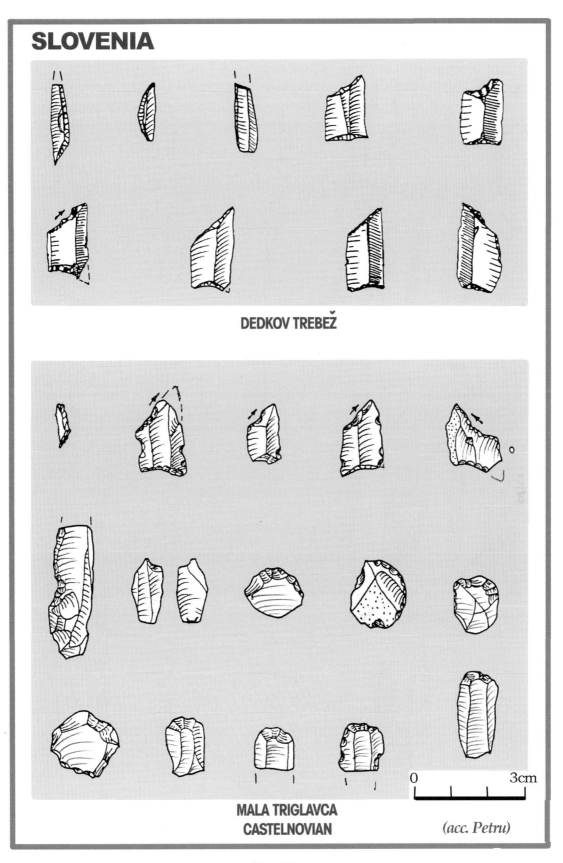

Fig. 7.2c

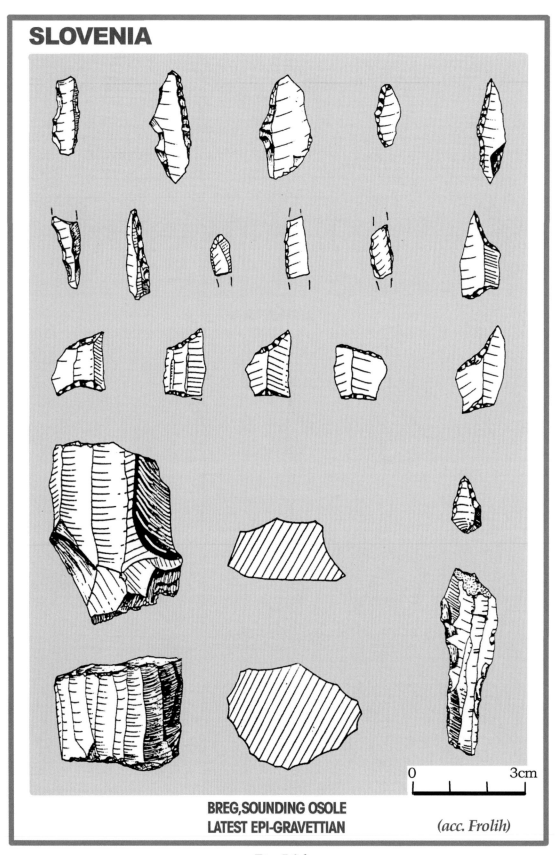

SLOVENIA

BREG, SOUNDING OSOLE
LATEST EPI-GRAVETTIAN

(acc. Frolih)

0   3cm

Fig. 7.2d

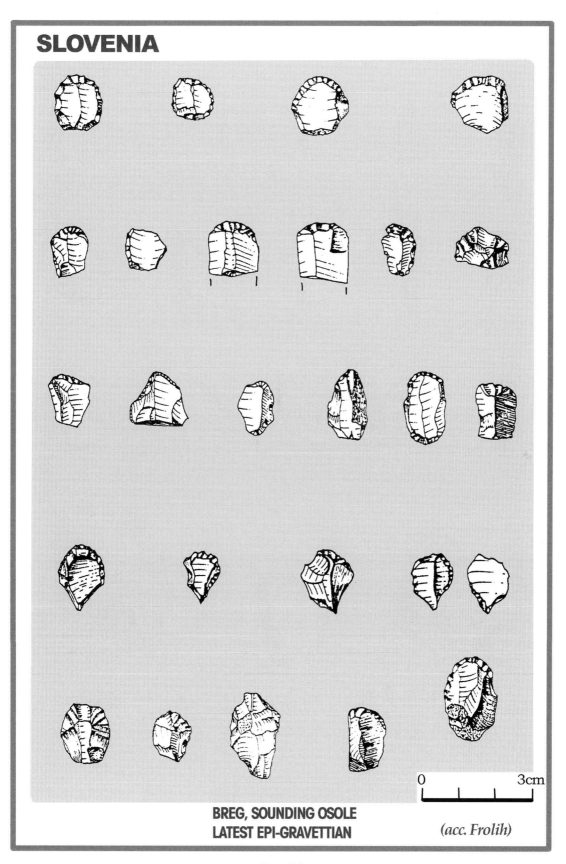

SLOVENIA

BREG, SOUNDING OSOLE
LATEST EPI-GRAVETTIAN

(acc. Frolih)

0   3cm

Fig. 7.2e

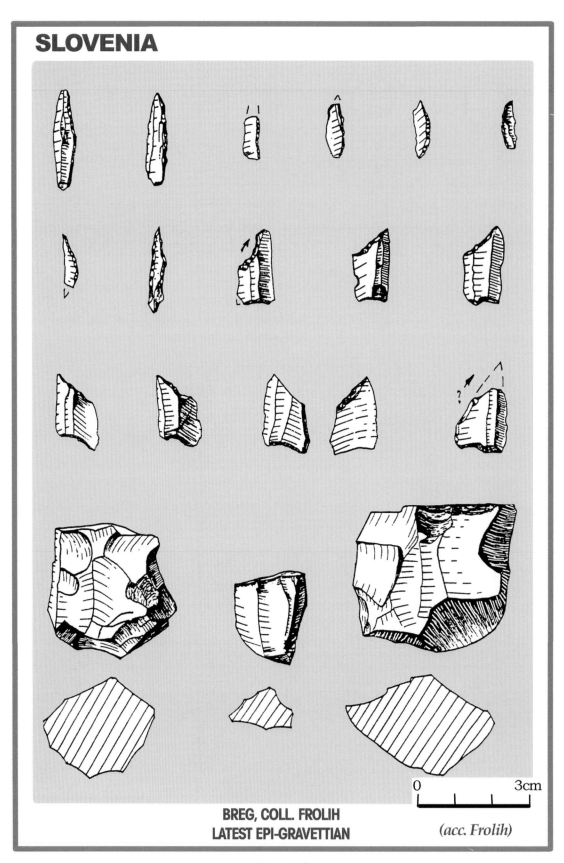

SLOVENIA

BREG, COLL. FROLIH
LATEST EPI-GRAVETTIAN

(acc. Frolih)

0   3cm

Fig. 7.2f

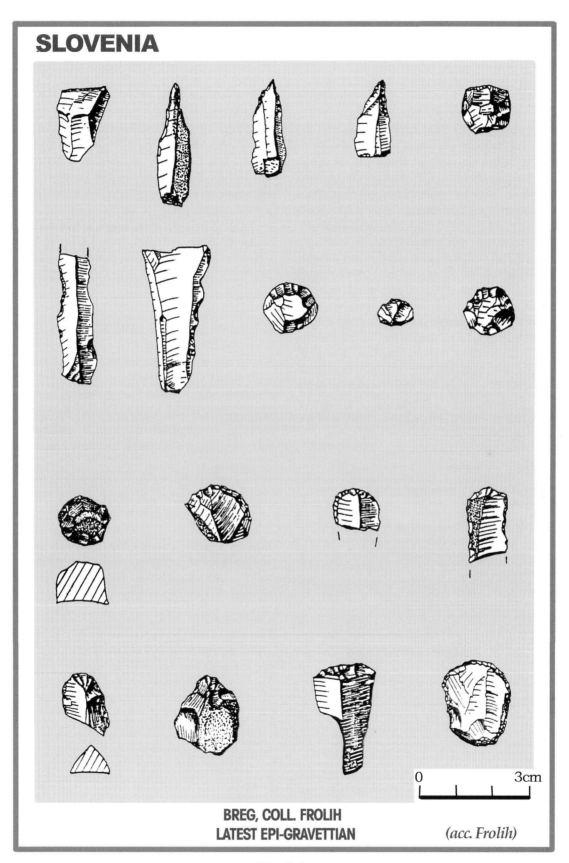

Fig. 7.2g

Frea II and III, Tartaruga 2, etc.). The material from Pod Črmukljo is also very similar to that from Mala Triglavca (cf. below). The classical Italian sites and also Mala Triglavca in Slovenia failed to provide the fourth element: narrow symmetric trapezes that were not formed with the microburin technique. It is thus to be surmised that these trapezes are part of some other unspecified assemblage.

Together with Boris Kavur, then archaeology student at the University of Ljubljana, we decided to check whether these trapezes are distinct from the Castelnovian material in terms of planigraphy or raw material. The surviving field records kept by Mitja Brodar appear to suggest that the Castelnovian trapezes (executed with the microburin technique) were confined to a different area than the narrow trapezes whose planigraphic range is perhaps similar to that of the ceramics (?). The raw material analysis consisted in macroscopic determination of the variety and color (mostly of radiolarites) in the assemblage to which the characteristic cores, tools and waste were later assigned. To enable the evaluation of the taxonomic position of the narrow trapezes, I present in the table below the raw material determinations in the context of the division proposed above (showing the second, third and fourth elements). This table, featuring only a small series of artifacts, does not warrant entirely univocal conclusions but does suggest that the raw material structure of the group of narrow trapezes is slightly different than in the case of Castelnovian finds. In addition, interestingly, the data suggest that the Sauveterrian points (PD) do not necessarily have to belong to the Castelnovian assemblage, possibly being remnants of a separate Late-Sauveterrian assemblage (?).

Pod Črmukljo – raw material

Raw material	Sauveterrian elements (microliths)	Castelnovian element (trapezes made with microburin technique and microburins)	Narrow trapezes
olive	4	2	1
gray	5	5	2
gray sheen	5	8	1
light gray	1	2	–
dark gray	–	5	–
reddish	–	–	1
Banded reddish	–	–	1

On the other hand, simple trapezes appeared in very late Sauveterrian at Montclus in France and at Pradestel in Italy (information from Paolo Biagi).

Mala Triglavca
This multilayer rockshelter in a small cave was partly excavated by F. Leben between 1979 and 1985 and only briefly presented in his 1988 publication. The collection is partly available at the National Museum in Ljubljana and I studied part of it together with Boris Kavur and Simona Petru. Some micro-wear studies of the chipped industry were performed by Petru (1997) as part of her MA thesis (Department of Archaeology, Ljubljana University). Recently, I. Turk published the material, but without any information on stratigraphic subdivisions, which no doubt existed.

The chipped industry presented below comes from a c. 1.50-meter thick cave sediment, which was excavated mostly by horizontal layers of 10, 15 or 20 cm, and not fully sieved. The two topmost "Neolithic" layers (280–349 cm) included ceramics in addition to the flint industry. The "Mesolithic" layers yielded, parallel to the lithics, also bone and antler artifacts, such as spindle-shaped points/*sagaies*.

The flint industry of the upper part of the stratigraphic sequence described here, appears to be highly homogeneous, with the following characteristic features (table below):

Firstly:
- discoidal cores,
- small end-scrapers on flakes (circular/subcircular and very short),
- small end-scrapers on blades (long, short and very short),
- perforators.

Secondly:
- regular bladelets, frequently sectioned or notched (Montbani bladelets) originating from preformed cores,
- trapezes formed with the microburin technique (asymmetric, rhomboidal and symmetric); the microburins themselves are present in all layers.

Mala Triglavca. Typology and technology of the Castelnovian in the upper layers (from the original material)

Artifact	*Layer*					
	280/300	320/340	340/360	360/375	375/385	410/430
Discoidal core	□		□	□	□	
Regular bladelet	□	□	□	□	□	□
Sectioned bladelet		□		□	□	
Notched bladelet			□	□		□
Round end-scraper		□			□	
Very short end-scraper		□		□	□	
Long end-scraper on blade		□	□	□		□
Very short end-scraper on blade			□	□	□	□
Perforator				□	□	
Short asymmetric trapeze		□		□		□
Rhomb					□	
Symmetric trapeze	□					□
Microburin	□	□	□	□	□	□

Turk's publication adds new types in the trapezes and rhombs group, as well as identifies new types of Sauveterrian affinity.

The two groups of morpho-technological features described above provide definite indications regarding the taxonomical position of the Mala Triglavca collection. The first suggests Mesolithic cultures of the region (Sauveterrian, Castelnovian), while the second points univocally to the Castelnovian.

In Slovenia, similar materials were recovered by Mitja Brodar at Pod Črmukljo (cf. above). One must also mention the site of Dedkov Trebež and Viktorjev Spodmol, while in neighboring areas there is Romagnano III, AA, AB, Plan de Frea II and III and some sites around Trieste (Tartaruga 1–2, Azurra 1, Edera, Benussi 3, etc.). In most of these sites trapezes are accompanied by small geometric and non-geometric points of Late Sauveterrian character.

Similar points (backed, crescents – DD, Sauveterrian – PD, isosceles – TN and scalene – TH, TE triangles), which the present author has not seen, have been published by I. Turk, but without describing their stratigraphic position; they could constitute evidence for a transitional, Sauveterrian-Castelnovian complex or a Late Sauveterrian complex.

Viktorjev Spodmol

A similar situation occurred in a collection published by Turk, which the present author again has not seen. Turk shows the classical Late Sauveterrian with discoidal cores, circular/subcircular small end-scrapers (also tectiform) and fine *lamelles à dos*, Sauveterian points PD, rare isosceles TN, and the more numerous Montclus/scalene TE triangles, as well as a few rectangles RA; symmetrical trapezes are very seldom encountered.

Dedkov Trebež

The surface collection from this site is kept at the Department of Geology of the University of Ljubljana. A small part of it was published by Mitja Brodar and analyzed in greater detail by D. Josipovič in his MA thesis.

The collection contains the following elements:
i discoidal cores;
ii very short, small end-scrapers on flakes and blades;
iii small retouched truncations on blades;
iv two small backed pieces with straight back;
v isolated small segment;
vi isolated small scalene triangle with short base;
vii regular pre-formed cores for blades;
viii regular bladelets, including notched (Montbani type) and sectioned specimens;
ix trapezes: symmetric (formed with the microburin technique) and asymmetric (formed with a different technique).

The first seven of these elements have good analogies in Sauveterrian and Early-Castelnovian or in the youngest Epi-Gravettian assemblages. The rest are indicative of the Atlantic period and have Castelnovian analogies; however, the trapezes formed without using the microburin technique may be somewhat younger and/or not Castelnovian (dating to the early ceramic period (?), cf. Pod Črmukljo).

Sites on the Ljubljana Plain

Breg

An extensive subsurface site surveyed (Mark Frelih) and later tested by F. Osole and Mark Frelih in 1983/84 and by Michai Budja in 1996.

The surface collection and material from Osole's explorations are kept at the Department of Geology and Palaeontology of the University of Ljubljana, while Budja's materials are at this University's Department of Archaeology.

A. The surface collection includes, among other things:
i small, very short end-scrapers on flakes (including circular/subcircular specimens), accompanied *inter alia* by very short specimens on blades;
ii perforators;
iii backed pieces with straight and arched back, including larger (older ?) and smaller forms;
iv preformed cores for regular bladelets;
v regular bladelets, also sectioned and notched (Montbani type). This collection, provided it is homogeneous (cf., e.g., some of the backed pieces!), constitutes a composition typical of the inland trans-Dynaric province (latest Epi-Gravettian elements combined with elements of Castelnovian affinity). A similar composition is to be observed in materials excavated by Osole (see below).

B. The collection from the 1983/84 excavations (layer 3/3a), which is yet to be published in full (included in our description is information from the analysis of the original material), features elements similar to those in the surface collection, namely:
i discoidal cores,
ii small, very short end-scrapers on flakes (including circular ones) but also on sectioned blades (very short and long),
iii small arched and straight backed pieces (with no large specimens in evidence);
iv small segments (crescents DD),
v isolated small points with double back (Sauveterrian PD),
vi small retouched truncations,
vii perforators,
viii pre-formed cores for regular bladelets,
ix numerous regular bladelets, also sectioned and notched (Montbani),
x asymmetric trapezes and rhomboids, some formed with the microburin technique.

Contrary to suggestions by Mark Frelih, there are no burins in the collection, but the appearance of small splintered pieces merits note, these apparently being typical of the Mesolithic in the area north of the Dynaric Alps and south of the Carpathians (cf. "Lepensky Vir" and "Vlasac"). As in the surface collection described above, it is just as easy here to isolate the local base of the assemblage represented by elements (i)–(vii), with backed pieces dominating over geometric forms (a feature of the latest Epi-Gravettian tradition) and the Middle Holocene element, in this case fairly strong Castelnovian. However, it would be hard to describe the 1983/84 inventory from Breg as classical Castelnovian, since Castelnovian in the west is a development of Sauveterrian rather than Epi-Gravettian, but on the other hand in Odmut, it derives rather from Epi-Gravettian.

According to the plates in Frelih's publication, the material in trenches I and II (with touching corners) and in the layers distinguished in them (1–2 and 3–3a; 60–80 and 12–30 cm thick respectively!) is homogeneous, and that is why I describe it collectively. The exception here are backed pieces and segments which, according to the explorer, occured only in the lower (3–3a) layer in trench II.

The flint industry in layer 3–3a was accompanied by a rich collection of spindle-shaped points/*sagaies* made of bone and antler (with the best parallels in local Epi-Gravettian), as well as primitive ceramics (possibly Early Neolithic according to Budja's opinion). Charcoal from layer 3a yielded a ^{14}C date of c. 5900 cal. BC (Z-1421).

C. The collection recovered by Michai Budja also comes from two test trenches sunk several dozen meters away from Mark Frelih's excavations.
Trench I yielded layer 1 with the following material:
i   small and very short end-scrapers (but with no circular forms);
ii   small arched and straight backed pieces;
iii   symmetric trapeze formed without using the micro-burin technique. The material included also Early-Neolithic ceramics.

Trench II was dug to a depth of some 190 cm and several of its layers (18, 16, 12, 11, 8, 7, 5, 3, 2) contained archaeological material. The most numerous collection came from layer 2.

Layer 2 (10–20 cm thick) yielded the following flint industry:
i   small, very short end-scrapers on flakes;
ii   small backed pieces with arched and straight backs, and one larger (Paleolithic?) specimen;
iii   small segments DD;
iv   single scalene triangle with short base TH;
v   single isosceles triangle TN;
vi   small dihedral burin on a flake;
vii   small retouched truncations;
viii   single regular core fragment;
ix   infrequent regular bladelets, also sectioned specimens and some bearing traces of retouch;
x   symmetric trapezes, one of which was possibly made with the microburin technique.

The flint artifacts were accompanied by spindle-shaped bone points.

Like Osole's and Frelih's collection described above, Budja's assemblage comprises very late Epi-Gravettian (items i–vii) and "Late-Mesolithic/Early-Neolithic" elements or, generally speaking, elements of Atlantic age (= after 7000 cal. BC). In Budja's collection, these Atlantic elements are even "less Castelnovian" than in Osole's collection.

Also noteworthy is the presence in Budja's collection of splintered pieces, which may be the consequence of the truly dismal quality of the local raw material on this site; in Osole's collection the raw material is clearly superior. Similar artifacts occur in at least some of the microlithic industries in the Pannonian Basin (Sered'), in the region of the Iron Gates (Lepenski Vir, Vlasac) and the Ljubljana Plain (Breg, Vrbičev Hrbec, Zamedvedca) suggesting that we are dealing with a supraregional cultural feature.

Zamedvedca

This large surface collection is kept at the Department of Archaeology, University of Ljubljana, and was studied by D. Josipovič. The following elements merit attention:
i   very short, small end-scrapers on flakes (including circular ones) and end-scrapers on sectioned blades;
ii   small retouched truncations;
iii   arched and straight backed pieces, which are the most numerous, small, but also larger specimens (the latter perhaps Paleolithic?);
iv   single finds of small segments;
v   isolated small scalene triangles with short base;
vi   symmetric trapezes;
vii   regular bladelets, sectioned and with retouch (but lacking notches of the Montbani bladelets type).

The inventory consists of the same set of elements found in Breg with the small end-scrapers accompanied by small points, most of which are backed. This is a set typical of local Epi-Gravettian. Epi-Gravettian elements occur alongside late (Atlantic) trapezes (symmetric, formed without using the microburin technique) and regular bladelets. The collection resembles those from Breg (Budja's collection).

Vrbičev Hrbec I/II

D. Josipovič's surface collection from this site is kept at the Department of Archaeology, University of Ljubljana. It features:
i   very short, small end-scrapers on flakes, including circular specimens; also very short, small end-scrapers on blades (with some long pieces, too);
ii   small retouched truncations;
iii   straight and arched backed pieces;
iv   one scalene triangle;
v   cores for regular bladelets;
vi   regular bladelets, including retouched and sectioned specimens;
vii   one symmetric trapeze formed without using the microburin technique.

Elements (i)–(v) are Epi-Gravettian while the others date to the Atlantic period. In general, this inventory is similar to the inventory from Breg, Michai Budja's collection. Needless to say, its homogeneity is uncertain.

Conclusions

1. The small number of Slovenian microlithic inventories described above (isolated microliths of the kind discussed here occurred also in Kambrce, Podmol pri Kostelcu and Ovcja Jama) are grouped in two zones separated by the Dynaric Alps:

- southern, extending over the Adriatic coastal zone, and continuing to sites in the Trieste Karst (Samatorza, Benussi, Edera);
- northern, comprising the Ljubljana Plain with the upper course of the Sava river and being the extreme southwestern extension of the Great Pannonian Plain.

2. A cautious analysis of the available mostly Middle-Holocene material suggests that they may be divided into two groups differing with regard to the morphology of tools, "descendants" of Early-Holocene industries:

- in the south, the Middle-Holocene assemblages display Late Sauveterrian features typical of the region (small backed points, mostly elongated triangles accompanied by backed pieces and Sauveterre points); the best analogies are the assemblages from Benussi, Romagnano III and Gaban (cf.) in Italy;
- in the north, the latest Epi-Gravettian elements appear to predominate, namely small backed pieces (the most numerous category) occurring with small armatures resembling the ones described above (triangles, backed pieces, Sauveterre points) which, however, are clearly less numerous.

In all, the differences here are of a very detailed nature since other early technological and typological elements are in both cases similar (small discoidal cores, very short, small end-scrapers). After all, the Sauveterrian appeared in the south as a result of local evolution of the Italo-French Epi-Gravettian!

Elements very similar to the latest Epi-Gravettian described here are also known from Slovakia (Dolna Streda), central Hungary (Pečs) and Romania (Gîlma), as well as from the Iron Gates (Lepenski Vir, Vlasac, cf.). Overall, we are dealing with an intra-Carpathian phenomenon connected with the Pannonian Plain and dated to the Early (Padina in Serbia) and Middle Holocene (sites with trapezes; the Early Holocene phase is as yet unknown from Slovenia).

3. Elements of the traditional Epi-Gravettian substratum described above are joined in both cases by Middle-Holocene "additions", such as preformed-core technique for regular bladelets, regular bladelets (often sectioned or notched) and, finally, trapezes.

In the south, these Middle-Holocene "additions" combined with the "old" Sauveterrian elements gave rise around 7000 cal. BC to the classical north Italian Castelnovian (Romagnano III, Gaban, Plan de Frea, Benussi, Edera, Samatorza, Mala Triglavca = model A, cf. "Pre-Neolithic/Castelnovian"). In the north, the "additions" are diverse, the trapezes may be Castelnovian or not (without the microburin technique, like in Lepensky Vir and Vlasac = model B, cf. "Pre-Neolithic"), but the old substratum is always retained. Further north, trapezes of the Castelnovian type are not to be found at all.

7.3. Lepensky Vir lithics

(co-author – J. K. Kozłowski)

Lepenski Vir, the lithic industry of which is presented here, was a great sensation in studies of European prehistory in the late 1960s, offering as it did hope for a local neolithization of the Balkans. There were two things fascinating about Lepensky Vir: spectacular stone sculptures and the presence of a stable (or rather long-lasting, perhaps permanent) "village" with numerous "houses", which were huts in fact, built on a trapezoid plan. Years later, we are prepared to assume that the site was a stable and prospering semi-permanent community. It lies in the Iron Gates area on the Danube, in Serbia, and was investigated by Dragoslav Srejović. No sieving was done. Radiocarbon dating places it in the 7th millennium cal. BC.

The material presented here is from layer I, which was contemporaneous with a few dozen of the trapezoid houses. It has recently been reported that Starćevo-type pottery (!) had been found on the floors of these houses.

General Structure of the Assemblage (Fig. 7.3)

The flint material from Lepenski Vir (layer I) presented below (854 items) possesses exact vertical and horizontal localization related to the dwelling structures discovered in this level. It includes:

Cores and splintered pieces	73	8.56%
Flakes and fragments	604	70.89%
Blades and fragments	118	13.84%
Retouched tools	59	6.69%

The above structure is typical of "home"/base camp sites where all of the stoneworking was done on the spot and mostly local raw material was used. Almost 91.03% of the products were manufactured of local raw material.

Blades

Transversal platforms/butts are typical. Their edges are straight and parallel. Punctiform platforms are in the majority. Parallel interscar edges appear usually on the dorsal face. Some of the whole blades have transversal and slightly oblique ends; they are heavier than those described above and demonstrate negatives of core preformation on the dorsal face. Some of the blade-like flakes, which may have not been subject to core processing, could be trimming blades. The standard size of whole blades and

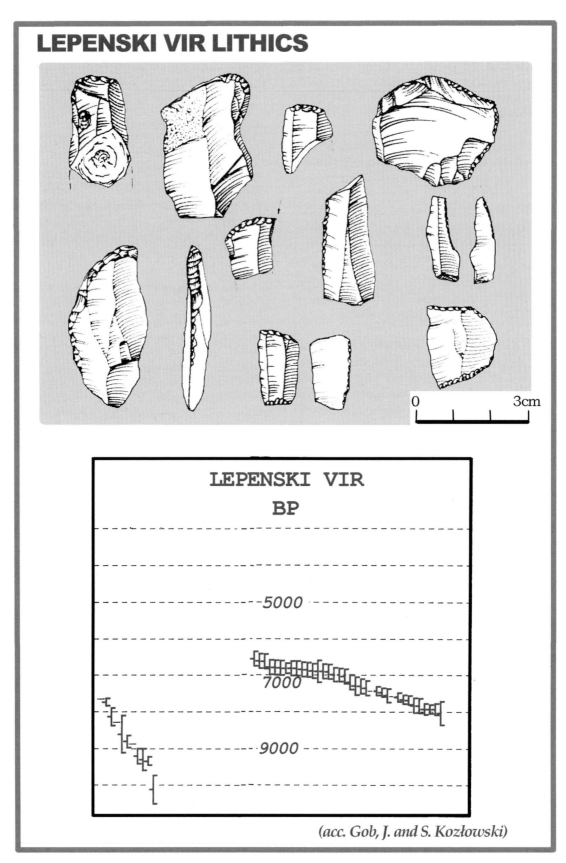

(acc. Gob, J. and S. Kozłowski)

Fig. 7.3

bladelets was 21 to 40 mm in length and 8 to 20 mm in width in proportions of from 2:1 to 4:1.

The blades and bladelets from the comparable Vlasac site (cf.) are shorter and narrower, but the standard width of artifacts from Lepenski Vir is the same as that from Vlasac. Somehow, however, the comparison does not fit the accepted framework. Lepenski Vir has no narrower pieces.

Irrespectively of all the mentioned differences, the technical standard of blades and bladelets from Lepenski Vir is close to that of Vlasac. The same concerns typometric features (proportions are the same).

Blade and bladelet fragments

Whole blades (but not trimming blades) were the initial form. Breakings on the described fragments seem to be intentional in most cases and are the effect of blade sectioning (cf.), a technique often used in Late Mesolithic industries based on regular blades (e.g. Janislawician, classical Castelnovian, cf.) or even in the Early Mesolithic (e.g. Butovian and Kunda, cf.). These objects correspond to similar pieces from Vlasac.

Retouched Tools

General Structure of the Assemblage

The Lepenski Vir I assemblage contains 59 retouched tools. They are shown in the table (numbers of typological groups from 1–12 as in Vlasac, cf.).

The presented diagram shows the major tool classes: A – end-scrapers; B – retouched flakes; C – burins; D – truncations; E – retouched blades; F – combined; H – macroliths; I – leaf-points; J – tanged points; K – armatures; L – splintered pieces; M – others. The general structure of the Lepenski Vir I assemblage obviously corresponds to Vlasac assemblages. All typological groups encountered in Vlasac appear at the site in almost identical order, i.e. retouched flakes (B) and retouched blades (E) predominate, but end-scrapers (A) and armatures (K) are quite numerous as well. Not a single typological group absent from Vlasac occurred in Lepenski Vir.

Detailed Typology

When comparing the typological structure of Lepenski Vir I and Vlasac assemblages in detail, we arrive at the following conclusions: Lepenski Vir I typology is poorer than that of Vlasac, which may be explained by a lesser number of studied pieces. Nevertheless, certain typological convergences between the two sites can be noticed. Among 70 types distinguished at Vlasac (cf.), 26 (i.e., 37.1%) occurred in Lepenski Vir and only 3 types strange to Vlasac appeared in Lepenski Vir.

Further analysis of the retouched tools from the two sites implies that Lepenski Vir I and Vlasac are typologically similar due to the similarity of such characteristic forms as end-scrapers (A), retouched flakes (B), retouched blades (E), chisel-like tools, splintered pieces (L), backed blades and microliths/armatures (K – trapezes and micro-

retouched bladelets). Moreover, an arched backed blade/knife, identical with the specimen from Vlasac occurred at our site. Its stratigraphic position is not entirely clear, but its Mesolithic position is virtually unquestioned.

Thus, typological differences between the two sites mostly concern not exemplified types, i.e., truncations, burins and perforators. These account for 5–11% at Vlasac and 11.84% at Lepenski Vir. One should mention a burin having its analogy in Vlasac, with stratigraphically uncertain, but most likely Mesolithic position.

Concluding, the assemblages of retouched tools from Lepenski Vir I and Vlasac are very much alike and represent the same cultural unit, referred to here as Lepenski Vir culture (cf. also "Slovenian Mesolithic").

Considerable typological convergences between the two discussed sites do not obliterate certain differences between some artifacts concerning typometric aspects rather than morphology. Not only some of the blades from Lepenski Vir, but also a few of the retouched tools (end-scrapers and retouched blades) from this site are much larger than their equivalents in Vlasac and this could be due perhaps to a difference in the raw material used.

Typological group	Vlasac %			Lepenski Vir	
	I	II	III	N°	%
1	9.08	13.41	15.65	5	8.47
2	15.23	20.73	20.86	10	16.94
3	1.32	2.42	–	–	–
4	19.86	19.51	17.39	7	11.86
5	2.64	2.43	3.47	2	3.38
6	7.94	3.04	4.34	2	3.38
7	1.98	–	3.47	4	6.77
8	12.58	15.85	21.73	14	23.72
9	1.32	2.43	0.86	1	1.69
10	9.27	8.53	4.34	3	5.08
11	1.98	1.21	0.86	3	5.08
12	12.58	10.36	6.95	8	13.55
Total N°	152	164	115	59	99.89%

These typometric differences, however, fail to shake our conviction that the two sites reveal a close similarity of the tool assemblages.

Composition of major tool classes in Vlasac and Lepenski Vir (for numbers, cf. text on Vlasac)

Conclusions

The analysis of chipped artifacts from Lepenski Vir presented in this paper implies the following conclusions:

1. Chipped stone artifacts from Lepenski Vir I should be classified as a separate taxonomic unit, which Janusz Kozłowski and I have described together with Dragoslav Srejović as Lepenski Vir culture (Vasile Boroneanţ refers to this same unit as the Schela Cladovei culture). Next to

material from Lepenski Vir, this unit includes collections from the three layers of the Vlasac site, from Icoana, Schela Cladovei and Ostrovul Corbului and much more to the west, perhaps from the Slovenian sites in the Ljubljana Plain (e.g. Breg, excavations of Michai Budja ?).

2. The inventory of Lepenski Vir I is of Mesolithic style and comes from a local Late-Paleolithic/Mesolithic tradition of the Cuina Turcului/Padina type, but goes together with Early Neolithic pottery.

7.4. Vlasac

(co-author – J. K. Kozłowski)

The most characteristic and the richest site of the Lepensky Vir/Schela Cladovei culture, apart from Lepensky Vir itself, is Vlasac (Serbia). It is an open, multi-layer site in the Iron Gates region, explored in 1969–1974 by Zagorka Letica and Dragoslav Srejović. The excavations revealed trapezoidal huts, numerous inhumations, ornaments and bone industry C$_{14}$ datings are placed around 7000–5000 years cal. BC. Letica published a monograph of these finds, while Janusz K. Kozłowski and Stefan K. Kozłowski contributed a separate discussion of the flint industry (Fig. 7.4a–h).

Below is a description of the retouched tools (without the stratification).

1. End-scrapers (A)
(according to the letter markings for typological groups used in this volume)

Vlasac yielded 61 end-scrapers, subdivided into 15 types as follows:

1.1. Very short arched end-scrapers (6) on small flakes with convex, occasionally irregular front, and semi-steep or steep retouch; four pieces have the front in the distal part, the remaining two in the lateral part of the flake; one specimen has a slight base retouch.

1.2. Short arched end-scrapers (2) on heavy blade-like flakes; one has a slightly convex and the other two a strongly convex, steep or semi-steep front.

1.3. Short, arched end-scrapers with unilateral retouch (8), on flakes with slightly convex and semi-steep or steep fronts. The edges have fine and quite steep retouch.

1.4. Short, arched end-scrapers with bilateral retouch (2), made on blade-like flakes; one has an oblique semi-steep working end, the other a steep convex one. Edges with partial semi-steep retouch.

1.5. Short end-scrapers with oblique front (4), on flakes; fronts steep, slightly convex, and slantwise with the axis of the tool.

1.6. Elongated arched end-scrapers (3), on heavy blades; fronts convex or denticulated, with fine, interrupted, denticulated retouch on the longer edge. The fronts are semi-steep, one is localized in the proximal part.

1.7. Elongated, arched end-scrapers with lateral retouch (3), made on blades; straight, semi-steep transversal fronts, one specimen fully retouched on one, the second on both sides of the length; two pieces with fronts in the proximal parts.

1.8. Very short, straight end-scraper (1), on flake; steep front, irregular, somewhat denticulated.

1.9. Very short end-scraper with oblique front (1); steep, straight and slightly undulating front.

1.10. Very short end-scrapers with unilateral retouch (2), made on flakes; steep or semi-steep straight fronts, edges completely retouched.

1.11. Circular and subcircular end-scrapers (7), on flakes; short with steep or semi-steep retouch; one fully retouched, another has undulated retouched edge with two distinct nosed convexities.

1.12. High end-scrapers (6), short or very short, on flakes, two varieties: nosed (4) and wide, straight fronts (2); steep retouch, usually thick and occasionally with retouch on one of the longer edges. 1.13. Atypical nosed flake end-scraper (1), with steep retouch of the front.

1.14. Double end-scraper (1), on flake with convex fronts; steeply and semi-steeply retouched.

1.15. End-scrapers on splintered pieces (4); two different categories: two simple arched, one double and one arched specimen with convergent retouched sides, all pieces short and steeply retouched.

1.16. Fragments (9).

2. Irregular Scrapers (= Retouched Flakes) – B

2.1. Straight lateral irregular scrapers (19), on simple flakes or blade-like flakes or on splintered pieces (5). They have simple dorsal (14), ventral (3) or alternate retouch (2) at an angle of 70–80°(12) or 50–65°(8). In two cases the retouch was slightly denticulated and in another two rather high. Apart from the retouched lateral edge, the end of one artifact was thinned by splintered retouch (showing wear ?); another specimen has a notch on the other side, and a transversal breaking was found in one case; the majority are short pieces.

2.2. Lateral undulated irregular scrapers (4), on flakes; simple retouch (60–70°), denticulated (80°) or fine interrupted (60°).

2.3. Straight, transversal irregular scrapers (7), on flakes, with fine (80–90°), simple (65–75°), slightly denticulated (75°) or keeled retouch (60°); two pieces with dorsal, and five with ventral retouch.

2.4. Undulated, transversal irregular scrapers (4), three on flakes, one on an unworked piece of flint; transversal edges shaped by notched (72–85°) or denticulated retouch (50°).

2.5. Transversal, oblique irregular scrapers (5), four on flakes, one on an unworked piece of flint; retouch denticulated (50–80°), one case of simple (65°) and multiserial (95°).

2.6. Lateral and transversal irregular scrapers (15), on flakes (9), splintered pieces (4) or unworked splintered pieces (2); retouched on the transversal, mostly distal and on one of the lateral edges, in four cases alternated, mostly denticulated (50–70°), or simple fine (50–85°), and only exceptionally multiserial (80°).

2.7. Double lateral irregular scrapers (3), on heavy flakes with multiserial, denticulated or keeled retouch

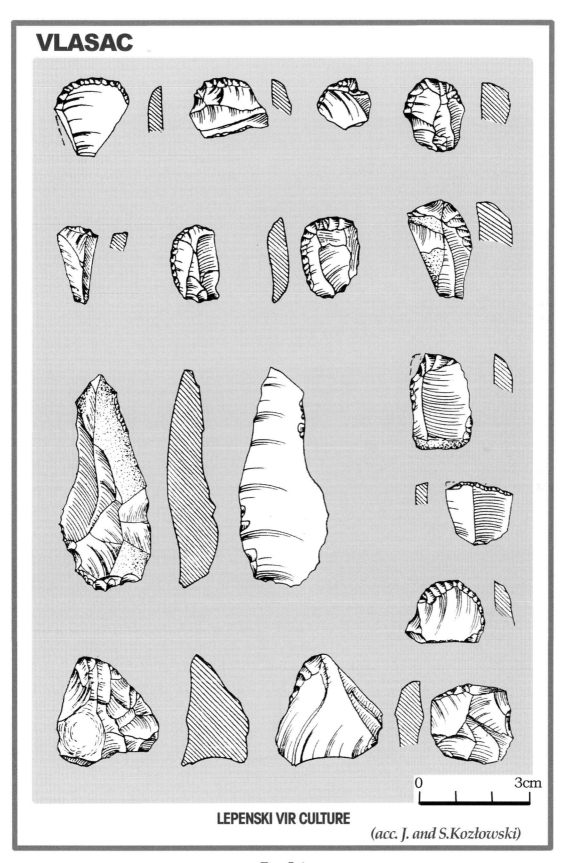

VLASAC

LEPENSKI VIR CULTURE

(acc. J. and S.Kozłowski)

0   3cm

Fig. 7.4a

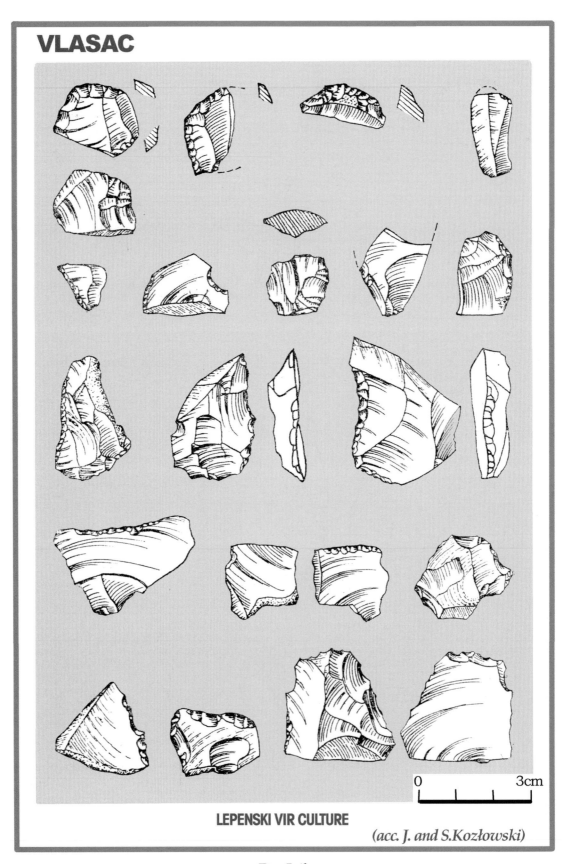

Fig. 7.4b

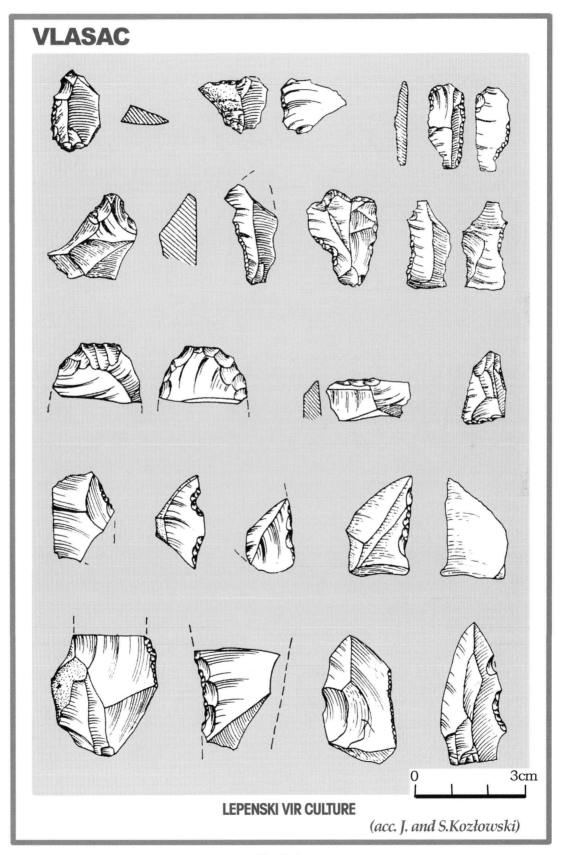

VLASAC

LEPENSKI VIR CULTURE

(acc. J. and S.Kozłowski)

Fig. 7.4c

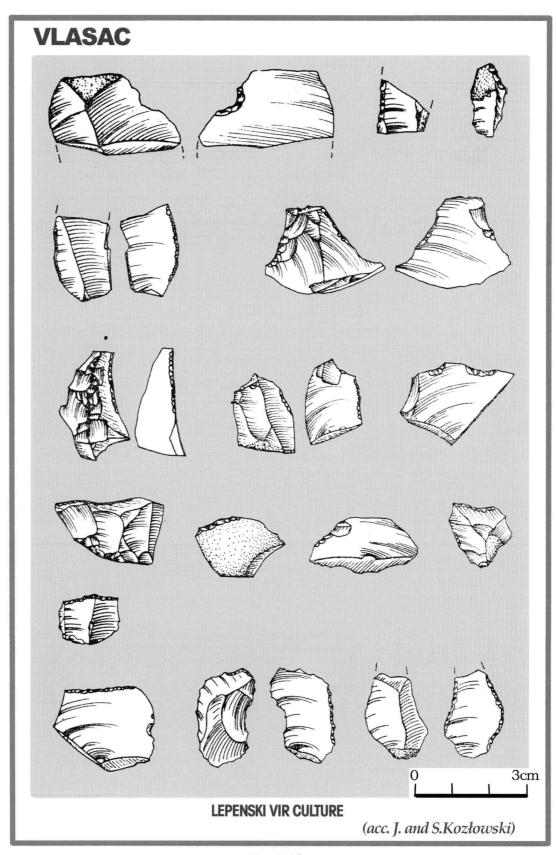

Fig. 7.4d

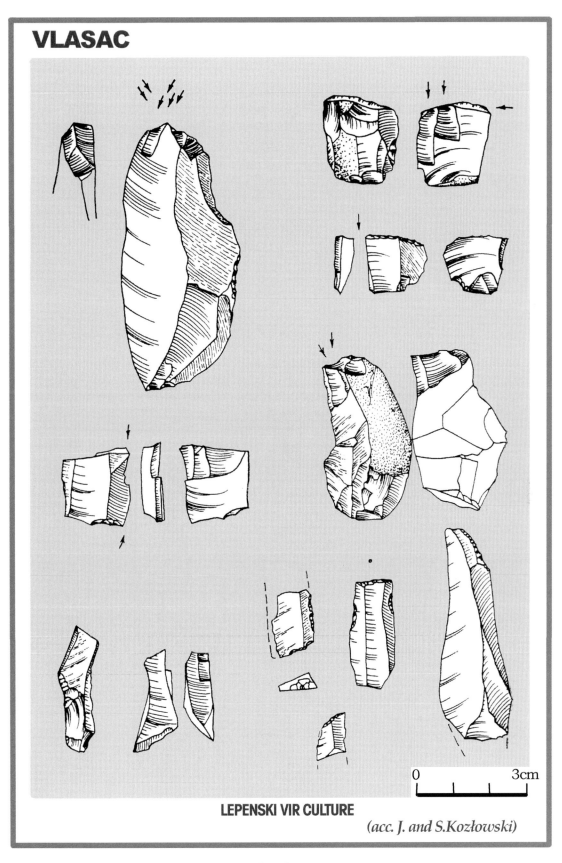

Fig. 7.4e

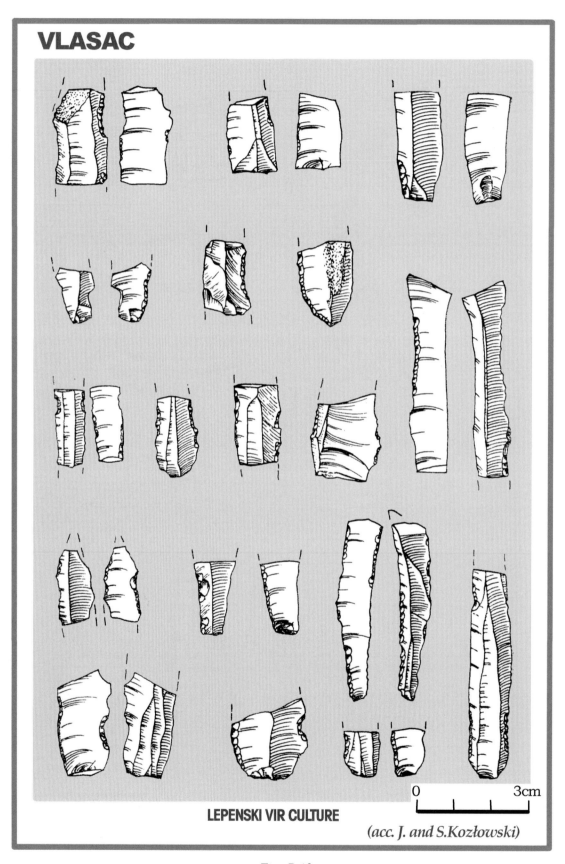

VLASAC

0   3cm

LEPENSKI VIR CULTURE

(acc. J. and S.Kozłowski)

Fig. 7.4f

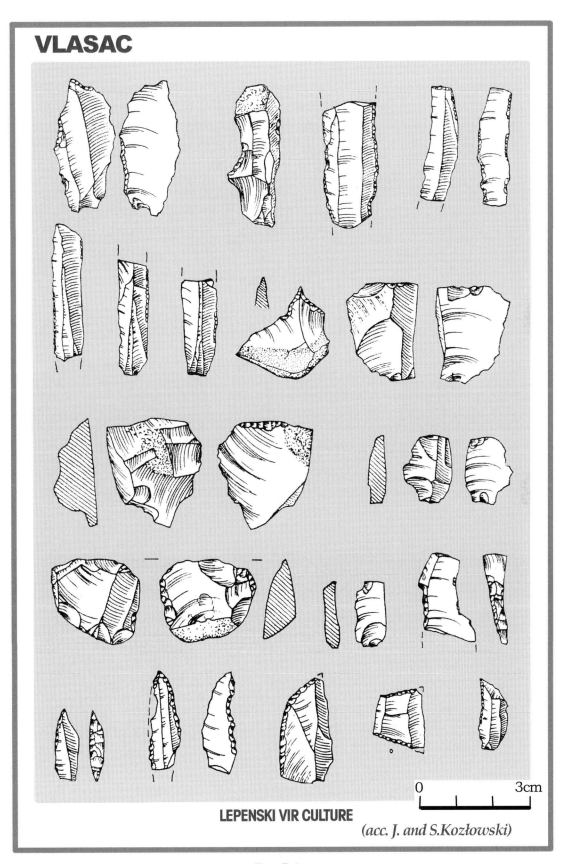

VLASAC

LEPENSKI VIR CULTURE

(acc. J. and S.Kozłowski)

0   3cm

Fig. 7.4g

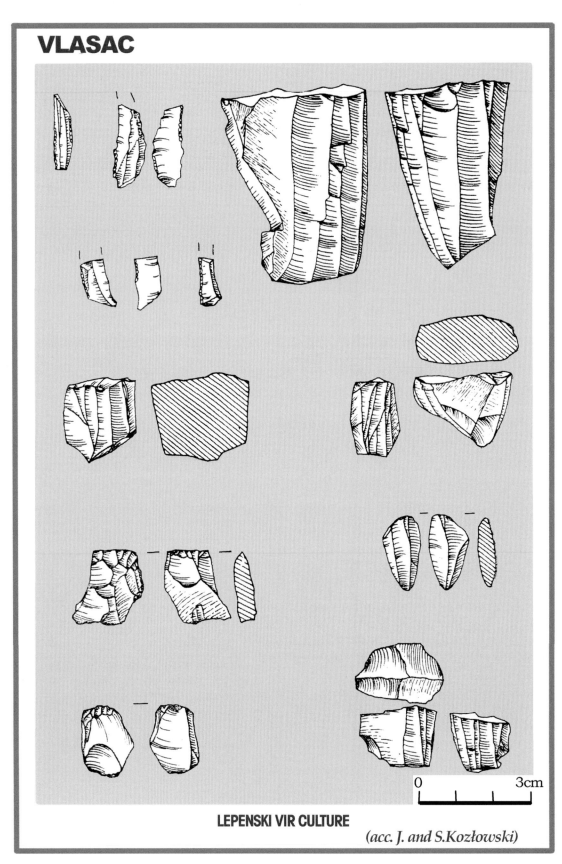

VLASAC

LEPENSKI VIR CULTURE

(acc. J. and S.Kozłowski)

0   3cm

Fig. 7.4h

(70–80°) on both edges, not covering, however, the entire length of the edges.

2.8. Convergent irregular scrapers (2), on flakes, although formed at the intersection of two notches (60–76°) producing a kind of protrusion.

2.9. Irregular scrapers on splintered pieces (22), made on excessively worked splintered pieces; retouch covers the end (6), one lateral edge (11), two lateral edges (1) or both the end and one side (4). The retouch on seven tools is simple and steep, on three specimens denticulated, on four notched; three artifacts have flat retouch, two have simple semi-steep retouch, and in one case the retouch is multiserial.

3. Side-scrapers (B)

The collection includes six side-scrapers, four made on flakes, one on a splintered piece, and one on an unworked piece of flint. They belong to four types: lateral convex (3), lateral undulated (1), partially retouched lateral (1), and lateral transversal (1); retouch is semi-steep, mainly fine and simple, in one case slightly notched.

4. Retouched Flakes (B)

Unlike irregular scrapers, they have only incomplete retouch, either intentional or the effect of use. Their typology has been based on the position of retouch in relation to the axis of the flake.

4.1. Flakes with unilateral retouch (34 full specimens and 8 fragments). According to the mode of retouch, they can be divided into the following groups: with fine simple retouch over a short section of one edge (19, including three inversely retouched); with similar retouch along nearly the entire edge (7, including one inversely retouched); with notched retouch (8, including two with inverse notch); and with denticulated retouch along a short section of the edge (2).

4.2. Flakes with bilateral retouch (11); retouch fine, simple, alternate (3), fine simple, dorsal (1), alternate interrupted (3), inverse interrupted (2), notched on one side and fine, interrupted on the other (2).

4.3. Transversally retouched flakes (17 complete specimens and two fragments), with incomplete, simple, fine retouch (7), similar retouch along the entire transversal edge (4, including one inversely retouched), flattish notched retouch (2, with one inversely retouched), fine interrupted (1), incomplete denticulated (1) and two retouched notches.

4.4. Flakes with lateral and transversal retouch (7), characterized either by simple fine retouch of the distal part and similar incomplete lateral retouch (4), or by fine retouch of the distal part and lateral notch (1).

4.5. Flakes with convergent retouched edges (1), retouch simple and fine, either on the dorsal face (1) or alternate (1).

4.6. Heavy flakes with denticulated retouch (2), one transversally retouched in the proximal part, while the other has transversal retouch on the distal part and a lateral notch.

5. Raclettes (B)

5.1. Simple *raclettes* (6), on flakes with retouch on the lateral (2), transversal (2), or both lateral and transversal edges (2). All of these specimens are characterized by very fine and steep retouch typical of *raclettes*, although unlike the classical specimens from Badegoulian their retouch never covers the entire circumference.

5.2. Inverse *raclettes* (6), with very steep and fine, ventral retouch, not covering the entire circumference.

6. Burins (C)

6.1. Central dihedral burins (2), on heavy flakes.

6.2. Lateral dihedral burins (4), three on flakes, one on blade. Multiple, partially flat burin scars are found on two pieces, one has a single burin scar, the last made on an elongated, narrow blade, one edge of which has a steep, inverse retouch, while the end is shaped with straight and bent blows.

6.3. Lateral burins on truncation (4), on flake with straight, transversal truncation, the other two are core-like specimens made on flat residual cores with transversal retouch, passing in one case into steep side retouch.

6.4. Burins on broken blade (2). One double specimen has on the other end a less distinct lateral burin on truncation. Apart from a lateral burin blow, both artifacts present evidence of a number of flat blows suggesting splintered retouch. Therefore, they can be considered as transitional forms between burins and chisel-like tools (cf. below).

6.5. Single blow burins (8), on flakes (5) or blades (3); the largest group comprises lateral artifacts (6, including a flat one). The remaining two include a transversal facetted burin on blade and a double burin on flake.

6.6. Burins on splintered pieces (1), single blow tool, the blow being situated on the side of a double-ended splintered piece or chisel-like tool.

6.7. Burin spalls (18).

7. Retouched Truncations (D)

7.1. Blades with transversal truncation (1), straight, steep truncation and lateral retouched notch.

7.2. Transversal truncations with lateral retouch (2) straight transversal truncation, situated in either the distal or the proximal part (the latter could be a double specimen).

7.3. Convex truncation (1), on elongated blank, with convex truncation.

7.4. Concave truncation (1), on broad blank.

7.5. Small (almost microlithic) truncation (2), transversal, convex, finely retouched, one on the proximal and the other on the distal part of the bladelet.

8. Retouched Blades/bladelets (E)

This category comprises all blades with lateral retouch. It includes a relatively small number of proper *lames retouchées*, and much more frequent blades with incomplete retouch of the edges, in many cases resulting from use.

8.1. One-sided retouched blades/bladelets (27); they can be further divided into three subgroups. The first consists of eight fragments (sectioning) and one complete specimen with continuous, simple, fine retouch on the dorsal (6) or ventral face (3). The second has specimens with interrupted retouch on the dorsal (6) or alternately dorsal and ventral face (10); retouch is steep or semi-steep, rarely denticulated. The third subgroup includes two blades with lateral steeply retouched notches.

8.2. Two-sided retouched blades/bladelets (29); for lack of artifacts with continuous retouch, the first subgroup consists of specimens with interrupted, frequently denticulated, simple fine, steep and semi-steep, exclusively dorsal retouch (13 specimens). The second subgroup includes artifacts with interrupted, but changeable retouch (on the ventral and dorsal faces), in six cases alternate. The type of retouch is similar to that of the previous subgroup. The last subgroup is represented by only one inversely retouched specimen with continuous retouch on one face and notched retouch on the other.

8.3. Retouched bladelet with transversal retouch of the end (1); resembles the two-sided blades of the third subgroup; its end, however, has a simple, fine, steep, transversal retouch.

8.4. Retouched bladelet with tang (1); retouched on both sides of the base on the dorsal face, retouch simple and quite steep.

8.5. Retouched bladelet fragment (1) of a transversally and longitudinally broken retouched blade.

8.6. Microretouched bladelets (11) with fine, interrupted, rarely denticulated retouch, along one or both edges. Retouch could have been effected by the use of unworked blades.

It should be noted at this point that most of the transversal breakings of the described blades resulted from intentional sectioning (cf.). As for retouch, in this group it is very often the effect of intense use and not intentional flake retouching.

9. Perforators (F)

The assemblages under discussion consists of 7 perforators, including one artifact on blade and six on flake. The perforator on blade has a poorly defined working end, shaped with semi-steep retouch in the distal part of the blade. Among the perforators on flake, one straight artifact has a clear-cut tip, the remaining four have lateral working ends formed by converging retouch of transversal and lateral edges. Only one artifact has no transversal retouch, and its working end is formed at the intersection of two notches.

10. Chisel-like/Splintered Tools (L)

10.1. Single chisel-like tools (18). This group includes flakes and blades with retouch of one edge or extremity. These tools resemble either the so-called Kostienki truncated blades/knives or unfinished splintered pieces on flake, or else they come close to flat, multiscar burins. The group, therefore, is not homogeneous and can be further subdivided into three subgroups, according to the position of retouch: tip-retouched (10), base-retouched (6), and side-retouched tools (2). The first subgroup consists of artifacts on flake (8) and on blade (2).

10.2. Double chisel-like tools (15), most closely related to splintered pieces although their working seems to be less advanced than that of proper bipolar splintered pieces. Most specimens have splintered retouch on both ends of the flake, except for three cases with lateral but also symmetrical retouch.

11. Backed Blades/Knives

Backed blades (6) stand out among the backed pieces in terms of size, reaching a length of up to 60 mm and width from 16 to 25 mm. Three are characterized by arched, though never high backs, not taking up the entire length of the pieces. The back is placed in the proximal part of the blank. One of the items, half-preserved, had a back which probably covered its entire length.

They are analogous to the Sauveterrian specimens of northern Italy and southern France (couteau type Rouffignac).

12. Microliths/Armatures (K)

This group of tools, probably the most characteristic for a majority of Mesolithic assemblages, has been classed following a list proposed by Stefan K. Kozlowski in his "Atlas of the Mesolithic in Europe" (cf. in this volume). The present paper employs not only names corresponding to particular classes of artifacts but also their corresponding letter symbols (e.g. DA; DB, AZ, AA, etc.). The small number of microliths appears to be due to excavation technique (no sieving done).

12.1–3. Backed pieces (D)

These tools were made on bladelets, often quite irregular. They are characterized by one steeply retouched back. The Vlasac assemblage includes 7 backed pieces, which are morphologically quite diverse.

First there is a small form with a straight back taking up the full length of the tool (DA). Another class includes asymmetric, slightly arched tools (DB). The latter are broad and similar to the Vlasac backed blades. Furthermore, there are two backed pieces (DC) with slightly arched backs not taking up, however, the entire length. Finally, there is a large stubby crescent with strongly arched back (DD-DE).

12.4. Isosceles (TN)

Specific to Vlasac is a large, broad, single isoscele triangle. This slightly damaged tool is made on flake or large blade. Two shorter, slightly concave edges have steep, high retouch. The piece is bent in section.

2.5. Sauveterrian points (PD)

Single very long and damaged specimen of this type,

particularly big (> 30 mm). It is characterized by convergent perforator-like steep and high retouch.

12.6. Rectangles (R)

Represented by one, nearly complete piece belonging to the RA class. Its back and two transversal truncations have steep retouch. The tool is slightly bent in section.

12.7–10. Symmetric trapezes (A)

All pieces in this group are made on regular bladelets with an average width of 11–12 mm. They are characterized by two symmetric slightly convergent, steeply or semi-steeply retouched truncations, placed transversally to the axis of the blade.

Simple trapezes (AZ) are the most numerous in the Vlasac assemblage (4), either with straight or slightly undulated truncation, and proportions approximating 1:1. One piece is particularly massive.

One piece is similar to these trapezes in terms of proportion and the type of retouch, but different in its concave, "Castelnovian" truncations (AF).

Moreover, two specimens of narrow trapezes (AA) were found; the length of the specimen in this case exceeds the width by more than 1.5 times. Their slightly concave truncations are more oblique than in the case of simple trapezes (AZ); one specimen has a truncation retouched on the ventral face.

12.11–13. Micro-retouched bladelets/inserts (WA-C)

These are delicate, slightly bent bladelets with straight, sometimes slightly undulating edges. Their average width is between 6 and 7 mm. Retouch is low, semi-abrupt with very fine negatives. It extends either along the entire length or along part of it, rarely forming a transverse truncation. Micro-retouched bladelets are divided into pieces with one or two retouched edges, sharply pointed and with a single base retouch.

Considered together with fragments, artifacts retouched on one edge prevail in the material under discussion.

One-edge bladelets are represented by seven specimens, of which five are retouched on the dorsal and two on the ventral face.

Two-edge bladelets are represented by seven pieces, which can be classified into three variants: specimens with dorsal, ventral and alternate retouch.

The Vlasac industry compared to Iron Gates Mesolithic assemblages

It has been noted already that the Vlasac industry had counterparts in assemblages coming mostly from Iron Gate sites on the Romanian-Serbian border. Two distinct phases prior to the local Neolithic can be observed in this territory:

– Epigravettian phase (or Romanellian according to Vasile Boroneanţ) represented, for example, by layers I and II of the Late Pleistocene Cuina Turcului rockshelter in Romania, as well as by the Early Holocene assemblage from Padina A (lower layers)

from Serbia, dating from the 11th (Cuina Turcului, layer I) to the 10th–8th millennia cal. BC (Padina – the lower burials; Cuina Turcului layer II);

– Lepenski Vir phase (from c. 7000 cal. BC), represented by layers I and II from Lepenski Vir, as well as by Icoana I, Vetereni-Terasa, Schela Cladovei and Ostrovul Banului. The Vlasac site should be assigned to this phase.

The transition from the first to the second phase was unbroken and must have taken place at the end of the 8th/beginning of the 7th millennium cal. BC. It was the time of the origin of specific local groups, including the "Lepenski Vir Culture", which sprang up within the widespread Late Pleistocene/Early Holocene Epigravettian tradition of the Balkan type, differing from the Italian one by the presence of numerous and different arched backed points.

The Balkan Epigravettian culture is characterized satisfactorily thanks to A. Paunescu who described the assemblages from Cuina Turcului and Ivana Radovanović who published Padina (cf. "South-East"). These assemblages are characterized by a predominance of very short and short end-scrapers, accompanied by quite numerous microliths (lanceolate backed points and crescents, isosceles and scalene triangles), while burins and splintered pieces are infrequent. The blade technique is still prevalent (cf. also Frankhthi and Medena Stijena industries).

Nearly all these traits, though with lesser intensity (unsieved material ?), are found also in Lepenski Vir culture and so, too, in the Vlasac assemblages, which also comprise very short and short end-scrapers, lanceolate points (DB), crescents (DD), rectangles (RA) and isosceles (TN). Furthermore, burins and a great number of splintered pieces, much more numerous than in the classical Balkan Epigravettian phase, have been observed.

There can be no doubt then that we are dealing with a continuation of the local tradition and a transition from Epigravettian to Lepenski Vir culture, although there are still gaps in the evolutionary sequence, not the least because of an incoherence of C[14] dates with regard to the litostratigraphic and paleoclimatic sequences.

Let us also quote Vasile Boroneanţ who observed a great share of flakes in the assemblages prior to the Lepenski Vir phase (an early phase of his Schela Cladevei culture). This, in our opinion, proves the local origin of this phase.

Despite numerous similarities between Lepenski Vir culture and classical Balkan Epigravettian, there is sufficient evidence to define this phase as a separate taxonomic unit. It concerns the Vlasac assemblages foremost, whereas a lack of quantitative data prevents conclusive determinations on the probably earlier (c. 8000 cal. BC) assemblages from Veterani-Terasa and Icoana I. Thus, our definition of Lepenski Vir culture cannot be a strict counterpart either of the "Schela Cladevei culture" as conceived by Boroneanţ or of the "Lepenski Vir culture" as defined by Srejović. A detailed analysis of the assemblages dating from c. 8000 cal. BC is needed for a more precise approach to the question (in order to clarify the question of the emergence of retouched bladelets, the appearance of splintered pieces in such numbers and the significant increase (if at all) in the frequency of irregular scrapers (B).

In analyzing traits of the Vlasac industry not connected with classic Epigravettian tradition, the following elements should be considered in a division into regional and pan-European:

1. Regional Balkan elements include numerous splintered pieces (known also from Slovakia and Slovenia, cf.) and prevailing irregular scrapers (popular also in Greece, cf. Frankhthi in). These elements are typical of many Balkan pre-Neolithic groups (e.g. Frankhthi – "Upper Mesolithic", Kytnos, Sered', Breg – Budja collection, cf. "Slovenian Mesolithic").

2. Also regional probably (though rather in the Pontic range?) are microretouched bladelets with counterparts in Dekilitazh (Bulgaria) and perhaps also in Ukraine (Kukrek culture bladelets, cf.).

3. The third original element in the Vlasac assemblage is the regular blade/bladelet technique which formed the basis for the production of characteristic retouched blades and trapezes.

A combination of these three elements emerged in the broadly conceived Mediterranean basin about 7000 cal. BC (cf. "Les courants interculturelles" = Castelnovization model B, cf. "Pre-Neolithic/Castelnovian"). Being (together with trapezes) an intercultural element in northwestern and central Europe as well, they acted as an additional stimulus for the formation and development of the latest regional Epigravettian tradition. At the same time, they appear to be a useful chronological indicator for dating the lower extent of Lepenski Vir culture from c. 7000 cal. BC or slightly later.

It follows from the above that the Vlasac industry together with the entire Lepenski Vir phase in the Iron Gate region belongs to the Mediterranean cultural province which evolved from an Epigravettian base. From the Late Glacial period onwards, the province underwent internal locally specific differentiation which led, *inter alia,* to the emergence of the Balkan Epigravettian culture, independent in its development of the Italian variants of this tradition; the latter, unlike the Balkan one, finally gave the Sauveterrian. The differences, already visible in the Late Glacial phase, consist in the numerous occurrences of arched backed points in the Balkan assemblages (as opposed to their scarce occurrence in northern Italy, except for the tenth layer at Riparo Tagliente in the north). The further development of the Balkan group followed even more divergent lines, leading to the rise of regional elements in the fields of tool technology and morphology. These technological novelties, however, have nothing in common with the Sauveterrian tradition from the more western regions. It is not clear, however, what the relation was between Lepensky Vir culture and the Epi-Gravettian complex of Gîlma type (Romania, Hungary, Slovakia). It can also be assumed that the complex from Breg (Michai Budja's excavations) from Slovenia (cf.) was very near to Lepensky Vir culture.

Table 7.1 Vlasac. General structure of the major tool classes (in %)

Major Class		Layer		
Typological groups	According to the classification in the present study	I	II	III
A End-scrapers	1	9.08	13.41	15.65
	2	15.23	20.73	20.86
B Irregular scrapers	3	1.32	2.43	–
	4	19.86	19.51	17.39
	5	2.64	2.43	3.47
C Burins	6	7.94	3.04	4.34
D Truncations	7	1.98	–	3.47
E Retouched blades	8	12.58	15.85	21.73
F Perforators	9	1.32	2.43	0.86
K Backed blades and microliths	11–12	1.98	1.21	0.86
L Splintered pieces	10	12.58	10.36	6.95
L Chisel-like tools	10	9.27	8.53	4.34

8

The West and the Centre

In the cultural sense, the Centre and West of Europe are subdivided latitudinally. In the early and middle period, the Beuronian spread across the uplands from the Belgian Ardennes and the Paris Basin to Moravia, southwestern Poland and the northern piedmont of the Alps, while the Maglemosian in the broad sense occupied, at least in the beginning, a belt from Britain in the west to the Polish Plain in the east. Later, the picture changed, when the "West" moved northward, crossing over this northern demarcation line (cf. "Mapping the Mesolithic").

This is why the two differing technocomplexes of West and Centre are discussed in a single chapter. In some periods of the Mesolithic, their fate was very strongly intertwined (cf. "Les courants interculureles") while the evolution of microliths throughout the Mesolithic was very similar or even the same (cf. "Rhythms" and "Koine").

In the chapter on territory (cf. "There") the reader will find papers treating on some of the spatial aspects of the Mesolithic in Western and Central Europe (cf. "Stories").

8.1. Les Courants interculturels dans le Mésolithique de l'Europe Occidentale

Cette étude est consacrée à un phénomène qui intervient à deux reprises dans le Mésolithique de l'Europe Occidentale aux 8e et 7e millénaires cal. A.C., englobant de vastes étendues de territoires. Il se manifeste par la présence de "composants", dits "sauveterrien" et "castelnovien" dans des inventaires considérés comme appartenant à des entitées taxonomiques différentes. Nous nous proposons dans cette étude d'effectuer une analyse chronologique et spatiale de ces composants (nommés dans le texte respectivement : composant "SVT" et composant "CST") et de tenter l'effort d'une explication des mécanismes qui déterminent le phénomène en question (Fig. 8.1a–b).

La définition des composants "SVT" et "CST"

Dans le rapport présenté au symposium international "The Mesolithic in Europe" qui s'est tenu à Varsovie en 1973, (cf. "Warsaw '73"), l'auteur du présent article suggérait que l'industrie lithique de chacune des cultures mésolithiques européennes était la somme d'un certain nombre de "composants". Ceux-ci, diffèrent entre autres par leur universalité, c'est-à-dire par leur importance et leur développement différents dans le temps et dans l'espace, leur genèse étant, par ailleurs, très variée. Il y a donc des "composants" qui tirent leur origines de sources locales et subsistent sur un terriroire donné dans tous les inventaires qui apparaissent au cours d'une période déterminée. Radicalement opposés sont les composants "marginaux" (dans le sens territorial) et "éphémères" (dans le sens chronologique), empruntés souvent à des milieux étrangers. Il convient en outre de souligner que les mêmes éléments typologiques et techniques peuvent dans un milieu culturel donné jouer le role de composants indigènes (fondamentaux) et dans un autre un rôle marginal ou éphémère. Le lecteur trouvera dans le présent ouvrage les exemples de cette différentiation.

Le composant "SVT"

Dans les inventaires mésolithiques de l'Holocène ancien d'Europe Occidentale on voit assez souvent apparaitre simultanément:

1. des triangles étroits scalènes à base courte de petites dimensions (TH)
2. des triangles similaires, mais avec 3 bords retouchés (TE)
3. les pointes de Sauveterre (PD)
4. de petites pointes et lamelles à dos (D)
5. de petits segments de cercle (DD)
6. la technique de la lamelle étroite

Certains types de cette liste apparaissent le plus tôt dans le Tardiglaciaire de la région occidentale du Bassin méditerrannéen, dans l'Epi-Gravettien régional. Toutefois, ce n'est que dans le Sauveterrien (Le Martinet, Montclus, Rouffignac, Culoz, Vionnaz, Romagnano III, Isola Santa,

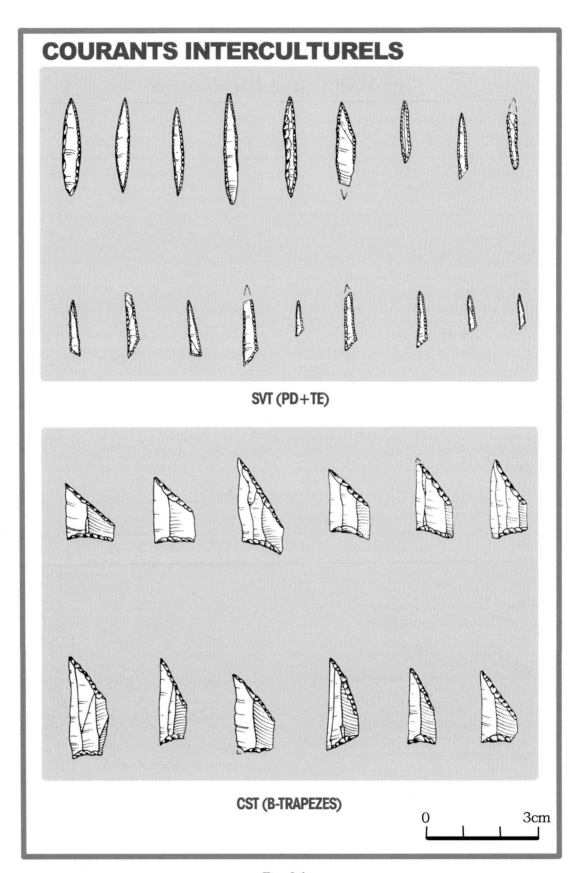

Fig. 8.1a

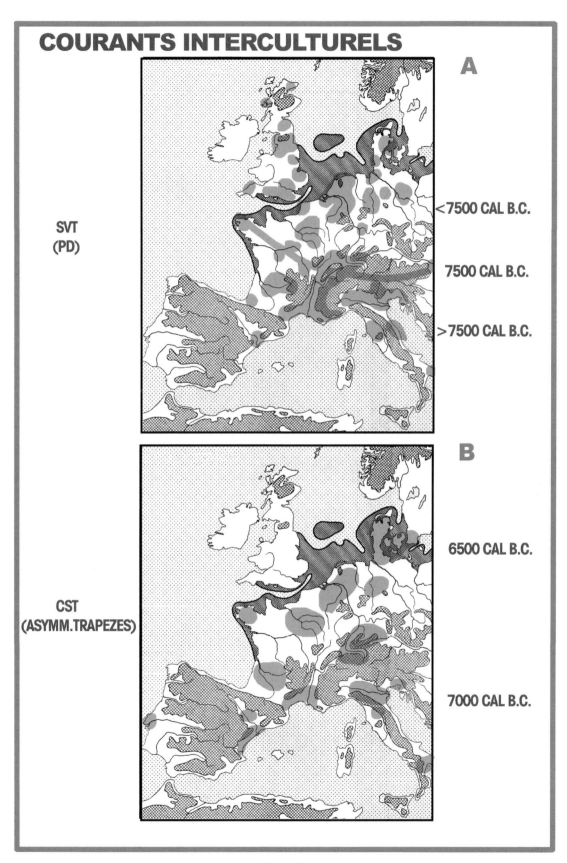

Fig. 8.1b

Gaban, Margineda, Vatte di Zambana, Pod Ćrmukljo, etc;) que la liste des éléments ci-dessus mentionnée s'est pleinement cristallisée, devenant dans le Midi ouest-européen typique pour son époque (env. 9000–7000 ans cal. A.C.).

Il est rare que le Sauveterrien ainsi défini possède les armatures ne figurant pas dans la liste présentée (par ex. les triangles isosceles = TN, TM). Nous pouvons alors à juste titre appeler cette liste "sauveterrienné" (ou "SVT").

L'analyse des industries mésolithiques ouest-européennes connues des régions non-sauveterriennes, montre qu'une partie d'entre elles, bien que ne pouvant être considérées sauveterriennes, contienent entre autres des armatures "sauveterriennes".

Les industries citées possèdent donc des propriétés que nous considérons comme caractéristiques du composant "SVT". Mais, tandis que sur le territoire sauveterrien le composant "SVT" était presque dépourvu d'éléments supplémentaires, sur les territoires s'étendant au nord et au nord-ouest des Alpes, jusqu'aux Iles Britanniques et le Danemark, il semble constituer lui-même un "supplément" venant s'ajouter dans un temps precis à d'autres éléments dont l'origine est locale. Citons à l'appui quelques exemples:

1. Dans le Beuronien de la Belgique, du Basin Parisien, de la Suisse et de l'Allemagne méridionale, à côté de la liste des formes caractéristiques (pointe de Tardenoix – XA-E, pointes à micro-troncatures distales, triangles scalènes – TN, pointes à dos courbs – DB), depuis une époque (dans le Beuronien C) apparaissent des éléments "SVT".

2. La situation est analogue aux Pays Bas et en Allemagne du nord-ouest, où dans le Beuronien tardif local (C) prend naissance la culture/groupe de Boberg (cf.), qui contient entre autres un fort composant "SVT"; elle est datée depuis avant c. 7000 cal. A.C.

3. En Grande Bretagne, le composant "SVT", identifié pour la première fois par Grahame Clark en 1955 comme élément "sauveterroid", s'accompagne aux éléments locaux du type "maglemosien" (du type Broxbourne, cf.), pour former, conjointement avec eux, la culture de Shippea Hill, cf. (= Narrow Blade Industry selon les auteurs anglais), depuis la moitié du 8e millénaire cal. AC.

L' analyse typologique et chronologique montre (cf. plus loin remarques détaillées relatives à la chronologie) que sur les territoires mentionnés aux points 1–3 le composant "SVT" apparait nettement plus tard que dans le Sauveterrien. Les conséquences de cette observation seront analysées plus loin.

Il serait utile de souligner alors que le composant "SVT" remplit dans le Sud le rôle de composant fondamental (sauveterrien) tandis que dans le nord son importance n'est que secondaire en comparaison avec les composants "indigènes". La logique nous porte à admettre que ce second milieu était, dans ce cas, un milieu "prenant" par rapport au premier.

Le composant "CST" (cf. "Pre-neolithic/ Castelnovian")

Il possède les caractéristique suivantes:

1) lamelles denticulées du type Montbani,
2) trapèzes asymétriques (AF) et rhombes/losanges dans plusieurs variante (BH, BW, BJ, BV, BC, BZ, BY, etc., cf. "Atlas"),
3) certains trapèzes symétriques: surtout les types à troncatures obliques et concaves (AF, cf. "Atlas").
4) débitage du type Montbani (cf. "Bladelets").

Selon l'opinion générale, les éléments cités, et en particulier les trapèzes, se rattachent à la phase récente du Mésolithique et on les considère comme étant de bon indicateurs chronologiques de cette phase.

Dans sa forme la plus pure, le composant "CST" apparait dans le complexe Castelnovien (Châteauneuf-lez-Martigues, Montclus, sup., Cueva de la Cocina, Moita do Sebastiao, Romagnano III, Gaban, Frankhthi, Mala Triglavca etc., cf. "Pre-Neolithic/Castelnovian" dans ce volume). On le retrouve aussi dans quelques groupes mésolithiques situés plus au nord et dérivant d'ailleurs du substrat local (Retzien, Montbanien, Téviècien, Cuzoulien etc.). Au debut le composant "CST" constitue là-bas uniquement un supplément venant s'ajouter, p. ex. dans le Rhenanien (est finalement le dominer) en formant un Montbanien nord) à différents composants locaux. En voici les principaux exemples:

1. Sur un substrat sauveterrien prennent naissance des industries du type Cuzoul (ou le Pre-Roucadourien de Julia Roussot-Laroque – sites de Cuzoul-de-Gramat, couches III–IV, Le Martinet, couches III–IV, et Rouffignac, couche 3C). Leurs origines sont donc assez proches de ceux du Castelnovien classique. Ce dernier est fondé également, sur la tradition sauveterrienne (sequences stratigraphiques de Montclus, de Romagnano III, de Gaban, cf., etc;), sur laquelle se sont superposés/formés des éléments castelnoviens).

2. Au sud-ouest le phenomene "CST" se developpe d'un Epi-Gravettien local (Levant espagnol avec Cocina et l'estuaire du Tag avec Moita do Sebastiao ; dans ce dernier cas l'origine Epi-Gravetienne/Epi-Azilien n'est pas encore pleinement attesté). Il est aussi possible, qu'un certain Asturien/Epi-Gravettien cantabrique passe vers une industrie du type Castelnovien, local.

3. Plus au nord, sur le substrat du Beuronien C et D et Rhénanien belge se sont formées, avec la participation du composant "CST", les entitées suivantes: de Montbanien méridional (Birsmatten-Basisgrotte, couches 1 et 2, Jägerhaushöhle, couches 6 et 7, Montbani 13), le Tévicien (Ty-Nancien, Pointe-de-la-Torche, Téviec, Hoëdic) et le Monbanian belge, ou septentrional.

4. Par contre, sur le territoire englobant les Pays-Bas, l'Allemagne nord-occidentale, le Danemark et la Suède méridionale, le composant "CST" apparait (sous la forme des seuls trapèzes) depuis env. 7000 ans cal. A.C. dans les groupes locaux (Boberg, De Leien-Wartena, Oldesloe) liés plutôt aux vieilles traditions du Mésolithique de la

Plaine, sans les dominer. Il est représenté seulement par les trapèzes, constituant un élément tout à fait marginal. C'est seulement depuis env. 6500 ans cal. A.C. q'il se manifeste pleinement dans le Kongemosien danois.

De même qu'il en a été du composant "SVT", le composant "CST" dénote lui-aussi de grandes irrégularités dans le rythme de son développement/proliferation, son rôle et sa variante perduration sur les différents territoires (cf. modèles A et B de la castelnovisation dans "Pre-Neolithic/ Castelnovian").

Chronologie

Dans cette partie de notre étude nous avons essayé de définir le cadre chronologique dans lequel ont existé et se sont développés sur différents territoires les deux composants décrits plus haut. Il s'agit entre autres d'établir s'ils ont apparu partout en même temps. Dans le cas d'une réponse négative, nous aurons à déterminer les dates des éventuelles différences chronologiques, et ceci tant en ce qui concerne l'apparition que la persistance du composant sur le territoire donné.

Les séquences stratigraphiques des grottes et des abris (cf. "Rhythms"), relativement nombreuses en Europe occidentale, prouvent que dans le sud-ouest européen le composant "SVT" apparait toujours avant le composant "CST" (Montclus, Le Martinet, Cuzoul-de-Gramet, Roquefure, Gramari, Rouffignac, Grande Rivoire, Charmate, Romagnano III, Gaban, Birsmatten-Basisgrotte, Jägerhaushöhle, etc). On est à même de prouver que dans le sud il persiste dès le début de l'Holocène (cf. "South"), alors qu'au nord des Alpes il apparait avec un considerable retard.

Toutefois, les séquences stratigraphiques citées n'englobent pas tout le territoire qui nous intéresse et, par ailleurs, ne fournissent pas toutes les dates necessaires. C'est pourquoi, en s'appuyant sur le catalogue des dated ^{14}C, publié par André Gob (cf. aussi les datations des different cultures sur les planches), nous sommes arrivés aux conclusions suivantes:

On peut distinguer:
1) les inventaires à composant "SVT" dépourvus en meme temps de composant "CST";
2) les inventaires à composant "CST" dépourvus du composant "SVT"

Y ont été incluses sous réserve les dates de Birsmatten-Basisgrotte qui nous semblent trop jeunes surtout lorsqu'on les confronte avec la datation de Mannlefelsen et Rochèdane,sites famillés par André Thévenin, ainsi que celle de Jägerhaushöhle (fouilles Wolgang Taute).

Les trapèzes datés du composant "CST"

B – Belgique: Coleoptère 5, Weelde-Paardsdrank; nord de la France: Poine-de-la-Torche, Hoëdic; Pays-Bas: De Leien, Luiksgestel, Wartena, Duurswoude I, III, Maarheze, Hatert, Oirschot V.
C – Espagne: Botiqueria 2; Portugal: Cabezo da Aruda 83, Cabezo de Amoreira 39, Moita do Sebastiao.

D – sud de la France: Rouffignac C2, C3 , Puechmargues II/2, Châteauneuf-lez-Martigues 7, 8, Gramari 3B, Montclus 14, 15–16.
E – Italie: Benussi 3, 3–4, 4–5, Passo della Comunella, Covoloni di Broion 6, Pradestel D_{1-3}, Romagnano III AA, AB_{1-2}, AB_3, Gaban.
F – Serbie: Vlasac I, II, III, Lepensky Vir I,II; Montenegro: Odmut V Ib, IIa, IIb,; Grèce: Franchti.
G – Suisse: Birsmatten-Basisgrotte 2, Schötz 7, Liesberg-mühli VI; Allemagne (sud): Inzigkofen-oberes Drittel, Falkenstein-oberes Drittel, Jägerhaushöhle 7.
H – Pologne: Jastrzębia Góra I, Krzekotówek 8, Całowanie VII, Tomaszów II.
I – Danemark: Kongemose, Villingebaek Ost A, Vedbaek; Suède: Ageröd I:B, I:D, V, VI, Segebro.

L'analyse du matériel daté nous amène aux conclusions suivantes:

1. Dans le sud de la France et en Italie le composant "SVT" apparait généralement dans des inventaires Sauveterriens classiques (Rouffignac, Isola Santa, Culoz-Abri etc.) c. au debut du 9e millénaire cal. A.C. En dehors du territoire sauveterrien, ce composant apparait vers la moitié du 8e millénaire. Dans la région située au nord des Alpes et du Massif central iI constitue le "supplément" de différentes industries de vieille tradition locale (p.ex. Coincy II et Montbani II en France, Birsmatten-Basisgrotte, couches inferieures, en Suisse et Jägerhaushöhle superieur en Allemagne). A la même époque, des éléments sauveterriens apparaissent en Grande Bretagne dans la culture de Shippea Hill, qui prenait alors naissance; formée d'éléments locaux (du type Broxbourne) et "sauveterriens".

Etant donné la continuité territoriale et chronologique incontestable de tous les éléments du composant "SVT" sur les territoires de I'Europe occidentale (cf. plus loin remarques concernant l'expansion territoriale, mais aussi "Atlas"), on peut admettre comme très vraisemblable la thèse de la prolifération du dit "composant" du Sud vers le nord. La datation de ce phénomène peut se situer vers la moitié du 8e millénaire cal. A.C.

2. Le composant "CST" est, par soucis de simplification, representé dans notre ouvrage par les differents trapèzes (A et B pour typologie cf. "Atlas"). Ils apparaissent, soit accompagnés par toutes les nouveautés technologiques et typologiques (nucleus, style de debitage, lames retouchées et à troncatures – model A, cf. "Pre-Neolithic/Castelnovian"), soit non accompagnés (model B). Le premier apparait a l'Occident pour la première fois au sud, autour de 7000 cal. A.C., puis se prolifère vers le sud-scandinave l'atteignant un peu plut tard (comme modèle complet vers 6500 cal. A.C., comme trapèzes singuliers, vers 7000 !). Le second semble précéder au sud le premier (Montclus en France et Pradestel superieur en Italie).

Developpement spatial

Notre première carte montre la répartition spatiale du composant "SVT" en Europe (représenté par la pointe de Sauveterre – PD). L'analyse spatiale et chronologique du composant "SVT" nous amène aux conclusions suivantes:

1. Le territoire sur lequel le composant "SVT" s'est développé le plus tôt (9e et la première moitié du 8e millénaires cal. A.C.) est limité à la France du sud/centre et à l'Italie.

2. Dans la moitié du 8e millénaire cal. A.C. le composant "SVT" pénètre la Plaine ouest-européenne jusqu'a la Grande Bretagne (devenue peu après une île, cf. remarques relatives au composant "CST") et l'Irlande.

3. Au cours de la période ultérieure (7e millénaire cal. A.C.) on note une disparition des éléments sauveterriens sur leur territoire d'origine, alors remplacés par le composant "CST". Ils subsistent, le plus longtemps en Grande Bretagne, peut-être parce que les éléments castelnoviens n'ont pu arriver jusque-là.

4. Quant à la carte, elle montre la diffusion du composant "CST", on en déduit qu'en principe, cette diffusion coincide, dans ses lignes générales, avec la portée du composant "SVT" (l'axe Sud-Nord). Mais on'y relève aussi des différences essentielles: l'absence d'éléments "castelnoviens" en Grande Bretagne, insulaire à cette époque; par ailleurs, pénétration de ces éléments "CST" jusqu'en Suède méridionale où l'on ne note pas d'influences sauveterriennes ; au début les trapèzes singuliers, puis le phénomène du Kongemosien (cf.).

5. Les datations du "CST" dans son modèl A au sud semblent être plus anciens (?) (env. 7000 ans cal. A.C.), qu'au Nord (env. 6500 cal. A.C.). Faut-il nous alors admettre deux phases dans le développement spatial du composant "CST"? Dans ce cas, les inventaires les plus anciens (autour l'an 7000 cal. A.C.) contenant des éléments "CST" – modèl A (cf. "Pre-Neolithic/Castelnovian") – seraient groupés dans la partie occidentale du Bassin méditerranéen, puis (après l'an 7000), aurait eu lieu l'expansion/la proliferation du composant vers le nord. Mais au Frankhthi (Grèce) et à Murzak-Kobra (?) (Crimée) le "CST" est encore plus ancien (cf. "Pre-Neolithic/Castelnovian").

L'histoire du composant "CST" varie évidemment en fonction du milieu culturel dans lequel il se développe ou à lequel il arrive. Dans le sud, non seulement il est apparu le plus tôt, mais c'est également là que son rôle diminue le plus vite (?), cf. séquences stratigraphiques de Montclus et Châteauneuf-lez-Martigues. A l'ouest (Le Martinet, Rouffignac, Cuzoul-de-Gramat) le composant "CST" apparait vers l'an 7000/6500 et disparait au 7e millénaire ; à peu près à la même époque ou un peu plus tard (cf. André Gob), les éléments castelnoviens font leur apparition dans le Bassin Parisien, en Belgique, aux Pays Bas et sur l'avant-terrain des Alpes. Néanmoins, ils y subsistent plus longtemps que dans le sud et l'ouest. Le composant "CST" ne pénètre pas jusqu'en Grande Bretagne, séparée par La Manche, par contre, à l'extrémité nord-est de l'espace couvert par sa présence il apparait d'une façon éphémère, de courte durée, vers l'an 7000 dans les Post-Maglemosien de la Scandinavie sud et s'installe pleinement vers 6500, comme le Kongemosien.

Courants interculturels dans le Mésolithique d'Europe occidentale

Ainsi que nous l'avons indiqué plus haut, au cours de la période du 8e au 7e millénaires cal. A.C., sur le territoire de l'Europe occidentale apparait à deux reprises un phénomène qui englobe de vastes étendues du territoire et s'infiltre à travers les barrières interculturelles:

1. Le composant "SVT", lequel dans l'Holocène le plus ancien n'était connu que dans le sud, est apparu à la suite de son expansion au cours d'une période en env. 7500 années cal. A.C. vers le nord, dans les inventaires de toute une série de cultures occidentaux (Beuronien, Boberg, Broxbourne, Maglemosien), mais pas centre-européennes.

2. Le composant "CST", lequel – il se peut – est apparu le plus tôt en Provence et en Italie du nord environ 7000 ans cal. A.C. a pénétré jusqu'en Hollande, Allemagne du Nord et Suède méridionale. On le connait à cette époque dans les cultures suivantes: Castelnovien français et nord-italien, Montbani sud et nord, Cuzoul (depuis 7000/6500 cal. A.C.), et Tévicien, Boberg, RMS/Rhenanien, Oldesloe et De Leien-Wartena, Post-Maglemosien sud-scandinave, le Kongemosien.

Les phénomènes décrits ne sont evidemment pas isolés dans la préhistoire; il suffit de rappeler l'expansion du composant "azilien" (cf. "Azilianization") à la fin du Tardiglaciaire sur le territoire compris entre l'Espagne et la Pologne. Nous appelons ce genre de phénomène les "courants ("modes") interculturels".

Pour éviter toute confusion, nous aimerions souligner que bien que l'on admette l'existence d'un droit de convergence agissant dans la préhistoire, celui-ci n'est pas à même d'expliquer des phénomènes aussi compliqués que ceux décrits dans la présente étude (un "composant", voir tradition, est une structure représenté par la technique du débitage et tout un jeu d'outils). Ces phénomènes, dénotant par ailleurs une compacité territoriale incontestable sur une immense étendue de territoire depuis sud de l'Europe jusqu'en Scandinavie et Iles Britaniques, se caractérisent par une continuité chronologique et territoriale, et apparaissent simultanément (ou non) sur la majorité du territoire mentionné. Nous pouvons, par contre, admettre la thèse, selon laquelle l'expansion éventuelle du composant au-delà de son milieu natal a pu être favorisée par des faits écologiques (?). Et enfin, il est opportun de rappeler, que si dans certaines cultures (dans ce cas celles du sud) les éléments considérés ont un caractère d'exclusivité ou dénotent une supériorité numérique, autant en dehors de celles-ci ils ne constituent parfois qu'un supplément à divers autres éléments locaux (model B du "CST", cf. "Pre-Neolithic/Castelnovian"), apparaissant là d'ailleurs assez tard.

Ce caractère complémentairé des composants "SVT" et "CST" dans les inventaires d'Europe nord-occidentale, ainsi que les données concernant leur datation expediement plus ancienne, soit prouvée, soit possible, dans le sud, suggèrent une affluence des éléments considérés sur les territoires situés au nord des Alpes et massif Central. D'ailleurs, le manque d'une différenciation territoriale et typologique des deux composants constitue un important argument contestant leur genèse locale (septentrionale). Un substrat différencié devrait engendrer par voie d'évolution locale une différenciation typologique évidente du composant.

Il semble que le phénomène des "courants interculturels" ici analysé présente en général plusieurs phases, dont les deux premières nous intéressent particulièrement:

1. Phase initiale – un composant déterminé prend naissance au sein d'une communauté donnée et pendant un certain temps, plus ou moins long, il est réduit à cette communauté.

2. Phase d'explosion/prolifération – le composant mentioné enfreint les barrières qui séparent sa communauté maternelle des communautés voisines. Au cours d'une période relativement brève (dans notre cas 50–100 ans) le composant se propage largement englobant graduellement de sa portée de nombreuses communautés différenciées (p.ex. le Rhenanien belge). Si l'on parvient à saisir et dater cet instant, on obtient un bon indicateur typologique de chronologie.

3. Phase de disparition – fortement différenciée; en général, la disparition du composant donné commence dans les régions ou il est apparu le plus tôt (une bonne analogie – le style gothique en architecture européenne !).

Il est souvent difficile de reconstituer d'une manière tout à fait claire les causes qui ont amené à la phase "explosive" du phénomène qui nous intéresse. A notre avis, il faudrait rejeter l'idée des migrations massifs d'importants groupes de population, car longtemps encore le substrat typologique fondamental des territoires "prenants" n'est pas entièrement étouffé. Ceci ne signifie pas, néanmoins, que nous devons rejeter toute possibilite de déplacement vers le nord de différents groupes d'individus, comme suggère André Thévènin pour le Sauveterrien ancien français. Finalement, si nous admettons le rapport génétique supposé qui existe entre les éléments "sauveterriens" et "castelnoviens" connus sur la Plaine et les territoires du sud, nous admettons par cela même la thèse sur les influences provenant de cette direction. Et comme les trapèzes n'ont pas de jambes, assurément quelqu'un a aidé à leur expansion.

La Palaeohistoire de l'Europe occidentale entre 10ᵉ et 7ᵉ millénaires cal. A.C.

Tous les faits établis dans le courant de la presente étude permettent de faire avancer quelque peu notre connaissance sur l'histoire de la partie occidentale de notre continent dans la période entre 10ᵉ et 7ᵉ millénaires cal. A.C. Il nous semble pouvoir la reconstituer de la manière suivante:

1. Au debut de l'Holocène l'Europe occidentale se divise en deux provinces écologiques et culturelles. Dans la première, existent les communautés Post Epigravettienes, Post Epi-aziliennes et Post Epi-magdaleniennes (Sauveterrien en France méridionale et en Italie du nord, Beuronien entre le Bassin Parisien et la Moravie). La seconde province comprend aussi la partie nord-ouest du continent. Elle s'est formée sur les traditions des communautés tardiglaciaires des plaines (l'Ahrensbourgien

et le Federmesser). Dans cette province prennent alors naissance le Maglemosien ancien: Star Carr (Grande Bretagne), Duvensee (Allemagne, Danemark) et Komornica (Pologne). A cette époque le composant "SVT" existe déjà au sud de la France et en Italie.

2. Au début du 8ᵉ millénaire cal. A.C., sur la base de Star Carr et de Duvensee, prennent naissance les nouvelles entitées locales nordiques – Maglemose 3 du Danemark et Broxbourne en Grande Bretagne.

3. Vers la moitié du 8ᵉ millénaire cal. A.C. le courant sauveterrien entre dans sa phase "explosivé". Le composant "SVT" apparait alors dans les inventaires de Beuronien (= Beuronien C de Wolfgang Taute, Tardenoisien – facies sauveterroide du Claude Barrière). Sous son influence également (un peut plus tard) se forment les groupes locales d'Allemagne du nord, Hollande et Angleterre: le Boberg (= composant Beuronien/pointes de Tardenois, plus triangles "SVT" – TE-TH, plus tard également "CST"); le Shippea Hill (= composant Broxbourne + "SVT"), le Svaerdborg (= Maglemose 3 + "SVT"). L'Europe occidentale subit une certaine unification culturelle ("sauveterrisation", cf. "The Sauveterrian Commonwealth").

Autour 7000 cal. A.C., apparaisse le courant castelnovien et peut après cette date (quand ?) il arrive à sa phase "explosivé". Le composant "CST" pénètre jusqu'en Scandinavie méridionale; une image culturelle de l'Europe, tout à fait nouvelle, est formée (cf. "Pre-Neolithic/ Castelnovian"). Disparaissent complètement les vieilles structures (Sauveterrien, Beuronien méridional ; au Nord un peu plus tard), remplacées par des structures nouvelles, dans lesquelles le composant "CST" se manifeste fortement (Castelnovien = composant "CST" + parfois "SVT"; Cuzoul = "SVT" + "CST"; Montbanien = composants RMS et Beuronien, plus graduellement "CST") etc. Une importante unification culturelle de cette partie du continent s'accomplit. Seule l'Angleterre, isolée, vit de sa propre vie (persistence de la culture de Shippea Hill, cf.).

Les éléments du composant "CST" atteignent également la Plaine, pénétrant et finalement dominant les Boberg et RMS/Rhenanien, et apparaissent enfin dans le milieu maglemosien. Là toutefois, ils ne sont pas capables d'amener à une unification aussi poussée que dans la province méridionale q'après un certain temps (le Kongemosien, vers 6500 ans cal. A.C.) ; mais les premières trapèzes du style "CST" apparaissent des env. 7000 cal. A.C.

***

Sur l'exemple du Mésolithique de l'Europe occidentale nous avons essayé d'examiner un intéressant phénomène culturel, qui constitue l'un des moteurs des changements dans la préhistoire du continent. Evidemment, ce type de phénomène ne se rapporte pas uniquement au Mésolithique, ni à la partie occidentale de notre continent; il se répète à maintes reprises au cours de l'histoire (cf. "Mapping the Mesolithic"), et parmi les causes qui déterminent sa naissance se trouvent aussi les transformations écologiques.

Aux deux courants interculterels examinés plus haut, a succéde, dans l'ordre chronologique, un autre courant venant également du sud, qui a conduit à la ceramisation (cf.), puis la néolithisation progressive de cette partie de l'Europe.

Addenda 2006

Le phenomène "CST" (modèle A) existe aussi à l'Est du continent (Kurzak-Kobien en Crimée, Grebenikien en Ukraine, en Moldova et en Moldavie roumaine, Janislawicien en Ukraine, Pologne, Belorussie et Lituanie, Odmut et Frankhti dans les Balcans. Parfois (Crimée ?, Grèce) il semble être plus ancien que 7000 cal. A.C. (cf. "Pre-Neolithic base").

8.2. The West: Beuronian and Rhenanian (Fig. 8.2a–d)

The first of the great cultural units discussed here, called the Coincy facies of the Tardenoisian by Jean-Georges Rozoy (also André Thévenin separates the northern Beuronian – although he fails to call it so – from the southern Sauveterrian), was named the Beuronian by Wolfgang Taute, who also suggested a periodization for it (cf. "Rhythms"). Taute distinguished three phases for southern Germany: A, B, and C (replaced there by South Montbanian or *spätes Mesolithikum*); André Gob added a fourth phase, D, occurring only in the north (cf. "Beuronian recent, Coleoptère").

The rhythm of change of the Beuronian, based on assemblages and dates from South German sites (Zigeunerfels, Schuntershöhle, Jägerhaushöhle and Falkensteinhöhle) is as follows (cf. "Rhythms"):

Earliest Mesolithic:
Tardenois (= X) points, distal micro-truncations
Beuronian A:

> The same types, but also new ones (double micro-truncations PE and Tardenois points with ventral retouch – XE))

Beuronian B:

> Same types plus Tardenois points with concave base (XA) but without the double micro-truncations (PE)

Beuronian C:

> Tardenois points mostly with concave base (XA), broad scalene triangles (TO) plus short base scalene triangles (TH, TE).

All phases also have DB backed points and TN triangles. This rhythm fits in well with the changes occurring parallely in the central and western European Mesolithic *koine* (cf. "Koine", "Rhythms" and "South"). The evolution ends with the northern Beuronian D with trapezes.

A similar line of evolution has been reconstructed for northwestern Europe by Jean-Georges Rozoy and for Belgium by André Gob and Pierre Vermeersch.

***

In the territorial sense, an observable stylistic differentiation distinguishes, among others, the eastern variant (Smolín) in Czechia, Moravia and Polish Lower Silesia. There is no "Sauveterroid" element in Bohemian and Moravian assemblages. There has also been talk of a northern Beuronian (Fernand Spier for Luxemburg), etc.

The origins of the phenomenon still remain unclear. Wolfgang Taute is of the opinion, based on his own research at Zigeunerfels among others, that the Beuronian developed from the local south German Epi-Magdalenian (layer D at the site), while André Thévenin points to Ahrensburgian roots, at least for the western Beuronian.

In the geographical sense (cf. "La cartographie du Beuronien"), the Beuronian with its fairly numerous multi-layer cave sites is backed up on the south against the Alps and the Sudeten and Czech Mountains further to the east; its eastern border is on the White Carpathians, which separate Moravia from Slovakia. It is mainly an uplands culture (piedmont of the Alps in Austria, Czech Republic, northern piedmont of the Sudeten, Belgian and French Ardennes, Bavaria, Svabia, Schwarzwald), although it extended also into the Lowland (e.g. Flanders in Holland and close to the Beuronian, the Boberg group, cf. "Sauveterrian Commonwealth"). It is surprising to see the settlement in the lowland parts of northern France, including the Paris Basin, as well as the apparently geographically unjustified border with the Sauveterrian on the Loire (no specially difficult barriers exist there, cf. "Pyrenees, Alps"). In the northwest, the English Channel constitutes the border.

About 7000/6500 cal. BC, the South Montbanian (part of the Castelnovian complex, cf.) started to appear in the territory occupied before by the Beuronian. In the northwest, however, the nord Beuronian was in its phase D at this time (cf. "Beuronian recent, Coleoptère").

The northwestern border of Beuronian territory was already on the Lowland (cf. "Mapping the Mesolithic"), where taxonomic and chronological issues are much more intricate and difficult to resolve. Hybrid groups dominated in France, Belgium, the Netherlands, northwestern Germany, often of unknown nature, but no nordic elements of any distinction (like, for example, chipped axes and adzes) can be observed in the Beuronian layers despite the presence in this region of Haltern-like assemblages similar to Duvensee and Star Carr (already described by Hermann Schwabedissen). These hybrid cultures include the late Boberg culture/group in Friesland and Lower Saxony. Beside casual "Sauveterrian" elements (PD, TH, TE) and "late" pieces (trapezes), the inventory included rare Tardenois points (X). Thus, Boberg could also be a late and peripheral variant of the Beuronian (?)

Rhenanian (Fig. 8.2b)

The Rhein-Meuse-Schelde culture of André Gob (also called the Lower Rhine culture by Raymond R. Newell) is a cousin or side branch of the Beuronian in the far northwest. It was entirley lowland in nature and differing from the classic Beuronian in having unique points with surface retouch (FA–C) and rectangles (RA). It is a fairly late phenomenon (from the end of the 8th until at least the end of the 7th millennium cal. BC), and a regional continuator of Beuronian. It was later replaced gradually by a local North Montbanian. The famous quartzite from Wommerrum was probably mined by this group and exported over long distances.

8.2.1. La Cartographie du Beuronien (Culture Beuron-Coincy)

Le but de cet texte est la presentation d'une carte de repartition du Beuronien ou la culture Beuron-Coincy. Cette entité taxonomique apparait et se développe pendant le Mésolithique inférieur, moyen et début du recent dans une grande partie de l'Europe occidentale et centrale.

Definition

La notion de "Beuronien" a été introduite par Wolfgang Taute pour dénommer une variante locale du Mésolithique du sud de I'Allemagne, aux 10/9ème – debut 7ème millénaires cal. A.C (Fig. 8.2.1a–c).

A la même époque, des industries très similaires au Beuronien ont été dénommées en fonction de leur localisation géographique (le "facies Coincy" du Tardenoisien de Jean-Georges Rozoy, le "Sauveterroide Komplex" de René Wyss, etc.). Plusieurs autres dénominations ont également été proposées pour le Beuronian; citons par exemple l'"Ardennien", le "Birsmattien" (Jean-Georges Rozoy), les groupes de "Hambach", de "Billinghausen",de "Teveren" (Surendra K. Arora) etc.

J'ai repris la définition de Taute en l'élargissant toutefois au concept plus vaste de la "culture de Beuron-Coincy" qui englobe dans ce "Beuronien" certaines (anciens et recents) industries "Tardenoisiennes" de l'Europe nord-ouest. La nouvelle denomination souligne l'existence, aux 10/9ème et 8/7ème millénaires, d'une unification culturelle dans le vaste territoire situé entre le Bassin Parisien et la Moravie en République Czeque et même la Basse Silesie polonaise, c'est-à-dire surtout dans la zone de collines et plateaux au nord des Alpes.

La culture de Beuron-Coincy (Beuronien) se caractérise par les traits suivants:

1. Une technique de débitage de nucléus à un plan de frappe ou à plans de frappe multiples, aussi opposées. De ces nucléus ont été extraites des lamelles trapues et peu régulières (style Coincy, cf. "Blade/bladelet").
2. Une série de plusieurs types de microlithes souvent assez larges:

    a) pointe du Tardenois, ou "C-point" de A. Bohmers and A. Wouters (4 variétés à base retouchée transversale: droite, concave, convexe, et à retouche inverse: XA, XC, XD et XE, dans ce volume)
    b) pointe de Zonhoven/microtroncature distale/pointe B des auteurs hollandais: K, dans ce volume, cf. "Atlas")

c) triangle isocèle court (TN)
d) pointe à dos court souvent légèrement arqué et trapue (DB)
e) triangle scalène court (TO)
f) triangle scalène allongé à angle obtus/ouvert (TR)
g) segment large (DD)

Les autres types de microlithes constituent soit une addition locale aux séries typiques du Beuronien (quelques rectangles ou microlithes à retouche couvrante dans le nord-ouest), soit un élément commun, mais limité dans le temps (les doubles troncatures PE dans les phases anciens, les éléments occidentaux sauveterroides depuis la deuxième moitié du 8ème millénaire, ou les trapèzes dans le Beuronien recent (= D) du début de 7ème millénaire cal. A.C.

3. Des grattoirs courts ou très courts, souvent sur éclat, peu réguliers avec une tendance à la denticulation.
4. Des éclats retouchés, souvent denticulés.
5. Des lames à troncature.
6. Des burins trapus, le plus souvent d'angle sur troncature.

Les différences de pourcentage dans le groupe des microlithes signifient surtout:

> a) une subdivision chronologique du Beuronien, décrite par Wolfgang Taute pour l'Allemagne ("Rhythms"), puis par Docteur Rozoy et André Thévenin pour la France et finalment André Gob pour la Belgique,
> b) une différenciation régionale.

Ceci ne modifie en rien le fait que la Beuronien est une entité largement répandue dans la carte "culturelle" du Mésolithique européen et comme un concept transfrontalier remplace plusieurs dénominations locales encore et toujours utilisées dans la litérature.

En préparant la carte du culture Beuron-Coincy, j'ai utilisé les sources rassemblées dans mon "Atlas du Mésolithique de l'Europe" (cf.).

Chaque point sur la carte signifie soit une série hétérogène, soit un outilage homogène contenant :

a) au moins une variété de pointe du Tardenois (X) et plus ou moins 3 types de microlithes mentionnés plus haut au paragraphe 2.
b) éventuellement plus d'une variété de pointe du Tardenois (X) (ou bien un grand nombre de pièces d'une même variété) plus deux types de microlithes de la liste présentée plus haut.

Dans son article sur le Mésolithique français publié dans les Actes des Colloques du Congrès de Forli (Italie), André Thévenin à obtenue pour la France les resultats comparables aux notres.

Comment 2006

In the original article, I had included at this point a list of sites. Since its first publication, the map has been updated with new sites published for the Czech Republic by Jiři

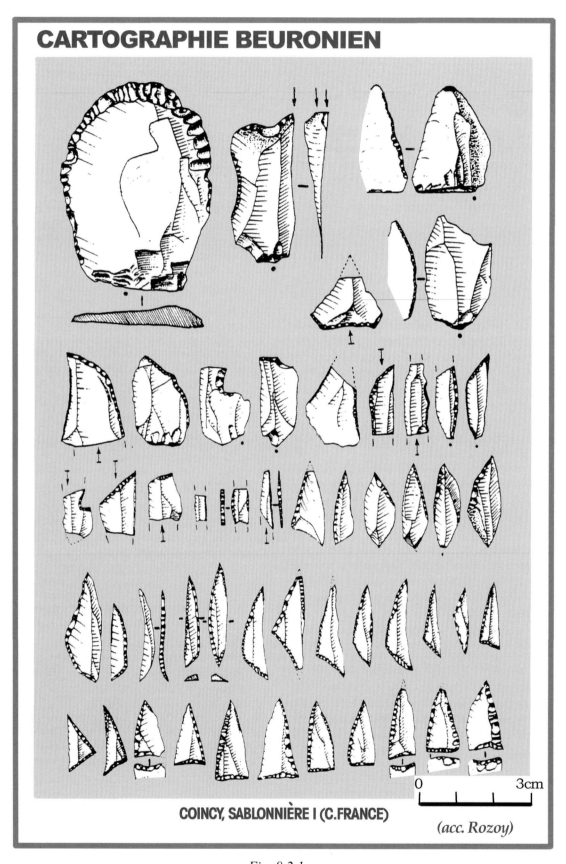

CARTOGRAPHIE BEURONIEN

COINCY, SABLONNIÈRE I (C.FRANCE)

0   3cm

(acc. Rozoy)

Fig. 8.2.1a

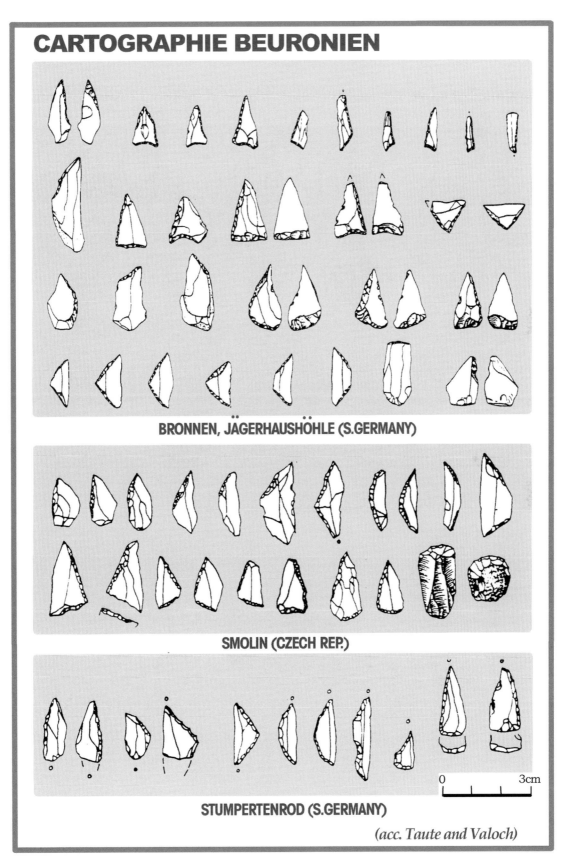

Fig. 8.2.1b

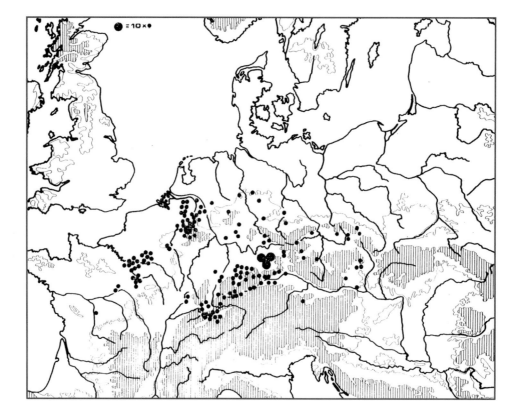

Fig. 8.2.1c

Svoboda and for southwest Poland (Kłodzko Dale) by Jarosław Bronowicki. New material has also been published for Germany by Michael A. Joachim, Surendra K. Arora and Erwin Cziesla. Only a few of these, more specifically the eastern ones, have been incorporated into the present map.

A cursory comparison suggests the possibility of dividing the Beuron-Coincy culture into two internal territorial units (Western Beuronian and the eastern variant of Smolín type, the latter with the slightly less typical, because less symmetrical, Tardenoisian (X) points and without the "SVT" component (cf. "Les courants").

8.2.2. Ost Beuronien und Ost Sauveterrien
Grundlagen der kulturellen Stellung
Nur wenige tschechische und slowakische Fundstellen haben geschlossene Funde erbracht (Barca I, Tašovice, Kůlna-Höhle – Schicht 3, Sered' – "Mačanské vršky" B, Smolín, Přibice). Das erschwert die Klassifikation der Materialien von zweifelhafter Geschlossenheit, da zum Beispiel keine Gewissheit darüber besteht, ob sämtliche Kulturvarianten, die einst im Mesolithikum des erörterten Gebietes vertreten waren, uns schon aus den genannten Komplexen bekannt sind. Um deshalb die Möglichkeit eines Fehlurteils zu verringern, seien auch territorial entfernte italienische oder schweizerische Vergleichsfunde sowie solche aus Deutschland in die Betrachtung einbezogen.

Im folgenden seien für das in Frage kommende Gebiet zwei mesolithische Kulturen herausgestellt, die an das schon an anderer Stelle vorgelegte Kulturschema anknüpfen (Fig. 8.2.2a–d).

Beuronien
Ihre Synonyma war unter anderem "Fazies Coincy" (Jean-Georges Rozoy), "Sauveterroider Horizont" (Hans-Georg Bandi) und "Komplexe von Smolin-Typus" (Stefan K. Kozłowski).

Im hier behandelten Gebiet wird diese Kultur durch folgende Komplexe repräsemtiert:

1. Smolín, Bez. Židlohovice
2. Tašovice, Bez. Karlovy-Vary
3. Přibice, Bez. Břeclav
4. Kůlna, Schicht 3, Bez. Sloup.

Ihre Élémente sind ausserdem aus solchen Inventaren bekannt wie Kůlna 2, Putím, Putím-Pikarna, Komařin, Dolni Véstonice und Kozly in der Tschechische Republik sowie Bisamberg, Kamegg NÖ, Limberg-Mühlberg und Salzburg-Maxglan in Österreich. Einzelne Artefakteformen vom wahrscheinlichen Beuronien-Typus treten an weiteren Fundplätzen auf.

Ähnliche Komplexe erscheinen im süd-ostliche Deutschlands, so Mücheln-Möckerling und Jüchsen im Sachsen/Thüringen, ferner im Süden Deutschland – Ensdorf, Jägerhaushöhle, Wunkendorf, Stumpertenrod und in der Schweiz – Birsmatten-Basisgrotte. Weiter im Westen sind solche noch aus Frankreich sowie aus Belgien und den Niederlanden bekannt (cf. "Cartographie du Beuronien").

Die Übereinstimmungen betreffen sämtliche Werkzeuggruppen, also die Mikrolithen – A-, B- und C (= Tradenois – X)-Spitzen, gleichschenklige (TN) und ungleichschenklige (TR, TO) Dreiecke in einigen Varianten, Segmente, seltener Sauveterrien-Spitzen (PD), die Kratzer – unter anderem Scheibenkratzer, schliesslich die Klingen vom Coincy-Typus.

Die tschekishe Materialien, die der so definierten Beuronien zuzuordnen sind, zeigen jedoch Besonderheiten, die regionale Differenzierung dieser Kultur bestätigen (regionale Varianten: Coincy, Ardenien, klassisch Beuronien und im Ost-Smolín). Die Variante Smolín weist beispielsweise sehr wenige und nicht sehr typische C/Tardenois-Spitzen und keine Eléménte der "Sauveterrien komponente" (cf. "Les courants") (= TH und TE Dreiecke) auf, ausserdem treten hier asymmetrische Trapeze auf.

Beim Versuch, die Verbreitung der Beuronien kartographisch darzustellen, zeigt sich, dass sie im Norden – wohl mit Ausnahme der Niederlande – nicht an das europäische Tiefland heranreicht und im Süden die Alpen nicht überschreitet (cf. "Mapping the Mesolithic"). Die tschekische und österreichischen Fundplätze schieben sich dagegen keilförmig zwischen die polnischen Komplexe der Komornica-Kultur (= Ost-Maglemosien) und die Epigravettien-Komplexe Ungarns, Rumäniens und der Slowakei bzw. die süd-west slowakischen Komplexe des Sauveterrien (cf. below).

Die Bestimmung der zeitlichen Stellung der Beuronien in ihrem Zentrum und im Westen ist kein Problem; im nördlichen Vorfeld der Alpen gehört sie dem 10/9. und 8. Jahrtausend cal. BC an, wie die Angaben für Jägerhaushöhle, Birsmatten-Basisgrotte, Zigeunerfels und Wunkendorf in Deutschland und Schweiz, ferner für Coincy II und Montbani II in Frankreich bezeugen. In einigen Regionen (zum Beispiel in den Ardennen und im Rheinland) hat die genannte Kultur bis zum 7. Jahrtausend cal. BC überdauert (Beuronien D), beispielsweise nach der Datierung der Grotte du Coléoptère in Belgien (cf.). Im östlichen Verbreitungsgebiet hingegen lässt sie sich wegen der geringen Zahl der Daten nicht so leicht zeitlich bestimmen. Wir wissen jedoch, dass die Beuronien dort schon im 8. Jahrtausend cal. BC bestanden hat, und zwar nach den Datierungen für Mücheln-Möckerling und Smolín. Ausserdem bestechen auch typologische Anhaltspunkte für die Datierung, zum Beispiel durch die Trapeze, die das Alter der sie enthaltenden Inventare auf das Atlantikum oder das ausgehende Boreal zu bestimmen erlauben. Angesichts dessen muss angenommen werden, dass die Beuronien in Böhmen/Mähren und in Österrreich zumindest an der Wende des 10/9. zum ende 8. Jahrtausend cal. BC. existiert.

Sauveterrien
In einem gewissen Gegensatz zu den Komplexen vom Typus Beuronien stehen die aus der süd-westlichen Slowakei bekannten Inventare der Fundplätze:

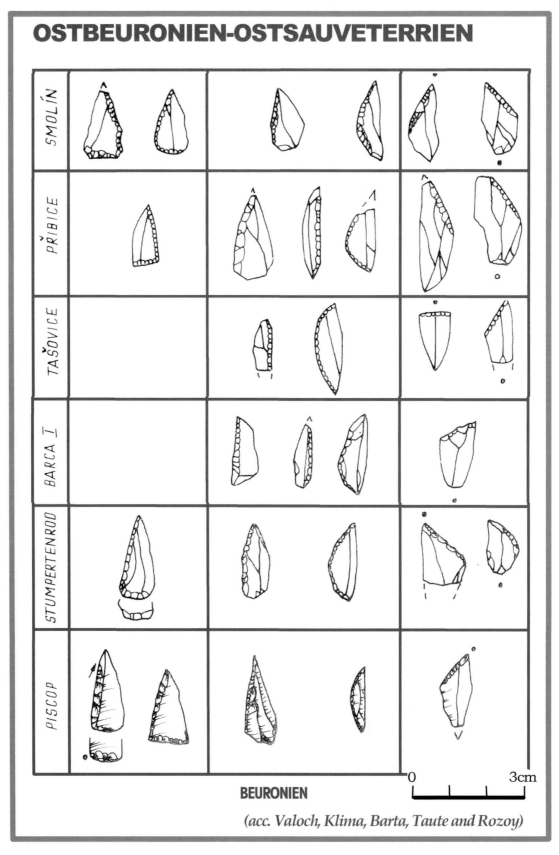

Fig. 8.2.2a

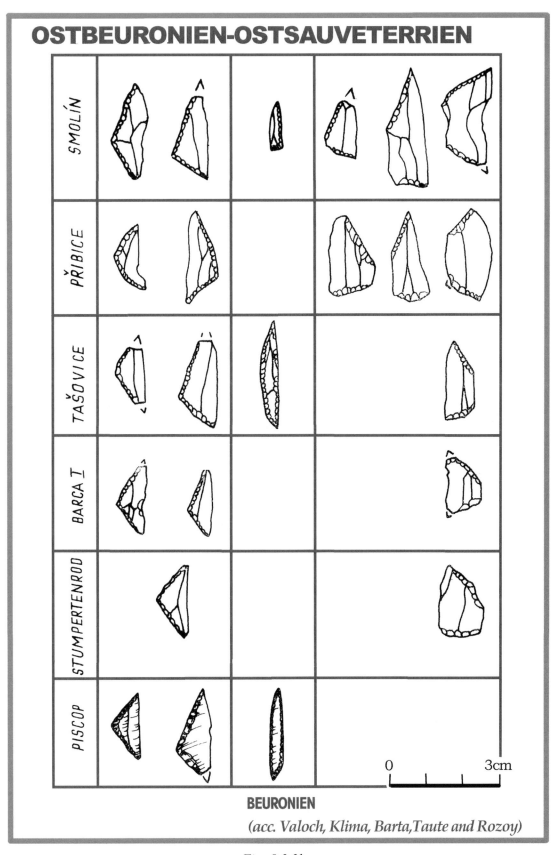

Fig. 8.2.2b

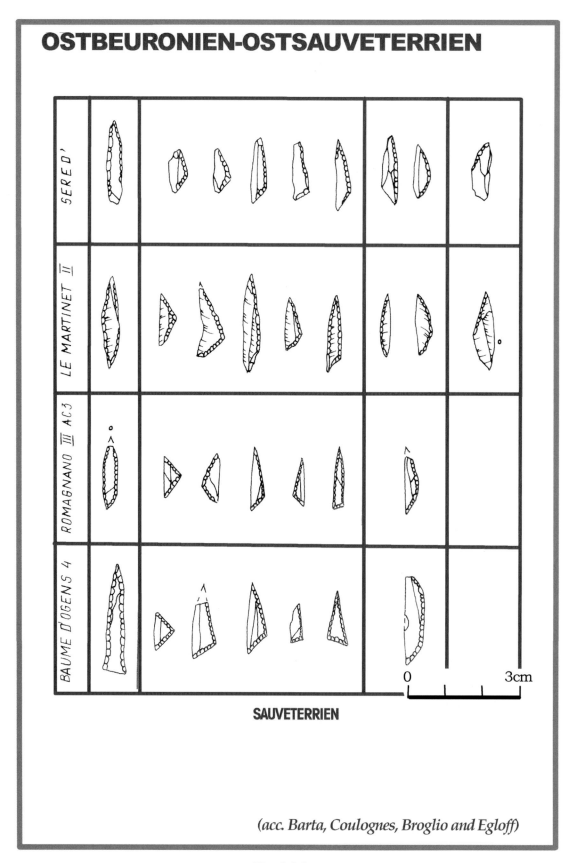

Fig. 8.2.2c

OSTBEURONIEN-OSTSAUVETERRIEN

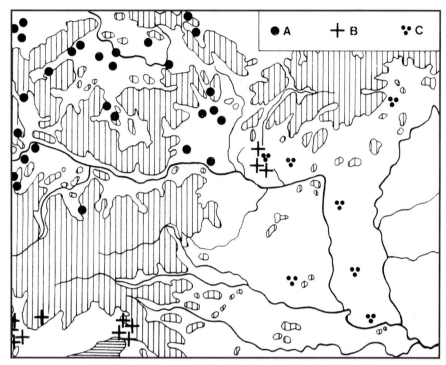

A-BEURONIEN B-SAUVETERRIEN C-EPI-GRAVETTIEN

SITES	◖	◗	◢	◗	▭	◁	◸	▱	▱	OTHER BLADELETS	END-SCRAPERS	BURINS	PERFORATORS
TARDIGRAVETTIAN													
CUINA TURCULUI /LOWER LAYER/	49	55	80	20	4	–	20	5	–	–	11	648	19	–
BĂILE HERCULANE	+	+	+	–	–	–	+	–	–	–	+	+	+	+
EPI - TARDIGRAVETTIAN													
CUINA TURCULUI	58	35	190	71	1	–	1	6	–	–	46	1151	56	–
SZŐDLIGET	+	–	+	–	–	–	–	–	–	–	+	+	+	+
HAJDUKOVO	+	+	+	–	+	–	–	–	–	–	+	?	?	?
GILMA	2	2	8	–	2	1	–	–	5	1	8	69	6	5
CREMENEA	–	–	+	–	–	+	–	–	+	+	+	+	+	+
CIUMEŞTI II	+	+	–	–	–	+	+	–	+	+	+	+	+	+
DOLNA STREDA	+	+	+	+	–	–	?	–	+	–	+	+	–	–
HURBANOVO	–	–	–	–	–	–	–	–	+	+	+	+	+	+

LATE EPI-GRAVETTIEN

(acc. J. and S.Kozłowski)

Fig. 8.2.2d

1. Sered' – Mačanske vršky B, Bez. Galanta
2. Mostová, Bez. Galanta
3. Tomašikovo, Bez. Galanta

Sie zeichnen sich durch folgende Merkmale aus: Regelmässige Mikroklingen, Ensembles charakteristicher sehr kleiner Mikrolithen, wie ungleichschenkelige (TR, TH, TE) und gleichschenkelige Dreiecke (TN), Sauveterrien-Spitzen (PD), Segmente (DD), Rückenmesser und B-Spitzen, sehr kleine Kratzer und Schaber, häufig mit gezähnten Rändern.

Diese Charakteristik beruht vor allem auf dem umfangreichsten und vermutlich geschlossenen Komplex vom Fundplatz Mačanske vršky. Wenn es sich tatsächlich um einen geschlossenen Fund handelt, dann kann man eine vergleichende Analyse wagen, welche überraschende Analogien aufzeigt, die ungeachtet, der Problematik durchaus real sind. Es zeigt sich nämlich, dass die oben aufgezählten grundsätzlichen Merkmale des slowakischen Inventars fast, genau übereinstimmen mit bekannten Merkmalskombinationen des Sauveterrien von norditalienischen und slovenischen Fundplätzen – so mit Romagnano III (cf.), Pradestel, Grotta Benussi, Vatte di Zambana, Pod Čmurkljo usw. Die Übereinstimmungen betreffen fast sämtliche Mikrolithen wie auch die Kratzer und Schaber; die Kongruenz ist somit vollständig (cf. "Pyrenees, Alps…").

Wenn die hier vertretene These richtig ist und das Vorkommen von Sauveterrien-Fundplätzen im Grenzgebiet der Slowakei und Österreichs seine Bëstatigung findet, dann muss noch geklärt werden, auf welche Weise sie mit dem klassischen Gebiet des Sauveterrien in Verbindung stehen. Diese Kultur tritt bekanntlich in Frankreich – zum Beispiel Rouffignac, Martinet, Culoz, Montclus, ferner in der Schweiz – Baume d'Ogens und Vionnaz, und schliesslich in Norditalien auf. Den slowakischen Fundplätzen liegen die italienischen sowie slovenischen (Pod Črmukljo, cf. "Slovenian Mesolithic") Fundplätze territorial am nächsten. Nur entlang dem nördlichen Vorfeld der Alpen oder über die Pforte von Ljubljana konnte das klassische Gebiet des Sauveterrien mit der Slowakei verbunden gewesen sein.

Noch einige Bemerkungen zur Chronologie. Das klassische Sauveterrien hat im 10/9. und 8. Jahrtausend cal. BC bestanden, sein Ende ist durch das Auftreten der ersten Trapeze – zum Beispiel Schicht 15–16 von Baume de Montclus – vermutlich um 7000 cal. BC gekennzeichnet. Der einzige reichere Sauveterrien-Komplex aus der Slowakei – Mačanské-vršky – enthält Trapeze, was ihn auf die Zeit um 7000 cal. BC oder später zu datieren erlaubt, also später als die Mehrzahl der klassischen Sauveterrien-Kultur. Doch all dies ist nur relevant, wenn es sich um einen geschlossenen Komplex handelt.

Comment 2006

Added to this is a unique Sauveterrian site in the Austrian Tyrol – Ullafelsen, excavated by Dieter Schäfer. It is, apart from Slovakian sites, certain proof of Sauveterrian penetration to the north. New Beuronian sites were recently discovered and excavated by Jiři Svoboda in the Czech Republic and by Jarosław Bronowicki in southwestern Poland. The Southern Czech Beuronian material was also recently published by Slavomir Vencl and his staff. All this Czech Beuronian differs slightly from the western Beuronian mostly by the lack of the "SVT" element (cf. "Les courants") and by the less typical X-points.

About 7000/6500 cal. BC, Castelnovian-style complexes appeared in Austria and in the southern part of the Czech Republic (e.g. Mikulčice, published by Bohuslav Klima), including, among others, a new coring technique, trapezes, *lamelles* Montbani (cf. "Blade/bladelet") and flat harpoons. These are most likely in a general Montbani style.

8.2.3. Le Beuronien recent

Coleoptére (Fig. 8.2.3a–b)

The small cave in the Belgian Ardennes, tested by J. Hamal-Nandrin and excavated by Michel Dewez and the present author in 1974–1976, yielded a Beuronian D assemblage (layer 5a), dated c. 6000 cal. BC.

Le Matériel archéologique

Inventaire

L'outillage de la couche 5a peut être considéré comme homogène, ce fait étant prouvé par l'analyse stratigraphique, par l'analyse de la répartition des pièces, par l'analyse typologique et par l'état de conservation des pièces.
On distinguera les groupes d'objets suivants:

– les nuclei	15 ex.
– les lamelles (aussi corticales, etc)	138 ex.
– les éclats et déchets	455 ex.
– les outils retouchés	44 ex.
– les déchets caractéristiques	6 ex.
Total	658 ex.

Les nuclei

II s'agit uniquement de nuclei à lamelles, provenant de petits rognons couverts de cortex.

Dans la phase initiale (phase du pré-nucleus), les nuclei ont été aménagés par des enlèvements latéraux et dorsaux.

La phase d'exploitation lamellaire se caractérise par des nuclei coniques et subconiques. Afin de permettre une exploitation exhaustive, il arrive qu'un second plan de frappe ait été aménagé sur certains pieces. Cette phase est aussi caractérisée par la technique de ravigage du plan de frappe et du front.

Le débitage

Le débitage a été réparti comme suit:
–   Lamelles provenant de la phase de formation des nucleus:

lamelles corticales	5 ex.
lamelles de la 1ère serie	11 ex.

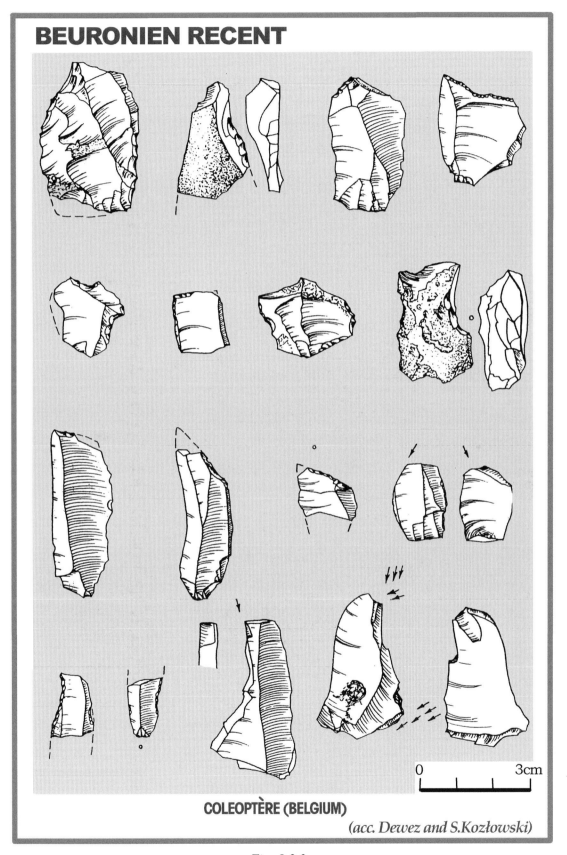

BEURONIEN RECENT

COLEOPTÈRE (BELGIUM)

(*acc. Dewez and S.Kozłowski*)

Fig. 8.2.3a

BEURONIEN RECENT

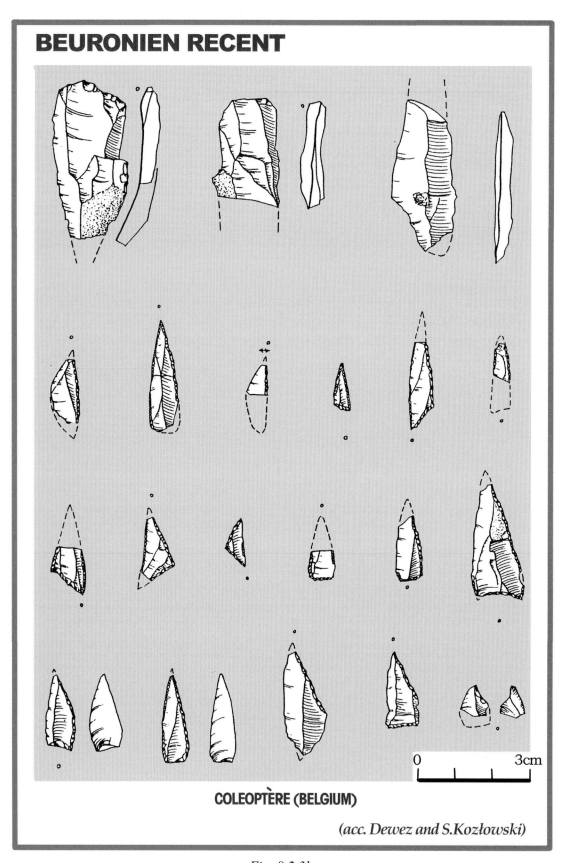

COLEOPTÈRE (BELGIUM)

(acc. Dewez and S.Kozłowski)

Fig. 8.2.3b

lamelles à crête		5 ex.
Total		21 ex.

Il s'agit de lamelles assez massives; de section sub-triangulaire, de profil courbe, qui sont les dernières débitées avant l'enlèvemenl de lames utilisables pour la fabrication d'outils.

– Les supports:

lamelles entières à talon large	5 ex.
lamelles entières à talon étroit	2 ex.
lamelles entières	3 ex.
fragments proximaux de lamelles à talon large	31 ex.
fragments proximaux de lamelles à talon étroit	14 ex.
fragments proximaux de lamelles	6 ex.
fragments médians de lamelles	38 ex.
fragments distaux de lamelles	18 ex.
Total	117 ex.

Les éclats
(provenant de la formation et du ravirage des nuclei)

éclats massifs d'aménagement des pré-nuclei	8 ex.
éclats d'aménagement parallèls à l'axe des nuclei	74 ex.
éclats d'aménagement perpendiculairs à l'axe des nuclei	12 ex.
fragments d'éclats d'aménagement	35 ex.
éclats de ravirage de toute la surface de débitage	14 ex.
tablettes	2 ex.
petits éclats et esquilles (longueur inf. à 1 cm)	310 ex.
Total	455 ex.

Les lames/lamelles
On compte dans ce groupe 138 pièces débitées dans le style de Coincy (cf. "Blade/bladelet"). Elles se répartissent en deux sous-groupes: le premier comprend les lames d'aménagement des nuclei (lames à crete, lames corticales, etc) et le second les supports d'outils ou les outils fonctionelles non-retouchés eux même.

Les supports laminaires/lamellers sont très souvent cassés perpendiculairement. Nous pensons qu'il ne s'agit pas de cassures accidentelles, mais plutôt d'une technique particulière de fracture propre à certaines traditions mésolithiques (cf. "Sectioning"). Certaines lames/lamelles du Coléoptère présentent une retouche dite d'utilisation.

Les éclats
Le groupe des éclats (455 ex.) est moins homogène que celui des lames et lamelles. Ce sont principalement des déchets de la formation et du ravirage des nuclei laminaires et lamellaires. Ces éclats peuvent parfois servir de support à certains outils.

Les outils retouchés
Les rares microlithes ont été répartis selon la classification de notre "Atlas" (cf.).

–	Lamelles a dos	4 ex.
	DB, court	1 ex.
	DB, longue	1 ex.
	DA, court	1 ex.
	fragments	1 ex.
–	Triangles	6 ex.
	TE, court	1 ex.
	TE, long	1 ex.
	TE, ?	1 ex.
	TO	2 ex.
	TN, petit	1 ex.
–	Pointes a base transversale	6 ex.
	XA	1 ex.
	XC, longue	1 ex.
	XD	1 ex.
	XE	2 ex.
	X ?	1 ex.
–	Micro-troncatures	2 ex.
	K	1 ex.
	K?	1 ex.
–	Trapèzes	1 ex.
	BJ/BV	1 ex.
	Total	19 ex.

Nous ajouterons à cette série un microburin.

Parmi les outils, on a distingué les formes suivantes:

–	éclats retouchés	8 ex.
–	éclats micro-retouchés	2 ex.
–	encoche	1 ex.
–	lames à troncature oblique	3 ex.
–	lame retouchée	1 ex.
–	burins	4 ex.
–	piece écaillée	1 ex.
–	lamelles retouchées	3 ex.
–	fragments d'outils	2 ex.
	Total	25 ex.

A cette série s'ajoute 5 chutes de burins.

Interpretation taxonomique
Le matériel de la couche 5a, bien qu'il soit assez pauvre, est néanmoins suffisamment caractéristique pour etre classeé dans une tradition bien définie.

La combinaison des classes de microlithes: D (A–B) + T (N–O) + K + X (A–E), associée au style de Coincy, est connue dans de nombreux sites du bassin de l'Ourthe (Mazures, la Roche-aux-Faucons, Durbuy). Elle est également bien connue dans des régions plus éloignées comme le Bassin Parisien (Coincy I et II, Piscop M1, Montbani II), le Nord-Est de la France (Roc-la-Tour II, Rochedane A2, A3, Oberlarg Q), la Suisse (Birsmatten-Basisgrotte 5–3), l'Allemagne (Ensdorf IV, Jägerhaushöhle 13–8, Stumpertenrod, Mücheln-Möckerling) et dans les Pays-Bas (Aardhorst-Vessem II–III).

Cette combinaison caractérise le Beuronien (cf.), appelée aussi facies Coincy du Tardenoisien (nom proposé par Jean-Georges Rozoy), qui s'est développé au Nord des Alpes pendant les 10/9ème et 7ème millénaires cal. B.C.

Rappelons toutefois que cette association peut s'enrichir d'éléments supplémentaires en fonction de ça position chronologique.

Premièrement les triangles TE s'y ajoutent pendant la deuxième moitié du 8ème millénaire et caractérise la phase récente du Beuronien (phase C de Wolfgang Taute).

Deuxièmement, les trapèzes asymétriques s'ajoutent à cette combinaison vers 7000 cal. B.C. (surtout dans le Bassin du Rhin inférieur et dans les Ardennes ; Beuronien D d'André Gob).

II est à souligner que vers 7000 cal. B.C., l'évolution du Beuronien ne suit pas partout la même direction: dans le Basin Parisien, la Suisse et sur le Danube supérieur allemanique il est remplacé par un Montbanien méridional (ou *"Spätes Mesolithikum"* de Wolfgang Taute) et à l'Est du Rhin par un Beuronien D à trapèzes.

Conclusion

En conclusion, la couche 5a du Coléoptère est attribuable à la tradition Beuron-Coincy (phase D) qui a évolué dans notre region. La présence d'un trapèze permet de dater cet outillage après 7000 cal. A.C. alors en concordance avec la date radiométrique.

8.3. The "Sauveterrian Commonwealth" or the West between the South and the Centre (Fig. 8.3a–d)

The five different cultures: Sauveterrian, Beuronian C, Boberg, Shippea Hill and Svaerdborgian, the first early and in the south, the other four more northerly and later, are characterized (in different degrees) by a pronounced presence of microliths, which can be considered as "sauveterrian" or "sauveterroid" (term proposed by Grahame Clark and used later by Hans-Georg Bandi and René Wyss) – original and unique in the south and apparently secondary in the north (cf. "Les courants interculturels").

The units described below have different genealogy: Sauveterrian originated from the Mediterranean (cf. "South") Epi-Gravettian and Epi-Azilian, Boberg can be part of the evolution in the northern reaches of the Beuronian, and Shippea Hill and Svaerdborg are yet another phase of local Maglemosian, transformed by southern influences. For a full picture, we can add here the slightly less sauveterrianized Beuronian C (the western variant).

The "Sauveterrian Commonwealth" (cf. "Les courants interculturelles") is characterized by a typical set of small and fine microliths, including short (TN, TM) and long triangles (TO, TD, TR and TH) and a variant with retouch on three edges (TE), Sauveterrian points (PD), and, finally, small delicate backed points and small crescents (DD).

Characteristic of sauveterroid cultures
Sauveterrian (Fig. 6a)

Name from the site Sauveterre-la-Lemance-le Martinet in France. The complex developed in territory from the Apennine Peninsula to the Pyrenees from the 10th/9th to the end of the 8th millennium cal. BC (cf. "Trentino sequence", "South" and "Rhythms" in this volume).

STONE INDUSTRY. "Sauveterrian" is characterized by original structure (high index of microliths K, medium or high index of end-scrapers A, medium index of burins C, truncated blades D and retouched blades E), as well as a specific structure of the very small and hyper-microliths group, in which relatively the same role is played by backed forms (including arched ones DD, DE), isosceles (TN, TN) and scalene (TO, TR, TH) triangles, Sauveterrian points (PD) as well as rectangles (RA). Also the characteristic group of denticulates on flake (B) should be mentioned.

BONE INDUSTRY is characterized, among other things, by the presence of spindle-shaped points/*sagaies*, often called *poinçons* in French srudies.

HISTORY. The Sauveterrian Culture derived probably from Epi-Gravettian *milieus* in the east and Epi-Azilian ones in the west. In particular, the assemblages from La Tourasse, Abri Cornille, Cuzoul-de-Gramat in France or Piancavallo in northern Italy, speak in favour of this proposition, as well as the fact that Sauveterrian points (PD), small backed points, small triangles (TN, TM, TR, TO) and spindle-shaped bone points are present in assemblages of the regional, pre-Sauveterrian, Epi-Gravettian. It is possible that also the Late Pleistocene, Provencal "Montadian" (described by Max Escalon de Fonton) characterized by denticulates and hyper-microliths is one of the initial forms, especially of the western/French variant of the Sauveterrian. It seems that already after full formation, which took place mostly in northern/central Italy and southern France probably in the 10th millennium cal. BC, the Sauveterrian spread northwards, among others through the Rhône valley, reaching as far as the Loire and Brittany (André Thévenin's idea). The Sauveterrian can be divided into several regional variants, among others, the Southern and Southwestern French, North Italian, Carstic and Tuscanian. The differences between them derive probably from the different cultural substratum (cf. also "South"). The evolution of the culture under discussion can be traced in the stratigraphical sequences of such sites as Rouffignac, Montclus and Fontfaurés in France, and Romagnano III and Isola Santa in Italy. The following tendencies result: disappearance of micro-truncations and backed points, as well as of crescents (DD, DE) in the youngest phase with simultaneous increase in the number of Sauveterrian points (PD). The last phase is characterized by numerous short-base triangles (TH, TE) and narrow trapezes at the end (Montclus). Further development goes in the direction of various Castelnovian mutations (the Cuzoul in the west and the classic French and Italian Castelnovian in the east).

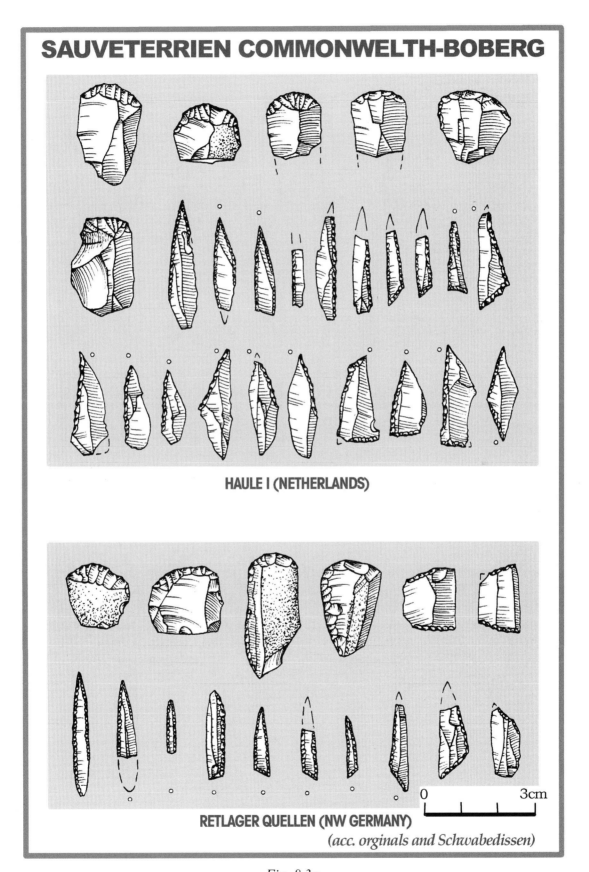

Fig. 8.3a

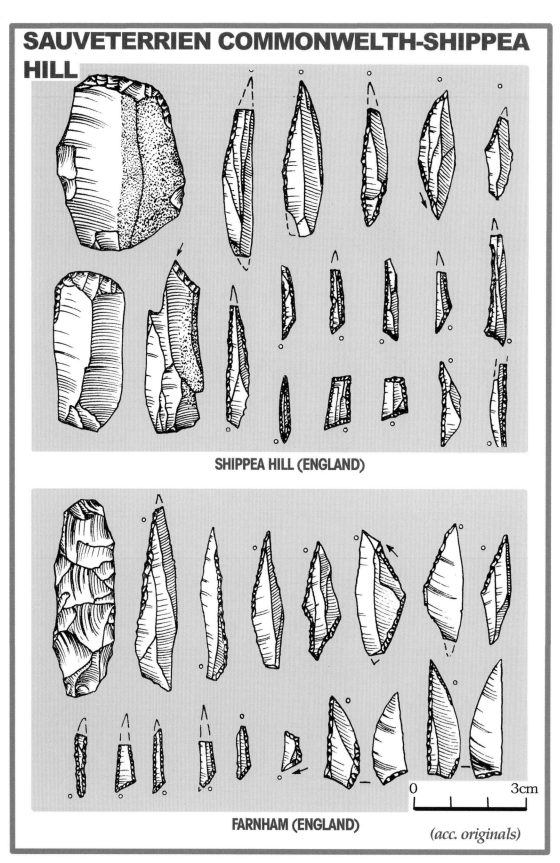

SAUVETERRIEN COMMONWELTH-SHIPPEA HILL

SHIPPEA HILL (ENGLAND)

FARNHAM (ENGLAND)

0   3cm

(acc. originals)

Fig. 8.3b

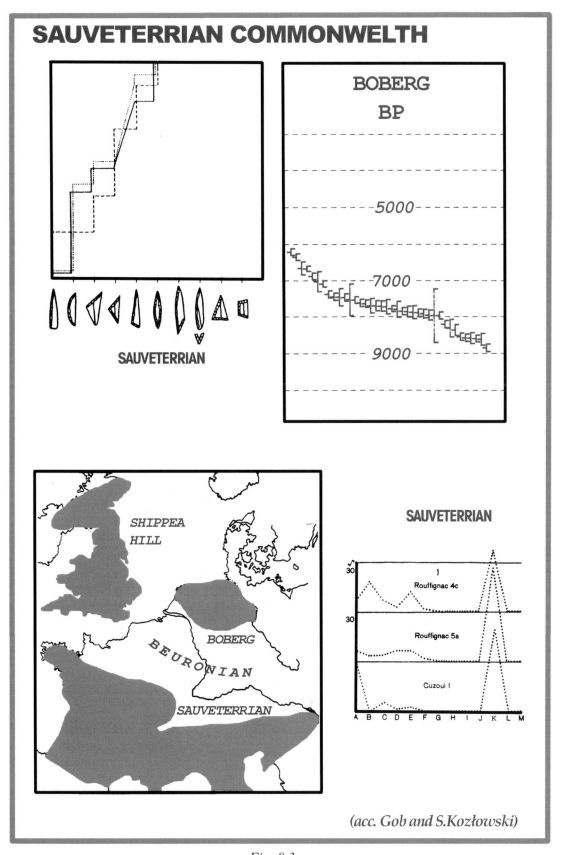

Fig. 8.3c

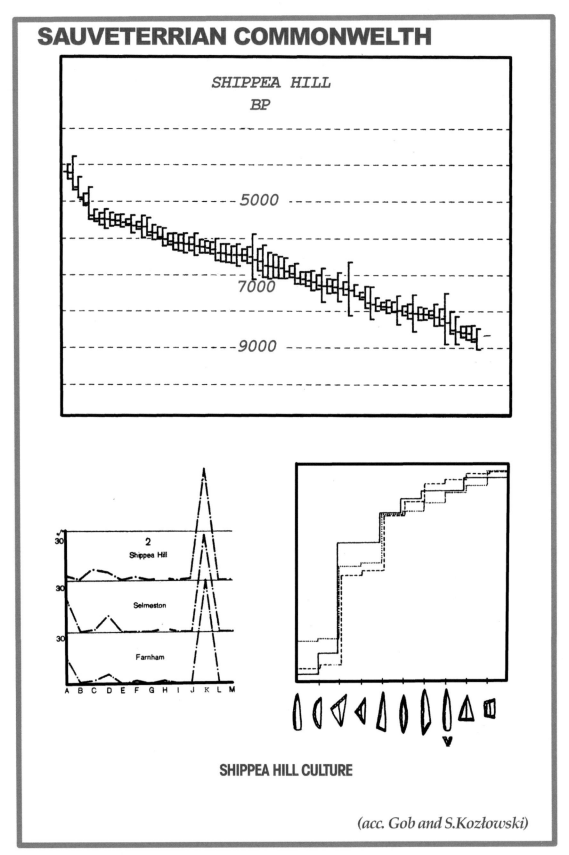

SAUVETERRIAN COMMONWELTH

SHIPPEA HILL
BP

5000

7000

9000

2
Shippea Hill

Selmeston

Farnham

A B C D E F G H I J K L M

SHIPPEA HILL CULTURE

(acc. Gob and S.Kozłowski)

Fig. 8.3d

Boberg (Fig. 8.3a)

Name from the Boberg site in Germany, proposed by Hermann Schwabedissen, also known as the Nollheider Group (Surendra K. Arora), developed in the territory between the lower Elbe and Rhein rivers, from the second half of the 8th millennium cal. BC.

STONE INDUSTRY. Apart from the above-described common properties of the "Sauveterrian Commonwealth", it is additionally characterized by original structure (high index of microliths K, and end-scrapers A, low index of burins C, perforators F and irregular scrapers B), as well as by original structure of the microliths group (most numerous are the backed points, next to quite numerous Tardenoisian (X) points and scarce micro-truncations, B-points (K), scalene (TR, TO, TH) and isosceles (TN) and trapezes (AA, AZ).

HISTORY. Boberg is probably the sum of local late Beuronian elements, represented by backed points and micro-truncations (K), crescents (DD), isosceles (TN), and Tardenoisian points (X) and the Sauveterrian elements originating from the south (small triangles and backed and Sauveterrian points), testifying perhaps to a northward migration (?) of the population of Sauveterrian tradition in the middle/second half of the 8th millennium cal. BC. The developed, 7th millennium phase of Boberg sports trapezes and lasted in its base territory at least until the emergence of the first Neolithic farmers. There are those who would like to see it as an extremely sauvetterized northern variant of Beuronian C and D in the Lowland.

Shippea Hill culture (Fig. 8.3b)

Name from Shippea Hill-Peacock's Farm in Great Britain, also called the Narrow Blades Industry (Roger Jacobi). The unit developed in the territory of Britain and northern Ireland from the middle of the 8th millennium cal. BC.

STONE INDUSTRY. Apart from the common properties (already remarked by Grahame Clark) of the "Sauveterrian Commonwealth" cultures (cf. above), it is additionally characterized by original structure (high index of microliths K, medium or high index of burins C, truncations blades D, and chipped axes H), as well as by specific structure of the microliths group: numerous micro-truncations (K), quite numerous isosceles (TN) and scalene (TO, TR, TM) triangles, scarce backed points, crescents (DD) and Sauveterrian points (PD) and unique backed points with ventral retouch and short rectangles (RB-RC).

HISTORY. The phenomenon is a sum of two elements: local one of the Maglemosian (namely Broxbourne) type (lanceolate DB and retouched base DF points, single (K) and double (PE) micro-truncations, unpolished axes) and outside one originating probably, from the continental Sauveterrian (small elongated triangles TH, TE, and backed points, Sauveterrian points PD), and added to this the narrow-bladelet technology. This could be evidence of northward migrations (?). Shippea Hill can be subdivided into regional variants, the Horsham in the southeast among others (with specific XH points), the classical and recently described one, such as that for Man Island and western Britain.

Two other "victims" of Sauveterrianization are the Beuronian (cf.) in phase C (western variant) and the Svaerdborgian (cf.) in southern Scandinavia. The first one appears to have been a less sauveterrianized version of Boberg (a crossing of Beuronian tradition with "Sauveterrian" elements), while the second one is an eastern, weak, analogy to Shippea Hill. After all, with Dogger Bank Shelf still constituting a land bridge the territories of Britain and Denmark remained immersed in a common Maglemosian tradition and continued to draw on it.

8.4. After sauveterrization

Larnian/Irish Late Mesolithic (Fig. 8.4)

This Late Mesolithic unit, identified by Hallam C. Movius, is found in Northern Ireland and the Isle of Man. Peter Woodman dated it from c. 7000 cal. BC. The people specialized in a littoral economy, although not to the exclusion of all other forms. It was based on procuring marine molluscs (shell middens, cf., are known), as well as hunting seals on the coast and big game inland. Sites include: Larne-Current Point, Cushdun.

The curious stone industry is characterized by big blade technique, with big tanged knives/flakes/points, "blade points" and end-scrapers, finally polished and unpolished axes/adzes and picks.

Obanian

Poorly studied local cultural unit on the western coast of Scotland and the Orcade Islands, dated to the 5th millennium cal. BC (among others, Clive Bonsall's AMS dates for flat bone harpoons), exploiting sea resources (seals, fish, mollusk) more than inland ones. Shell middens are found in seashore caves, but also on open sites.

The tool inventory features flat, double-row harpoons with big barbs and stone and bone "pegs" (retouchers? weights?). Poorly studied and not well represented, the stone inventory also contains picks. Classic sites: Risga, Cnoc Shigeach.

8.5. The Centre: Maglemosian

The situation is much more complex in the north of the European Plain, marked by Maglemosian tradition. This is more or less the Lowland, that is, land lying usually below 200 m a.s.l. (cf. "Relief", "Inland", "Lake and river").

Firstly, it offers no important territorial barriers, thus it is open to communication. A developed river network with water courses generally flowing northward, connected by numerous small rivers and streams of various sizes and a series of postglacial circum-Baltic lakes (cf.) also favored interregional communication, thus fomenting an exchange of ideas. It was excellent subsistence for communities of hunters and gatherers (cf. "Inland").

Some regions (West, cf. "Les courants intercultureles")

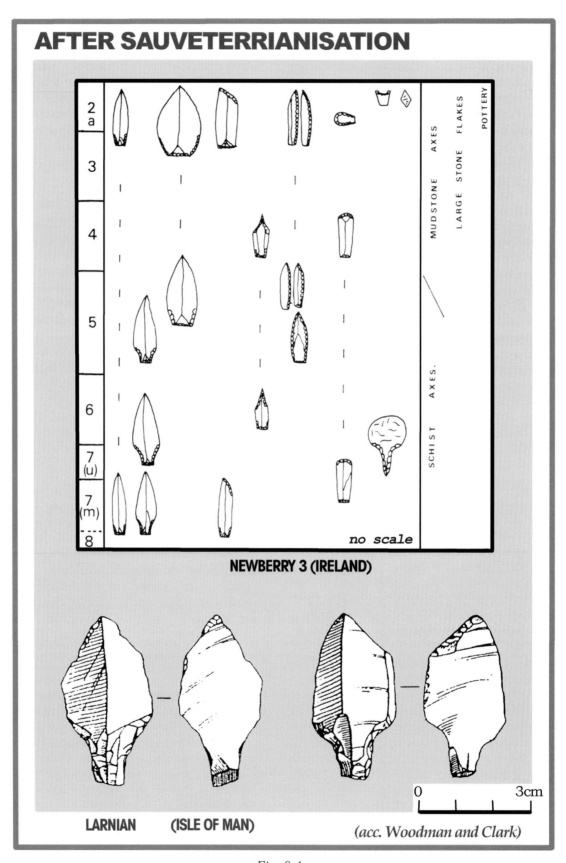

Fig. 8.4

were also open to influence from the south (called "sauveterrization" in this volume, cf.) which hastened changes, while others, as in the east, were protected from such changes by barriers like the Czech Mountains, the Sudeten and Carpathians, but also by the distance; their peripheral situation also helped to limit change.

Hence, the uneven rhythm of change (cf. "Rhythms") in an area that had previously been fairly uniform in terms of style. Hence also misunderstandings between Erik Brinch-Petersen and the author on the meaning of the term "Maglemosian" and the internal divisions and sequence of this phenomenon.

Overall, two or even three lines of evolution can be observed: western, northern and eastern. In all three, the point of departure are industries with broad geometric microliths (isosceles TN, broad large scalenes TO and TR, crescents DD, double (PE) and single (K) truncations, backed points DA, DB, etc.), each with regional variants: Star Carr – Thatcham, Duvensee – Klosterlund, and Komornice – Całowanie, which tend to evolve (or not), but in fairly different directions. And at different speed, too.

The Star Carr variant in the west was replaced quickly (when?) by Broxbourne-type assemblages (the youngest radiocarbon dates refer to material of this kind from Mother Groundys Parlour, upper layer, excavations by Charles McBurnay!), where various backed points predominated (DB, DF) together with microtruncations (K), unpolished axes and very short end-scrapers.

The same situation is encountered in southern Scandinavia (Svaerdborg I and II assemblages from the middle and second half of the 8th millennium cal. BC) and in Polish Pomerania and Kuiavia (excavations by Zbigniew Bagniewski and Lucyna Domańska respectively), but most certainly not further inland and west of Poland, in Brandenburgia, where the old style continued *en vogue* (cf., e.g., the Friesack sequence, excavations of Bernhard Gramsch).

About the middle of the 8th millennium cal. BC, the west of Europe, including the northwestern part of Maglemosian territory, was sauveterrized (cf. "Les courants"). This meant basically a change of technique: coring (narrow bladelets) and the appearance of more (Great Britain) and less numerous (southern Scandinavia) "Sauveterrian" types (scalenes with short base TH and TE in the west and north, Sauveterrian points PD in the west) the East (Poland) adapted scalenes with short base residually at best and at a later time (in the trapeze phase).

Great geographical perturbations took place at the same time and slightly later. The gist of the changes was a gradual submerging under sea of land lying to the north (Dogger Bank and the Western Baltic bridge). The final step in this process was the isolation of the British Isles from the continent (in the middle and second half of the 8th millennium cal. BC), which automatically left it out of the "Maglemosian game". The phenomenon caused a population shift with peoples from flooded territories pressing south, west, east and north, and obviously disturbing the existing *status quo*.

The results from different regions are not the same. In southern Scandinavia (c. 7000 cal. BC), the local Maglemosian adopted more numerous and finer scalenes (TH and TE) and related forms (PB, PC etc.), then trapezes (early Atlantic Scania assemblages, e.g. Ageröd I, H/C upper), and was finally completely castelnovized c. 6500 cal. BC (Kongemose Culture, cf. "Pre-Neolithic/Castelnovian").

The East continued in its Duvensee-Komornica tradition also after 7000 cal. BC, evolving after some delay (how long?) into Ageröd I H/C, upper layer, or Svaerdborg I (Becker's collections), Oldesloe, Jühnsdorf, Chojnice and Pieńki.

Whatever the perturbations taking place, the present author is convinced that the entire Maglemosian *sensu largo*, from the Vistula to Britain, should be considered as belonging to a Central-Western European Mesolithic *koine* (cf.), meaning that the same or similar development occurred there (broad microliths turning into narrow microliths and then into trapezes), although not in the same manner everywhere (cf. "Rhythms").

Meticulous reconstruction of regional sequences (Erik Brinch-Petersen for southern Scandinavia, Raymond R. Newell for northwestern Europe, Grahame Clark and Roger Jacobi for Great Britain, Peter Woodmann for Ireland, Hermann Schwabedissen and Bernhard Gramsch for northern Germany, Stefan K. Kozłowski for Poland) and attempts at correlation of the different sequences have been very difficult because of extremely numerous subsurface and often hopelessly mixed open sites which offer no stratigraphy and more often than not, no dating opportunities. Hence, the not always successful attempts at typological dating, hampered by regional variations.

Another issue at hand is understanding the origins of the Maglemosian phenomenon. Firstly, the submerging of Dogger Bank and the Western Baltic land bridge has deprived us of a part of the important sources, and secondly, regional cultures preceding the Maglemosian (Feldmesser-Tjongerian-Creswellian, Ahrensburgian and Swiderian) were distinguished, described and dated based on similarly uncertain subsurface or surface sources. Thirdly, another reason for the difficulties in interpretation is the controversy over the mechanisms triggering the change from a tundra to a forest model of subsistence at the turn of the Pleistocene and Holocene (especially as after calibration the Preboreal period turns out to be very long!, cf. "Chronology"). On one hand, population shifts are suggested at the turn of these two periods (Romuald Schild's very probable migration hypothesis concerning the settling of Scandinavia by Lowland inhabitants and the Swiderians moving northeast, as well as Bernhard Gramsch's opinion about southern backed points complexes having their share in the settling of the Lowland in the Early Holocene), but on the other, there is a quiet local evolution taking place, nicely confirmed in the available evidence from nothern Europe (theories by Erik Brinch-Petersen and André Gob on the Epi-Ahrensburgian roots of the Maglemosian or André Thévenin's similar idea about the local Ahrensburgian giving rise to the Beuronian).

8.5.1. the South Scandinavian sequence

Excellently described by Erik Brinch-Petersen, the south Scandinavian sequence (Klosterlund-Sønder Hadsund-Bøllund-Svaerdborg) assumes the homogeneity of the "transitional" phase to Svaerdborg I (Bøllund site in Jutland), despite material originating from two distant areas and hence not necessarily homogeneous (Lars Larsson), although it could be. Despite everything, the hypothesis put forward once by the present author (opposition between Duvensee and Svaerdborg cultures) remains sound, even though Søren H. Andersen has attempted to distinguish a separate, early culture called the Klosterlund; same opinion of Bernhard Gramsch!

8.5.2. The Northern or Maglemosian Complex

Division, chronology, territorial range (Fig. 8.5.2a–n)

The Maglemosian Complex includes nine cultures, classified in three separate groups:
1) Duvensee Culture Group (Star Carr in the west, Duvensee in the centre and Komornician in the east);
2) Maglemose Culture Group (Broxbourne in the west and Svaerdborgian in the east);
3) Postmaglemosian Culture Group (De Leien-Wartena, Oldesloe, Chojnice-Pieńki and Nøstvet/Lihult Cultures).

The Maglemosian Technocomplex (for Poland, cf. "Eastern Maglemosian", with more developed subdivisions) developed in the territories of North-Central and Northwestern Europe from the end of the 10th until the 6th/5th millennium cal. BC. (also "Nord").

Basic similarities

End-scrapers (A) and unpolished/chipped axes/adzes/picks (H) are the basic stone tools bringing together the Maglemosian regional entities. In the first group, very short flake end-scrapers ("Azilian") predominated especially in the early stages. They were constantly accompanied by short end-scrapers, more numerous in the later stages. Macrolithic tools formed another characteristic element: mainly flint axes, adzes and picks. Proximal microtruncations (K) constituted the third common element (at least in the early and middle stages). Apart from these, certain similarities have been traced in the bone industry, namely, the domination of barbed points (cf. "Points/*sagaies*"). Similarities occur also in the ornamentation of bone tools ("Maglemosian Style", cf. "Art and ornaments").

The Duvensee Culture Group is additionally characterized by short and massive burins (C) mostly on truncation, and presence of perforators/becks (F). Also double micro-truncations (PE), short (TO) and obtuse-angled triangles (TR), backed points (DA) and broad isosceles triangles

(TN) occur. Another common element are double-platform cores giving short, irregular bladelets of Coincy style (cf. "Blades/bladelets").

The Maglemose Culture Group was characterized principally by lanceolates (DB), Maglemosian backed points (DB-C), retouched base bladelets (PB) in the east and rhomboidal points (RB, RC, cf.). Cores (keeled, conical), giving long, regular bladelets are another common feature, especially in the Svaerdborgian.

The Postmaglemosian Culture Group was distinguished by the uninterrupted presence of long, narrow and rather small microliths made on microbladelets; long triangles with short base (TH) should be mentioned here, including a variant with three retouched edges (TE), followed by bladelets with retouched base (PB, PC) and, finally, trapezes (AZ, AA), as well as some pieces from the trapeses B group.

The similarities manifest themselves also in core shape (subconical, conical cores, which are the final shapes of keeled forms for narrow, regular bladelets).

Differences

The above-described common elements of Maglemosian as a whole are not represented equally in all nine cultures. For instance, very short/flake end-scrapers are more numerous in the Duvensee and Maglemose Culture Groups, whereas short and even long (on blades) pieces dominate in Postmaglemosian cultures. Moreover, macrolithic tools (H) are better represented in southern Scandinavia, as well as in Britain and in the territory between the Elbe and Oder rivers. There are fewer east of the Oder (and they are rather absent from southern Poland). Also important differences can be traced in the proportions of the microliths group. The recognizable entities/cultures of the Maglemosian/Northern Technocomplex are as follows.

Star Carr Culture (cf. "Le Komornicien") (Fig. 8.5.2a)

Name from the site Star Carr 4 in Great Britain. Also known as Proto-Maglemosian Culture (Grahame Clark), developed in the territory of Great Britain and the Dogger Bank Shelf in the 10/9th millennium cal. BC.

STONE INDUSTRY. Characterized by common Maglemosian and specifically Duvensee Culture Group features, it also has original structure (high or medium index of end-scrapers A and microliths K, medium or low index of burins C, low index of truncated blades D, perforators F and axes H, as well as specific structure of the microliths group: numerous microtruncations K and rather high index of double micro-truncations PE and isoscele triangles TE, also backed points D and scalene triangles TO and TR. Single Lyngby points are an individual feature of the Star Carr Culture in its earliest stage.

BONE INDUSTRY. Characterized among other things by the presence of barbed points, the barbs being small and numerous.

HISTORY. Star Carr Culture is possibly a continuation of

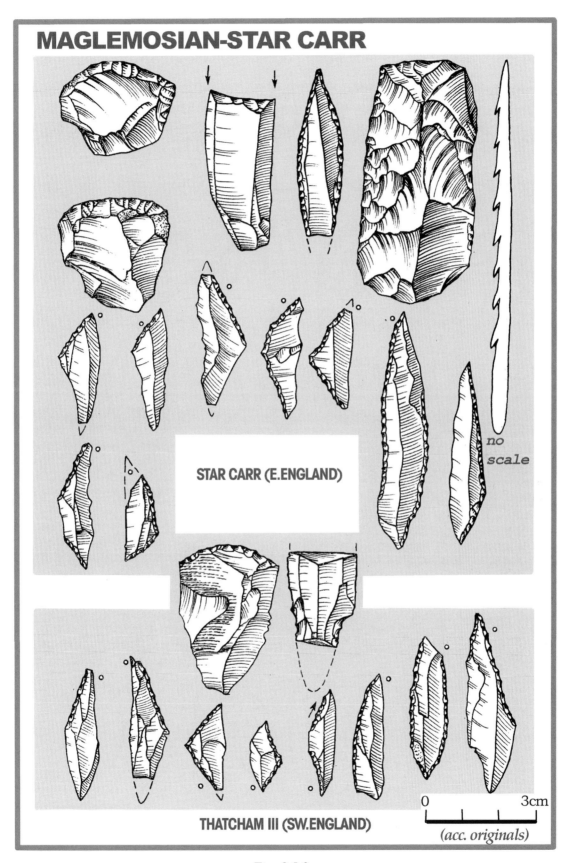

Fig. 8.5.2a

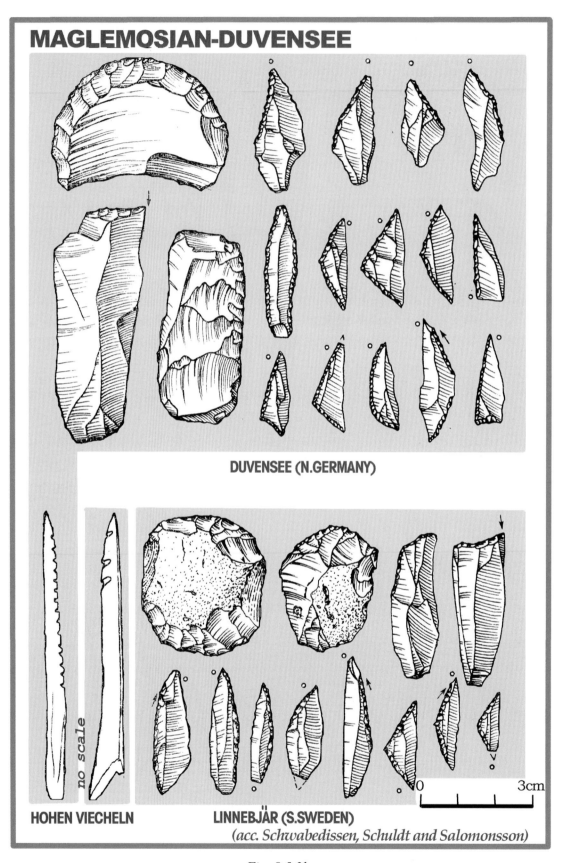

Fig. 8.5.2b

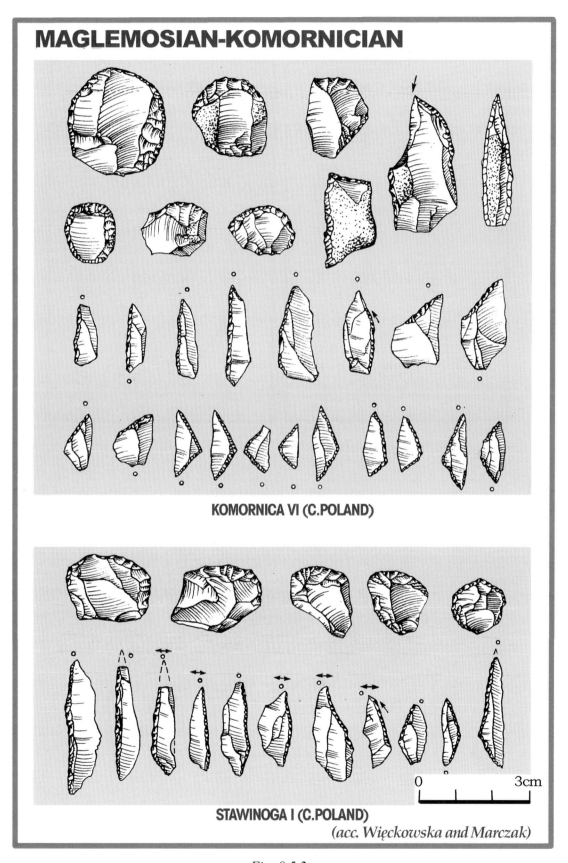

MAGLEMOSIAN-KOMORNICIAN

KOMORNICA VI (C.POLAND)

STAWINOGA I (C.POLAND)

(acc. Więckowska and Marczak)

Fig. 8.5.2c

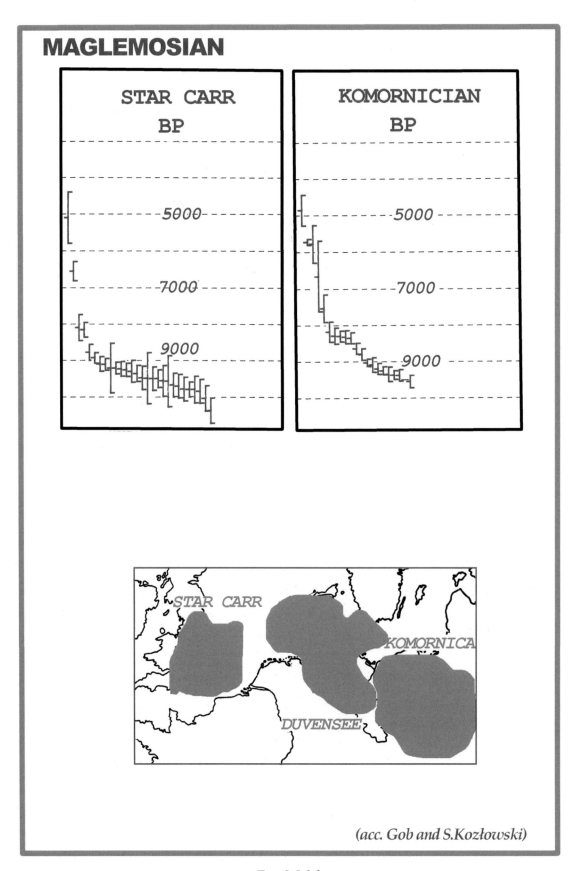

Fig. 8.5.2d

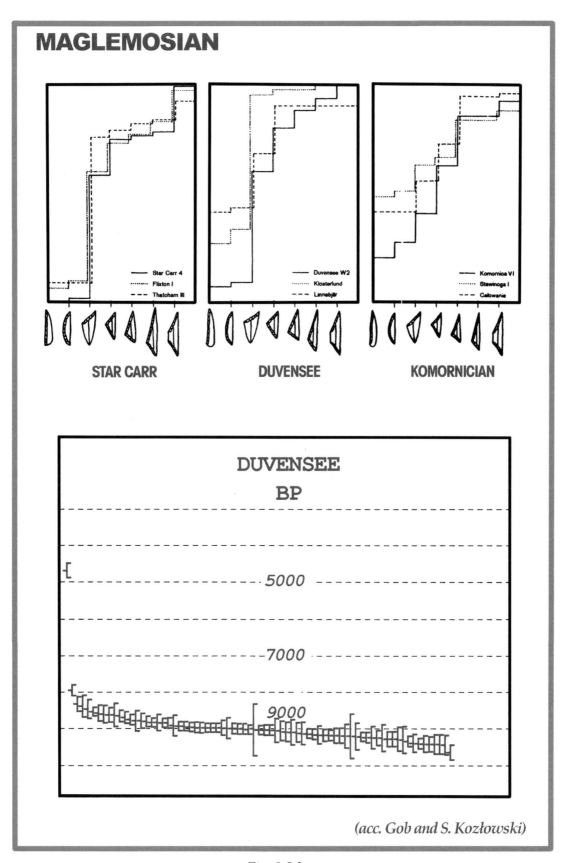

Fig. 8.5.2e

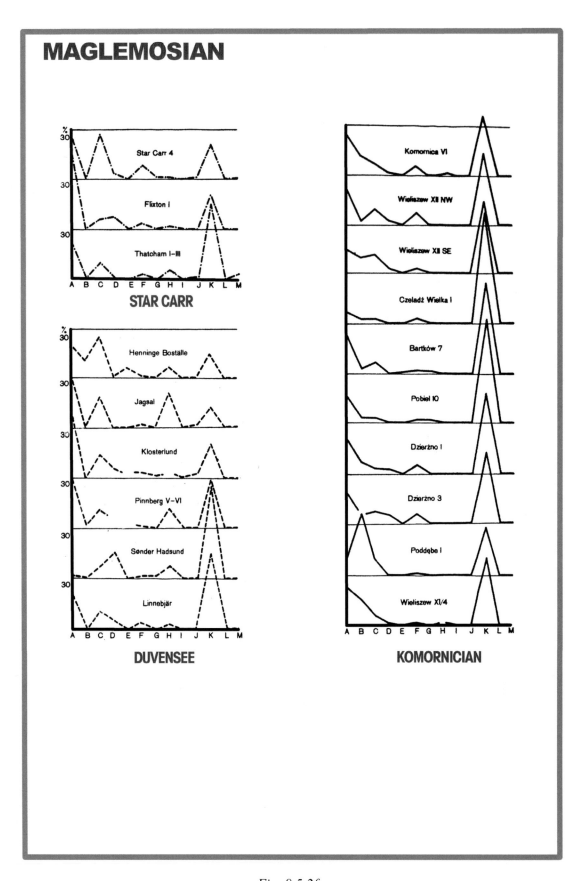

Fig. 8.5.2f

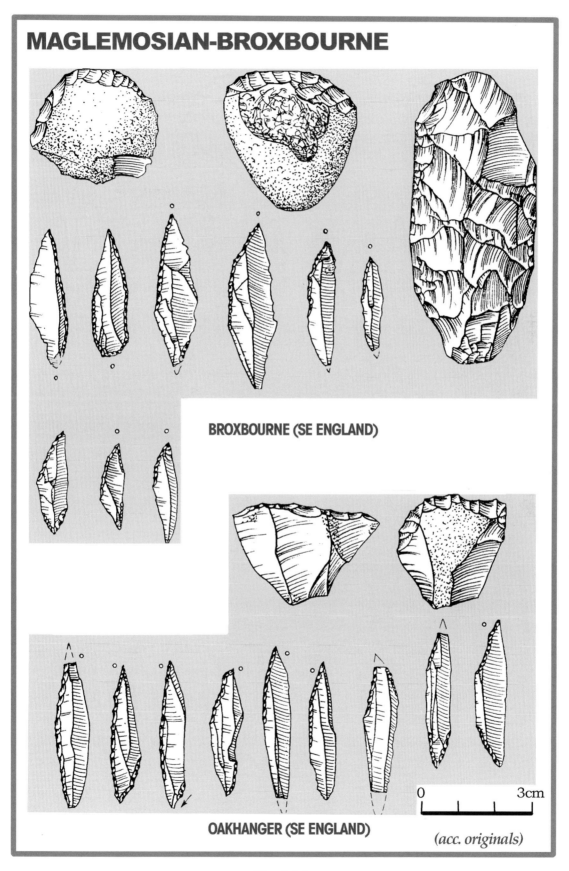

MAGLEMOSIAN-BROXBOURNE

BROXBOURNE (SE ENGLAND)

OAKHANGER (SE ENGLAND)

0   3cm

(acc. originals)

Fig. 8.5.2g

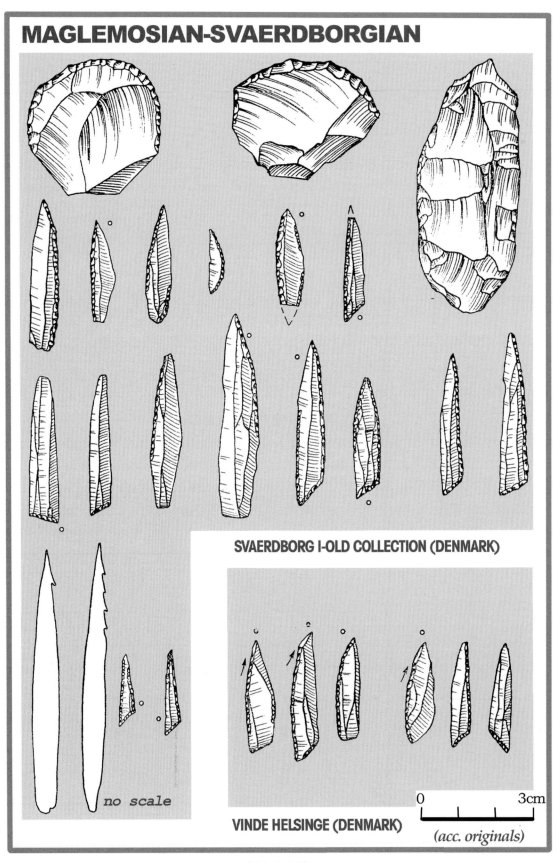

Fig. 8.5.2h

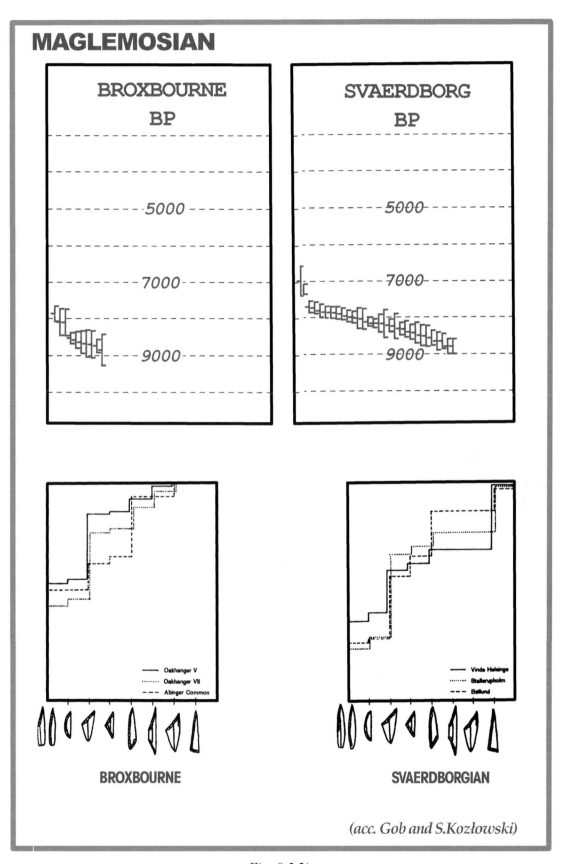

Fig. 8.5.2i

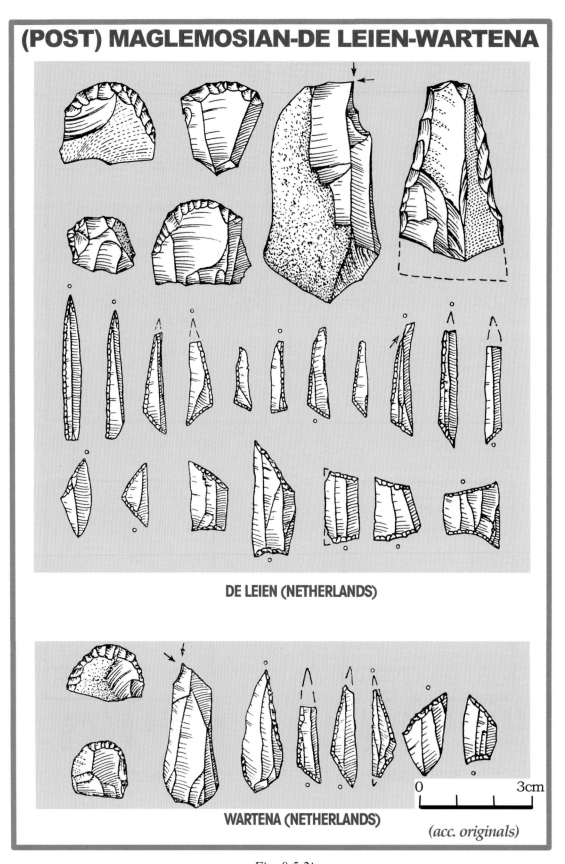

Fig. 8.5.2j

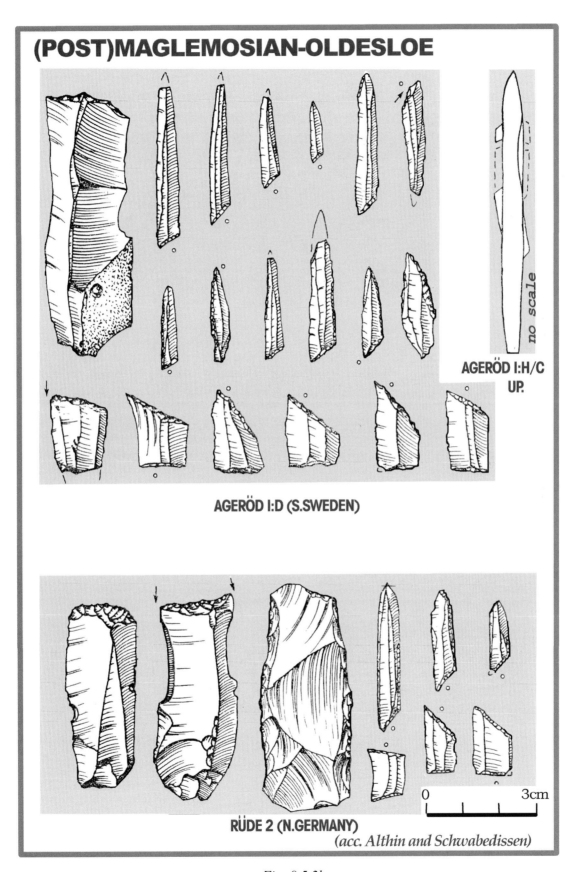

(POST)MAGLEMOSIAN-OLDESLOE

AGERÖD I:H/C UP.

no scale

AGERÖD I:D (S.SWEDEN)

RÜDE 2 (N.GERMANY)

(acc. Althin and Schwabedissen)

0   3cm

Fig. 8.5.2k

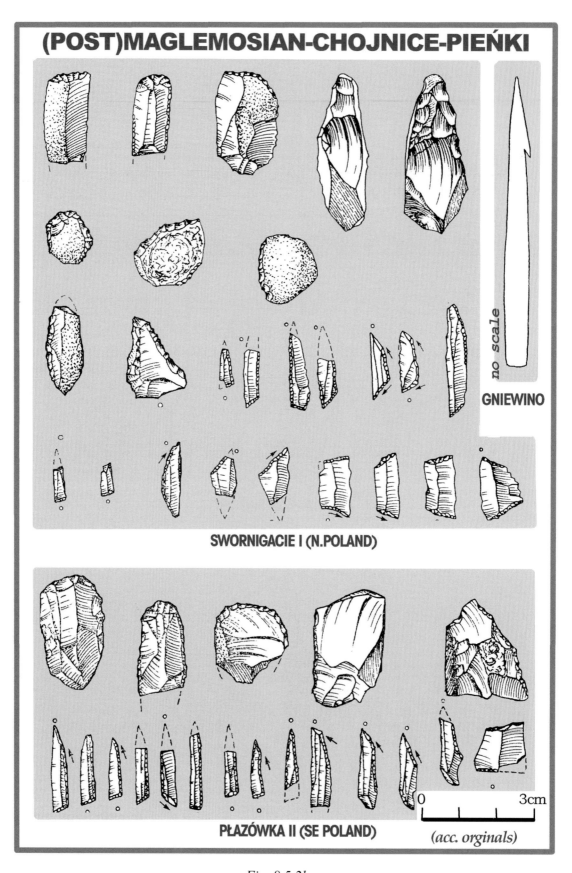

Fig. 8.5.2l

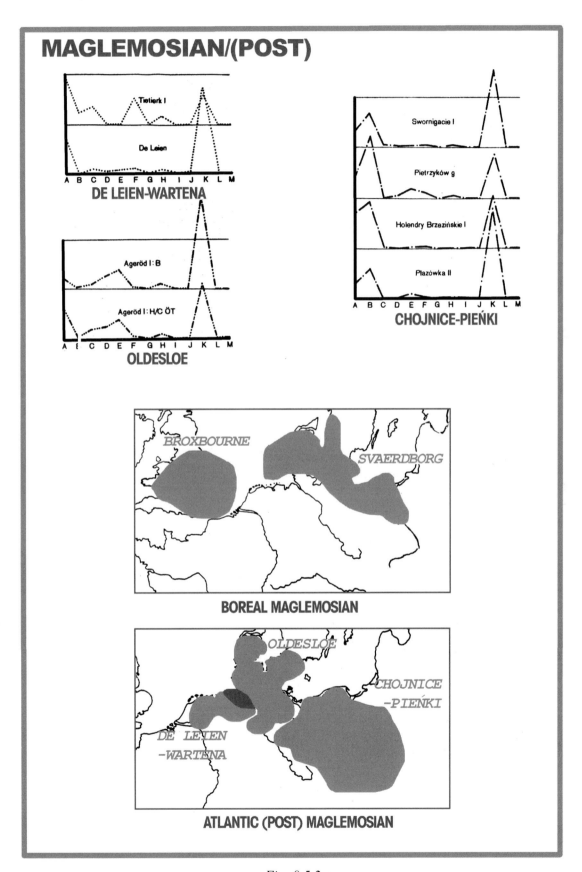

Fig. 8.5.2m

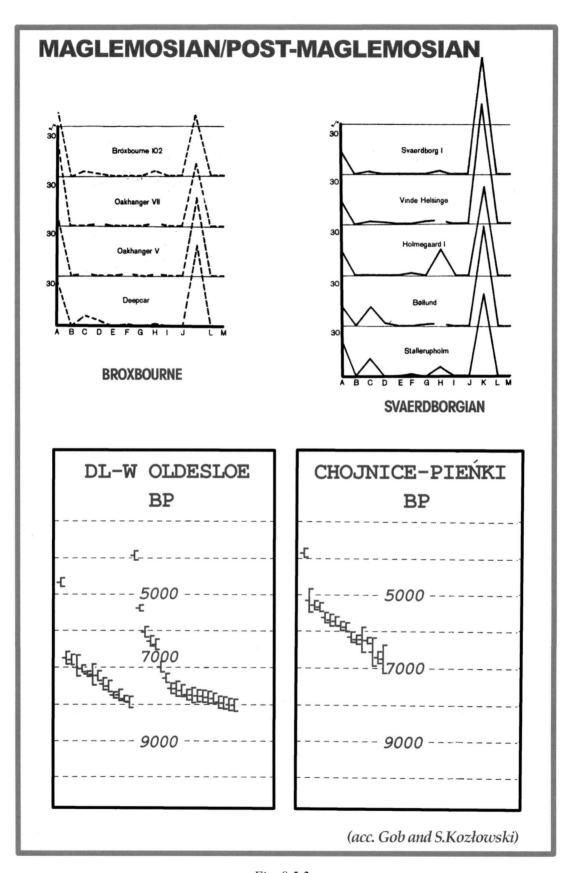

Fig. 8.5.2n

the western variant of the Ahrensburgian (double-platform core technique, short and very short end-scrapers, burins, truncated blades, Lyngby points, micro-truncations K), which migrated northward or evolved in East Anglia. This evolution could have gone through the Epi-Ahrensburgian (cf.). Later it evolved in the direction of the Broxbourne Culture.

Duvensee Culture (cf. "Le Komornicien") (Fig. 8.5.2b)

Name from the Duvensee W 2 site in Germany. Known in Bornholm as the Melsted Group (Carl J. Becker) and in Denmark as the Klosterlund industry (Søren H. Andersen). It existed in southern Scandinavia for a short period of time (as Maglemose 1, according to Erik Brinch-Petersen) and in the German Lowland (Hermann Schwabedissen, Bernhard Gramsch) for much longer from the second half of the 10th to the beginning of the 7th millennium cal. BC (cf. "Rhythms").

STONE INDUSTRY. Common Maglemosian and specific Duvensee Culture Group features were supplemented with original structure (high or medium index of end-scrapers A, burins C, and microliths K, medium or low index of axes H, low index of truncated blades D, and perforators F), as well as pecific structure of the microliths group (high index of microtruncations K, quite numerous backed points D and isosceles triangles TN, also crescents DD and scalene triangles TO and TR).

BONE INDUSTRY. Characterized by the presence of harpoons of Duvensee (no. 2), Dobbertin (no. 4) and Pritzerbe (no. 8) types (classification according to Grahame Clark).

HISTORY. Duvensee Culture comprises the following elements: 1) element common to Star Carr Culture, the Western variant of Ahrensburgian, as well as Epi-Ahrensburgian cultures: microtruncations (K), isosceles triangles (TN), double truncations (PE), very short end-scrapers, burins; 2) element related mostly to Star Carr Culture or some unknown milieu (perforators, harpoons), and finally 3) element with fairly numerous backed points related perhaps to the Federmesser *milieu* (remnants existing (?) in Dogger Bank Shelf and surely in northern Holland during the very Late Pleistocene and very early Holocene; information from Raymond R. Newell) or the Western variant of Ahrensburgian Culture. It seems that the Duvensee was formed either under the influences of cultures from the Dutch-British territories or was of local origin (from Epi-Ahrensburgian Culture), as suggested by Danish researchers. The Duvensee Culture is divided into a number of groups from the very beginning: Haltern, Melsted, Klosterlund, Classical and Fien, and this could also be rooted in their origins. The first group did not possess axes (and was not classified in the Northern Technocomplex by Hermann Schwabedissen), the second was distinguished by more lanceolate points, and the fifth had a clearly smaller tools and some Tardenoisian (×) points. The first two groups relatively quickly changed into the Svaerdborgian industry; the German entities lasted

longer and, at the turn of the 8th and 7th millennia cal. BC, they gave birth to some Post-Maglemosian Cultures: Oldesloe and Jühnsdorf in northern Germany.

Komornician

Cf. separate text in this volume.

Broxbourne Culture (Fig. 8.5.2g)

Name from the Broxbourne 102 site in Great Britain. It existed in Britain and on the Dogger Bank Shelf from the beginning (?) to the middle of the 8th millennium cal. BC. Not distinguished by Roger Jacobi, who divided the British Mesolithic into "Early" and "Late".

STONE INDUSTRY. Apart from the common Maglemosian characteristics, it features additionally original structure (high index of end-scrapers A and microliths K, low index of burins C, truncated blades D, perforators F and axes H), and unprecedented microlith structure: high index of lanceolate and similar points (DA, DB, DC, etc.), presence of isoscele triangles (TN), microtruncations with perforator-like tips (KA) and narrow double microtruncations (PE).

HISTORY. As indicated by many elements, Broxbourne Culture originated directly from local Star Carr Culture. One cannot resist the impression, however, that also outside elements (Federmesser/Creswellian?) might have had their share (slowly disappearing from Dogger Bank Shelf); they could have been the source (?) of numerous backed points so characteristic of Broxbourne. A similar differentiated D backed points should be noted as appearing at the same time in Denmark (cf. "Atlas"), as demonstrated by Erik Brinch-Petersen. Also, the common shape of Creswellian and Broxbourne double truncations merits attention. Broxbourne ended with the appearance in its territory of Sauveterroid elements (middle of 8th millennium cal. BC) which made way for Shippea Hill Culture.

Svaerdborgian (Fig. 8.5.2h)

Name after the site of Svaerdborg I (old excavations) in Denmark. It developed from the middle to the end of the 8th millennium cal. BC in the territory of southern Scandinavia, the eastern part of Dogger Bank Shelf, northern Mecklemburg and Polish Pomerania and Kuiavia. Classified as Maglemosian 3 by Erik Brinch-Petersen.

STONE INDUSTRY. Apart from common Maglemosian features and those typical of the Maglemose Culture Group, it is also characterized by original structure (high index of microliths K, medium index of end-scrapers A, medium or low index of irregular scrapers B and axes/adzes H), as well as specific microliths structure (domination of lanceolate points DB, DC and DF, high index of microtruncations K, numerous long triangles with short base TE, TD, continuously present crescents DD and not very numerous isoscele triangles TN, as well as bladelets with retouched base PB and rhombs RB and RC. High keeled end-scrapers (= keeled cores) are also characteristic.

BONE INDUSTRY. Harpoons of Mullerup type (7) and single-barbed harpoons (5), as well as double-slotted points (type 21$_2$) (typology according to Grahame Clark).

HISTORY. The Svaerdborgian (Maglemose 3 according to Erik Brinch-Petersen) was formed by three factors. Firstly, the local substratum represented by the southern Scandinavian variant of Duvensee Culture, i.e., the Klosterlund/Melsted Group. Secondly, numerous lanceolate points in several variants, which developed in the Melsted Group and were probably the result of western influence (relics of the Backed Points cultures on Dogger Bank Shelf?). Thirdly, an element probably from the outside, represented by the technique of conical/keeled core, regular microbladelets, and among the microliths by long triangles TD and TE ("sauvetteroid" influence). The Svaerdborgian can be divided into two territorial variants: the Classical Group and the Ageröd Group distinguished by a clearly smaller number of triangles. This differentiation may indicate the direction from which the elements enumerated in third place arrived. According to Erik Brinch Petersen, Svaerdborgian evolution was characterized by backed pieces disappearing to be replaced by elongated microliths/triangles, PB and PC points (the Klosterlund-Sønder Hadsund-Bøllund-Svaerdborg sequence).

The Svaerdborgians took part probably in the formation of the Post-Maglemosian Culture Group (De Leien-Wartena, Oldesloe and Chojnice-Pieńki Cultures, cf.), but also in the push to the north of the microbladelet industry of Lihult/Nøstvet type (cf. "North"). The following facts speak in favour of this idea: the presence of long triangles, points with retouched base (PB), Nowy Młyn points (PC), lanceolate points and axes/adzes in the listed cultures, which are younger than the Svaerdborg Culture, as well as weak typological continuation in the following Kongemose Culture. Following from this is the theory about the Svaerdborgians' shifting south and north at the turn of the 8th and 7th millennium cal. BC. The cause of this migration was the sinking of the West-Baltic and Jutland-British land-platforms. Forced to leave southern Scandimavia, the Svaerdborgians settled in the lakelands of the Plain and along the west Scandinavian coast.

De Leien-Wartena Culture (Fig. 8.5.2j)

Name from the sites of De Leien and Wartena in Holland, proposed by Raymond R. Newell. Also known as Western Oldesloe, developed from the end of the 8th millennium (?) cal. BC in the territory between the lower courses of the Elbe and Rhein rivers.

STONE INDUSTRY. Apart from common Maglemosian/ Northern Technocomplex and Postmaglemosian Culture Group traits, it is also characterized by original structure (high or medium index of end-scrapers A and microliths K, medium or low index of irregular scrapers B, burins C, perforators F, low index of chipped axes H) and the presence of lanceolate points DB, DC, small backed points, isoscele triangles TN and asymmetric trapezes B. High end-scrapers/cores have also been recorded.

HISTORY. De Leien-Wartena is, according to Raymond B. Newell, the result of a superimposition of elements of Maglemose type (lanceolate points DB, long triangles TD, TI, TH, points with retouched base PB, Nowy Młyn points PC, very short end-scrapers, high end-scrapers or keeled cores, unretouched axes, subconical cores, bladelets, (cf. "Les pointes PB et PC") originating most probably from the Dogger Bank Shelf, on a local Boberg-type substratum (Tardenois points X, backed points DA, microtruncations K). Trapezes were added to this (representing southern influence, cf. "Les courants..."). The southward migration idea is motivated environmentally; at this time the Dogger Bank Shelf was nearly entirely submerged, forcing the local population (mostly Svaerdborgians) to migrate to the south (but also to Britain?) where it settled especially in Friesland lake territory closely resembling the base environment.

Oldesloe Culture (Fig. 8.5.2k)

Name from the site of Oldesloe-Brennermoor in northern Germany. Sometimes referred to mistakenly as Gudenaa Culture in Denmark, this unit existed in southern Scandinavia for a short period of time (e.g. Svaerdborg I – Becker's collection or rich mixed collections from Jutland) and for a longer time in the German Lowland (Jühnsdorf and Kobrow groups of Bernhard Gramsch), from the beginning of the 8th millennium cal. BC (some inventories with trapezes from Ageröd mose).

STONE INDUSTRY. Presents all the common Maglemosian and Postmaglemosian features and additionally an original structure (high index of microliths K, low index of end-scrapers A, irregular scrapers B, burins C, and unpolished axes H, nearly medium index of retouched blades E, as well as asymmetric trapezes of group B and long and short end-scrapers on blades.

BONE INDUSTRY. Finely toothed harpoons and double-slotted points.

HISTORY. The Oldesloe is typologically the result of the mixing of several elements: firstly, local Duvensee Culture (isosceles TN and microtruncations K, backed points, axes/adzes); secondly, arriving Svaerdborgian elements (lanceolates DB/DC, long triangles TD, TE, points with retouched base PB, Nowy Młyn points PC, subconical and keeled cores, slotted bone points, harpoons); and finally trapezes, which are a southern invention. The earliest phase (with trapezes but without the Duvensee elements) started forming still in Svaerdborgian territory, but the actual development of Oldesloe Culture took place only after the alleged southward migration (Hermann Schwabedissen's idea but some traces could still continue in the basin of Jutland's Gudenaa river); it was forced by environmental change (at the beginning of the 8th millennium cal. BC) (cf. also remarks on the Svaerdborgian). The culture under discussion existed there regionally (the coast became Ertebøllian) at least until the appearance of the first Neolithic farmers on the lower Oder river.

Chojnice-Pieńki Culture

Cf. more detailed text on the Polish Post-Maglemosian entities in this volume.

Nøstvet-Lihult Culture

(cf. "Nord").

8.5.3. Epi-Ahrensburgian

This industry from northwestern Europe (Zonhoven in Belgium, Pinnberg in northern Germany, Baremose and Aabenraa in Denmark), described by André Gob and referred to as Maglemosian 0 by Erik Brinch-Petersen, is dated to the turn of the 10th and the 9th millennium cal. BC and was in all likelihood an evolutionary stage between the Late Pleistocene Ahrensburgian (with tanged points) and the assemblages rich in microliths but devoid or almost devoid of tanged points of Star Carr, Klosterlund, Haltern and Duvensee types, perhaps also Komornica type, in northwestern and central Europe.

8.5.4. Local and foreign elements in the British Mesolithic (Fig. 8.5.4a–b)

This article was written independently of Roger Jacobi's "Britain inside and outside Europe". It points out Britain's original ties with the continent via Dogger Bank: Maglemosian connections with numerous elements identical to ones from the European Lowland (e.g. axes/adzes, DA, DB, DC, DD, DE and K-points, triangles TN, TO, TR, etc., cf. "Atlas"), as well as "Sauveterrian" elements (PD points, TH and TE short-base triangles) that are concurrent with the Mesolithic of western Europe. These contacts were broken off around the second half of the 8th millennium cal, BC when the English Channel was formed. Hence, the absence of trapezes which never made it to the Isles from the Continent (cf. also the successive paper).

Introduction

The multilateral continental connections of the British Mesolithic have been discussed repeatedly by Grahame Clark and thus need not be described again herein. Nonetheless, as far as the author can remember, there has never been an attempt to examine the problem against a broader background. Neither has it been attempted to explain the historical processes taking place over huge territories of northern and western Europe. A cartographic presentation covering such an extensive area would have been particularly useful for the purpose.

The aim of this essay is to show and interpret territorial and chronological frames for important typological elements of the British Mesolithic: mostly Early Mesolithic backed points DF and Sauveterrian points PD (cf. "Atlas"), which could be treated as synonyms of respectively the Early and the Late Mesolithic in Britain. The different origins of the two types, and the different chronology and territorial ranges are in some sense symbolic of the two different worlds towards which Great Britain gravitated at different times.

Distribution maps for the classes of tools mentioned above are integral to this paper. The maps are supplied with commentaries presenting the definitions of both classes of tools and their territorial and time analysis.

Sources have already been listed in the author's original publication of the "Atlas of the Mesolithic" (cf.).

Discussion

Sauveterrian points (= points PD)

1. The most complete definitions were provided by Claude Barrière and Jean Georges Rozoy, agreeing to a large extent; the author has adopted their definitions herein.

2. A spatial analysis of PD points indicates that at the time of their maximum range they were an intercultural element (cf. "Les courants interculturels"), occurring from northern Italy and southern France up to Scotland and northwestern Germany. The range shown on the map constitutes a sum of ranges from different periods of time and thus one may attempt a chronological division.

3. Having considered the factor of time variability, it appears that the primary, i.e., earliest, range of Sauveterrian points may be reconstructed first of all as the area south of the Loire (from the Latest Pleistocene up to c. 7700/7500 cal. BC). The second stage of the spatial development is marked by the extension of the range of Sauveterrian points (PD) to the north followed by its gradual disappearance in "native" territories (from c. 7000 cal. BC, cf. "Mapping the Mesolithic").

4. The thesis presented above assumes the existence of a true genetic connection between the Anglo-Dutch pieces and the Franco-Italian ones.

5. These connections are justified by:
   a) typological homogeneity of all the pieces in question,
   b) their territorial homogeneity (cf. detailed map),
   c) continuity of occurrence (no marked time gaps) in the Mesolithic of western Europe (Sauveterrian and early Castelnovian or Cuzoul cultures in the south, Beuronian, Boberg, Rhein-Meuse-Schelde, De Leien-Wartena and Shippea Hill Cultures in the north, including the Irish Early Mesolithic of Peter Woodman).

6. Assuming this idea, we must share the opinion about the allochtonic origin of the earliest British PD points and the accompanying small, fine scalene triangles TH and TE with short base, which the author believes to be a manifestation of strong southern influences in the Mesolithic of the Netherlands and Great Britain, commencing about the middle of the 8th millennium cal. BC.

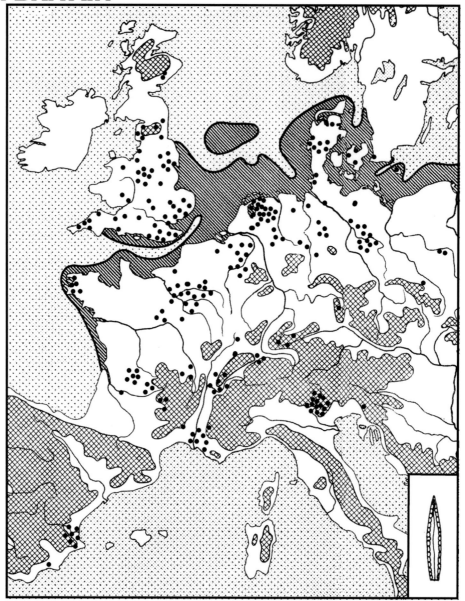

Fig. 8.5.4a

LOCAL AND FOREIGN ELEMENTS IN BRITAIN

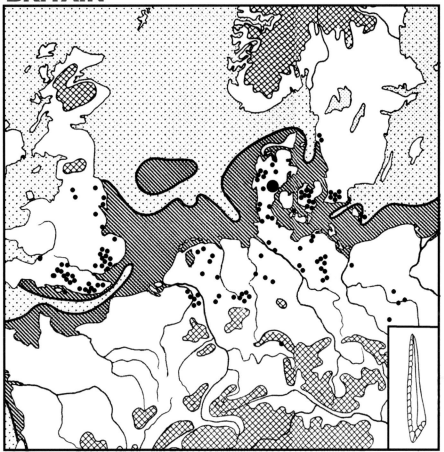

- **BACKED POINTS WITH OBLIQUELY RETOUCHED BASE (DF) CONNECT S.SCANDINAVIA, BRITAIN AND NORD EUROPEAN PLAIN**

Fig. 8.5.4b

7. These changes were manifested in northwestern Europe, among others, by the introduction of a new, narrow-bladelet technique, small scalene triangles with short base (sometimes with retouch on the third edge), rectangles (RA), Sauveterrian points and finally some (nonexistent in Britain) rhomboids/trapezoids (the latter not earlier than c. 7000/6500 cal. BC).

8. This presumed southern influence led to the emergence of new taxonomic units across northern Europe: Shippea Hill in Great Britain, perhaps the Svaerdborg in Denmark (?) and the Boberg variant of the latest Beuronian in the Netherlands and northwestern Germany.

Backed points with an oblique, retouched base (= DF).

1. They have been defined by Grahame Clark as types of C1b and C1d. T. Mathiassen called them "Lancetter no. 6" and Erik Brinch Petersen "pointes à dos abattu et base tronquée No. 4" (first variant). The discussed microliths differ from the Pleistocene pieces mainly as regards more delicate blanks and a smaller size.

2. Territorial analysis indicates that in the Early Holocene they were in use from Britain to Scania, Dogger Bank Shelf included, and that they were known mainly from assemblages of Star Carr, Broxbourne, Shippea Hill (all in Britain), Duvensee, Svaerdborgian and De Leien-Wartena (Netherlands, Germany, Denmark, Sweden) and earlier (more massive examples) from Azilian, Gravettian and Federmesser and Creswellian cultures.

    In the south, they reached as far as the German Plain (inland, up to 200 m a.s.l.); pieces from Poland are scarce to the extreme.

3. Unlike Sauveterrian points (cf. above), the northern range of DF points did not change much over the entire period of their existence (Late Pleistocene up to Atlantic time). In any case, they were characterized by great territorial stability between Great Britain and Denmark, as they can be traced there in the Mesolithic back to at least the 10th/9th millenium cal. BC (Thatcham I/V, Star Carr, both sites in England; Klosterlund in Denmark; Duvensee in Germany, all from the 10th–8th to the 7th millennium cal. BC, when the last Scandinavian pieces disappeared, i.e., Ageröd Mosse in Scania, but the British ones were still in existence, i.e., Shippea Hill, Culverwell, Wawcott, etc.); the situation is somewhat different further to the south, where DF points are of relatively late origin (Siegerswoude, Hatert, Le Leien, all sites in the Netherlands, dated to the 7th millennium cal. BC).

4. The chronological and spatial analyses permit the assumption that backed DF points were, at least from the 10th/9th millennium cal. BC, an important and permanent element of the Mesolithic of N-W Europe stretching over considerable territory from Great Britain to southern Sweden. They could be considered as proof of close relations among Early Mesolithic cultures of the areas in question (Star Carr, Duvensee) and this remains in conformity with Grahame Clark's theory.

5. This British and southern Scandinavian uniformity (cf. also "Rectangles...") from the second half of the 8th millenium cal. BC underwent slow and gradual disintegration, firstly because of the gradual sinking of the Dogger Bank landbridge and, secondly, because of differentiation caused by outside influence (cf. "Les courants"), the beginnings of which go back to about 7500 cal. BC (cf. above, remarks on Sauveterrian points).

6. Consequently, the same cultural background, represented here by backed DF points, gave rise to Sauveterrian/Sauveterroid (after Clark) elements in the northwest (PD points, scalene triangles, backed points, etc.) and elements more loosely (?) connected with the Sauveterrian *milieu* in southern Scandinavia (narrow bladelet technology, scalenes). These processes led to the development from a single, uniform background of two completely different traditions/cultures: Shippea Hill in Britain and Svaerdborgian in Denmark.

7. At the beginning of the 7th millenium cal. BC, DF points disappeared from Scandinavia (earlier from the Dogger Bank Shelf), appearing instead in Friesland and Schleswig-Holstein. Hermann Schwabedissen and Raymond R. Newell believe this to be connected with people moving away from flooded land and migrating south.

Conclusions

First of all, in the 10th/9th and the first half of the 8th millenium cal. BC, the territory of Britain was admittedly part of the same cultural "niche" as southern Scandinavia and northern Germany. This is proved for the 10th/9th millennium cal. BC by, among others, assemblages of the Star Carr, Klosterlund and Duvensee type and by DF points for a somewhat later period, the latter becoming gradually more numerous in the territory discussed.

Secondly, the eastern connections weakened in the second half of the 8th millennium cal. BC and the West was supposedly superseded by influences coming from the south, most probably from a Sauveterrian *milieu*. These influences were very strong but fairly short-lived, since Britain was turned into an island soon afterwards. This led to the "Sauveterrian style" being present in Britain much longer than on the continent, thus extending the longevity of the "Sauveterrian Commonwealth" (cf.) there.

8.5.5. Le Komornicien et ces liens occidentaux (Duvensee–Star Carr–Komornica)

L'étude traite de certaines cultures rattachées au Komornicien (cf.)/Maglemosien polonais. L'auteur a tenté d'établir:

1. une caractéristique typologique de Komornicien (Fig. 8.5.5a–c, 8.5.2d);

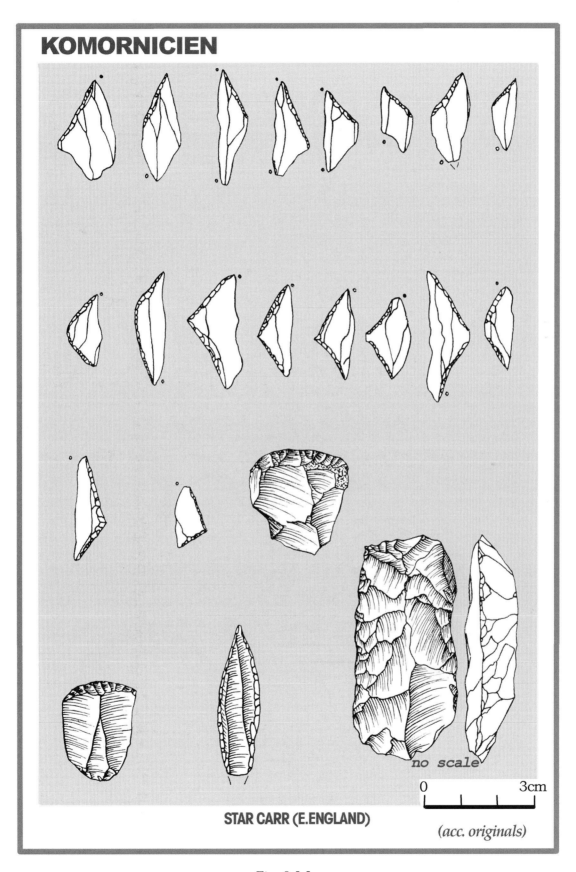

KOMORNICIEN

STAR CARR (E.ENGLAND)

no scale

0 3cm

(acc. originals)

Fig. 8.5.5a

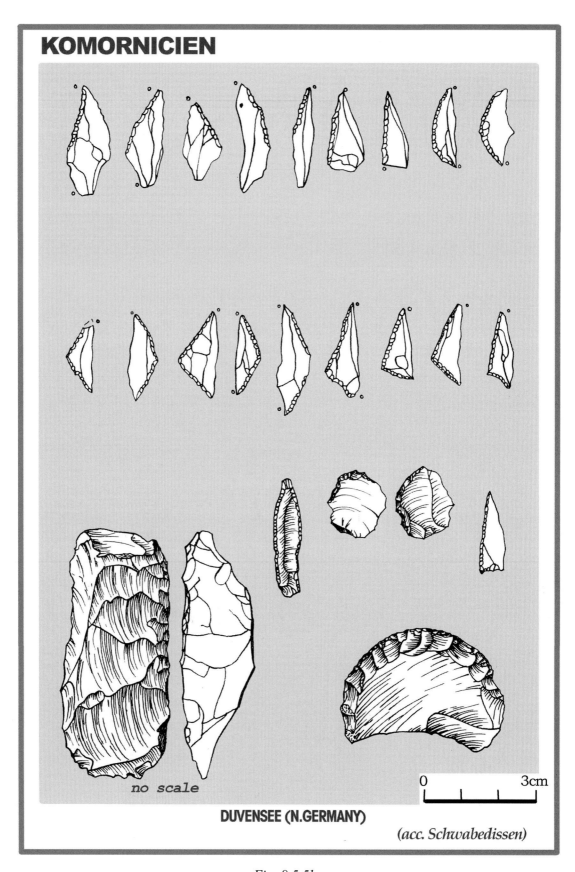

KOMORNICIEN

no scale

0   3cm

DUVENSEE (N.GERMANY)

(acc. Schwabedissen)

Fig. 8.5.5b

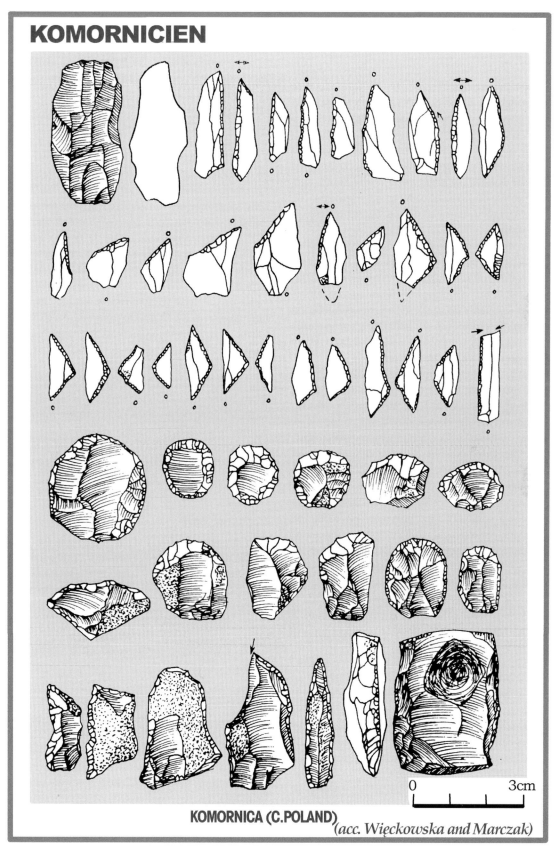

KOMORNICIEN

KOMORNICA (C.POLAND)
(acc. Więckowska and Marczak)

0   3cm

Fig. 8.5.5c

2. un essai de comparaison entre les outillages représentant le Komornicien et les cultures Maglemosiennes classiques voisines;

3. l'étendue du domaine territorial de Komornicien.

Au début, je place le Komornicien au Mésolithique inférieur et moyen. L'ancienneté de cette culture raportée au Préboréal, au Boréal et au début de la période Atlantique, est confirmée par la présence des microtroncatures doubles (PE), des segments de cercle (DD), des triangles isocèles (TN), des pointes à dos type DA, des micro-lamelles tronquées proximales (K), et depuis plusieurs dates ^{14}C, etc.

Je présente ensuite tous les éléments caractéristiques des outillages appartenant au Komornicien, en s'appuyant à cet effet sur les trouvailles les plus classiques de Stawinoga, district de Pułtusk, de Komornica VI et de Wieliszew XI, district de Nowy Dwór, et de Całowanie, district d'Otwock (Pologne centrale).

L'analyse de ces outillages permet d'y constater l'existence de six types caractéristiques de microlithes (pointes à dos DA, micro-troncatures K, triangles isocèles TN, triangles scalènes obtusangles TR, microtroncatures doubles PE et segments de cercle DD. Leur retouche est abrupte et haute. Ces formes sont d'habitude accompagnées de grattoirs très courts sur éclat et de burins masives de petites dimensions, ainsi que de perçoirs.

Il se trouve cependant, que cette caractéristique du Komornicien peut aussi bien être appliquée aux cultures de Duvensee et de Star Carr (cf.), ainsi qu'à celles du Maglemosien ancien du Danemark (Klosterlund). Les cultures du Mésolithique inférieur et moyen de l'Allemagne du nord et du Mésolithique ancien de l'Angleterre présentent tous les types d'outils que l'auteur vient d'énumérer; à Duvensee, ainsi qu'à Star Carr on constate, de plus, la présence des tranchets/haches non-polies, types rares au Komornicien. La caractéristique présentée ci-dessus, en montrant touts les liens exterieurs du Komornicien, n'englobe pas encore toutes les particularités du Komornicien, et en conséquence, il est nécessaire de le compléter en y intégrant des traits typiques supplémentaires.

Ces traits supplémentaires qui différencient le Komornicien de ses voisins occidentaux consistent surtout dans la divergence des rapports numériques entre certains indices statistiques.

Dans le Komornicien le nombre de pointes à dos (DA) prédomine toujours celui de micro-troncatures (K); c'est un trait caractéristique de cette culture. On n'observe ce rapport ni en Allemagne, ni en Angleterre, où les micro-troncatures sont d'habitude plus nombreuses que les pointes à dos. Cette divergence d'indices statistiques permet à elle seule d'établir une ligne de démarcation entre le Komornicien d'une part, la culture de Duvensee de l'autre.

Ce trait distinctif se trouve souligné par des différences métriques, observées dans le groupe de microlithes: en Allemagne et en Angleterre, on a réussi à constater une prédominance marquée des microlithes dépassant 20 mm de longuerre (86 pourcent du total des pièces de ce type), à l'opposé du Komornicien, où prédominent les microlithes

qui n'atteignent pas 20 mm (60 pourcent du nombre total de microlithes). Il ne faudrait pas oublier que ce ne sont pas là des différences causées par la nature de la matière première dont ces outils sont faits: en Petite-Pologne, par exemple, on connaît des microlithes de Komornicien, dont la matière première peut aussi bien servir à la production des pièces de grandes dimensions (même des bifaces).

En s'appuyant sur les types des microlithes, il faut donc admettre une proche parenté entre le Komornicien et le Duvensee; la différence statistique et métrique qui accompagne cette parenté des deux cultures, permet de les distinguer l'une de l'autre.

Ayant établi les traits distinctifs du Komornicien, l'auteur a pu définir l'étendue approximative de l'espace, où cette culture a été la plus typique. À en juger d'après les matériaux publiés à ce sujet, le domaine du Komornicien s'étendait sur le territoire de la partie orientale de la Grande-Pologne, sur celui de la Mazovie en Pologne centrale, de la Haute-Silésie et d'une partie de la Basse-Silésie, enfin sur la partie ouest de la Petite-Pologne, et en Poméranie occidentale. Quelque rares sites existent aussi en Ukraine du nord.

La partie ouest de ce territoire semble particuliérement intéressante; c'est là que le domaine du Komornicien se touche avec l'extension territoriale maximum de l'aire où apparaissent les tranchets/haches mésolithiques nombreux, tellement caractéristiques du Duvenseen. Cette concordance de deux extensions territoriales suggère l'existence d'une zone d'influences/contacts réciproques, dans le territoire de la partie ouest de la Grande-Pologne, entre le Komornicien et le Duvenseen.

A l'est la frontière du Komornicien suit plus ou moins la frontière oriental du pays; le Komornicien se trouve là-bas en voisinage avec la culture de Kudlaevka (cf.).

Comment 2007

This is a resumé of an old essay showing the "horizontal" connections within Maglemosian, emphasizing the very uneven lasting of this "Early" unit. Both the "early" and the "late" age of Komornician have been confirmed now by carbon dating.

8.5.6. The Early/Middle (and Late) Eastern Maglemosian

Komornician (Fig. 8.5.2c, 8.5.5a–c)

A. History of studies. Distinguished by the present author and named after the Komornica VI site near Warsaw. Hanna Więckowska and Maria Marczak identified it independently as the Narvian cycle (after the Narew river in Poland).

B. Cultural framework. The Komornician is an eastern branch of the early and middle phase of the Maglemosian *sensu largo* and is typologically close to the German Duvensee and British Star Carr cultures (cf. "Le Komornicien"). Its assemblages also resemble those of the early phase of the South Scandinavian Maglemosian, as understood by Scandinavian authors (Klosterlund, Sønder Hadsund, Melsted).

C. Assemblages and inventories. Over one hundred certainly Komornician sites are known from Poland, more than 30 of which have been excavated.

The classical Komornician inventories in Mazovia include, among others, Stawinoga I, Całowanie III, Komornica VI, Poddębe I, Wieliszew IX, XI, XII and XVIIc; in northeastern Poland we have Grądy-Woniecko 1, in Upper Silesia Dzierżno 1 and 3, in Little Poland Grzybowa Góra IV/57 and VIII/59; in Lower Silesia Ługi C, Lubiatów, Pobiel 10, Bartków 7 and Czeladź Wielka 1. Great Poland yielded inventories from Chwalim 1, Lasek 2a, Mosina 3/1 and 3a; Kashubia, Swornigacie IV, Męcikał 6 and 11, and Zbrzyca 2; in central Poland there is Witów 1, and in the eastern extremities of Poland Luta 1; finally, in western Pomerania, there is the site of Tanowo.

D. Territorial range. Komornician sites occupy the big-valleys belt, entering the low-lying regions of the upland (Sandomierz Valley, Nida Basin) in the south. The northern limit appears to coincide with the Pomeranian front moraines. The Pripet river basin in the east (Belarus) has yielded backed pieces similar to the Komornica ones (DA and DB) which in a number of cases, however, are related to inventories of the local Mesolithic culture (Kudlaevka, cf.). In fact, two poor inventories (among them Msta in northern Ukraine) could be considered as Komornician there. The western limit of the Komornician is placed in the belt separating Brandenburg from Great Poland. This division line was established on the basis of rather small differences between the Komornician and Duvensee assemblages, both statistical (dominance of microtruncation K points over DA–DB points west of the Oder, cf. "Le Komornicien") and metrical (greater size of artifacts west of the Oder).

E. Chronology. The chronology of the Komornician is fairly well known since we have a series of ^{14}C dates for its sites. Most of these date the culture mainly to the end of the 10th and the 9th and 8th millennia cal. BC. These datings are corroborated by typological markers; most of the Komornician assemblages lack trapezes and this fact allows them to be dated to before 7000 years cal BC. There is finally strong evidence that the last phase of Komornician may be dated to the beginning of the 7th millenium. This is suggested by some datings from Lower Silesia (Pobiel 10) and central Poland (Witów 1, layer 7), and also by the presence of small numbers of trapezes in some assemblages of Little and Great Poland, Kashubia, northeastern Poland, Mazovia and Silesia, this chronology being in good accord with the chronological position of the related German Duvensee culture.

In the 7th millennium, the Komornician begins to disappear. In the east, it was locally replaced by the Post-Maglemosian Pieńki group (cf.), and later (c. 6500 cal. BC) by the Janislawician. In Great Poland and Lower Silesia, it was transformed into the local Post-Maglemosian (cf.), but locally it could have survived even longer, as apparently suggested by radiocarbon dates and typological features

from Stara Wieś and Chwalim 1 in Great Poland, Męcikał 6 and 11 in Kashubia, and Komornica I in Mazovia, as well as some Silesian concentrations of sites (Barycz river valley). In such isolated enclaves it might not have been transformed into the Post-Maglemosian and could have lasted up to the 6th/5th millenium cal. BC.

F. Settlement network (cf.). Given the big-valley character of the Polish Lowland in which the Komornician existed, its settlement network was based primarily on a system of latitudinally running proglacial/marginal stream valleys (Toruń-Eberswalde, Warsaw-Berlin and Barycz-Głogów) and secondarily on longitudinal gorges of rivers connecting these latitudinal valleys. The slightly less irrigated patches of ground moraine were clearly shunned. We may distinguish a number of Komornician site concentrations which partly reflect the actual settlement structure of those times. Noteworthy among these concentrations are the well documented ones from Kashubia, the Poznań area, those on the Obra, Nida, Czarna and (especially) Barycz rivers, from the vicinity of Warsaw and Krakow, Upper Silesia and the middle Warta course. Traces of other concentrations are apparent on the middle course of the Kamienna, upper Bzura, upper Warta, middle Bug, and in the Sandomierz Valley. The concentrations enumerated above form narrow belts along water courses; they are 20–50 kilometers long on the average and may be further subdivided into smaller structures.

In the direct hinterlands of the concentrations, the sites are somewhat scattered, and they are absent altogether from drier or more elevated ground.

The Komornica sites are located mainly on sandy edges of the lower terraces or on small intravalley elevations, i.e., on dunes and remnants of terraces. In the latter case, the vicinity of old river beds was a favourite choice of locality (e.g. Pobiel 10). Medium-sized sites of an area of several ares dominate and these have yielded either unscattered concentrations (e.g. Dzierżno 3) or groups of several such concentrations or "kshemenitsas" (Wieliszew XI). We cannot be sure whether the separate concentrations were contemporary. The next site type is that of extensive camps stretching along terrace edges, as a rule devoid of flint scatters (Smolno Wielkie 1, Pobiel 10, Luta 1). The sites certainly contain mixed material and their inventories usually present the sum of a number of Komornician settlements. Finally, there are small and poor single-concentration or non-concentration sites (e.g. Witów 1, layer 21); in the former case, they are probably traces of single settlements, and in the latter traces of brief penetrations of uninhabitable beaches on the river shores. Zbigniew Bagniewski signalled the discovery in Lower Silesia of a number of Komornician habitation structures (Siedlnica 6, Czeladź Wielka I, Bartków 7). These were allegedly oval or circular semi-sunken huts. However, in the light of Raymond R. Newell's studies, hollows left by windfallen trees look very similar in the archaeological record. At Grzybowa Góra IV/57 site, on the other hand, a depression was discovered, about 2 m in diameter, filled with hematite; it could be the bottom of a hut of unknown structure.

Recently, a very interesting oval structure with thin long wooden sticks serving as a wall was discovered by Marian Marciniak in Mszano in Polish Pomerania.

G. Environment. As Krzysztof Cyrek claimed, the Komornician population utilized primarily local flint as raw material (from deposits up to about 50 km away), and imports from distant places were rare. Thus, in most of the area local erratic and surface raw material was chiefly exploited, while in northern Little Poland the industries were based on "chocolate" flint, and in the upper Vistula on the Jurassic-Krakow raw material and the Cretaceous Świeciechów flint (these, however, being usually accompanied by local erratic flint). Despite the dependence on local raw materials, the assemblages are usually composed of two to four different kinds of flint (with a predominance of local ones), especially in the Vistula river basin, and this testifies to the contacts and perhaps even to the mobility of people within a given macroregion (several dozen km).

H. Flint inventories. (a). Technology. Core processing based on small flint nodules which did not usually go through the pre-core phase. The cores were thus usually unformed. Small flattish cores were used for irregular bladelets, single- or double-platform ones or cores with changed orientation, small in the final stages, for short and not very regular bladelets, and then, in the final phase of the processing, also flakes. The use of flake blanks in tool production is quite substantial; they were used for most of the end-scrapers and burins, as well as axes/adzes and irregular scrapers. Micros' retouch is usually steep.

(b). Retouched tools. The most numerous category are the end-scrapers (20–30%) and microliths (over 40%). The first index is constant for the entire Komornician, while the latter is probably due to the "domestic" rather than the "hunting" function of the described sites. Mention should be made also of irregular scrapers (5–15%) and the rare perforators that are always present in these assemblages.

(c). Principal tool groups for the Komornician as a whole include:

- very short and small end-scrapers on flakes, also short specimens;
- short and very short burins with various massive tips, usually made on flakes;
- slim becks-perforators with continuous retouch along the entire length of both edges;
- backed pieces DA, DB and DC as well as crescents DD (always more numerous than K-points);
- K-points, that is, proximal micro-truncations;
- triangles TN, TM, TO and TR.

I. Bone inventories. There is no direct evidence in this respect. The bone assemblages ought to be close to those typical of Duvensee culture, including, among others, Pritzerbe-type and Dobbertin harpoons (respectively, types 8 and 4 in Grahame Clark's system), as well as mattocks with Maglemosian ornament (cf. "Art and ornaments"), e.g. piece from Woźniki.

J. Territorial division. Relying on cartographic data (dis-tribution of the various classes of microliths and axes, cf. "Atlas") verified on the basis of homogeneous assemblages, it may be assumed that the known Komornician territory is divided into at least two zones. The northwestern zone, comprising the area north of the Barycz proglacial stream valley, as well as Great Poland, is characterized by the presence of axes/adzes and the more numerous backed pieces DB, while the southeastern zone by the more numerous segments DD and backed pieces DA. Added to this are less distinct elements of territorial differentiation (e.g. segments DE) not found in assemblages in Mazovia and central Poland, where the backed pieces DD are in fact also less numerous.

K. Chronological division. Given the fact that many Komornician sites may constitute the aggregate remains of a sum of settlements spanning several centuries (e.g. Całowanie with its series of datings spanning about 1500 radiocarbon years! – information of Romuald Schild), it is at this stage difficult to study the internal evolution of this culture by seriation as applied by many scholars to the Mesolithic. There is, however, a good measure of probability in the conviction that the rare double micro-truncations PE occured in the early Komornician, while the long scalene triangles with short base (TE, TH) appeared towards the end (in Poland: beginning of the 7th millennium cal. BC). In the Early Atlantic phase there were also PB and PC micro-truncations, and not very numerous trapezes (mostly AA).

The latest phase consists of a gradual but regionally differentiated transition to local Post-Maglemosian units (decrease of K, TN, DD and DA microliths, increase of TH and TE and trapezes).

The outlined internal evolution of the Komornician generally follows the evolution trends of classical Maglemosian, but with some retardation (cf. "Rhythms").

L. Origin. It is extremely difficult to recreate the origins of the early units of the Maglemosian complex, Komornician included. This is chiefly due to the fact that they are characterized by elements occurring in the Late Pleistocene over large territories of broadly understood central Europe and in various cultural environments. The "northern" backed pieces (DA, DB) and K-microtruncations, for example, are known in the Final Paleolithic from both the central European Uplands (Epi-Magdalenian) and the Carpathian Basin (Epi-Gravettian), as well as from some areas on the Lowland (Creswellian and Federmesser in northwestern Europe). This is even more true of the very short end-scrapers on flakes, core processing techniques and even geometrics which are known in the Balkans from Epi-Gravettian sites, among others (cf. "Southeast"), but also occur in the Ahrensburgian in the nord-west, as well as in Mediterranean environments.

The most logical hypothesis at this stage would be that the early units of the Maglemosian evolved on the Lowland between Poland and Great Britain in the first half of the 10th millennium cal. BC, as a result of, on one hand, the northward shift and adaptation to lowland environments of Final Paleolithic groups inhabiting upland areas (also those inside the Carpathian arc) and, on the other, of the adaptation of a part of the Ahrensburgians to the forest environment of the Early Holocene (= Epi-Ahrensburgian of André Gob). This could mean that the territorial differentiation of the Komornician was the result of genetical differences existing in it from the very beginning. The northern branch could have resulted from the adaptation of some Ahrensburgians (and later migration to the east), while the southern could have been due to the northward migration of Epi-Gravettians from the Carpathian Basin (idea proposed by Bernhard Gramsch).

M. Disappearance. As already stated, the Early Atlantic phase of the Komornician is an evolutionary transition to Postmaglemosian units but only in part of Komornician territory. Intercultural trends at the beginning of the Atlantic period (the introduction of long triangles with short base and trapezes) brought evolutionary changes in the northern tradition (more in the west, less in the east). The alleged southward migration of the Svaerdborgians from their Scandinavian homeland (forced to move by the marine transgression gradually flooding the West-Baltic land bridge) began also more or less at that time. Typological evidence suggests that the Svaerdborgians or post-Svaerdborgians migrated at least as far as the northern (lakeland) part of the Lowland (bringing with them narrow bladelets technology) and apparently mixed with the local respectively Komornica or Duvensee people creating Post-Maglemosian groups (cf. below). According to Zbigniew Bagniewski and the present author, Komornician could have survived for a long time in local enclaves.

N. Art. The single finds of antler axes carrying Maglemosian ornamentation from Woźniki on the Bug river, Nitki in Mazuria and Ostrołęka on the Narew may be Komornician.

8.5.7. The Eastern Post-Maglemosian (Fig. 8.5.2l)

A. History of studies. I originally called this unit the "Chojnice-Pieńki culture". New discoveries in Poland demonstrated the elements I included in this unit to be more differentiated territorially than expected. Moreover, similar elements are known from Mecklenburg (Oldesloe-Kobrow, Jühnsdorf and Ahlbeck of Bernhard Gramsch), southern Scandinavia (early Atlantic Ageröd of Lars Larsson, also Svaerborg I, Becker's collection, also Gudenaa in Jutland), Schleswig-Holstein (Oldesloc of Hermann Schwabedissen) and Holland (De Leien-Wartena of Raymond R. Newell, micro-bladelet tradition in Scandinavian Peninsula). Now, it is advisable to replace the local notion by a more general one proposed in the title of this chapter.

B. Cultural background. As said already, the Post-Maglemosian groups belonged to the Maglemosian complex as its late phase and they ranged territorially from Friesland to Polish Mazovia, not everywhere reaching the Lowland limit in the south.

Typologically, the Post-Maglemosian materials are characterized by a structural combination of older (short microliths and lanceolates) and younger elements (long

microliths on narrow bladelets plus trapezes), axes/adzes and end-scrapers, the very short and short, but also the very long.

C. Assemblages and inventories. There are at least 70 Post-Maglemosian inventories in Poland. About a dozen or so of them are homogeneous, e.g. Jezierzyce 19, Dąbki, Jastrzębia Góra 4 and Swornigacie I–III, V and VI in Eastern Pomerania; Holendry Brzezińskie I, Ruda Komorska 1 and Białobrzegi in Great Poland; Telążna Leśna I in Kuiavia; Świdry Małe 3 and Poddębe VII in Mazovia; Krzekotówek 8, Świętoszyn I and Siedlisko 16 in Lower Silesia; and finally Czernichów I and Płazówka II in Little Poland.

D. Territorial range. The Post-Maglemosian groups in Poland occupy almost all of the territory, but are best represented along the Warsaw-Berlin proglacial stream valley. It seems that they will not be found in northeastern and eastern Poland, mostly east of the Vistula.

B. Chronology. The dating of the Post-Maglemosian in Poland is based primarily on infrequent radiocarbon age estimates, which all indicate the 7th and the 6th millennia cal. BC. The dates pertain to Lower Silesia (Krzekotówek 8) and Pomerania (Jastrzębia Góra 4 and Dąbki 9), i.e., to two extremities of the territorial range of the Polish Post-Maglemosian. Judging by typology, the majority of its Polish assemblages ought to belong generally to the Atlantic period, since they almost always contain trapezes. However, there are also a few assemblages without trapezes (Świdry Małe 3, Holendry Brzezińskie I) which, if the absence of trapezes is not merely a question of statistics, may theoretically be very late Boreal. The generally young age of the Polish Post-Maglemosian is also indicated by its characteristic core processing technology, using subconical cores (relics of keeled cores, in fact) for regular bladelets, and slim microliths, including TH and TE short-base scalene triangles, as well as PB and PC points (cf. "Pointes PB et PC"). This chronological position is in fact confirmed also for territories west of Poland where we have a number of decidedly Atlantic radiocarbon dates (the oldest are from Holland, c. 6800, and from Swedish Scania, c. 7000 years cal. BC). From the viewpoint of the logic of evolution trends (cf. "Rhythms") valid in the entire Maglemosian complex, all the "Post-Maglemosian" groups must of course be younger than the Star Carr-Duvensee-Komornica complex (cf. "Le Komornicien") and the Svaerdborgian from which they partly stem.

The dating of the beginning of the Post-Maglemosian in Poland has yet to be settled conclusively. On the one hand, there is fairly reliable data about the survival (at least locally) of the Komornician into the 7th millennium and we are convinced that this unit (or parts thereof) contributed to the formation of Post-Maglemosian groups (at least some of them) in Poland. On the other hand, faced with the presence of infrequent Post-Maglemosian assemblages without trapezes, we are led to believe that the late Boreal Svaerdborg group (end of the 8th millennium cal. BC) may have played a part in their formation (especially in Pomerania). We thus admit the possibility that these assemblages did not appear quite synchronously; e.g. in Pomerania – given the similarity of the materials there to Carl J. Becker's collection from Svaerdborg I – they might have emerged earlier (about 7000 years cal. BC?) than in the south. In any case, we do not have reasonable grounds for dating these southern assemblages to before the end of the 8th millennium cal. BC and the actually available C_{14} dates in Poland are not earlier than the beginning of the 7th millennium cal. BC.

In the light of the available archaeological record, the upper chronological limit for the Post-Maglemosian in Poland may locally be as late as in the 5th millenium, when even in isolated environmental niches (e.g. Lower Silesia, Kuiavia and central Pomerania) the first ceramics appear (Dąbki 9 with its Ertebølle pottery), or local Neolithic cultures (Funnel Beaker from Chwalim) stemming, at least partly, from these groups. Although a long persistence, up to the emergence of local Neolithic cultures (i.e. practically up to the 5th millennium cal. BC), is probable in the case of the described unit in western and northern Poland, the chronology of the Pieńki group has to be different ("shorter"). This is because the Vistula river basin, at least from the middle of the 7th millenium cal. BC, was almost completely dominated by the Janislawician (cf.), thus leaving little time for the existence of the Pieńki group. This is in good agreement with the very small number of sites of the group in question. We would date it to the early stage of the Post-Maglemosian, i.e., somewhere around the first half of the 7th millennium cal. BC, between the disintegration of the traditional structures of the local Komornician and the appearance of the Janislawician tradition.

F. Settlement network. The settlement network was based primarily on latitudinally running proglacial stream valleys, and longitudinally oriented river gorges and lake troughs, differing in this respect from the Komornician network. The sites are very clearly grouped in a number of concentrations (20–50 kilometers long) lining the banks of water courses. Concentrations include Szczecin, central Pomerania, Puck, middle Noteć, Oborniki, Poznań, middle-Warta (this concentration perhaps divided into two parts), Obra, Kashubia, Bydgoszcz, Toruń, Bóbr, Warsaw and Nida.

The sites are most often situated on terrace-sandy forms, and not only on river banks but also on lake shores (mainly Great Poland).

G. Natural environment. The fauna of Post-Maglemosian territory apparently no longer includes the elk, or else the animal is extremely rare. The large mammals that are present include roe deer, red deer and wild boar, as well as occasional *Bos*. The Post-Maglemosians exploited mainly local erratic flint raw materials, but the situation in the middle and upper Vistula river basin was different; exotic "good" flint was used alongside the local raw material. The assemblages of this zone, according to Krzysztof Cyrek, usually contain at least three different raw materials, sometimes coming from as far away as 100 kilometers, and in roughly equal proportions at that. This assertion as well as the observations of cortex surface on

artifacts appear to support the supposition on potential Post-Maglemosian flint mining.

H. Flint inventories. (a) Technique. The Post-Maglemosian core produced very regular bladelets, which were (according to Karol Szymczak, cf. "Blade/bladelet") first of all distinguished by parallel edges and a standard width of 6–8 mm. Bladelets were obtained most probably with the pressure technique applied to single-platform cores, which are usually subconical in their final stages, but in their origin keeled/carenoidal cores and actually preformed. The bladelets were fashioned into long and narrow microliths, often formed with the microburin technique. Trapezes, on the other hand, were made of bladelets obtained from bigger cores.

(b) Retouched tools. Only three typological groups are important among flint tools, namely end-scrapers, irregular scrapers and microliths. End-scrapers and irregular scrapers together comprise 30–60% of the retouched tools.

The microliths index varies from 40 to 70%. (c) The basic tool group of the Polish Post Maglemosian comprises:

– small end-scrapers on blades, long, short or very short, often retouched on the edges,
– small very short end-scrapers on flakes,
– irregular scrapers,
– long scalene triangles with short base (TH, TE, TI),
– elongated micro-truncations PB,
– a few microtruncations K and not very many backed pieces (DA, DB).

(d) Elements of facial and chronological differentiation. Only a few of these will be mentioned as knowledge of the regional differentiation of this cultural phenomenon is still inadequate.

Characteristic of the northern branch are double asymmetric micro-truncations (PC), axes/adzes and picks. The TK scalene triangles have an even more limited territorial range, being found chiefly in northwestern Poland (cf. "Atlas").

Narrow PI points (with *piquant trièdre*) occur in the middle and upper Vistula river basin, while axes/adzes are present in northwestern Poland.

Chronologically significant elements include micro-truncations K, regarded as indices of the old tradition (Komornician) theoretically diminishing in number in the later assemblages; this, however, has not been proved. The younger elements are naturally the long triangles and points with a short base, as well as the AA (narrow) and AZ (regular), and, slightly later, the AC (high) trapezes. Trapezes are dominant in the late phase.

Here we come to the question of the typological and statistical boundary between the Komornician (and, more broadly, the Lower/Middle Mesolithic) and the Post-Maglemosian, arising first of all from the fact that the latter evolved among others from the Komornician environment. At this stage the boundary is drawn arbitrarily, regarding as Post-Maglemosian assemblages that are characterized by a predominance of microliths with short base (especially long triangles).

I. Bone inventories. The few bone points and harpoons of Mesolithic character found in Pomerania have the nearest typological parallels among southern Scandinavian specimens connected with the Late/Post-Maglemosian tradition (mainly harpoons of types 5, 6 and 7, according to Grahame Clark's classification). All of these artifact types may of course be "Maglemosian" (i.e. Boreal) or Post-Maglemosian, which in the case of points and harpoons from Góra Orle in Polish Pomerania is indicated by the Early Atlantic pollen date from that site. On the other hand, the ornamented antler axes from Pomerania are undated and could belong to either the Komornician or the Svaerdborgian, or even Post-Maglemosian.

J. Ceramics. Some sites yielded "forest-type" pottery sherds which Zbigniew Bagniewski refers to the Post-Maglemosian tradition. This is still a much discussed issue, contested by some, but there are no logical reasons to deny that pottery could have been associated with the youngest assemblages, something that is confirmed by stratified and well dated finds from the Dąbki 9 site in Pomerania; the well stratified Post-Maglemosian material from this site was accompanied by Ertebølle ceramics (information from Jacek Kabaciński). On the other hand, some Lower Silesian Post-Maglemosian sites yielded Funnel Beaker sherds (e.g. Dąbrowa Krepnica excavated by Zbigniew Bagniewski or Chwalim excavated by Michał Kobusiewicz).

K. Territorial division. The facial elements in Polish Post-Maglemosian groups make it possible to divide them into at least four territorial units, slightly differentiated among themselves by the presence or absence of single artifact types.

The most distinct is the Chojnice group occupying a large territory between Kashubia and the Warsaw-Berlin proglacial stream valley. It is characterized by the presence of axes/adzes, picks, TK triangles, PB and PC elongated points, and AD trapezes among others. The second territorial branch is the Pieńki group (middle and upper Vistula river basin) which lacks the mentioned triangles, axes and PC points, but is marked by the presence of PI points. The third group may be named after the Bóbr river in western Lower Silesia. It has chipped axes, JJ (= short Janislawice-like) points and big retouched truncations on blades, but lacks the PB and PC microliths and has very few PI points. Finally, a separate group is apparently formed by the coastal (?) Pomeranian sites (e.g. Jastrzębia Góra excavated by Lucyna Domańska) which are distinct in having carenoidal/keeled cores (in the west) and very regular conical cores, as well as apparently the most elegant shape of bladelets and slimness of microliths. There are no PI and JJ points, but some RA rectangles are present.

M. Origin. The origin of each of the Polish Post-Maglemosian groups seems to be slightly different. The Pomeranian variant appears to be most similar to Late/Post-Maglemosian (end of the 8th millennium cal. BC)

materials from southern Scandinavia, northern Germany and Pomerania, which stem from local traditions there. It is now certain that Polish Pomerania and Kuiavia featured Svaerdborgian settlement at least locally at the time (Nowy Młyn, Wierzchowo 6, Dąbrowa Biskupia), known also from northern Mecklemburg, Vor-Pommern and Bornholm. This settlement also occurred, as it seems, on the West Baltic land bridge, and we thus believe that the Pomeranian group is simply an evolutionary successor of the local variant of the Svaerdborgian. The local traditions are apparent chiefly in the slimness of the backed pieces, in the short end-scrapers, carenoidal cores and axes.

The Chojnice group is a combination of local Komornician and foreign Svaerdborgian elements (cf. "Les points PB et PC"). Its origin may be connected with the alleged southeastward migration of the south Baltic population to the lakeland environments where they came into contact with late Komornician communities.

The remaining two groups are far removed from the region where southern Scandinavian peoples could have begun their migrations. In the Bóbr group there are virtually no clear traces of migrations from the north, since the axes there may have been a legacy of the local variety of the Komornician. There are also none of the distinctly "Maglemosian" (= northern) PB and PC points (cf.). For this reason we regard this group rather as the outcome of local evolution of the Komornician exposed to traditions bearing the idea of narrow bladelets and long triangles.

The situation is different with the Pieńki group which does have some Scandinavian elements (PB points). The group might be a trace of the penetration of Maglemosian elements along the Vistula valley to the south and their superposition over the Late Komornician substratum.

N. Disappearance. As mentioned already, the author believes that the Post-Maglemosian tradition survived locally up to the 5th millennium cal. BC. It even reached the ceramic phase (Dąbki 9 in Pomerania with Ertebøllian ceramics, Dąbrowa-Krępnica with FBK in Lower Silesia; Chwalim in western Great Poland with FBK). It could have happened first of all in western Poland, i.e. in the Bóbr, Pomeranian and Chojnice groups (cf. "Ceramization"). The first Neolithic cultures appeared on the margins of these groups in the second half of the 6th millennium cal. BC, and the occupation of some Post-Maglemosian environmental niches took place as late as in the middle of the 5th millennium cal. BC (part of the Chojnice territory) or even in the 4th millennium cal. BC (part of the Pomeranian group area?). It was only then that the full acculturation of the western and northern Post-Maglemosian was completed (transition to Funnel Beaker culture).

The disappearance of the Pieńki group was of course a different matter: it was absorbed or replaced by the Janislawician at a fairly early stage (c. 6500 cal. BC).

9

The East

Eastern Europe extends for 2700 km from east of the Vistula basin and the Eastern Carpathians all the way to the Ural Mountains. It has more than 3000 km from north to south and covers c. 5.5 million square kilometers. It is a huge lowland with no distinct territorial barriers of any kind, except Valdai and Nord Belarusian plateaus. Even so, it is subdivided into a number of latitudinal climatic zones that are reflected in the geosystem, starting with the tundra in the north, turning into the taiga or coniferous forest, then mixed forest, forest-steppe and steppe. Each zone is also characterized by its own specific fauna, which in the Mesolithic consisted of the reindeer in the northernmost tundra, very popular elk in the taiga, and mixed/broad-live forest animals more to the south, also in the forested big and deep river valleys in the southern steppe; they spread slightly to the north of this in the Atlantic period. The area is further differentiated by hydrography: Vistulian/Würmian lakelands in the north, more to the south the flat landscape with the great rivers (Volga, Kama, Don, Dnestr, Dnieper and their tributaries) and a distinctly poorer network of medium-size rivers and streams (Oka, Donetz, Boh, Pripiat, etc.) separating the dry stretches of uplands in between.

This extensive area in the north has been studied (Lev V. Koltsov, Mikhail Zhilin, Rimute Rimantiène, Svetlana Oshibkina, Georgi Burov, Alexander Sorokin, among others) insufficiently and unequally. Datings are rare, especially for regions in the far east and north, while for other areas there are virtually no source materials.

Generally speaking, the zone lying north of the steppe is characterized by rather poorly differentiated industries, typical of the very typologically and technologically uniform Northeastern Technocomplex (conical core, pressure exploitation, very regular bladelet, sectioning, burins on broken blade, end-scrapers on blades, microretouched inserts WA-C) or, less correctly, Kundian (classic Kunda culture in the Baltic lakelands in Estonia, Latvia and Karelia, and even in Finnish Lapland (!), and respectively, the western variant of this culture in Lithuania and northeastern Poland and northern Belarus, and the Kudlaevka culture in central Belarus and northern Ukraine). The huge inland territory, especially the upper Volga basin, was occupied by the Butovian. All these entities were characterized by the presence of specific tanged points, called (how correctly?) Post-Swiderian by Russian researchers.

The internal regionalization of this westernmost branch of the Northeastern Mesolithic in terms of the flint industry is insubstantial and almost undetectable (even though cultures other than Kunda and Butovo have been distinguished for particular regions: Kama–Vychegda and Romanovka–Ilmurzino in the east, Sukhona or Veretie in the north; not all researchers are of the same opinion in these matters). It is better observable in the bone industry with classic Kunda having barbed points (type 6 and 17 after Grahame Clark) and Havel-like harpoons, while Western Kunda featured points triangular in section (type 13) and the Butovian had single-barbed, flat harpoons of type 17. Where studies could be undertaken (Eastern Baltic region), the bone industry (cf. "Points") was observed to change over time (for Latvia, Ilge Zagorska has noted a gradual replacement of Havel-like harpoons) and in the stone industry, big elongated tanged points with very short pedoncule (type LF, cf. "Atlas") were replaced by smaller willow-leaf-shaped and rhomboidal specimens (respectively types LA, LB and LE); it seems that this observation holds true for the entire region (cf. "No rhythms").

This very long and uninterrupted existence was crowned by the appearance at the very end of ceramics in the last stage of development (Narva on the Baltic and Upper Volga inland, both from the 6th millennium cal. BC, described respectively by Adomas Butrimas and Nina N. Gurina, cf. "Ceramicization").

To the east and northeast of the tanged-points zone there appear less well studied complexes of Kama-Vychegda culture, which is identical technologically (blades sectioning, pressure core exploitation) and close typologically (microretouched bladelets WA–C, burins on broken blade) to assemblages from the western part of the Eastern European Lowland. Further to the east, there are the better known but poorly dated southern Ural complexes of Yangelka type, discovered by Gerald Mathiushin. Beyond the Ural, the phenomenon extended far to the east.

The first complex (Kama-Vychegda, described by Georgi Burov) was devoid of tanged points (assuming the reason is not merely in the statistics!), while Yangelka is distinguished by specific, broad triangular points, formed by the microburin technique; this last industry is accompanied by flat harpoons.

One gets the impression that the entire northeastern complex was rooted in the Upper Paleolithic of Siberia (Afontova Gora, Verkholanskaia Gora, Kokorievo, all in the Angara basin). It is to be assumed that the basic technologies reached the Russian Lowland at the close of the Pleistocene and in the very Early Holocene (the oldest known radiocarbon dates from the Baltic region and upper Volga are of Pre-Boreal age). It probably spread quite quickly to the eastern borders of Poland. The origins of the typically Eastern Mesolithic tanged points, which the Russians once called "Post-Swiderian", remain unresolved, the points resembling (but not the oldest ones) morphologically Swiderian specimens, while having been produced with non-Swiderian technology. The newcomers from the East appear to have had the opportunity to see these Swiderian points on the western fringes of the Eastern European Lowland.

The southern fringes of the Kunda complex in the Early and Middle Holocene are flanked in Belarus and northern Ukraine by the poorly dated forest Kudlaevka culture (cf.), which is characterized by numerous fine backed bladelets and points, and by small tanged points in its north. The former could have linked the Kudlaevka with Komornician (similarly as the few perforators and very rare triangles), but they could have also originated from Epi-Gravettian/Molodovian *milieu* (in any case, such backed points also occur in the Kunda culture to the west, e.g. Miłuki in northeastern Poland, information from Jerzy Siemaszko). The Kudlaevka tanged points may have something to do with Western Kundian. The Kudlaevka culture is followed by Janislawician as a neighbor to the south of the Northeastern Complex.

The steppe-forest and steppe zones in the south are entirely different from the forest belt. They are characterized by considerable dynamics of change in terms of style and distinct ties with the south, that is, the Caucasus and Balkans. At the beginning (Latest Pleistocene, Earliest Holocene), according to Volodymyr Stanko, the dominating forms are big geometrics, and pencil like cores and the later sequence is generally as follows:

Middle Holocene
    Kukrek and Grebeniki
    Kukrek and Murzak-Koba (?)
Early Holocene
    Zimnikovtsy-Shan-Koba-Belolesye

The first and the Kukrek tradition refer to the Caspian-Caucasian, the third rather to the Mediterranean (cf. "Castelnovian").

The chronology of some of these cultural phenomena is not entirely clear at present, while huge empty spaces on the map are often a source of embarassment. Even so, Ukrainian researchers and especially Dmitri Telegin, Leonid Zalizniak and Volodymyr Stanko should be commended for having done so much recently to radically improve the situation.

9.1. The Northeastern flint tools (Fig. 9.1a–o)

Kunda or Post-Swiderian tanged-points/arrowheads

Post-Swiderian tanged points were formed on broad and narrow blades, straight in profile as a rule, seldom on trimming blades, very seldom on flakes. Common to these specimens was a ventral, most often semi-abrupt retouch of the base (or pedoncule) and almost as frequent of the tip. Flat ventral retouch is rare. Some types have entirely or almost circumferential retouch on the ventral face. Retouch forming the base or pedoncule on the dorsal face was less frequent. A group of these points has becks or truncations on the tip. The pedoncule could be formed with alternate retouch. These points were arrowheads as indicated by the finds from Oleni Ostrov (cf.).

The East European arrowheads can be subdivided as follows:

1. Willow-leaf shaped points (nonpedonculate, LA–B, for typology cf. "Atlas"). Big, medium and small, most often of average size. All are slender, more likely to be broad. The base is pointed as a rule, but blunt bases occur as well. The edges are commonly left unworked. These specimens come in a) classic leaf-shaped variant, and b) with sharp-angled base, which appears to have been distinguished to some extent by a bending of the edges.
2. Rhomboid tanged points (LE). Mainly medium-size and small, occasionally even microlithic, usually very broad, in proportions either slender (but close to squat) or squat. Bases and tips pointed. Ventral retouch covers most or all of the tool's circumference. Dorsal retouch is usually poorer. Some of the specimens from this group were made on flakes.
3. Pedonculated points (LC–D). Mainly average and small in size, slender, poorly retouched, the pedoncule either quite pointed or blunt, the tip always sharp. Pedoncules are 1/4 to 1/3 of the specimen length. Two variants can be distinguished: a) mostly broad specimens with a broad, indistinct pedoncule (LC), a bit like the rhomboid ones (convergent edges, the same concerns the pedoncule) and b) narrow specimens with a fine and more distinct pedoncule than in the previous variant, having parallel edges (LD).
4. Points with short tang (= Pulli type – LF). Always big and slender, not much retouch at both ends, more seldom on the dorsal face. Both narrow and broad. The pedoncule formed as a short and pointed, often strongly undercut tang, which is usually just 1/8 of the specimen length.

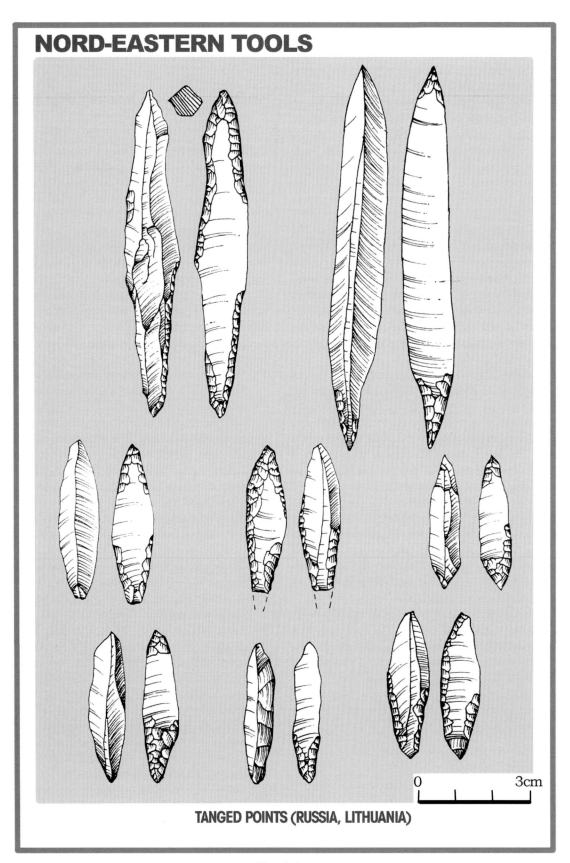

NORD-EASTERN TOOLS

TANGED POINTS (RUSSIA, LITHUANIA)

0   3cm

Fig. 9.1a

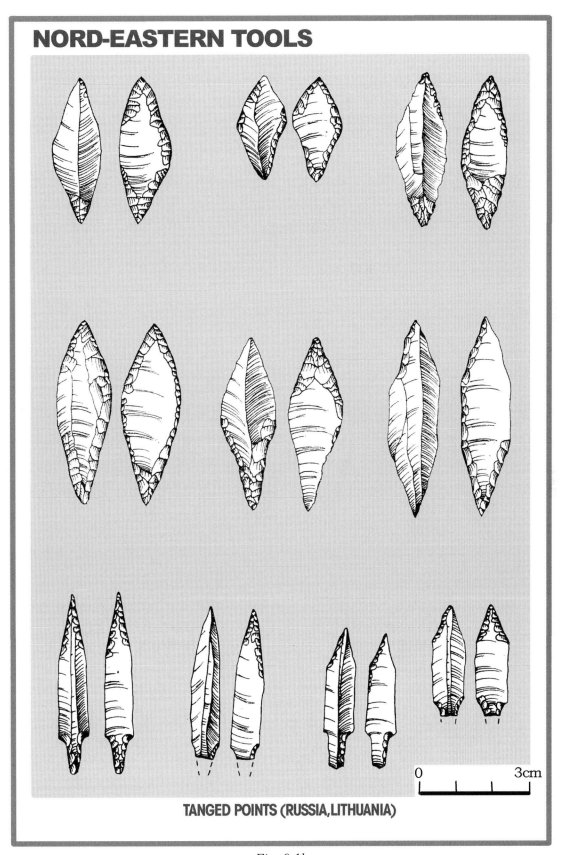

NORD-EASTERN TOOLS

TANGED POINTS (RUSSIA, LITHUANIA)

0   3cm

Fig. 9.1b

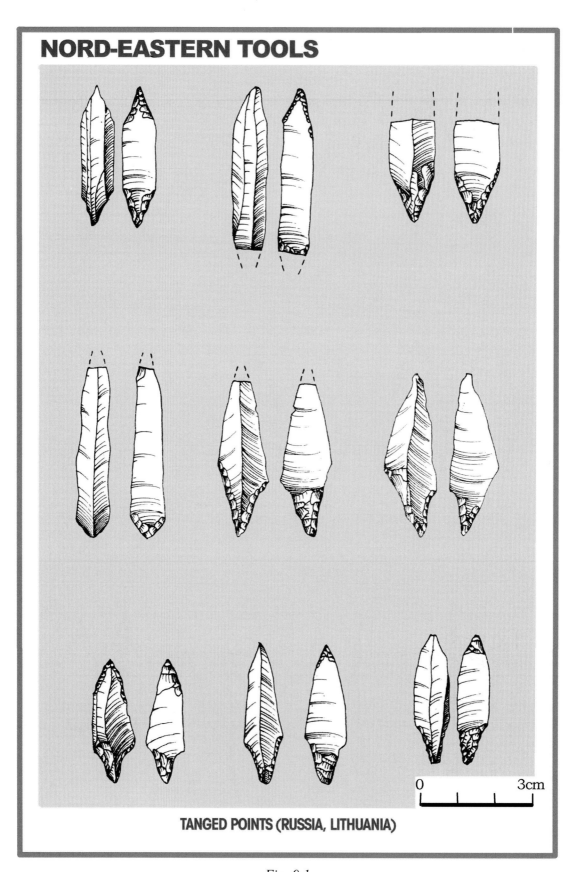

NORD-EASTERN TOOLS

TANGED POINTS (RUSSIA, LITHUANIA)

Fig. 9.1c

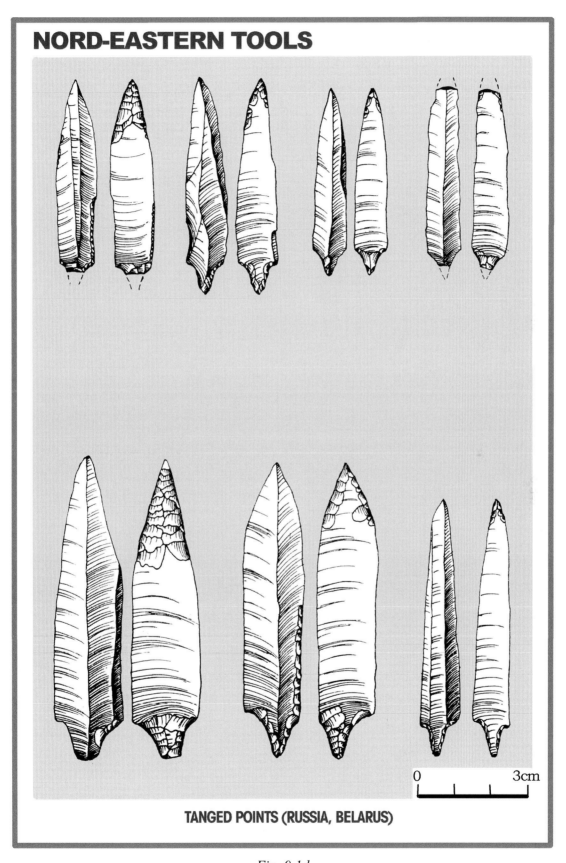

NORD-EASTERN TOOLS

0   3cm

TANGED POINTS (RUSSIA, BELARUS)

Fig. 9.1d

NORD-EASTERN TOOLS

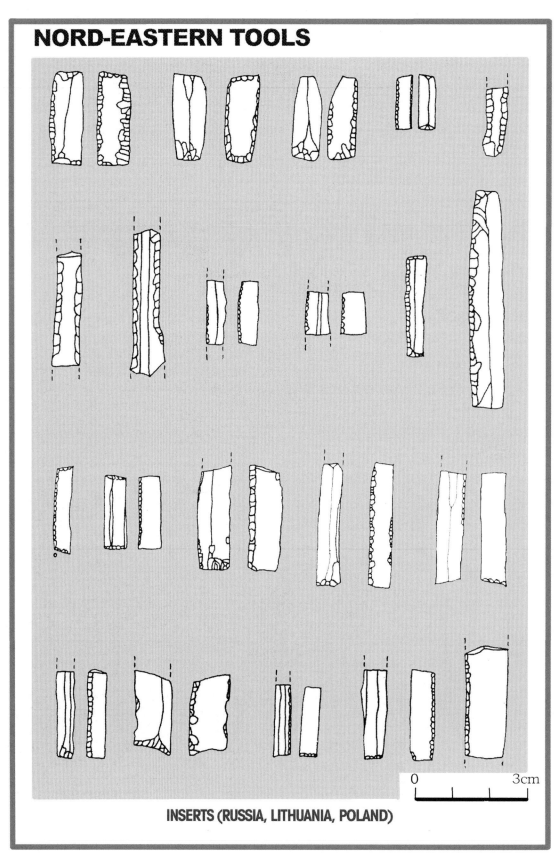

INSERTS (RUSSIA, LITHUANIA, POLAND)

Fig. 9.1e

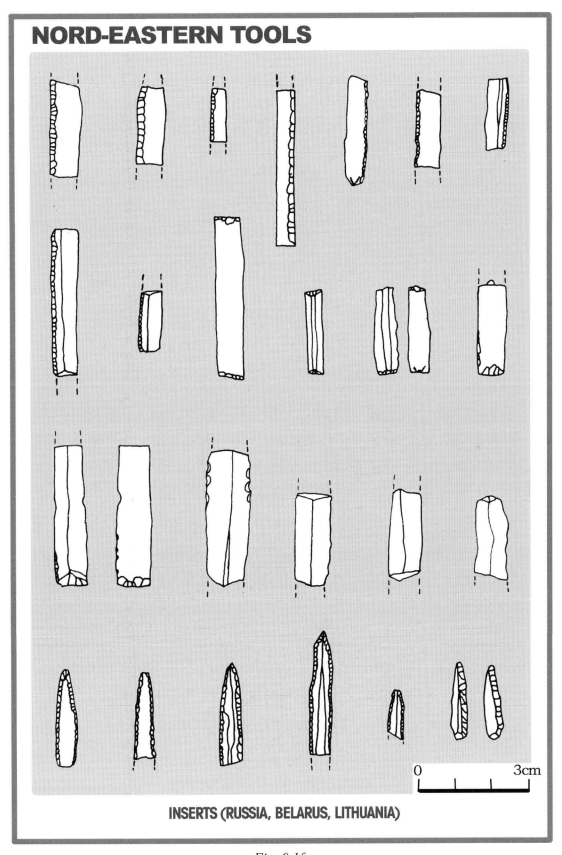

NORD-EASTERN TOOLS

INSERTS (RUSSIA, BELARUS, LITHUANIA)

Fig. 9.1f

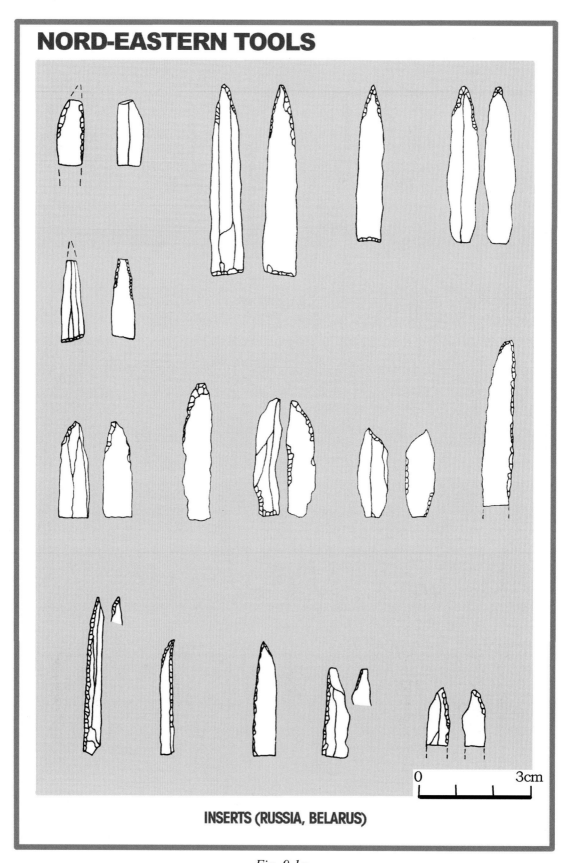

NORD-EASTERN TOOLS

INSERTS (RUSSIA, BELARUS)

Fig. 9.1g

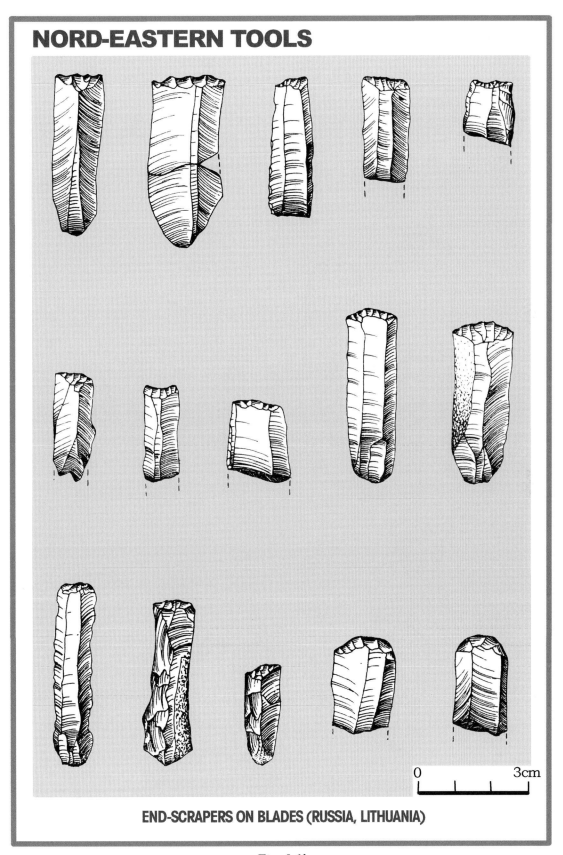

NORD-EASTERN TOOLS

0   3cm

END-SCRAPERS ON BLADES (RUSSIA, LITHUANIA)

Fig. 9.1h

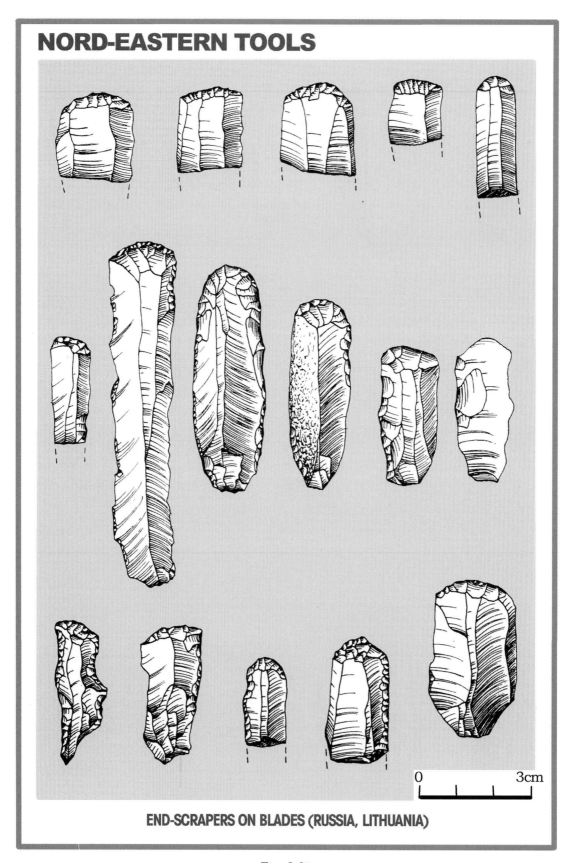

Fig. 9.1i

NORD-EASTERN TOOLS

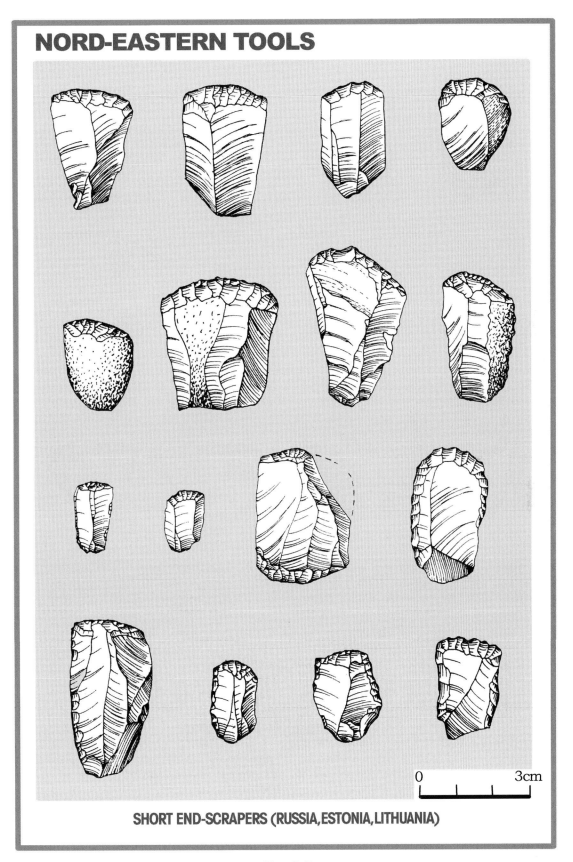

SHORT END-SCRAPERS (RUSSIA, ESTONIA, LITHUANIA)

Fig. 9.1j

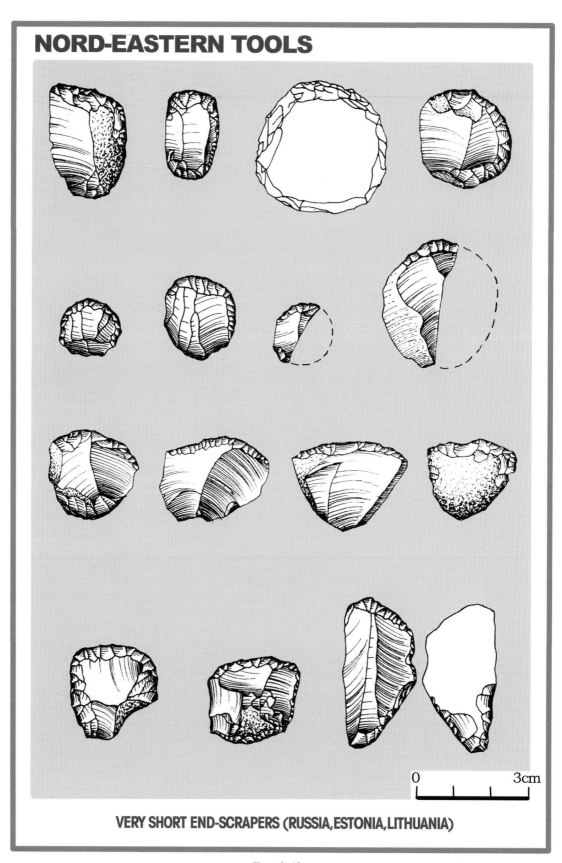

NORD-EASTERN TOOLS

0   3cm

VERY SHORT END-SCRAPERS (RUSSIA, ESTONIA, LITHUANIA)

Fig. 9.1k

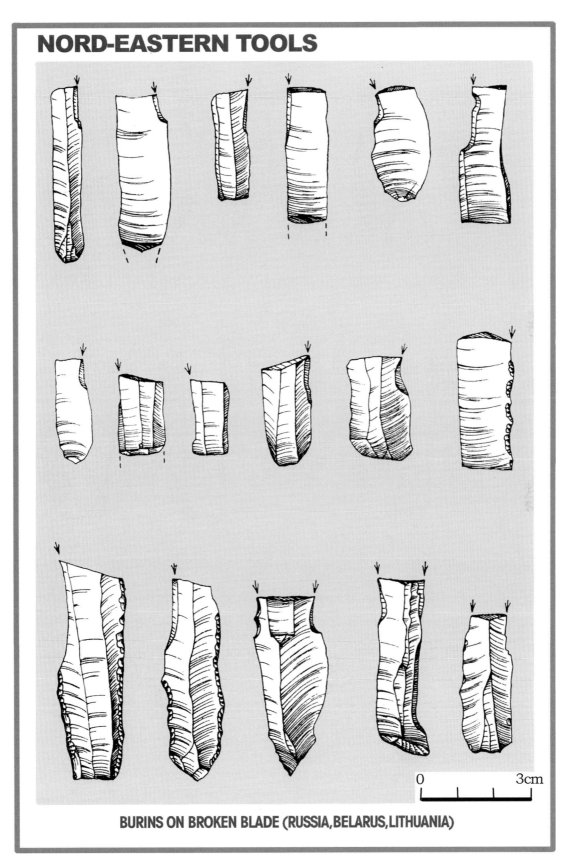

NORD-EASTERN TOOLS

BURINS ON BROKEN BLADE (RUSSIA, BELARUS, LITHUANIA)

Fig. 9.1l

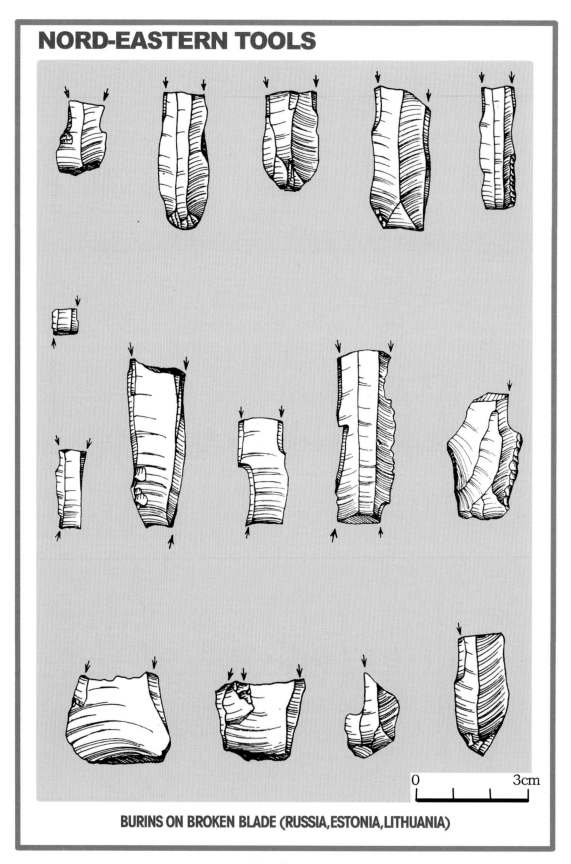

NORD-EASTERN TOOLS

BURINS ON BROKEN BLADE (RUSSIA, ESTONIA, LITHUANIA)

Fig. 9.1m

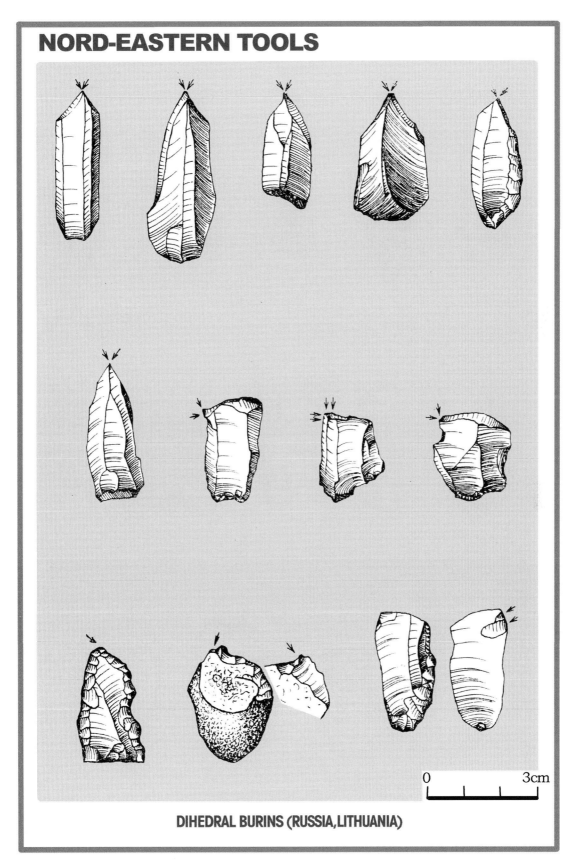

NORD-EASTERN TOOLS

DIHEDRAL BURINS (RUSSIA, LITHUANIA)

Fig. 9.1n

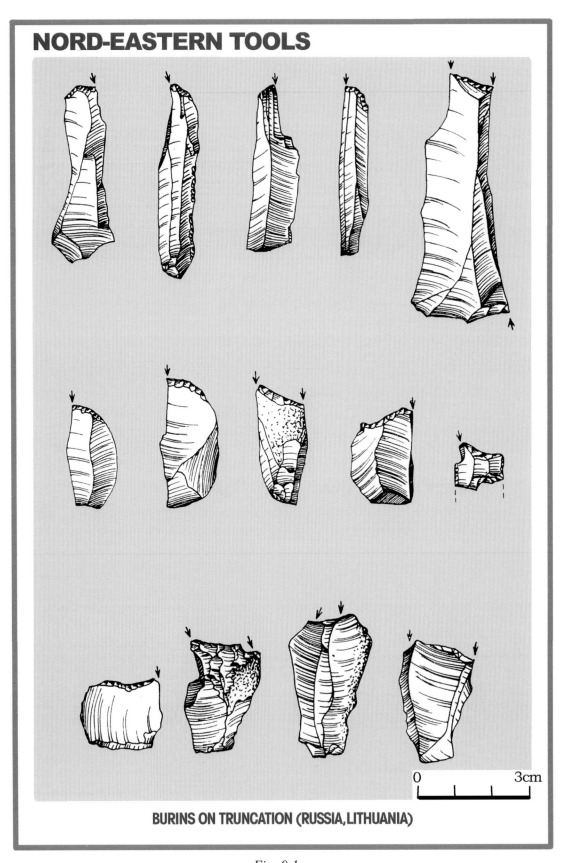

NORD-EASTERN TOOLS

BURINS ON TRUNCATION (RUSSIA, LITHUANIA)

Fig. 9.1o

Retouched inserts (cf.)

Made commonly on delicate and elongated, very regular bladelets, seldom on blades, struck of conical or pencil-like cores. Mostly fine, semi-abruptly retouched, rarely flattish; retouch is not always continuous, sometimes it concerns only part of the length. They fall into the type proposed by Romuald Schild as Borki bladelets, and armed daggers (Kunda) and slotted points (cf.). The retouch covers the lateral edge(s) of specimens or fragments of these edges, less often the shorter edges/bases. It can be found on the ventral and dorsal faces, very seldom alternate. A large group of these microliths has the shorter edges (bases) intentionally broken. In size, these are mostly microlithic, very small and small; in proportions, they are elongated as a rule, rarely squat.

Subdivision by shape is as follows:

1. Rectangular inserts, with a number of variants, the most popular one being indisputably a specimen with one long edge retouched (WA), either ventrally or dorsally, broken or retouched at the base and tip. Almost as popular were specimens with two long sides retouched (WB), either ventrally or dorsally, rarely alternate, the short sides being formed by breaking. Other variants are clearly less frequent.
2. Pointed (WC) inserts. Different from the rectangular ones mainly in shape. One broken end/edge, retouched or not, the other ending in a beck or point. The most common variant is retouched on the entire length of the long sides, the retouch often being alternate. The others have only parts of the edges retouched.

The group of inserts should include also blank, intentionally broken (cf. "Sectioning") bladelets. Like the above described retouched inserts, they were used for slotted-bone points and daggers (type 21 in Grahame Clark's classification).

End-scrapers

The most numerous group in Mesolithic tool inventories of the forest zone in eastern Europe. The most important types are presented below in the order suggested by their quantities.

1. Slender blade end-scrapers. Of big and medium size mainly. Made of slender, regular, rather broad blades (seldom trimming blades), usually as variously arched specimens, occasionally with almost straight, rarely oblique, straight front. Retouch of edge(s) is along the full length or just part of the length.

   The type also includes specimens on transversally broken blades, which are short and even very short in proportions. The blanks were probably intentionally shortened/sectioned, hence these scrapers should be moved respectively to the short and very short end-scrapers group.

   There are two principal variants of this type: a) slender arched specimen (or almost straight), with blank edge, and b) slender arched scraper (or almost straight) with retouched edge(s).
2. Short blade end-scrapers. From very small to big in size with the majority being medium and big. Almost always (few exceptions) made of broad blades. Scraping edges are arched as a rule, sometimes oblique, frequently weakly arched, often almost straight, occasionally doubled. They occur in the following variants: a) short arched pieces, single with blank edge, and b) short arched scraper, with retouched edge(s).
3. Circular and semi-circular end-scrapers. Made on flakes, the scraping edge taking up most often about half the circumference. Mostly very small and small.
4. Very short arched end-scrapers. From small to medium in size, most frequently made of flakes. Scraping edges weakly arched, rarely double. Edges occasionally retouched. The most frequent variants include: a) very short fan-shaped type with blank edges, and b) short arched, single with retouched edges.
5. Extremely short arched scrapers. On blade, very small and small.
6. Single specimens of other scrapers occur as well, including pedonculated specimens.

Burins

Burins are a key and characteristic tool group in Mesolithic inventories of northeastern Europe. The relative distinctness and clarity of particular types is also characteristic of the region. The presentation follows the number of particular specimens that the author is aware of.

1. Lateral burins on broken blade. Blanks used for the purpose are almost always blades, slender and broad more often than not. Specimens on flakes are very rare. The burin is practically always formed by breaking a blank transversally or occasionally at an angle (at one or both ends) and making one or a few burin blows, always lateral. The negatives are commonly short, rarely corresponding to the length of the specimen. Occasionally, they are somewhat twisted, flattish or entirely straight. In some cases, the edge(s) are retouched fully or in part, before striking a burin spall. The angle of a burin tip is usually near to straight, the tip narrow. The following variants can be distinguished: a) burins on broken blade, slender, seldom squat, most often small and medium in size, b) burins on broken flake, usually squat and short, broad and small, and c) specimens combined with other tools.
2. Lateral burins, on retouched truncation, slender. Usually oblique retouched truncation, sometimes transverse, made on blades, slender, either narrow or broad. Burin angle is usually sharp, tip narrow.
3. Lateral burins, on retouched truncation, short and very short with transversal truncation. Specimens on blade and flake, small and very small, broad. The truncations are usually slightly concave, the angles close to straight, tips rather broad.

4. Lateral burins on truncation, short and very short with angled truncation. More often on flake, broad, small or very small. Burin angle is c. 60°, tips are narrow.

5. Central dihedral burins. Made on broad blades and flakes, slender or short, often very short, small. Burin angle usually sharp, tips broad.

6. Transversal dihedral burins. Made on flakes, short and very short, very small. Burin angle close to straight, tips broad.

Other flint tools

Apart from the most characteristic flint tools presented above, the East European forest Mesolithic has yielded a number of flint tools that do not occur in such numbers, indeed are sometimes unique. One should mention the fairly characteristic truncations, of which some have ventral retouch near the tip. Slender becks/perforators, resembling the said knives, have also this ventral retouch.

Finally, one should mention mostly use-retouched blades (*skobieli* in Russian) and presumably few unpolished axes/adzes.

Comment in 2006

This paper was written in 1965 and was based on the published evidence available at the time. Later research trips to the then Soviet Union and numerous new publications have not had any significant impact on the characteristic presented above.

9.1.1. The Northeastern technocomplex

The Northeastern or Kunda Technocomplex is a regional exemplification of the adaptation of man to the forest environment; it formed and developed in the lowland of eastern Europe and Siberia. The population of this cultural unit/tradition based its living mainly on hunting forest game (mostly elk), as well as on exploiting the lake environment (e.g. Kunda Lammasmägi in Estonia, Yangelka, Zamostye, Ozerki, Veretie, all in Russia). They inhabited small multi-huts open camps (e.g. Borki, Koprino, Žemiai Kaniukai, etc.) and they buried their dead on cemeteries (e.g. Oleni Ostrov and Popovo in Russia, and Zvejnieki in Latvia).

Division, chronology, territorial range

There are five/six European taxons in the Northeastern Technocomplex (Fig. 9.1.1a–f); also some of the Pleistocene and Early Holocene cultures of Western Asia could belong here. The accessible material makes it possible to distinguish with certainty a big western unit, which is referred to here as the Kunda Culture Group (Lithuanian/Western Kunda, Classical Kunda, Butovian and Kudlaevka cultures) apart from which two other European units have been found: the Kama-Vychegda in the northeast and the Yangelka culture in the southern Ural mountains. All started probably in Siberia in the Late Pleistocene; the Eastern European development began probably in the 10th millennium cal. BC, in the territory between the Ural mountains and the Baltic Sea.

Note: Some authors (R. Indreko) included nearly all of the known East European Plain Mesolithic units in the Kunda Culture.

Basic similarities

The technological and typological homogeneity of assemblages of the Northeastern or Kunda Technocomplex is astonishing. Long and short end-scrapers on regular blades as a rule and with an arched front, are distinguished in this category (cf. "The Northeastern flint tools…"). Next come end-scrapers on broken/sectioned blade and mostly short specimens. Sometimes retouch of edges appears. Among burins, pieces on broken blade dominate. Moreover, long angle burins on truncation always occur (although they are less numerous) as well as short angled burins on truncation. The third very characteristic group is constituted by the so-called Borki microretouched bladelets – inserts (WA-D), i.e. specimens with semi-abrupt microretouch on the edge or edges with one or two transversal bases (broken or retouched).

Cores deserve special attention; they are represented by long conical specimens (in pencil form, hence *karandash* in Russian) for the production of very regular blades and bladelets (by pressure); they are in fact probably the final phase of keeled cores (finds from Veretie I). Finally, there is the highly popular technique of intentional blade sectioning which is characteristic of the entire Technocomplex.

Also some of the elements of bone industry (Shigirskoe points-Grahame Clark's type 16) are common to the whole Technocomplex.

The Kunda Culture group is additionally characterized by differentiated tanged points (cf. "The Northeastern flint tools…"). They are partially Swiderian or Ahrensburgian, but mainly Kunda types (LA–D, cf. "Atlas"), distinguished by semi-abrupt, ventral retouch.

Differences

A general trait of the Kunda/Northeastern Technocomplex as a whole is a considerable prevalence of blade-tools over flake-tools, but there seem to be some local differences. Also the percentage of particular types or typological groups is not the same everywhere. The Kunda culture is characterized, among other things, by a high percentage of very short, often circular end-scrapers on flake and a low percentage of burins on broken blade, also the number of Swiderian-like points – compared to Kunda points – is large. The Butovian from the upper Volga region is nearly devoid of end-scrapers on flake and the number of axes, characteristic for the Lithuanian Kunda, is very small there.

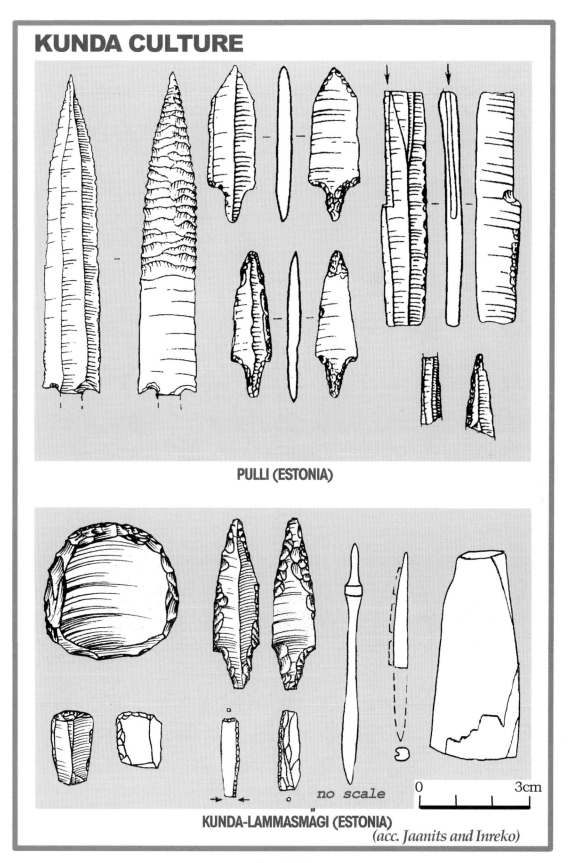

KUNDA CULTURE

PULLI (ESTONIA)

KUNDA-LAMMASMÄGI (ESTONIA)

(acc. Jaanits and Inreko)

Fig. 9.1.1a

KUNDA CULTURE

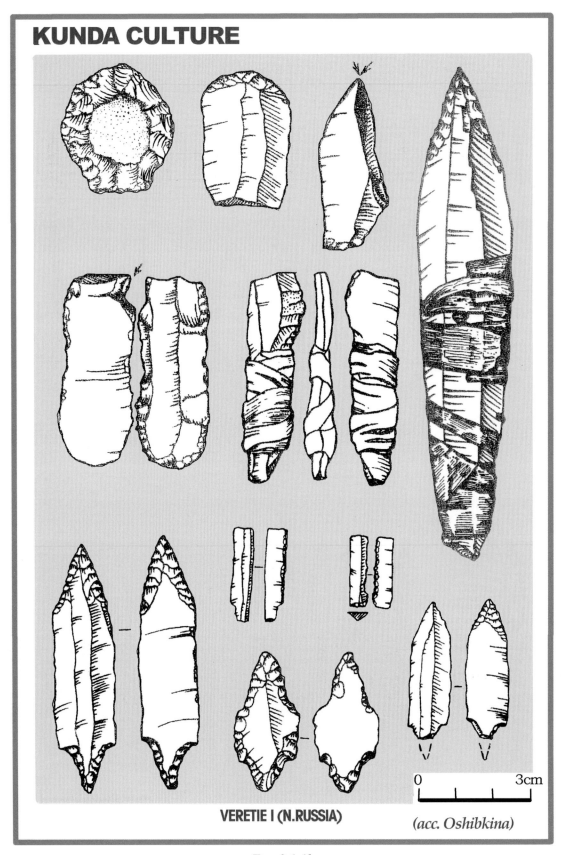

VERETIE I (N.RUSSIA)

(acc. Oshibkina)

0 _____ 3cm

Fig. 9.1.1b

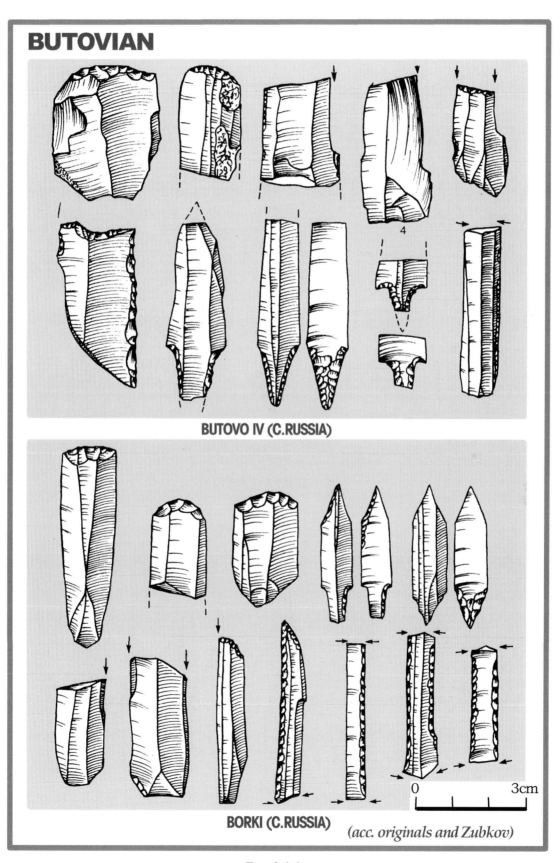

BUTOVIAN

BUTOVO IV (C.RUSSIA)

BORKI (C.RUSSIA)

(acc. originals and Zubkov)

0   3cm

Fig. 9.1.1c

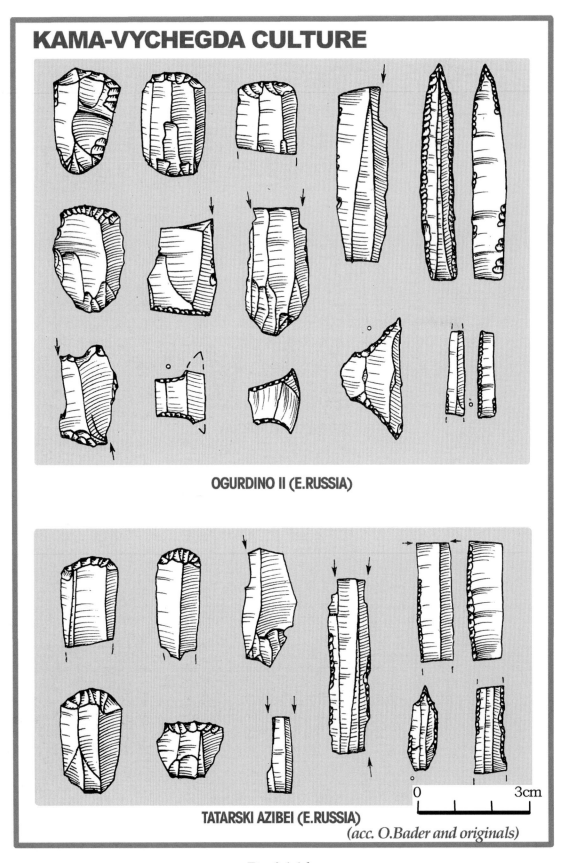

KAMA-VYCHEGDA CULTURE

OGURDINO II (E.RUSSIA)

0 3cm

TATARSKI AZIBEI (E.RUSSIA)

(acc. O.Bader and originals)

Fig. 9.1.1d

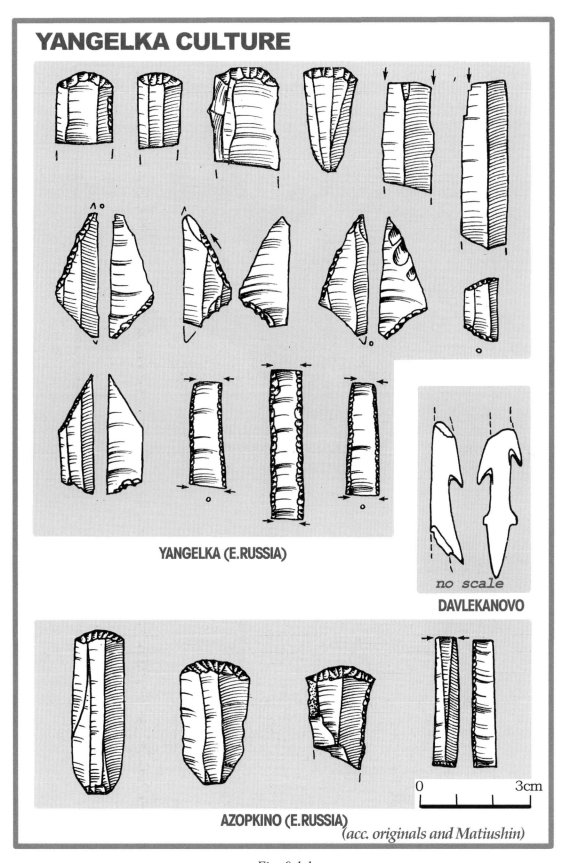

YANGELKA CULTURE

YANGELKA (E.RUSSIA)

no scale

DAVLEKANOVO

AZOPKINO (E.RUSSIA)

(acc. originals and Matiushin)

0   3cm

Fig. 9.1.1e

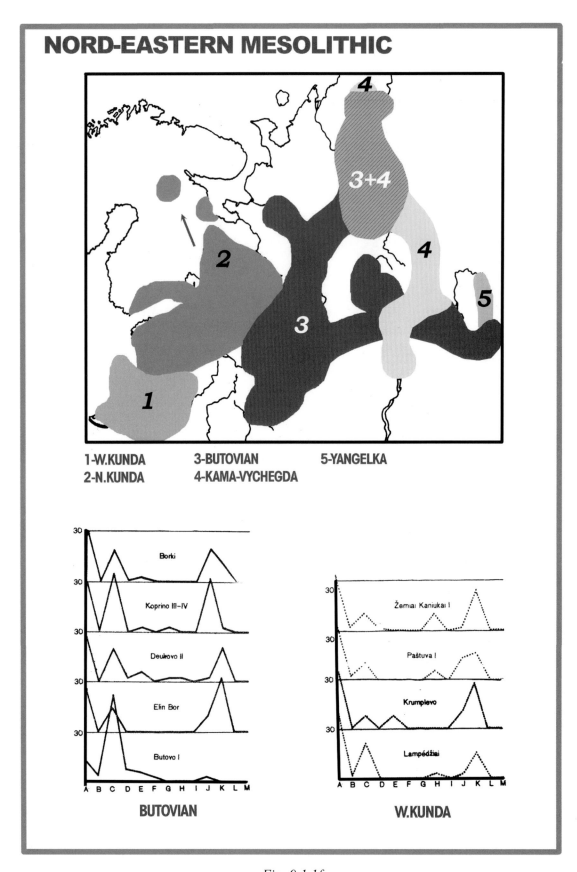

Fig. 9.1.1f

The Cultures of the Northeastern Technocomplex

Western or Lithuanian Kunda Culture

The culture existed in the territory between the lower Vistula and Western Dvina/Daugava rivers from the end of the 10th to at least the 7th millennium cal. BC.

STONE INDUSTRY. Apart from the described common properties of the Northeastern Technocomplex and the Kunda Culture Group, it is additionally characterized by original structure (high index of end-scrapers A, high or medium index of microliths K, low index of irregular scrapers B, burins C and axes H), some backed pieces (DA–DB!), few Janislawician points (JA–C) and trapezes in the later phase and very short end-scrapers.

BONE INDUSTRY. Points with triangular section (Grahame Clark's type 13), Shigirskoe points (type16) and single-slotted points (type 21_1).

HISTORY. The Western Kunda Culture could be a sum of the local Swiderian elements (Swiderian points ?, very short end-scrapers) and Eastern elements (Borki microretouched bladelets/inserts, long end-scrapers, elongated burins on broken blade and on truncation, the technique of conical core, Shigirskoe points and single-slotted points). Backed pieces (earlier) and the Janislawician points, as well as trapezes later, were added gradually.

Classical Kunda Culture

Name from the site Kunda-Lammasmägi in Estonia. Culture known from the territory between the western and northern Dvina rivers, as well as from Russian Karelia, southern Finland and even Finland's Lapland, from the 10th to the 6th/5th millennium cal. BC. Svetlana Oshibkina has also proposed separate Sukhona and Veretie cultures far in the north, which we consider as being Kunda.

STONE INDUSTRY. Apart from the common features of the Northeastern Complex and the Kunda Culture Group, it could be additionally characterized by the presence of polished axes, slate daggers (comparable to the Finnish Suomusjärvi, cf.), as well as irregular scrapers (B) and very short, often circular end-scrapers (A).

BONE INDUSTRY. Havel-type harpoons (Clark's class 12A), Pentekinnen-type points (type 17), Lohusu-type harpoons (type 18), and Shigirskoe (type 16), single-slotted points (21_1) and, in Kunda, very numerous barbed points of the Kunda type (6).

Kunda culture could be the result of mutual influence of two elements: local Swiderian (Post-Swiderian points LA–LF?, very short end-scrapers, Havel harpoons, Pentekinnen bone points) and eastern elements, possibly of Siberian origin, represented by inserts WA-C, long end-scrapers, burins on broken blade, the technique of conical/keeled core, very regular blades and bladelets and finally single-slotted points. The third element is a common creation which could have developed from the Swiderian, but was executed with non-Swiderian technique – the Kunda/Post-Swiderian tanged point. It seems that part of the Swiderians played a direct role in the formation of the

Kunda culture, when groups of hunters coming from the East reached the Baltic Sea (10th millennium cal. BC). Kunda culture is additionally characterized by elements common with the Suomusjärvi culture neighboring with it on the north (daggers of slate, polished axes and chisels). L. Jaanits demonstrated that Kunda served as the basis for the formation of the earliest ceramic Estonian culture of Narva.

Butovian Culture

Name from the site of Butovo in the upper Volga basin in Russia. Also known as the Upper Volga or Oka-Volga culture, evidenced in the basin of the upper Volga from the 10th to the 6th millennium cal. BC.

STONE INDUSTRY. Common properties of the Northeastern Complex and the Kunda Group, plus original internal structure (high or medium index of end-scrapers A and burins C, medium or low index of tanged points J and microliths E).

Butovian consists of two components: the Eastern, represented by WA-C inserts, long end-scrapers on blade, burins on broken blade and angled on truncation, technique of conical/keeled core for bladelets, pressure manufacture and the Postswiderian component (Kunda tanged points LA-LF). Thus, the entity under discussion could be the result of the interaction of the Swiderian (alleged migration to the northeast) with human groups which in the very Early Holocene conquered the basin of the upper Volga. They probably came from the East where characteristic elements of these groups are present in the local Upper Paleolithic (Verkholanskaia Gora and Kokorievo in Siberia). Added to this is a local tradition (Resetta-type industry?). Butovian gave rise to the local ceramic culture (Upper Volga culture).

The recent discoveries of Mikail Zhilin and Vladimir Lozovski have yielded some information on the evolution (preponderance of LF tanged points at the beginning), as well as bone industry (16, 17, 18, 21_1 and 24 in Grahame Clark's classification).

Kama-Vychegda Culture

Name from rivers in Russia, known also as Kama Culture (described by Georgi Burov). This poorly researched entity developed in the basins of the Kama, as well as the extreme northern reaches of the Vychegda and Petchora rivers in the Early (rather in the south) and Middle? (also in the north) Holocene (the unit is poorly dated).

STONE INDUSTRY. Consists of the common features of the Northeastern/Kunda Mesolithic, but without the Post-Swiderian/Kunda points.

The Kama-Vychegda Culture draws from an alleged migration west and northwest of a Siberian population probably at the beginning of the Holocene; this group responded to influence from the South as confirmed by some double truncations and the presence in the region of flat harpoons known from the southern fringes. Also belonging to this unit is the famous site of Vis I from the 7th millennium cal. BC with a fantastic collection of well preserved bows (cf.).

Yangelka Culture

Name from the river Yangelka in southern Ural in Russia, described by Gerald Matiushin. The culture developed in the territory of Southern Ural at the turn of Pleistocene and Holocene (no precise dates available).

STONE INDUSTRY. Northeastern/"Siberian" elements plus, among other, narrow trapezes and trapezes with concave edges as well as Yangelka points, assymmetric trapezes in fact (rather Late Mesolithic?), with microburin scar.

BONE INDUSTRY. Flat single- and double-barbed harpoons (Dovlekanovo).

The Yangelka Culture is a sum of Siberian (long end-scrapers, burins on broken blade, Borki bladelets (WA–C), technique of conical core, pressure-made blades) and Southern (Yangelka points, trapezes, flat single- and double-barbed harpoons) elements.

9.1.2. The Lithuanian variant of Kunda Culture (Western Kunda)

Distinguished by Rimute Rimantiéne as Neman culture, recently reworked by Thomas Ostrauskas. The currently preferred name is Lithuanian or Western group/variant of Kunda culture, proposed by S.K. Kozłowski.

CULTURAL FRAMEWORK. This taxonomic unit is one of the the the westernmost members of the Northeastern/Kunda Mesolithic technocomplex which could have also included Kudlaevka culture (cf.) in the region and further to the east, the classic Kunda, Butovian, Kama-Vychegda, etc. in the Baltic countries and Russia (Fig. 9.1.2).

ASSEMBLAGES AND INVENTORIES. About 50 flint inventories from Lithuania, Belarus and northeastern Poland may be regarded as belonging to the Lithuanian Kunda culture, some of them being homogeneous but of various significance (Krumplevo and Semenov Khutor from northern Belarus; Lampédžiai, Žemiai Kaniukai, Paštuva and Niatesai 1 from Lithuania; Pianki, Puchówka 10 and Miłuki 4 from Poland). Moreover we include in this entity some isolated finds of bone points from Lithuania and the Mazurian lakeland zone. The alleged association of these sites with the Lithuanian Kunda is suggested by cartographic analysis.

TERRITORIAL RANGE. It extends mostly over the southern sandy part of Lithuania, but also is poorly represented in the western, base morainic part (information from Thomas Ostrauskas) and covers the northern and the north-western part of Belarus (investigations of Nina N. Gurina and V. Ksendzov) as well as a fragment of northeastern Poland (explorations by Jerzy Siemaszko and Karol Szymczak).

The southern and the southwestern range of the cultural unit under consideration seem to coincide with the northern limits of the partly contemporaneous Kudlaevka and Janislawice cultures (the latter in the Late Mesolithic). And since typically Janislawician elements are always present in Late Kunda Lithuanian assemblages (while the Kunda elements are found in some Janislawician assemblages) it is difficult to draw the border line between the two units on the basis of numerous but uncertain material.

CHRONOLOGY. There are only a few absolute dates for the discussed taxonomic unit, but the oldest (Miłuki 4 combining tanged and backed points) come from the 11th/10th millennium cal. BC. Geomorphological data (the situation of sites on the second and third terraces of the Neman river in Lithuania) indicate the Atlantic age of most of the known material, and this is well confirmed by the presence of trapezes in most of the Lithuanian Kunda assemblages and inventories, and thermophylic nut species *Trapa natans* at Lampédžiai site. However, some of the assemblages (Paštuva, Miłuki, etc. new yet unpublished site in Lithuania, excavated by Thomas Ostrauskas) did not contain trapezes but had backed pieces instead; they are older.

SETTLEMENT NETWORK. The Western Kunda settlement network is based on a frame formed by the Neman, Neris and Dvina/Daugava rivers together with their tributaries, as well as by the Biebrza and Narew with their tributaries and the Mazurian lakes system in Poland. The sites are not found on the weakly irrigated elevated areas occupying a large part of the region in question (ground moraine and fluvioglacial). There exists one major concentration of sites, tens of kilometers across, on the Neman and Neris river junction. Other concentrations are indistinct, but extensive surveying on the Lega river in Poland has provided several dozens of Kunda-type collections (information from Jerzy Siemaszko).

Flint inventories

a. Technology. The flint technology is based on the exploitation of fairly large single-platform cores for blades and bladelets. There are two varieties of cores: conical, and pencil-shaped with circumferential flaking surface. The latter cores are typical for the northeastern Kunda tradition. Also present are more massive subconical or even carenoidal/keeled specimens; their flaking face usually does not take up the entire perimeter. Both core classes bear extensive pre-core preparation and were exploited with the pressure technique. Very regular bladelets, 10–11 mm wide on the average, were obtained, while the smaller specimens gave blanks of an average width of 5–7 mm. Bladelets were the most important blanks for tools production, especially tanged points (LA–LF), microretouched inserts (WA–C), rare Janislawician points (JA–E) and trapezes (AA–AC), and some of the burins and end-scrapers. The conversion of blanks into tools frequently consisted in intentional sectioning. Innumerous backed pieces (DA, DB) are present in the older assemblages. Finally, the countless microburins deserve mention. Some tools were made on flakes left-over from the core preparation process. Rare unpolished axes/ adzes were made from natural flint tablets or large flakes.

b. Flint tools. All Western Kunda flint inventories include a set of typological groups comprising end-scrapers

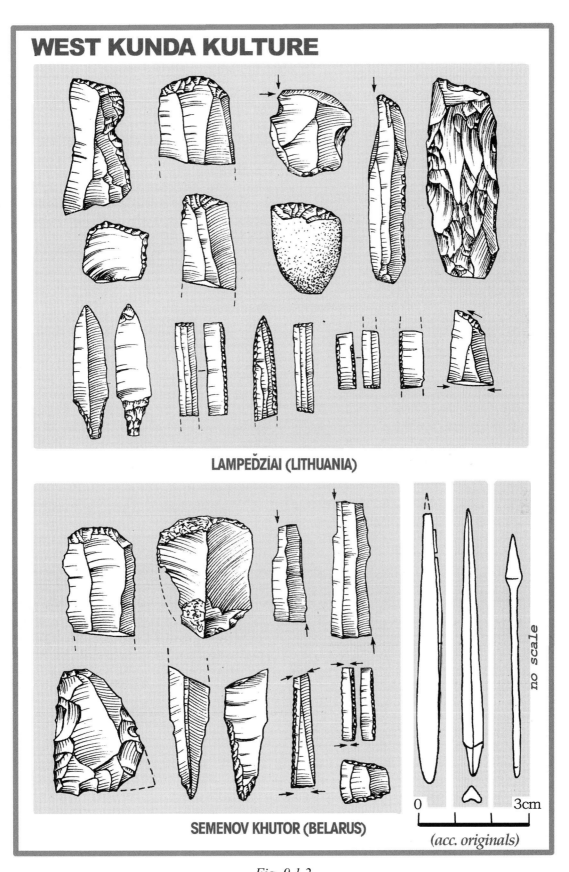

Fig. 9.1.2

(A), burins (C), irregular scrapers in the late phase (B), retouched bladelets (E), unpolished axes (H) and microliths (K); all these are accompanied by tanged points (J). The most numerous category are end-scrapers (A) which usually account for more that 30% of the implements. Irregular scrapers (B) are fairly numerous (10–25%), while other groups are always unabundant, with the exception of tanged points (J) which in Lithuania and Belarus may comprise even over 30% of the assemblages.

c. The characteristic tool group consists of:

–   Post-Swiderian tanged points (LA-F),
–   retouched inserts (WA-WC),
–   Janislawician points (JA-JE) and trapezes (AA, AZ, AC) in the late phase,
–   arched end-scrapers on blades (often retouched edges),
–   short flake end-scrapers,
–   various irregular scrapers in the late phase,
–   slim burins on truncations,
–   burins on broken blades,
–   rare unpolished axes,
–   rare backed points (DA-DB, in older assemblages)
–   retouched blades or bladelets with retouch due to use.

BONE INVENTORIES. Among the finds from the area between the Vistula and the Dvina/Daugava rivers, the slotted bone points with one groove armed by unretouched bladelets (21_1, all type references after Grahame Clark's classification), bowling-pin shaped points (16), points with triangular section (13) and perhaps some Havel-type harpoons with large barbs (e.g. specimen from Łękno, dated by H. Gross to the Boreal period) could be regarded as belonging to the Western Kunda tradition.

CERAMICS. Data from Lithuania and Belarus, as well as some finds from Poland (e.g. Pianki) indicate that in its later phase the West Kunda culture could have adopted ceramics of the Dubičiai/Neman type.

9.1.3. Kudlaevka culture

The unit was first distinguished by the present author on the basis of material from the Ukrainian site of Kudlaevka and the Belarussian site of Kozhangorodok (Fig. 9.1.3).

CULTURAL FRAMEWORK. Given the presence of many retouched inserts (WA-WC) and locally some Post-Swiderian tanged points (L), I have included this unit in the northeastern (Kunda) tradition. However, this hypothesis will be verifiable only after more homogeneous assemblages are discovered. We must bear in mind that some elements of this culture (end-scrapers, some cores, microliths) are of clearly "northern" (= Maglemosian) or southern (= Epi-Gravettian) character.

ASSEMBLAGES AND INVENTORIES. At present we have a mere two dozen or so inventories of the Kudlaevka type, of which only those from Kudlaevka and Tatsenki in Ukraine and Burdeniszki 1c and 1d in northeastern Poland are probably homogeneous (information from Thomas Ostrauskas).

TERRITORIAL RANGE: Sites occur mostly in southern Lithuania, Belarus and northern Ukraine, extending to the Desna and Sosh river basins in the east. In Poland, the unit is known from the northeastern part of the country. It is perhaps noteworthy that in Belarus, the Kudlaevka and Janislawice inventories practically never occur in the same places, possibly indicating that the two units are chronologically distinct. Recently Thomas Ostrauskas published a complete map of the culture, including also north Ukrainian material described by Leonid Zalizniak.

CHRONOLOGY. Kudlaevka chronology is based almost eclusively on typological and geomorphological data which suggest a generally older date than for the Janislawician, not the least being different site localization. Many inventories are known to include trapezes; even so, a few trapeze-less inventories have been noted and the combination of backed pieces and tanged points has been dated in the north to the very Early Holocene (Miłuki 4, which is an assemblage more Kundian than Kudlaevkian in nature, includes both tanged points and backed pieces).

Flint inventories

a. The core processing technique involves the exploitation of fairly small double-platform cores for bladelets and apparently larger single-platform specimens for the production of regular bladelets. The bladelets (both regular and not regular) were fashioned into microliths (K), regionally tanged points (J) and retouched blades (E), and rarely into end-scrapers (A), most of which are on flakes, similarly as irregular scrapers (B) and burins (C). The majority of microliths (DA and DB backed pieces) carry abrupt retouch, but the WA–C inserts bear fine and semi-abrupt treatment.

b. Retouched tools. There is virtually no reliable information about the percentages of the separate tool classes. Nevertheless in the case of north-eastern Poland (Burdeniszki, excavated by Karol Szymczak) we may say that irregular scrapers dominate in the assemblages, amounting to about 30% of the implements. Burins and retouched blades are less numerous while end-scrapers, microliths and tanged points are still fewer. The Belarussian and Ukrainian inventories, which are, however, surface collections, are marked by a dominance of irregular scrapers, a moderate content of microliths, end-scrapers and retouched blades, and lower amounts of burins, perforators and tanged points.

c. The basic tool group of the Kudlaevka culture consists of DA, DB and DD backed pieces, retouched inserts WA–WC (locally?), as well as AZ and AC trapezes (in the late phase), irregular scrapers and short end-scrapers on flakes, regular retouched blades and perforators.

d. The facial indicators consist of differentiated and not very regular small tanged points unknown in the eastern and southern assemblages (Tatsenki-type) which, in their turn, are apparently distinguished by the presence of *pointes* and *lamelles à dos*.

TERRITORIAL DIVISION. In the present poor state of research

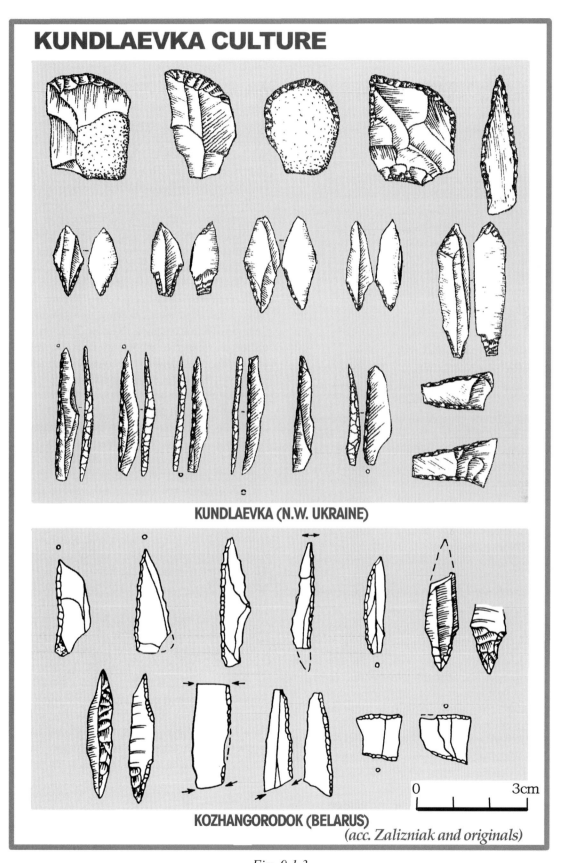

KUNDLAEVKA CULTURE

KUNDLAEVKA (N.W. UKRAINE)

KOZHANGORODOK (BELARUS)

(acc. Zalizniak and originals)

0   3cm

Fig. 9.1.3

of Kudlaevka, we may divide the phenomenon (after Leonid Zalizniak) into the classical Kudlaevka group with tanged points, occurring in the area between the Biebrza river in Poland, the middle Neman and upper Dnieper (in Lithuania and Belarus), and the more southerly Tatsenki group (backed points and bladelets, few or no WA–C inserts?); the latter group existed only along the lower Pripet and the middle Dnieper rivers.

ORIGIN. As it seems, the emergence of the Kudlaevka culture was the result of influence either of the Maglemosian or Molodovian/Epi-Gravettian environments on the Belarus and north Ukrainian Final Paleolithic environment. This not local tradition is represented by the DA, DB and DD backed pieces (cf. "Atlas") as well as the very short flake end-scrapers and characteristic perforators (very Komornician!, cf.). It might have come mainly from the Komornician which left evident traces of its influence in Volhynia (Midsk and Kukhari sites). The East-Gravettian source of these elements (especially of the perforators) is less probable.

The successors of Kudlaevka are the Belarussian and Ukrainian Janislawice assemblages (eastern and Rudoi Ostrov groups).

9.1.4. Push to the extreme North

Recent Finnish and earlier Russian research (Heikki Matiskainen and Mikhail Zhilin, but also Georgi Burov) has shown that the northeastern Mesolithic hunters (Kunda, Butovian and related) penetrated, most likely during a climatic optimum (?), also the far north of the continent. Testifying to this are the Finnish Lapland site of Sujala, as well as the finds from beyond the Polar Circle in Vychegda and Pechora basins, including Vis I site, famous for its bow (cf.) collection. This Atlantic-period (?) push to the far north has its more westerly counterpart in the appearance of the microbladelets industry (Nøstvet/Lihult) on the west Swedish and Norwegian coast.

9.1.5. The Early and Middle Holocene Cultures of the western part of Eastern Europe

Natural environment
It is obvious that such a vast area as the one under consideration, and one stretching for about 1800 km from north to south, must have been highly diversified environmentally. This is indeed the case today, and may be inferred for the past.

The differentiation is of zonal character and the different zones are arranged latitudinally, this being conditioned on the one hand by climate, and on the other by ground relief, geological structure, soils and hydrology.

The combined effect of all these factors led to the appearance of three main floral-faunal and landscape zones in the western part of Eastern Europe in the Early and Middle Holocene (Fig. 9.1.5a–d):

A. lowland zone of young lakelands in the north;

B. lowland zone of great river valleys in the central part; and

C. upland-lowland steppe zone in the south.

Each of these zones, still discernible today, significantly influenced the character of Early and Middle Holocene settlement, creating determinants for its further development.

Zone A
The zone of young lakelands covers the areas of the east Baltic states and is bounded in the south by the front moraines of the Vistulian/Valdai/Würmian Glaciation maximum, which is the water-divide between the Baltic and the Black Seas. This epi-glacial landscape declines in both relief and altitude towards the Baltic Sea.

Almost all of zone A is covered by boulder clays, which are sometimes sandy. This type of cover does not favour the discovery of Mesolithic sites. The geological substratum was of course one of the fundamental factors conditioning the dominant soil types of this zone. These are podzol-grassland soils with some sandy islands (Estonia) and the borderland well developed, consisting, on the one hand, of medium-sized rivers flowing directly into the Baltic: Southern Dvina/Daugava, Neman, and, on the other, of numerous small rivers flowing either into the sea or into one of the mentioned rivers, together with many shallow lakes which are frequently connected by the dense river network.

This type of drainage system provides very favourable conditions for hunter-gatherer-fishing settlement. In zone A, settlement is confined either to sandy river terraces (mostly Lithuanian sites) or to lake terraces, islands and river confluences (Latvia, Estonia).

The present-day climate of zone A is transitional between oceanic and continental. Mean July temperature ranges from 15 to 20°C, the figure for January ranging from 0 to -10°C; in this respect zone A does not differ from zone B (cf. below). Annual precipitation is 600–1000 mm. There are many indications (mainly from pollen analyses) that zone A was also relatively distinct in the Early and Middle Holocene.

Zone A belongs mainly to the vast province of taiga-type European lowland coniferous forests. The composition of the forest is of course conditioned by the climate and by soil type. Around 9500 cal. BC Estonia was covered by birch forests, and Lithuania and Latvia by birch-pine formations. Around 8100 cal. BC the birch-pine forests expanded northwards, partly eliminating the birch forests from Estonia. Latvia and Lithuania were overgrown by northern conifer-deciduous mixed forest (*Pinus* variant), while the remaining area was already overgrown by mixed deciduous forest.

Large-mammal fauna is known in zone A from Mesolithic sites in Estonia, Latvia and Poland. Throughout the period the elk dominates among large mammals. On sites belonging to the 10th and 9th millennia cal. BC, elk bones comprise over 95% of large-mammal bones, and in a later period the figure remains over 50%. Early sites

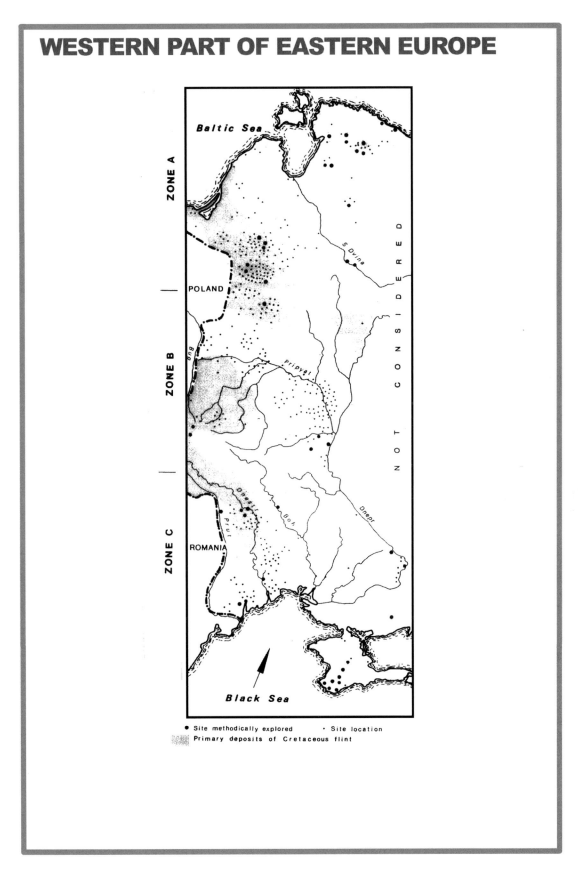

Fig. 9.1.5a

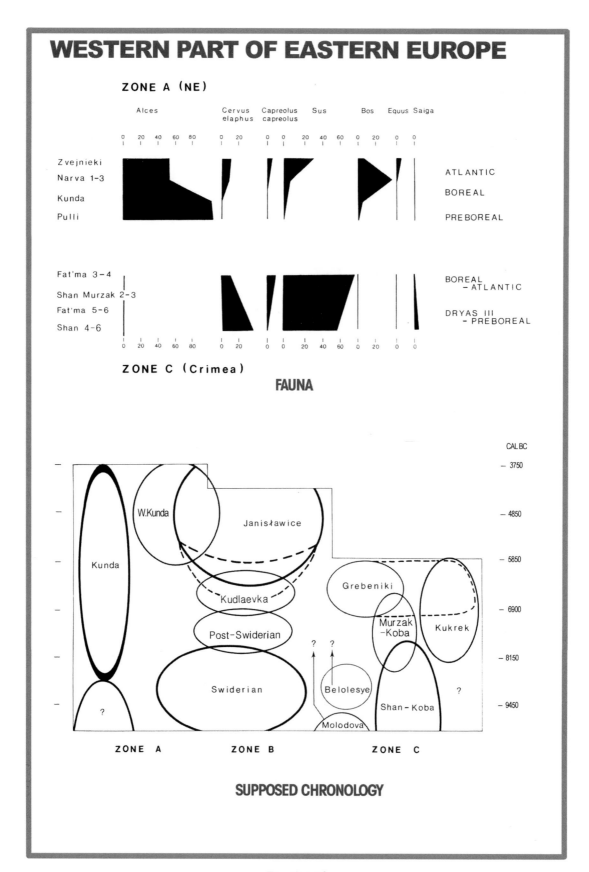

Fig. 9.1.5b

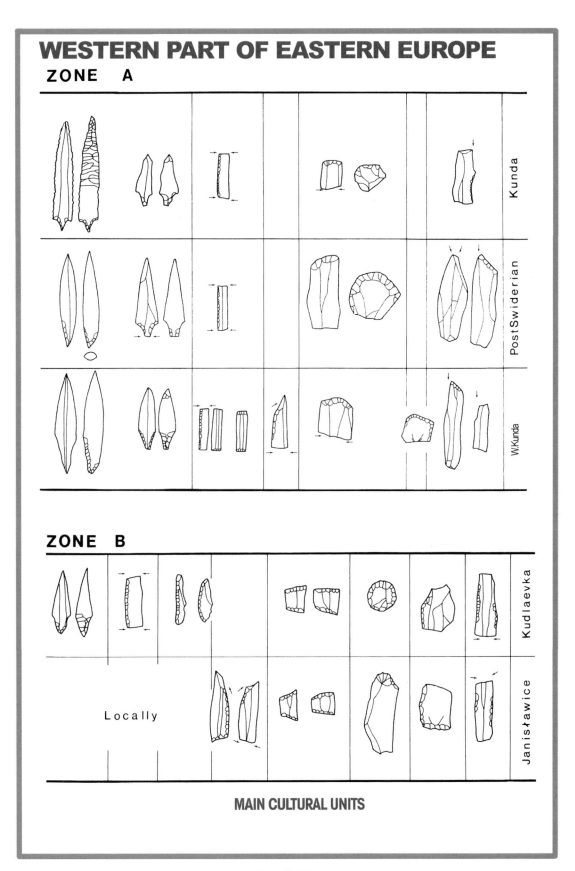

Fig. 9.1.5c

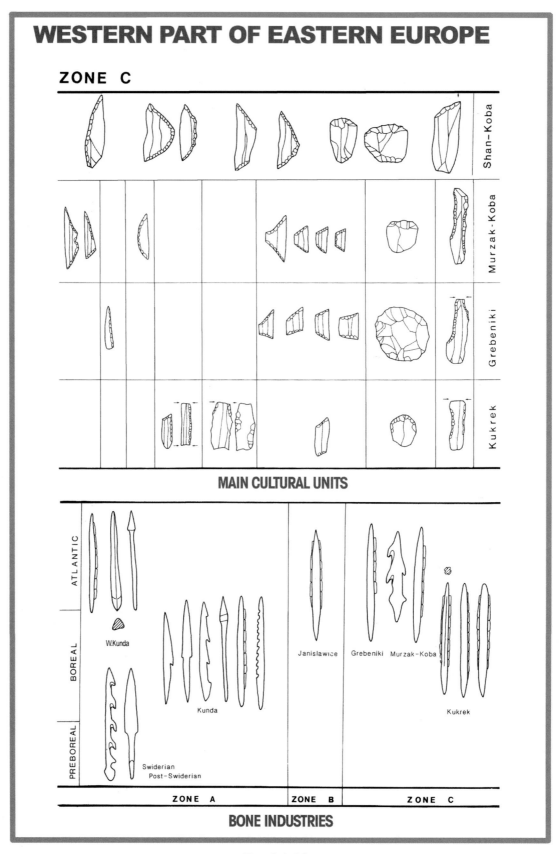

Fig. 9.1.5d

contain small numbers of bones of red deer, roe deer, wild boar, *Bos*, and wild horse. On later (= Atlantic) sites, the numbers of these bones increase, with boar and *Bos* bones becoming particularly numerous.

H. Gross once suggested that in this area (strictly speaking, in what was formerly East Prussia) reindeer and elk were present not only in the late Pleistocene but also in the very early Holocene (especially the Pre-Boreal period). This idea about the local survival of the reindeer till a relatively late period is theoretically acceptable given that it correlates well with data concerning the possible survival of the Swiderian culture in Lithuania and northern Belarus well into the 10th millennium BP. It must be added that Gross substantiated his theory with results of pollen analysis. New evidence from well-dated sites appears to show that the reindeer could have survived (if it did at all!) well into the Holocene only in the southwestern part of zone A, vanishing in the northeastern part by the mid 9th millennium cal. BC (personal information from Ilge Zagorska).

Finally, mention should also be made of the lithic raw materials which had an obvious bearing on the local culture. The availability of raw materials in zone A varies considerably. In Lithuania there are abundant deposits of good Cretaceous flint, while Latvia and Estonia (with some "black" flint) are almost totally devoid of good raw material; this led, on the one hand, to partial substitution of flint by other materials (quartz and slate in Estonia) and, on the other, to a much greater use of bone and antler as material for tools (cf. "Bone and stone cultures"). A theory, now obsolete, was even propounded in the literature (Nina N. Gurina) that unique "bone cultures" existed in this area. The raw material situation not only affected the form of the tools, but also had a direct bearing on the settlement network, with sites visibly concentrated around raw material outcrops (e.g. Lithuania).

As is evident from the above description, zone A is distinct in certain respects, but similar to zone B in others; in some periods both zones were characterized by a similar culture.

Zone B
The zone of big east-west orientated river valleys coincides mainly with Belarus and some of the northern extremeties of the Ukraine. It is a natural extension of a similar zone in Poland and Germany. In the north it is bounded by the front moraines of the Valdai/Würmian Glaciation and in the south by the loess uplands of Volhynia and Podolia. It is a distinctly lowland area overall, called Polesye, made up of depositional landforms of the Rissian (Dnepr) and the Warta (Moscow) Glaciations. These include sandy forms of ground moraine, uplands, outwash, and elevated loess patches (rising to over 200 m a.s.l.) of northwestern Belarus. The soils of zone B developed on sandy substrata are mostly of the grassland-podzol variety, as in zone A, whereas on heavier substrata (e.g. loess) brown earth soils dominate. The entire area is drained by a dense network of small and medium-sized rivers flowing into the major

river of this zone, the Pripet, which flows latitudinally to join the Dnepr (Black Sea catchment area). The Pripet is obviously a marginal valley of one of the Pleistocene glaciations (Moscow) and has all the attributes of such a feature (extensive marshlands, lakes, etc.).

The dense drainage network of zone B and especially its medium-sized rivers (Styr, Khoryn, Uborch, Uzh, Ptych, Shchara, upper Neman, and Pripet) with their sandy terraces formed an excellent framework for Early and Middle Holocene settlement which, it seems, developed along different lines from that in zone A (at least in its northeastern part). The settlement map shows "chains" of sites localized in valleys of at least the medium-sized rivers; the valleys of small water courses, the uplands, and even the relatively low-lying areas of ground moraine were avoided (the latter are poorly watered in the sense of having a low density of surface drainage). The river valleys were not only the most attractive settlement niche, but appear to have been the only environment exploited by the hunters and gatherers of those times. The same might apply to a part of zone A (southern Lithuania). The climate of the big valley zone is continental, with less annual precipitation than in zone A (500–600 mm) but with similar temperatures (15 to 20°C in July and 0 to -10°C in January).

Zone B is, of course, a forest zone of lowland taiga type, differentiated territorially according to differences in soil substratum. By c. 9500 cal. BC the area was already overgrown by mixed forests which, about 1500 years later, were replaced in southwestern Belarus by northern conifer-deciduous mixed forest (*Pinus* variant). The river valleys thus provided a particularly rich environment.

The forests were inhabited by large mammals. The only direct evidence of this fauna comes from the ceramic site of Zatsenye on the River Tsna (excavated by Mikhail Cherniavski) in central Belarus, dated to the 5th millennium cal. BC. Elk was the dominant species (comprising over 50% of large mammal bones); also fairly plentiful were boar (c. 30%) and red deer (c. 20%).

Finally, a few words about the stone raw material from zone B. Readily accessible flint raw materials, mainly of Cretaceous age, dominate. These were obtained from various sources, both from primary chalk deposits and from Cretaceous rafts transported by the Rissian glacier to the south. Primary chalk deposits crop out all over northern Belarus (upper Neman and upper Dnepr river basins) and also in Volhynia. These deposits were cut by the larger rivers (Neman, Dnepr, Desna, Styr, Khoryn). The other source of flint raw material is the so-called Cretaceous rafts with flint nodules, scattered practically all over Belarus as a result of ice sheet transport; these rafts are especially plentiful in Polesye. The flint raw material from both these sources is usually of good quality. An inferior raw material (occurring as small nodules, often with cracks) is Cretaceous erratic surface flint which is scattered through glacial deposits over practically all of Polesye. It also seems that nodules of good Cretaceous flint from the primary deposits of Volhynia were transported towards the Pripet valley by its southern/right tributaries, and were extracted from river alluvia. The more important outcrops of better-quality raw materials naturally attracted Mesolithic settlement. This is evidenced by the particularly numerous Neman sites (information from Wiktor Obuchowski), the sites on the Desna river and probably also some of the Pripet sites. Mesolithic studies were carried out mostly by Vladimir Isaenko, V. Ksendzov and recently by Wiktor Obuchowski.

Zone C
This is the vast area between the line of Volhynian loess uplands and the coast of the Black Sea. It is principally an upland but flat area (the Moldavian upland in Romania, the Bessarabian, Podolian and Dnepr uplands in western Ukraine) bounded in the south by the Black Sea lowland and the Crimean mountains. It is of plate structure (the Black Sea plate) bounded in the west by the eastern Carpathians, and is built of loess and loess-like deposits on which chernozem-type soils (locally differentiated) have evolved.

Zone C naturally belongs to the Black Sea catchment area and is cut by large (Dnestr, Dnepr, southern Bug/Boh) and medium-sized rivers, often flowing in deep canyons. The river network is much less dense than in the other two zones. There are few small water courses, and so the zones of Mesolithic settlement, concentrated in valleys (terraces and edges of the uplands), are split up and separated by poorly watered stretches of loess uplands, often devoid of traces of human activity. It seems that owing to its specific hydrological features, zone C had smaller settlement capacity than zones A and B. This situation appears to be due to the local climate which today is characterized by relatively high mean January temperatures (0 to -5°C), high mean July temperatures (20 to 25°C), and modest annual precipitation (400–500 mm). This type of continental climate must have also obtained in the Early and Middle Holocene when zone C was overgrown by steppe-like vegetation mixed with some forest elements. In the 9th and 8th millennia cal. BC, Volhynia and Podolia were overgrown by deciduous mixed forests of continental type; further south there was forest-steppe and steppe proper. In the 7th and 6th millennia cal. BC, most of zone C became dominated by continental-type deciduous forest, bounded in the south by a narrow belt of steppe (reconstruction by Pavel M. Dolukhanov). Throughout the Early Holocene the valleys of the big rivers were overgrown with rich gallery forests.

The zone C fauna is marked by local differentiation and is known primarily from 7th and 6th millennia cal. BC archaeological sites. On the Black Sea coast, at the site of Mirnoe near the Danube delta (excavated by Volodymyr Stanko) the dominant large mammal is *Bos* (over 80% of large mammal bones) with the horse (14%) in second place. There are infrequent bones of red deer, boar and ass. Elsewhere, in the middle Dnestr river basin, the dominant animal on Mesolithic and early ceramic but not Neolithic sites is red deer which is accompanied locally by numerous roe deer (over 30%) and in other cases by numerous *Bos* or

boar. This indicates that the generally similar fauna of the southern zone is locally differentiated into open landscape and forest assemblages. The former occurs mainly on the Black Sea lowland and uplands, the latter in forest-covered big river valleys. The composition of the upland fauna is similar to the local latest Pleistocene fauna from layer Ia at the site of Molodova V in Moldova, although, of course, the proportions of the species in Holocene layers are different from those in the Final Pleistocene layers.

A full sequence of large mammals is known from the Crimea. The fauna is composed of three thermophilous species (red deer, roe deer and boar) which were probably still accompanied by saiga antelope at least in the Late Pleistocene.

In the Shan-Koba development phase (final Pleistocene and probably early Holocene, according to Vadim Koen and Volodymyr Stanko), the dominant species in the Crimea was the boar (60%); red deer accounts for over 30% of the fauna, but roe deer and saiga antelope were scarce. Subsequent periods saw an increase in the importance of boar (up to 80%) and roe deer (up to 10%), the gradual disappearance of red deer, and the complete disappearance of saiga. The zoological evidence does not permit a distinction to be made between Boreal and Atlantic faunas, since they tend to be lumped together in publications dealing with bone assemblages of the Murzak-Koba and Grebeniki phases (statistics by Elena Vekilova). It is reasonable to suppose, however, that the role of red deer was greater in the 8th millennium cal. BC than in the 7th and 6th millennia cal. BC.

Zone C also abounds in good quality flint raw materials which, however, was not evenly distributed throughout the territory. Richest in this respect is the western part with *in situ* Cretaceous flint close to the ground surface, known from Volhynia, Podolia, the eastern Carpathians (Prutul, Ibanești), and the upper and middle course of the Dnestr. The Cretaceous rocks in these areas are cut by river valleys, and the rivers carry raw material nodules which can therefore be found in the alluvia of these rivers. In the Crimean mountains there are also good Cretaceous flints that can be transported by the local rivers. The eastern part of zone C has fewer sources of lithic raw materials, but there are siliceous rocks along the middle course of the Boh/southern Bug river and erratic flint along the middle Dnepr (Nadporozhye). In this zone, too, the settlement network is in part influenced by the distribution of raw material deposits, and Mesolithic settlement in the eastern part of zone C is less intense not only, it seems, because of the less thorough exploration of this area.

Archaeological evidence
The Early and Middle Holocene evidence from the western part of Eastern Europe differs considerably as regards its cognitive value and is unevenly distributed. This is due to several factors which include, on the one hand, the geological structure of the various regions (resulting in differences in raw material availability) and, on the other, the different activities of archaeologists, not all of whom

are specialists in collecting evidence of the social activities of hunter-gatherer communities. For example, the sandy regions of Lithuania and Belarus have produced numerous collections but, since these are largely the products of surface exploration, there are very few well documented homogeneous assemblages. This is because Stone Age settlement in this region was generally confined to small dry sandy elevations in river valleys where sedimentation had ceased already by the end of the Pleistocene. Thus, repeated settlement in the same locations led to the appearance of mixed sites which should be explored very methodically indeed, if homogeneous assemblages are to be obtained. It should also be stressed that the highly elevated sandy plateus of Belarus seem to be devoid of Mesolithic sites.

The situation is different in Estonia and Latvia where rare sites are located on clayey lake and river terraces. Several of these sites were covered by layers of organic sediments. The result is that in these countries known sites are few but have often been excavated methodically, yielding homogeneous assemblages and numerous radiocarbon and/or pollen dates, as well as organic material.

In the southern regions (Ukraine and Moldova) the situation is different again. The sites are admittedly few, but they often contain homogeneous assemblages. This appears to be due to the less intensive settlement of the area and to the undoubtedly smaller potential for choosing sites, compared to the sandy zone of Belarus and Lithuania. In effect, the loess-covered southern zone provides a fair number of homogeneous assemblages and, as in Estonia and Latvia, data about fauna, bone implements and chronology.

Separate mention should be made of the multi-layered cave sites of the Crimean peninsula which provide a basis for the relative chronology of this part of the Ukraine.

As will be appreciated from this brief review, the state of research into Early and Middle Holocene materials from the western part of Eastern Europe varies, hence many of the conclusions proposed in this paper continue to have the value of working hypotheses. It is fortunate, however, that there are several valuable assemblages from outside the region, and these add to the evidence at our disposal.

To conclude these remarks about the archaeological evidence, some consideration must be given to the reconstruction of Early and Middle Holocene settlement in the western regions of Eastern Europe. Although this task is very difficult in view of the previously mentioned disparities in the exploration of the region, the following points can be made:

a)   In the young lakelands (Estonia, Latvia, northern Lithuania, Mazuria) the probably sparse settlement was concentrated around numerous, shallow post-glacial lakes, and also spread onto terraces of medium-sized rivers.

b)   In the sandy regions of southern Lithuania (zone A), Belarus, northwestern Ukraine and northeastern Poland (zone B), settlement was confined to terraces of medium-sized rivers (Neman, Pripet, Shchara, Lega, Neris).

c)   The upland regions of Würmian and Rissian ground moraines of northern Belarus and Lithuania were not settled at all (?); the same is true of the southern loess uplands.

d)   The loess uplands of the western Ukraine were also probably sparsely settled or not at all (on the other hand, material is known from the sandy region of Small Polesye); the same applies to the eastern Carpathians bend.

e)   The Black Sea lowland and the lower part of the lower Dnepr river basin featured settlement mainly along the few big and medium-sized rivers (Dnestr, Boh/ southern Bug) and around the shallow lakes (limans) of the Black Sea coast.

f)   The Crimea is characterized primarily by cave sites/ rock shelters in the mountain zone.

The settlement network was thus based on an entire system of medium-sized rivers characterized by an exceptionally rich environment, and on the lake system in the north. It clearly avoided the poorly watered and elevated areas of loess and of frontal and/or ground moraines.

The drainage network in the western part of Eastern Europe is, of course, highly differentiated along the north-south axis – from the lakeland belt in the north, through the system of great river valleys, through the upland belt where rivers are rare, to the poorly watered zone of the Black Sea uplands and lowland in the south. The exceptional density of settlement in the sandy soils of the northernmost zones (Lithuania, northern Belarus) is therefore understandable.

The settlement network was certainly influenced by the distribution of stone raw material outcrops. This is particularly evident on the middle Neman and Pripet rivers and also along the Dnestr. It appears that the exceptional concentration of sites there may be due to outcrops of good quality lithic raw materials found in deposits on the river terraces.

Chronological foundations
One of the main difficulties in the study of the Mesolithic of this part of Europe stems from the fact that, with the exception of Latvia and Estonia, very few sites could and have been dated. The situation is so serious that several large taxonomic units have not been carbon-dated at all. In spite of this, a basic chronology may be derived, relying in part on dates based on typological analysis and site stratigraphy. It is also possible to make use of existing dates for sites in neighbouring regions – Poland, Hungary, Romania, or the upper Volga area.

The situation has naturally improved since the first publication of this text; new dates have appeared for Lithuania, Latvia and northeastern Poland, as well as entire series of dates by the Kiev Laboratory for Ukraine. Some of the latter are difficult to interpret and accept, inclining the author, together with Paolo Biagi, Leonid Zalizniak and Volodymyr Stanko to develop a program for radiocarbon verification of Ukrainian Mesolithic chronology by the Groningen Laboratory. Still, no dates have yet become available for the Mesolithic in Belarus.

Table 9.1. Stratigraphy and relative chronology on the major sites in zone C, according to stratified sites

NORTH CAUCASUS SLOPES		CRIMEA				CULTURE
Gubski Naves	Sosruko	Shan-Koba	Fat'ma-Koba	Zamil-Koba	Kukrek	
–	–	layer 2	layer 3/4a	–	–	GREBENIKI
upper layer	–	layer 3	layer 4b	upper layer	upper layer	MURZAK-KOBA
–	layer 1	–	–	–	lower layer	KUKREK
–	–	layer 4	layer 5	–	–	IMERETINSKA
lower layer	layer 3	layers 5/6	layer 6	lower layer	–	SHAN-KOBA

The Crimean peninsula (cf. above) provides data for relative dating of Mesolithic assemblages based on stratified cave and rock-shelter sites. Unfortunately, many of the assemblages from this area do not have absolute dates, having been excavated before World War II.

The table contains the most important data concerning the stratigraphy of the Crimean and north Caucasian sites. Generally speaking, the first Final Paleolithic/Early Mesolithic assemblages to appear in this area were those with arched-backed pieces (Shan-Koba-Belolesye culture, cf.), which were succeeded by quasi-Gravettian assemblages (Imeretian culture of the Caucasian tradition); the latter, however, appears to have been a brief episode connected with a short-lived northwestward penetration of Caucasian peoples. Nevertheless, it seems that the tradition of arched-backed pieces (Shan-Koba) survived in this area (e.g. the uppermost layer of the site of Siuren II). The tradition of arched-backed pieces probably originated in the final phase of the Pleistocene (evidenced by the presence of the antelope, *Saiga tatarica*, indicating a cool continental climate, and the presence of Swiderian elements in some assemblages); the Shan-Koban probably survived until the appearance of cultures with trapezes – this is indicated, among others, by the presence of infrequent arched-backed pieces in assemblages of the trapeze-Murzak-Koba culture.

The assemblages with arched-backed pieces are succeeded by assemblages with trapezes. These assemblages (which are mainly those of the Murzak-Koban) are characterized by an entirely new ("Castelnovian", cf.) technology of carefully preformed core reduced by the pressure technique, regular blades/bladelets, denticulated (= Montbani) bladelets, and finally the presence of trapezes. Problems arise, however, when it comes to dating the emergence of these elements. On the one hand, we know that similar technological and typological elements appeared in central, southern and western Europe only c. 7000 cal. BC (cf. "Pre-Neolithic base"); on the other, there are radiocarbon determinations from the site of Laspi 7 (Murzak-Koba culture), which suggest an earlier date (8th millennium cal. BC) for such elements. We also know of 8th millennium cal. BC datings for comparable material from Frankhthi, phase 8, in Greece (published by Cathérine Perlèz). Since there are no grounds for questioning the above datings, it may be supposed tentatively that the intercultural trend with trapezes (cf.) was generally earlier

than 7000 cal. BC in the Black Sea zone. But the dates for the Murzak-Koba culture may also be wrong (they come from shell middens), and the change in Crimea could have occurred at exactly the same time as elsewhere, that is, c. 7000 cal. BC.

The Murzak-Koban is followed in Crimean sites by assemblages of Grebenikian and preceded and/or paralleled and followed by the Kukrekian. The time of their emergence is uncertain, with the radiocarbon dates from Igreń 8 on the Dnepr (Kukrekian) indicating a date perhaps as early as the 8th millennium cal. BC.

Relatively good chronological data has been obtained for zone A. There is a full sequence of dates from Estonia and Latvia (completed with comparable dates for central and northern Russia and Russian Karelia) for the Kunda and comparable Butovo cultures (cf.), as well as pollen dates for single bone and antler artifacts from the local Late Paleolithic and Mesolithic. Added to these are a few radiocarbon dates from nearby Poland and Lithuania.

The cultural sequence of zone A begins in the Dryas 3 period and the very early Preboreal when the Swiderian is documented in Poland (youngest dates = c. 9000 cal. BC), and also in Lithuania and the Kaliningrad district (pollen dates for Lyngby-type axes, Havel-type single-barbed harpoons, and processed reindeer antlers, all dates according to H. Gross, ^{14}C datings for flint inventories collected by Romuald Schild). It is difficult to date the moment of disintegration of the Swiderian culture, i.e. when the classic structure of the reindeer hunters' culture breaks down, giving way perhaps to the ephemeral, forest-based Post-Swiderian (?). If it is true that the reindeer survived in what was formerly East Prussia till the early Preboreal period, then this point in time might be hypothetically assumed to be the moment of transition to the rare Post-Swiderian assemblages (Karol Szymczak's idea), which cannot be dated directly.

The latter should be younger than the Swiderian assemblages (having evolved from them) and older than the Lithuanian and classic Kunda culture assemblages which occurred in Estonia and northeastern Poland from c. 8900–8600 cal. BC (Pulli, Miłuki) and which existed until the Late Mesolithic, as indicated by numerous C_{14} dates from Estonia (Narva), Latvia (Zvejnieki, Osa), Karelia (Oleni Ostrov) and northern Russia (Veretie, Vis, Popovo) and in turn the late Lithuanian (Lampedžiai) inventories. The Lithuanian sites contain chronologically diagnostic elements such as trapezes or Janislawice points, which are of Atlantic age.

A separate problem is presented by sites of the Janislawician (cf.) occuring mainly in southern Lithuania. The Polish dates for this culture suggest that it was already in existence in the 7th millennium cal. BC (rather second half), and this is in accord with its technological and typological characteristics ("Castelnovian", cf., regular cores and blades, trapezes, retouched blades). The problem to be solved is its position with respect to the late Lithuanian/Western Kunda culture (cf.) which dominates more to the north. Relying more on intuition than on facts, the present author is inclined to believe that the two cultures (Late West Kunda and Janislawician), which shared only part of their territorial ranges, developed in parallel, perhaps with the Janislawician dominating earlier in the south, and at the end also in northern Lithuania (this is why the ceramic Narva culture of the region has trapezes, cf. Zedmar = Serovo excavated by Vladimir I. Timofeev).

The chronology of Mesolithic sites from zone B is the most difficult and least reliable, since there are no direct datings from this area. One must thus make use of information from zones A and C and also from the Polish equivalent of zone B.

The final phase of the Pleistocene (Dryas 3) is characterized in Poland by the presence of the Swiderian; the same is true of the very beginning of the Pre-Boreal period (cf. remarks about zone A). It may thus be assumed that the Swiderian assemblages in Belarus, identical with Polish ones, date to the same period. They are paralleled in the east by Desnian (cf.) settlement. These are probably succeeded by Post-Swiderian and Post-Desnian assemblages corresponding to the hypothetical ones from Lithuania.

The next developmental stage in the Mesolithic of zone B is represented by assemblages of the Kudlaevka (cf.) type, characterized by the presence of backed pieces with a straight back and (but not always) of tanged points. Judging by their morphology, the rare tanged points are of Post-Swiderian origin. The backed pieces, on the other hand, are related either to some relatively unknown late Gravettian tradition (e.g. Molodova-Lipa Epi-Gravettian from the south) or to the "Maglemosian" Komornica (cf.) culture from Poland. In both cases, they could have appeared in zone B already in the Early Holocene.

It is noteworthy that the backed point/tanged point composition is known from the region already from the 9th millennium cal. BC (Miłuki in northeastern Poland, as well as the undated, trapezeless Lithuanian Paštuva). On the other hand, trapezes might suggest an early Atlantic age for some assemblages.

After the Kudlaevka-type assemblages comes the Janislawician, the emergence of which is dated in Poland to the mid 7th millennium cal. BC. It features trapezes and regular bladelets, and therefore appears to be generally of Atlantic (= "Castelnovian", cf.) age, a conclusion confirmed by Polish radiocarbon dates for this culture.

The chronological evidence may be summarized as follows:

1. The western areas of Eastern Europe are characterized by a latitudinal zonal structure which had considerable influence on the development of local Early and Middle Holocene cultures.

2. In the latest Pleistocene/Earliest Holocene, Zones A and B were dominated at first by the Swiderian and/or Desnian and related cultures (in general, these were traditions associated with tanged points) and later by traditions at least partly connected with them (Kunda, Kudlaevka). Zone C was dominated by the arched-backed pieces and geometrics traditions of Caspian-Caucasian origin.

3. In the 8th millennium cal. BC (?), there occured in zone C a technological and stylistic change, which, among other things, saw the introduction of trapezes and a new blade technology, associated with the Murzak-Koban (?) and Kukrekian.

4. In the 7th millennium cal. BC, a new technology with trapezes appeared in zone B, signifying a complete cultural change (Janislawician) which undoubtedly originated in the south and spread also finally to zone A where, at the beginning, it introduced mostly slight modifications in the local cultural environment based on the tanged point tradition existing here from the Preboreal period (Western Kunda) before actually dominated the region. Similar changes occured at the time in the flint industry of zone C (the Grebeniki of the 7th millennium cal. BC).

5. The evidence presented above favors the idea of a constantly "pulsating" process of pushing northward from the south.

Taxonomic divisions

The following makes an effort to present the basic elements of the stylistic and technological differentiation of Mesolithic materials, together with information about their place in time and space and about their environmental conditioning.

Tanged point technocomplex

The technocomplex with tanged points is represented in the Latest Glacial/Earliest Holocene, in the southwestern part of zone A and in all of zone B by the Swiderian and Desnian cultures and perhaps by Post-Swiderian assemblages evolving from it (Karol Szymczak's theory). The supposed Post-Swiderian assemblages are found (if?) only in the northeastern part of Poland and in Lithuania (cf.).

The Post-Swiderian assemblages could still retain some of its stylistic and technological features, but they differ considerably from one another. The few data from northeastern Poland place them generally in the Preboreal period.

Technologically, the Swiderian and the Post-Swiderian are similar; the double-platform core technique dominates in both, the difference being that in the Post-Swiderian assemblages the cores are often small. This is due to replacing mined flint with erratic rock, which is one of the features of the disintegration of the Swiderian model and its adaptation to new conditions.

The dominant stylistic elements in both units are non-pedonculate and pedonculate tanged points, slim and short scrapers, and burins. Post-Swiderian assemblages often, but not always, include other forms of tanged points, e.g. forms with semi-abrupt (vs. flat) retouch on the ventral face, or forms with an intentionally truncated pedoncule. Also found in these assemblages are finely retouched bladelets, undoubtedly of east European origin (e.g. Ełk, excavated by Jan Trzeciakowski).

Northeastern technocomplex (cf.)

The Late Pleistocene/very Early Holocene Swiderian could perhaps be partly responsible (?) for the emergence of the western section of the Mesolithic Northeastern (Kunda) technocomplex, which in the area under consideration is represented by three taxonomic units: in zone A there is the classical Kunda culture, developing further to the north since at least the beginning of the 8th millennium cal. BC, and in the southwest the Lithuanian variant of Kunda; while in zone B there is the Kudlaevka culture. The latter two cultures are also known from northeastern Poland, while the Kudlaevka (cf.) is additionally present in northern Ukraine and east of the Dnepr. The relatively early chronological position (Preboreal period) of both entities was recently established (Miłuki, Poland).

The three taxonomic units differ in terms of the technology. The Kudlaevka still retains elements of Post-Swiderian technology, but both the units from zone A are based on the technique of single-platform core for blades and bladelets, probably of eastern, even Siberian origin. The blade sectioning technique is present in all three units, and in the zone-A units such blades were used to produce numerous end-scrapers and burins, retouched blades and finely retouched bladelets/inserts.

The link between all three units and the forest environment is beyond doubt. The main hunted animal was the elk; the people lived in small temporary camps, chiefly on lake shores in the northeastern part of zone A, and on river banks in the other areas.

Stylistically, all three units are characterized by the presence (Kudlaevka only in the north) of non-pedonculate/willow-leaf-shaped and pedonculate tanged points with local variations. Some of these may have a post-Swiderian origin (?). The tanged points are accompanied by finely retouched bladelets, very characteristic of the entire Mesolithic between our zones A and B and the Ural mountains, slim and short end-scrapers (the former often on broken blade), and burins (often on broken blade or on truncations), as well as retouched blades. The remaining elements are specific to the separate units. In the Lithuanian Kunda culture there are few backed pieces at the beginning and at the terminal stage infrequent Janislawice points (JA–C) and irregular scrapers (cf.) together with trapezes. The Kudlaevka culture is marked by the presence of numerous backed points and backed bladelets, segments, as well as short end-scrapers and in the late phase trapezes. The classical Kunda assemblages could also occasionally contain partially polished axes.

JanisLawician (cf.)

A separate taxonomic position is occupied by the Janis-lawician, which occurs mainly in zone B but also in the southwestern part of zone A. This entity is also known from the Vistula river basin in Poland, and from the northern part of western Ukraine (zone C), as well as Trans-Carpathian Ukraine (Kamyanitsa, excavations of Leonid Matskevoi). The radiocarbon dates from Poland, the presence of trapezes in the assemblages and different geomorphological position compared to Kudlaevka place this unit in the Late Mesolithic, after Kudlaevka culture.

Technologically, the Janislawice culture is distinct from the units with tanged points described above. The dominant technique is that of regular single-platform pre-formed (keeled) core, which, however, differed from those of Kunda culture for example. The bladelets from such cores are regular and fairly large, and this forced the Janislawicians to seek better quality raw materials, often of mined origin. These bladelets were used in the production of truncations, Janislawice points (JA–C) and trapezes, rarely of end-scrapers. The flakes were used to make irregular scrapers. The Janislawician must be genetically related to a southern environment (zone C) from which the technological and typological innovations (e.g. trapezes) spread northward, probably around the mid 7th millennium cal. BC, to become superimposed on local substrata. In conclusion, it is worth mentioning that various other types of tools characterize the Janislawice assemblages depending on the local substratum (cf. "Pre-Neolithic"): in Poland, scalene triangles with short base (TD, TI), and narrow trapezes (AA); in central Belarus and Lithuania, broad/high trapezes (AC); further to the east, tanged points (remains of Kudlaevka tradition); and in Lithuania, Janislawice points with obliquely truncated base (JE). Camps usually occured on river terraces, and the people hunted elk and red deer.

Zones A and B are marked by broad similarities in cultural taxonomy, undermined only in the late period by the successive waves of southern influences (regular blade technology, trapezes); but zone C is markedly distinct typologically (cf. below).

Shan-Koba and Belolesye-type assemblages

The transition from the Pleistocene to the Holocene is poorly studied in zone C, but it is known that at that time there were two closely related cultural units: the Shan-Koban and Belolesye-type assemblages. Both of these, as well as the typologically similar east Ukrainian and Caucasian units (cf. "Caspian-Caucasian"), appear towards the end of the Pleistocene. There are some indications that they could have survived until the Early Holocene. Genetically, they are probably related to Caspian/Caucasian origin (e.g. industries of Trialetian type in the Caucasus, southeast Turkey, south and east Caspian) and the maximum range of industries of this type originally covered at least the southern belt of all of zone C. The technology of the Shan-Koban and of Belolesye-type assemblages is based on fairly wide, not very regular blades, and often also on flakes. Dominant in the assemblages are large segments and isosceles triangles or double truncations, as well as short end-scrapers mostly on flakes and finally big lanceolates (= Federmesser).

The early Holocene environment inhabited by the hunters of zone C was mainly steppe cut by valleys of the big rivers which were overgrown by gallery forests; the fauna of these forests included red deer, *Bos*, boar, and horse.

Local cultures of zone C

The Murzak-Koban, Kukrekian and Grebenikian are cultures that developed after the phase described in the previous section. The first and the last of these appear to be partial genetic successors of the local early Holocene cultures, suggested by the diversified backed pieces and segments present in some (earliest?) of their inventories. The Kukrekian appears to be unrelated. Elements shared by all three cultures include: slim, conical, single-platform cores for regular bladelets with circumferential flaking face, denticulated blades and very short end-scrapers. The trapezes known from the Murzak-Koban and Grebenikian are probably of southern origin. The features which distinguish these cultures among themselves are the special, notched elongated triangles of the Murzak-Koban, the finely and ventrally retouched bladelets and retouched inserts of the Kukrekian, and the very rare Gravettian backed pieces of the Grebenikian.

The range of the Murzak-Koban is very local, but the other two units occupy all of zone C (the Grebenikian in the west up to the Carpathians, and the Kukrekian in the east of these mountains as far as the foothills of the Caucasus, with the upper layers of Caucesian Sosruko site), upper layer. They are thus steppe and deciduous forest cultures based on hunting red deer and *Bos*.

A separate problem is presented by the dating of both the Kukrekian and Murzak-Koban cultures, which apparently appear in zone C as early as the 8th millennium cal. BC (cf. section on chronology), which is perhaps not how it really was, for the Murzak-Koban.

As regards settlement, the network is not as dense as in zones A and B or perhaps less studied (?) The settlement sites include terraces of large and medium-sized rivers, the edges of loess uplands, and caves and rock-shelters. Large open sites are known (Mirnoe) which are either remains of large settlements (less portable) or traces of repeated visits by settlers to the same spot.

Grebenikian has his own ceramic phase, known as the Bug-Dniester culture, once erroneously considered as Neolithic.

Bone industries (cf. Chapter 12)

The distribution of bone and antler artifacts in the western part of Eastern Europe is very uneven. Vast regions are devoid of them, due to the character of certain Holocene sediments which do not favor their survival. It must also be borne in mind that such artifacts are very often accidental finds without stratigraphic or cultural contexts. For this reason, emphasis should be placed on classes of artifacts with diagnostic features that make it possible

to reconstruct their original cultural context with a high degree of probability, especially as single specimens of these artifacts are known from systematically excavated and explored sites – specifically, harpoons, points and ornamented axes/adzes. It is worth noting that the study of bone and antler artifacts is particularly important in zone A (especially in its northeastern part) where good lithic raw material was not always available and where organic materials had to replace it at least in part (cf. also "Bone and stone cultures").

The bone points and harpoons known from the region under consideration are very varied morphologically; their territorial ranges differ (cf. "Points, *sagaies*"), as does their popularity. Some classes appear to have inter-regional character; others are confined to one zone, or even to a fragment thereof.

The most widespread type are spindle-shaped points/*sagaies* with a single slot or *reinure*, and unretouched bladelets as inserts (type 21_1 in Grahame Clark's classification). These occur in zone C and are connected with the local cultures there (Murzak-Koban, Kukrekian, Grebenikian), i.e. with cultures of the 8th/7th millennium cal. BC. One specimen of this type is known from zone B, while in zone A the points with a single slot are fairly numerous and are characteristic of the middle and late Kunda culture, both the Lithuanian and classic variants.

Another interregional type are biconical points (Clark's type 16) known from vast areas of the Eastern European forest zone, reaching as far west as northeastern Poland, and in the east spreading beyond the Ural mountains (Shigirski Torfianik). In our area they occur mainly in zone A but also (rarely) in B. From the very beginning of the Holocene (Pulli in Estonia, c. 8800 cal. BC) they are characteristic of the Kunda *milieu*, and later (?), in Lithuania, of the Lithuanian/Western Kunda; they exist from the beginning and continue to be present in the Russian forest "Neolithic" (= early ceramic Mesolithic cultures). In general, they appear to be among the key elements characterizing the Russian Mesolithic taiga/coniferous forests.

All the other types are of local or regional character only. In all of zone A there occur since the beginning of the Holocene single-barbed harpoons with large barbs, probably derived from the Final Paleolithic Havel-type specimens (Clark's types 9, 10 and 12A); points with small barbs (Clark's type 6) appear a little later (8th millennium cal. BC). In Latvia and Estonia, the first type belongs to the classic Kunda tradition, while in Lithuania it is perhaps post-Swiderian (?) and early Western Kunda (?). The second type is attributable to both Kunda traditions.

Also from zone A, we should mention points of Clark's types 17 and 18, linked with the classical Kunda tradition (but also with upper Volga Butovian) from the 9th/8th millennium cal. BC, and points with triangular cross-section (Clark's type 13) which are undated but probably belong to the western Kunda tradition. These points are also known from northeastern Poland. The cultural affinities of the various types of points are confirmed by their occurrence on Kunda culture sites (Kunda-Lammasmägi,

Pulli, Zvejnieki, Veretie I, Oleni Ostrov, etc.), several pollen dates for single finds, and by their geographic position.

The last type characteristic of zone A, or rather mainly of its western part, is the spindle-shaped point with two slots armed with broken bladelets, sometimes even retouched (variant 2 of Clark's type 21). However, its territorial range in the west is markedly different from that of the Western Kunda types 13, 16, and 21_1. This suggests a potential link with the Janislawician or even Komornician, which accords with the cartographic context of a similar specimen discovered in Belarus.

Finally, in zone C, the characteristic, flat double-barbed harpoons with widened base appear, probably by the 8th/7th millennium cal. BC (Murzak-Koban), in addition to the points with a single slot described at the beginning of this section. Similar specimens (but single-barbed), unfortunately undated, are known from the Mesolithic of the Caucasus (Kvachara), the middle Volga, and the southern Ural mountains (Davlekanovo, here with Yangelka-type material). The type apparently originates from the south. The subsequent elements of this phenomenon could be the Mesolithic flat harpoons from the Balkans (e.g. Vlasac, Odmut) and the Alps (e.g. Birsmatten-Basisgrotte, Liesbergmühli, etc.) dated to the 7th millennium cal. BC (cf. "Points, *sagaies*").

9.2. Caspian-Caucasian industries

These related geometric although not very microlithic industries occurred around the Caspian and Black seas, as well as in the Crimea and southern Ukraine up to the lowest course of the Danube, the Caucasus, including Georgia, Uzbekistan, Turkmenia, Iran, northern and southeastern Turkey, and even north Iraq. Unfortunately, sites are few and often poorly dated (but stratified in exchange!) (cf. Shan-Koban culture, also sites of Dam-Dam-Cheshme in Turkmenia, Edzani in Georgia, Chokh in Azerbaijan, Belt and Ali Kosh in Iran, Hallan Çemi in Turkey).

Their origins are dated overall to the 12th/11th (?) millennium cal. BC and they are thought to have developed from local Gravettoid industries. Their disappearance is variously dated depending on the region: 10th (or later) millennium cal. BC in Crimea, c. 7000 cal. BC in northern Iran, middle of the 9th millennium cal. BC in southeastern Turkey. They are divided into a number of branches or local cultures, including the Trialetnian south of the Caucasus (with local variants of Edzani, Chokh and Belt) and the Shan-Koban (Shan-Koba site in Crimea) to the northwest of it, as well as the less well studied and undated local variants occurring on the northern slopes of the Caucasus (e.g. Kholodnyi Grot) and in the Ochakov steppe in the West (Belolesye). They are usually found in caves, although open sites are also known (Edzani in Georgia), not to mention whole villages (Hallan Çemi in Turkey).

A description of the Ukrainian variant (Shan-Koba) of the discussed phenomenon follows.

9.2.1. The Shan-Koban

The unit is attributed to the Caspian-Caucasian industries (cf.) and existed in Crimea and the northern piedmont of the Caucasus (Sosruko), as well as in the Ochakov steppe near the mouth of the Danube (Belolesye), in the 12th/11th millennium cal. BC (and how much later?). Distinguished by Gennadi P. Grigoriev, it was named after a site in Crimea (Ukraine). The more important sites are listed as: Shan-Koba, Buran-Kaia I and II, Siuren II, Zamil-Koba in Crimea and Sosruko (lower level) on the northern slopes of the Caucasus – all cave sites or rock shelters, and finally Belolesye (Fig. 9.2.1a–b).

The flint industry is based on large and short prismatic cores used to produce broad blades/flakes. The tools inventory is dominated by short and very short scrapers on blade, arched-backed blades, and finally large geometric microliths, broad segments, big double backed truncations, big isosceles triangles. It undoubtedly originated from Caucasian and Ukrainian (?) industries of "Gravettian" type, being part of the overall Azilianization (cf.) and geometrization (cf.) processes occurring at the close of the Pleistocene. The evolution clearly leads to point miniaturization and microlithization (upper layers at Siuren II), effectively becoming Murzak-Koban (cf.)

The Zimnikovtsy type industry existing between the Shan-Koban in the south and the Desnian (cf.) zones has massive trapezes of comparable style and similar problems with datation.

9.3. "Model A" Castelnovian cultures in the East

Included here are such eastern European units as:

- Murzak-Koba in Crimea,
- Grebenikian in western Ukraine, Moldova and Romanian Moldavia,
- Janislawician in central and eastern Poland, southern Lithuania, Belarus, and the northern part of Ukraine,
- possibly also the Donetz group in eastern Ukraine (?)

It is not clear whether Kukrek culture belongs here.

All these units have been presented in the chapter devoted to the "Pre-Neolithic/Castelnovian" (cf.). Let it be noted here, however, that the chronology of Murzak-Koba culture, which is based on several radiocarbon dates all coming from a single laboratory and said to reach back to before 7000 years cal. BC, is singularly in doubt. But on the other hand, phase 8 at Frankhthi (Greece) with its industry of Castelnovian style is dated similarly (already published by Cathérine Perlèz).

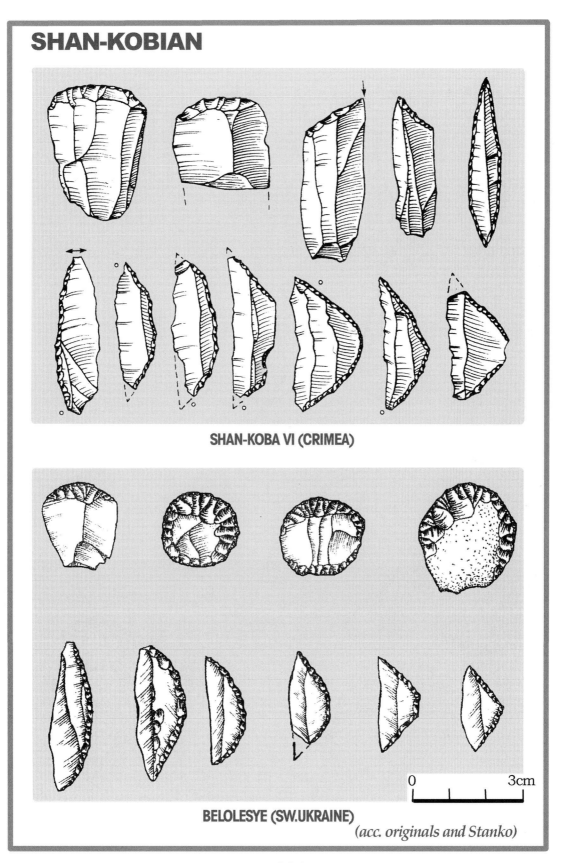

SHAN-KOBIAN

SHAN-KOBA VI (CRIMEA)

BELOLESYE (SW.UKRAINE)

(acc. originals and Stanko)

Fig. 9.2.1a

TRIALETIAN

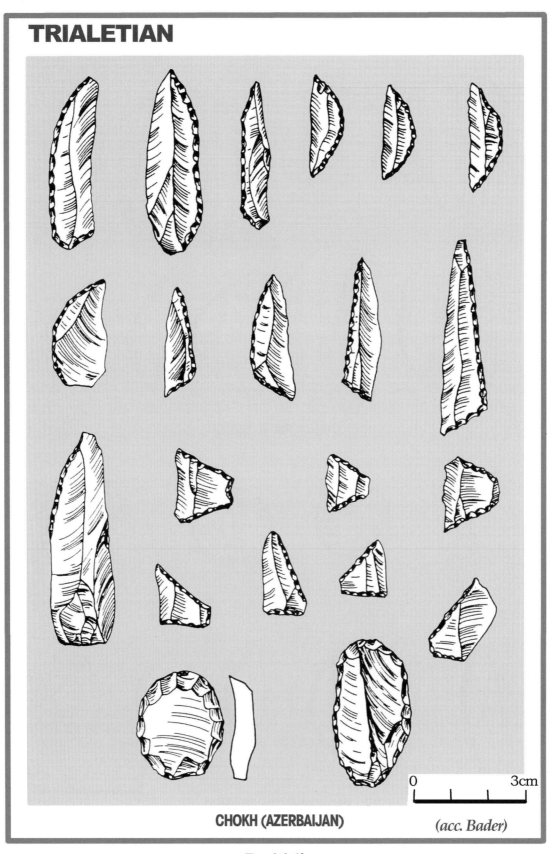

CHOKH (AZERBAIJAN)

(acc. Bader)

0   3cm

Fig. 9.2.1b

10

The North

The North, meaning Scandinavia (with the exception of Scania), was settled later than the southern regions owing to the longer presence of the glacier and a different, cold climate. Man did not appear here before the beginning of the Holocene and when he did, he was obviously mostly descended from the Dryas 3 reindeer hunters coming with and from the tundra in the European Lowland, who had moved gradually northward in the wake of the reindeer. A late phase of the Tanged Points Complex developed there (cf. below), in the west, south and far north, mainly coastal sites and a few up in the mountains in the west – Fosna/Komsa (= Early Mesolithic = Ahrensburgian), Suomusjärvi in the east, but also sporadically Kunda in Karelia and southern Finland. In the far south, around Swedish Göteborg, the "Maglemosian" Sandarna group (cf.) appeared not very much later (cf. recent book by Bernd Nordquist).

The few finds of bone on these sites and the rock art of the Atlantic face of Norway and petroglyphs of Kola Peninsula demonstrate the domination of elk in these times (deer will appear later, reindeer is rare). It should be kept in mind that the glacier was still covering most of the interior of Scandinavia. The connections between the Mesolithic of Finland and central and northern Sweden have not really been identified. This Swedish region has not been studied in any great extent and difficulties are also due to the raw material used here (mostly quartz!). Nevertheless, Stig Welinder has already published one Swedish flake oblique trapeze identical with Finnish specimens.

Generally, the local raw materials (quartz, quartzite, slate etc., with the exception of the far south where good flint is available) have a strong influence on a proper techno-typological picture of the assemblages.

The parallel development of eastern (local Suomusjärvi and exotic Kunda culture from the southeast to Finland and Karelia) and western regions (within the frame of the Tanged Points tradition) broke off about 7000/6900 cal. BC, when a new tradition emerged in the West (microbladelets tradition or Lihult/Nøstvet) cancelling any traces of TPC on the west Swedish and Norwegian coasts, while in the

east Suomusjärvi culture continued to exist, developing according to the pattern described by Heikki Matiskainen. The ceramization of this culture occurred finally in the Sperrings phase.

Around c. 7000 cal. BC the West seems to have experienced the migration of people escaping from the gradually flooded areas (Dogger Bank and Western Baltic land bridges), going in various directions, including to the north. The new culture, Lihult/Nøstvet, which reached along the western coast up to Norland (but also into the mountains of southern Norway), bore many Late Maglemosian features (microbladelets, keel-cores, crescents, scalene triangles, lanceolates, bladelets with retouched base PB, etc.). Further motivation for such migration to the north was the Atlantic optimum, causing the climate to warm up and thus making northern territories more hospitable (dissapearence of the glacier). This migration was paralleled in the east by Kunda penetration into the Finnish Lapland Sujala and the Russian far north (Vis).

10.1. The Scandinavian Tanged Points

The name is connected with characteristic, mostly tanged/pedonculated points (cf.), and the phenomenon is a continuation of the Tanged Points Complex (TPC) of the Late Glacial European Plain in the Holocene. It existed in the northern Baltic countries (Norway, Finland, western, central and northern Sweden, Russian Karelia and Kola Peninsula), in the coniferous forests (northern fringes) and tundra, as well as Norwegian high mountains environments, inhabited mostly by elk and reindeer. Seal appears on the beaches. The region's strongly pronounced zonation is due not only to climatic conditions, but also to morphology (high mountains vs. coastal regions), as well as the gradually disappearing glacier in the inland; this limited the settlement mostly to the coastal zones, the mountains being visited only seasonally during the summer and of course afer deglaciation.

The morphology of local stone industries is strongly influenced by low quality raw material: quartzite and quartz. Some implements were also made of crystalline (different polished axes, e.g. Lihult, Limhamn, *Walzenbeil*) and soft rocks (Olonetz slate).

A large number of sites is known from the region, but most of them have yielded only surface collections; recent rescue excavations have provided good assemblages. The excavated sites come mostly from Finland and Norway, a few are known from central Sweden, Russian Karelia and Finnmark. The first attempts at datation were based on geological observations (position of fossil sea shore), but in the last decades several ^{14}C dates have been published.

The phenomenon is technologically and typologically strictly linked to the Late Pleistocene/very Early Holocene industries of central and eastern Europe (Ahrensburgian, Brommian, Desnenian), especially the presence of pedonculated/tanged points, but also the morphology of end-scrapers and burins, as well as core reduction strategies. These features seem to prove a southern/Lowland migratory origin of the Scandinavian complex (reindeer hunters leaving the European Plain).

The early phase of the phenomenon (from the 10th/9th millennium cal. BC) is characterized by the tanged points industries and unpolished axes. Regional variants: Komsa in the north, Fosna in the west (in fact, one entity!) and very Ahrensburgian and Brommian-like (at least in their earliest stage) and Suomusjärvi in the east. The last unit also has polished adzes, ornamented maceheads and finally daggers/points, all made of different kinds of rock.

Some undated engravings of Norwegian coastal rock art should perhaps be associated with the Mesolithic settlement/people, the same perhaps could be said of the "petroglyphs" of the White Sea. It seems also that the sculpted elk heads (stone, antler, wood, cf. "Art zoomorphique") already known from the East European Mesolithic as well as from a later contexts, could characterize the Scandinavian Tanged Points Mesolithic, which additionally has some geometric ornamentation of stone (macehead) implements.

10.2. The TPC in its younger phase

Communities living in the tundra and its forest taiga border zone were one of the most fascinating cultural phenomena in the prehistoric period under discussion. There are similarities between them not only in the sphere of economy but also, and symptomatically, in the sets of tools they used. These similarities are probably the result of a common cultural tradition, for they manifest themselves not in single forms, but in whole sets; moreover, it is known from elsewhere that the simple functions of the artifacts in question were fulfilled by entirely different tools in other territories and in other times. Thus, the existence of kinship relations between the communities which lived on the fringes of the Northern European tundra should be accepted and they have to be included in one big cultural unit which is called the Tanged Points Technocomplex.

Division, Chronology, Territorial Range (Fig. 10.2a–e)

The Tanged Points (cf.) Technocomplex includes cultures divided into two groups:

1 Lowland Culture Group (Brommian, Ahrensburgian and Swiderian);
2 Scandinavian Culture Group (Fosna/Komsa, Suomusjärvi and Desnenian).

The beginnings of the phenomenon go back as far as the 12th millennium cal. BC and are connected with central and part of eastern Europe, where the entities of the Lowland Culture Group existed until the end of the 10th millennium cal. BC. The second stage of TPC is represented by the Scandinavian Culture Group from the 10th/9th millennium cal. BC.

The TPC displays substantial morpho- and technological homogeneity, which defines what we call the TPC standard as follows:

i   diverse tanged points (cf.), among others, Bromme, Ahrensburgian, Swiderian points and Desnian flake, oblique trapezes,
ii end-scrapers on blades and flakes (very short, sometimes even circular, short, long), and
iii blade and flake burins (dihedral and on truncation).

These implements are usually medium-sized, on average smaller than the Upper Paleolithic finds which they resemble stylistically, and markedly larger than their Holocene non-tanged counterparts in the Lowland. Their dimensions could reflect adaptation to the generally inferior quality of the raw material found on the Lowland, material which was sometimes mined and occasionally distributed over large distances.

The blanks, in addition to blades, include in this period a clearly larger proportion of flakes.

The standard also comprises:

iv diverse harpoons, (mostly of Havel 12A and 12B types, cf. "Pointes…"), and
v   Lyngby-type "axes" (of reindeer antler).

The Scandinavian Culture Group is not as well known as the Lowland one yet; moreover, the stone raw material such as the often used quartz and quartzite, both difficult to process and giving less typical forms, must have influenced considerably the shape of tools (especially in central and northern Sweden). For this reason, the remarks below, especially with regard to burins and end-scrapers, should be treated as working hypotheses. The above mentioned two typological groups seem to manifest certain connections with elements of the Lowland Culture Group: for the Fosna/Komsa culture, these are the elongated end-scrapers, and for the whole Scandinavian Culture Group the very short, subcircular and circular end-scrapers. Some burins of the Fosna/Komsa and Desna (cf.) cultures also manifest connections with Lowland ones. Kinship between cultures of the Scandinavian Group is confirmed by such common elements as the discoidal core technique and presence of

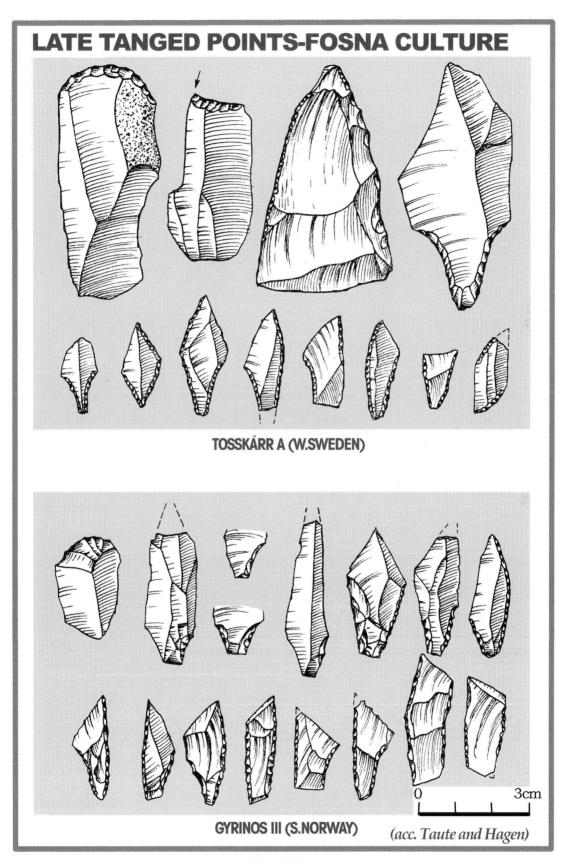

Fig. 10.2a

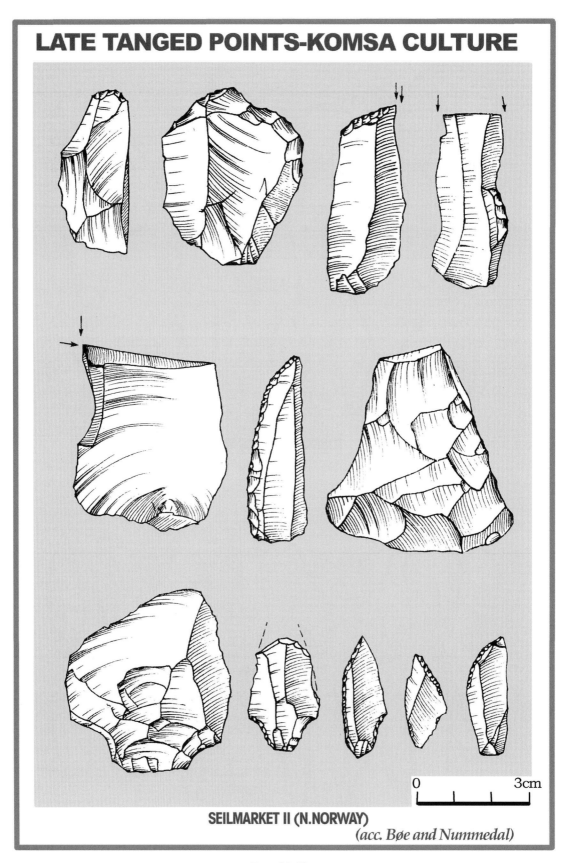

Fig. 10.2b

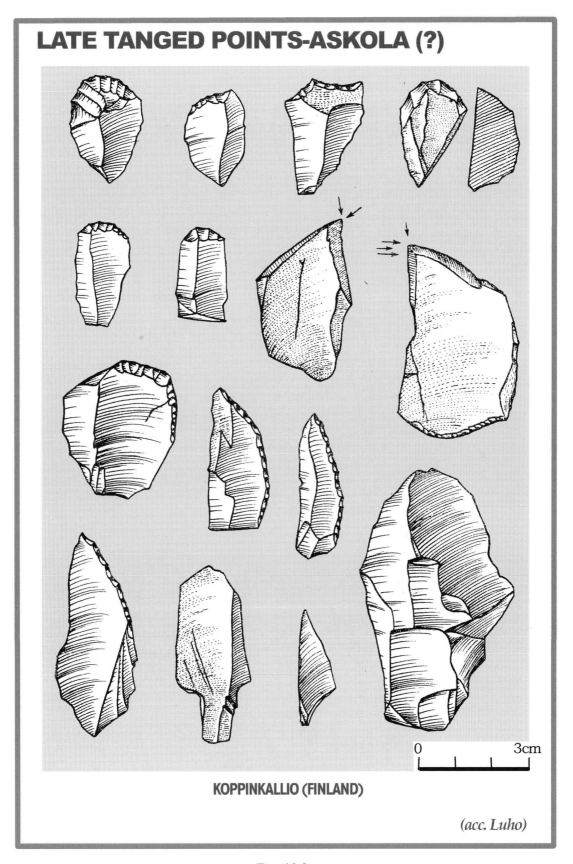

LATE TANGED POINTS-ASKOLA (?)

KOPPINKALLIO (FINLAND)

0 3cm

(acc. Luho)

Fig. 10.2c

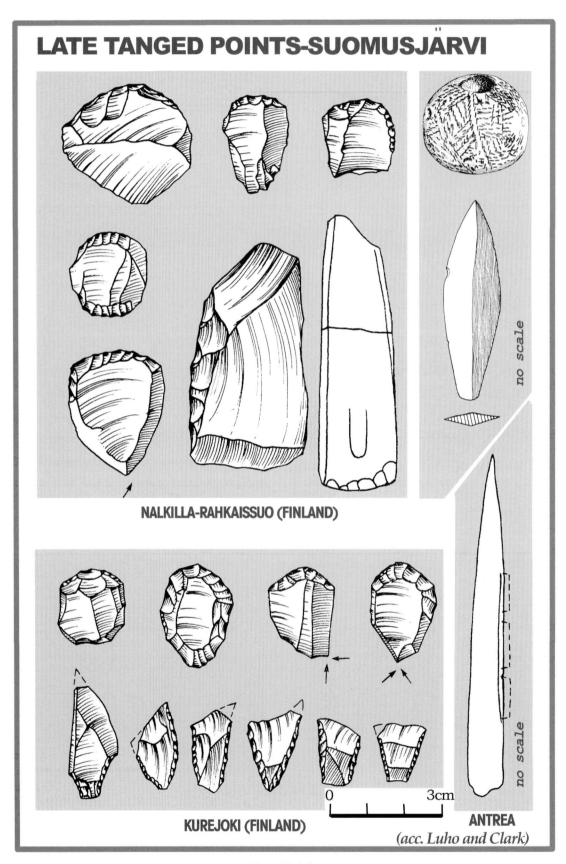

Fig. 10.2d

LATE TANGED POINTS

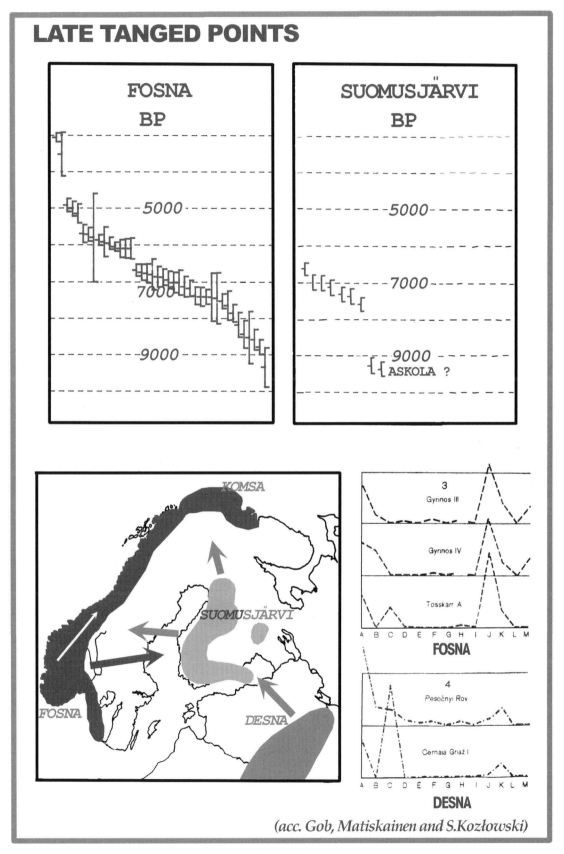

(acc. Gob, Matiskainen and S.Kozłowski)

Fig. 10.2e

unpolished axes, and finally, the oblique, mostly flake trapezes of Desnian type (Fig. 10.3b).

Differences

The common elements are represented in different proportions in particular cultures/entities. For instance, long end-scrapers and long burins are most numerous in the Late Pleistocene Brommian; the same concerns Lyngby tanged points, which are ever present in the other cultures but are less numerous there. On the other hand, very short end-scrapers are characteristic of especially the Ahrensburgian, Swiderian and Desnian located south of the Brommian. Moreover, long burins occur in quite large numbers in the three mentioned cultures.

Fosna Culture

Name from an island in Norway, also sometimes known as the Hensbacka Culture. It existed in western Norway until the end of the 8th millennium cal. BC (or shorter?), when it was replaced by the microbladelet phenomenon (or local Post-Maglemosian).

Stone Industry. Apart from the above described common TPC properties, it has original structure (high index of microliths K, high or medium of end-scrapers A, low of side-scrapers B, axes H and tanged points J). It also has, among others, microtruncations K, rhombs, tanged points with semi-abrupt retouch on the ventral surface, as well as Ahrensburgian points and Desna flake oblique trapezes.

Fosna is the sum of Ahrensburg-Bromme and "Desna" elements (= trapezes). The presence of the first two elements in this part of Scandinavia can be explained well enough by the supposed northward migration of the East Ahrensburgians and Brommians. The Desna element (cf. "Desna Culture") would have had to move from eastern Europe to Finland and then via the Aaland Islands (from Suomusjärvi Culture) to West Scandinavia (?) but the trapezes could have also developed from Ahrensburgian tanged points. In its territorial development, Fosna Culture spread very early towards the North, the result of which is the Norwegian Komsa Culture, in fact identical with Fosna.

Style IV of Norwegian rock paintings could possibly go with Fosna culture.

Komsa Culture

Name from Komsa mountain in Norway, also known as the Finnmarkian. It existed in northwestern and northern Scandinavia parallel and in connection with Fosna.

Stone Industry. Apart from the common elements of the TPC, it also has a few lanceolate points, rhombs and polished axes-chisels among other things.

A techno-typological uniformity between Fosna and Komsa cultures, now even physically connected along the Atlantic coast of Norway, has recently been accepted

Suomusjärvi Culture

Name from lake Suomusjärvi in Finland. It existed in eastern Scandinavia and the Kola Peninsula (Rybachyi Polostrov) from the end of the 9th millennium cal. BC. The so-called Askola Culture of V. Lucho is considered as belonging to the Suomusjärvian.

Stone Industry. Apart from the common TPC and Scandinavian Group elements, it also comprises, among others, lanceolate points, polished daggers of slate, decorated stone maceheads and polished axes/adzes; they dominate in different phases of the culture's existence, which started from what was once called the Askola culture.

History. Suomusjärvi could be a younger reflection of the earlier inland Desna Culture (cf.) (tanged and shouldered points, long and very short end-scrapers, oblique flake trapezes, lanceolate points). Thus, it is possible that in their migration after game Desnian reindeer hunters reached Finland at the beginning of the Holocene and even influenced the formation of the Fosna/Komsa phenomenon (flake oblique trapezes).

The enormous territorial gap existing between the Desnian and Suomusjärvi territories in the north (cf. "Desna culture") remains a major issue to resolve.

10.3. Desna culture

1. This East European cultural unit (Fig. 10.3a–c) was described by the author and Janusz K. Kozłowski when its Final Paleolithic chronology was proposed and it was recognized as part of the Tanged Points Complex (TPC). Earlier studies (Vladimir Bud'ko – Grensk culture) and later (Leonid Zalizniak – Pesochnyi Rov and Krasnosilsk cultures; Lev Koltsov, Mikhail Zhilin – Yenevo culture) had positioned it either in the Final Paleolithic (Bud'ko, Zalizniak for Krasnosilsk) or the very Early Mesolithic. The matter was later summed up by the author in a separate article, which included the first comprehensive map of this new territorial unit. In view of new material being available today, it is worthwhile to recapitulate the matter.

The Desnian fits the TPC standard perfectly; in other words, characterizing its assemblages is a fairly regular joint occurrence of medium-sized tools (3–5 cm), such as big and medium Lyngby points, short and very short end-scrapers and dihedral burins, as well as burins on truncation.

The Desnian is distinct from related TPC units (Swiderian, Ahrensburgian, Brommian) in that it regularly yields shouldered (less frequent) points and oblique trapezes on flakes, which brings it very close to the Scandinavian variant of TPC of the Early Holocene (Suomusjärvi, Fosna/Komsa).

2. To the author's best knowledge, the map represents the east European territorial extent of the said points and trapezes, demonstrating their indeed supraregional character. It further shows that they are characteristic of regions in the eastern part of central and eastern Europe and that they partly overlap with Swiderian territory.

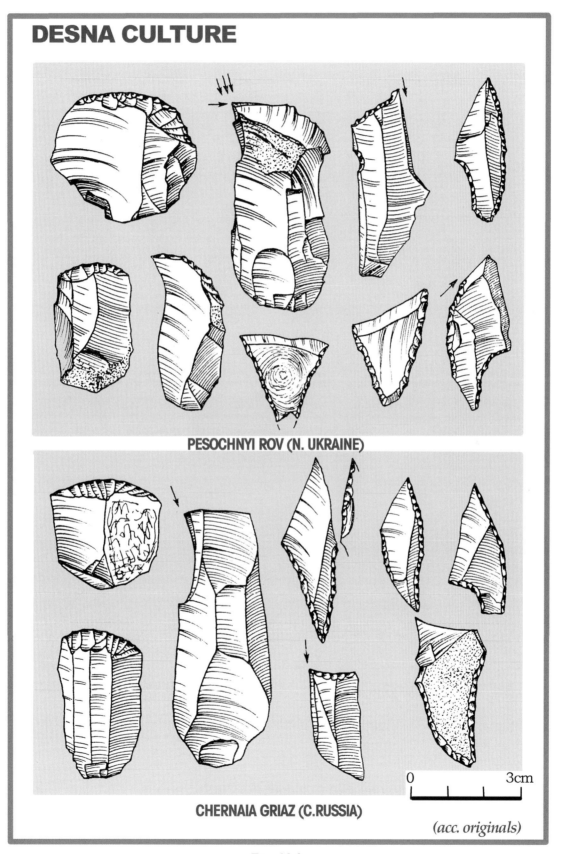

DESNA CULTURE

PESOCHNYI ROV (N. UKRAINE)

CHERNAIA GRIAZ (C.RUSSIA)

0   3cm

(acc. originals)

Fig. 10.3a

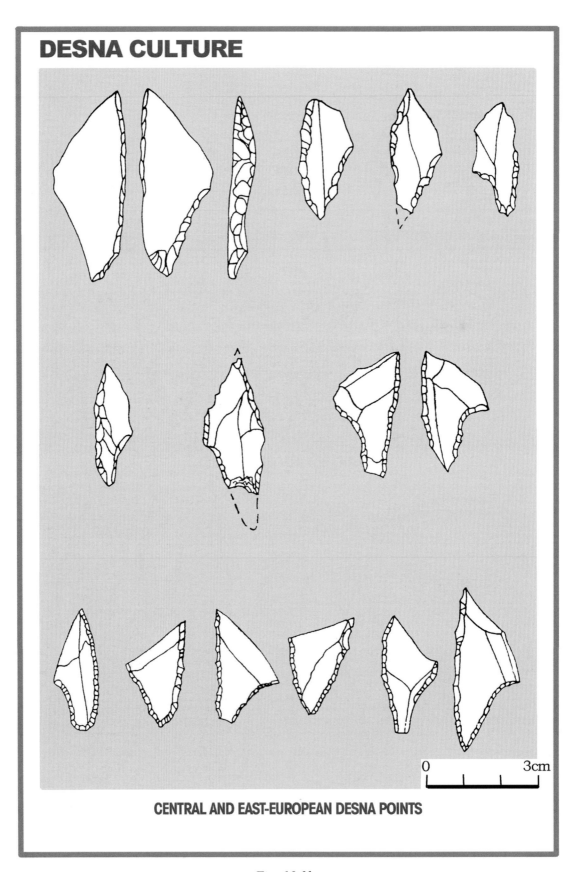

Fig. 10.3b

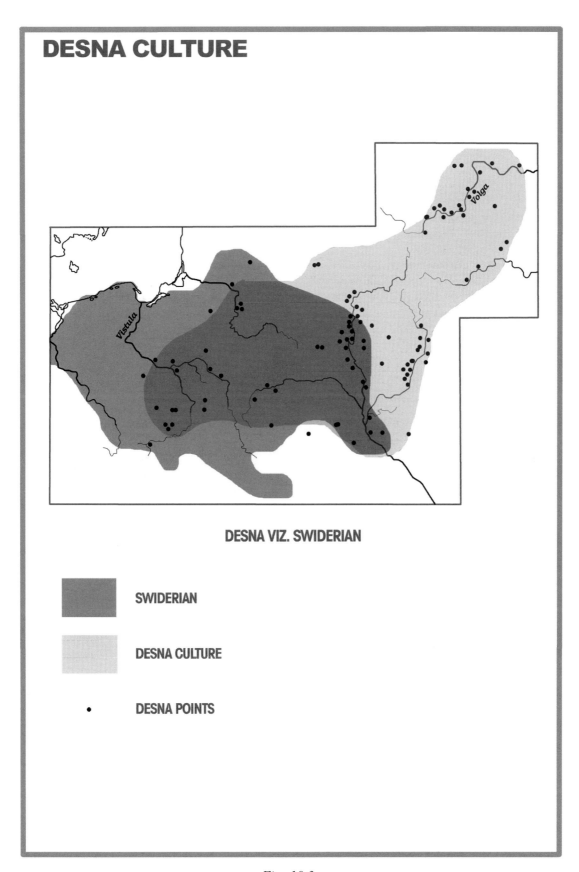

Fig. 10.3c

3. Desnian chronology has been the issue of debate with Eastern European colleagues opting rather for the Early Holocene (10th–early 9th millennium cal. BC, similar ^{14}C dates published for central Poland by Romuald Schild), contrary to the earlier opinion of the present author, who like Bud'ko before him, now prefers the Late Glacial and more specifically Dryas 3 (stratigraphical context of the assemblage from Witów-concentration II and typological ones from the same Witów, Jacentów and Stańkowicze III, all sites in Poland). As far as the typological context is concerned, the author is referring to Late Paleolithic arched points being present in Witów and Jacentów, and Swiderian tanged points in Stańkowicze, always together with Desnian elements.

Perhaps there is actually no controversy and the Desnian simply covers both mentioned periods, similarly as the related Swiderian (the ^{14}C datings from Believo 4A are generally of the 10th/9th millennium cal. BC; they go together with several pollen datings).

4. Initially, there could have existed a territorial connection between the Desnian territory and the earliest cultures of Scandinavia (?), which resembled it closely (especially the nearest territorially Suomusjärvi culture); then Desnian elements should be expected in northern Belarus, Latvia, Estonia, and even northwestern Russia. Unfortunately, these regions have hitherto yielded virtually no Final Paleolithic/Early Mesolithic assemblages (except for the Swiderian site of Salaspils Laukskola in Latvia), although a few harpoons of other than Swiderian type have been found (Havel type 12A$_3$ cf. "Points") there. Final Paleolithic sites situated in the Vistulian/Würmian glaciation zone, especially on the base moraine clays, are especially difficult to detect.

5. Climatic changes at the turn of the 11th and the 10th millennia cal. BC replaced the tundra in the European Lowland with forest formations. One consequence of this was the northward migration of fauna dominated by the reindeer and its replacement by forest fauna. Some of the animals belonging to the latter, such as the elk, were already to be found in this area earlier. Faunal migrations were a gradual process, and the reindeer could have still been known (?) in northern Poland or Lithuania at the very beginning of the Holocene (H. Gross' theory). It retreated northwards, via the East Baltic countries, through Denmark and southern Sweden, the northern-European shelf and the future English Channel.

Climatic change resulted in altered biotopes and corresponding changes of adaptive models, as well as a gradual opening up of northern Europe to human settlement. Two scenarios are possible for further development and both seem to have taken place:

a. The reindeer-dependant populations with tanged points abandoned their native territories and followed the animal into new ecumenes, preserving their way of life and range of implements;

b. People adapted on the spot to new conditions and existing adaptive models disintegrated.

Regarding the first scenario, it is very probable that part of the Brommians and Ahrensburgians and perhaps also part of the Desnenians migrated in the direction of Scandinavia where they continued their respective traditions in the west (Fosna/Komsa) and east (Suomusjärvi). The north European industries are generally younger than their close equivalents in central and eastern Europe.

As regards the other scenario, it involves local adaptation to new conditions on the northern fringes of the Ahrensburgian, Swiderian and Desnian zone (i.e., with a shift in a generally northern direction and "outside", towards the Epi/Post-Ahrensburgian industries of the Zonhoven/Bare Mosse/Pinnberg/Star Carr/Duvensee/Haltern type or the hypothetical post-Swiderian industries in Polesye and Lithuania, as well as the post-Desnian (?) industries from the upper-Dnieper region).

This scenario leads to a rapid disintegration of the existing systems (e.g. raw material procurement) and the emergence of entirely new formations which are already typically Mesolithic.

The Epi (Post)-Ahrensburgian industries (cf.) did away with tanged points (although single specimens were still found in Star Carr and Thatcham) and they attached increasing importance to geometrical microliths, which in fact were known earlier in the West Ahrensburgian tradition. In the east, the Swiderian tradition gradually vanished by the end of the 10th millennium cal. BC from Poland (the latest datings from Całowanie VI B are for 9000 cal. BC), apparently without leaving any local continuation, perhaps evolving in Lithuania and Belarus (as suggested by Karol Szymczak) into as yet poorly researched hybrids which departed from the previous cultural standard; however (e.g. Kudlaevka?, cf.), they retained severely modified tanged points for quite some time yet.

It may be that the phenomenon of Holocene industries with tanged points characterizing the Mesolithic of Eastern Europe (Butovian, Kunda, cf. "East") generally east of the lower Vistula, Neman, Dvina/Daugava and Dnieper rivers is somehow connected with the described process (?). Russian researchers have sometimes referred to this Mesolithic as "Post-Swiderian" (not to be confused with the strictly chronological term used above, in this case it means the supposed origins), assuming that the tanged points known from these industries originated from the Swiderian tradition.

10.4. Sandarna

A local Mesolithic culture of western Sweden, closely related to the Maglemosian (cf. "West and Center") and originating from Federmesser?, occupying in the Early and Middle Mesolithic the coastal zone on the eastern shore of the Danish straits. The name comes from a site near Göteborg, Sweden. It is characterized by short and very short end-scrapers, unpolished axes, borers and burins, but especially specific shouldered points; microliths include lanceolates with totally or partly retouched back (DB, DC) and fine microtruncations, but not triangles (Dogger Bank's possible Federmesser connections, Fig. 10.4).

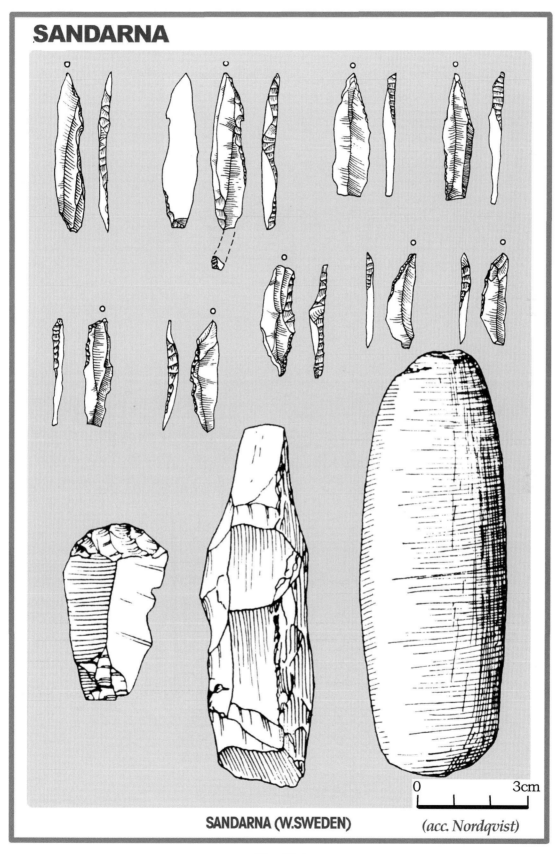

SANDARNA

SANDARNA (W.SWEDEN) *(acc. Nordqvist)*

0 — 3cm

Fig. 10.4

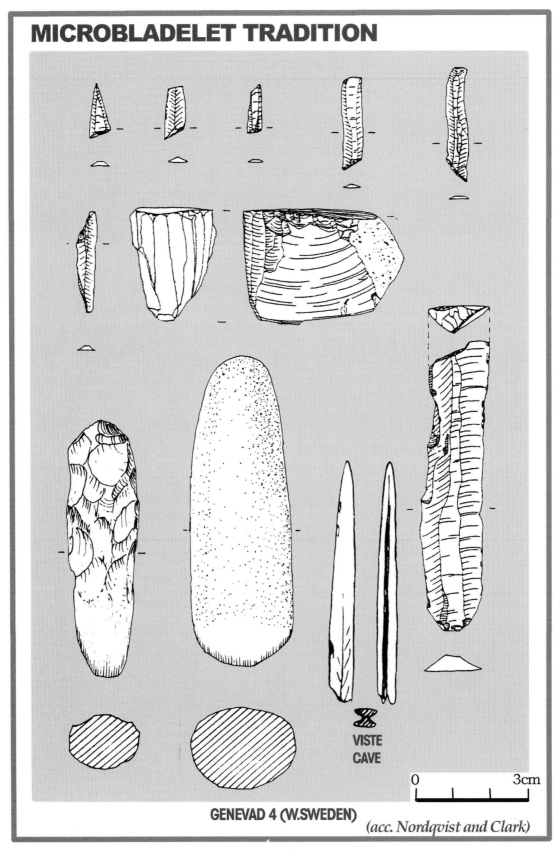

Fig. 10.5

10.5. Microbladelets (Lihult in Sweden, Nøstvet in Norway)

Late Mesolithic (from c. 7000 cal. BC) culture of southern and western Norway and western Sweden, mainly coastal (although mountain sites are known as well), showing clear Late Maglemosian links (cf. "West and Center") (keeled cores, microbladelets, PB and PC – cf. "Les pointes PB et PC") microliths, DB backed points and other narrow microliths, etc. and based on new (flint) raw material. Moreover, polished axes of Nøstvet type, as well as unpolished flint specimens (but no trapezes), making it possible to date this alleged effect of Post-Maglemosian northward migration (escape from flooded areas in northwestern Europe) around c. 7000 cal. BC. H. B. Bjerck has suggested a pre-Nøstvet, local Maglemosian settlement in the region.

11

Castelnovian/Pre-Neolithic

In Europe, the end of the 8th and the beginning of the 7th millennium cal. BC witnessed a rapid and almost momentous change occurring across the continent from the Atlantic to the Black Sea. Considerable techno-typological uniformization took place with the emergence of what the author believes were the Pre-Neolithic industries of the Castelnovian complex/style. The Late Mesolithic had begun.

Researchers still find it difficult to ascertain the mechanisms of this phenomenon, elements of which can be discerned also outside Europe (North Africa, Mesopotamia, Central Asia with their trapezes), but it can be described. We do know that this was the Big Bang that brought about the ceramization (cf.) and later neolithization of the Continent.

The Castelnovian phenomenon can be divided into the western, "more Castelnovian" variant and the eastern "less Castelnovian", the border between the two running across the Balkans (Croatia serving as a border between Slovenian and Montenegro sites).

11.1. The Pre-Neolithic (Castelnovian) base of the Early Neolithic Stone Industries in Europe

Introduction

The aim of the present paper is to describe an important cultural process transpiring between the 8th and 5th millennium cal. BC in most of Europe (and North Africa). The process is characterized by the introduction of a number of technological and stylistic innovations in the Mesolithic chipped industries of those areas. It is my conviction that the innovations described here had far-reaching consequences as they were the key to the deep adaptive transformations awaiting the communities on the continent. These technological and typological transformations shall be referred to as "pre-neolithization", since it was precisely this event that preceded and brought on the actual, although usually local neolithization of Europe, especially with regard to the lithic industries, and in some parts of

the Continent the social organization and even economy (the classical process of neolithization derived genetically from it).

In terms of the hitherto existing taxonomy of stone industries, the "Pre-Neolithic" is chronologically equivalent to some extent with the "Late Mesolithic" (Fig. 11.1a–d).

Technology and typology of pre-neolithization/ castelnovization

From the point of view of lithic technology "pre-neolith-ization" is characterized by the appearance and extensive spread of big, mostly single-platform cores of locally differing shapes, used to manufacture regular blades and bladelets by means of either pressure or punch technique. The cores were usually carefully prepared (back and sides, occasional heating) and so were the platforms which could also be rejuvenated. According to Jacques Pellegrin, at least in the West the cores were exploited by means of the pressure technique. The shape of these specimens was locally differentiated, e.g. pencil-like cores with circumferential flaking face (in their final stage) predominated on the Black Sea and Pontic steppe (cf. "East"), whereas more to the west conical and subconical cores being the final stages of keeled specimens were in ascendancy (classical Castelnovian, Montbanian, but also more eastern Janislawician, the Thessalian Late Mesolithic and preceramic Neolithic etc.). As said already, core processing produced in this case very regular, slender parallel-edged blades and more numerous bladelets. These bladelets served further to obtain retouched tools or were used as *in posteriori* tools, i.e., the blade was transversally broken (cf. inserts) so that it could be used as a knife or knive/sickle insert, for example. Another technique typical of pre-neolithization is the microburin technique, but it is not represented everywhere (absent from some industries in the East and the Balkans, e.g. Odmut and Grebeniki).

The new type of industry demanded large-size raw material which was not always locally available. This prompted long-distance imports of material (obsidian from

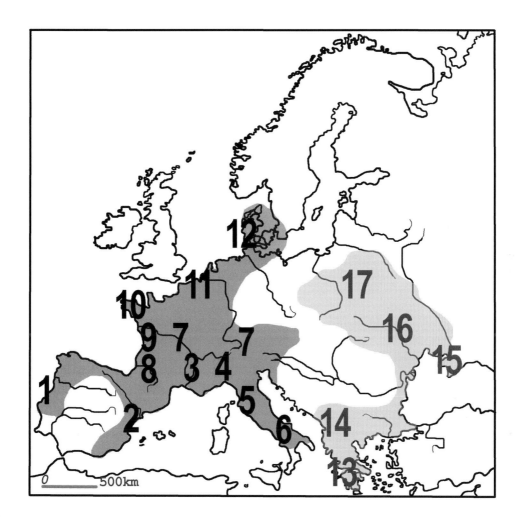

Fig. 11.1a

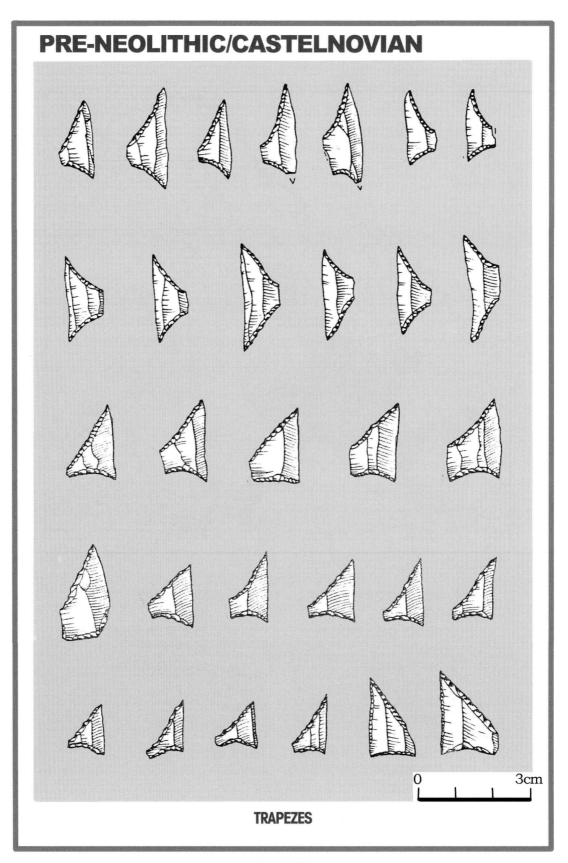

Fig. 11.1b

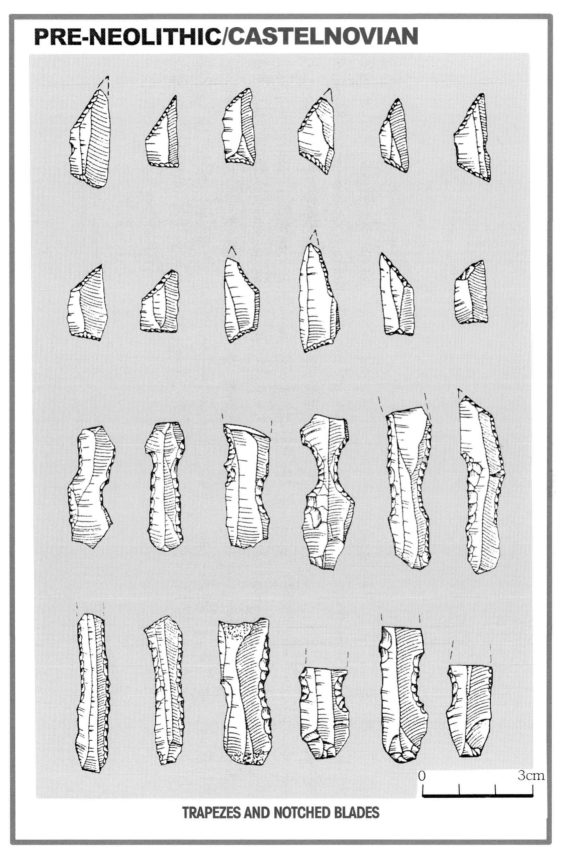

Fig. 11.1c

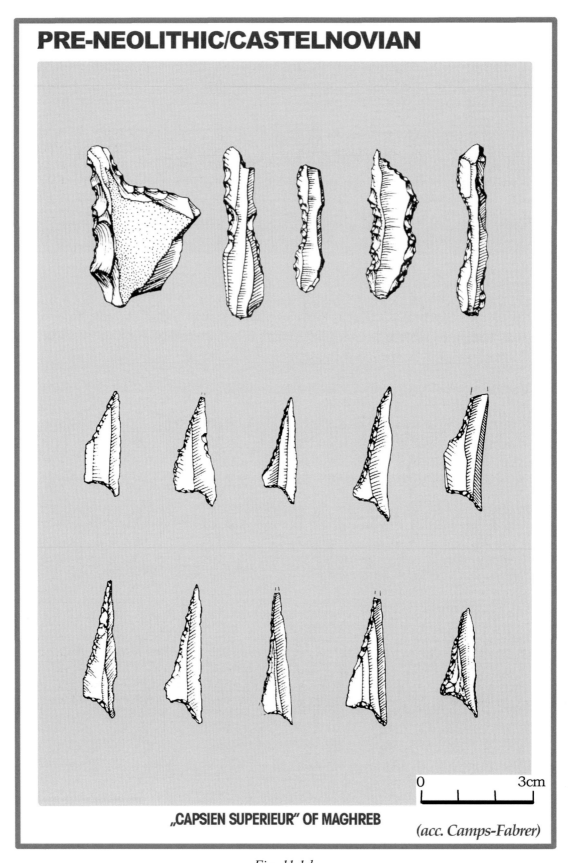

Fig. 11.1d

Melos found in Frankhti, quartzite from Wommerssom in North Montbanian and RMS, "chocolate" flint in Janislawician, Balkan "honey" flint in industries of the Southeast) and even mining exploitation of sources (e.g. Tomaszów in Poland and the pre-Alpine moraine outcrops in southern Germany, information from Wolfgang Taute).

The group of retouched tools included:

1) symmetrical (A) and/or asymmetrical (B) trapezes and rhomboids present in abundance and territorially differentiated (cf. maps in the "Atlas");

2) elongated retouched truncations on blades/bladelets – not in all industries, occasionally double (later functioned as sickle inserts);

3) elongated arched end-scrapers on blades, locally differentiated, accompanied regionally by short and very short/circular specimens;

4) retouched bladelets falling into two groups: denticulated and notched implements (= *Montbani bladelets*, according to Jean-Georges Rozoy), the second group containing specimens with discontinuous, mostly use retouch;

5) some of the Pre-Neolithic cultures are associated with flat harpoons with one or two rows of barbs. They are found in some Pre-Neolithic industries in the Alpine regions (pre-Alpine South Montbani, Gaban "Neolithic", Udinese Castelnovian) and the Carpathian Basin, in the Dynaric Alps (Odmut), Crimea (Murzak-Koba) and Slovenia (Spehorka), but are absent from other territories.

The map presents in detail the pre-neolithization process in various industries distributed over Europe and North Africa from the 8th to the 5th millennium cal. BC. As we can see, the listed set of attributes is repeated over a big part of the Continent. Although there is a general similarity between the "Pre-Neolithic" assemblages, they differ in the details. Consequently, various combinations of locally variable sets of attributes are obtained, all the result of the impact of one and the same event upon differing "recipients", backgrounds and cultural traditions. If we take into account the fact that the process of "pre-neolithization" is chronologically logical and probably coherent (cf. below), then it is highly plausible to hold that these similarities were not accidental. In other words, they reflect a process which, for reasons unknown, had spread consistently over large areas of Europe and which demonstrates some correspondence with the Early Neolithic of the same areas.

Local and regional differentiation of Pre-Neolithic phenomenon, apparent from the mapping of trapezes, for instance (cf. "Atlas"), appears to be due to the influence of ideas coming from outside ("givers") on a specific local community ("takers") characterized by own traditions, know-how and customs. The outcome is individual, meaning the emergence of regional and local reactions in the form of different cultures of the Castelnovian complex/ style, from which a local evolution then proceeded.

Chronology

Pre-Neolithization with its characteristic typological and technological features occurred probably asynchronously in the areas under discussion. The earliest records of it are outside Europe, in the Maghreb, which yielded a number of C^{14} datations from the 8th and even 9th millennium cal. BC (*Capsien superieur*). On the Black Sea shore (Murzak-Koba culture), elements of pre-neolithization could also emerge equally early (?). The stratigraphic data (caves in Crimea) and C^{14} determinations appear to date the phenomenon in this area to as early as the 8th millennium cal. BC (?). The same could be said of Frankhthi, where the first trapezes (phase 8) appeared in the second half of the 8th millennium cal. BC. But in central, western and most of southern Europe (but not southeastern), Pre-Neolithic industries did not develop before the beginning of the 7th millennium cal. BC (in the south) or later, that is, c. 6500 cal. BC (in the north) (cf. numerous C^{14} dates for the West and Italy, reaching up into Belgium, Poland and southern Scandinavia in André Gob's catalogue). The evidence of radiocarbon dates confirms that Pre-Neolithic components spread fairly quickly throughout Europe.

The emerging picture is of a three-stage development of the phenomenon:

1) stage I, dated to the second half of the 8th millennium cal. BC (Greece, perhaps Crimea?);

2) stage II–III, starting from the beginning of the 7th millennium cal. BC and covering most of Europe, earlier in the south (II, from c. 7000 cal. BC) and later in the north (III, from c. 6500 cal. BC). This stage is the object of our special attention.

Territory

The presented map gives a schematic idea of the extent of the pre-neolithization phenomenon, the mapping also presents the territorial range of the event, which in Europe did not actually spread to the forest zone of the Russian Plain. Most of the Scandinavian Peninsula and Great Britain (because of the Channel!) also remained outside of its range.

Complications begin on the border between eastern and western Europe, where the classical *Castelnoviano Italiano* with microburins reaches no further than Slovenia and Istria; central Croatia knows no Castelnovian, which then appears in the form of the (Para)-Castelnovian Odmutian (without microburins) in Montenegro, Albania and Thessaly. The connection between the two territories went either along the Dalmatian coast or not at all. And if so, then what?

Most likely we are deling here with two parallel, similar but independent phenomena: "Castelnovian" for the west and "Para-Castelnovian" for the east.

Assimilation of Pre-Neolithic elements

If the thesis on the southern or Mediterranean origins and

northward spread of Pre-Neolithic/Castelnovian elements is accepted, their assimilation by local European Mesolithic cultures needs to be looked into. Investigations of the European industries of that period show that none of the Mesolithic central and western European communities was able to withstand the pressure of pre-neolithization once a given community found itself within its influence. But the reaction was varied. It should be borne in mind that in respect of technology and typology pre-neolithization created an apparent and incomplete techno-typological uniformity of European Mesolithic cultures. Firstly, local differentiation of assimilation can be observed, manifested by the emergence of two different models of industry: Mediterranean (model A) and Lowland (model B). In the northern Mediterranean and Atlantic littoral, as far as the Paris Basin and up to Belgium and southern Germany, lithic inventories underwent more or less rapid and complete transformation in the 7th millennium cal. BC. The same happened in the Balkans and Pontic steppes. The newly formed industries contained almost no finds typical of the earliest stage of the local Mesolithic, whereas finds with sets of attributes typical of Pre-Neolithic/Castelnovian industries occur in large quantities. The Mediterranean model (= A) is represented by, among others, the classical French and Italian Castelnovian, Montbanian (both South and North), as much as Odmutian, Cuzoulian and Teviecian, and finally, Frankhti group in Greece. A different (=B) model is represented by the Late Mesolithic cultures in northern Europe (Post-Maglemosian, Lower Rhine/RMS/Rhenanian, Boberg, Beuronian, Komornician, etc.) where Pre-Neolithic components (mostly trapezes, accompanied by the 'old' microliths; more likely "influence" rather than "change" or "adaptation") were present but did not dominate in inventories of the 7th millennium cal. BC and did not eliminate locally characteristic types. Full technological and typological pre-neolithization of the North European Lowland units did not take place before the 6/5th millennium cal. BC. Beside the general and regional zonal variations in the reaction of the Mesolithic environment to pre-neolithization reflected in the models distinguished above (A – full and rather rapid pre-neolithization, B – selective and slow process), differences occur within the framework of each model. They are of secondary importance pertaining to measurable attributes, morphology and technology of trapezes/rhombs, blades/bladelets or retouched blades and retouched truncations. These nuanced variations on a regional scale are best accounted for by the different traditions of "recipient" cultures, each assimilating Pre-Neolithic components in a specific way. The sources of these differences can also be sought in the original differentiation of the Pre-Neolithic event into Post-Sauveterrian (west) and Post-Epigravettian (east) variants. However, analyses based on the latter assumption would be premature.

In a few cases (Pradestel in Italy, information from Paolo Biagi; Montclus in France; Scania and Poland), model B appears immediately and only locally before model A.

Some aspects of social organization of Pre-Neolithic communities

Discussed here are some of the social and economic aspects of communities with Pre-Neolithic/Castelnovian industries. First of all, in areas of distribution of assemblages with Pre-Neolithic components, independent cemeteries or graves inside settlements appeared, bearing witness to settlement stability (Moita do Sebastiao, Téviec, Hoëdic, Arruda, Amoreira, Vasilyevka, Skateholm, etc.).

These Pre-Neolithic groups also organized a highly developed raw material supply system operating from remote deposits in order to procure high-grade lithic raw material (cf.) required by the new technology. The problem of ownership of deposits must have arisen at about this time. The Janislawicians (cf.) in Poland are a classic example, having mined "chocolate" flint and transported it over c. 300 km. Another good example id provided by Frankhti where obsidian was imported from the island of Melos some 130 km away. Other communities of the Pre-Neolithic complex, e.g. the Castelnovian in Italy, also organized raw material supply from distant deposits to ensure the availability of high-quality raw material. Rhenanian/RMS and North Montbanian constitute another example, using as they did imported quartzite from Wommersom. The emergent picture, especially in the Mediterranean model (= A), is that of a wealthy community, stable and sedentary or semi-sedentary, living in a rich forest environment with plentiful food. In view of this, it is not surprising that attempts at local ceramization (cf.) and later neolithization could be anything but successful after some time. These processes were facilitated both by the environment and by the degree of man's control over it. It is not without reason that Mesolithic ceramics appeared in a number of different places in Europe as further proof of considerable stabilization and sedentarization.

The typological features of the period, especially in the Mediterranean model, do not seem to depart conspicuously from the classical culture of the Neolithic as an economic model. Close similarities can be seen with regard to the lithic industries (cf. "Ceramization"), social organization, settlement pattern and the system of raw material supply, whereas subsistence patterns differed.

Early industries of Southern Europe – Latest Mesolithic/Early ceramic/Neolithic

There is considerable evidence to show that as far as typology and technology are concerned the main bulk of early industries of the south European Neolithic/ceramic Mesolithic are for the most part a continuation of the evolution of the local Pre-Neolithic. Let us look at some examples in support of this thesis.

In eastern Europe, notably in the Black Sea region, two early ceramic cultures are distinguished: Bug-Dniester and Kamennaya Mogila (?). They have pre-ceramic phases (7th millennium cal. BC), respectively Grebeniki and Kukrek. Subsequently, these two cultures developed a ceramic phase. Both Kamennaya Mogila (?) and Bug-Dniester are derived from the local Pre-Neolithic.

The alleged pre-ceramic Neolithic in Greece (7th millennium cal. BC: Argissa Magula, Frankhthi) displays features that are common with the Pre-Neolithic. In former Yugoslavia, the local typically pre-Neolithic cultures (Odmut, 7th millennium cal. BC) could have their continuation in local early ceramic cultures with impressed and Starčevo wares (Odmut, upper layers, Mehtelek).

In northern Italy, in turn, the industries of early ceramic cultures show features in common with the local Castelnovian (6th millennium cal. BC; Gaban, Vho, impresso, etc.). The situation seems slightly different in France where the Pre-Neolithic cultures (Castelnovian, Cuzoulian, south Montbanian) are followed by Neolithic assemblages with cardial ware and local Post-Castelnovian industries, mostly tied in with the latest Mesolithic. In the Spanish Levant, similar developments have been recorded (Cocina and Botiqueria sequences). Both Spanish and French local early ceramic/Neolithic groups are characterized, as a rule, by flint industries derived from the Pre-Neolithic but slightly changed.

To sum up, this first stage of the evolution of early ceramic, sometimes Neolithic industries, dated from the beginning of the 7/6th millennium cal. BC and later, is a direct or indirect continuation of local Pre-Neolithic industries. These processes are frequently associated with ceramics and occasionally with incipient elements of a food-producing economy.

As far as the lithic industries are concerned, changes affected the size of blades which grew bigger (= "second standard", e.g. Starčevo/Körös in the Balkans), while the tool kit became impoverished mainly because of the disappearance of arrowheads.

Stages of pre-Neolithization (typology and technology) and Neolithization (economy)

The above considerations have led to the following conclusions.

I) The Pre-Neolithic/Castelnovian/Para-Castelnovian components in lithic industries, later typical of most early ceramic and/or Neolithic industries in Europe are first recorded in three regions (8th millennium cal. BC): North Africa (Upper Capsian), Peloponnese and perhaps the Black Sea (Murzak-Koban?).

2) Around the beginning of the 7th millennium cal. BC, Pre-Neolithic elements occupied the northern fringes of the Mediterranean and spread quickly north and northwest (via two different routes) to cover half of the European continent by the middle of the 7th millennium cal. BC. The phenomenon can actually be divided into the western and eastern with the great void of central Croatia in the middle. It cannot be excluded that climatic changes at that time and possibly demographic pressure may have caused the migrations (?).

3) Local Mesolithic cultures responded variously to the influence or pressure from outside. Generally, assimilation of the phenomenon occurred, although in individual ways. On the northern Mediterranean littoral, the new patterns were assimilated almost completely (model A), whereas in the Lowland industries at the same time (7th millennium BC) assimilation was selective (model B). Two models of assimilation of the Pre-Neolithic idea (respectively, A and B) can be observed, each model having its local variants which reflect different relations between the recipient environment and external influence.

4) The Pre-Neolithic/Castelnovian populations/communities appear to have introduced, at least in the Mediterranean zone (Mediterranean model A), a more advanced social organization (further sedentarization of life, cemeteries, trade in raw materials over large distances, possibly ownership of flint deposits), and locally, a Neolithic economy or at least new technologies (cf. "Ceramization").

5) The Mediterranean model (A) shows a tendency towards northern expansion reaching new territories in the northern European Lowland. The first stage of this expansion is marked perhaps by the emergence in the middle of the 7th millennium cal. BC of the Cuzoul and Montbani (both southern and northern) cultures in France and Switzerland, southern Germany and Belgium, and the Grebeniki culture in Ukraine. Later in the north (from 6500 cal. BC), the Kongemosian of southern Scandinavia appeared, as well as the Janislawician of Poland and Belarus.

6) At the turn of the 7th millennium cal. BC a Neolithic expansion took place in the direction of the Carpathian Basin and the Central Europe, represented by the Starčevo-Körös and subsequently by the Linear Band Ceramic cultures, this expansion reached most of western and central Europe. By the 6th millennium cal. BC these areas were covered by a modified Mediterranean model of pre-neolithization (Mehtelek-type industry) with broader blades of imported raw material and trapezes associated in a number of cases but not always, with Neolithic economy and ceramics.

7) Consistent evolution of the Pre-Neolithic phenomenon finally imposed the Mediterranean model and induced uniformity of Late Mesolithic cultures in a large part of the Central European Lowland previously dominated by model B. The process was more or less completed by the 5th millennium cal. BC. The early Funnel Beaker chipped industries thus emerged.

8) A typical tendency in the course of the process of transition from the Pre-Neolithic into the Neolithic/ ceramic industries is that the elimination of some classes of tools (like the differentiated microliths and very short end-scrapers, for example) makes them typologically poorer, while from the viewpoint of technology blade and core size increases to meet new demands. This could be due in part to the emerging "market", where not only raw materials, but also

ready products were traded, meaning that they were produced, transported and sold by specialized artisans (?).

9) The above data suggest that many European Early Neolithic industries were in fact a more or less direct continuation of European Pre-Neolithic industries. In other words, in many cases the beginnings of the European Neolithic were at least partly a local event.

10) Importantly, the Pre-Neolithic/Castelnovian formation was commonly ceramicized (cf.) before becoming ultimately neolithized (Italy, France, Iberia, southern Scandinavia, Balkans, Pontic steppe, eastern part of central European Lowland).

Conclusions

Concluding, the hypothesis put forward in the present paper broadens the view of neolithization as a process by demonstrating its temporal extent as well as local aspects. The long process of pre-neolithization/Castelnovization obviously provided at a very early moment in time, a material and organizational base for the technological (ceramics) and economic advances described as Neolithization. The latter event was an outcome of a long and consistent process.

One final remark – the actual mechanism operating the described phenomenon, which spread like wildfire over vast expanses within a rather short period of time (2–3 million square kilometers for model A), still escapes our full understanding. It appears to be homogeneous, because every time and at the same time it leads to similar, although not identical techno-typological results. What are we to do, however, with the African finds and with the trapezes appearing in the Iraqi "Neolithic" around 7000 cal. BC? Could direct links have existed at the time between the Maghreb, Mesopotamia and southern Europe? Or is it simply convergent cultural development?

11.2. The Castelnovian Complex

The Castelnovian complex (Fig. 11.2a–p) is characterized by single-platform core technique giving long, regular blades and bladelets (Montbani style of Jean-Georges Rozoy), the Montbani denticulated and simple use-retouched blades, as well as various trapezes (cf. "Les courants interculturels", "Atlas"), both asymmetrical and symmetrical, sometimes rhombs, Montclus and Vieille trapezes among others, etc.

The percentage of particular types mentioned above and common to the entire Technocomplex is not constant. Short forms occur among end-scrapers (more often in western Europe) and end-scrapers on blade are more common in the south. Some microliths characteristic of the Sauveterrian can be found, for example, in early assemblages in the south (Cuzoulian and classical western Castelnovian), while Beuronian types appear in the north (both Montbanians and Téviecian). Similar observations can be made for the eastern regions (e.g. elements of the

Epi-Gravettian in Frankhthi and Odmut, and of Shan-Kobian in Murzak-Kobian). These presences are all indicative of differentiation and regional roots of particular entities making up the Technocomplex as such.

Substantial technological differences are to be observed in microliths formation. The West prefers the microburin technique to sectioning which is more common in the East (except for the Janislawician).

Classic Castelnovian (Fig. 11.2b top and base)

Named after Châteauneuf-lez-Martigues in France by Max Escalon do Fonton, previously known as the Provencal Group of the Tardenoisian. It existed in France and Italy from the beginning of the 7th millennium cal. BC.

STONE INDUSTRY. Apart from the above described common elements of Castelnovian Complex it is additionally characterized by original internal structure (medium or high index of retouched blades E, microliths K and irregular scrapers B, medium or low index of end-scrapers A, burins C and truncated blades D), as well as by an almost absolute, except for the earliest inventories, lack of microliths apart from those characteristic of the Castelnovian Complex.

BONE INDUSTRY. Spindle-shaped points/*sagaies*; flat harpoons in northeastern Italy and Slovenia.

Classical Castelnovian differs regionally with regard to the end-scrapers (e.g. north Italian *tettiforme* absent from central Italy, but present in south Italian Latronico, (cf.), regional features of trapezes, ventral retouches of French asymmetrical trapezes, absence of *picqant trièdre* in France, etc. In Italy, four regional groups exist: northern, northeastern, Tuscanian and Latronico.

Iberian "Castelnovian" (Fig. 11.2b mid)

The littoral of the Iberian peninsula (Cocina in Spain and Moita do Sebastiao in Portugal) and since recently also the interior (Botiqueria in the Ebro basin) reveal a local industry close to the classical Castelnovian, existing from the middle (?) of the 7th millennium cal. BC, although developing, unlike in France and Italy where Castelnovian grew from Sauveterrian, from a local Epi-Gravettian or else the "sauvetterianized" industry from Filador. For these reasons, among others, it is difficult to consider any one of these industries as true classical Castelnovian. Recent research at Kobeaga II appears to confirm what has been assumed already that the local late Asturian also had serious links with Castelnovian.

Heir to this Iberian "Castelnovian" was the local Muge culture from the 6th millennium cal. BC, localized from the mouth of the Tag River in Portugal to the Spanish Levant (cf. "Rhythms").

Montbanian (Fig. 11.2f)

Name from the site of Montbani 13 in France, proposed by Jean-Georges Rozoy, also known as the Montbani Group of Tardenoisian Culture. It developed from the middle (?)

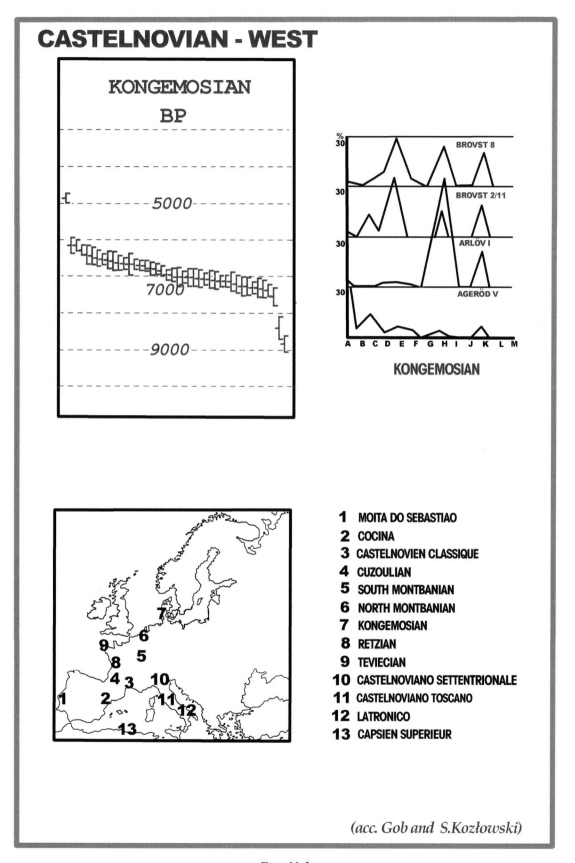

Fig. 11.2a

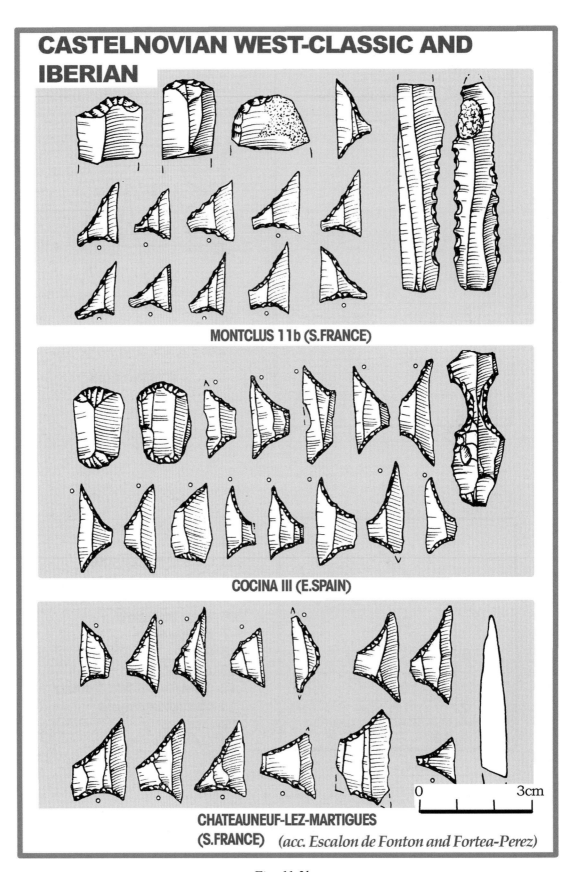

CASTELNOVIAN WEST-CLASSIC AND IBERIAN

MONTCLUS 11b (S.FRANCE)

COCINA III (E.SPAIN)

CHATEAUNEUF-LEZ-MARTIGUES (S.FRANCE) *(acc. Escalon de Fonton and Fortea-Perez)*

0   3cm

Fig. 11.2b

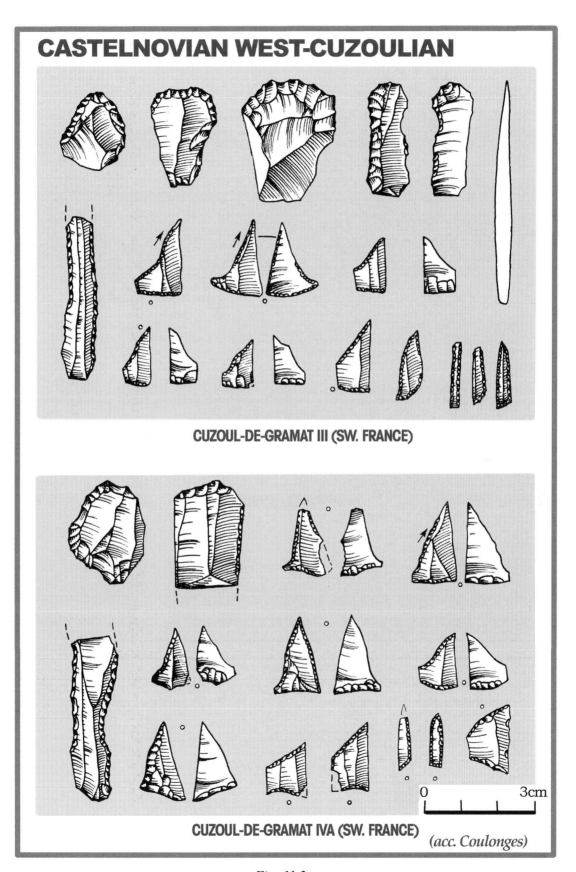

CASTELNOVIAN WEST-CUZOULIAN

CUZOUL-DE-GRAMAT III (SW. FRANCE)

CUZOUL-DE-GRAMAT IVA (SW. FRANCE)

(acc. Coulonges)

0   3cm

Fig. 11.2c

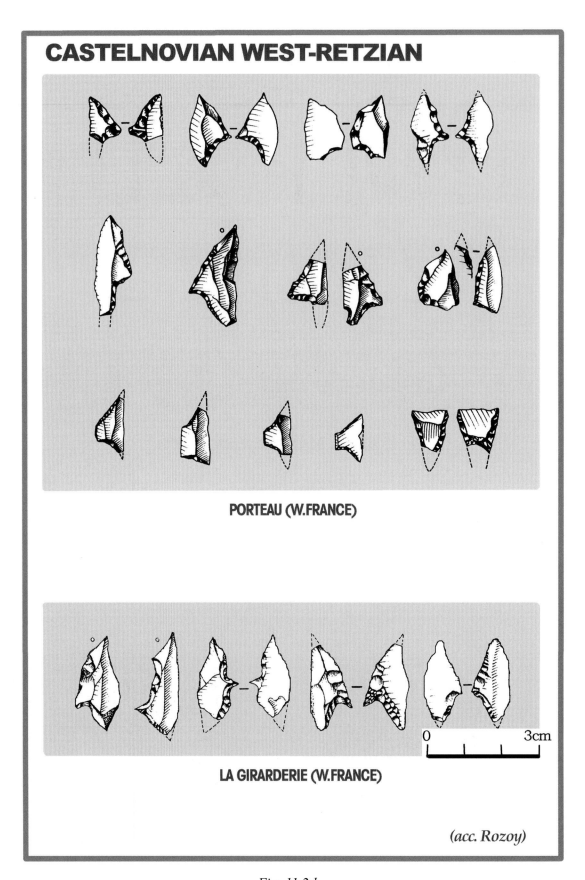

Fig. 11.2d

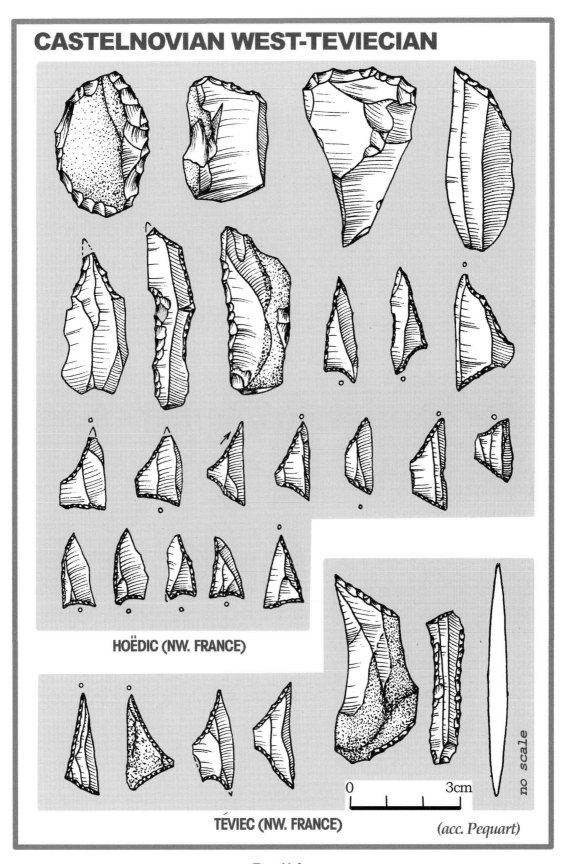

CASTELNOVIAN WEST-TEVIECIAN

HOËDIC (NW. FRANCE)

TÉVIEC (NW. FRANCE)

0   3cm

no scale

(acc. Pequart)

Fig. 11.2e

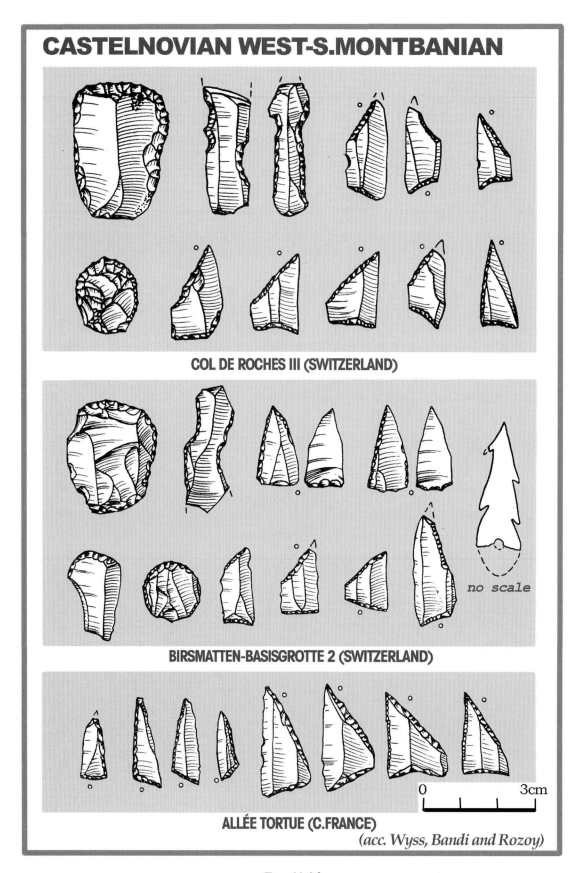

CASTELNOVIAN WEST-S.MONTBANIAN

COL DE ROCHES III (SWITZERLAND)

BIRSMATTEN-BASISGROTTE 2 (SWITZERLAND)

no scale

0   3cm

ALLÉE TORTUE (C.FRANCE)

(acc. Wyss, Bandi and Rozoy)

Fig. 11.2f

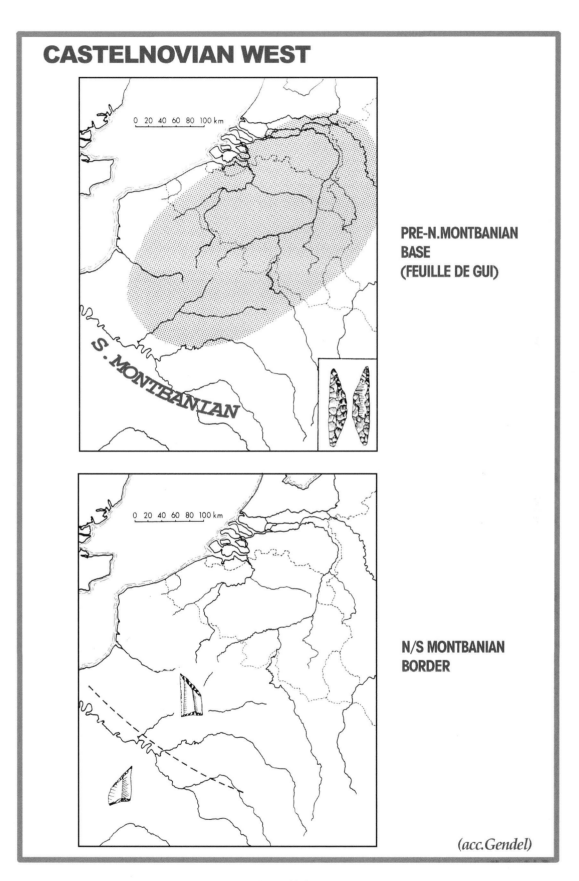

Fig. 11.2g

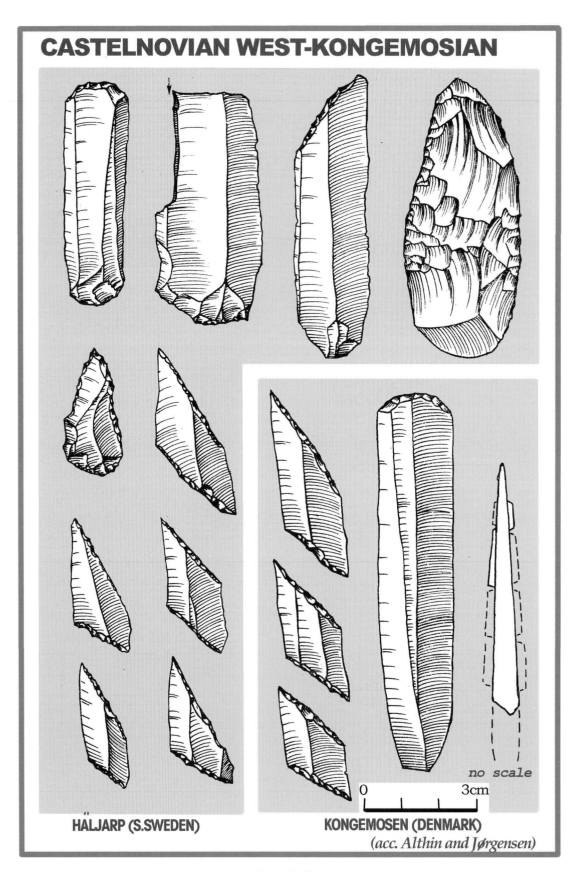

CASTELNOVIAN WEST-KONGEMOSIAN

HÄLJARP (S.SWEDEN)

KONGEMOSEN (DENMARK)
(acc. Althin and Jørgensen)

no scale

0   3cm

Fig. 11.2h

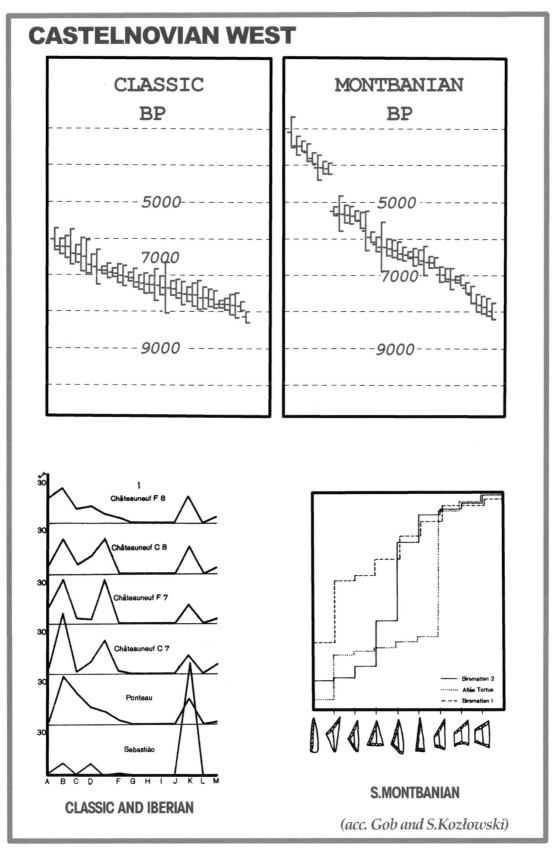

Fig. 11.2i

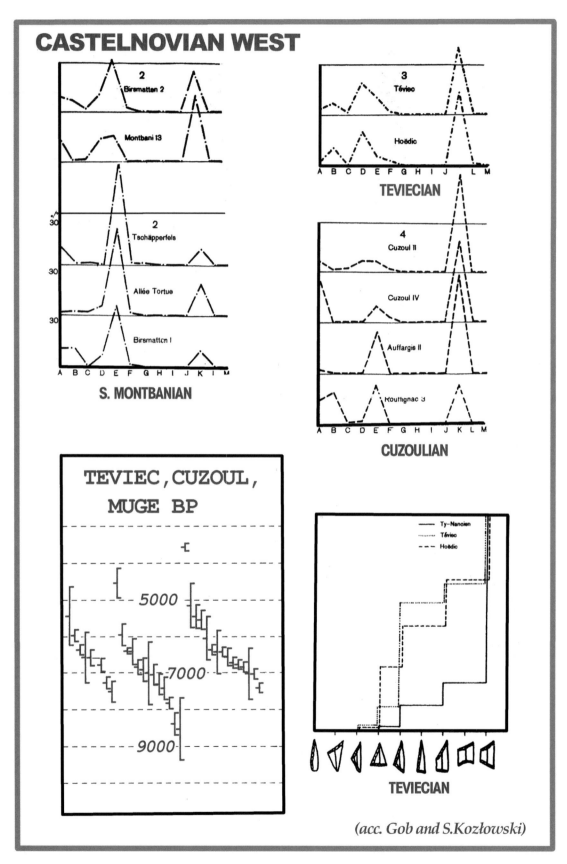

Fig. 11.2j

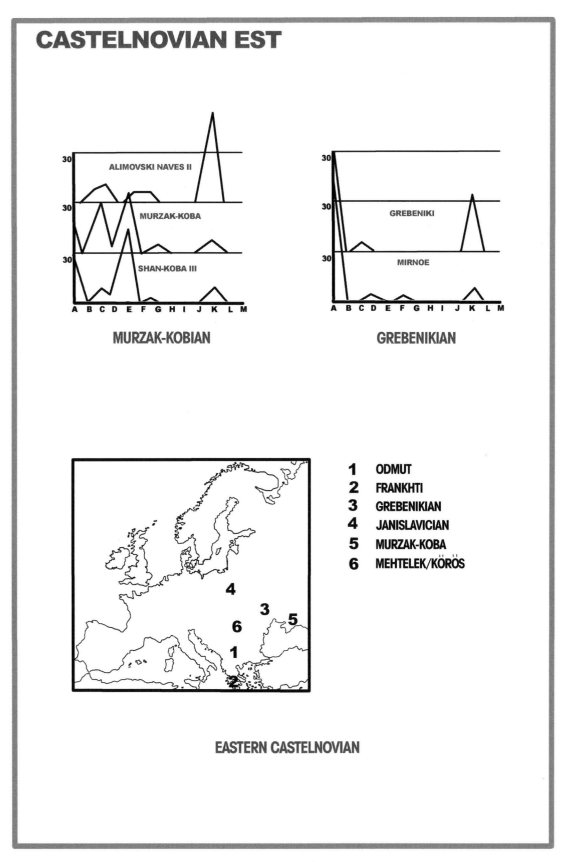

Fig. 11.2k

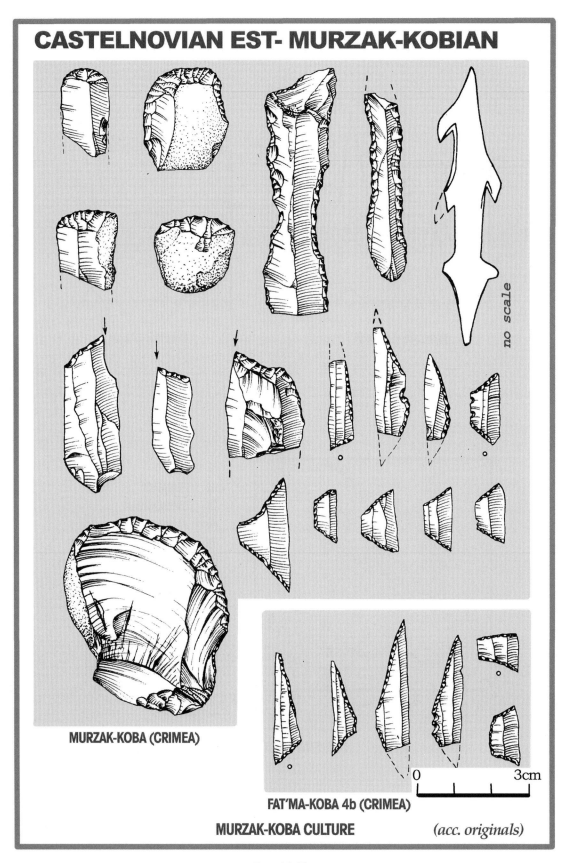

Fig. 11.2l

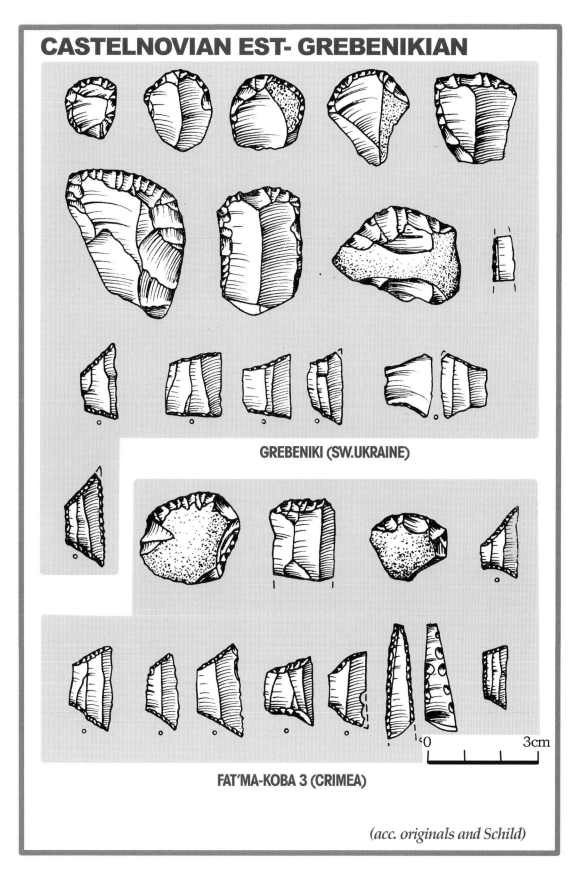

CASTELNOVIAN EST- GREBENIKIAN

GREBENIKI (SW.UKRAINE)

FAT'MA-KOBA 3 (CRIMEA)

(acc. originals and Schild)

Fig. 11.2m

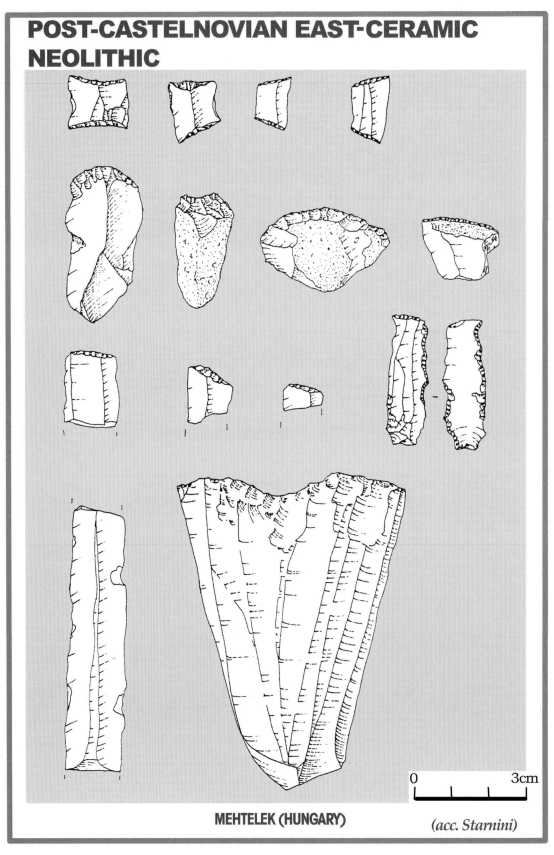

POST-CASTELNOVIAN EAST-CERAMIC NEOLITHIC

MEHTELEK (HUNGARY)

0   3cm

(acc. Starnini)

Fig. 11.2n

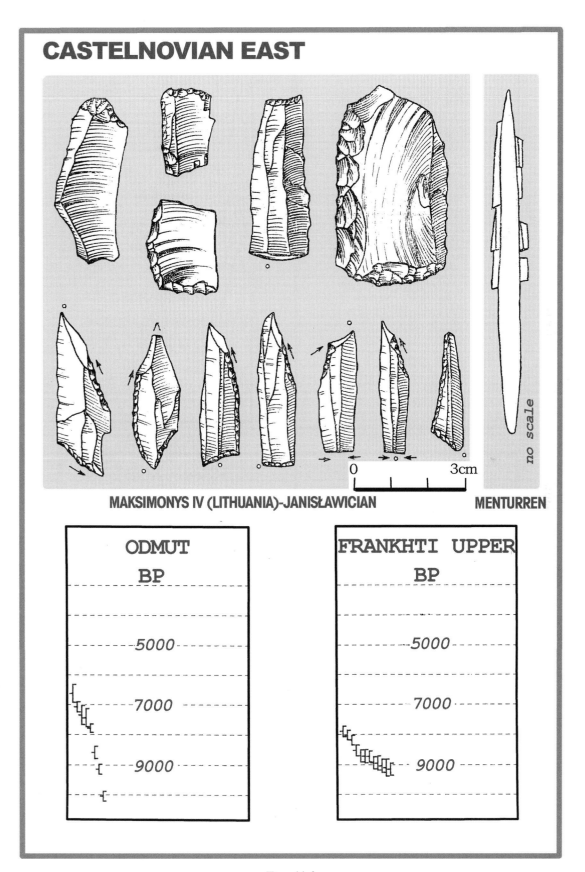

Fig. 11.2o

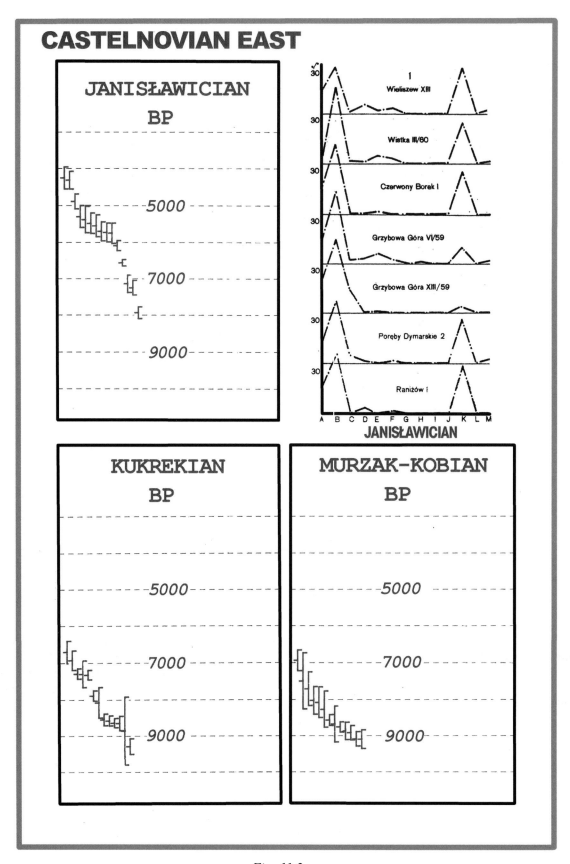

Fig. 11.2p

of the 7th millennium cal. BC in the foothills of the Alps, the Paris Basin and Belgium, also Austria and Bohemia, from Late Beuronian in the south (= South Montbanian) and Rhenanian in the north (= North Montbanian).

STONE INDUSTRY. Apart from the above described common features of the Castelnovian Complex, it is additionally characterized by original structure (high index of retouched blades E, medium index of end-scrapers A, and microliths K, low index of burins C, and irregular scrapers B), as well as original structure of the microliths group among which various trapezes (mostly of group B, differently oriented in the north and in the south) occur; backed points (D), B-points (K), isosceles triangles (TN), Tardenoisian points (X) and long scalene triangles (TR, TO) are present in the south, flat retouched microliths in the north.

BONE INDUSTRY. Spindle-shaped points/*sagaies* and flat harpoons of Birsmatten type (in the south).

HISTORY. Montbani Cultures are the outcome of Castelnovian "trends" (symmetric and asymmetric trapezes, Montbani retouched bladelets, core-exploitation technique, long end-scrapers) being superimposed on a local substratum represented by the Beuronian C and more to the north by Beuronian D and the RMS cultures (Tardenoisian points X, isoscele triangles TN, backed points D, B-points K, *feuilles de gui*, core-exploitation technique, bladelets of the Coincy style, very short end-scrapers on flakes). The hypothesis is confirmed, for example, by stratigraphical sequences in Jägerhaushöhle (Germany) and Birsmatten-Basisgrotte (Switzerland). The formation process of the new unit might have been connected with the northward migration of human groups? (cf. "Mapping the Mesolithic"). Some Montbanian assemblages preserve many elements of the Beuron-Coincy or RMS type (e.g., layers 1 and 2 in Birsmatten, Switzerland), while the Castelnovian element prevails in others (Montbani 13 and Allée Tortue, France). This may be connected with the evolution leading to the territorial differentiation of the culture under discussion. Notably, Peter A. Gendel has demonstrated Montbanian to be dividable into two territorial groups (north and south) on the grounds of, for example, the territorial distribution of asymmetrical trapezes (left- and right-hand truncations = lateralization); the boundary runs between the Paris Basin and Belgium and repeats the line dividing the Beuronian from the Rhenanian. Montbanian is the base of the Neolithic cultures of France and Switzerland.

Téviecian

Name after the site of Téviec in northern France, proposed by Jean-Georges Rozoy, also known as Hoëdic Culture and the Armorique Group of Tardenoisian Culture. It existed in Brittany on the Atlantic coast from the mid (?) 6th millennium cal. BC (why so late a beginning?!).

STONE INDUSTRY. Characterized by common Castelnovian features plus original structure (high index of microliths K and truncated blades D, medium of irregular scrapers B and retouched blades E, low of end-scrapers A and burins C), also of microliths: isosceles triangles TM, Tardenois points

X, numerous scalene triangles TH, and numerous trapezes. Retouched flakes are also present on a continuous basis. Altogether the Téviecian was born from a local Beuronian (continuation of some microliths).

BONE INDUSTRY. Spindle-shaped points (= *sagaies*).

HISTORY. The Téviecian is a sum of allochtonous Castelnovian elements (asymmetric and symmetric trapezes, Montbani bladelets, core-exploitation technique, debitage style) and Beuronian tradition (Tardenois points X, isosceles triangles TM). Moreover, the numerous enough presence of retouched truncations and irregular scrapers, as well as denticulated end-scrapers links it with the western variant of the Sauveterrian (e.g. local site of Pointe de Bertheaume, excavated by Pierre Gouletquer). French researchers originally assumed that the said culture had formed in the south and had spread to Brittany along the Atlantic coast; from the present perspective, this does not seem such a bad idea (cf. works of Grégor Marchand).

Cuzoulian

Name proposed by the author after Cuzoul-de-Gramat in France, known also as "Pre-Rocadourian" (Julia Roussot-Laroque). It emerged in the basins of the Garonne and Loare rivers at about the middle of the 7th millennium cal. BC. Later it evolved into the Rocadourian.

STONE INDUSTRY. Apart from common Castelnovian features, it is additionally characterized by original structure (medium or high index of retouched blades E and microliths K, and constant presence of end-scrapers A and few burins C, as well as Martinet points BM, Vielle and symmetrical ΛZ trapezes, short-base scalene TH and TE triangles, and Sauveterrian points PD).

BONE INDUSTRY. Spindle-shaped points (*sagaies*).

HISTORY. The Cuzoulian industry is a sum of local Sauveterrian elements (triangles TN, TH, TE, backed and Sauveterrian PD points, denticulated end-scrapers, spindle-shaped bone points) and Castelnovian "trend" that had previously been foreign to its territory (trapezes, Montbani bladelets, core-exploitation technique, blanks). Its local roots (Sauveterrian) are confirmed by the lower layers at Rouffignac, Cuzoul-de-Gramat and Le Martinet in France, its originality by the so-called "Martinet points" (asymmetric trapezes BM). Both basic elements lasted simultaneously in the early phase of the Cuzoulian, then the Sauveterrian element disappeared (Le Martinet), until finally the trapezes with flat, ventral retouch appeared, already accompanied by ceramics.

Retzian (Fig. 11.2d)

Most likely a Late Mesolithic facies of the Western Castelnovian on the French Atlantic littoral, perhaps even continuing into a ceramic phase. It was first distinguished in France by Jean-Georges Rozoy on the grounds of surface collections (including La Girarderie and Le Porteau). The name comes from Pays de Retz between the estuaries of the Loire and Seine rivers.

STONE INDUSTRY. Concentrates on regular blade debitage. Blade sectioning is present and Montbani *lamelles* appear, as well as many retouched flake-scrapers. Microliths are distinguished by the presence of *armatures à éperon* with *piquant tièdre* and *flèches du Chatêlet*, plus the odd asymmetrical trapeze. Added to this are the finds from Le Porteau which are proof of a highly organized raw material economy. No datings are available.

Kongemosian (Fig. 11.2h)

Name after the site of Kongemosen in Denmark (Svend Jørgensen), first described by T. Mathiassen as the Older Coastal Culture. The culture appeared in the Western Baltic region in the mid 7th millennium cal. BC and was replaced by the Ertebøllian.

STONE INDUSTRY. Characterized by big, regular elongated blades and the elongated tools made on them: arched end-scrapers (A), dihedral burins (C), truncated blades (D), quite numerous retouched blades (E), numerous or quite numerous unpolished axes (H), rhomboids (BH) and some oblique trapezes (B).

BONE INDUSTRY. Characterized by wide, double-slotted points.

HISTORY. It is likely that the Kongemosian is the final stage of the Castelnovian "push" to the north (cf. "Mapping the Mesolithic"). It was "announced" by isolated finds of asymmetrical trapezes of group B in Post-Maglemosian assemblages from Scania and northern Germany around 7000 cal. BC (e.g. Ageröd I:D and Rüde 2) (cf. "Pre-Neolithic").

Odmutian (cf. Odmut, Fig. 11.8a–b)

Named after the site of Odmut (cf.) in Montenegro. It has all the technological and typological attributes of the "Castelnovian trend" and is dated from the middle of the 7th millennium cal. BC (dates for Odmut) and later (ceramic layers at Odmut, then Méhtelek on the Tisa river, Donja Branievina in Serbia, ceramic sites of Turkish Thrace). It has been recognized in Montenegro (Crvena Stijena, Medena Stijena, Odmut), Albania (Konispol), Thessaly (Argissa Magula), Hungary (Méhtelek), Serbia (Donja Branievina) and northwestern Turkey.

STONE INDUSTRY. The few and rather banal distinctive elements include ordinary (AZ) and narrow (AA) trapezes formed by sectioning and very short and short, small end-scrapers; seldom encountered backed pieces confirm an Epi-Gravettian origin. The percentage structure in the tools group has been presented already in the part concerning the Odmut site. It comes very close to what is represented by the Moldavian-Ukrainian Grebeniki Culture. The Odmutian is separated from the Italian-Slovenian and Istrian classical Castelnovian by a surprising gap (c. 400 km); on the other hand, it could have some connection with Italian Puglia through the Ormuz Strait (?).

Frankhti

The Frankhti sequence (Frankhthi group, cf. "Southeast") shows an uninterrupted development of the local Epi-Gravettian tradition from about the 22nd–23rd millennium BP until the 8th millennium cal. BC, when the eastern Castelnovian/Odmutian marched in to replace it. According to Cathèrine Perlez, the early forms of the Late Pleistocene (layers 4–6 = 13th–11th millennium BP) are characterized by an industry with small backed points of Gravettian type, small triangles (scalene and isosceles), finally segments and small, short and very short flake end-scrapers. Starting from the Late Pleistocene, geometric microliths and classical scrapers are phased out, being replaced gradually by backed bladelets and denticulate irregular scrapers. This particular change resembles the situation in this group of tools in the Iron Gate on the border of Romania and Serbia (cf. "Southeast").

Before 7000 cal. BC a Castelnovian-style industry (phase 8) appeared, quickly losing the backed forms (which, however, were still there in phase 8) and presenting specific trapezes (including B, types AZ and AA) and entirely unique forms of armatures *à tranchant transversal* and *lamelles à dos et troncature proximale* (phases 8–10). The latter distinguish the Frankhthi Castenovian from the Odmut variant.

Murzak-Koban

Name after the site of Murzak-Koba in Crimea, first described by M.V. Voevodski. Known only from the Crimea, it is dated there to the 8th millennium cal. BC (?), although the present author retains his doubts.

STONE INDUSTRY. Characterized, among other things, by small end-scrapers on sectioned blade, short and very short end-scrapers on flake, angled burins on truncation, denticulated bladelets of the Montbani type, and among the microliths by narrow (AA) and normal (AZ) trapezes and trapezes with concave edges (AF), as well as by characteristic Murzak-Koba notched triangles.

BONE INDUSTRY. Characterized by double-barbed flat harpoons.

HISTORY. Murzak-Koban Culture follows and is partly related to Shan-Kobian (cf.) (burins on truncation, some microliths), but most of its elements are of either Caucasian (?) (flat harpoons, long triangles) or Castelnovian derivation (debitage, trapezes, Montbani bladelets).

Grebenikian

Name from the site of Grebeniki in Ukraine, proposed by Volodymyr N. Stanko. The unit developed in Crimea and western Ukraine, Moldova and Romanian Moldavia in the 7th millennium cal. BC and later.

STONE INDUSTRY. Characterized by small very short end-scrapers, as well as normal symmetric (AZ), narrow (AA) and asymmetric (BH) trapezes. Also retouched bladelets of Montbani type occur.

Deriving from the Grebenikian is the ceramic Bug-

Dniester Culture, originally believed by Viacheslav.I. Markevich to be a Neolithic culture (alleged but now questioned early pig breeding). What is surprising is the close similarity of the Grebenikian with that of Balkan Odmutian (cf.). Should this be construed as evidence of close kinship?

Janislawician (cf. below).

11.2.1. Janislawician

Janislawician is obviously Castelnovian *sensu largo*. The name comes from a well-known Mesolithic grave discovered in Janisławice in central Poland (6th millennium cal. BC). "Vistulian cycle" is a term used alternately with "Janislawician" in Polish studies (Hanna Więckowska). In Ukraine, Leonid Zalizniak once wrote of the Rudoi Ostrov culture having this culture in mind.

CULTURAL CONTEXT. Following Maria Chmielewska's suggestion, I originally assumed that this unit belonged to the northern or Maglemosian tradition; today this classification is unacceptable. The possible similarities of some Janislawice and northern elements pertain only to phenomena that are of secondary or local importance (e.g. chipped, unpolished axes, long triangles TI, and few JA-like points in Holmegaard I, Denmark).

Elements regarded as typically Janislawician (Fig. 11.2.1a–e, 11.2o–p) were spread across a wide territory ranging from central Greater Poland (western Poland) to central Ukraine. Their territorial extent thus equaled in size that of the Maglemosian technocomplex, for example. Throughout this vast area there is a uniform basic tool group that is regionally augmented by various elements internally differentiating this unit into several regional groups.

ASSEMBLAGES AND INVENTORIES. The greatest number of homogeneous Janislawician assemblages is known from Poland where they are grouped in Mazovia (Wistka Szlachecka I, III, VI; Wieliszew XIII), Kuiavia (Deby 29), in central Poland (Ciołki-Zagłoba, Janisławice, Osjaków, Łykowe 1), Little Poland (Jawornik-Czarna, Tomaszów II, Grzybowa Góra VI/59, Dąbrówka 3, Raniżów 1, Poręby Dymarskie 2, Gwoździec 9, Baraki Stare), in eastern (Słochy Annopolskie I and II, Nieborowa 1) and north-eastern Poland (Grądy Woniecko), and in Lower Silesia (Świętoszyn II). In all, we know at least 80 Janisławician inventories which are grouped mainly in the middle and upper Vistula river basin extending westwards into the Warta section of the Warsaw-Berlin proglacial stream valley and occasionally into the Barycz proglacial stream valley.

To the east of Poland a few homogeneous Janislawice assemblages occur in southern Lithuania (Maksimonys IV), northern Belarus (Niesilovichi VII, Belitsa II) and along the lower Pripet (Vishorod DVS, Rudoi Ostrov), as well as in Trans-Carpathian Ukraine (Kamyanitsa). There are 50–60 Janislawician inventories east of the Polish border. To this we can perhaps add single bone points from northeastern Poland and the Pregola river basin.

TERRITORIAL RANGE. The territorial range of the basic markers of Janislawician inventories, i.e. JA, JB and JC points, slightly exceeds that of the actual range of the Janislawician. This is due to the demonstrable impact of this complex on adjacent units (e.g. the Chojnice group along the middle Warta and late Western Kunda in Lithuania and Belarus). The same in fact may be said of the second important marker, the irregular scrapers on flakes which are known, e.g., from sites of the Western Kunda and Komornician. Without going into details, it may be claimed safely that in northeastern Poland the Janislawician certainly reached northern Mazovia and southern Pomerania, as well as the Narew river basin, and in the south it did not spread beyond the Carpathians (except for the site of Kamyanitsa I in Trans-Carpathian Ukraine!); Silesia is almost completely devoid of Janislawician settlement. In the west, the infrequent sites in proglacial stream valleys do not go beyond the Poznań meridian with the not very dense network of sites in this region going as far as the upper Warta course. In any case, the western limit of Janislawician could have been conditioned by the rather elevated barriers separating the Vistula basin from the Oder basin (Kraków-Wieluń Jura and the Łódz upland). The southern limit of Janislawician elements in eastern Europe practically coincides with the 200 m contour line which marks the actual border between the upland and lowland zones in western Ukraine (water divide between the Baltic and the Black Sea, cf. "Pontic elements"). The northern limit of these elements in Belarus virtually extends along the Valdai (=Würm) front moraine, although locally it seems to reach northwards beyond it along the middle Neman course. Further east, the sites with JA–C points keep mostly to sandy soils and therefore the northern limit of their occurrence in this area follows the lower course of the Pripet all the way to Kiev. However, Janislawician proper is confined in the east to the upper Neman course and the upper Pripet river basin.

CHRONOLOGY. The dating of the Janislawician is based on a limited number of radiocarbon age estimates for Poland (mostly) and Ukraine, on typological indicators of chronology and on stratigraphy. The C^{14} dates place it in the 6th (Tomaszów II) and in the mid 7th millennium cal. BC (Dęby 29), at least as far as Poland goes. Some new dates (Łykowe 1) come from the 5th millennium (the same for Sośnia with its mid 5th millennium date). Certain typological and technological (= Castelnovian) elements of the inventories also place the unit in the Atlantic period. We have in mind here mainly trapezes and the regular blade technology. At the same time we know assemblages from Janisławice and Nieborowa 1 which have no trapezes, and these, theoretically, might be slightly earlier. The same goes for Maksimonys IV in Lithuania. In any case, the Janislawician elements are known from the late western Kunda assemblages in Lithuania and northern Belarus.

The rare stratigraphic and topographical data prove in general that in Poland the Janislawician is younger than the Komornician (Janislawician elements in layer 3 in Witów are later than the Komornician layer 7; the situation in Grądy-Woniecko 1 near Białystok (northeastern Poland)

JANISŁAWICIAN

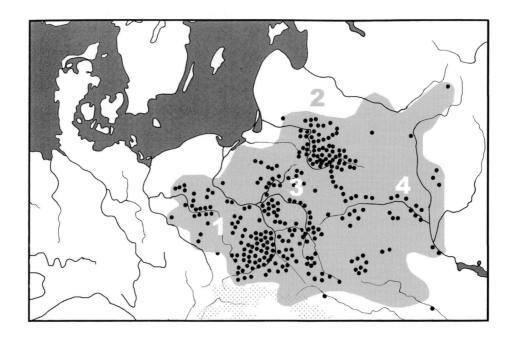

TERRITORIAL GROUPS:

1-WISTKA
2-MAKSIMONYS
3-EASTERN
4-RUDOI OSTROV

Fig. 11.2.1a

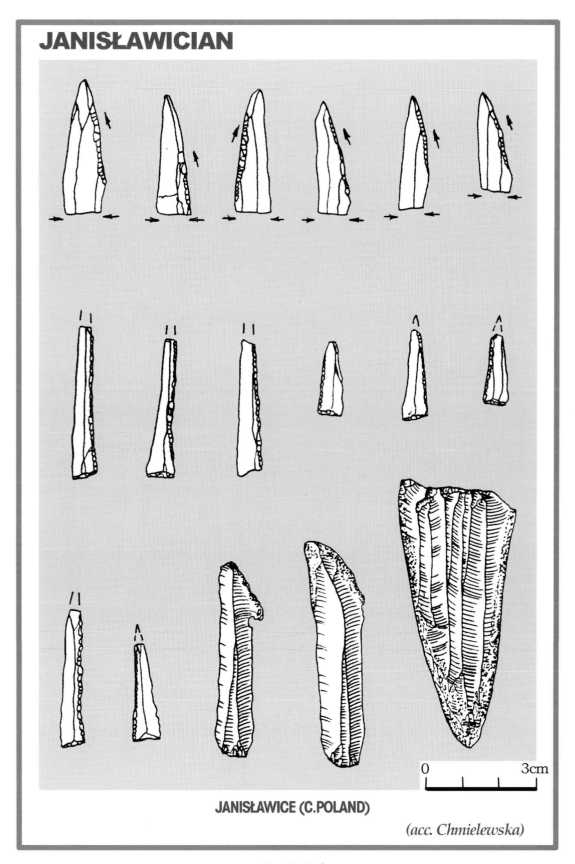

JANISŁAWICIAN

JANISŁAWICE (C.POLAND)

(acc. Chmielewska)

0 3cm

Fig. 11.2.1b

JANISŁAWICIAN

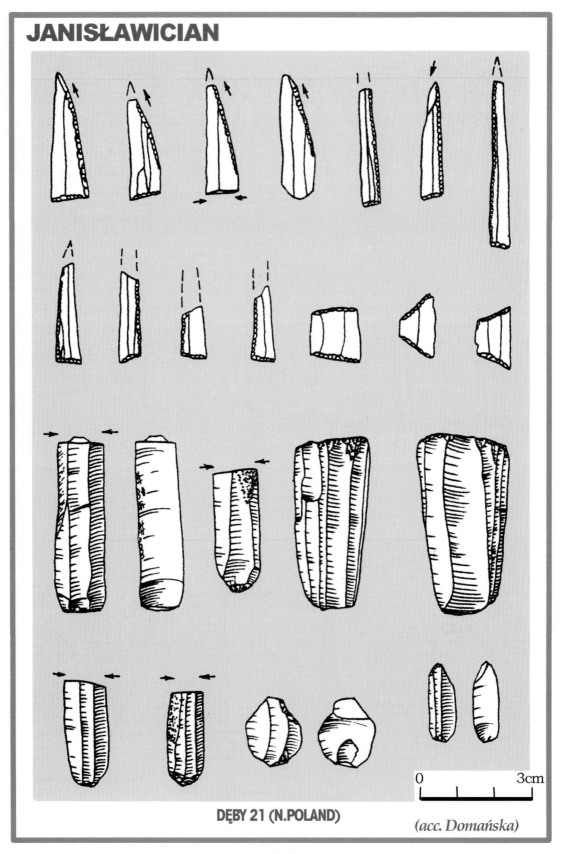

DĘBY 21 (N.POLAND)

(acc. Domańska)

0   3cm

Fig. 11.2.1c

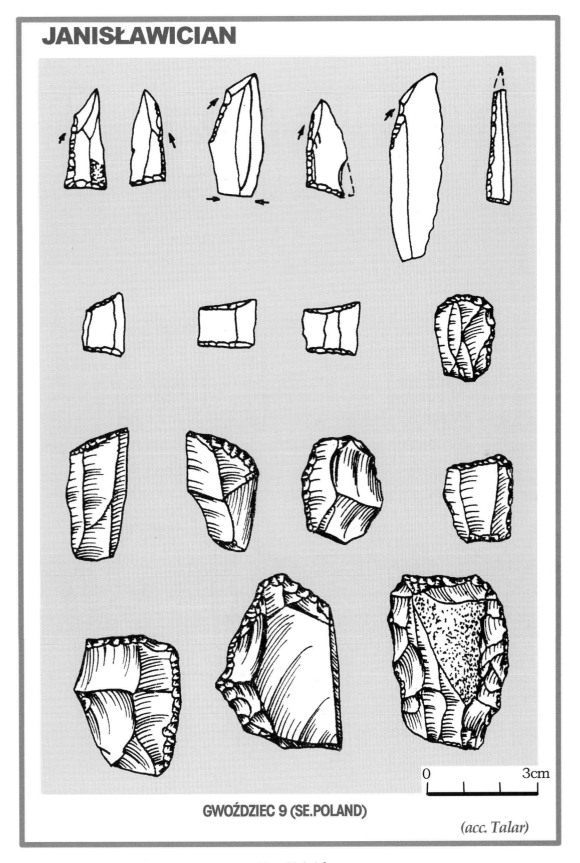

JANISŁAWICIAN

GWOŹDZIEC 9 (SE.POLAND)

(acc. Talar)

Fig. 11.2.1d

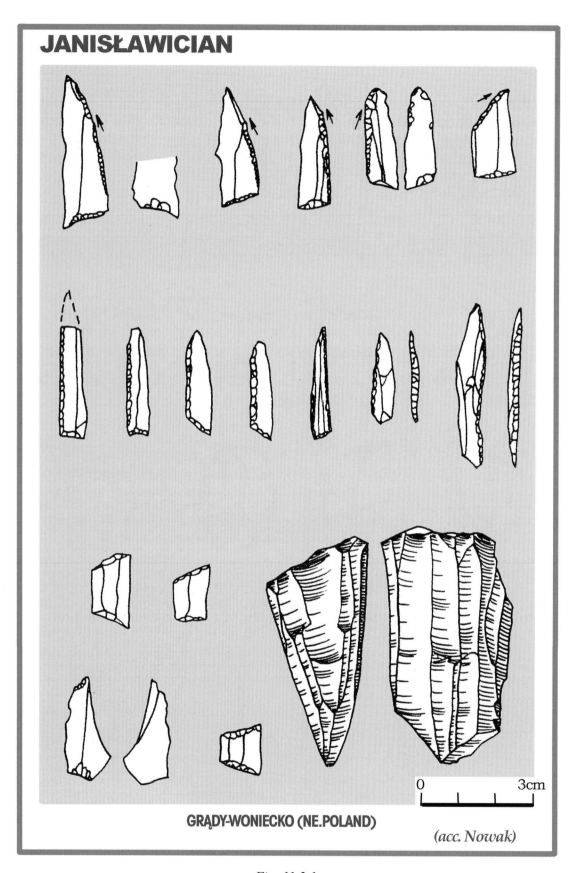

JANISŁAWICIAN

GRĄDY-WONIECKO (NE.POLAND)

(acc. Nowak)

Fig. 11.2.1e

and the topography of Belarussian sites of Kuklaevka type viz. Janislawice is similar). The Janislawician can thus be assumed as appearing in central Europe at least in the mid/end of the 7th millennium cal. BC, this being additionally indicated by the fact that in the middle and upper Vistula basin there should be time for the late (trapezes!) phase of the Komornician and for the Early Atlantic Post-Maglemosian (cf.) Pieńki group and in the east for late Kudlaevka (cf.).

In southern Poland, a few early Janislawician obsidian artifacts (Raniżów 1, Grzybowa Góra XIII/59) show them to be perhaps contemporaneous with the Danubian cultures from that area (middle of the 6th millennium). In their first stage, the south-Polish Neolithic cultures probably had no access to sources of "chocolate" flint which seem to have been at that time in the hands of the Janislawicians. This could be documented by the C^{14} date from one of the shafts in the flint mine in Tomaszów I.

There are also some other indicators of the contemporaneity of the Early Neolithic and Janislawician populations. There exist in Little Poland, also in Janislawician contexts (?), some flint implements (rhombs BH) which are of southeastern provenance (cf. "Pontic elements"). These are dated in their original environments to the second half of the 7th (?) and 6th/5th millennia cal. BC.

In any case, the Boreal phase of the Janislawician seems to contradict the logic of developmental trends in the European Mesolithic, since Janislawician technology is manifestly young and no doubt belongs to the "Castelnovian style". The final phase of the Janislawician complex may survive (at least locally) even as late as the 5th/4th millennium cal. BC: along the Neman and Pripet rivers and also in Poland (Mazovia), some Janislawician assemblages are apparently accompanied by forest-type ceramics (of Dubičiai-Neman type, cf. "Ceramicization").

A few of the Janislawice-like assemblages (e.g. Korzecznik in Kuiavia and Łykowe 1 in central Poland) are carbon-dated to the 5th and even to the turn of the 5th millennium cal. BC. Such assemblages are characterized among others by a reduced typological diversity in the microliths group in which trapezes dominate (e.g. also Wistka Szlachecka VI).

SETTLEMENT NETWORK. Janislawician sites, naturally grouped in river valleys, form a number of concentrations, 30–50 kilometers long on the average. The most important concentrations are: Włocławek, Łęczyca, Warsaw, middle Bug, Skarżysko, upper Warta, Nida, Kolbuszowa, Dębica, Cracow, Włodawa; and to the east of Poland: Styr, Brest, Pinsk, Grodno, Lida, Merkis, middle Pripet, etc. Janislawician sites are sometimes situated higher than the older (Komornica or Kudlaevka) ones.

The sites occupy mainly river terraces and sometimes sandy dunes. An oval-shaped sunk dwelling with a hearth laid out with flat stones is known from the Grzybowa Góra XIII/59 site in Little Poland.

ENVIRONMENT. Janislawician forests were inhabited by mixed fauna, with elk dominating in the east, and red deer, roe deer, *Bos* and wild boar in the west. Particularly

important for the Janislawicians was good-quality flint raw material needed for the broad bladelets used in tool production. Accordingly, mined raw material was preferred, especially "chocolate" flint, which, being a local raw material of preference in other (Post-Maglemosian) cultural groups of the Polish Late Mesolithic, became for the Janislawicians a raw material that they brought in mass quantities from as far away as 200 kilometers and more. A probable Janislawician "chocolate" flint mine and the workshops that went with it are known from Tomaszów. Given that "chocolate" flint could not be used exclusively, Janislawician groups distant from deposits of the flint had to remain content with local raw material, utilizing mostly, as may be presumed, *in situ* outcrops (e.g. Cretaceous "rafts" in northeastern Poland and Lithuania).

FLINT INVENTORIES.

a. Technology. The Janislawician core formation involved the exploitation of fairly large subconical, conical specimens deriving from carenoidal/keeled single-platform cores. The sides, back and platform of these specimens were often carefully prepared. The cores went through the phase of pre-core, usually horse-shoe shaped. Pressure technique was applied to produce regular, fairly long bladelets, 8–11 mm wide. These were reworked with microburin technique into microliths, usually using semi-steep retouch. Bladelets were sectioned frequently (information from Marcin Wąs). The fairly numerous tools (mainly scrapers) were made on flakes from the core preparation process, although rare flake cores occur as well.

b. Retouched tools. The tool structure of the Janislawician assemblages is characterized by numerous irregular scrapers (B: 40–54%, very characteristic rectangular specimens, often with ventral retouch), moderately numerous end-scrapers on blades (A: 3–24%) and microliths (5–33%), and by the constant, albeit few retouched truncations (D) and mostly use-retouched blades (E). Characteristically, microliths content in Janislawician assemblages is markedly lower than in Komornician and Postmaglemosian ones. This is due to arrow construction, which changed from the earlier variant of being armed with more than one microlith to one with only one arrowhead mounted on a shaft (JA–JC point or trapeze).

c. Facial indicators. To the west of the Vistula these included TD and TI scalene triangles with short base and AA and AZ symmetrical trapezes. From the Vistula up to the Khoryn river in Ukraine and the upper Neman in Belarus we have TD triangles and AZ and AC trapezes, as well as some WA–C inserts. In the upper Neman river basin, the facial tools are JE points (with oblique base), TD triangles, WA–C inserts, unpolished axes and AC trapezes, as well as some backed pieces. Finally, along the middle and lower Pripet we have AC trapezes, WA–C retouched inserts, some tanged points (LA–D) and few Kukrek inserts. A local element southeast of the middle Vistula are BH rhombs, and in northeast Poland WA–C inserts.

It also seems that one might find elements of chronological differentiation in the Janislawician assemblages. These would be backed pieces for the earliest phases in northern Belarus, and perhaps Komornician microliths occurring in various quantities in Poland (e.g. Dąbrówka 3, Grzybowa Góra VI/59). This, however, is far from being proved.

BONE INVENTORIES. I once considered it possible that the double-slotted bone points (type 21$_2$ of Grahame Clark) armed with sectioned, unretouched bladelets were associated with the Janislawician, but I am less sure of it today.

CERAMICS. The connection of the Dubičiai-Neman-type pottery with the youngest assemblages in Poland and Belarus was suggested by Mikhail Cherniavski, and is possible.

TERRITORIAL DIVISION. I have divided the Janislavician into several territorial variations.

a. The Wistka group was identified almost exclusively in Mazovia, central Poland and northern Little Poland; in addition to elements of the basic tool group it is also characterized by long triangles TI and TD, and trapezes AA and AZ. It also contains TH and TE triangles on occasion. The oldest Wistka assemblages may contain some rare Komornician elements.

b. The eastern group occupies the eastern and central Vistula river basin, the upper Neman and the upper Pripet river basins. It is characterized primarily by AC trapezes and few TD triangles, as well as AZ trapezes, WA–C inserts and some rare unpolished axes. In this zone the oldest assemblages may contain single backed pieces, if the Janisławice complex was preceded in the area by assemblages of Kudlaevka culture.

c. Further east, triangles vanish altogether but backed pieces (DA, DB) appear along with tanged points (LA–D), and this justifies the recognition of a separate Rudoi Ostrov group, which has also several Kukrek (Pontic) elements, like the characteristic inserts.

d. Finally, the Lithuanian Maksimonys group, characterized by JE points, few backed pieces and unpolished axes, should be placed in Lithuania.

CHRONOLOGICAL DIVISION. If a trapeze-less phase of the Janislawician actually exists (Maksimonys, Nieborowa), then it would be the oldest. In the Vistula river basin, it ought to contain elements of the preceding cultures (Komornician and/or Post-Maglemosian Pieńki). Such elements are certainly present in some assemblages with trapezes (e.g. Dąbrówka 3) and these could constitute phase II. The final phase (Wistka Szlachecka VI, Łykowe) could be characterized by the presence of ceramics. At that time a gradual loss of typical features occurs, and the flint industry acquires numerous trapezes.

DISAPPEARANCE. As already mentioned, it is possible that there exist assemblages containing Janislawician elements and ceramics (e.g. Łykowe in central Poland), and because of the latter such assemblages are sometimes called "Neolithic" or "para-Neolithic". However, they do not exhibit all of the "classical" Janislawician features (though always having JA–C points); what is more, they sometimes contain a number of "Neolithic" flint (e.g. flatly retouched blades).

INHUMATIONS. The well known grave from Janisławice containing a sitting skeleton of a Laponoidal male is connected with the Janisławice complex. The grave goods included numerous (21) microliths, an animal-tooth necklace, cores, a pre-core, blades and numerous bone and antler tools.

11.3. Pseudo-Castelnovian (?) cultures of the Pontic Steppe

Two related cultures, Kukrek and Donetz, are believed to have existed respectively in the lower and central basin of the Boh/southern Bug and Dniester, as well as the northern piedmont of the Caucasus following the Shan-Koban/Belolesie episode, which ended in the 8th (?) millennium cal. BC (that is, of course, if the radiocarbon datings are not erroneous). Both are characterized by regular blade/bladelet technique using pencil-like conical cores, retouched blades and bladelets (including Montbani type in Kukrek) and trapezes (only in the younger Kukrek-type assemblages). The relationship of the two cultures with the Castelnovian phenomenon has not been proved. The following is a brief description of these two units (Fig. 11.3a–b).

Kukrekian

Named after the Kukrek site in Crimea. The culture existed in the Pontic steppe from the 8th to the 6th millennium cal. BC.

STONE INDUSTRY. Described by Elena A. Vekilova, the industry is characterized by very short, also small end-scrapers on flake, massive very short transversal flake burins and sometimes retouched bladelets of the Montbani type (in younger assemblages). The microliths group includes microretouched inserts/bladelets of WA–B type, rare narrow rhombs, rare scalene triangles, microtruncations, and rare trapezes (not in all assemblages). Also retouched on the ventral surface so-called Kukrek inserts (i.e., blades with flat splintered retouch on the ventral face) are characteristic.

BONE INDUSTRY. Single and double slotted points.

Donetz group

Described by Dmitri Y. Telegin, a flint industry of the eastern Ukrainian/Russian border, named after the Severski Donetz river. It combines features of the Black-Sea-steppe industries, e.g. Kukrek (conical pencil-like cores, AF trapezes, WA–B inserts) and para(?)-Janislawician ones (JB–C points, AA, AZ trapezes). Rather late than early Mesolithic. It has not been resolved whether the tanged points (LA–D) occurring in the region are an integral component of this industry.

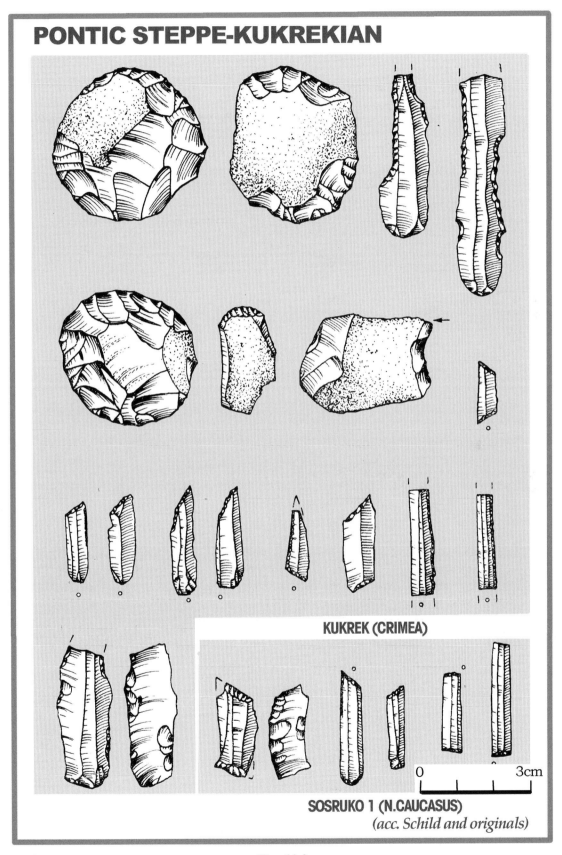

Fig. 11.3a

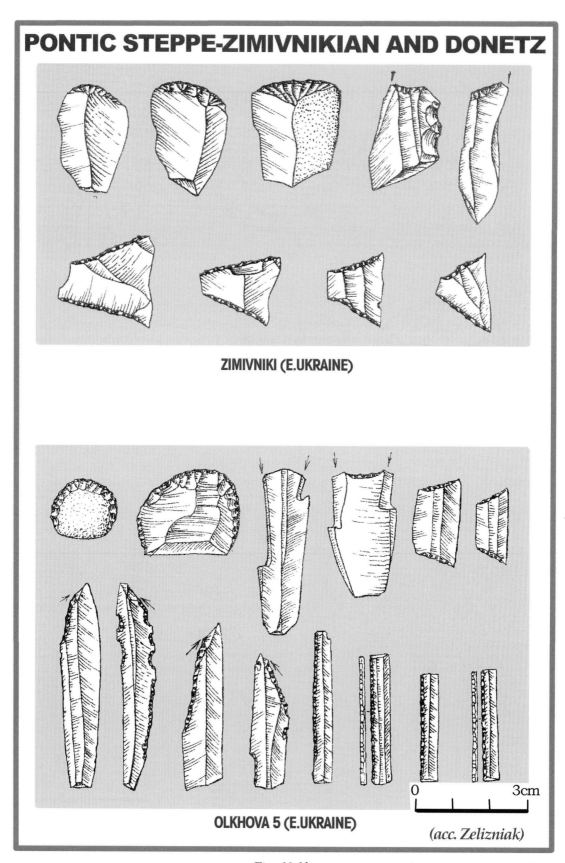

Fig. 11.3b

11.4. Pontic elements in the Late Mesolithic of the Vistula and Boh (southern Bug)-Dniester basins

Introduction

Although the basic outline of the "cultural" differentiation of flint assemblages regarded as "Mesolithic" has already been established for the Central and Eastern European Mesolithic (Kozłowski, Zalizniak), we are still far from full knowledge of the territorial and chronological differentiation of microlithic flint materials in this part of the Continent in the Early and Middle Holocene. Particularly troublesome gaps are to be noted in the knowledge of those regions which are not covered or which are only partly covered by sandy deposits: among others, the steppic-loess areas in southeastern Poland and the western and southern Ukraine. It is with these regions that the present contribution is concerned (Fig. 11.4a–b).

The said region is characterized by differentiated geological and geomorphological structure. There are on one hand the mostly loess uplands of Lublin, Volhynia, and Podolia, and on the other, the lower plains and river valleys in the upland region which are mostly sand formations (Sandomierz Basin, Polesye and Little Polesye, valleys of the longer Ukrainian rivers like Dniester, Boh/southern Bug, Dniepr etc.). Naturally, the land formation is reflected in the state of research in the region in question as far as Mesolithic flint inventories are concerned. A number of such inventories have been exposed by wind in the sandy areas, but none have been found in the loess. This is not so much evidence of no Mesolithic settlement in the region as the apparent covering of the originally frequented valleys with loess deluvia "liberated" as a result of Neolithic deforestation. This idea is supported by observations made on the northern border of the loess plateaus in Poland and Ukraine (Mesolithic sites in sandy valleys traversing the northern ridge of the plateaus, e.g. material from the upper courses of the rivers Bystrzyca, Bug, Styr and Khoryn), as well as by the relatively well known Mesolithic sites in the loess regions between the rivers Prut, Dniester, Boh (= southern Bug) and Seret etc. in Ukraine and Romanian Moldavia. Therefore, there seems to be nothing that would contradict the possibility of Mesolithic settlements existing also in the uplands or, more precisely, in the smaller valleys traversing them. As we shall see later on, traces of such settlements of quite an individual character do exist.

Rhomboid Microliths of the BH class in Poland and Ukraine

At the end of the 1960s and the beginning of the 1970s, while working on a monograph study of the Mesolithic in Little Poland and then in the whole country, I distinguished a distinct class of microliths with a shape close to a rhomb (I referred to them as PH at the time), occurring sporadically in Mesolithic collections of doubtful homogeneity, mostly east of the Vistula river. I even provided an inventory of those collections, although I drew no conclusions based on that material. My further studies on the Mesolithic on an

European scale this time led through the stage of charting particular classes of finds (cf. "Atlas"), so that I also charted the rhomboid microliths, changing their symbol from PH to BH on the way. And then it turned out that the Polish finds are grouped mainly in the southeastern part of the country and are not cartographically connected with the southern Scandinavian (= Kongemose) and Belgian (= north Montbani) concentrations of comparable finds. Today I know that the Polish finds are simply a logical continuation of the concentrations of BH microliths known from the "corridor" formed by the Boh and Seret in Ukraine, where they occur in assemblages of late Grebenikian, Bug-Dniester and early Trypolye cultures.

Therefore, one should now ask whether the BH microliths known from southeastern Poland are not evidence of the presence of at least one of these cultures in the territory of Poland? In order to answer this inquiry it was necessary first to establish types of other finds usually accompanying the rhomboid microliths in the Grebenikian, Bug-Dniester and Trypolye cultures; then, it had to be checked whether these cultures also occured in southeastern Poland; and finally, whether by chance they were not typical of the classical Polish Mesolithic cultures.

Characteristic of Grebenikian and Bug-Dnester flint inventories, chronology and territorial range

The flint industry in the two cultures is virtually identical or if differing, then only in minor details; the Bug-Dniester culture is no more than a ceramic phase of the Grebenikian. It is based on conical cores for regular blades and bladelets. Predominating among the retouched tools are small squat, very short end-scrapers (many made on flakes); retouched blades with discontinuous, sometimes alternate retouch are also present; less frequently one encounters denticulated bladelets (Montbani type). Apart from that, there occur symmetrical (AA, AZ and AF) and asymmetrical (BJ, BV, BZ, and BY) trapezes, as well as the rhomboidal microliths BH mentioned above.

Both cultures cover an area from the eastern Carpathians to the Crimea, their range reaching the Danube delta in the south and the watershed between the Polish Bug and the Ukrainian Dnester rivers in the north. Available radiocarbon datings place both units between the 7th and 5th millennium cal. BC, which is in keeping with the character of the flint industry revealing the predominance of the two main features common to a majority of European Late Mesolithic industries (cf. "Pre-Neolithic"), namely, the regular bladelet technique and the trapezoid microliths.

Typological elements known from the Pontic cultures in the area of southeastern Poland

The presented map shows that in southeastern Poland, that is, east of the upper Vistula, there is a concentration of rhomboid microliths of the BH class.

Still, there are indications other than the BH microliths of Pontic connections in the same region, namely:

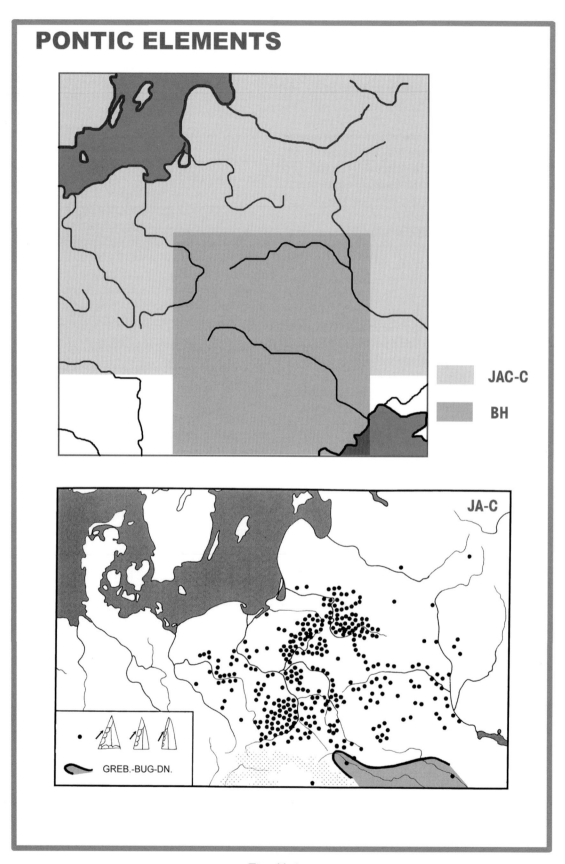

Fig. 11.4a

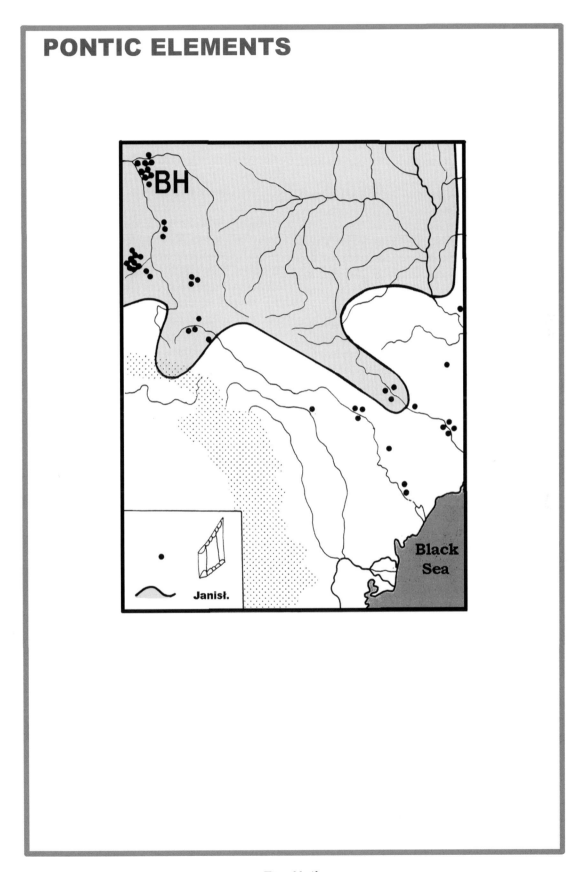

Fig. 11.4b

1. In southeastern Poland, one encounters infrequent symmetrical trapezoids of the AF class (with concave truncations), unknown from central and western Poland, but characteristic of the Mediterranean-Pontic province;
2. Jan Machnik announced the presence of Bug-Dniester type pottery in Łukawica (southeast of the country).

Concluding, we can confirm the concentration in southeastern Poland of a number of elements which cannot be placed as a whole within the standard of classical southeastern Polish Late Mesolithic (Janislawician, cf.), but which refer rather to the Grebenikian/Bug-Dniester complex, a statement strongly supported by cartographic arguments.

In the introduction to the present paper I mentioned the differentiated geological structure and geomorphology of both southeastern Poland and western Ukraine. The area is a transitional zone from the sandy-loamy Great European Plain to the loess-chernozem areas of the steppic Pontic plateaus. Moving still further, on the one hand we encounter such landscape elements as the sandy Sandomierz Basin or the equally sandy Polesye, both in the north, and on the other, strongly sculptured loess uplands (Volhynian, Podolye, Bessarabian, Moldavian, as well as Lublin plateaus) in the south, traversed by infrequent but fairly large and deep river valleys (Bug, Dniester, Boh, Prut, Seret).

The forest cover reconstructed for the sandy-loamy plains in the 7th–5th millennia cal. BC features a predominance of pine, accompanied by alder, *Quercetum mixtum*, and birch. On the other hand, for the areas of the Boh and Dniester basins in the Atlantic period, Pavel M. Dolukhanov suggests deciduous forests with a predominance of *Quercetum mixtum* and coniferous formations in the deep river valleys.

If we accept the interpretation by the cited author and recall the earlier remarks about the Lublin Upland belonging to the zone of uplands of the Pontic Plain, we shall have to accept, too, that is was covered by deciduous forests in the Atlantic period. Thus, we obtain another indication justifying the thesis about the presence of Grebenikian elements in the Lublin region.

Therefore, from the middle of the 7th millennium cal. BC, the Polish plains were already occupied by Janislawician settlement, while in the deep valleys of the Ukrainian upland area there existed settlement in the Grebeniki/Bug-Dniester tradition.

It also looks as if it will be difficult to discern the presence of Late Mesolithic of the Pontic type in the basin of the Vistula; we are dealing there with a border zone between the Baltic and Pontic cultures or simply between the Mediterranean and northern zones. This zonation separates cultures but the extent of mutual influences has yet to be estimated.

11.5. The Mesolithic: between East and West

The stage

Two contrasting worlds in terms of climate (cold in the North, warm in the South), geomorphology (flat and low in the North, hilly in the South, then flat and low again), soil (clays and sands in the North, loess in the South) and vegetation (forests, potatoes and rye in the North, forest-steppe and steppe, corn, wheat, grapes, watermelons and melons in the South), and fauna (saiga antelope in the South, wisent in the North). Two entirely different regions – the Mediterranean and the Baltic, the "Roman" and the "Barbarian", apparently mutually impermeable and completely foreign.

Nothing further from the truth! Prehistory and history have demonstrated constant penetration, a watershed boundary between the Black Sea and Baltic that was no more than symbolic, the river network of the two regions – the Polish (San, Bug, Vistula) and the Ukrainian (Prut, Dniester, Boh) – being complementary and the inhabitants of the two regions expressing mutual interest. Moreover, the two regions attracted outside interest as well, of friends and foes alike, the outcome being frequently a more or less natural shift of the barriers in the "Pontic-Baltic corridor" and an ethnic, cultural and religious mosaic of Ukrainians, Poles, Jews, Armenians, Valachians and Tartars, no longer in existence but once so powerful in the region... (Fig. 11.5).

Theatrum minus

The cartograms of the "Atlas of the European Mesolithic" (cf.) suggest (e.g. DA backed points map) a certain territorial continuity between the basins of the Vistula, Neman and Pripet, a continuity that is not quite in keeping with the overall Mesolithic division into the East and West observed for the 9/8th millennium cal. BC and expressed on the map by the opposition: Kunda tanged points + retouched inserts (East) – various microliths, i.e., geometrics/triangles/ segments (West), (cf. "Mapping the Mesolithic"). Once mapped, the two elements show a border zone for the 9/8th/ early 7th millennium cal. BC running from lower Vistula to eastern Little Poland generally east of the Vistula and west of the Bug. It is the border zone between the northern Mesolithic (Maglemosian) and the northeastern Mesolithic (Kunda) and it is one of the principal cultural borders of the European Mesolithic for it divides two contrasting worlds. It will disappear, at least to some extent, in the Late Mesolithic, once the Janislawician (cf.) is formed, that is, in the middle of the 7th millennium cal. BC (cf. *infra* "Theatrum maius", also the "Atlas", cf., maps AZ and AC; also cf. "Mapping the Mesolithic").

How is it then that the DA and DB backed points typical of the Northern/Maglemosian Mesolithic are found east of the Bug as one of the elements defining a local cultural unit, the Kudlaevka (cf.) culture (= combination of Kundian elements with the said backed points) and had they arrived from the west at all, as assumed by Leonid Zalizniak?

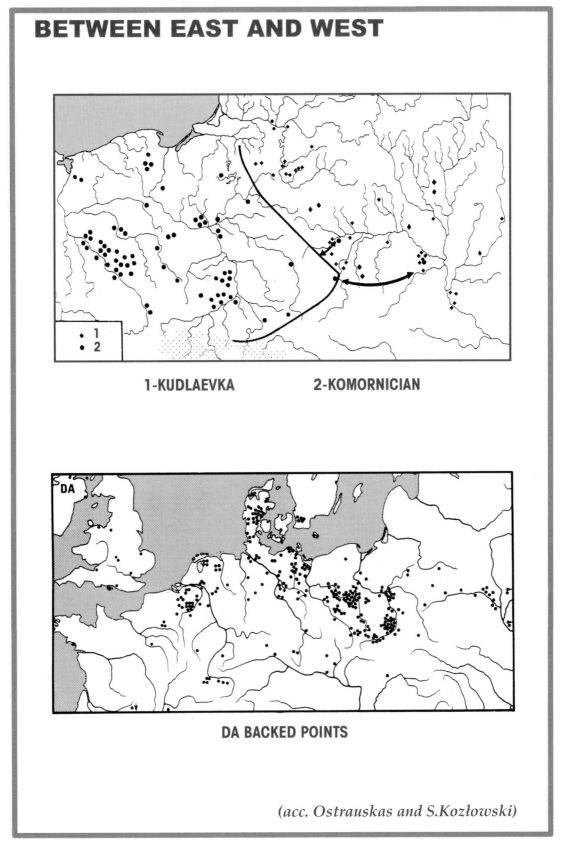

Fig. 11.5

The answer depends on whether you prefer to deal with western "influence", coming from the Komornician milieu, or you wish to see the origins of Kudlaevka backed points in the south, that is, in the Late Paleolithic communities of Volhynia (Lipa), Podolya (Halich) and the basin of the Dniester (Molodowa V, topmost layer).

The latter interpretation appears to be favored by the virtually total absence in Kudlaevka assemblages of triangles which were unknown in the Moldavian and Volhynian region, while being typical of Komornician assemblages. Limited numbers of reliable datings for Kudlaevka assemblages (combination of backed point and tanged point at Preboreal Miłuki 4, Poland-information of Jerzy Siemaszko) make the interpretation even more difficult, especially as in northeastern Poland and Belarus, and partly also in Ukraine, they occur in geomorphologically different position compared to Janislawician ones, which would indicate that they are of different (earlier) than Janislawice age. A similar phenomenon is known from Polish territory (Witów and Grądy-Woniecko with Komornician material lower down and Janislawician above). The existence of Kudlaevka assemblages with and without trapezes would suggest a pre-Atlantic age for the latter and an Early Atlantic age for the former.

Hence the "Komornician-Kudlaevkian case" is not clear enough not to be taken for a "Moldavian-Kudlaevkian case", too.

Theatrum maius

In 1715, the Armenian Krzysztof Szadbey, a forefather of the present author, came from Istanbul to southeastern, then Polish Pokutye, to establish the town of Kuty (a charter granted by King Augustus II the Strong). In doing so he followed in the footsteps of countless forbearers traveling between the warm Black Sea and the colder north. His progeny, the Osadca line, all bearing the telling nickname of the "Settler", wandered further north in the 20th century, settling in Lvov (the author's mother). Later, the winds of war threw them even further north and west, to Warsaw.

In reality, the wanderings of the author's family repeated the ancient trail of the Tartars and Turks, of the great hetmans of the Polish armies Żółkiewski and Chodkiewicz, of King John III Sobieski, of the Cossacks, the Armenian merchants from Kaffa and the Valachian shepherds. Naturally, it was traced way back earlier, at least in the Middle Paleolithic (Levalloisian and Micoquian); here, I will be concerned with its operation in the Late Mesolithic.

Contacts at this time between the southeastern region (basins of the Prut, Dniester and Boh) and the Northwest (eastern part of the Vistula basin) are documented by flint rhomboids (BH) on one hand and Janislawician microliths (JA-C) on the other. In the south, BH rhomboids appeared in a late (?) phase of Grebenikian, most likely in the second half of the 7th – beginning of the 6th millennium cal. BC or a bit later, and continued in the early and middle phase of the Bug-Dniester culture, reaching even early Trypolye. Outside the Ukrainian-Moldavian environment, the BH rhomboids are seldom encountered in Central Europe, a mere few on the upper and middle Vistula (Lublin uplands, Nida Trough and eastern Mazovia, cf. "Pontic elements"), where they are allochtonous and rare, hence atypical. The local contexts they appear in (if identifiable at all) are mainly Janislawician and in one case Funnel Beaker Culture (Karmanowice, information from Jerzy Libera); they are entirely unknown from the Early Danubian (information from Janusz K. Kozłowski and Vitali Konopla) and Late Danubian (information from Anna Zakościelna) of Poland and Ukraine.

West of the Vistula (with the exception of the Nida Trough) they never appeared and they are not found in the Pripet basin either (information from Leonid Zalizniak). Similar specimens of the BH type, also of possible southern/Mediterranean provenance, contemporary (or slightly earlier?) with the Central European, are encountered in northern France and Belgium, also in Denmark and Scania (cf. "Pre-Neolithic").

These specific elements are part of a greater phenomenon of pre-Neolithization/castelnovization (cf.), covering the Mesolithic from c. 7000 cal. BC (enforced demand for blanks of large parameters, change of core exploitation reduction strategy, raw material mining, long-distance distribution of raw materials and semi-products, complex core preforming, change to pressure technique, new tools, mainly trapezes and rhomboids, but also retouched blades and truncations, cf. "Pre-Neolithic"). The phenomenon originated in the Mediterranean zone and spread to the north, taking over much of Europe, including the region under study here (Grebeniki/Bug-Dniester, Kukrek, Murzak-Koba, Donetz (?) and Janislawician cultures).

Assuming the described model is not false in any extent, in our case the South would have been the "giver" and the North the "taker".

The question now is where to draw the boundary between the alleged "givers" and the alleged "takers". The answer comes from mapping data, more specifically from an analysis of the southern extent of Janislawician elements contemporary with the BH rhomboids. Based on the chief Janislawician representative, that is, JA–C points (cf. "Atlas"), it can be said that in the southeast the Janislawician reached the sandy regions of Volhynia (Small Polesye) and the vicinity of Przemyśl (Sierakośce), Trans-Carpathian Ukraine (Kamyanitsa I), vicinity of Lvov (Brzuchowice VI) and the upper course of the Dniester (Weren), and Koniecpol on the Boh. As for Grebenikian, its northern extent reached the upper Dniester (Radelichi near Drogobych).

We are dealing therefore with a typical, partly super-imposed extent of the elements of two neighboring cultural regions, which is most likely due to neighborly interaction with occasional "visits" to the "neighbors". The BH rhomboids suggest even far-reaching penetration. Individual characteristic elements penetrated into the neighbor's territory via the river network (Boh, Dniester, Prut, Bug, San, Vistula).

The situation was much the same on the peripheries of

the Kukrek and Janislawician cultures, slightly further to the east (penetration of the so-called Kukrek inserts along the Boh and Dniester, in the latter case in the direction of the Pripet basin).

This model of mutual contacts, interactions and opposition in the border zone between the Black Sea and the Baltic, as exemplified here by the Late Mesolithic relations between the Janislawician and the Grebeniki/Bug-Dniester culture, was repeated a number of times in the prehistory of the region: Levalloisian – Micoquian, Magdalenien – Molodovian, Funnel Beaker – Trypolye, etc., and the same is to be said of historical periods... The seasonal shifts of boundaries, facilitated or provoked by changes of the environment among others, was part of the picture.

From one stage to the other

The Late Mesolithic connections and relations described above (*Theatrum maius*) passed down the "corridor" linking the Ponticum with the Balticum. The eastern Carpathians rising a few hundred meters above sea level close off this corridor on the west; enclosed inside this ridge is the Carpathian Basin which is apparently isolated from Little Poland and Ukraine (cf. "Southeast"). But the isolation is not absolute, as indicated by not numerous Late Mesolithic material of both "Polish" and "Ukrainian" origin occurring inside the Basin, as well as Transcarpathian elements found in Poland.

Firstly, there is purely Janislawician material in Transcarpathian Ukraine (Kamyanitsa I) and typically Kukrek material (mainly Kukrek-type inserts) in local contexts in Polish Orava (Lipnica Wielka, information from Paweł Valde-Nowak). Mention should also be made of a double-slotted armed bone point from Slovakia (Medvežia, published by Juraj Barta), closely resembling finds from Ukraine which are considered as Mesolithic.

Originating from the Carpathian Basin in turn is obsidian (mainly on its way to Poland?); the raw material is found residually mostly in Late Mesolithic assemblages in western Upper Silesia (Late Komornician Dzierżno of Bolesław Ginter), and in the east (upper and middle Vistula basin) in Janislawician contexts (Raniżów 1 excavated by the author, and Grzybowa Góra XIII/59, excavated by Romuald Schild).

The Carpathian barrier is thus obviously hardly impermeable at this time and the relatively low passes (c. 900 m a.s.l. – Uzhok, Tartar, etc.) are not impassable. However, the following issues need to be resolved:

– exact chronology of the appearance of obsidian from the south (7th or 6th millennium cal. BC?);
– procurement model for this raw material (directly or at least partly through the Early Danubians and if the latter, then in the 6th millennium cal. BC).

Finally, it is not clear how the Kukrek elements passed into non-Kukrek cultural context. On one hand, they are encountered far to the north in the basin of the Lower Pripet, where they occur together with Janislawician material, and on the other hand, they spread north all the way to Orava in the Western Carpathians. Perhaps they are a more easterly equivalent of the BH rhomboids described above?

11.6. Gaban

(co-author – G. Dalmeri)

Introduction

The following publication presents the results of the archaeological investigation in the Mesolithic layers at Riparo Gaban, near Trento, northern Italy. The excavations, begun by Bernardino Bagolini in the early 1970s, were continued by him and by the author, together with Alberto Broglio, Giampaolo Dalmeri and Michele Lanzinger in the early eighties. Here we publish the Mesolithic material.

Research

In the study of the Romagnano III (cf. "Trentino sequence") Mesolithic series, a detailed Sauveterrian sequence was found. However, the final part of this sequence was missing and it was impossible to reconstruct a detailed sequence in the Castelnovian series, which was divided in Romagnano into two phases: ancient (dated to the first half of the 7th millennium cal. BC) and recent, at the turn to the Neolithic (= ceramic) about 5500 cal. BC. This consideration brought our attention back to Riparo Gaban which offered more developed Castelnovian sequences (Fig. 11.6a–e).

Site

The Riparo Gaban site is a multilayer (from the Middle Mesolithic until the Early Iron Age) rock shelter, located on the western slope of Monte Calisio in Piazzina di Martignano, Trento, Italy. Exposed on the east, it is elevated about 80 m above the valley of the Adige.

^{14}C dating

Altogether nine charcoal samples, coming from the Bagolini-Broglio-Dalmeri-Kozłowski excavations (sector IV), were dated by the Laboratory of the Christian-Alberts University in Kiel, Germany, giving the following results in Table 11.1.

The archaeological comment is as follows:
– The datings follow (with two exceptions: GAB 2 and GAB 4) established site geological and cultural stratigraphy;
– They also clearly confirm the dating of the Sauveterrian-Castelnovian transition, established on the neighboring site of Romagnano III at around 8000 years BP (c. 7000 cal. BC);
– They confirm the uninterrupted continuation of the settlement at that time;
– The dates suggest the existence of a Late Sauveterrian occupation (GAB 7, layer FB), little known on other

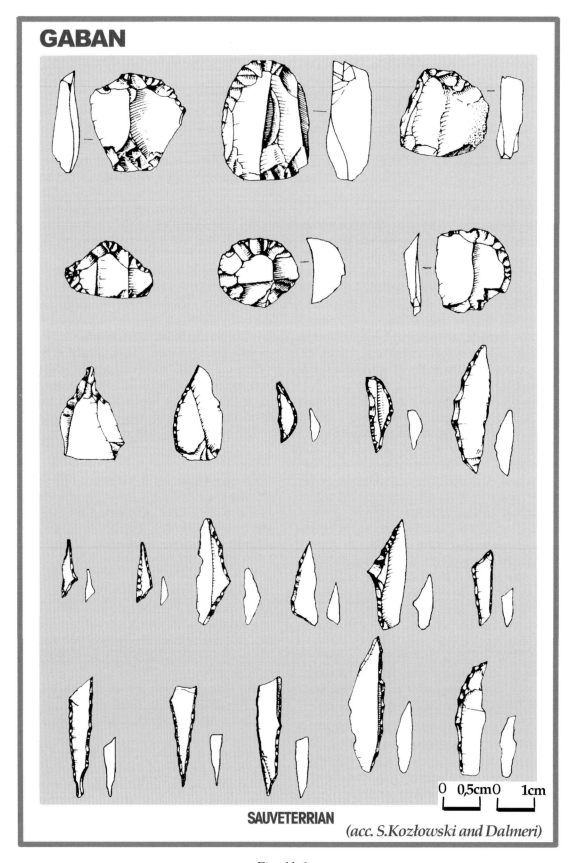

Fig. 11.6a

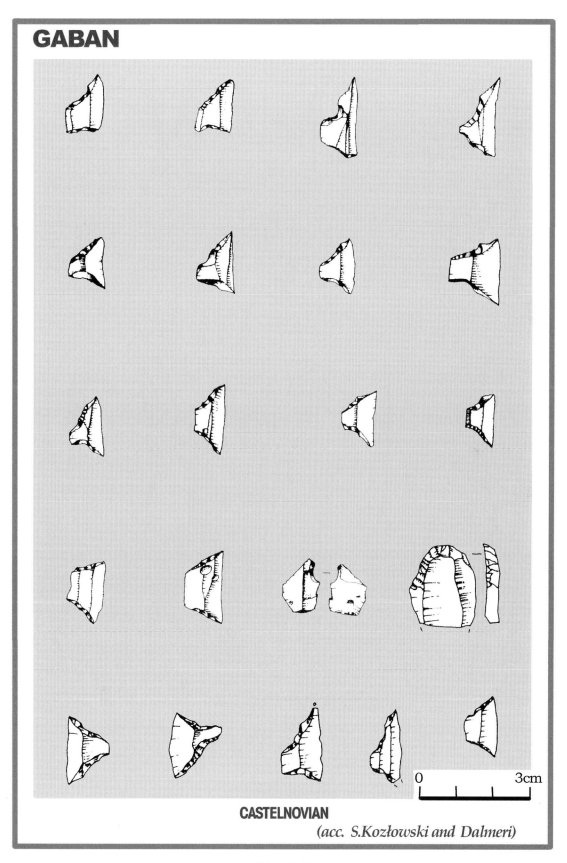

GABAN

CASTELNOVIAN
(acc. S.Kozłowski and Dalmeri)

Fig. 11.6b

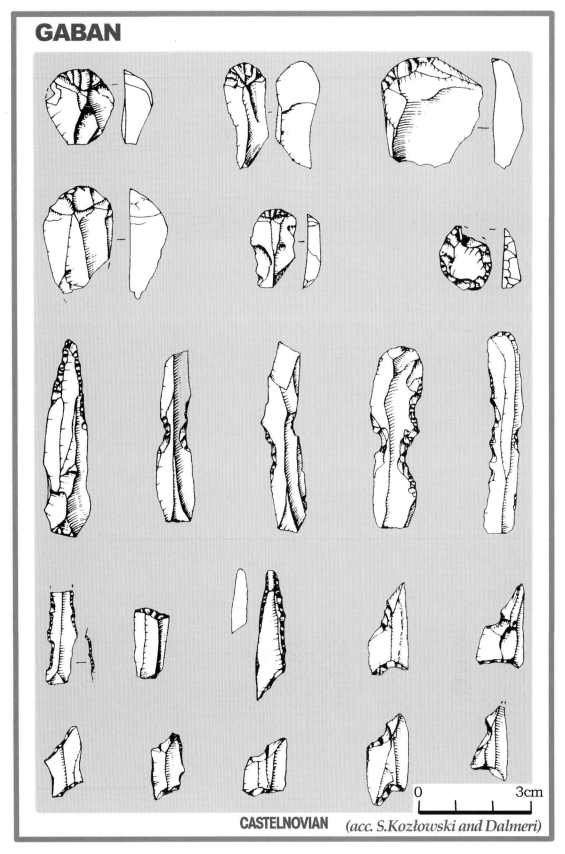

Fig. 11.6c

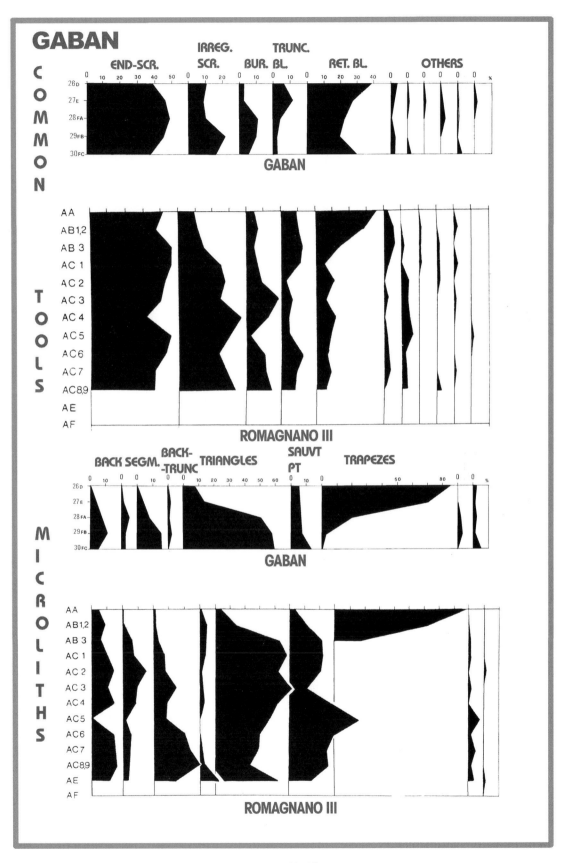

Fig. 11.6d

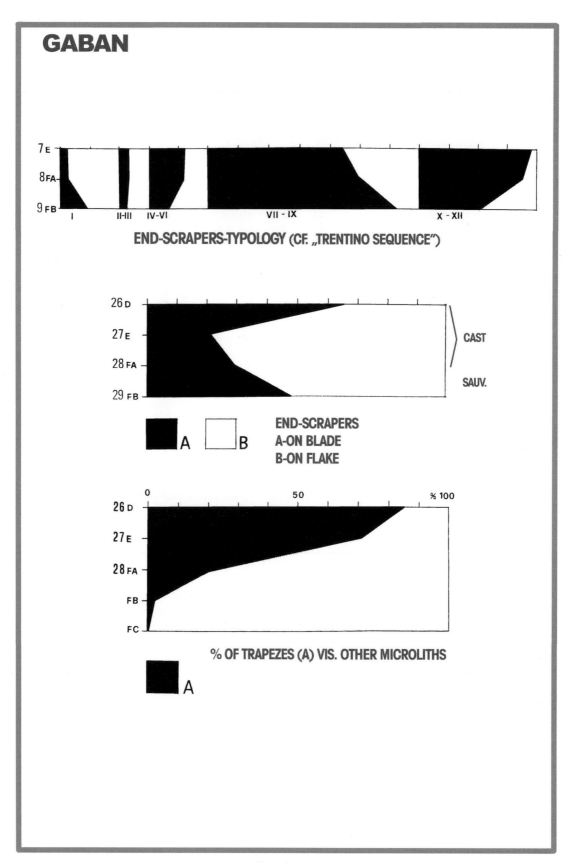

Fig. 11.6e

Table 11.1

Sample no.	Laboratory Code	Layer	Radiocarbon age BP	Culture
GAB 1	KIA 10362	D	7283±38	Early Neolithic
GAB 2	KIA 10363	E	6968±41	Castelnovian
GAB 3	KIA10364	FA	7971±42	Early Castelnovian
GAB 4	KIA10365	FA	8323±63	Early Castelnovian
GAB 5	KIA10366	FA	7725±49	Early Castelnovian
GAB 6	KIA10367	FA	7902±55	Early Castelnovian
GAB 7	KIA10368	FB	8193±66	Latest Sauveterrian
GAB 8	KIA10369	FC (F13)	8509±44	Middle Sauveterrian
GAB 9	KIA10370	FC (F16)	8847±57	Middle Sauveterrian

sites of the Conca di Trento (e.g. small collection from Vatte di Zambana).

Typologie des industries

L'analyse a été effectuée sur la base de la liste typologique crée pour l'étude des industries mésolithiques de Romagnano III (cf. in this volume). Aux types déjà décrits nous avons ajouté quelques types non existants à Romagnano:

A. Grattoirs.

Grattoir sur lame, court, intègre, à front arqué; grattoir sur lame, double, sans retouche latérale; grattoir sur lame, double, avec retouche latérale; fragment de grattoir sur lame; grattoir frontal court sur éclat, à front arqué oblique et retouche latérale; grattoir frontal très court sur éclat à front arqué oblique et retouche latérale; grattoir ogival à ogive large, à retouche latérale.

B. Eclats retouchés. Racloir à retouche inverse.

C. Burins. Burin sur lame fracturée, double; burin dièdre sur lame mince; burin dièdre *à biseau* carénoïde; burin court et massif *à biseau* carénoïde; burin court et massif *à biseau* carénoïde opposé à burin dièdre; burin court et massif à un enlèvement opposé à burin sur troncature.

C1. Groupe des "Burins de Ripabianca". Le "Burin de Ripabianca" a été decrit comme un burin sur retouche latérale. Plusieurs types ont été définis, selon différents critères: localisation et profil de la retouche de préparation; orientation de la retouche; association de plusieurs enlèvements ou types.

D. Lames tronquées. Lame très large (> 20 mm) à troncature retouchée.

G. Couteaux à dos courbe. Couteau à dos marginal très court; couteau à dos marginal très étroit; fragments de couteaux à dos.

K. Composites. Grattoir-perçoir, grattoir-eclat retouché.

N. Pointes sur lame ou éclat laminaire. Fragment de pointe-troncature.

T. Trapèzes. Trapèzes asymétriques courts, trapèzes symétriques.

Structure des catégories des outils et des armatures

A l'intérieur de la catégorie des outils, les grattoirs (38–49%), les becs et les perçoirs (< 5%) présentent une certaine stabilité dans toute la séquence. Les couteaux à dos et les composites sont toujours caractérisés par des pourcentages très faibles (environ 2% maximum). Les autres groupes montrent des changements des indices: diminution des indices des éclats retouchés (16/21–8/10%) et des burins (5/10–2%), accentuée surtout au passage du Sauveterrien au Castelnovien; paralellément à une augmentation des indices des lames tronquées (2/9–5/11%) et des lames retouchées (19/20–22/38%).

A l'intérieur de la catégorie des armatures on remarque une certaine stabilité dans la séquence mésolithique pour les pointes à dos et les dos tronqués (toujours inférieurs à 5%) et, dans toute la séquence, pour les pointes à deux dos (toujours inférieur à 10%). D'autres groupes montrent des tendances évolutives, comme, par exemple, la disparition graduelle des pointes sur éclat laminaire et des segments; la forte diminution (au Castelnovien) des triangles; et l'augmentation progressive des trapèzes qui au stade céramique/Néolithique arrivent jusqu'à 84% des armatures. Cela correspond à une rarifaction, puis disparition des armatures sauveterriennes, remplacées par des castelnoviennes (trapèzes).

Structure des groupes d'outils

A. Grattoirs. L'indice des grattoirs sur support laminaire varient entre 22 et 65%, sans toutefois mettre en évidence une tendance uniforme. Dans le Sauveterrien (FB-29) la fréquence est de 48%; elle diminue au Castelnovien jusqu'à 29–22% et au "Néolithique Ancien" atteint le maximum (65%). Néanmoins, dans les deux secteurs considérés, en ce qui concerne le niveau E-27, la situation est différente, aussi bien pour les grattoirs sur lame que pour les trapèzes: dans le secteur V les grattoirs sur lame sont presque absents et on constate une grande concentration de trapèzes (différentiation fonctionnelle entre les deux secteurs?). Les autres groupes de grattoirs ne montrent aucune tendance évolutive.

C1. Burins de Ripabianca. Ils sont présents, en faible quantité (2 pièces), seulement à partir du "Néolithique Ancien".

D. Lames tronquées. Au cours du "Néolithique" on assiste à l'introduction d'un type de troncature sur support laminaire grand et massif inconnu au Mésolithique.

E. Lames retouchées. Dans la séquence castelnovienne et au "Néolithique Ancien" on a observé une augmentation progressive de l'indice des lames retouchées (surtout les lames à encoche et denticulées) présentes déjà au Sauveterrien.

G. Couteaux à dos. Ils sont présents dans toute la séquence mésolithique.

Structure des groupes d'armatures microlithiques
N. Pointes sur éclat laminaire. Le nombre des pièces est très faible. Néanmoins, on observe, dans le Sauveterrien, un équilibre entre les deux classes (troncatures viz. dos).

P. Segments. Dans ce groupe aussi, le nombre de pièces est très faible: on remarque au Sauveterrien, la dominance constante des types allongés (12.2%).

R. Triangles. Les triangles sont toujours présents, même au "Néolithique Ancien". Les scalènes dominent (90–98%) et les isocèles semblent presque disparaître. L'indice des scalènes longs à base courte augmente suivant la séquence au détriment de ceux à base longue. Les triangles scalènes à trois côtés retouchés (TE), considérés dans leur ensemble, augmentent au Castelnovien (jusqu'à plus de 50% en E-27).

S. Pointes à deux dos. Elles sont peu nombreuses. Au Sauveterrien on observe une prédominance des formes longues (PD–7.2%).

T. Trapèzes. On enregistre une tendance à l'augment-ation de l'indice des types asymétriques courts, qui sont toujours les plus nombreux (40–55%), une diminution des romboïdes (23–16%) et une certaine stabilité des types asymétriques longs et symétriques (10–15%). A l'intérieur du groupe des asymétriques on note une tendance évolutive pour le type 10, qui au court du temps, devient plus allongé, ses troncatures sont plus concaves et le côté court plus petit.

Comparaisons avec la séquence du bassin de Trento

La comparaison de deux séquences voisines, celle de Romagano III et celle de Ripano Gaban permet de constater l'existence au Gaban d'une phase sauveterrienne se situant après la fin de la séquence sauveterrienne de Romagano III et avant le début du Castelnovien.

Ces considérations se fondent sur les datations ¹⁴C et sur l'indice élevé des segments longs par rapport aux courts, constaté au Gaban.

Les différences entre les deux séquences mises en évidence entre les deux sites sont les suivantes:

– le bas pourcentage des triangles scalènes longues avec base courte de Gaban (triangle de Montclus) contraste avec les valeurs élevées connus de Romagnano (faute de description?);

– l'index plus élevé, des grattoirs, sur éclat à Gaban par rapport à Romagnano.

En ce qui concerne le Castelnovien, on remarque une grande similitude structurale entre les deux séries appartenant au Castelnovien ancien (couche FA-28) et moyen/récent et la longue perduration des microliths sauveterriens dans cette industrie.

Le "Néolithique Ancien" de Gaban est une continuité technique, typologique et structurale du Castelnovien recent local.

Conclusion
1. Riparo Gaban is a typical, small multi-layer site presenting part of a local cultural sequence: Middle-Late Sauveterrian-Castelnovian-Early Neolithic. Romagnano III and Pradestel, all localized in the same region, are similar in type.
2. The Sauveterrian is represented here in its middle and latest phase; the Castelnovian could be divided into two phases.
3. The Riparo Gaban Mesolithic industries, typologically similar to those from Romagnano III differ from their neighbours in some aspects:

• The raw material structure in the Sauveterrian period differs considerably from that of Romagnano III (distance of only 8.50 km) and Pradestel (distance of 4 km); in the Castenovian period the raw material structure of Gaban is similar to that of Romagnano, but still different from that of Pradestel;

• Some typological and statistical data of the Gaban Mesolithic are also slightly different from that known for Romagano III (almost the entire Mesolithic, except Latest Sauveterrian, sequence of Conca of Trento) and Vatte di Zambana (the late phase of the Sauveterrian). The difference is visible in the group of end-scrapers, where the flake forms predominate in Gaban (except in layer 27/E) on blade pieces (which is the opposite of the situation seen in Romagnano III). The second difference is clearly visible in the group of triangles, which are more numerous here (except layers 27/E and 26D) than in Romagnano III. In the group of triangles, Gaban with its latest Sauveterrian also seems to differ from the late Sauveterrian of Romagnano. While, long base scalene triangles are in equilibrium with the short base pieces on this last site (the same in Vatte di Zambana), the Gaban latest Sauveterrian shows the domination of the long-base variety, and the equilibrium of these two varieties appears only in the Early Castelnovian. All this could mean that the Mesolithic industries of Gaban, which seem to be more or less contemporary with the upper part of the Romagnano III sequence (layers AC2–AA, but the Gaban latest Sauveterrian phase from layer FB does not occur in Romagnano) constantly differ from those of Romagnano and Pradestel in the raw material economy, end-scrapers structure and triangles structure, and internal composition of the microliths group (absence of some types).

All this cannot be accidental, depicting instead a permanent difference existing between the industries of the two compared sites. This could mean that inside the Conca of Trento, just between Romagnano III (+ Pradestel?) on one hand, and Gaban on the other (distance of 4–8.50 km), there existed a real (tribal?) border in the Mesolithic period.

11.7. Latronico (Fig. 11.7)

Excavated by G. Cremonesi, this multilayer cave of southern Italy presents a local variant of the Castelnovian phenomenon, not linked with the preceding Marisa-type (cf.) tradition. It appears c. 7000 cal. BC and exists until local ceramicization (cf.)

Excerpts from a publication prepared together with Carlo Tozzi appear below.

Grattoirs

Ils sont généralement allongés (classes I, IV et V dans la typologie de Broglio et Kozlowski) et assez courts (classe XVI); les pièces très courtes (classes IX–XV) sont rares (6 sur 95). Les pièces allongées, généralement sur lame, prédominent: les grattoirs à front arqué (36 sur 61) et grattoirs a front tectiforme (25 sur 61) sur lame entière ou lame sectionnée, parfois avec la retouche sur un bord. Suivent les grattoirs plus courts, généralement sur éclats (28 pièces), majoritairement à front tectiforme, rarement à museau. Les pièces très courtes, sur éclat, ont un front arqué (6 pièces).

La proportion entre grattoirs sur lame et grattoirs sur éclat est de 61 pièces contre 34. Elle est constante tout au long de la séquence. Mais la proportion des grattoirs sur lame évolue : en nombre égal à la base, les grattoirs à front arqué dominent à la fin de la séquence.

Les grattoirs de Latronico se distinguent de ceux des autres sites castelnoviens italiens: si les pièces à front arqué et tectiforme se rapprochent des sites septentrionaux (Romagnano III, Gaban), Latronico se distingue par l'absence des pièces très courtes et circulaires, caractéristiques du nord. En Italic centrale (Piazzana, Lama Lite, Passo della Communella), on ne connaît pas les grattoirs sur lame à front arqué ou tectiforme, mais les grattoirs courts et très courts sont abondants. Dans le sud, Latronico ne suit pas la tradition locale antérieure représentée par Grotta Marisa, (cf.) comme le montre l'absence des petits grattoirs circulaires romanelliens.

Conclusion

Latronico se distingue clairement du Castelnovien du nord et du centre de l'Italie, et ne semble pas dériver du Mésolithique local précédent.

Les armatures

Typologie

A l'exception de quelques (5 sur 263) lamelles à dos abrupt marginal, toutes les autres sont des trapèzes. Une partie d'entre eux entre dans la classification proposé par Broglio et Kozlowski pour l'Italie septentrionale:

trapèzes asymétriques de types 1, 2, 4, 5, 7, 9 et 11 fabriqués par la technique du microburin, à piquant trièdre conservé. Les autres trapèzes – symétriques – sont fabriqués par sectionnement sur des supports plus étroits. Seule une toute petite partie d'entre eux se rapproche du type 11. On peut les subdiviser en quatre catégories (cf. "Atlas").

AA: trapèzes étroits à troncatures concaves;
AC: trapèzes larges à troncatures concaves;
AZ: trapèzes réguliers à troncatures concaves (cf. type 11 du nord);
AF: trapèzes réguliers à troncatures concaves profondes et piquants trièdres;

Si les trapèzes asymétriques entrent dans la tradition castelnovienne, les formes symétriques semblent locales (sud de l'Italie).

Structure statistiques

Au debut de la séquence, les trapèzes symétriques dominent tandis qu'à la fin, ils sont en nombre presque égal aux asymétriques. Le gabarit des pièces augmente avec le temps: dans la phase F, les trapèzes voient leur taille augmenter, résultat d'une augmentation en nombre des types asymétriques. Les trapèzes symétriques restent de petite taille jusqu'à la fin de la séquence, mais les proportions changent: le type AZ augmente au détriment des autres types. Le type AF apparaît dans la partie médiane de la sequence, pour devenir un des fossiles directeurs du Mésolithique récent et du Néolithique du Mezzogiorno.

Conclusion

A l'exception du type AZ, proche du type 11 septentrional, les autres armatures ne trouvent pas d'analogie dans le Castelnovien italien. Les analogies connues manquent de cohérence: AZ est connu dans le Mésolithique récent des Balkans (Odmut et Franchti supérieur), AA se retrouve dans le Languedoc (Baume de Monclus, couches du Sauveterrien récent), tandis qu'AF est connu dans le Castelnovien français. A part des contacts possibles avec les Balkans, les autres rapprochements semblent être des convergences. Au contraire, les armatures asymétriques trouvent leur place dans le Castelnovien du nord et du centre de l'Italie. Le type 7 est dominant (environ 50%), les autres types restent stables tout au long de la séquence, contrairement, à ce que l'on observe au nord de l'Italie.

11.8. Leduc 2 (Fig. 11.8)

An open-air Late Mesolithic site in Wallony (Belgium), excavated by André Gob, and dated to c. 6000 cal. BC. This text is a small excerpt from the original publication prepared by the excavator and the author. We describe

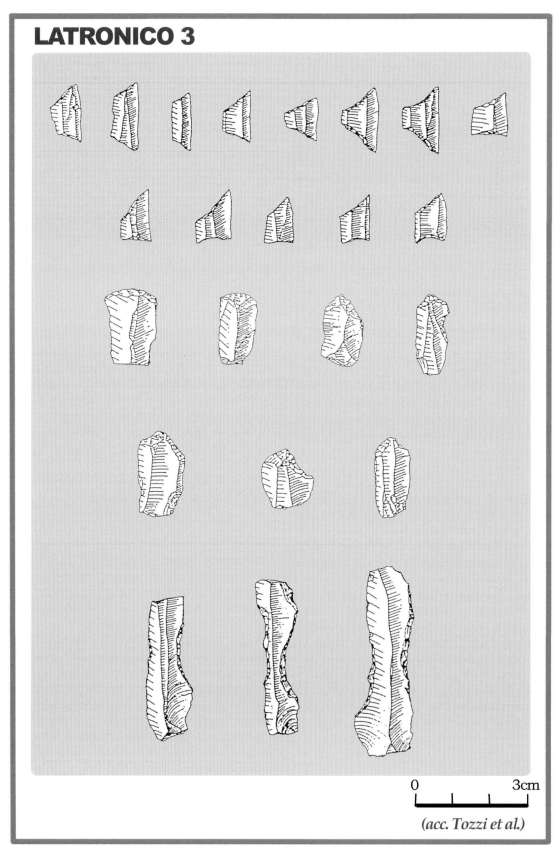

LATRONICO 3

0   3cm

(acc. Tozzi et al.)

Fig. 11.7

LEDUC 2

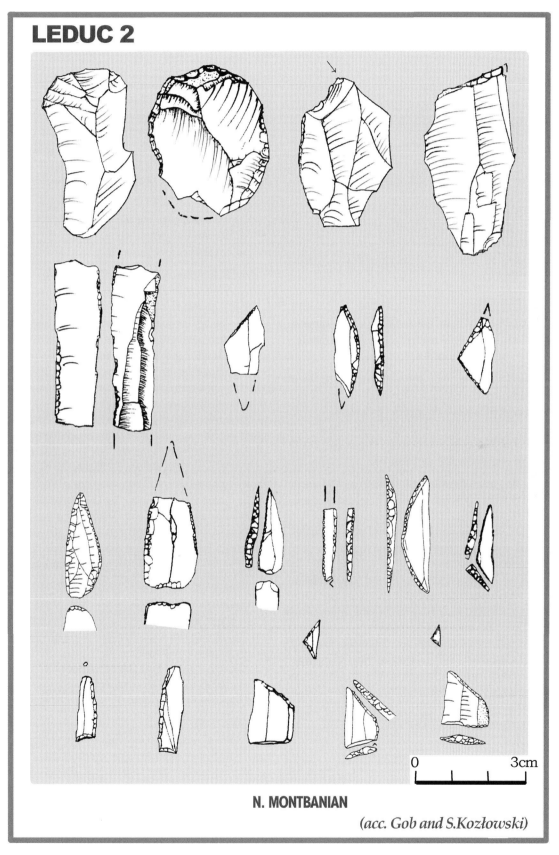

N. MONTBANIAN

(acc. Gob and S.Kozłowski)

Fig. 11.8

here only part of the Mesolithic material, omitting the Neolithic collection.

Nucleus

22 pièces ont été trouvées à Station Leduc, dont 4 mésolithiques et 19 néolithiques.

Nucleus mésolithiques

Ils sont très peu nombreux, petits (en dessous de 5 cm), et plus exploités (achèvés ou dans un état d'exploitation avancé). Chaque pièce représente un type different:

• nucléus à lames à un plan de frappe,
• nucléus caréné (*handle core*) à deux plans opposées,
• nucléus subcirculaire, à deux plans de frappe (1 préférentiel).

Les lames

Le site a fourni en tout 562 lames, dont env. 414 dans l'ensemble mésolithique.

Lames mésolithiques

Total -env. 414 pièces, dont 101 entières, 114 fragments proximaux, 118 distaux et 74 mesiaux. Les dimensions des pièces entières sont les suivantes:

• longueur: 10–72 mm (avec une dominante entre 14–30 mm), parmi les exemplaires plus longs on observe un pourcentage plus elevé de pièces corticales.
• largeur: 2–24 mm (avec une dominante entre 5–12 mm), parmi les exemplaires plus larges les pièces corticales sont aussi plus nombreuses.

Les proportions varient entre 2:1 et 4:1 (avec une dominante autour de 3:1) et le poids moyen d'un exemplaire est de 0,8 gr.
Tout l'ensemble est dominé par les pièces non-corticales.

Les lames sont peu courbées, le maximum de cette courbure est placé vers la moitié de la longueur, les bords sont relativement parallèles, le talon large, souvent lineaire, le bulbe punctiforme, proeminent, l'extremité distale pointue, la section transversale plutôt triangulaire (43 pièces) que trapezoidale (13 pièces).

On doit aussi mentionner ici les fragments mesiaux de lames, qui semblent être le résultat final d'un fractionnement intentionnel (cf. "Sectioning"). Ces pièces se distinguent par leur forme rectangulaire ainsi que par leurs dimensions (10 a 15 mm de longueur, 6–11 mm de largeur) et leurs proportions (2,5:1–1:1) recurrentes.

Outils rétouchés

Le site a livré 106 outils retouchés (entiers et fragments), dont env. 84 font partie de l'ensemble mésolithique et env. 22 semblent etre plus récents.

Outils rétouchés mésolithiques
Nombre total: env. 84 pièces, dont

7 grattoirs,
5 burins (plus chûtes de burins),
6 troncatures retouchées,
5 lames retouchées,
57 microlithes (plus 6 microburins et formes apparentées),
1 pièce esquillé (?),
31 fragments d'outils.

Les grattoirs a front arqué sont courts, effectués sur éclats, provenant en majeure partie de la phase de preformation du nucléus. Il existe un unique exemplaire de grattoir sur lame sectionnée. Un grattoir semble avoir été formé sur éclat fragmenté, un autre possède un front double.

Les éclats retouchés sont amorphiques et leur retouche semble etre fortuite, due a leur utilisation.

Parmi les rares burins on retrouve des types suivants:

• transversales sur surface naturelle,
• d'axe sur troncature, et
• d'angle sur troncature.

Les troncatures retouchées (6 pièces) sont des specimens elancés et ont été faites sur lames. L'unique exemplaire trapu a été effectué sur éclat. Les troncatures sont droites.

Les lames retouchées (parfois sous forme de lames sectionées) ne sont pas trop nombreuses dans l'inventaire mésolithique (5 pièces). Il s'agit de lames régulières, mais leur retouche est irregulière, courte, interrompue, parfois ventrale ou alterne. Elle serait presque toujours le résultat d'une utilisation de lames brutes.

La seule pièce qui presente des caracteristiques différentes devrait etre classifiée comme lamelle Montbani et se distingue par la presence de deux encoches opposées.

Les indices de grattoirs, de burins, de troncatures et de lames retouchées sont assez bas (env. 28% au total).

Les microlithes forment un groupe très important, car leur indice atteint plus que 70% des outils.

Typologiquement, les microlithes peuvent être bien decrites a l'aide de la liste typologique de A. Bohmers et A. Wouters. Ainsi, on renconre a Station Leduc 2 les:

• pointes de type A,
• pointes de type B,
• segments,
• triangles isoceles,
• triangles à angle obtus,
• lamelles à dos sur support sectionné,
• lamelles à dos à base retouchée,
• trapèzes asymétriques,
• feuille de guy.

Tous les types de microlithes mentionnés ci-dessus coexistent dans les outillages mésolithiques de la region et forment un outillage coherent a caractere Mésolithique récent locale type representant le passage Rhénanien-Montbani variant séptentrional.

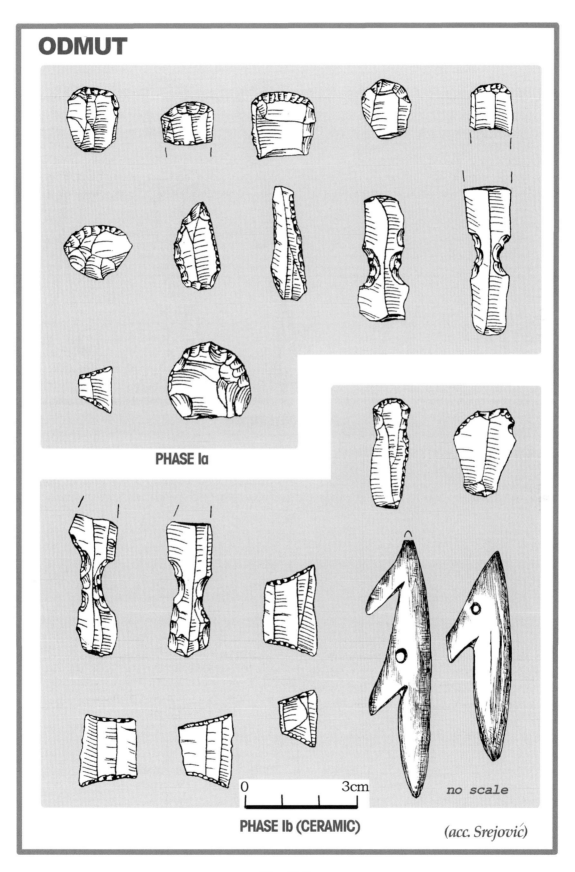

Fig. 11.8a

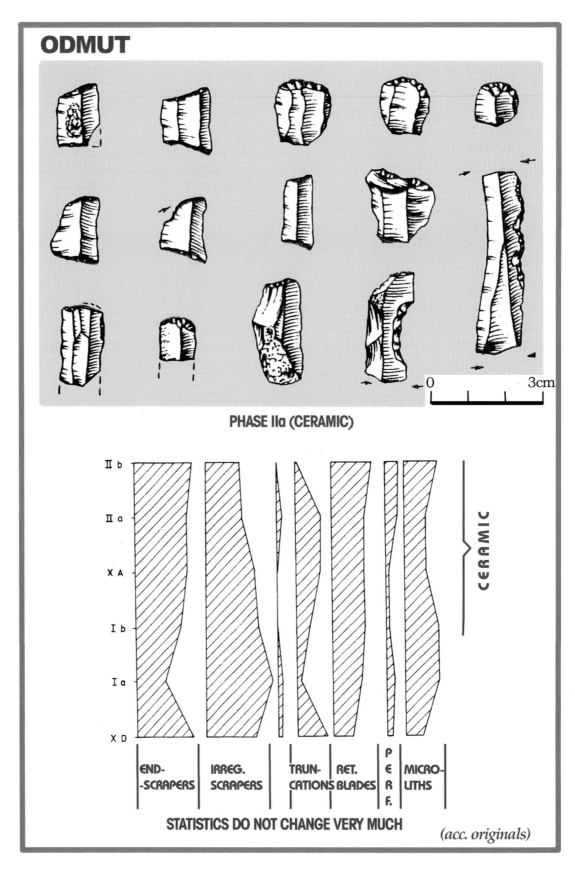

Fig. 11.8b

11.9. Odmut

(co-author – J. K. Kozłowski and I. Radovanovic)

This multi-layer cave site from the mountains of Montenegro (Fig. 11.8a–b), excavated by Dragoslav Srejović, yielded a Castelnovian-type industry carbon-dated to the 7th millennium cal. BC. The site, published by Janusz K. Kozłowski, Ivana Radovanović and Stefan K. Kozłowski, gave the name to Odmut culture/group (cf.), one of the Castelnovian units.

Starčevo-type and impresso wares were among the finds from the upper layers. The following is a presentation of the typical assemblages (layer IIa).

Layer IIa

GENERAL STRUCTURE

The assemblage yielded 632 flint artifacts. The tools index amounts to 15.4%. Unlike the preceding layer XA, the blade index of IIa drops to reach the level from the lower layers.

CORES

Only 27 cores were recovered from layer IIa. Single-platform specimens are entirely blade cores. Also present are conical specimens (7.4%). The categories of splintered pieces (14.8%) and double-platform cores (3.7%) are distinctly on the decline.

FLAKES

Flakes amount to 60.3% of the whole assemblage.

WASTE

Waste accounts for 8.7% of the whole assemblage.

BLADES

The total number of blades/bladelets in this layer is 66 (10.66%). The frequency of complete specimens had not changed from layer Ib and an increase in proximal fragments can be observed.

The ratio of cortical blades/bladelets is slightly higher (27.27%); on the other hand, there are no changes in the frequency of cortical flakes. This might possibly be explained by a tendency to obtain blades in the early phase of core processing without previous decortication.

From the point of view of the blade cross-sections, there is a conspicuous increase (compared to the earlier phase) in triangular ones (51.52%).

The parallel-sided bladelets are on the increase (54.55%); this trend was observed already in layer Ib.

The average length of blades is 25.2 mm, with a standard deviation of 5.22; the average width is lower than in layer XA, being 8.94 mm with a standard deviation of 2.57; and the average thickness is also lower – 2.29 mm with a standard deviation of 0.92.

TOOLS

In layer IIa end-scrapers represent 29.0% of the tools assemblage. All the implements occurring in the stratigraphical sequence are found in this assemblage as well. A tendency can be observed for the index of blade forms to become higher than before (altogether 52% of all specimens).

Similarly to the preceding layer XA, irregular scrapers/retouched flakes are few (20.0%) and follow the local tradition (transversal, lateral, convergent).

The occurrence of two single-blow burins in layer IIa is unprecedented in Odmut.

The retouched truncation index is fairly high in this layer (14.0%). Morphological features of truncations closely resemble those of specimens from the underlying layer XA. Specimens with a concave truncation are slightly fewer than before.

The group of retouched blades (18.0%) comprises, similarly to layer XA, specimens with opposite notches, as well as all types known from the lower layers.

Perforators are fairly well represented (6.0%). These are mainly short becks on blades with lateral retouch, and fine alternate perforators.

The set of microliths (11.0%) is standard, limited to trapezes (AF, AZ, AA without *piquant tièdre*).

Stratigraphical sequence and seriation of assemblages

Absolute dating

From the site of Odmut twelve radiocarbon dates are available for the sequence which is the object of our interest. The dates come from the following layers: XD (SI-2221), Ib (four dates: SI-2228, SI-2224, SI-2226, SI-22279),IIa (SI-2221, SI-2220, SI-2217, SI-2219), and layer IIb (Z-12, SI-2222, SI-2223).

The diagram of ^{14}C determinations has basically confirmed the succession of layers. Of special importance is the series of dates obtained for layers IIa and IIb, which place these layers within the time ranges of c. 6700/6200 and 6000/5700 years cal. BC respectively.

The dates obtained for layers XD and Ib also make up a sequence, although some of them cannot be accepted without reservations.

Layer XD has only one date: c. 9500 cal. BC. This date cannot possibly determine the age of materials in layer XD, the main bulk of which is characterized also by trapezes.

Layer Ib yielded four dates, of which two (SI-2226 and SI-2227) correspond well with the stratigraphic sequence, and are slightly later than the dates from layer IIa. This has been additionally supported by the evidence of Starčevo ceramics in the top of layer Ib. The two earlier dates obtained from layer Ib, viz. SI-2224, are questionable; they differ considerably from the two later dates.

The series of ^{14}C determinations under discussion shows that layers Ib (top) and IIb form a sequence which may be dated feom c. 6900 to c. 5650 years cal. BC.

Numerous data are available both for the Balkans and for the entire northern coast of the Mediterranean (Frankhthi, Romagnano III, Chateauneuf-lez-Martigues, Vlasac, Lepenski Vir) indicating that trapezes appeared in this area c. 7000 cal. BC (but earlier in the Frankhthi cave). For this reason, we have decided to date the lower boundary of the sequence at Odmut to the turn of the 8th millennium cal. BC or slightly later. Consequently, Odmut represents a sequence enclosed within the time block from around 7000 to at least 5700 cal. BC (layer IIb), or only slightly later (layers XB and XC). Thus, the whole sequence of the site of Odmut is contained within a time range of c. 1000–1300 calendar years and at its end enters into the Stačevo ceramic period.

General features of the stone industry at Odmut

All the levels of the site of Odmut (from XD to XC) are characterized by the same industry. The general structure of the sequence has been calculated on the basis of a series of 4426 artifacts (without layers XB and XC, which have provided too small samples) and shows proportions typical of Mesolithic habitation sites. Flakes predominate (63.5%), constituting, together with waste, 71.6% of the total inventory. Such a high index indicates that complete processing of raw materials was carried out on the site (part of decortication, core preforming, blank detachment, core rejuvenation and other repairs, and tools retouching).

The next group in size is made up of blades or bladelets (11.4%) showing a fairly high index for a site where flakes are used as blanks as well. The contemporaneous site of Vlasac (cf.) contains only 7–8% blades, while flakes are more numerous (75–77%) than at Odmut.

The indices of tools (9.8%) and cores (7.1%) are not very high, they tally with the average for sites in which cores were processed on the spot.

Retouched tools

Analysis of six assemblages of different ages from Odmut (from XD to IIb) has shown unquestionably that retouched tools are identical in all the assemblages, in terms of morphology as well as statistics. For this reason, we can talk about a uniform aceramic and later ceramic (Starčevo) lithic industry at Odmut, which is characterized by the following stable features:

1. End-scrapers are, as a rule, about 30% of all retouched tools, retouched flakes/irregular scrapers being at about 10–20%. Temporal variability consists in the gradual replacement of the latter by end-scrapers. In the group of retouched flakes, flake specimens (short, robust, very short arched, and discoidal) give way to blade specimens (primarily short and slender arched scrapers).

2. The presence of typical burins at Odmut is questionable.

3. The group of retouched truncations (on blades/bladelets: straight and concave, transversal and oblique, and specimens with a retouched back), retouched blades (simple, notched, and microretouched), and blade perforators (*becs*) are stable at the level of c. 10, 18 and 5% respectively. In the group of retouched blades, in the top part of the sequence appear specimens with opposite notches.

4. The group of microliths, too, shows stability of index (ca. 12%) and typological composition (backed pieces, trapezes AF, AZ and AA and microretouched bladelets). It is likely that in the upper part of the sequence the number of backed pieces drops.

Seriation of assemblages

Neither the indices of the general structure nor the frequency of flake categories, classified in terms of dorsal patterns, show variations in time. Similarly, retouched tools show no significant quantitative or qualitative changes.

The Odmut sequence compared to the Balkan and Mediterranean Mesolithic and Neolithic industries

The lithic industry at Odmut is striking for its surprising long stability over a span of c. 1000–1300 calendar years, this with regard to technology (cores, blades) and morphology of retouched tools, as well as the quantitative structure of major tool classes. Minor changes occurring in the sequence are statistically insignificant and are mainly due to raw material economy.

Nonetheless, the homogeneity of the Odmut industry is relative as the sequence can be divided into four stages in terms of the relationship between the major tool class indices. Thus, the first stage is represented by layer XD, the second by Ia and Ib, the third by layers XA and IIa, the fourth by layer IIb. This differentiation is partly functional and partly reflects the real temporal variability of the Odmut industry.

The weak changeability of the Odmut site industry sets it apart from the sequences of Slovenia (cf.) and northern Italy (cf.). In these two areas, the first pronounced techno-morphological changes can be observed (as in Montenegro) in the transition from the Middle to the Late Mesolithic, simultaneously with the emergence of the Castelnovian phenomenon (cf. "Pre-Neolithic"). The second came at the close of the Late Mesolithic and in the beginning of the Neolithic proper (more ceramic than agricultural in this area). The changes at the transition from the Middle (Sauveterrian) to the Late (Castelnovian) Mesolithic in the west have been well described for the Trentino sequence (cf.). Changes which took place in this sequence at the transition from the Castelnovian to the local ceramic "Neolithic", also the analogous modifications observed in the Riparo Gaban (cf.) and Pradestel sequences, are not equally apparent. Technological tendencies initiated in the classical Italian Castelnovian became widespread only in the Neolithic proper (Romagnano III T4–T3, Gaban N, Pradestel B-A). Interestingly, a new technology (*seconde mode/standard*) of blade production is incipient in classical Castelnovian with blades becoming larger and technologically more elaborate. These blades were to become widespread in the true Neolithic.

Some of the aspects of this technological change (viz. large number of blades with facetted platforms, replacement of irregular cross-sections by triangular or trapezoidal ones, parallel blade edges) are identical with the modifications which can be observed in the transition from layer Ia to Ib at Odmut, i.e., before pottery made an appearance. Thus, the vital technological *caesura* at Odmut precedes the appearance of ceramics, whereas in Italian sequences technological innovations appear to parallel the emergence of pottery (cf. "Ceramization").

It should not be overlooked that in the north Italian sequence, the passing of the Late Mesolithic into the "Neolithic" is reflected in a changed structure of retouched tools, with particular tool types undergoing changes (e.g. trapezes, appearance of elongated rhombs). These modifications are not always the consequence of developmental tendencies in classical Castelnovian (such as the increase of the trapezes index at the expense of other microliths, steady increase in the proportion of retouched blades).

By contrast, the Djerdap sequence (in the Iron Gates, cf. "Southeast") on the Serbian-Romanian border witnessed evolution that proceeded from the local Epi-Gravettian of the Cuina Turcului-Padina type to Lepenski Vir culture. This change introduced new blade technology, trapezes, retouched truncations and retouched blades, while triangles, backs and truncations, and backed pieces gradually disappeared. Moreover, a specific (for this region) development of splintered technique took place, and the frequency of irregular scrapers/retouched flakes increased conspicuously. Neolithic assemblages with ceramics of the Proto-Starčevo-Gura Bacului-Circea type with developed technology of slender and large blades emerge following Lepenski Vir culture (or parallel to it), if the presence of Starčevo pottery in trapezoid houses of Lepenski Vir will be confirmed (and it is!) and in all likelihood also contemporaneously with it. These assemblages cannot be regarded as a continuation of Lepenski Vir technology, but rather as the effect of migrations of population groups with the white painted ware from the territory of Thessaly and Macedonia (e.g. Méhtelek in Hungary and Donja Branjevina in Serbia).

The region of the Iron Gates is characterized by considerable stability of the Lepenski Vir culture lasting c. 1000 calendar years. This was terminated by a distinct techno-morphological change at the time that the ceramic Neolithic emerged, it is in the time of main settlement in Lepenski Vir.

The situation differed on the southern slopes of the Dynaric Alps and on the Adriatic coast, now partly submerged. Successive to the Early Holocene Epi-Gravettian of the type represented in layers VII–VI at Crvena Stijena in Montenegro are the industries of para-Castelnovian type, e.g. layer IV at Crvena Stijena. They seem to be very close or identical to Odmut. These industries are still in evidence at the time that the *impresso* ware appears (layer III of Crvena Stijena); they were also found in Albania and Greece (Argissa Magula). On the grounds of the incomplete data at our disposal, it would seem that the para-Castelnovian tradition of Odmut type underwent only minor modifications when the *impresso* or Starčevo ware appeared; these modifications were manifested by a slight increase in blade dimensions and the occurrence of types of trapezes and especially rhombs (BH) unknown until then.

Moving on to Greece, we should stress that we do not know of any early Holocene industries of northwestern Greece, and the Neolithic is poorly represented there.

Sequences of Epi-Gravettian industries are known only from the Peloponnese and Thessaly, and are particularly well-documented in the Frankhthi Cave (cf. "Southeast"). The beginning of the Holocene in this sequence is marked, contrary to the rest of Europe, by a growth in flake component (*phase lithique* VII according to Cathèrine Perlès), followed in the "Upper Mesolithic" by an increase in the proportion of geometric microliths, primarily trapezes. These are (*phase lithique* VIII) earlier than in other parts of Europe (second half of the 8th millennium cal. BC). These tendencies persisted into phase IX at the end of the 8th millennium cal. BC, when the only new element are microliths with semi-step bifacial retouch.

The pre-ceramic Neolithic (phase X) in the Frankhthi sequence displays a twofold technology: alongside flake specimens (c. 70 %) carefully made blades occur, produced using the pressure technique. These blades are a novelty and have no roots in the Early Holocene technologies in this area.

The blade character is even more pronounced in the industries of the pre-ceramic Neolithic in Thessaly, first of all at Argissa Magula (its industry is comparable to Odmut), where trapezes are still present, although less frequently. When the Proto-Sesklo ceramics appeared, this strongly blade-oriented industry continued, but with the adoption of an important technological innovation in the form of tools with surface retouch.

In Bulgaria, the modest Mesolithic material (Dekilitash, described by Ivan Gatsov) contains Epi-Gravettian elements and the new blade technology with trapezes. The connection between the two elements is not clear as there are only surface collections available from this area. It would seem, however, that the Late Mesolithic in Bulgaria does not represent the Castelnovian tradition, but rather the latest Epi-Gravettian model. The earliest ceramic Neolithic in Bulgarian territory, of the Chavdar-Kremikovci type, has a blade industry with larger irregular blades, which were occasionally transformed into retouched tools, primarily end-scrapers and retouched blades. This industry has no links with the local Mesolithic base. In northeastern Bulgaria (e.g. Usoye 1), on the other hand, blade-flake industries (with ceramics) are found and observed to be more closely affiliated with the local Epi-Gravettian tradition.

As far as the taxonomic position of the Odmut industry is concerned, the view we have put forward earlier about the strict, classical Castelnovian character of this industry has not been fully confirmed by an analysis of the material and should be revised.

Representative of the classical Castelnovian and territorially closest to Odmut are the sites of Romagnano III and Riparo Gaban in northern Italy, as well as Mala Triglavca in Slovenia (cf.). The Odmut industry differs from the classical Italian Castelnovian in tool groups structure and details of technique and morphology. Major tool classes of the classical nord-Italian Castelnovian invariably show a high index of end-scrapers (c. 40%), whereas at Odmut the index of these tools does not exceed 30%. End-scrapers at Odmut are outnumbered by retouched flakes/irregular scrapers.

Retouched blades of the classical Castelnovian are more numerous than at Odmut, while the frequency of retouched truncations is similar in the two industries; burins, well known from the Castelnovian, are absent from Odmut. With regard to the morphology of particular tool groups, the classical Castelnovian is characterized (especially in its early phase) by the presence of single microliths of the Sauvetarrian type (e.g. Sauvetarrian points, triangles); occurring among the trapezes are asymmetrical specimens and rhombs unknown at Odmut. It should be noted that the classical Castelnovian commonly employed the microburin technique to produce trapezes (*piquant trièdre*), while this method was not used at Odmut, where trapezes were formed by sectioning (cf.).

Differences can be found also in the end-scrapers group. The Castelnovian industry of northern Italy contains a rich group of blade forms (more numerous than at Odmut), in Trentino additionally also specimens with angular (*tettiforme*) fronts and lateral retouch. These types were not found in the Odmut industry. Moreover, retouched blades in classical Castelnovian comprise a larger proportion of notched forms. But we should remember that they are unknown also from the Castelnovian of Carsto Triestino.

We note also a territorial gap between the westernmost sites of the Odmut type (Montenegro) and the easternmost Castelnovian ones (Slovenia).

The Odmut industry also shows certain dissimilarities in comparison to Late Mesolithic and Early Neolithic industries in Greece. On the other hand, some features of blade technology (e.g. *seconde mode/standard* from Frankhthi) are similar. Analogies, however, do not go beyond the general common denomination of the "Mediterranean Pre-Neolithic" style, which comprises not only the classical Castelnovian but also *Capsien superieur* in Africa, Montbanian in the West, the industry from Murzak-Koba in Crimea and many other late industries. In other words, this extensive circum-Mediterranean cultural territory is linked in the Late Mesolithic by a certain techno-morphological standard (cf. "Pre-Neolithic"), while preserving individual features, such as the set of retouched "home" tools.

The culture of Lepenski Vir deviates markedly from Odmut industry. In the Lepenski Vir industry, (cf.) irregular scrapers/ retouched flakes outnumber end-scrapers(40%:10%). Truncations on the Danube are much fewer, but the index of retouched blades is the same or higher than at Odmut. Disparities can be seen as well in the coring technique (plate cores and exceptionally numerous splintered pieces at the Irona Gates). Essential differences are observed in the morphology and stylistics of retouched tools: smaller proportion of blade end-scrapers and notched blades, many Djerdap types not present among microliths from Odmut, micro-retouched bladelets found on both sites.

The review of parallels between the Balkan and middle Mediterranean industries shows that Odmut industry can be ascribed to a broadly understood Castelnovian complex (cf.) and can be treated as a separate culture/group within this complex.

Two more issues to close with. For one thing, it cannot be excluded (?) that Odmut and the East European/North Pontic Grebenikian industries (cf.) may be identical or very close (although core technique is apparently different). If the close kinship between these two units is not merely apparent (possibly due to the considerable techno-typological simplicity of these two industries), we would be dealing with a northward proliferation (cf. "Pontic elements"), including east of the Carpathians but also along the inside of the Carpathian Arch, of an uniform phenomenon of Pre-Neolithic nature (cf. "Pre-Neolithic"). It could also be assumed that the Odmut industry proliferated (or at leash show links) toward the west (?) through the narrower than today Ormuz strait in the direction of the Italian Mezzogiorno, this time together with the earliest Neolithic ceramics (cf. "Latronico" also "Ceramization").

Appendix

Odmut. Numbers of retouched tools after the list constructed for Vlasac (cf. "Southeast").

Tool category	XD	Ia	Ib	XA	IIa	IIb	XB	XC
1. End-scrapers								
1.1.	4	2	6	6	5	2		
1.2.	5	4	7	9	11	9	1	
1.3.	1							
1.4.				1				
1.5.								
1.6.			1	2	3	1		
1.7.								
1.8.	3							
1.9.	2			1				
1.10.				1				
1.11.	2		1	1	1	1		
1.12.	1			3	1			
1.13.	2		1	1	1	2		
1.14.	1		1	1	3	1		
1.15.			1					
1.16.					2	3	2	
1.17.					2			
Total	21	6	18	26	29	19	3	1

Tool category	XD	Ia	Ib	XA	IIa	IIb	XB	XC
2. Irregular scrapers								
2.1.	1	1						
2.2.	2	2	2	2	1	1		
2.3.		1						
2.4.	2	1		1	1	1		
2.5.	2		2		1			
2.6.			2	3				
2.7.								
2.8.								
2.9.								
2.10. (oblique)	1							
2.11. (fragment)	2					1		
2.12. (denticulated)	2	2	2		1	2		
Total	13	7	10	6	5	5		

Tool category	XD	Ia	Ib	XA	IIa	IIb	XB	XC
3. Side scrapers								
4. Retouched flakes	6	9	9	18	15	6		1

Tool category	XD	Ia	Ib	XA	IIa	IIb	XB	XC
5. *Raclettes*								
5.1.								
5.2.								

Tool category	XD	Ia	Ib	XA	IIa	IIb	XB	XC
6. Burins								
6.1.								
6.2.	1							
6.3.								
6.4.								
6.5.					2			
6.6.								
6.7.		1						
Total	1	1			2			

Tool category	XD	Ia	Ib	XA	IIa	IIb	XB	XC
7. Retouched truncations								
7.1.	2	1	1	3	9			
7.2.	3			2	1	1		
7.3.	4		1	3	2			
7.4.	1		1	2	2			
7.5.	1			2				
7.6. (ventrally retouched			2					
Total	11	1	5	12	14	1		

Tool category	XD	Ia	Ib	XA	IIa	IIb	XB	XC
8. Retouched blades								
8.1.		2	3	2	2	2		
8.2.			1					1
8.3.								
8.4.	1	1						
8.5.	3	2	3	2	1			
8.6.	2	1	1	3	10	9	1	1
8.7. (notched)	1	1	4	8	5	2		
Total	7	7	12	15	18	13	1	2

Tool category	XD	Ia	Ib	XA	IIa	IIb	XB	XC
9. Perforators								
9.1.		1	1	1	5	4		
9.2.	2							
9.3.		1			1			
Total	2	2	1	1	6	4		

Tool category	XD	Ia	Ib	XA	IIa	IIb	XB	XC
10. Chisel-like tools								
10.1.	1	1				1		1
10.2.		1	1					
Total	1	2	1			1		1

Tool category	XD	Ia	Ib	XA	IIa	IIb	XB	XC
11. Backed blades								

Tool category	XD	Ia	Ib	XA	IIa	IIb	XB	XC
12. Microliths								
12.1.						2		
12.2.	1	2	1	1				
12.3.		1						
12.4.								
12.5.								
12.6.								
12.7.		2	1	1	3	3		
12.8.	1	1	3		4	1		
12.9.	2		1	3	1			
12.10.			1	2				
12.11.	1	1	3	2	1	4		
12.12.	1	1	1	2				
12.13.						1		
12.14.								
Total	6	8	11	9	11	11		

12

Bone, Antler and Amber

12.1.1. Pointes, sagaies et harpons du Paléolithique Final et du Mésolithique en Europe du Centre-Est

(co-author – J. K. Kozłowski)

Introduction

On se propose, dans cette étude, de présenter les principaux types de pointes, sagaies et harpons en os et bois d'animaux, qui apparaissent sur l'étendue de l'Europe centrale et orientale, entre la mer Baltique et Adriatique et entre le Rhin et le Dnieper. N'ont pas été prises en considération les variétés et les types représentés par des pièces isolées.

Du point de vue chronologique on a tenu compte des pièces du Paléolithique final et du Mésolithique.

Dans sa première partie, l'étude contient une liste des groupes typologiques et leur division selon les différents types, illustrés par les figures (cf. les numéros des divers types conformes au texte).

La seconde partie de l'ouvrage montre la place que les différents types et ensembles de types divers occupent dans le temps et dans le cadre des entités taxonomiques Fig. 12.1.1a–e).

A. Typologie des pointes, sagaies et harpons (cf. "Late/Final Paleolithic Points and Harpooons")

1. Pointes à reinures armées
Classification
1.1 – 1.6: deux rangées d'armatures,
1.7: une rangée d'armatures,
1.1 aplaties, section biconvexe,
1.2 aplaties, section plano-convexe,
1.3 assez larges, bipointues, aplaties (= *Vogelpfeile* des auteurs allemands, type 21_2 d'après Stefan K. Kozłowski),
1.4 type Ageröd, étroites, à base pointue, section circulaire ou carrée (= type Stora Dode de Grahame Clark),
1.5 type Svaerdborg d'après Clark, comme 1.4 mais, en plus, microbarbelure à la base,
1.6 type Søholm, large, aplatie, base droite, partie distale élargie, porte souvent des ornementations,
1.7 type 21_1, étroite, à reinure sur toute la longueur ou sur une partie de la pièce, section circulaire ou ovale.

Classification métrique
Les pièces de grandes dimensions: 12–20 cm de long; les valeurs les plus fréquemment rencontrées oscillent aux environs de 20 cm. Le type 1.3 ne dépasse pas d'habitude cette longueur; le type 1.4 la dépasse toujours.

2. Pointes en forme de pelle
L'extrémité distale en forme de pelle posée sur un fût cylindrique. Base biseautée ou pointue.

Subdivision
2.1 type Pentekinnen ou 17 d'après Clark, la tête douce-ment marquée atteint 1/3–1/2 de la longueur de la pièce,
2.2 type Zvejnieki, la tête (facettée parfois) bien marquée, un fût court: jusqu'à 1/3 de la longueur,
2.3 type Torvala, courte tête à ailerons, parfois des ornementations.
Le type 2.1 exécuté aussi en bois de renne.

Classification métrique
a) Pièces de grandes dimensions: 12–25 cm;
b) Pièces de très grandes dimensions: au-dessus de 25 cm.
Le type 2.1 se situe dans la zone supérieure des "grandes" et parmi les "très grandes" pièces.

3. Pointes à section triangulaire (ou demi-circulaire)
3.1 type 13 de Clark, sveltes, étroites, pédoncule court, pointues,
3.2 comme 3.1 mais, en plus, incisions microbarbelures sur deux bords,

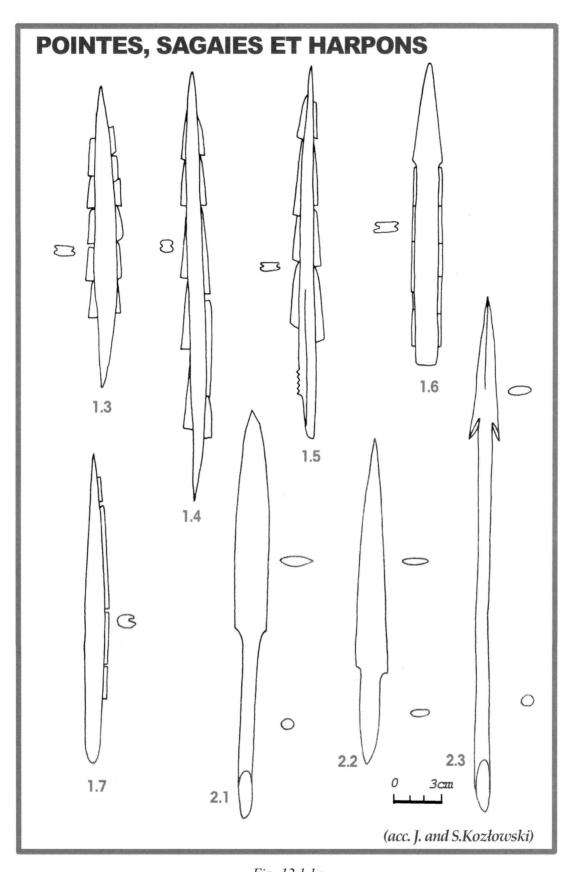

Fig. 12.1.1a

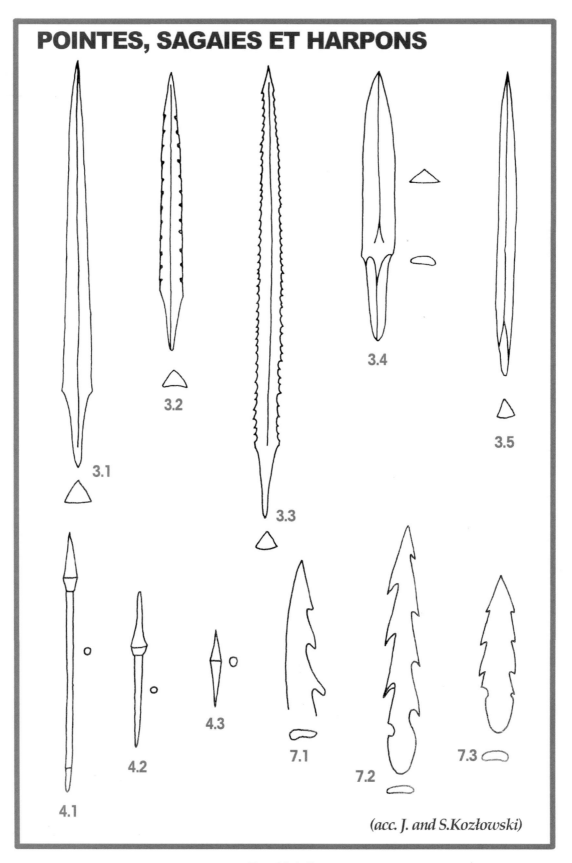

Fig. 12.1.1b

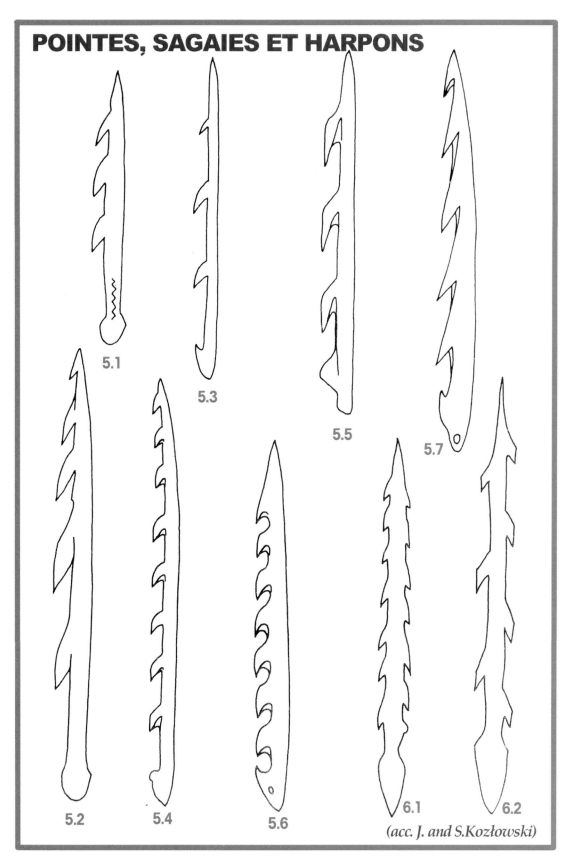

Fig. 12.1.1c

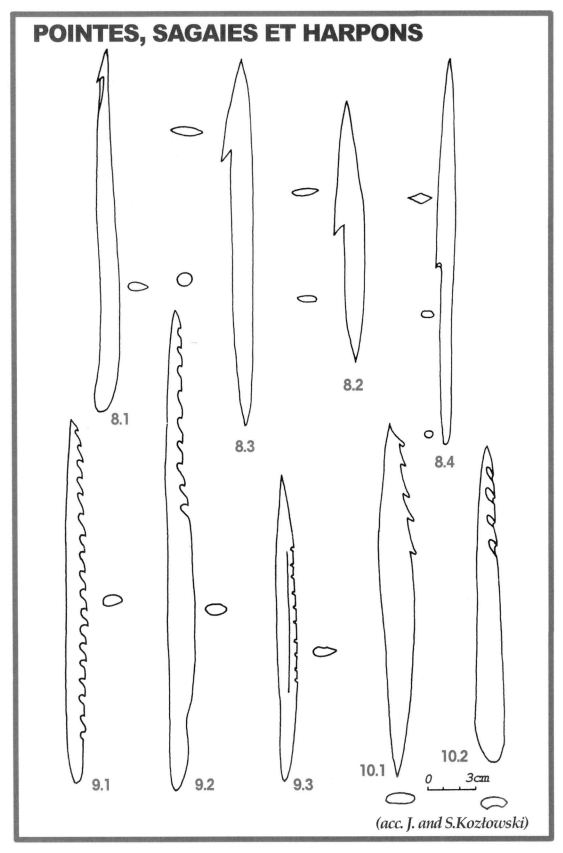

Fig. 12.1.1d

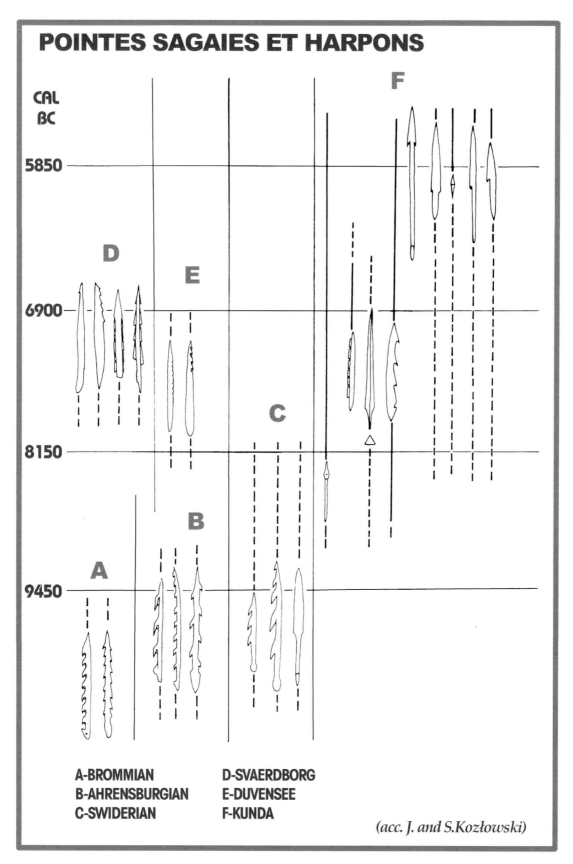

Fig. 12.1.1e

3.3 type 20 d'apres Clark, comme 3.1 mais, en plus, deux bords denticulés,

3.4 type Drusken, large, pédoncule court, massif,

3.5 type Lisiogon, svelte, étroite, les deux extrémités pointues dans la même mesure, absence de pédoncule.

Classification métrique
a) Pièces de grandes dimensions: les plus nombreuses, d'une longueur de 14 à 25 cm;
b) Pièces de très grandes dimensions: jusqu'à 31 cm.
Manque de corrélation entre les classes morphologiques et métriques.

4. Pointes biconiques (= type Shighirskoe des auteurs russes ou 16 de Clark).
Biconiques, souvent fixées sur un fût cylindrique, pointu ou biseauté.

Subdivision:
4.1 type Pulli, tête asymétrique par rapport à l'axe transversal, fût long (3/4 de la longueur),
4.2 comme 4.1 mais le fût plus court, 1/2 à 2/3 de la longueur,
4.3 courtes, biconiques, symétriques par rapport à l'axe transversal, dépourvues de fût ou à fût très court, base pointue.
Remarque: Paraléllement ils existent des rares exemplaires en bois! (Veretie I en Russie séptentrionale).

Classification métrique
a) Pièces de petites dimensions: 3–6 cm de longueur;
b) Pièces moyennes: 6–12 cm de long;
c) Pièces de grandes dimensions: au-dessus de 12 cm, les plus nombreuses.
Le type 4.3 est en corrélation avec la classe des "petites" pièces et les valeurs inférieures des "moyennes". Les types 4.1 et 4.2 se situent dans les classes des "moyennes" et des "grandes".

5. Harpons à une rangée de barbelures
Quelques grandes barbelures nettement marquées sur un fût massif s'étendent sur plus de 1/2 de sa longueur. Base élargie. Clark les classifie principalement comme type 12A (nos. 5.2, 5.4) ou 10 (no. 5.6) et 9 (5.7).

Subdivision
5.1 type Rękawczyn ("12A" de Clark): 3–4 barbelures triangulaires, larges, couchées, éloignées d'une base renflée; section ovale; parfois ornementées,
5.2 type Nowe Juchy d'après Clark: 4–6 barbelures couchées, larges, éloignées de la base renflée, section ovale,
5.3 type Lubana d'après Clark: 3–4 barbelures griffues, non couchées, base asymétrique, section ovale ou carrée,
5.4 type Weseram comme 5.3 mais 6–8 barbelures anguleuses;

5.5 type Løjesmølle d'après Clark comme 5.3 mais les barbelures larges et fortement recourbées;
5.6 type Törning d'après Clark: 4–8 barbelures fortement recourbées, anguleuses, larges, serrées, base asymétrique,
5.7 type Góra-Orle d'après Clark: 4–8 barbelures faiblement marquées, fortement couchées, base asymétrique, souvent avec un cran.

Matières premières
Une bonne partie des pièces 5.1, 5.2, 5.3, 5.4, 5.5, 5.6 est formée de bois de renne. Les pièces du type 5.7 ainsi qu'une partie des pièces appartenant aux types indiqués ci-dessus, sont exécutées en bois d'élan. Certains sont datés au Dryas III (Stellmoor, Wojnowo) et Preboreal (Rudninkiai en Lituanie). Certains types sont aussi differentiés géographiquement? (5.6 au Scandinavie, en Allemagne, et 5.1 en Pologne et Lituanie).

Classification métrique
a) Pièces de grandes dimensions: 12 à 25 cm de longueur, les plus nombreuses;
b) Pièces de très grandes dimensions: dépassant 25 cm, peu nombreuses.
Du point de vue métrique se distingue le type 5.1 (valeurs inférieures des "grandes"), tandis que les types 5.2, 5.3, 5.4, 5.5 et 5.6 oscillent dans les limites des valeurs supérieures de cette classe métrique.

6. Harpons à deux rangées de barbelures
Subdivision
6.1 type Lachmirowice, barbelures couchées, peu marquées, sortant d'un fût aplati,
6.2 type Stellmoor, barbelures non couchées, nettement marquées à la sortie du fût, anguleuses, alternées, base renflée.
Le plus souvent bois de renne, parfois aussi d'élan.

Classification métrique
a) Pièces de grandes dimensions: longues de 16 à 25 cm, les plus nombreuses;
b) Pièces de très grandes dimensions: d'une longueur au-dessus de 25 cm, moins nombreuses.

7. Harpons plats
7.1 larges, une rangée de barbelures couchées, serrées,
7.2 type Birsmatten, larges, deux rangées de barbelures couchées, alternées, base renflée, parfois avec une perforation; arrondie ou droite, parfois perforée,
7.3 type Bernaufels comme 7.2 mais à barbelures non alternées.
Généralement en bois de cerf.

Classification métrique
a) Pièces moyennes: longues de 8 à 12 cm, assez nombreuses;
b) Pièces de grandes dimensions: de 12 à 16 cm de long.

Les pièces du type 7.3 sont plus courtes que celles du type 7.2.

8. Harpons/pointes à une barbelure
Subdivision:

8.1 type 5 d'après Clark, fût très long, large, base arondie ou pointue, une barbelure courte, petite, section lentiforme,

8.2 fût mince et long à section circulaire ou rectangulaire, large, barbelure plate, base pointue,

8.3 type Oleni Ostrov comme 8.2, mais la barbelure atteint 1/2 de la longueur de la pièce, suivie par une reinure armée des lamelles non retouchées,

8.4 type Lohusu d'après Clark, fût à section cylindrique ou rectangulaire, une barbelure aplatie, longue (1/2 de la longueur de la pièce), large, base pointue ou biseautée.

Classification métrique

a) Pièces moyennes: longues de 8 à 12 cm;

b) Pièces de grandes dimensions: d'une longueur de 12 à 25 cm;

c) Pièces de très grandes dimensions: dont la longueur dépasse 25 cm (apparaissent rarement).

Le type 8.2 est en corrélation avec la zone supérieure de la classe des "grandes", le type 8.3 avec la zone supérieure de la classe des "moyennes" et le type 8.4 se situe dans toute la classe des "grandes".

9. Harpons microbarbelés

9.1 microbarbelures sur plus de 2/3 de la pièce, section lentiforme, base pointue, (type 6 d'après Clark; en bois au Veretie I en Russie septentrionale),

9.2 comme 9.1 mais les microbarbelures s'étendent sur 1/3 à 2/3 de la longueur de la pièce,

9.3 type Duvensee-Dobbertin (2 et 4 d'après Clark), incisions serrées sur un bord, section lentiforme.

Classification métrique:

a) Pièces moyennes: 6–12 cm de long, rares;

b) Pièces de grandes dimensions: longues de 12 à 25 cm, nombreuses;

c) Pièces de très grandes dimensions: dont la longueur dépasse 25 cm, assez nombreuses.

Manque de corrélation entre les classes métriques et morphologiques.

10. Harpons à barbelures dans la partie distale
Subdivision

10.1 type Mullerup (7 de Clark), une rangée de 2–5 petites barbelures couchées couvre 1/4–1/2 de la longueur de la pièce; fût long, large, à section lentiforme, pointu ou arrondi,

10.2 type Pritzerbe (8 d'après Clark), une rangée de barbelures couchées, faiblement marquées, délimitées par des incisions larges et profondes; fût long, arrondi, à section concave-convexe.

Type 10.2, os longs de l'aurox (d'où la section caractéristique).

Classification métrique:

a) Pièces moyennes: 9 à 12 cm de longueur;

b) Pièces de grandes dimensions: longues de 12 à 25 cm.

Il n'y a pas une nette corrélation entre les classes métriques et typologiques.

B. – Position taxonomique et chronologique des pointes, sagaies et harpons

Le Maglemosien (cf. "West and Center")
Cet complexe "nordique" est appelé le plus souvent "Maglemosien" (*sensu largo*). Pour certaines cultures qui le composent (Duvensee, Svaerdborg, Oldesloe, Chojnice-Pieńki) on peut reconstituer partiellement l'ensemble caractéristique des pointes et harpons.

1. Le Duvensee
Pointes et harpons co-apparaissent avec les outillages lithiques au moins dans trois inventaires de cette culture: Duvensee, Hohen Viecheln et Friesack en Allemagne. En se fondant sur ces outillages et sur l'analyse cartographique, Hermann Schwabedissen et Bernhard Gramsch ont établi comme étant caractéristiques de cette culture en premier lieu les harpons 9.3 et 10.2. Par ailleurs, à la culture considérée se rattachent le plus probablement les harpons 9.1 et 9.2, de même que – en tant qu'élément périphérique peut-être – les harpons 8.1 et 10.1. Néanmoins, il est difficile de déterminer si les harpons 5.6, comme le suggère p. ex. J. Brøndsted se rattachent au Duvensee de Danemark (= Klosterlund).

On peut faire dater l'ensemble fondamental des types au IXe et VIIIe millénaires cal. BC.

2. Le Svaerdborgien
Nous connaîssons nombre d'inventaires du type Svaerdborg à harpons et pointes (p. ex. Mullerup I, Vinde Helsinge, Svaerdborg I et II, Holmegaard I, Øgaarde, Verup), aussi n'y a-t-il pas de difficultés à reconstituer leur ensemble caractéristique. Parmi les harpons, il y a lieu de faire mention en premier lieu des types 8.1 et 10.1 ainsi que 9.1 et 9.2; par contre, les pointes représentent principalement les types 1.4, 1.5 et 1.6.

La datation de l'ensemble osseux du type Svaerdborg est fondée sur de nombreuses dates palynologiques et radiometriques. Elles se situent dans le cadre de la seconde moitié du VIIIe millénaire cal BC.

3. La phase tardive du Maglemosien
Le nombre des inventaires lithiques avec des objets en os est dans ce cas fortement limité (AgERöd I: H/C, Rüde 2). Cependant, il est fort probable qu'aux cultures Oldesloe en Allemagne et en Scanie et Chojnice-Pieńki en Pologne se rattachent les harpons 8.1 et 9.1 et il nous faut indiquer

additionnellement – pour la première les pointes 1.4, et pour la seconde – peut-être les harpons, 5.7 (?).

Autres cultures de l'Europe centrale
Janislawicien – il se peut que s'y rattachent les pointes du type 1.3, ce qui ne trouve qu'une confirmation cartographique partielle, mais deux spécimens du type 1.3 de Menturren et de Tłokowo semblent être datées du Boréal.

Le Kongemosien – certains inventaires (p. ex. Kongemosen) ont fourni des pièces du groupe 8.

Le Mésolithique nord-oriental (Kunda au sens large, cf. "East")
Dans ce technocomplexe (cultures de Kunda et le Boutovien) apparaissent les groupes suivants: 1, 2, 3, 4, 5, 8, 9 et 10. Sur le territoire qui nous intéresse se développaient à l'époque de l'holocène inférieur quatres cultures mésolithiques: celle de Kunda en Estonie et Lettonie, celle du variant Lituanien (occidental) de Kunda, celle de Kudlaevka, plus au sud, et le Boutovien sur la Volga supérieur.

Le nombre des inventaires qui réunissent en soi des instruments en pierre et des instruments en os est assez grands dans les cultures indiquées (Pulli I, Oleni Ostrov, Kunda-Lammasmägi, Veretie I, Zvejnieki, Osa, Narva Zamostie, Ozerki, etc.).

1. La Kunda classique et le Boutovien
La phase ancienne représentée par le site de Pulli I en Estonie se caractérise par des pointes du groupe 3 (sans définition précise) ainsi que du type 4.1 et les harpons 5.7.

La phase moyenne, connue de Kunda-Lammasmägi, fournit: des pointes du type 1.7, 9.1, 9.2, 3.1 et 4.1, 4.2 et des harpons 5.7.

La phase développée est représentée par des sites tels que: Osa, Zvejnieki en Lettonie, Oleni Ostrov, Veretie I et Narva en Russie septentrionale. Elle se caractérise par des pièces continuant la tradition (types 4.1 et 5.7), avec, en même temps, l'apparition de types tout à fait nouveaux: 2.2, 2.3, 4.3, 8.2, 8.3 et 8.4.

La chronologie de la phase ancienne peut être fixée à la limite du XIe et X^e millénaire cal. BC, la phase moyenne oscille aux environs du VIIIe millénaire (Kunda-Lammasmägi). La phase la plus recente est datée à Narva approximativement à 5000, et à Osa environ 6000 ans cal. BC.

Il semble que les dates liées au Boutovien sur la Volga supérieure sont identiques.

2. Le variant Lithuanien/occidental de Kunda
On connaît seulement de nombreuses pièces isolées. L'analyse cartographique et les coïncidences évidentes de l'inventaire du silex avec celui de Kunda classique suggèrent l'appartenance à cette entité des types suivants: 4.1, 4.3, 1.7, 3.1, 3.2 et 3.5. Parmi les harpons, citons les types 8.1 et peut-être 8.2, et aussi quelques pièces du groupe 5.

Deux pièces appartenant le plus probablement à cette culture, possèdent des datations palynologiques: la pointe biconique de Zedmar/Serovo est datée à la limite du Boréal et de l'Atlantique, et la pièce à reinure d'ex Zinten à la première moitié de l'Atlantique. Ces datations sont conformes à la chronologie admise du variant Lithuanien de Kunda.

Le Mésolithique occidental et méridional
Ils touchent de ses extrémités l'étendue visée par la présente élaboration. Ses plus anciennes cultures occidentaux et méridionaux (Le Beuronien, le Sauveterrien et le Epi-Gravettien du Balcan) sont caractérisées par la présence des "poinçons" qui semblent très bien se situer dans le groupe de sagais à section ronde ou ovale.

Dans certains inventaires de la phase tardive, considérés comme appartenant à ce qu'on appelle le Montbanien (cf. faciès Montbani des auteurs français), ou plus à l'Est l'Epi-Gravettien recent, apparaissent en Suisse et en Allemagne méridionale, mais aussi au Liechtenstein et en Autriche, la Sérbie, Le Montenegro et la Slovenie et en Italie nord-est les harpons du type 7.2 et 7.3.

On peut fixer la chronologie de ces harpons à la période après 7000 cal. BC.

12.1.2. Late/Final Paleolithic and Mesolithic Bone/Antler Points and Harpoons in Central Europe (cf. "Pointes, sagaies…")

(co-author – E. Sachse-Kozłowska)

1. The area of Central Europe extending from the Baltic and Adriatic seas to the Elbe and Dnieper rivers has yielded so far several hundred bone/antler points and harpoons that can be dated with varying degree of probability to the very end of the Pleistocene (starting from the Bølling) and the early and middle Holocene (Fig. 12.1.2a–b).

2. These are mostly accidental and isolated finds outside their cultural context, although there are cases when points/harpoons were discovered in well dated contexts (e.g. Stellmoor, Friesack, Ulkestrup, Svaerdborg, Hohen Vieheln, sites in southern Germany and Switzerland, east Baltic and upper Volga finds, Cuina Turcului, Vlasac, Lepenski Vir, Odmut in the Balkans and others). These finds facilitate a more reliable cultural and chronological interpretation of the considerably more numerous group of artifacts without contexts.

3. Also helpful in such classifications are some of the isolated finds which, although lacking clear "cultural" contexts, were individually dated by ¹⁴C or pollen methods, as was the case with British finds which Clive Bonsell dated by the AMS method, or with harpoons from former East Prussia pollen-dated by Hugo Gross. Neither should one forget the raw material criterion, important in chronological determinations, especially in the north. It permits the following division into finds:

- older than the Preboreal, made primarily of reindeer and less frequently of elk antlers; and

BONE/ANTLER POINTS AND HARPOONS

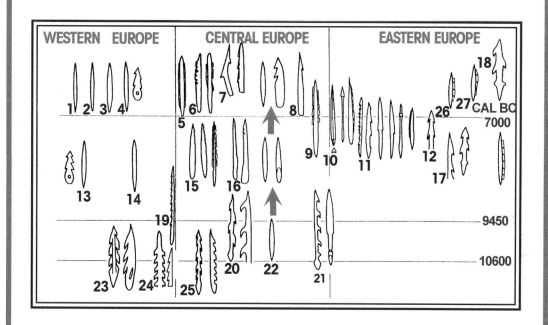

1-CASTELNOVIAN
2-TEVIECIAN
3-CUZOULIAN
4-MONTBANIAN
5-KONGEMOSIAN
6-OLDESLOE
7-ERTEBØLLE
8-CHOJNICE-PIEŃKI
9-JANISLAWICIAN

10-WEST KUNDA
11-NORD KUNDA
12-KAMA-VYCHEGDA
13-SAUVETERRIAN
14-BEURONIAN
15-SVAERDBORGIAN
16-DUVENSEE
17-YANGELKA
18-MURZAK-KOBA

19-STAR-CARR
20-AHRENSBURGIAN
21-SWIDERIAN
22-EPI-GRAVETTIAN
23-AZILIAN
24-CRESWELLIAN
25-BROMMIAN
26-GREBENIKIAN
27-KUKREK

Fig. 12.1.2a

BONE/ANTLER POINTS AND HARPOONS

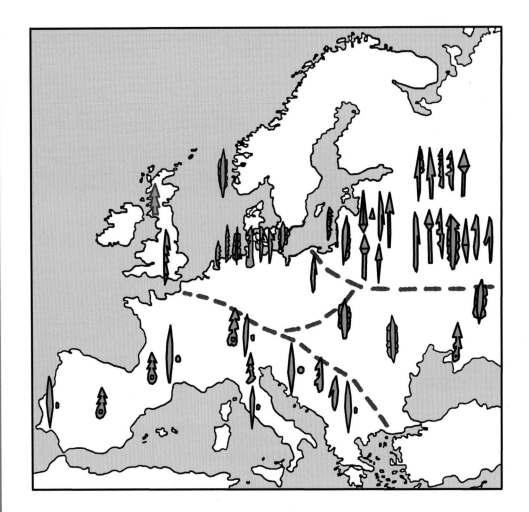

CF. 12.1.2a

Fig. 12.1.2b

- younger (from the Preboreal onwards), made mainly of the bones and antlers of forest animals.

4. In the north, points and harpoons occur mainly in the circum-Baltic lakelands (Scania, Zealand, Schleswig-Holstein, Mecklenburg, Brandenburg, Pomerania, Masuria, coastal areas of Lithuania, Latvia and Estonia), being virtually unknown in neighboring inland sandy territories (Jutland, Brandenburg, Great Poland, Mazovia, interior of Lithuania, Belarus etc., but known from the upper Volga lakeland. This has to do more with the contrasting preservation potential of cultural layers in the two regions (maximal in lakelands, minimal in sandy areas) than with actual deposition history. One cannot rule out, however, that the above dychotomy, which is also of environmental character (well irrigated lakelands vs. drier inland areas), had impact on local cultures, in the quantitative sense, but perhaps also functional.

5. In the area in question, points and harpoons exhibit both chronological and functional differentiation which seems to be the result of different territory "histories" (different local traditions expressing themselves in different chipped industries) and in many cases of different object function (hunting weapons, fishing spears, etc., cf.).

The folowing is a discussion of both the morphological differentiation of points and harpoons (territorial and over time) and their relationship to flint industries known from the area of interest to us. Such a reconstruction is deemed possible despite serious gaps in material from inland territories. We will conclude with a synthetic presentation of provinces/territories characterized by permanent features of their bone/antler industries.

In the case of finds from lowland areas, Grahame Clark's traditional typology was employed in suitably modified form; when describing artifacts from southern/upland areas this terminology was augmented with traditional terms borrowed from literature dealing with the Upper Paleolithic (cf. "Pointes, *sagaies*").

We now present the principal groups of Central European points and harpoons.

6. Spindle-shaped points *sagaies*/"*poinçons*". Notably banal in shape, these points are known from numcrous early contexts (such as Italian and Balkan Epi-Gravettian, Magdalenian, the Tardiglacial of the northern European Lowland, but also of Crimea and Caucasus!), occurring also in clearly younger contexts (e.g. Holocene industries of western and southeastern Europe).

Practical considerations have limited our analysis to areas/periods/taxons for which the described points are characteristic with no or almost no competition. We have thus left out specimens from, generally speaking, sites north of the Alps and Carpathians (they present sets of much more complicated forms, cf. below), going on to consider the broadly understood northern Mediterranean region.

A brief observation before we proceed. There is a tendency, not always justified, among the older French authors (Max Escalon-de-Fonton already not among their number) to describe the points considered here as "*poinçons*" or perforators/awls. Most of these specimens are in fact spindle-shaped points/*sagaies*.

In central Europe, spindle-shaped points occured during the Tardiglacial in the Italian and Balkan Epi-Gravettian (Polesini, Cuina Turcului, Climente, Sandalja, Ovčja Jama etc.), surviving in this area and further west and south (France, Switzerland) in the Early/Middle Holocene in the Sauveterrian tradition (e.g. Le Martinet), Lepenski Vir culture (e.g. Vlasac, Lepenski Vir), the Latest Epi-Gravettian (Breg in Slovenia), Castelnovian (e.g. Mala Triglavca in Slovenia, Gaban in Italy or Châteauneuf-lez-Martigues in French Provence), Beuronian (e.g. Birsmatten-Basisgrotte in Switzerland), the Montbani tradition in southern Germany and Switzerland, but also Late Mesolithic industries of southwestern (Cuzoul) and northwestern France (Hoëdic).

Meriting separate mention are the *sagaies*/points *à biseau simple* which sometimes accompany the said spindle-shaped points. They are found only in Epi-Gravettian context in Italy and the Balkans, in the latter case up to the Middle Holocene (e.g. Vlasac and Lepenski Vir in Serbia).

One gets the impression that the discussed phenomenon exhibits territorial and chronological homogeneity, and on a macroregional scale at that. Such homogeneity is in good accord with the Late Glacial uniformity of the Mediterranean Epi-Gravettian (from Spain to Greece and Romania) which at the turn of the Pleistocene and Holocene gave rise to two of the main post-Epi-Gravettian traditions: the Sauveterrian in the west (with the Late Mesolithic industries of Castelnovian, Cuzoul, Montbani and Téviec types stemming from it) and the Latest-Epi-Gravettian in the east (Frankhthi, Crvena Stijena, Breg, Odmut, Dekiltash, Jaszbereny, Jasztelek, etc.)

7. HARPOONS AND BARBED POINTS

7.1. Harpoons with large barbs occur in northern central Europe and in northwestern Europe, in the northern foreland of the Alps and in the circum-Baltic belt of young Würmian/Vistulian lakelands. They differ as to morphology and raw material, mainly reindeer antler and/or (slightly later?) elk antler, but also share a number of features, most importantly:

- massive stems
- several massive, usually widely spaced barbs

The differences include:

- manner of treating the base (symmetric or asymmetric broadening, no broadening)
- number of rows of barbs (one or two)
- shape of the barbs and the distance between them

Culturally, this group of artifacts is mainly Late Magdalenian/Hamburgian/Creswellian at the beginning. The dominant forms of that time are rather diversified single-barbed specimens with no distinct base and various barb morphology, made from reindeer or elk antlers. Better known, and slightly younger in age, is the circum-Balticum group of finds which, firstly, can be dated quite well (mainly to the Allerød-Dryas III-Preboreal period, and to slightly later times in the east); secondly, its morphology is better described (among others, Törring and Havel types as defined by Grahame Clark); thirdly, the group displays territorial differentiation and, finally, it appears to be an obvious continuation of Magdalenian/Creswellian/Epi-Magdalenian evolution.

First of all, there are the double-barbed harpoons of the Havel type (12B in Clark's classification) which dominate in eastern Germany and Denmark, with one specimen also being known from Polish Pomerania. Next we have several variants of single-barbed harpoons (Havel types $12A_4$ and $12A_6$ in Scania, Denmark and northern Germany; Havel $12A_1$ and $12A_2$ in northern Poland; Havel $12A_3$ in Latvia, and derivatives of Havel 12A in Estonia and Karelia).

The problem of chronology and "cultural"/taxonomic attribution of the described harpoons does not seem to be insurmountable. They appeared in Meiendorf in Germany (Hamburgian-Bølling), in Ahrensburgian Stellmoor (Germany) and Wojnowo (Poland, probably Swiderian) and are dated in the latter case to the Dryas III period; specimens from Rudninkiai (Lithuania) and Pulli (Estonia) are dated to the Preboreal. The harpoons are made of reindeer antler more often than elk antler. All this suggests ties between these harpoons and the Hamburgian and Creswellian (cf. High Furlong in Britain), but foremost the Tanged Points Complex tradition and its immediate successors.

The presence of single harpoons of the Havel group in the eastern Baltic region, in the Kunda *milieu* with suspected Swiderian connections (Pulli, Kunda-Lammasmägi, Oleni Ostrov), does not come as a surprise, the more so since such harpoons are known in the Lubana region in Latvia most probably since the end of the Pleistocene (are they connected with the Desnian? cf. "North"). The Holocene barbed points of the Central European Lowland appear to be a true continuation of this group (cf. below).

7.2. Barbed points of the Central European Lowland. Unlike the harpoons described above, which were used rather for hunting game on land, barbed points served the purposes of fishing (cf. "Pike from Kunda"). The beginning of the postglacial period witnessed considerable changes in the style of Central European materials, also the bone/antler industries. The general trend of the time, particularly visible in the Lowland, was for glacial environmental elements to be replaced with boreal ones. Among other things, the old fauna (reindeer, elk) gradually gave way to new species (red deer, roe deer, aurochs, wild boar, etc.). In bone/antler industries, this resulted in the switch from antler to bone (cf. "Game"), with consequences for tools morphology. It also seems that around this time a fundamental functional change took place: the harpoon, which was a land hunting weapon, became a fishing spear.

Nonetheless, an important element of lowland tradition survived: the northern part of the Central European Lowland (and no other region besides) continued to be characterized by barbed harpoons/points. Continuity of the tradition was maintained until very late in fact (cf. remarks on flat harpoons below). The new points had much finer barbs than the Havel group preceding them. These barbs were usually grouped in the distal part of implement, the base is never distinct.

Barbed points are characteristic mainly of the Maglemosian with some being present also in the eastern Baltic regions (Kunda-Lammasmägi). In the early phase (Star Carr) these locally and chronologically diversified artifacts are a delicate version of the massive specimens (perhaps in its Creswellian variant?). Later, depending on their position in time and space, they may exhibit several more massive barbs (Clark's type 7/Pritzerbe in eastern Germany, belonging to the Duvensee culture) or one-to-several finer and more delicate ones (Clark's types 5 and 7 in Ulkestrup Lyng, Svaerdborg I and II in Zealand and in Pomerania, connected with the Svaerdborg group and possibly derivatives thereof ?).

The Kunda type (Clark's type 6), featuring very fine and numerous barbs, appears to be slightly more widespread, occurring from Scania (Ageröd) all the way to Estonia (Kunda) and northern Russia (Veretie I) and being present also in the northern Mesolithic Maglemose (even Dogger Bank!).

The Late Mesolithic flat harpoons known from the Baltic zone appear to be a continuation of the described barbed points (cf. below).

The morphological similarities between Late Magdalenian harpoons of Central Europe and the circum-Baltic harpoons of the Havel group may be surmised as not accidental, and the same may be said of similarities between specimens of this latter group and the numerous barbed points succeeding them in the same area.

What we thus have north of the Alps and Carpathians, right up to the Baltic and North Sea, is a province characterized by a tradition of barbed points and harpoons.

7.3. Flat harpoons

This is a fairly heterogeneous group, distinct most importantly in:

- proportions of finds (specimens are usually broad)
- flat cross section
- raw material (in most cases red-deer antler, hence the flat cross section)
- very large barbs

Many formal, chorological and chronological attributes divide this group of implements into several classes, definable in various degrees. Outside our territory we have Azilian, middle Volga, south Ural, Crimean, Caucasian and even Natufian harpoons.

Disregarding the single find from the Late Paleolithic site at Szekszard-Palank in Hungary, flat harpoons occur in Central Europe in three chronological/territorial zones:

- southern Scandinavia, northeastern Germany, northwestern Poland
- northern foreland of the Alps (southern Germany, Switzerland, Liechtenstein, Austria)
- lower and middle Danube and its tributaries, plus the Dynaric Alps region (Serbia, Montenegro, Slovenia)

In all three zones they are a Late Mesolithic (Middle Holocene) phenomenon, taxonomically connected with, respectively, Ertebølle culture, South Montbanian (*Hirschhorn harpunen Horizont* of René Wyss/*Spätes Mesolithikum* of Wolfgang Taute respectively), and the Latest Epi-Gravettian of Lepenski Vir and/or Castelnovian of the Odmut type. The harpoon traditions in the second and third zones may have continued locally into the Early Neolithic.

8. NON-BARBED POINTS

8.1. SLOTTED ARMED POINTS (GERMAN *VOGELPFEILE*)

These are known mainly from the circum-Baltic zone (Norway, Scania, Zealand, northeastern Poland, eastern Baltic countries), but also from Belarus, central and northern Russia, Karelia, Ukraine and Slovakia (single finds in the latter two cases). They are characterized by a slotted stem, armed with mainly unretouched flint inserts. The older tradition of mounting flint inserts in grooves/*reinures* is know from the Uper Paleolithic/Eastern Gravettian cultures (Molodova, Amvrosievka, Mezin) and from the Upper Paleolithic in the Ural Mountains (Talitski site) and Siberia, as well as Middle Magdalenian (La Garenne and Pircevent in France). In Central Europe they are confined to the southern and western fringes of the Baltic, dating mostly to the Early and Middle Holocene (Menturren, Tłokowo, Kunda-Lammasmägi, Veretie I, Ageröd, Kongemosen, Svaerdborg I) and differing morphologically, territorially and "culturally". They characterize also the "microbladelet tradition" of the Norwegian western coasts.

Generally speaking, in southern Scandinavia and in the center (up to the Neman river) the most frequent forms feature two grooves. In Denmark and Scania these include the more sophisticated Maglemosian and post-Maglemosian Svaerdborg type, as well as the more simple type 21_2 in Clark's classification (as many as several dozen specimens in Scania). The latter may be connected, in Poland for example, with the Janisławician (inserted in grooves of the point from Tłokowo were retouched triangles, among other flints). Single-groove specimens start to dominate east of the lower Vistula course. In our area these are represented by the simple 21_1 type, most probably belonging to the Kunda (*sensu largo*) tradition. The "*vkladishi*" (inserts, cf., retouched and unretouched), plentiful in the eastern European Mesolithic, served, among other things, to arm the slotted eastern European points (and also daggers, cf. "Slotted objects").

Surprising in this context is the Bear Cave in Slovakia, most probably a brown bear killing site. The two-groove point resembles the circum-Baltic specimens but seems to originate from a different world (e.g. from the Kukrek or other eastern European steppe tradition).

8.2. STEMMED POINTS

This is a rather heterogeneous group which we distinguish here merely for our own convenience: it comprises morphologically diverse artifacts, some of which are clearly of eastern, while others are of central European character.

We include among the central European types points with triangular cross section (Clark's type 13), known from former East Prussia and Great Poland, among other places, and also the spatulate specimens of Pentekinnen type (Clark's type 17), occurring between Klaipeda (Lithuania) and Brandenburg but exhibiting some similarity to specimens discovered further east (Kunda tradition in Latvia, Estonia, Karelia, northern Russia and along the upper Volga, among others).

The oldest of all the finds is likely a spatulate point with broad, short stem and triangular cross-section from ex Drusken in former East Prussia, dated by Hugo Gross to the Allerød period (between the Pentekinnen type and type 13). Pentekinnen-type (17) specimens were as a rule made of reindeer or elk antler, a fact indicating their fairly old age (Late Glacial-Preboreal), while the typical points with triangular cross section (Clark's type 13) were made of the bones of forest animals, pointing to their younger age. Pentekinnen points could have been associated with the Tanged Points or Backed Points Late Glacial Complex, while their later forms, mostly with the Kunda tradition *sensu largo*. The taxonomical position of the points with triangular cross section is uncertain (Lithuanian/western Kunda?).

The last form in the stemmed points group are points of the Shigirskie type (16 in Clark's classification), also known in their wooden version (Veretie I in northern Russia); these were most probably arrows or arrowheads (cf. similar wooden forms!). In central and eastern Europe, they are represented by numerous specimens, discovered along the lower Vistula and in former East Prussia, as well as on Kunda sites in Estonia (Pulli, Kunda-Lammasmägi), Karelia (Oleni Ostrov), northern Russia (Veretie), as well as along the upper Volga (Zamostie), and beyond the Ural Mountains (Shigirski Tofianik, there numerous isolated finds). This is the flagship point of the Mesolithic (and the earliest regional ceramic "Neolithic") of the forest zone of the eastern European Lowland. In Central Europe it is most probably associated with the local (= Lithuanian) variant of the Kunda tradition.

9. CONCLUSION

9.1. The described antler/bone harpoons and points of Central Europe are strongly diversified territorially, culturally, chronologically and functionally. It is possible to distinguish at least three regions or provinces with a degree of harpoons/point morphological homogeneity in the Late Pleistocene/Early-Middle Holocene:

(a) Alpine-Baltic with Magdalenian/Havel-group harpoons and Holocene barbed points

(b) northern Mediterranean with simple, not barbed points/ *sagaies*

(c) eastern-European with stemmed and slotted points

9.2 Harpoon and point function is diverse: at first they are used as hunting weapons (cf. "High Furlong"), turning later into fishing spears (cf. "Pike from Kunda"), but only locally in lakeland areas; they could also have served as arrowheads.

9.3 The surprising longevity of the three local traditions/ provinces prompts us to assume a considerable settlement stability (on a macroregional scale) in the Late Pleistocene and Early-Middle Holocene of central Europe.

12.2.1. *L'art zoomorphique mésolithique de la Circum-Baltique*

1. Le but de cet article est de présenter des objets d'art mésolithique zoomorphique des régions bordant la mer Baltique (Scandinavie méridionale, nord de la Pologne, Lituanie, Lettonie et la Plaine russe, Fig. 12.2.1a–c).
2. Le domaine qui nous intéresse, pendant l'Holocène ancien et moyen, était assez diversifié écologiquement:

a) A l'ouest et au sud, dans la zone de climat océanique, se développe, dans un premier stade, une forêt de bouleaux et de pins (10e–9e millénaires cal. BC) qui se poursuit par une forêt de pins, pour aboutir à une forêt mixte. Cette forêt était habitée par une faune de grands mammifères (cf. "Game") avec prédominance du cerf élaphe et par une présence bien marquée du chevreuil et du sanglier; on trouve enfin l'auroch et l'élan; l'ours est rare (il s'agit de données fournies par les sites de la Suède, du Danemark, et de l'Allemagne). Il est permis de supposer que ces régions présentent des variations géographiques, régionales et "micro-régionales", ainsi que des variations chronologiques, au point de vue tant de la végétation que de la faune.

b) Sur la côte orientale de la mer Baltique, apparaît un milieu fortement influencé par un climat continental. La séquence évolutive des forêts est généralement comparable à celle de l'ouest, mais on observe toutefois une certaine abondance d'épicéas et un retardement par rapport aux régions plus occidentales. Dans le groupe des grands mammifères, l'élan prédomine et est sporadiquement accompagné du cerf et du chevreuil.

3. La différenciation taxonomique durant l'Holocène inférieur et moyen, suit assez bien la diversification écologique décrite au point 2. Sur les côtes occidentales et méridionales de la mer Baltique se développe le complexe Maglemosien (cf. – au sens large), tandis que sur les côtes orientales on trouve les cultures appartenant au complexe nord-oriental (culture de Kunda, cf. "East" – dans le sens large).
4. Les régions occupées par les entités culturelles des deux complexes mentionnés ont livré quelques objets d'art zoomorphique dont l'attribution au Mésolithique n'est pas certaine dans tous les cas. Ces objets varient au point de vue des matériaux utilisés, des techniques et du style.
5. Le Maglemosien est caractérisé par la présence des deux groupes d'objets attribuables au Mésolithique:

a) Le premier groupe, comportant de petites statuettes d'ambre, se localise essentiellement au Danemark et au nord de la Pologne, c'est-à-dire à proximité des dépôts naturels d'ambre. Remarquons toutefois que les régions où les gisements d'ambre sont les plus riches (péninsule de Sambie) n'ont livré qu'un seul objet attribuable à ce groupe (Juodkrante en Lituanie).

Si l'on considère l'homogénéité stylistique de ce groupe, on constatera que celle-ci dépend d'avantage des traditions culturelles que du milieu. Néanmoins, ce fait n'exclut pas une influence exercée par les caractéristiques de la matière première. Ceci est visible non seulement dans les dimensions des objets (celles-ci ne dépassent pas en principe quelques cm), mais également dans la sélection des animaux représentés. On constate la présence de représentations réalistes complètes, fortement simplifiées d'ours (trois exemplaires), de sanglier et peut-être de cheval (n'est-il pas plus ancien?), donc d'animaux dépourvus de bois. Les représentations de cervidés sont exceptionnelles et seulement partielles (dépourvus de bois; exemple: une tête d'élan du Danemark). On trouve aussi des exemples difficiles à interpréter (par exemple la tête de Juodkrante en Lituanie).

Trois faits sont encore à préciser:

- certains objets d'art peuvent constituer des fragments d'une composition plus grande (c'est le cas des têtes-contures perforées décrites ci-dessus, p. ex. celles d'élan)
- certaines statuettes comportent un décor de pointillés, de zigzags ou de quadrillés (traces d'un pelage?)
- toutes les pièces sont des trouvailles hors-contexte et ne sont attribuables au Mésolithique que par la présence du décor décrit plus haut, caractéristique du style dit "maglemosien"

b) Un second groupe de cet art zoomorphique nordique comporte des outils en bois de cervidés gravés. Ils sont moins nombreux (deux objets seulement). On trouve ici une "hache" en bois de cerf à décor du style "maglemosien" ("squelette d'hareng") provenant de Szczecin-Grabowo, en Pologne nord-occidentale, qui présente schématiquement un petit cervidé ou un cheval. Le second objet est également une "hache" (Ystad en Suède méridionale), présentant deux cervidés dans un style plus réaliste, associés à l'ornement "maglemosien".

L'étonnant contraste thématique qui existe entre les groupes "a" et "b" peut être expliqué par une plus grande habileté de la technique de gravure pour représenter des figures plus élaborées (par exemple les cervidés – Ystad en Suede, Szczecin-Grabowo et Podjuchy en Pologne: humains ou les insectes). Ce n'est toutefois pas la seule explication possible de cette différence stylistique.

6. Sur le territoire occupé par le complexe nord-oriental on trouve certains ensembles homogènes mésolithiques contenant des objets d'art (Vis au nord de la Russie, Oleni Ostrov en Carélie, Zvejnieki en Lettonie, et Zamostie sur la Volga supérieure, etc.). Ils se différencient nettement des objets connus plus à l'ouest. Ce sont principalement des statuettes en bois de cervidés (mais à Vis la sculpture est en bois!), réalistes ou stylisées, présentant l'élan (surtout la tête de cet animal) soit sur en "baton" (Oleni Ostrov), soit comme element decoratif (les skies, cf., de Vis), soit une statuette à part. On trouve parfois ces "batons", plus ou moins réalistiques, dans les sépultures (Zvejnieki, Oleni Ostrov) et on peut supposer qu'elles avaient une signification symbolique, peut-être d'attribut social.

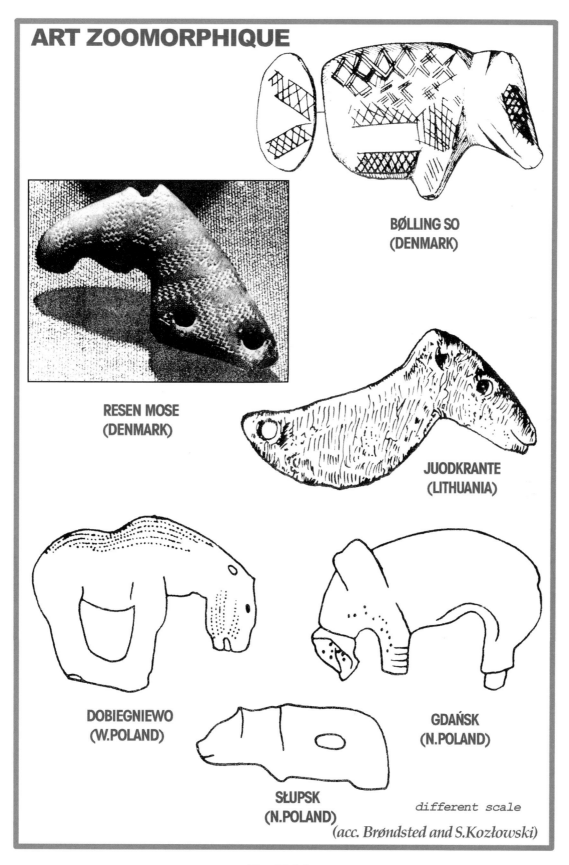

ART ZOOMORPHIQUE

BØLLING SO
(DENMARK)

RESEN MOSE
(DENMARK)

JUODKRANTE
(LITHUANIA)

DOBIEGNIEWO
(W.POLAND)

GDAŃSK
(N.POLAND)

SŁUPSK
(N.POLAND)

different scale

(acc. Brøndsted and S.Kozłowski)

Fig. 12.2.1a

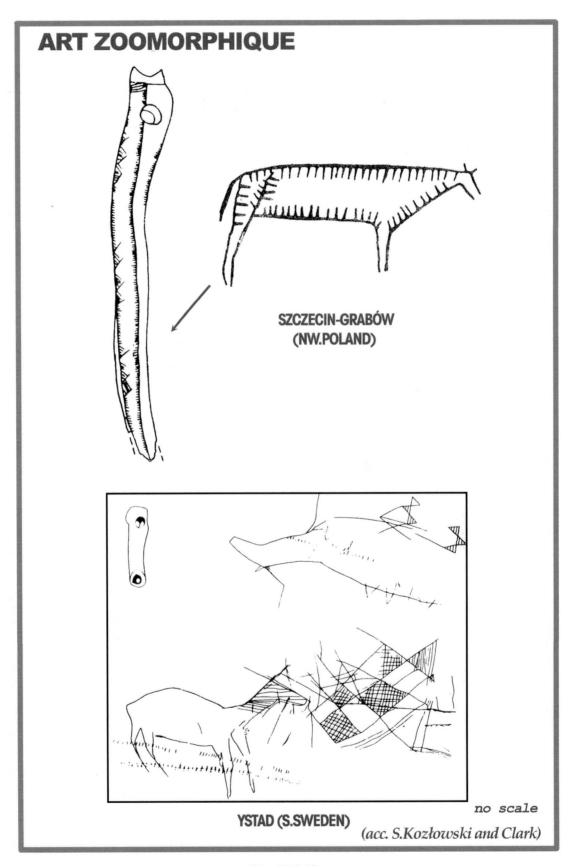

ART ZOOMORPHIQUE

SZCZECIN-GRABÓW
(NW.POLAND)

YSTAD (S.SWEDEN)

no scale

(acc. S.Kozłowski and Clark)

Fig. 12.2.1b

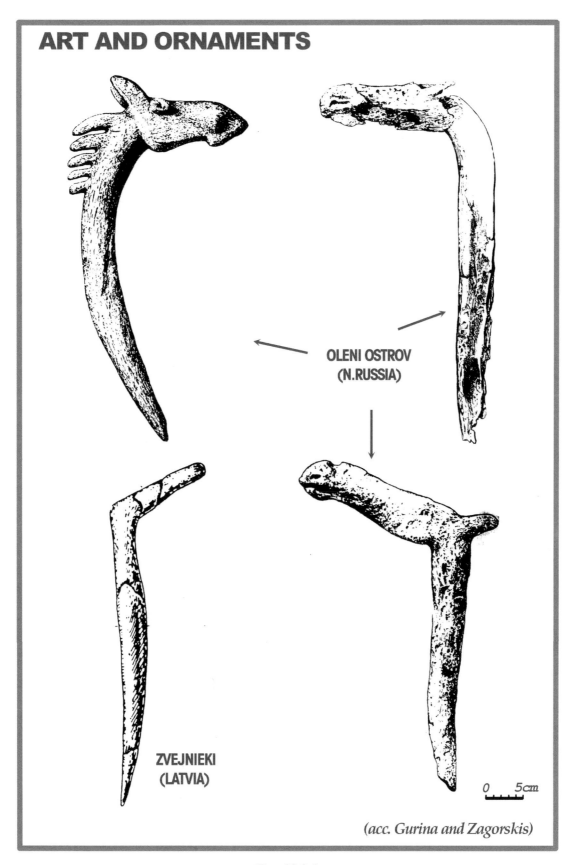

ART AND ORNAMENTS

OLENI OSTROV
(N.RUSSIA)

ZVEJNIEKI
(LATVIA)

0   5cm

(acc. Gurina and Zagorskis)

Fig. 12.2.1c

On peut remarquer que les trouvailles mentionnées ci-dessus constituent une périphérie occidentale et méridionale de l'ensemble de l'art de l'âge de la pierre caractérisé par les differentes représentations d'élan. Rappelons les gravures rupestres de la Norvège et de la Suède, ainsi que les petroglyphes de la peninsula Kola, mais aussi têtes sculptées en pierre.

7. Pour conclure ces remarques concernant les objets d'art zoomorphique mésolithique, trouvées autour de la mer Baltique, nous soulignons que:

a) cet art ne reflète que partiellement la différenciation territoriale de la faune de cette époque (par exemple l'importance des représentations de l'ours dans l'art de la zone occidentale);

b) la différenciation de la matière première utilisée par l'artiste mésolithique est due à la tradition culturelle;

c) la diversification des thèmes suivant la matière première peut s'expliquer par l'adaptation du sujet aux possibilités techniques offertes par cette matière;

d) certaines matières premières (comme par exemple l'ambre) limitaient fortement les possibilités de l'artiste;

e) les animaux figurés sont dans la plupart des cas assez bien discernables. Peut-être certains décors essayent de présenter le pelage de l'animal.

12.2.2. Woman's statuette from Gaban

In 1974, Bernardino Bagolini's excavations of sector III at Gaban (cf.) revealed a female representation. It was found in the base layer of the Castelnovian pit. The figurine was hardly a full statue, but rather a combination of incised relief and polishing on the surface of a red-deer tubular antler. The anatomic details are very realistic (body, legs, hands, breast) except for the head and face, which are almost invisible (Fig. 12.2.2).

Compared to figurines of the Paleolithic "Venus" type, the Gaban representation is rather flat (especially in the breasts section). It was never planned to follow this style, being rather determined by raw material structure. The 5.5 mm thick hard layer suitable for carving, backed by *spongiosa*, permitted nothing but "silhouette" depiction at best (with flat back). It is also possible that the relief was never to be cut from its original red-deer antler base (the tip of the piece is formed into a kind of handle, perhaps to be suspended).

It is not clear whether the item was considered as finished. The lack of head and face is hardly proof of unfinished work, as Upper Paleolithic examples of "Venuses" demonstrate.

If the "Venus" from Gaban was never planned in the Paleolithic style (and this is probably the case), it can hardly be considerd as descendent from this specific style (as suggested by Paolo Graziosi). The piece from Gaban should be viewed as unique, and it has in fact no parallels either in the Paleolithic or in the Neolithic, except, of course, for the female subject, already well known in both periods.

Our piece is clearly Castelnovian, and rather late (Layer E-27) than early, which means that it should be placed after 6500 (dates for layer FA) and before 5500 cal. BC.

12.2.3. Art and ornaments of the European Mesolithic

Mobile art

Like his Paleolithic ancestors, Mesolithic man had a penchant for matters other than material. His spiritual side remained as important as the physical one. Evidence of this aspect of Mesolithic life is limited, but frequently telling, in the form of art objects found throughout Europe. Obviously, not all or even many of such objects have survived down to our times. Most have disappeared , having been made of perishable, organic material. Rock art is rare in the period and when it does occur, it is extremely difficult to date.

The most prolifically represented category of mobile art (especially numerous in northern and northeastern Europe, due to conditions favorable for the preservation of organic material) is dominated by objects of everyday use, mainly tools (adzes, daggers) and hunting weapons, covered with an engraved or drilled ornament, which is appropriately either linear or dotted (cf. description by Grahame Clark). The composition of the ornament is perfectly suited to the morphology of a piece.

Rare anthropomorphic and zoomorphic representations occur as well. These can be images of animals or humans (cf. "L'art zoomorphique") carved in bone or antler or actual figurines in the round carved in antler (Zamostie in Russia), wood (Vis in Russia) and amber (Fig. 12.2.3a–f).

The two abovementioned provinces richest in objects considered as art are stylistically different. Maglemosian art is best known: tools decorated with rich engraved and drilled ornaments (adzes, handles, daggers and projectile points). Motifs, described by Grahame Clark, are differentiated formally and perhaps also chronologically. Next are small figurines of forest animals (bear, elk, boar, horse, geese) made of amber, amber ornamental pendants, more (Ystad) or less (Podjuchy, Szczecin-Grabowo) realistic engraved animal motifs on antler adzes and mattocks.

Separate mention should be made of an Erteb øllian painted paddle from Tybrind Vig in Denmark, which was decorated with an extraordinary non-linear geometrical ornament.

The art of the northeast is represented by a tradition that is original in theme as well as style. The most spectacular pieces are figural representations of animals (mainly elk) and humans. Geometric ornaments on various objects of everyday use are also fairly abundant, e.g. zigzag ornaments on bone daggers (Estonia, Karelia) and stone maceheads (Finland).

The said images of elk are always realistically presented animals (Oleni Ostrov), having astounding parallels in the petroglyphs of Zalavruga on the White Sea. Then come the fascinating "maces"/"batons" topped with heads of elk (e.g. cemeteries at Zvejnieki in Latvia and Oleni Ostrov in Karelia) and finally, the unique tip of wooden skis (cf.)

GABAN

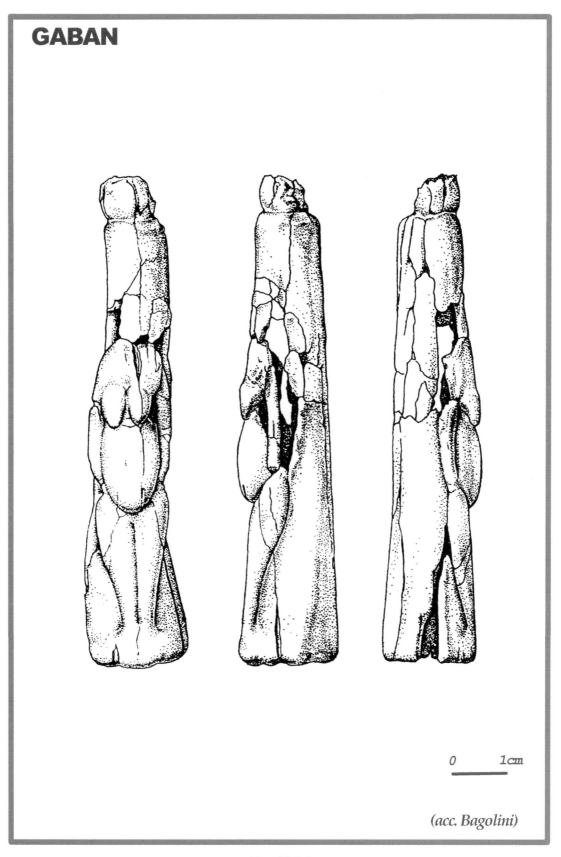

0   1cm

(acc. Bagolini)

Fig. 12.2.2

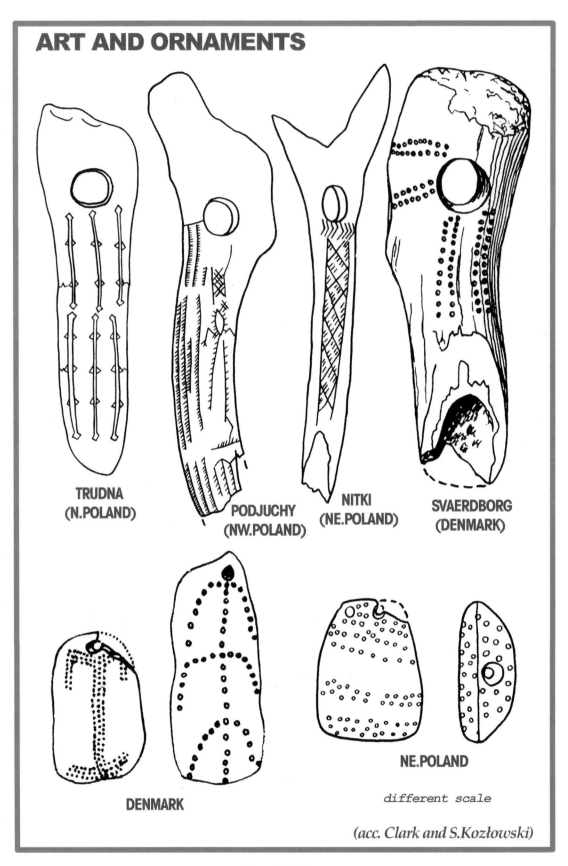

Fig. 12.2.3a

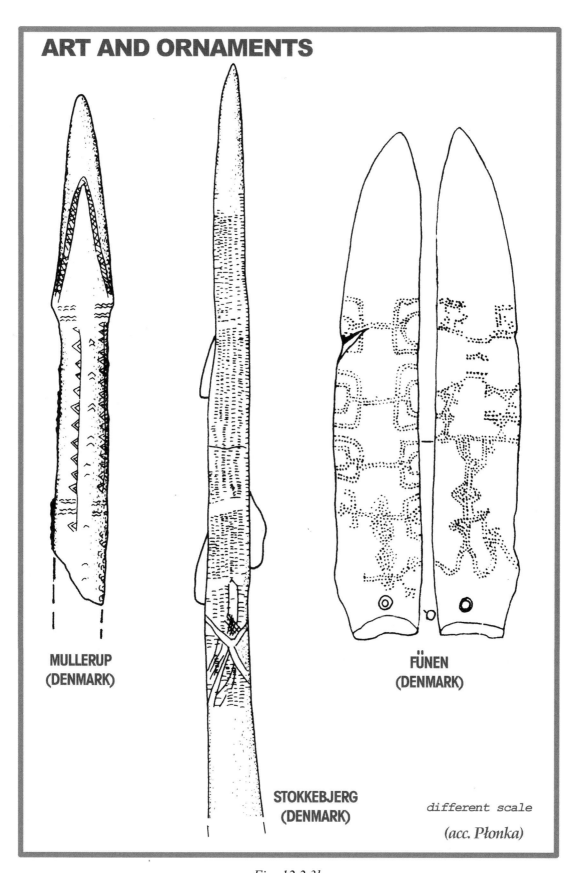

ART AND ORNAMENTS

MULLERUP
(DENMARK)

STOKKEBJERG
(DENMARK)

FÜNEN
(DENMARK)

different scale

(acc. Płonka)

Fig. 12.2.3b

ART AND ORNAMENTS

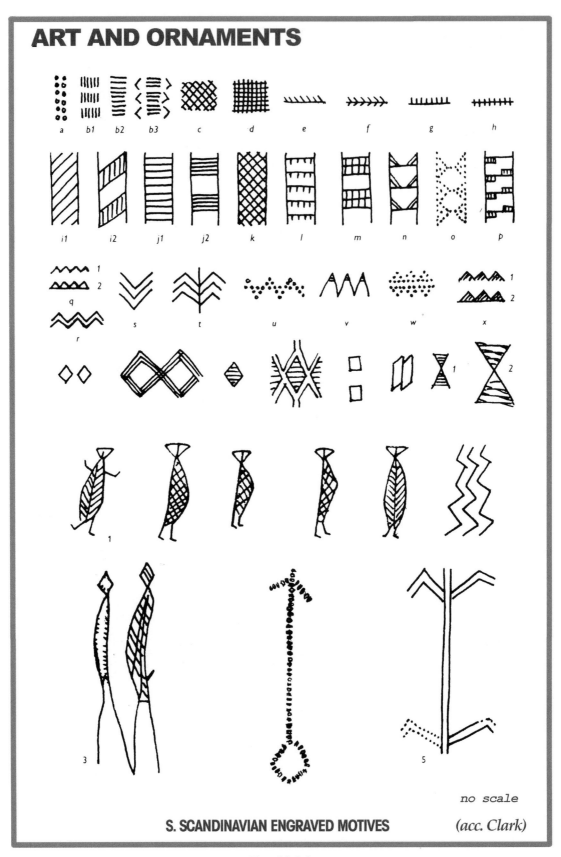

S. SCANDINAVIAN ENGRAVED MOTIVES (acc. Clark)

no scale

Fig. 12.2.3c

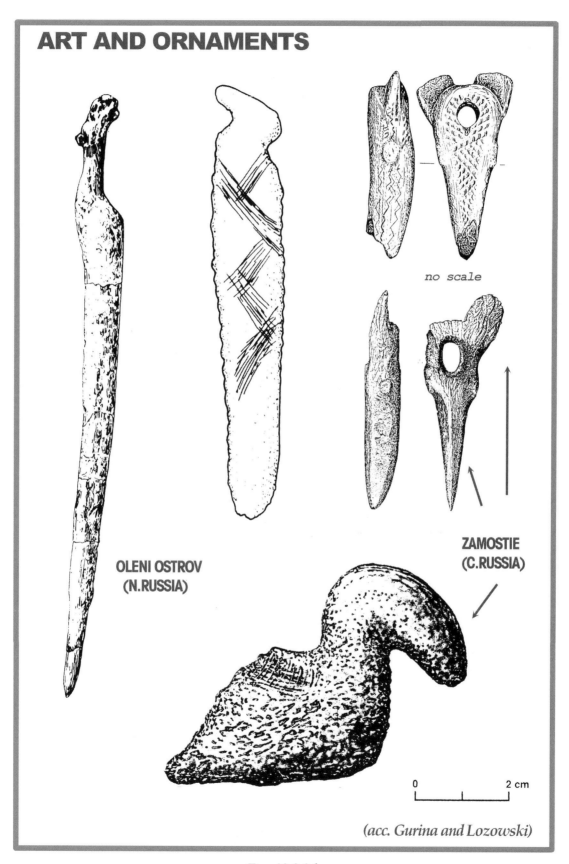

ART AND ORNAMENTS

no scale

OLENI OSTROV
(N.RUSSIA)

ZAMOSTIE
(C.RUSSIA)

0   2 cm

(acc. Gurina and Lozowski)

Fig. 12.2.3d

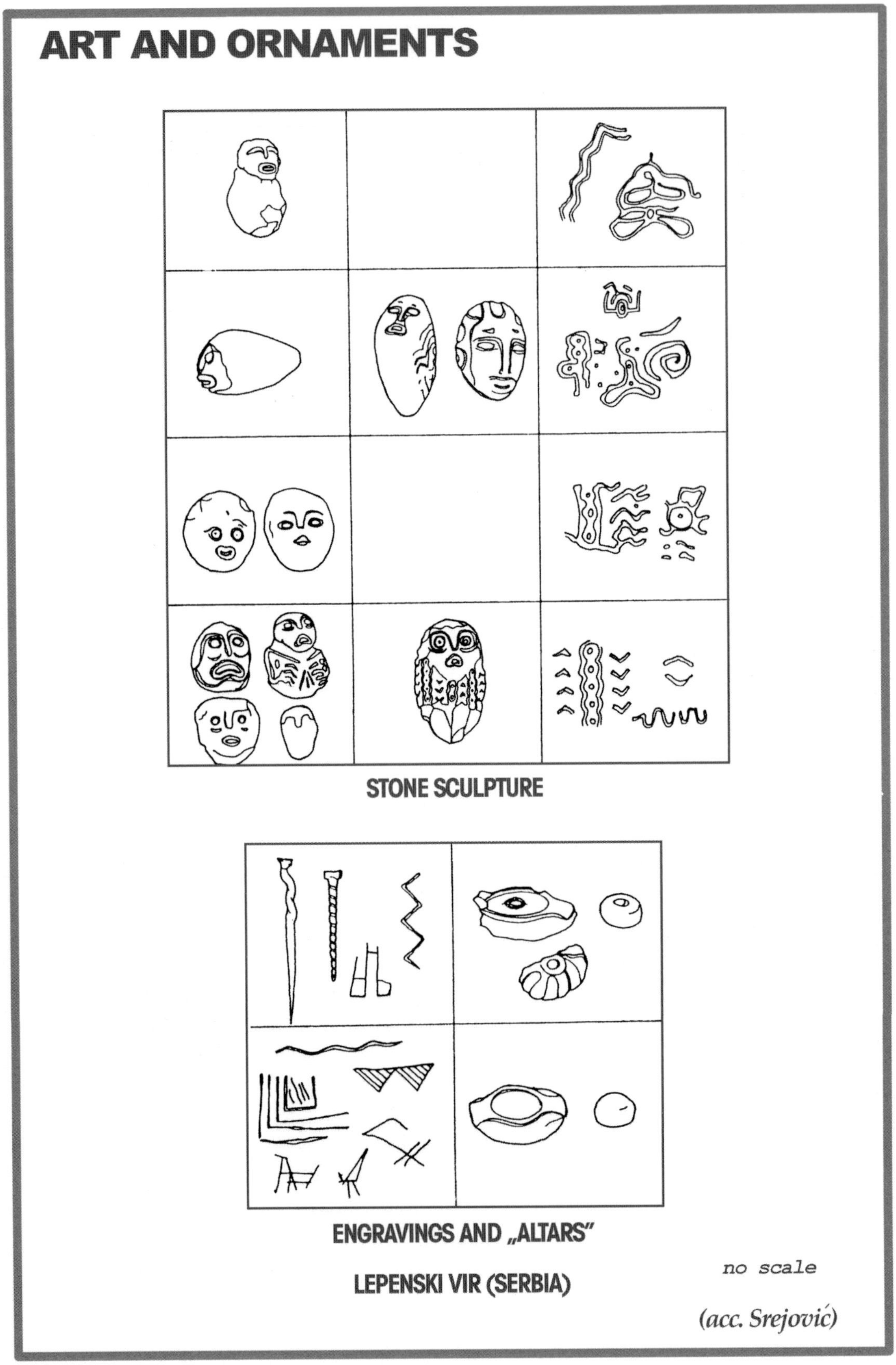

ART AND ORNAMENTS

STONE SCULPTURE

ENGRAVINGS AND „ALTARS"

LEPENSKI VIR (SERBIA)

no scale

(acc. Srejović)

Fig. 12.2.3e

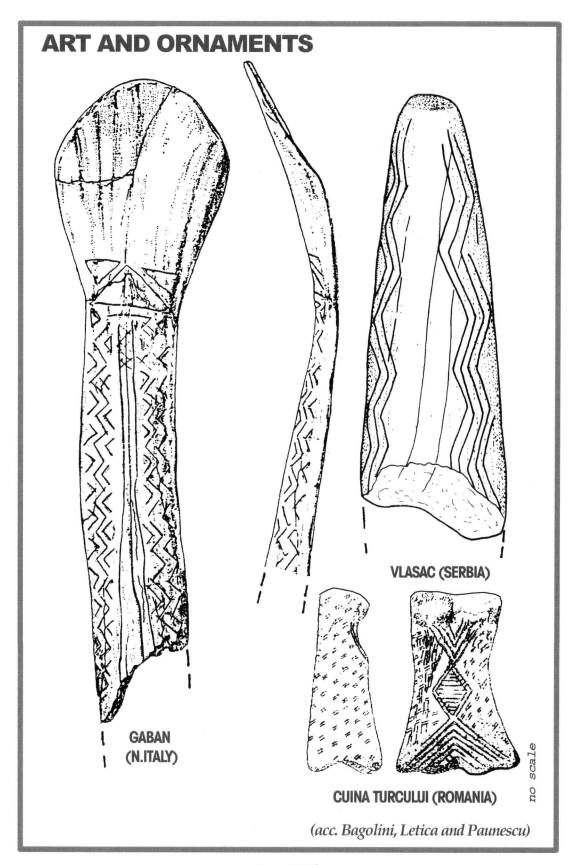

ART AND ORNAMENTS

GABAN (N.ITALY)

VLASAC (SERBIA)

CUINA TURCULUI (ROMANIA)

no scale

(acc. Bagolini, Letica and Paunescu)

Fig. 12.2.3f

from Vis I and "silhouettes" of elk from Zamostie on the upper Volga. Neither should one forget the human figurines from Oleni Ostrov and the representations of a snake from the same site.

Both the themes and the style of these objects find continuation in the local "Neolithic" (e.g. Sventoji I in Lithuania).

Another domain of artistic activities by the Mesolithic hunters of northeastern Europe are tools and weapons. The predominant form are engraved or drilled ornaments, resembling Maglemosian but not identical (zigzags, chevrons, parallel dashes and lines, "herring-bone" pattern).

A special case of mobile art, but very local at the same time, are the famous stone sculptures from Lepensky Vir in Serbia. These are mostly human heads depicted with an expression that borders on caricature, intended rather as images of local divinities. Relief geometrical ornaments are carved in stone, repeating similar motifs found on bone and antler, which refer to an engraved geometric Epi-Gravettian tradition (e.g. Vlasac and Cuina-Turcului, Dubova, similarly upper Gaban, cf.).

To remain in the Mediterranean zone, let us not forget at this point the "Venus" from Riparo Gaban (cf. "Woman's statuette...") in northern Italy. It is a fine example of realistic art connected with the Castelnovian tradition, naturally sharing nothing in common with the art of the Upper Paleolithic.

Rock art

Examples of rock art found in different regions merit separate discussion. They are usually difficult to date, but also distinctive in view of their subject matter concentrated on hunting, presenting individual animal or human figures, but also occasionally entire scenes (Fig. 12.2.3g–h).

Starting from the north there are the expressive carvings and petroglyphs of Scandinavia and Zalavruga on the White Sea, continued in the east by the numerous Siberian petroglyphs. The oldest styles are dominated by animal themes, including particularly realistic representations of elk, which was the biggest mammal in this part of the world at this time. Reindeer is less frequent, as are the big forest mammals. The hunting scenes of Zalavruga are exceptional for their vibrant expression, one example being hunters on skis trailing an elk.

The oldest objects from Scandinavia, as well as some from the Kola Peninsula could date from the Mesolithic. This conviction is grounded in the fact that very similar images of elk can be found in the mobile art of the northeastern Mesolithic (see above) and is further confirmed by the possible correlation of Fosna sites with neighboring rock art.

Another important and known concentration of Middle Holocene rock art is found in the Spanish Levant, painted on the walls of shelters. They represent two phases, the first one being characterized by geometrical ornaments and dated to the Mesolithic (7th millennium cal. BC?). The classic phase, which is better known as "Levantine art", originates from the 6th–5th millennium cal. BC (?) and is probably connected with local cardial pottery among others, meaning that it represents a culture still based on a hunting economy, but already with knowledge of ceramics (cf. "Ceramization"). The hunting theme dominates in Levantine art, but scenes of fighting between groups of warriors are also present. Representations of animals and people are painted in the silhouette technique in red and black. The animals are very realistic, but humans are rendered in a specific manner, and all the actors are in constant motion.

Perhaps of Mesolithic date as well are single representations of elk from Val Camonica, Italy, discovered by Emmanuel Anati. Neither can a Mesolithic date be excluded for the petroglyphs from Kamennaia Mogila in Ukraine, where antelopes and elks were represented.

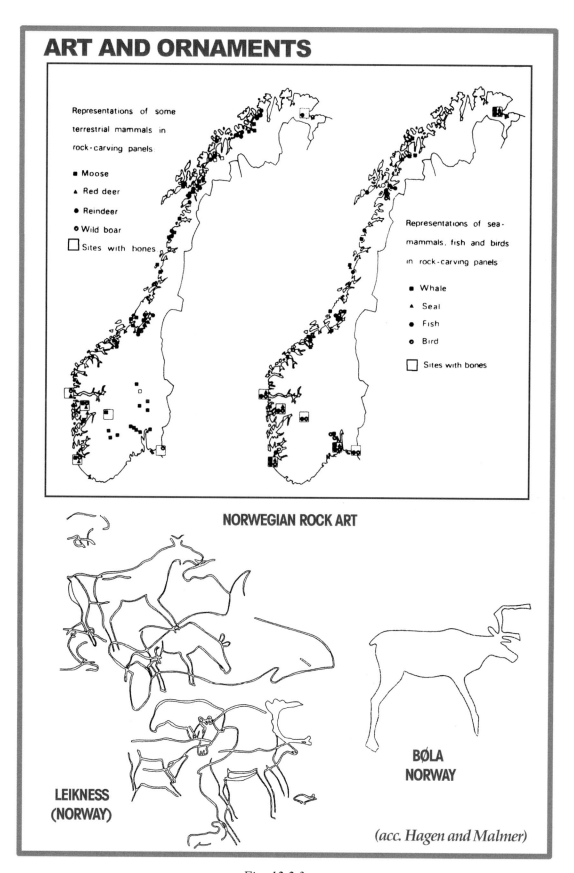

Fig. 12.2.3g

ART AND ORNAMENTS

CUEVA DE LOS CABALLOS (E.SPAIN)

(acc. Beltran)

Fig. 12.2.3h

13

The Final Score

In conclusion of this fairly lengthy book, I present a brief summing up, broken up into three parts: the sources – their possibilities and their limitations, the paradigms, the extent of our knowledge of Mesolithic culture, and the history of Mesolithic Europe. Indeed, that last part, although modest in volume, is surely the most interesting...

"Thinking Mesolithic" has led us to a series of conclusions which are on the whole banal to the extreme or else have been voiced already in the past. Yet there are new propositions as well. The following is a record of both.

Sources

Lithics are a mass and often surface or sub-surface source, especially in view of the less than intensive, or nonexistent sedimentation processes in the Holocene; for the same reason, they are characterized by uncertain or doubtful homogeneity. The material from the south of the continent is less numerous (and even poor for the Balkans), although "better", because it is frequently "sealed" inside a specific geological layer.

This dichotomy is of consequence for chronologization. Sites in the north, contrary to those in the south, are often sand sites with little opportunity for stratigraphy and "good" radiocarbon dating because of the inherent problem of establishing unquestioned links between the charcoal samples, nonexistent "layer" and archaeological material.

Added to this are questions of homogeneity, especially in the case of the biggest and richest sites where there is practically no way of knowing whether we are dealing with a single base camp inhabited for a longer period of time or a sum of successive settlements by groups representing the same (or not the same) cultural tradition and the sum of repeated occupations, occurring over the course of even several hundred years.

There is, finally, the handicap of gaps in the archaeological record, such as:

* the small number of sites that can be attributed to the Preboreal, an important transition period that lasted, after calibration, about two millennia(!). In the Lowland especially these sites are buried often quite deep
* less limited but still limited number of sites from the Boreal (8th millennium cal. BC)
* "unchartered (or unexplored) territories (gaps)" on the study maps of Mesolithic Europe

The case for non-lithics is even more difficult as far as sources are concerned, because of the following:

* bone/antler industries are known only from selected regions (circum-Baltic, upper Volga, some rock-shelters of southern Europe
* wooden industries are rare to the extreme and known only from a few microregions
* for reasons of questionable homogeneity (cf. above), the bigger camps are either poorly investigated or known, or understood
* little is known of dwellings due to the flimsiness of their construction.

Even more ephemeral and dispersed is the economic data (with the exception of big game hunting which has been not too badly researched and found to be zonally and chronologically differentiated, although there are still many gaps on the map), especially with regard to fishing and gathering.

These weaknesses of the source base are responsible for constructing generalizations that continue to be excessively banal, general and based mostly on common sense. On the other hand, they determine the choice of fields of research (cf. below), also such as the territorial and/or taxonomic aspects of the Mesolithic, which for reasons discussed in detail at the beginning of this book is treated by the present author as a purely chronological designation.

The Paradigms

Considering that taxonomy is one of the promising and as yet not fully explored research fields, it is essential at this point to comment on how it was treated in this book.

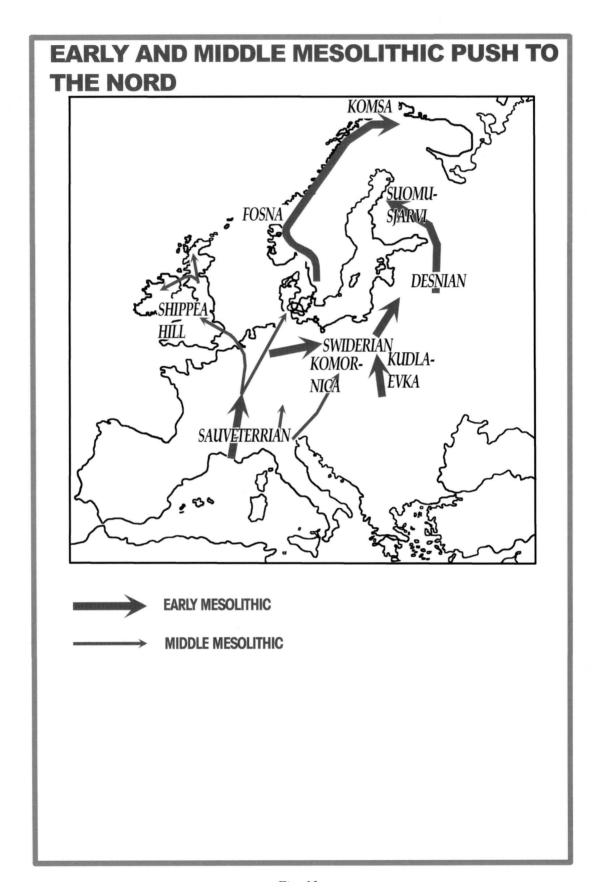

First and foremost, an effort has been made to treat observable differences and similarities of style in the spatial aspect, under the assumption that like any other cultural phenomenon or trait, it should have its spatial limitation, that is, bigger or smaller, but specified range, and of course a temporal one as well.

Upon analysis of the territoriality of thus conceived types/classes of artifacts and combinations of types (making up a given picture of tradition in given homogeneous assemblages or structures), we arrive at a series of smaller or bigger, differentiated territorial ranges for particular elements. Thus, we come to deal with "territory" with its limitations, we see the dichotomy between "filled" and "empty", we observe how some ranges, territories and borders could be repeated several times by different features.

Consequently, we are returning to an old European tradition of describing taxonomic units ("civilizations", "cultures", peoples, tribes, etc.) in territorial terms, graphically. We are following here the solutions proposed for the Late Paleolithic and Mesolithic already by Grahame Clarke, Hermann Schwabedissen, Wolfgang Taute, Jan M. Burdukiewicz, Stefan K. Kozłowski and Janusz K. Kozłowski, in opposition to the somewhat "Darwinian" French vertical evolutionary columns and numerous local Mesolithic "cultures" understood as sequences of industries (e.g. Jean-George Rouzoy's local taxonomy for France, and terrible references to the "Early-Middle and Late Mesolithic" in many regional studies).

In effect of our interpretation, an "archaeological culture" bonded by a shared, common tradition (technology, typology, internal statistical structure) must have its own defined "territory", which can be divided into smaller sub-territories or "cultural groups" distinguished by secondary stylistic traits. In turn, following D. Clarke, an archaeological culture may constitute part of a bigger whole, a "technocomplex" characterized by a common "history" and shared tradition. Finally, an archaeological culture thus understood as a material reflection of a specific living community, which has its "own" territory and guarded borders, will also have its own "history" because it appears to be a separate human organization or entity.

Organizations of this kind have their stability which in our case is based on the conservative and virtually unchanging or gradually changing character of a regional/local material culture/style. The element of change, which clashes with stability, usually draws from intercultural or interregional trends and fashions coming in naturally mostly from outside. The objective is thus to defend distinction, while adapting to new wherever it appears to be to the advantage.

A question for interpretation is the actual mechanism of proliferation/interpenetration and acceptance of new elements in successive environments and communities. In this regard, prehistory, not only of the Mesolithic, appears to be helpless.

Territories

Mesolithic territoriality is of twofold nature: cultural (discussed above) and settlement, of which below. Any given cultural territory needs to be organized in one way or another, hence there needs to be a settlement pattern of some kind, most likely dependent on geographic and social factors.

The former include the water network as contrasted with dry areas and the rich in game and warm river valleys as opposed to dry and poor in biomass cooler uplands. Then there are natural barriers and passes, deposits of raw materials, differentiated flora and fauna, and a differentiated climate. With regard to social factors, one should surely mention hierarchized segments of "tribal" organization which can be transposed into an observable segmentation of Mesolithic settlement with territories of a diameter respectively 30–50, 100–200 and 300 km constituting the principal units.

A common cemetery, uniting the people, could/should be placed in the center of such (which?) structure.

The smallest of these units, 30–50 km, is probably a closed and very isolated microcosmos, resistant to outside influence, conservative and virtually invariable (except for small, seasonal moves). It does, however, admit occasional change of a fundamental nature in the instrumentarium, as at the turn of the Pleistocene and Holocene and a second time at the turn of the Middle and Late Mesolithic. These changes tend to be quick (reasonably rapid mutation) rather than slow, and they are separated by usually very long periods of boring stability, not to say stagnation, in terms of tool style. In the western *koine*, changes in the group of microliths, resulting most probably from the consecutive inventions of new types of arrowhead construction, upset this longterm stability.

Moreover, changes of the described kind are supra-regional, hence also intercultural.

General and individual

Should one desire to characterize it somehow in general, Mesolithic culture will have some shared traits (although hardly a proliferation of these) which are not as unique as some would like to believe.

First of all, Mesolithic culture in general is a continuation of Upper/Late Palaeolithic culture with little or no change (local tradition without change, local tradition with change, migration of people without change of tradition, migration of people with changes). As such, it is naturally a specialized hunting-gathering formation with regional emphasis on different game hunting, intensive fishing (apparently a novelty) and perhaps a gradual increase (?) in the significance of regionally differentiated gathering.

The instrumentarium (not taking into account the almost unknown wooden tools) is straightforward:

- different arrows (with stone geometric/microliths or tanged arrowheads, but also with wooden tips) propelled with bows

BEFORE

Fig. 13b

- hurled harpoons and spears (made of bone/antler/wood)
- "domestic" tools, mainly of small size, e.g. stone scrapers, retouched-use-retouched and unretouched blades and bladelets, truncations, "axes" of antler and "daggers" of antler/bone, cervid spikes, knife-scrapers made of boar tusks, wooden dugouts and paddles
- regionally also stone axes-adzes, burins and perforators
- stone raw material quarried or collected mainly within the framework of local autarkic economies (distance of up to 50 km); real imports (radius of > 150 km) did not appear until the Late Mesolithic and made possible an increase in the size of flint tools. Prior to that, the autarkic character of the raw material economy generally forced a considerable miniaturization of stone implements; local raw materials occurred mostly as small-size nodules or as big but internally cracked ones

Even so, small geometrics and not very big tanged points, as well as other tools were quite effective as arrowheads despite their micro size. For the first time in the history of humanity man could make virtually everything out of practically nothing.

The impression of a certain stylistic uniformity of this equipment that lends itself from an analysis of the finds is also due to the simplicity of designs, forms (mostly single or multiple backs/truncations) and techniques of execution (sectioning or microburin), as well as the small size of blanks. A real stylistic or cultural differentiation can be observed often only with regard to rare/specific types.

Supplementing this Mesolithic inventory are fishing implements – hooks, traps, nets with floats – which, however, do not need to be pan-continental in nature, even though fish were naturally caught everywhere in the Europe of the time.

The inner structure of assemblages could reflect stylistic and/or cultural distinction, as well as their chronological position, but also the actual function of a site or complex of sites – whether it is a "base" or "satellite" camp, a workshop, butchering site, etc. – and whether the stone raw material was at all accessible.

The said functional differentiation of assemblages is occasionally reflected in the rare, well-documented but not very surely dated Mesolithic "camps" of different size and richness; their homogeneity (meaning a short-lasting and uninterrupted occupation), however, is seldom verifiable, especially with regard to the big features. Seasonality is also confirmed.

Cultural/territorial differentiation

The techno-typological differentiation of the Mesolithic is apparently more important, at least to the present author. On the whole, it seems to correspond to the different traditions separating people and communities and it appears to be verifiable cartographically. An analysis taking into consideration techno-typological and technical aspects of material/sites/assemblages demonstrates the differing territorial importance/value of various types and sets of types, which can be basically territorial, specific, individual (local or regional) or general (supraregional, intercultural) in a territorial sense. Therefore, such cartographic characteristics can be both completely banal or particularly typical. Finally, types and sets of types can indicate chronological horizons and in such cases, they are naturally characterized by a supraregional range.

Mapping of types and sets of types (controlled from the structural – assemblages, and chronological – datation point of view) reveals the existence of territorial structures exceeding the modern political boundaries, exhibiting own borders and featuring a common style and structure comprised of many types. It leads to generalizations on a continental scale: Europe can be divided into super-territories that are characterized by common techno-typological features (technocomplexes). These in turn are subdivided into smaller territories corresponding to particular "archaeological cultures".

Divisions of this kind are based in environmental factors like climate, fauna, flora, raw materials, geomorphology, barriers, gates, hydrography etc. Even so, they are mainly a genetic continuations, one way or another, of Terminal Paleolithic styles reinforced by the isolationism of small microcosmoses separated one from the other by vast distances (physical and mental) and kept apart by the above-mentioned environmental factors. Of just such microcosmoses Ryszard Kapuściński wrote:

> *For most people the world ends on the threshold of their own home, the outskirts of their own village, the borders of the valley they live in at the farthest*

To be brief, the Mesolithic is a very stable, one could even say petrified formation, strongly subdivided and structured regionally, featuring definitely the longest spans of stabilization in the techno-typological, but also territorial and "cultural" sense, complete (the East of the continent) or almost complete, lasting a few millennia at a time regionally (e.g. in the Russian Lowland). Preceding and possibly interrupting it are relatively brief moments of destabilization that result in significant techno-typological (but also behavioral) changes, instigated most frequently by drastic or at least significant ecological changes (turn of the Pleistocene and the Holocene in most areas of Europe, then the beginning of the Atlantic period), including climate, vegetation, fauna, but also geology, such as sinking of whole land formations. The changes could be adaptive (to a new local environment) or migratory (in search of a disappearing homeland). The end effect of processes understood in this way was a gradual and multidirectional disintegration of the "old" system, occurring over a certain span of time, even up to hundreds of years long, during which a "new" system developed.

Pulsating toward the north

A gradual but regular warming of the climate in the

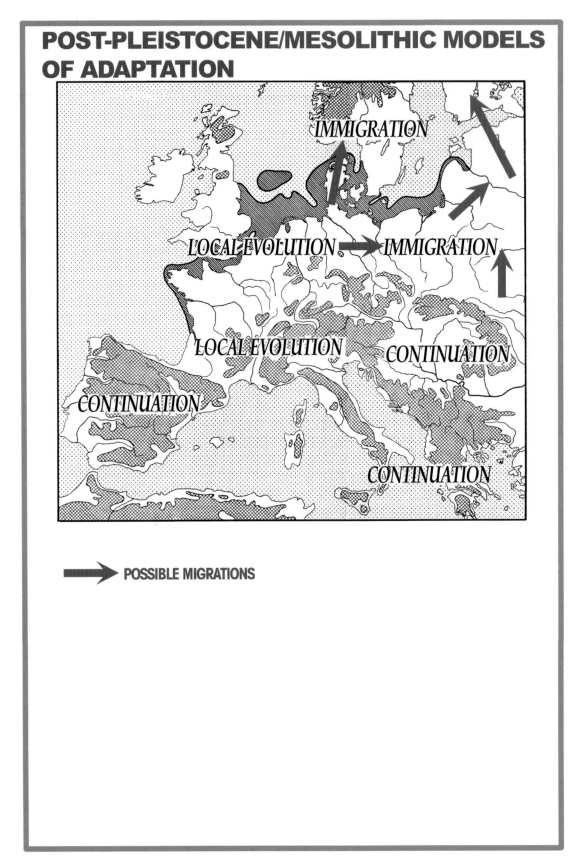

Fig. 13c

immediately post-Pleistocene period and the Early and Middle Holocene pushed the vegetation zones (tundra, taiga, mixed and finally deciduous forests) latitudinally to the north. With these zones went the faunal complexes (respectively, reindeer, elk, forest fauna).

This northward pulsating push appears to have significantly impacted several times the movements of human groups or at least the proliferation of certain ideas, as a rule from the south to the north.

1. The earliest "push" came in the end of the Pleistocene and beginning of the Holocene, which was a time of revolutionary ecological changes (first half of the 10th millennium cal. BC) marked by relatively rapid northward displacement of ecological zones and a gradual deglaciation of the north. According to the archaeological record, the Norwegian Arctic territories were settled already around this time (migration of hunters representing the Tanged Points tradition from northern Central Europe), and Finland even earlier (information from Heiki Matiskainen). At this point a big part of northern Europe (not including northern Russia?), so far uninhabited, seems to have started teeming with life.

Parallely in the same time we observe a clear proliferation to the north of Mediterranean or more broadly speaking, southern European elements:

- the Sauveterrian expands toward the north, following the French Rhône valley (see André Thèvenin's nicely documented idea);
- new types of microliths and geometrics known earlier from the south reach the European Lowland (important theory presented by Bernhard Gramsch);
- the southern German-French-Belgian Beuronian could have been a reminiscence of this proliferation (according to W. Taute's presumably correct theory, originating from the south German, if not a more widely considered Epi-Magdalenian, and not from the Ahrensburgian as A. Thèvenin would like);
- next the Polish Komornician (which could have, however, come from Germany), the German Duvensean (?) and Belarusian-Ukrainian Kudlaevka (with the West Ukrainian Epi-Gravettian/Maglemosian (?) of the Pleistocene, but also possibly the Polish Komornician?).

Nevertheless, the Early Mesolithic of Eastern Europe was probably not the effect of a migration or influence from the south, but possibly one from Siberia (although A. Sorokin would prefer to see its roots in the local/southern Epi-Gravettian).

2. The second paroxysm came in the second half of the 8th millennium cal. BC when the entire northwest of Europe was "sauveterrized", that is, it underwent a certain typological uniformization that originated most likely from the Sauveterrian/southern source. This change drew from the introduction of a new core-reduction technology and microbladelet blanks, imposing new types of microliths and forcing (or forced by) a change in arrowhead construction.

It could be correlated with significant ecological change in this region at this time, mainly the spread of deciduous (oak) forests. But this change obviously did not cause the phenomenon.

Simultaneously, the real Sauveterrian also ventured north beyond the Alps (into Austrian Tyrol) and the Dynaric Alps, western Slovakia and the Mesolithic reached the north of Britain. What's more, Sauveterrization does not look like actual human-group movement, contrary to the proliferation of the Sauveterrian described above (cf. pt 1).

At about the same time (?) elements of Kukrek culture, possibly from the Caucasus (?), appear to have pushed north into the Ukrainian steppes.

3. The third stage of the process was the "Castelnovization" of Europe, meaning the appearance over large parts of the continent of a new blade technology, system of long-distance distribution of raw materials and new types of geometrics (trapezes, rhomboids). The phenomenon appears to have spread gradually from the south (Frankhthi, before 7000 cal. BC) to the north (Kongemose, c. 6500 cal. BC), which nicely correlates with the northward expansion of forests in the Atlantic period and the domination of deer and boar in the center and west of the continent at this time.

The regionally differentiated phenomenon (western and eastern zones) becomes implanted more (model A) or less (model B) deeply, but on the whole slightly later in the north, but generally spreads from the southern "center" (Romagnano III, Odmut, Chateauneuf around 7000 cal. BC) to the peripheries (Botiqueria, Moita do Sebastiao, Rouffignac, Tévièc, Leduc, Kongemose, Dęby etc., etc., from around 6500 cal. BC!).

The ceramization of Europe will be a later counterpart of this phenomenon (in terms of the northward push), although spreading by different channels, and of course, it will be paralleled or followed by the Neolithization of the continent.

4. The phenomena that may have paralleled Castelnovization, but were at least partly caused by other reasons include:

- migration of the microbladelet tradition from southern Scandinavia to Sweden and Norway (although the causes of this migration may have been more complicated), pushing out Fosna culture to the north;
- settling the Russian Far North, marked by such sites as Veretie I, Olei Ostrov and Vis I (assuming there had not been an earlier push paralleling the first stage in Scandinavia described above) and the emergence of the Kunda tradition in Finnish Lapland (Sujala).

The final stages of the process witness the Neolithization of western (*impresso*/cardial), central and northwestern Europe (Band-ceramics) all the way to the external, western, central and northern regions of the continent.

The data at our disposal is still insufficient to give an understanding of which of these "pushes" can be considered as migration and which as acculturation.

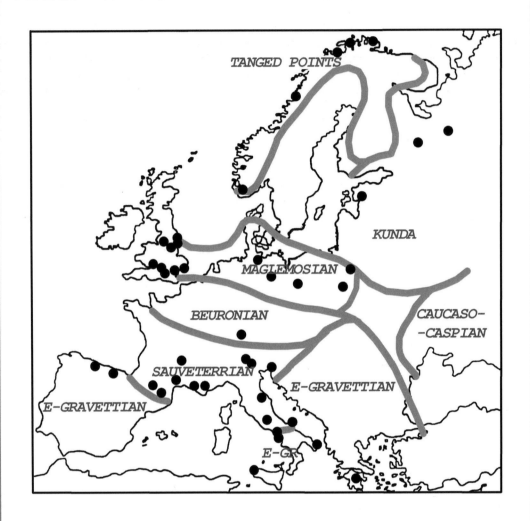

Fig. 13d

The Mesolithic history of Europe

Before

Mesolithic cultures did not come from nowhere and they are naturally a continuation and/or adaptation of cultures from the Dryas 3 period, the last cooling in the Pleistocene which occurred in the 11th millennium cal. BC, and the earliest Holocene (10th millennium cal. BC). During this period Europe was divided into four separate ecological zones which extended more or less latitudinally: 1. the glacier in the north and its foreland; 2. tundra, mostly on the Plain; 3. forests, mostly birch and pine more to the north and a mixed deciduous forest in the south; and 4. steppe in the Black Sea region.

The fauna inhabiting these zones was correspondingly differentiated as well. Reindeer ruled in the tundra, the elk was found in the northern stretch of forests, while the southern forests were replete with deer, auroch, boar, horse and the *equus hydruntinus*; finally, in the steppe, outside the valleys where forest animals lived, the saiga antelope was hunted.

The differentiated zonal hunting economy practiced for millennia (different animal habits, different ways of hunting, different hunting *instrumentarium*, different social organization) was supplemented with other kinds of activities, especially in the south of the continent (gathering mollusks, for example, and fishing).

Topping this in the cooler Dryas 3 were the strongly differentiated cultural traditions corresponding roughly to ecological and geographical zones. They were to give rise in the near future to the differentiated cultures of the Mesolithic.

Following are some remarks on this subject.

In the 10th millennium, the south of Europe (Spain, Italy, Balkans) preserved the most traditional Upper Paleolithic outlook (it was to be exactly the same in the beginnings of the Holocene – e.g. Romanelli in Southern Italy). In Iberia, Italy and in the Balkans the Epi-Gravettian of Mediterranean type underwent two parallel processes: microlithization of bladelets, geometrization of backed bladelets and points, and finally the miniaturization of other tools (Piancavallo in northern Italy, Montadian in Provence, Szekszard-Palank in Hungary, Molodova Ia in Moldova, Cuina Turcului in Romania, Lower-Middle Frankhthi in Greece, etc.).

At the same time, the Upper/Late Paleolithic cultures of the north and west (among others, Western Magdalenian and Western Creswellian, as well as some variants of the Eastern Gravettian) are "Azilianized" (introduction of very short flake scrapers and arched backed points), that is, they take on western Azilian (western and northern Europe) and northern Federmesser/Epi-Magdalenian (southern Germany), Epi-Gravettian (in the Balkans) or Shan-Kobian (Ukraine) characteristics, occupying for the most part the northern outskirts of the Epi-Gravettian.

During this time the Lowland North, but also the south of Scandinavia, was settled (from where?) by the newly emerging tundra peoples/cultures using recently invented tanged points. Some of the described phenomena lasted even into the Holocene.

The map of Europe in the Dryas 3 and the earliest Preboreal periods is relatively well established, showing latitudinal zonation, as described above, that is, in agreement with the environmental zonality of the continent. The southern belt was occupied by Epi-Gravettian entities: the Mediterranean type from the Balkans to the Pyrenean Peninsula, and the Eastern type east of the southern Carpathians all the way to the Don River (where dates are unfortunately few). In both cases, there was an "Azilianized" continuity of local development through the millennia. Both territories also reveal "azilianization" processes, in differing degrees for that matter (Italian Romanelli-type, French Azilian and German Federmesser assemblages in the west and Borshchevo II-type assemblages in the east). Both also exhibited (although in differing degrees) the phenomena of microlithization and geometrization (Piancavallo, Montade, Romanelli, Frankhthi, Molodova 1a etc.). In both cases we are dealing with hunters interested in forest game; in the south, the fauna also included *equus hydruntinus* and in the east, the reindeer, together with forest fauna, was still to be encountered in the forested valleys of the wooded steppe.

The Shan-Koban-Beloblesye culture of Ukraine and the northern piedmont of the Caucasus also belongs to this southern zone, although it does not seem to be autochthonous, but rather appears to be connected with the Caucasian-Caspian para-Gravettian tradition. This culture lives of forest game and the *saiga* antelope. Azilianization is also an observable process here, as well as partial geometrization but without microlithization pushed to the extreme.

The next zone to the north runs along the Alps from eastern France to Moravia. It is occupied by industries which refer to the Epi-Magdalenian (Rochèdane, Zigeunerfels, Kůlna, etc.). Azilianization is also an observable phenomenon in this area (very short scrapers, arched backed points). Hunted chiefly by these groups was forest game and reindeer.

The Lowland, as already mentioned above, constitutes the next zone. In the Dryas 3 period and the very beginning of the Preboreal, it is occupied by mostly tundra cultures/tribes with tanged points as a characteristic element of their stone tool industries. These are, starting from the west: Ahrensburgian, Brommian, Swiderian and Desnian, extending from eastern England all the way to the Upper Volga. The hunters preyed on tundra reindeer, occasionally also elk. Azilianization was also noted in this group (but not in northern Brommian) in the form of scrapers but devoid of arched backed points, geometrization and microlithization (with the exception of the western variant of Ahrensburgian).

In the northwestern part of the continent the local Creswellian entered also at this time its Azilianization stage (Dead Man's Cave). This culture based its hunting economy on forest game.

Its eastern neighbor on Dogger Bank Shelf and in northern Holland, also bearing distinct marks of Azilianization

Fig. 13e

was the latest phase of the Federmesser Culture (with sites in northern Holland dated to this period! – information from Raymond R. Newell).

There is no persuasive data for settlement of such age on the Lowland east of the Upper Volga river; relics of the Eastern Gravettian may have survived on the Upper Volga (Resetta Culture?).

Summing up, the ecological and cultural zonality described above should be emphasized, because it was largely to be repeated in the Mesolithic over most of the continent (parallels: western Mediterranean Epi-Gravettian = Sauveterrian, Balkan Epi-Gravettian = Epi-Gravettian Mesolithic of the Balkans, South German and Czech Epi-Magdalenian = Beuronian, Ahrensburgian + Creswelian + Federmesser = Maglemosian) with the exception of the northern reaches of Europe where migratory trends were present.

Thus, a general theory about the mostly local continuations of the Upper/Final Paleolithic into the local/earliest Mesolithic can be assumed with some potential, insignificant mobility. These continuations concern industries already azilianized in the terminal Pleistocene (almost all of Europe) and locally geometrized and microlithized (southern edge of the continent), as well as furnished with tanged points in the north. All of these characteristics will last into the Mesolithic, even if partly delocalized, and some of them (microlithization and geometrization) will develop and spread to larger areas, mostly to the north.

Finally, one should note that wherever significant techno-typological changes can be observed at the Paleolithic-Mesolithic transition, they do not occur at the turn of the Pleistocene and Holocene, but somewhat later (9500–8800 cal. BC in Crimea, Estonia, France, Italy, Poland, Norway, Britain, Finland and Germany), which means that regionally the Final Paleolithic traditions survived unchanged into the first half of the Preboreal (Swiderian, Desnian, Shan-Koban, Ahrensburgian in Sweden and Norway, Epi-Gravettian in the Balkans and Iberia, etc.).

Change and continuation

The Big Change

The turn of the Pleistocene and Holocene (c. 10,500/9800 ! cal. BC) in the opinion of many researchers was supposed to be the reason for the emergence of a new "cultural"/adaptive quality called the Mesolithic. This new quality was indeed revealed in many, but not all areas, and not at this time, but somewhat later (c. 9600–9500 cal. BC – cf. above). For this reason the Mesolithic cannot be described as a ubiquitous model, lifestyle or culture, but only as a period with a conventional beginning line.

It cannot be defied that the environmental shaking up that occurred at the beginning of a new interglacial period was sufficiently important to put the machine of history into motion, changing the fairly stable system known from Dryas 3. These relatively rapid changes concerned climate foremost. In the beginnings of the Holocene (10th millennium cal. BC) it moved rapidly from a glacial to an interglacial phase, leading to a number of significant changes of biotopes in Europe. One of these was the northward proliferation of the forest zone practically into southern Scandinavia, central England and southern Finland, thus reducing the tundra to a belt north of this zone (previously it covered practically all or at least a big part of the northern European Lowland). A parallel gradual melting of the Scandinavian glacier and perhaps the smaller one in the north of the British Isles lasted until c. 7000 cal. BC, slowly increasing the extent of the ecumene.

Forest expansion and receding of the tundra had its consequences for the migration of big mammals, constituting the main economic base of hunting-gathering societies of the period and for a long time yet. Reindeer moved up north to the areas where it lives today (in Scotland it was recorded in historical times), while forest game – deer, elk, reindeer, auroch, boar, horse – extended gradually its habitat toward the north while retaining an inner zonality with the elk keeping more to the coniferous forests in the north and the other species inhabiting the mixed and deciduous woods in the south. Much later, with improvement of the climate, forest fauna will expand more to the north.

The parallel evolution of marine reservoirs in northern Europe (Baltic and Northern Sea) changed to some extent the range of ecumenes in this period (a slow and gradual, but continuous reduction of territory).

All these changes could not have had no influence on the adaptive patterns of at least some Final Paleolithic human groups, especially those located in the northern part of the Dryas 3 ecumene. The adaptive reactions generally fall into two basic models:

- local adaptation to new conditions (regardless of what is meant by the term) without changing the place of residence
- migration in an effort to keep up with a receding familiar environment

It is also possible to imagine a more complicated process in which both strategies find application (for different parts of one community, e.g. the fate of the Ahrensburgian!). Whatever the case may be, any attempt at reconstructing the process based on the archaeological record presents considerable interpretational difficulties. The same is true of the origins of the Mesolithic cultures. It is due presumably to gaps in the record; after all, most sites are not well dated, while evolutionary change in archaeology can proceed quite rapidly at times. Hence caution is recommended in reading the remarks below.

It is possible that the first model (local adaptation) was realized more frequently in the south where the Pleistocene to Holocene environmental change may not have been as bitterly felt. The second model is more likely to have characterized northern regions, where the temptation to settle newly emerging land and to follow the disappearing beloved reindeer would have been much stronger. This

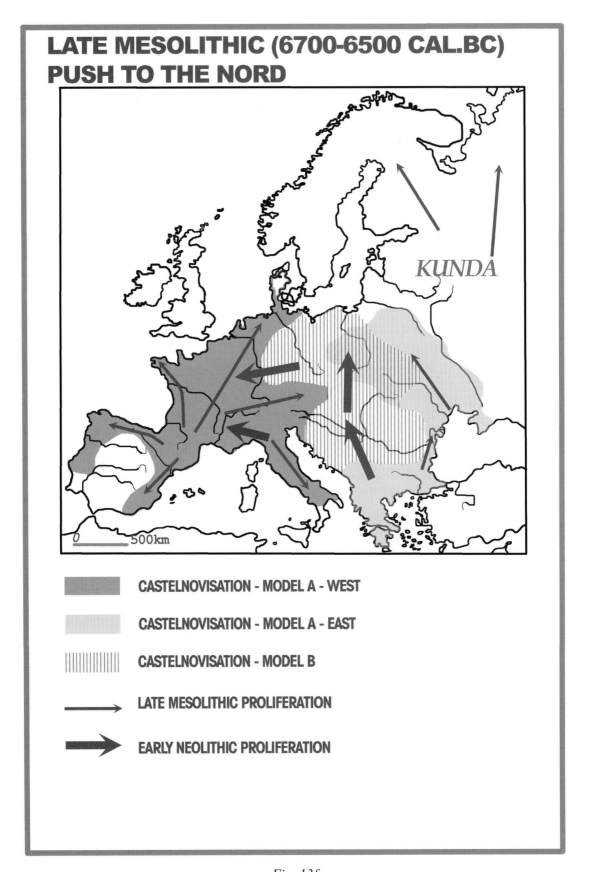

Fig. 13f

is generally confirmed in practice. Wherever significant changes in culture and tool style are noted, there are usually two other, significant phenomena:

- The changes, assuming they occur, take place not in the time traditionally considered by geologists as the transition from the Pleistocene to the Holocene, but quite a long time later, that is, around 9600–9500 cal. BC. At least some of the cultures of the terminal Pleistocene style survived into the Early Holocene (Ahrensburgian, Swiderian, Desnian, Balkan Epi-Gravettian, Shan-Kobian, etc.). It is possible, therefore, to speak of a certain retardation of the cultural and stylistic reaction (if it appears) to environmental change (the oldest dates for new cultures/taxons are placed around 9500 cal. BC)

- Classic new Mesolithic industries were preceded in at least a few cases by industries of veritable transitional style in which certain earlier characteristics disappeared (e.g. points in western Ahrensburgian) with the simultaneous increase in the importance of features that are a local attribute of the Mesolithic (e.g. geometrics and microliths). Examples include the Epi-Ahrensburgian of northwestern Europe, the "early Mesolithic" of Belgian Wallonia, the "Mesolitico Antico" of northern Italy, etc. This transitional phase of not fully transitional "Early Mesolithic" cultures was usually rather short and was followed by an eruption of "Mesolithic style" industries considered classic for given regions (e.g. Early Maglemosian type Star Carr-Klosterlund, Beuronian A and Early Sauveterrian respectively). It is another matter altogether whether this "transitional phase" means the same in all cases; in some instances it may well be nothing more than a cover for a paucity of sources in the archaeological record (small sample size translating into the limited typicality of assemblages that are *de facto* already of the "Mesolithic style")

- Cultures representing the classic ("new") Mesolithic of a given region started forming only after this initial "transitional" stage ? (cf. Stabilization)

The above remarks clearly demonstrate the futility of searching for a single root or cause for Mesolithic Europe. Even had it existed, there is no reason to assume that it would have led every time to the same effects. Therefore, it is possible to speak of important changes taking place on a regional and even macroregional scale, but never on a continental one, this because some regions, like the Balkans, did not experience any profound typological/technological transformation at this time.

This is naturally in agreement with the chronological definition of the Mesolithic proposed in this volume, from which it draws that everything that was taking place in Europe starting from around 9600/9500 cal. BC should be referred to as "Mesolithic" regardless of how "innovative" or "traditional" the nature of this "everything" was. Despite this there is no way of refuting that in a significant part of Europe the Mesolithic introduced an entirely new economic

and cultural quality, one that is definitely easier to recognize in the north than in the south. Specific technical designs, known from earlier times but much less widespread and applied, are proliferated to the north at this time. Moreover, new territories are discovered and settled, hence the shock to stability is immense in some regions.

Models for the emergence of Mesolithic cultures can be different, as I have already said in the introduction above. The following is a general presentation.

The *first model* is one of local environmental and economic, as well as stylistic continuation. It was applied at the southern edges of Europe where the transition from the Pleistocene to the Holocene had not brought any significant environmental change, the *caesura* provoking real changes having come earlier by 2000 years – in the Allerød. It initiated local adaptive patterns, including forest game hunting, development of fishing, miniaturization and local geometrization of stone tools, etc. In this way local units of the Late Mediterranean Epi-Gravettian were formed (among others, Azilian, Montadian, Romanellian, Balkan Epi-Gravettian of the Cuina Turcului type, Italian Piancavallo, and Iberian Maleates), as well as of the post-"Gravettian" cultures of the Caucasian-Caspian complex in the circumpontic area (Trialetian, Shan-Kobian-Belolesian).

Any potential cultural change in these regions where the transition from the Pleistocene to the Holocene had not been strongly felt in the environmental sense would need to have been caused by a different reasons, which is not to be fathomed at present. Neither would such change have covered the entire discussed territory. This was the case: regions that were particularly isolated, such as the southern ends of the Iberian and Apennine peninsulas, the Carpathian Basin and the northern Black Sea littoral escaped cultural/stylistic changes at this time. Others (south of France and central and northern Italy) passed through an evolution from the Epi-Gravettian to the Sauveterrian.

In the *second model,* in the area to the north of these "conservative" territories (except for the Sauveterrian), in a belt from the Pyrenees to the British Isles, southern Scandinavia and Poland, the 10th millennium featured a number of important cultural and stylistic changes which took place in the early Preboreal and which led to the formation of entirely new hunting-gathering-fishing cultures that were quite different from their predecessors. They were characterized by a modified or new *instrumentarium* that had undergone serious miniaturization and geometrization, finally losing some of the stylistic features as far as the flint tools were concerned. These new cultures or taxonomic units belonging to the western technocomplex (among others, the legendary western "Tardenoisian"/Beuronian and the equally famous northern "Maglemosian") have given shape to the traditional typological and stylistic definitions of the Mesolithic that are deficient, because they leave out at least a half of Europe from this time.

The described model was applied in three different climatic, environmental, landscape and cultural zones. In the south it was France south of the Loire, central and northern

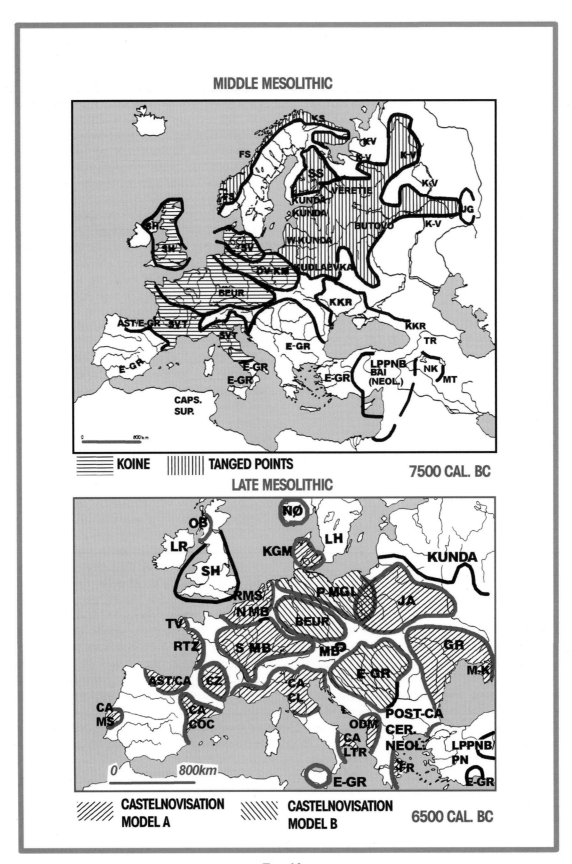

Fig. 13g

Italy, part of the Spanish Levant, Italian Mezzogiorno with local Late Pleistocene Epi-Gravettian and related industries (Montadian, Azilian, Italian Epi-Gravettian, including Piancavallo, Romanellian, etc.). To a lesser (in the extreme south and west) or greater degree, these cultures evolved and/or were transformed into the Mesolithic Sauveterrian, which enjoyed a very similar territorial range (from the Pyrenees to the Loire river, the Slovenian karst and Tuscany), or the para-Sauveterrian industries in the case of the Spanish Levant, Italian Mezzogiorno and the upper Hungarian Tisa river basin. This occurred through a change of core-reduction technology (introduction of discoidal cores) and an observable, rapid increase in the number of already known geometric and non-geometric microliths and their further microlithization occurring at the same time. The process is dated to around or after 9000 cal. BC. The as yet poorly investigated transitional phase is referred to by Alberto Broglio as "Mezolitico Antico".

Slightly further to the north and at the same time, the Mesolithic Beuronian A emerged in the western and central European uplands. In the south, this unit was considered by Wolfgang Tauté as a continuation of a southern German and Czech Epi-Magdalenian of the Zigeunerfels type. In turn, André Thèvenin does not exclude the possibility of the Ahrensburgian participating in the process (but only in the north), although this idea seems doubtful at the very least.

In the Western and Central European Lowland, the transition appears much more complicated as a process and it has yet to be fully understood. Even so, a few fairly certain remarks can be put forward.

In the 10th millennium cal. BC, the territory between eastern England, Belgium, northern Germany and Denmark was the arena for the emergence of a new cultural unit called the Epi-Ahrensburgian (Zoenhoven, Pinnberg I, Bare Mosse). This short-lasting culture which is devoid (or practically devoid) of tanged points was the possible effect of a local evolution (and adaptation to a forest environment) from the Ahrensburgian to the Maglemosian in its earliest form (Star Carr-Thatcham-Klosterlund-Duvensee type industries with sometimes the latest tanged points and numerous broad geometrics with an Ahrensburgian flavor to them). In the case of the Epi-Ahresburgian, the industry is a typically transitional one which will lead in time to the "true" Mesolithic.

The fate of Late Pleistocene peoples inhabiting the later submerged Dogger Bank Shelf of the Northern Sea is difficult to trace and understand. One should keep in mind, however, that apart from the very rare tanged points known from Epi-Ahrensburgian, there were also classic Maglemosian arched backed points (Bøllund, Broxbourne, Svaerdborg) that were slender and backed microliths (e.g. Klosterlund in Denmark, Oakhanger in England), possibly originating from cultures with backed tools (in northern Holland there is the site of Federmesser from the Dryas 3 period, and the Creswellian tradition is thriving in England of the times – e.g. Mother Groundy's Parlour, upper layer).

The last element of this still unclear puzzle (the role of backed pieces is particularly unclear to the present author) is the potential Maglemosian expansion to the east, to the territory of Poland (c. 9000–8000 cal. BC), only recently left by the disappearing (to the northeast?) Swiderians. However, one cannot exclude a southern/trans-Carpathian (at least in part) origin for the Polish Variant of the Maglemosian. It should be stressed that almost all Komornician types of microliths (TN, TO, TR, DD, DD), except K, are present in the inner Carpathian, Late Glacial Epi-Gravettian. Why then should we not imagine after Bernhard Gramsch, an Early Holocene "push" from the south to the north (southern Komornician does not know unpolished axes).

The *third model* is fully migratory in nature and was applied in the northern extremes of Europe, that is, in the Circumbaltic. It was characterized by two things, one of which was a northward wandering of part of the Tanged Point hunters (Ahrensburgian, Brommian, perhaps also Swiderian, Desnian?) who gradually settle Scandinavia as it is deglaciated at this time, giving rise to the local Mesolithic cultures with tanged points (Fosna-Komsa and Suomusjärvi). Up to this point things appear to be clear: the moving ecumene is followed by the most closely connected specialized hunters or at least part of them. The other case is much less obvious, although just as logical. Romuald Schild and Hanna Więckowska have demonstrated conclusively the absolute lack of any genetic (techno-typological) ties between the Late Pleistocene Polish Swiderian and the Polish early Mesolithic (Komornician). Schild has even suggested on the basis of ^{14}C dating from Całowanie near Warsaw in Poland that a gap of two-three hundred radiocarbon years existed between the end of the Polish Swiderian and the beginning of the Polish Maglemosian. It follows from this that the Swiderian reindeer hunters had abandoned their territory and the only possible route they could have taken ran along the eastern shores of the Baltic.

Some of the elements connected with the Swiderian can be traced later in the Mesolithic of eastern Europe (a few Havel-type harpoons – some in local Kunda context, the idea for the tanged point but produced in a different technology). The matter has yet to be explained in full as the Post-Swiderian (= Kunda/Butovo) of Russian researchers is not connected technologically with the Swiderian, although it has some tanged points that are very much Swiderian in appearance. The techno-typological connections between Ahrensburgian-Brommian and Fosna-Komsa are evident and the same could be said in the Desnian-Suomusjärvi-Fosna-Komsa case, even though here the problem is a lack of territorial connection between the mentioned entities. The Swiderians probably left their homeland and … disappeared.

Another unique model that may have been successfully implemented in the East European Lowland in the Early Holocene (?) was the sum of two components: pressure technology and sectioning (end-scrapers, burins on truncation and on broken blade, sectioned bladelets, retouched inserts) combined with tanged points resembling Swiderian ones in appearance but not technology (single-platform pressure technique different from the double-platform Swiderian one). The first component appears to be rooted in the Siberian Upper Paleolithic (Baikal and Angara Basins with Afontova Gora, Verkholanska Gora, Kokorievo, etc.). It is not clear when it first appeared in European Russia, meaning was it a local characteristic of the Russian Lowland from the Late Glacial or only from the Early Holocene ? Russian researchers used to imagine that this "Siberian" element was influenced by Swiderian neighbors, giving birth to the Burovo and Kunda cultures. Most Polish scholars reject this interpretation, but the present author is not quite that contrary to the idea (the earliest Kunda-Butovo tanged points come from 10th millennium cal. BC).

A.N. Sorokin puts the local Resetta culture originating from the Epi-Gravettian at the root of the Russian, Upper Volga forest Mesolithic.

To close these remarks, the author would like to reiterate the extensive differentiation of the beginnings of the Mesolithic in a highly regionalized Europe, the evident continuations, local adaptations/evolution, migratory models and ultimately acculturation. On the whole, however, the overall image of the continent already in the 10th millennium cal. BC appears to be entirely new from both the environmental and cultural point of view. The new units appearing next to surviving ones were generated by different adaptive potential with regard to the ecological novelties of the Early Holocene, realized in different ways by an already strongly differentiated population residing on the continent.

Stabilization

Starting with the 10th millennium cal. BC, the more or less complicated processes of adaptation and culture creation described above resulted in the emergence of a stylistic and territorial, meaning "cultural" system which was to last for centuries or regionally (in the east) for millennia and which was not disturbed by any regional or even supraregional trend or fad. It can be assumed that the technocomplexes and their local cultures of the end of the 8th and beginning of the 7th millennium cal. BC, took on their final shape around 9000 cal. BC (Jagerhaushöhle for the Beuronian, Romagnano III and Predestel for the Sauveterrian, Thatcham and Star Carr for Star Carrian, Friesack and Klostelund for Duvenseean, Całowanie and Chwalim for the Komornician, Pulli for the Kunda, new far-northern Norwegian sites for the Fosna-Komsa, Padina and Frankhthi for Balcanian Epi-Gravettian, etc. etc.). Several macro-territories/technocomplexes were formed at this time only to last for hundreds and even thousands of years within virtually unchanging natural borders which although penetrable, remained unpenetrated for very long periods on end. It was also at this time that the Mesolithic *koine* (geometrization and microlithization) was formed in the west, south and center of Europe in opposition to the oriental and Nordic tanged points traditions.

From the very beginning this formative period in the European Mesolithic was marked by a greater regional differentiation, expressed in the division of the technocomplexes created at this time into regional entities/cultures. The situation remained relatively stable until c. 7500 cal. BC when a transregional sauveterrization fashion occurred in the west (cf. below), in the face of a strong Mesolithic conservatism in the center and east. East of the Elbe river notable changes did not occur for another one thousand years, until c. 7000–6500 cal. BC, and in Russia and the circumBaltic area not before the 6th–5th millennium cal. BC.

At this point one should recall the supraregional post-Pleistocene adaptation models of the southeast of Europe, Italy and Iberia, characterized in this period by a virtually unchanged continuation of local Late Paleolithic (Epi-Gravettian) traditions/style. Moreover, the northern extremes of the European continent did not come to be settled before the Early Holocene when they were occupied by bearers of an unchanged or only little changed industries of the Bommian-Ahrensburgian-Desnian-Fosna-Komsa type. Between the two extremes, the most important and most revolutionary transformations were taking place in the west and in the center. These were the complicated social adaptation models, both local and not local, that Late Paleolithic communities were going through in their quest to adapt to their new environments (Ahrensburgian, Epi-Ahrensburgian, Epi-Magdalenian, Federmesser-Azilian, Epi-Gravettian, etc.). While we have still to understand the exact mechanism of these processes, we are aware of the fact that they contributed to the stabilization of the 10th–8th millennia cal. BC.

Changes in the west

Around the mid 8th millennium cal. BC or a little bit earlier, the flint industries of northwestern Europe from central-northern France and northern Ireland to southern Scandinavia and Germany west of the Elbe river, witnessed the introduction and spread of microbladelets, which had previously been either unknown or weakly distributed in this region. Along with the microbladelets came the narrow microliths made from them, especially the scalene triangles with short base (TH, TE, TI in our "Atlas", cf.), but also regionally Sauveterrian points (PD) and rectangles (RA).

Specimens of this kind appeared at this time in the Beuronian C in France, Germany and Belgium, in the Maglemosian of Britain and southern Scandinavia – mostly triangles in the latter case (but not in eastern Germany and Poland), causing a considerable transformation of the local and regional industries, including observable taxonomic changes like the emergence of Shippea Hill Culture in Britain and Ireland, Boberg in northwestern Germany and the Netherlands and the Svaedborgian in Denmark and southernmost Sweden and northwestern Poland.

All the above-mentioned, newly introduced elements in the local, northern cultural environment had their earlier counterparts appearing regularly and steadily in the neighboring Sauveterrian of southern Europe. Therefore, it is difficult to avoid the impression that the entire "sauveterrization" of the northwest, described above, originated in the south. We are incapable for the moment of reconstructing the mechanisms of this techno-typological change/phenomenon (improvement of arrowhead construction?) that swept through Europe, but at least we think we can describe it.

Anyhow, the previously existing latitudinal zonality in the west and center (starting from the south: Sauveterrian – Beuronian – Maglemosian) was disrupted at this time, mostly in the West; the new trend was limited to the west of the continent, totally avoiding the center where this particular triangle with short base (and only the triangle) did not appear until the very end of the 7th millennium cal. BC.

Collapse of the Maglemosian

From the beginning the Maglemosian *sensu largo* occupied a substantial stretch of the European Lowland from Britain to Poland, including the land bridge of Dogger Bank Shelf and the Pomeranian-Danish one. Following from postglacial processes of the period, ocean levels started to rise in the Early Holocene, paralleled by the simultaneous sinking of other regions in northwestern Europe. This gradually reduced the Maglemosian ecumene, leading finally to the isolation of the British Isles (the English Channel appeared in the second half of the 8th millennium cal. BC) and instigating natural migratory movements of the population living in the gradually submerged areas. This was first observed by Hermann Schwabedissen and later by Raymond R. Newell.

The appearance of new cultures in the Late Mesolithic of the European Lowland (De Leien-Wartena in Holland, Oldesloe-Jühnsdorf in Germany, Chojnice-Pieńki in Poland and Nøstvet-Lihult in southern and central Scandinavia (this last with an entirely different raw-material base than the preceding local Fosna culture) was the probable result of the "radial", decentralizing migrations and can be dated to c. 7000 cal. BC.

These new units, mostly descendants of Svaedborgian, are distinguished foremost by the microbladelet technique (known also from southern Scandinavia, cf. undated Svaedborg I site, coll. Becker) which is in all likelihood rooted in the earlier sauveterrization process. Secondly, they apparently "cancel" old structures existing in the newly acquired territories (correspondingly, Duvensee in the west and Fosna in the north, Komornician in the east). The castelnovization of the southern Scandinavian Mesolithic progresses at this time, first weakly (model B – Ageröd I:D) around 7000 cal. BC, then completely (model A – Konglemosian) around c. 6500 cal. BC. More to the south and north, the Post-Maglemosian will continue to last for even hundreds of years to come (in Polish Pomerania even up to the 5th millennium cal. BC! with Ertebølle ceramics in Dąbki). The population leaving Dogger Bank must have also retreated partly to the west, into Britain, but palpable evidence of this migration has yet to be recognized in the archaeological record.

Pre-Neolithisation (between 7000 and 6500 cal. BC)

This period is deemed, if not revolutionary, then at least of breakthrough nature in the history of Mesolithic Europe and for a variety of reasons at that. A number of successive supraregional phenomena takes place at this time, encompassing considerable areas of the continent and ultimately preparing the ground for the Neolithization of Europe. The breakthroughs that the author has in mind all had their genesis in the south, the Mediterranean part of Europe and all of them consistently developed toward the north, reaching in the end, frequently many hundreds of years later, almost to the extreme north of the continent. They were in chronological order: castelnovization, ceramization and Neolithization. In the north, between Britain and Poland, these processes were paralleled by observable environmental changes consisting of the spread of deciduous forest and related fauna from the south to the north, and from the west to the east.

Let us first take a closer look at the Mediterranean processes. Castelnovization in fact represents pre-Neolithization. It first appeared in the Middle Mesolithic communities of the northern (Frankhthi) and southern (Capsien superieur) shores of the Mediterranean already (locally) in the second half/end of the 8th millennium cal. BC. It encompassed all of the northern Mediterranean coast (and the Black Sea) from c. 7000 cal. BC (classical Castelnovian) or slightly later (Cocina, Moita do Sebastiao in the west, Odmut, Murzak-Koba, Grebeniki in the east) to penetrate northward into inland Europe by c. 6500 BC (Cuzoulian, South and North Montbanian, Retzian, Teviecian and finally Kongemosian in the west and Janislawician in the east).

This is model A of castelnovization, that is, a complete and relatively rapid techno-typological and raw-material transformation of preceding local Middle Mesolithic industries. The other contemporary model (B) was much less revolutionary and resulted in selective adaptation of only certain elements of model A (trapezes complementing practically only slightly changed local industries of more inland/northern Middle Mesolithic tradition Post-Maglemosian, Latest Epi-Gravettian, Late Beuronian). Model B frequently preceded a final slow introduction of model A (e.g. the Northern Montbanian after the Rhenanian). Model A had two territorial variants: western (Western Castelnovian) and eastern (Eastern Castelnovian), separated by the void of Croatia. The first was characterized, among others, by the microburin technique, the second, at least in the south, rather by sectioning of bladelets.

In fact, the change depended on a significant techno-logical matter that was modified for reasons as yet unfathomable for us: Boreal bladelets and microbladelets were replaced by bigger, broader and much more regular specimens which demanded better execution techniques and raw material of larger size. Techniques of sophisticated core-preforming were applied to produce relatively big single-platform cores, usually of the keeled type. Flint raw material frequently collected from the surface in previous times often could not satisfy requirements, prompting Mesolithic man to travel even considerable distances in search of better raw material and to develop mining techniques to acquire better and bigger-size material from original deposits. One effect of this demand was the development of an organized "market" with long-distance imports distribution (obsidian in Frankhthi, Wommersom quartzite in northwestern Europe, Balkan "honey" flint, "chocolate" flint in Poland, etc.) to areas where appropriate flint could not be acquired locally.

The technological change influenced far-going typological changes that meant mainly:

- typological simplification and standardization of lithic industries (replacing differentiated microliths with more monotone Late Mesolithic types of trapezes and less often rhomboids);
- simplification of internal industry structure (combinations of scrapers, truncations, retouched blades and trapezes).

The impression is of considerable standardization of Castelnovian flint industries, although in fact a closer analysis (cf. "Atlas") leaves no doubts as to the continuation of obvious earlier regionalisms. Indeed, one has the feeling that depending on the local community differently "accepting" the Castelnovian impulse coming from outside, the local or regional result of castelnovization differs, especially with regard to the shape of microliths-trapezes.

In later evolution the results of castelnovization became much more differentiated. Broader blades ("second standard") became a landmark of the Post-Castelnovian, mostly ceramic and Neolithic cultures of southeastern and southern Europe. At the other end, western Europe had, after castelnovization, its "baroque" microliths-trapezes, often with flat, covering retouches.

In any case, castelnovization in the technical sense was a natural point of departure (directly in Italy, the lands of former Yugoslavia and in Ukraine, indirectly in western Europe) for the earliest ceramization, as well as the earlier or later Neolithization, of western and southern Europe and the Pontic northern littoral. Also connected with castelnovization are most of the Mesolithic cemeteries (Moita do Sebastiao, Téviec, Hoëdic, Skateholm, Vasilevka) which testify to a semi-sedentary lifestyle or at least a high level of organization (ownership) of the then tribal territories.

It should be kept in mind, however, that similar features can be found at this time outside the impact zone of the castelnovization phenomenon (Zvejnieki, Popovo, Oleni Ostrov, Vlasac). Whatever the case may be, the appearance of a newer, higher technology based largely on a complicated organization of acquiring large-size concretions of better, often imported raw material, as well

as the higher level of organization of tribal territories with some common point of reference (cemetery) signify the coming of an evolutionary step forward that will eventually lead to the Neolithic.

This next step is the ceramization of some of the Late Mesolithic cultures (mostly post-Castelnovian, but also the non-Castelnovian ones). The phenomenon cannot always be identified with Neolithization – suffice it to recall the evidently non-Neolithic potteries of the Ertebøllian, Narva, Bug-Dniester, Upper Volga, impresso, Vho and Gaban cultures. These early ceramics appear at the earliest just after 7000 cal. BC in southern Italy, and later in southern France and Spain as far as the west is concerned, and in the Near East (Proto-Hassuna, Pre-Halaf – here they are Neolithic) with regard to the east. This is followed by a proliferation of ceramics often along with local Late Mesolithivc industry mutations toward the west (Muge) and north (Cuzoul) in Europe and toward the south (Yarmuk) and northwest (Anatolia) in the Near Eastern regions.

The Neolithic character of these entities is not always obvious (especially in the case of the western variant of the phenomenon, but also in the Polish and Russian Lowlands and southern Scandinavia), but it is clear that ceramization covers on one hand industries with clear Castelnovian style and typology (Odmut in Bosnia, Mala Triglavca in Slovenia, Soroki in Moldova), often in the broader (="second") bladelet size standard (Smilčić in Dalmatia, Gaban and Vho in Italy, Neolithic Mehtelek in Hungary and Donja Branjevina in Serbia), Post-Castelnovian of southern Germany, or representing the "baroque" microliths in France, Belgium and Holland, but also frequently of non-Castelnovian or Post-Castelnovian style (armatures of the Muge type) in the southwest.

At least some of these ceramization processes led in effect to the creation of a "ceramic Mesolithic".

Ceramization gradually spread to the north also in the east, reaching the Central and East European Lowland (Ertebølle, Dubičiai, Narva, Upper Volga) and eastern Scandinavia (Sperrings) at a slightly later date (5th millennium cal. BC).

The third and last phenomenon, for it ended the Mesolithic, was Neolithization, occurring in each case locally or regionally. It marked the transition, at least partial, of a given population to a production economy. On the whole, the phenomenon appeared first in the Near East and Anatolia in the late PPNB phase, spreading later to the Balkans (how? – the LPPNB/BAI industry is different from Castelnovian) and the northern Mediterranean coasts. Successive stages of its proliferation (the mechanisms of which continue to escape us) are the Körös/Kriš/Starčevo (with Post-Castelnovian industry!) and later classic Band-Ceramic, Lengyel and Polgar cultures, respectively of the 7th, 6th and 5th millennia cal. BC in central and western Europe, occupying the broadly understood northern piedmont of the Alps and Carpathians, and the Plain, and characterized by stone industries of the Post-Castelnovian type (second standard), and finally, the TRB culture (5th–4th millennium cal. BC) in the Lowland. The bearers of the former are considered allochthonous in the north (originating from model A of castelnovization) and coming from the south, while those of the latter are already autochthonous, meaning they should be descended directly from local Late Mesolithic cultures (model B occasionally passing into model A of castelnovization, and finally to Post-Castelnovian (?)).

In this way the world of the hunters-gatherers was gradually acculturated starting from the south, while in the north it faded out, making place for Neolithic (=Post-Castelnovian!) farmers and stockbreeders.

The three phenomena here described are in some regions mutually exclusive, while in others they overlap, hence the presented sequence going from both models of castelnovization through ceramization to Neolithization is not necessarily the rule everywhere.

In closing, it can be said that the emergence of the south European Neolithic (in the economic sense) was in reality local, differently progressing ceramization and a more or less selective, local adaptation of a Neolithic model of the economy without any Anatolian or Near Eastern influence to be discerned in the archaeological record (at least in the chipped industry). The processes are selective (e.g. only ceramization), on a Pre-Neolithic Castelnovian base (e.g. Odmut, Grebeniki) or Post-Castelnovian ("second standard" variant – Körös/Kriš/Starčevo, Gaban, Vho, impresso and Danubian, or a more "baroque" variant – Iberian and south French "cardial"). It is possible to speak in this case of a full techno-typological continuation from the Mesolithic to the Neolithic, concurrently with an undoubted proliferation to the north and west of a new technology (pottery) and a new economic concept.

What is the most surprising is the lack of techno-typological links between this European ceramic and Neolithic Castelnovian and Post-Castelnovian and the nearest Central Anatolian Neolithic entity – LPPNB.

The phenomenon will later spread to the north (Danubian proliferation) and will stimulate similar reactions (more often ceramization) to culminate in a full Neolithization of the local Late Mesolithic in the form of TRB culture.

The one general conclusion that one is readily left with at the end of the day – and with which I would like to close this text – is that there are in life things that even the philosophers have never dreamt about…

Bibliography

Abbreviations

AAL   Acta Archaeologica Lunden – sia, Sweden
AB   Aarbøger, Denmark
AI   Archaeologia Interregionalis, Poland
AR   Archeologické Rozhledy, Czech Republic
AUO   Arbok Universitets Oldsaksamling, Sweden
BAR   British Archaeological Reports, United Kingdom
BSPF   Bulletin de la Societé Préhitorique Française, France
ERAUL   Etudes et Recherches Archéologiques, Université de Liègé, Belgium
GZMS   Glasnik Zemljskog Musea – Sarajevo, Bosnia and Hercegovina
IPEK   Jahrbuch für Prähistorische Und Etnographische Kunst
JBHM   Jahrbuch der Bernischen Hist. Museum, Switzerland
KSIA   Kratkie Soobshchenija Instituta Arkheologii A. N. SSSR (also Kratkie, Soobshchenia Instituta Istorii Kultury Matierialnoi A. N. SSSR), Russia
KSIAUAN
    Kratkie Soobshchenia Instituta Arkheologii Ukrainskoj A. N., Ukraine
Lietuvos TSR
    Lietuvos TSR Akademijos Darbai, Lithuania
MIA   Materialy i Issledowania po arkcheologii SSSR, Russia
PPS   Proceedings of the Prehistoric Society, United Kingdom
PA   Preistoria Alpina, Italy
PZ   Prähistorrische Zeitschrift, Germany
RSP   Rivista di Scienze Preistoriche, Italy
SA   Sovietskaia Arkheologia, Russia
Slov. Arch.
    Slovenska Archeologia, Slovakia
SCIV   Studii Si Cercetării de Istorie Veche, Romania
SMYA   Suomien Museet, Finland
VP   Veröffentlichungen des Museums für Ur und Früchgeschichte Potsdam, Germany

Affolter, J., Grunwald, C. 1999. Approvisionements en matières premières dans les sites mésolithiques du Vercors. In: *Thèvenin, A. (ed.) 1999.*

Aimé, G. 1989. Les abris sous roche de Bavans (Doubs). In: *Aimé, G., Thévenin, A. (ed.) 1989.*

Aime, G., Thévenin, A. (ed.) 1989. *Épipaléolithique et Mésolithique entre Ardennes et massif alpin, Table Ronde de Besançon.* In: *Mémoire de la Société d'Agriculture, Lettres, Sciences et Arts de la Haute-Saône, Archéologie, 2.*

Aimé, G., Bintz, P., Cupillard, Ch., Cziesla, E., Gob, A., Le Tensorer, J-M., Löhr, H., Pion, G., Rozoy, J-G., Spier, F., Thévenin A., Ziesaire, P. 1989. Epipaléolithique et Mésolithique entre Ardennes et Alpes, Lignes des résultats actuels. In: *Aimé, G., Thévenin, A. (ed.) 1989.*

Albrethsen, S.E., Brinch Petersen, E. 1975. *Gravene på Bøggebaken Vedbaek.* Historisk topografisk Selskab for Søllerø rød Kommune.

Alin, J. 1955. *Förtecking över Stenalderbopladsen i Norra Bohuslan.* Goëteborg.

Alin, J., Niklasson N., Thomasson H. 1934. Stenalderbopladsen paa Sandarma vid Goëteborg. In: *Goëteborgs Kungl. Vetenskaps- och Vittrehets-Samhälles Handlingar.*

Althin, C.A. 1954. *The Chronology of the Stone Age Settlement of Scania, Sweden, 1: The Mesolithic Settlement.* In: *AAL, (series in 4°), 1.*

Andersen, S.H. 1981. *Stenalderen, Jaegerstenaldere.* In: *Danmarkshistorien-Oldtiden, 1.* Sesam, Copenhagen.

Andersen, S.H. 1995. Coastal adaptation and marine exploitation in Late Mesolithic Denmark – with special emphasis on the Limfjord region. In: *Fischer, A. (ed.) 1995.*

Andersen, S.H., Bietti, A., Bonsall, C., Broadbent, N.D., Clark, G.A., Gramsch, B., Jacobi, R.M., Larsson, L., Morrison, A., Newell, R.R., Rozoy, J.G., Straus, L.G., Woodman, P.C. 1990. Making Cultural Ecology Relevant to Mesolithic Research. IA Data Base of 413 Mesolithic Fauna Assemblages. In: *Vermeersch, P., Van Peer, P. (ed.) 1990.*

Andersen, K. 1961. *Hytter fra Maglemosetid.* Danmarks aeldste boliger. Nationalmuseets A B.

Andersen, K. 1961a. Verupbopladsen, en Maglemmose boplads i Aamosen. *AB.*

Aparicio Perez, J. 1979. *Il Mésolitico en Valencia y en el Mediterraneo occidental.* In: *Servicio de Investigaciones Prehistorica. 59,* Valencia.

Aspes, A. (ed.) 1984. *Il Vento nell'antichita*. Banca Popolare di Verona. Verona.

Astuti, P., Dini, M., Grifoni-Cremonesi, R., Kozłowski, S., Tozzi, C. 2005. L'industria mesolitica di Grotta Marisa (Lecce, Puglia) nel quadro delle industrie litiche dell'Italia meridionale. *RSP*, 55.

Arora, S.K. 1966. Ein mesolithischer Fundplatz auf dem Blockenberg bei Stolberg, Kreis Aachen. *Bonner Jahrbuch*, 166.

Arora, S.K. 1973. Mittelsteinzeitlichte Formengruppen zwischen Rhein und Weser. In: *Kozłowski, S.K. (ed.) 1973*.

Arora, S.K. 1976. Die mittlere Steinzeit im westlichen Deutschland und in den Nachbarge biten. *Rheinische Ausgrabungen*, 17.

Bader, O.N. 1951. Stoianki Nizhneadyshchewskaya i Borovoe Ozero na reke Chusowoi. *MIA*, 22.

Bader, O.N. 1953. Kamskaya archeologicheskaya ekspedicya. *KSIA*, 51.

Bader, O.N. 1961. O sootnoshenii kultury wierchniego paleolita i mezolita Kryma i Kavkaza. *SA*.

Bader, O.N. 1965. Varianty kultury Kavkaza konca vierkhnego paleolita i mezolita. *SA*.

Bader, O.N. 1966. Mezolit lesnogo Priural'ya i nekotorye obshchie voprosy izuchenia mezolita. *MIA*, 126.

Bader, O.N. 1970. Mezolit. In: *Kamiennyi vek na territorii SSSR. MIA*, 166.

Bagolini, B. 1980. *Introduzione al Neolitico dell'Italia settentribonale*. Grafsche Editoriali Artistici Pordenonesi, Pordenone.

Bagolini, B., Broglio, A., Lunz, R. 1983. Le Mésolithique des Dolomites. In: *Bagolini B. (ed.) 1983*.

Bagolini, B. (ed.) 1983. Il Popolamento delle Alpi in età mesolitica VIII–V Millennio AC *PA*, 19.

Bagolini, B., Dalmeri, G. 1987. *I siti mesolitici di Colbricon (Trentino). PA*, 23.

Bandi, H.G. *et al.* 1963. *Birsmatten-Basisgrotte. Acta Bernensia*. 1.

Bandi H.G. 1967–68. Untersuchung lines Felsschutzdaches bei Neumühle (Gemeinde Pleigne, Kt. Bern). *JBHM*, 47–48.

Bandi, H.G. *et al.* 1979. *La contribution de la zoologie et de l'éthologie á l'interpretation de l'art des peuples chasseurs préhistoriques*. Société Suisse des Sciences Humaines. Editions Universitaires Fribourg, Fribourg.

Bang-Andersen, S. 1988. Mesolithic Adaptations in the Southern Norwegian Highlands. In: *Bonsall, C. (ed.) 1988*.

Bang-Andersen, S. 1995. The Mesolithic of Western Norway: prevailing problems and possibilities. In: *Fischer, A. (ed.) 1995*.

Bang-Andersen, S. 1999. Les premiers chasseurs de rennes des montagnes du Sud de la Norvège. In: *Thévenin, A. (ed.) 1999*.

Barandiaran, J. 1978. El Abrigo de la Botiquerie del Moros, Mazaleon (Ternel). *Cuadernos de Prehistorie y Arqueologia Castellonense*, 5.

Barandiáraran, I., Cava, A. 1988. The Evolution of the Mesolithic in the North East of the Iberian Peninsula. In: *Bonsall, C. (ed.) 1988*.

Barandiáran, J. 1998. *Paleolitico y el mesolitico*. In: *Preistoria de la Peninsula Iberica*. Editorial Ariel S.A., Barcelona.

Barbaza, M. 1999. *Les civilisations postglaciaires*. La Maison des Roches, Paris.

Barbaza, M., Briois, F., Valdeyron, N., Vaquer, J. 1999. L'Epipaléolithique et le Mésolithique entre Massif central et Pyrénées. In: *Thévenin, A. (ed.) 1999*.

Barrière, C. 1956. *Les civilisations tardenoisiennes en Europe Occidentale*. Paris.

Barrière, C. 1965. Le gisement de la Grotte de Rouffignac (Dordogne). In: Atti del *Congresso delle Scienze Pre- e Protostoriche*. Roma.

Barriére, C. 1973. Roufignac. *Memoire de l'Institut d'Art Préhistorique*. Université de Toulouse, 'Le Mirail. Toulose, 2.

Bárta, J. 1957. Pleistocenné piesočne duny pri Seredi a ich Paleolitické a mezolitické osidleni. *Slov Arch*, 5.

Bárta, J. 1973. Le Mésolithique en Slovaquie. In: *Kozłowski, S. K. (ed.) 1973*.

Bárta, J. 1981. Das Mesolithikum im nordwestlichen Teil des Karpatenbeckens. In: *Gramsch, B. (ed.) 1981*.

Becker, C.J. 1951. Maglemosekultur paa Bornholm. *AB*.

Becker, C.J. 1953. Die Maglemosekultur in Dänmark. In: *Congrès International des Science Prèhistoriques et Protohistoriques – Actes de la IIIe Session – Zurich 1950*.

Beltrán, A. 1982. *De Casadores a Pastores. El Arte rupeste del Levante Español*. Ed. En Wentro, Madrid.

Benac, A., Brodar, M. 1958. Črvena Stijena – 1956. *GZMS*, 16.

Benac, A. (ed.) 1979. *Praistorija jugoslovenskich zemalja*, 1. Svjetlost, Sarajevo.

Berg, E. 2003. The spatial and chronological development of the Mesolithic Nøstvet period in coastal southeastern Norway from a lithic raw material perspective. In: *Larsson, L. et al. (ed.) 2003*.

Bergsvik, K.A., Bruen Olsen, A.B. 2003. Traffic in Stone Adzes in Mesolithic Western Norway. In: *Larsson, L. et al. (ed.) 2003*.

Bergtsson, L. 2003. Knowledge and Interaction in Stone Age: Raw materials for adzes and axes, their sources and distributional pattern. In: *Larsson L. et al. (ed.) 2003*.

Biagi, P., Castelletti, L., Cremaschi, M., Sala, B., Tozzi, C. 1979. Popolazioni e teritorio nell'Appennino Tosco-Emiliano e nel tratto centrale del bacino del Po, tra il IX ed il V millennino. *Emilia Preromana* 8.

Biagi, P., Maggi, R. 1983. Aspects of the Mesolithic Age in Liguria. In : *Bagolini, B. (ed.) 1983*.

Bibikov, S.N. 1940. Grot Murzak-Koba – nowaia pozdnepaleoliticheskaia stoianka v Krymu. *SA*, 5.

Bibikov, S.N. 1959. Raskopki w navsie Fat'ma-Koba w 1956 g. *KSIAUAN*, 8.

Bibikov, S.N. 1966. Raskopki w navesie Fat'ma-Koba i nekotorye voprosy izuchenia mezolita Kryma. *MIA*, 126.

Bibikov, S.N., Stanko, V.N., Koen, B.Y. 1994. *Final Paleolithic and Neolithic in the Crimea Mountains* (in Russian). Vest. Odessa.

Bicker, F. 1934. Dünenmesolithikum aus dem Fiener Bruch. *Jahresschrift für die Vorgeschichte der Sächsisch-Thüringischen Länder*, 22.

Binford, L.R. 1973. The Magic Numbers "25" and "500". In: *Man the Hunter*. Chicago

Bintz, P. 1989. Saint-Thibaud-de-Couz (Savoie-Chartreuse) et Choranche (Isère-Vercors). L'Epipaléolithique et le Mésolithique del Alpes françaises du Nord dans leur cadre chronologique et bioclimatique. In: *Aimé, G., Thévenin, A. (ed.) 1989*.

Bintz, P. 1991. Stations mésolithiques de plein air dans les massif subalpins du Vercors et de la Chartreuse. In: *Thévenin, A. (ed.) 1991*.

Bintz, P., Ginestet, J.P., Pion, G. 1991. Le Mésolithique et la néolithisation dans les Alpes françaises du Nord : donées stratigraphiques et culturelle. In: *Thévenin, A. (ed.) 1991*.

Bintz, P., Grunwald, C. 1990. Mésolithique et Néolithisation en Chartreuse et en Vercors (Alpes du Nord): Evolution culturelle et économie du silex. In: *Vermeersch, P., Van Peer, P. (ed.) 1990.*

Bintz, P., Picavet, R. 1994. Le Mésolithique et la néolithisation en Vercors: évolutions culturelles et approche territoriale. In: *Pion, G. (ed.) 1994.*

Bintz, P., Argant, J., Chaix, L., Pelletier, D., Thiébault, S. 1999. L'Aulp-du-Seuil un site d'altitude de Mésolithique et du Néolithique ancien (Saint Bernard-du Touvet, Isère): etudes préliminaires. In: *Thèvenin, A. (ed.) 1999.*

Birons, A. *et al.* (ed.) 1974. *Latvijas PSR archeologija.* Zinatne, Riga.

Bjerck, H.B. 1986. The Fosna–Nøstvet Problem. *Norwegian Archaeological Review,* 19.

Bjerck, H.B. 1995. The North Sea Continent and the pioneer settlement of Norway. In: *Fischer, A. (ed.) 1995.*

Bjørn, A. 1929. Studier over Fosnakulturen. In: *Bergens Mus. Aarb. Hist. Antiqu.,* series 2.

Blankholm, R.i E., Andersen, S.H. 1967. Stallerupholm. En bid rag til belysning af Maglemosekulturen i Østjylland. *Kuml.*

Blankholm, H.P. 1981. Aspects of Maglemose Settlements in Denmark. In: *Gramsch, B. (ed.) 1981.*

Bohmers, A. 1947. Jong-Palaeolithicum en Vroeg-Mesolithicum. In: *Memorial Book offered to Van Giffen.* Meppel.

Bohmers, A., Wouters, A. 1956. Statistics and Graphs in the Study of Flint Assemblages. A Preliminary Report on the Statistical Analisys of the Mesolithic in North-western Europe. *Palaeohistoria,* 5.

Bohmers, A., Wouters, A. 1962. Belangrijke vondsten van de Ahrensburg in de Gemeente Geldrop. *Brabants Heem,* 14.

Bokelmann, K. 1971. Duvensee, ein Wohnplatz des Mesolithikumsi in Schleswig-Holstein, und die Duvenseegruppe. *Offa,* 28.

Bonsall, C. (ed.) 1986, Gramsch, B. (ed.) 1981, Kozłowski, S.K. (ed.) 1973, Larsson, L. *et al.* (ed.) 2003, Théremin, A. (ed.) 1999, Vermeersch, P., Van Peer, P. (ed.) 1990, etc. – collected papers of international congresses and symposia.

Bonsall, C. (ed.) 1988. *The Mesolithic in Europe.* John Donald Publishers Ltd. Edinburgh.

Bonsall, C. 2004. The "Obanian Problem" – Coastal Adaptation in the Mesolithic of Western Scotland. In: *Gonzales Morales, M., Clark, G.A. (ed.) 2004.*

Bonsall, C., Smith, C. 1990. Bone and Antler Technology in the British Late Upper Palaeolithic and Mesolithic: the Impact of Accelerator Dating. In: *Vermeersch, P., Van Peer, P. (ed.) 1990.*

Brinch Petersen, E. 1966. Klosterlund-Sønder Hadsund-Bøllund. *Acta Archaeologica,* 37.

Brinch Petersen, E. 1972. Svaerdborg II. A Maglemose hut from Svaerdborg Bog, Zealand, Denmark. *Acta Archaeologica,* 42.

Brinch Petersen, E. 1973. A Survey of the Late Palaeolithic and Mesolithic of Denmark. In: *Kozlowski, S.K. (ed.) 1973.*

Broadbant, N.D. 1978. Prehistoric settlement in northen Sweden: a brief survey and a case study. In: *Mellars, P. (ed.) 1978.*

Brodar, M. 1992. Mezolitisko najdišče Pod Črmukljo pri Sembijah. *Archeolški Vestnik,* 43.

Broglio, A. 1976. L'Epipaléolithique de la Vallée du Pô, In: *Kozłowski, S.K. (ed.) 1976.*

Broglio, A. 1980. Il Paleolitico Superiore e l'Epipaleolitico del territorio veronese e dell'area circostante. In: *Fasani, L. (ed.) 1980.*

Broglio, A. 1983. L'Epipaléolithique de la Vallée du Pô, In: *Kozłowski, S.K. (ed.) 1983.*

Broglio, A. 1984. Paleolitico e Mesolitico. In: *Aspes, A. (ed.). 1984.*

Broglio, A., Kozłowski, S.K. 1983. Tipologia ed evoluzione delle industrie mesolitiche di Romagnano III. In: *Bagolini, B. (ed.) 1983.*

Broholm, H. C. 1926–27. Nouvelles trouvailles du plus Áncien âge de la Pierre – les trouvailles de Holmegaard et de Svaerdborg. In: *Mémoires de la Societé Royale des Antiquaires du Nord.*

Bøe, J. 1936. *Le Finnmarkien.* In: *Instituttet for Sammenlignende Kulturforsniesg, series B,* 32.

Brudiu, M. 1974. *Paleoliticul superior și Epipaleoliticul din Moldova.* Bucarest.

Burdukiewicz, J.M. 1986. *The Late Pleistocene Shouldered Point Assemblages in Western Europe.* E.J. Briel, Leiden.

Burov, G.M. 1965. *Vychegodski Krai. Ocherki drevei istorii.* Moscow.

Burov, G.M. 1973. Die mesolithischen Kulturen im äussersten europäischen Nordosten. In: *Kozłowski, S.K. (ed.) 1973.*

Burov, G.M. 1981. Der Bogen bei den mesolithische Stämmen Nordosteuropas. In *Gramsch, B. (ed.) 1981.*

Burov, G.M. 1988. Some Mesolithic Wooden Artificats from Site of Vis I in the European North East of the USSR. In: *Bonsall, C. (ed.) 1988.*

Burov, G.M. 1990. Die Holzgeräte der Siedlungsplätzes Vis I als Grundlage für die Periodisierung des Mesolithikums im Norden des europäischen Teils der UdSSR. In: *Vermeersch, P., Van Peer, P. (ed.) 1990.*

Burov, G.M. 1999. Le Mésolithique dans le Nord-Est de la Russie européene. In: *Thèvenin, A. (ed.) 1999.*

Burov, G.M. 1999. "Postwiderian" of the European North-East. In: *Kozłowski, S.K., Gurba, J., Zalizniak, L. (ed.) 1999.*

Cahen, D., Haesaerts, P. (ed.) 1984. *Peuples chasseurs de la Belgique préhistorique dans léur cadre naturel.* Institut royal des Sciences naturelles. Bruxelles 1984.

Campbell, J.B. 1977. *The Upper Palaeolithic of Britain.* Clarendon Press, Oxford.

Camps-Fabrer, H. 1975. Le faciès sétifien du Caprien superieur. In: *Camps, G. (ed.) 1975.*

Camps, G. (ed.) 1975. *L'Épipaléolithique méditerranéen.* Éditions CNRS. Paris.

Carlsson, T., Gruber, G., Molin, F., Wikell, R. 2003. Between Quartz and Flint. Material Culture and Social Interaction. In: *Larsson L. et al. (ed.) 2003.*

Charniavski, M.M., Kalechyts, A.G. (ed.) 1977. *Archaeology of Belarus, Stone and Bronze Ages* (in Belarussian). Belaruskaia navuka, Minsk.

Churchill, D.M., Wymer, J.J. 1965. The Kitchen Midden Site at Westward Ho!, Devon, England. *PPS,* 31.

Clark, D. 1969. *Analytical archaeology.* London.

Clarke, D. 1978. *Mesolithic Europe: The Economic Basis.* Duckworth, London.

Clark, G.A. 1976. *El Asturiense Cantabico.* In: *Almagro (ed.) Bibliotheca Prehistorica Hispana,* 13. Madrid.

Clark, G.A. 1977. L'Asturien des Cantabres. Etat de la recherche actuelle. In: *Escalon de Fonton, M. (ed.) 1977.*

Clark, G.A. 1983. The Asturian of Cantatria In: *Anthropological Papers of the University of Arizona,* 41, Tuscon.

Clark, G.A. 2004. The Iberian Mesolithic in the European Context, In: *Gonzales Morales, M., Clark, G.A. (ed.) 2004.*

Clark, G.A. 1999. Le Mésolithique de la côte atlantique ibérique: Tendances récentes. In: *Thévenin, A. (ed.) 1999.*

Clark, J.G.D. 1932. *The Mesolithic Age in Britain.* Cambridge.

Clark, J.G.D. 1934. A Late Mesolithic Settlement at Selmeston, Sussex. *The Antiquaries Journal,* 14.

Clark, J.G.D. 1934 a. Report on the Broxbourne Industry. *Journal of the Anthropological Institute of Great Britain and Ireland*, 64.

Clark, J.G.D. 1934 b. The Classification of Microlithic Culture. *Archeological Journal*, 90.

Clark, J.G.D. 1935. Report on recent Excavitations at Peacocks Farm, Shippea Hill, Cambridgeshire. *The Antiquaries Journal*, 15.

Clark, J.G.D. 1936. *The Mesolithic Settlement of Northern Europe*. Cambridge.

Clark, J.G.D. 1954. *Excavations at Star Carr*. Cambridge.

Clark, J.G.D. 1955. A Microlithic Industry from Cambridgeshire Fenland and other Industries of Sauveterrian Affinities from Britain. *PPS*, 21.

Clark, J.G.D., Rankine, W.F. 1939. Excavations at Farnham, Surrey (1937–38). *PPS*, 5.

Clark, G. 1967. *The Stone Age Hunters*. Thames and Hudson, London.

Clark, G. 1975. *The Earlier Stone Age Settlement of Scandinavia*. Cambridge University Press. Cambridge.

Clark, G. 1980. *Mesolithic Prelude*. University Press, Edinburgh.

Coles, J.M. 1971. The early settlement of Scotland: excavations at Norton, Fife. *PPS*, 37.

Conard, N.J., Kind, C.J. (ed.) 1998. Aktuelle Forschungen zum Mesolithikum, current Mesolithic Research. *Urgeschichtliche Materialthefte*, 12.

Costa, L., Vigne, J.D., Bocherens, H., Desse-Berset, N., Heinz, C., de Lanfranchi, F., Magdeleine, J., Ruas, M.P., Thiebault, S., Tozzi, C. 2003. Early Settlement on Tyrrhenian islands (8th millennium cal. BC): Mesolithic adaption to local resources in Corsica and Northern Sardinia. In: *Larsson, L. et al. (ed.) 2003*.

Coulonges, L. 1935. *Les gisements préhistoriques de Sauveterrele-Lémance*. In: *Archives IPH*.

Coulonges, L. 1954. Le sauveterrien. In: *Memorial Book of the SPF*. Paris.

Crotti, P., Pignat, G. 1991. La Transition méso-néolithique en suisse occidentale. In: *Thévenin, A. (ed.) 1991*.

Crotti, P. (ed.) 2000. *Meso '97 Actes de la Table ronde "Épipaléolithique et Mésolithique"*. *Cahiers d'Archéologique Romande*, 8.

Cuberg, C. The Hasslingehult Site. *Studier i Nordisk Arkeologi*. 10.

Cupillard, C., Perrenoud-Cupillard, N. 2003. The Mesolithic of the Swiss and French Jura and its margins: 10,150–6000 BP. In: *Larsson, L. et al. (ed.)2003*.

Cyrek, K. 1981. Acquisition and use of flint materials in the Mesolithic of the basins of Vistula and upper Warta rivers (in Polish). *"Prace i Materiały Muzeum Archeologicznego i Etnograficznego w Łodzi, Archeologia"*, 29.

Cziesla, E. 1992. *Jäger und Sammler. Die Mittlere Steinzeit im Landkreis Pirmasens*. Linden Soft Verlag, Brühl.

Cziesla, E. 1998. Die Mittlere Steinzeit im südlichen Rheinland-Pfalz. *Urgeschichtliche Materialhefte*, 12.

Daniel, R. 1932. Nouvelles études sur le Tardenoisien français. *BSPF*. 29.

Daniel, R. 1938. Le Tardenoisien classique du Tardenois. *L'Anthropologie*, 52.

Daniel, R.M. 1953. Les gisements préhistoriques de la vallée de Loing. *L'Antrpologie*, 57.

Daniel, R. 1965. Le Tardenoisien II de Piscop (Seine-et-Oise). *BSPF*, 62.

Daniel, R., Vignard, E. 1954. Le Tardenoisien. In: *Memorial Book of the SPF*. Paris.

David, E. 1999. Approche technologique des industries en matières dures animales du Mésolithique danois d 'après le matériel des gisements maglemosiens de Mullerup I (Sarauw's Island – 1900) et Ulkestrup Lyng II (1946). In: *Thévenin, A. (ed.) 1999*.

Desbrosse, R., Kozłowski, J.K. 1994. *Les habitats préhistoriques*. Editions de l 'Université Jagiellon de Cracovie. Cracow.

Djindjian, F. 1992. L'influence des frontières naturelles dans les déplacements des chasseurs-cueilleurs an Würm recent. *PA*, 28.

Dolukhanov, P.M. 1979. *Ecology and Economy in Neolithic Eastern Europe*. Duckworth, London.

Ducrocq, T. 1999. Le Mésolithique de la vallée de la Somme (Nord de la France). In: *Thévenin, A. (ed.) 1999*.

Egloff, M. 1965. La Baume d'Ogens, gisement épipaléolithique du Plateau Vaudois. *Jahrbuch der Schweizerischen Gesellschaft für Urgeschichte*, 52.

Egloff, M. 1967. Huit niveaux archéologiques à l'Abri de la Cure (Baulmes, canton de Vaud). *Ur-Schweiz*, 31.

Eriksen, B.V. 1990. Cultural Change or Stability in Prehistoric Hunter-Gatherer Societies. A Case Study from the Late Palaeolithic – Early Mesolithic in Southwestern Germany. In: *Vermeersch, P., Van Peer, P. (ed.) 1990*.

Eriksen, B.V. Change and Continuity in a Prehistoric Hunter – Gatherer Society: a study of cultural adaptation in Late Glacial-Early Postglacial southwestern Germany. *Archaeologia Venatoria*, 12.

Escalon de Fonton, M. 1954. Tour d'horizon de la préhistoire provençale. *BSPF*, 51.

Escalon de Fonton, M. 1956. Les industries mésolithiques en Basse-Provence. *Provence Historique*, 6.

Escalon de Fonton, M. 1956a. Préhistoire de la Bass-Provence Occidentale. *Préhistoire*, 12.

Escalon de Fonton, M. 1958. Quelques civilisations méditerranéennes du Paléolithique supérier au Mésolithique. In: *Memoires SPF*, 5.

Escalon de Fonton, M. 1971–1972. Les phénomènes de néolithisation dans le Midi de la France, In: *Schwabedissen, H. (ed.) 1971–1972*.

Escalon de Fonton, M. 1976. Les civilisations de l 'Epipaléolithique et du Mésolithique en Provence littorale. In: *Lumley, H. de (ed.)1976*.

Escalon de Fonton, M. 1976 a. Les civilisations de l 'Epipaléolithique et du Mésolithique en Languedoc oriental. In: *Lumley, H. de (ed.) 1976*.

Escalon de Fonton, M. 1976 b. La constitution de l 'Epipaléolithique et du Mésolitique dans le Midi de la France, In: *Kozlowski, S.K. (ed.) 1976*.

Escalon de Fonton, M. (ed.) 1977. *Congrès Préhistorique de France. XX e Session, Provence*. Sociètè Prèhistorique Française, Paris.

Escalon de Fonton, M. 1977 a. Le Montadien de Ponteau à Martigues (Bouches-du-Rhône). In: *Escalon de Fonton, M. (ed.) 1977*.

Escalon de Fonton, M. 1983. La constitution de l 'Epipaléolithique et du Mésolithique dans le Midi de la France. In: *Kozlowski, S.K. (ed.) 1983*.

Escalon de Fonton, M., De Lumley, H. 1957. Les industries à Microlithes Géometriques. *BSPF*, 54.

Falkenström, P. 2003. Mesolithic territorial behaviour in Central Scandinavia and adjacent regions. In: *Larsson, L. et al. (ed.) 2003*.

Fasani, L. (ed.) 1980. *Il territorio Veronese delle origini all'eta romana. Fiorini,* Verona

Feustel, R. 1961. Das Mesolithikum In Thüringen. *Alt-Thüringen,* 5.

Fischer, A. 1988. Hunting with Flint-Tipped Arrows: Results and Experiences from Practical Experiments. In: *Bonsall, C. (ed.) 1988.*

Fischer, A. 2003. Trapping up the rivers and trading across the sea-steps towards the neolithisation of Denmark. In: *Larsson, L. at al. (ed.) 2003.*

Forsberg, L. 1996. The Earliest Settlement of Northern Sweden – Problems and Perspectives. In: *Larsson, L. (ed.) 1996.*

Fortea Perez, J. 1971. *Le Cueva de la Cocina: ensayo de chronologie del epipaleolitico.* Servicio de Investigacion Preistorico.

Fortea Perez, J. 1973. *Los complejos micralaminares y geometricos del Epipaleolitico Mediteraneo Espanol. Universidad de Salamanca.* In: *Memorias del Seminario de Preistoria y Arqueologia.* Salamanca.

Fortea Perez, J. 1976. El arte parietal epipaleolitico del 6° al 5° milenio y su sustitucion por el arte levantino, In: *Kozłowski, S.K. (ed.) 1976.*

Foss, M.E. 1952. Drevneishaya istoria Severa evropeiskoi chasti SSSR. *MIA, 29.*

Fredsjö, A. 1953. *Studier i Västsveriges äldre stenalder.* Göteborg.

Frelih, M. 1987. Novo odkrita prazgodovinska plana najdišča na Ljubljanskem Barju. *Porocilo o raziskanju paleolita, neolite i eneolite v Slovenji, 15.*

Frelin-Khatib, C., Thévenin, A. 2000. Le Mésolithique du départament de l'Ain. In: *Crotti, P. (ed.) 2000.*

Froom, F.R. 1976. *Wawcott III, A Stratified Mesolithic succession.* In: *BAR – BS 27.*

Fugazolla Delpino, M.A. *et al.* 2003. *Civiltá dell'argilla.* Museo Nazionale Preistorico – Etnografico "Luigi Pigorini". Roma.

Freund, E. A. 1948. Komsa-Fosna-Sandarna. Problems of the Scandinavian Mesolithic. *Acta Archaeologica, 1.*

Garcia-Argüelles i Andreu, P., Nadal i Lorezo, J., Fullola i Pericot, J. 1999. L'Epipaléolithique en Catalogne: données culturelles et paléoenvironmentales. In: *Thévenin, A. (ed.) 1999.*

Garcia-Argüelles, 2004. Epipaleolithic Phases in the Northwest Coast of the Iberian Peninsula, In: *Gonzales Morales, M., Clark, G.A. (ed.) 2004.*

Gatsov, I. 1988. Early Holocene Flint Assemblages from the Bulgarian Black Sea Coast. In: *Bonsall C. (ed.) 1988.*

Gatsov, I. 1989 a. The archaeological cultures of the Late Pleistocene and Early Holocene in the western Black Sea region, and their significance for the formation of the Neolithic flint industries. In: *Kozłowski, J.K. (ed.) 1988.*

Geddes, D., Guilaine, J., Coularou J., La Gall, O., Martzluff, M. 1988. Postglacial Environments, Settlement and Subsistence in Pyrenees: the Balma Margineda. Andorra. In: *Bonsall, C. (ed.) 1988.*

G.E.E.M., 1969. Epipaléolithique-Mesolithique. *BSPF,* 66, 69.

Gehlen, B. 1999. Épipaléolithique, Mésolithique et Néolithique ancien dans les Basses-Alpes entre l'Iller et le Lech (Sud-Ouest de la Bavière). In: *Thèvenin, A. (ed.) 1999.*

Gendel, P.A. 1984. Mesolithic Social Territories in Northwestern Europe. *BAR – IS, 218.*

Gendel, P.A. 1988. The Analysis of Lithic Styles through Distributional Profiles of Variation: Examples from the Western European Mesolithic. In: *Bonsall, C. (ed.) 1988.*

Geupel, V. 1985–87. *Spätpaläolithikum und Mesolithikum im Süden der DDR, Katalog.* VEB Deutcher Verlag der Wissentschaften, Berlin.

Gietz, F.J. 2001. Spätes Jungpaläolithikum und Mesolithikum in der Barburg Höle, Dietfurt an der obern Donau. In: Landesdenkmalamt Baden-Württenberg. Konrad Theiss Verlag. Stuttgart.

Giraud, E., Vaché, C., Vignard, E. 1938. Le gisement mésolithique de Piscop. *L'Anthropologie, 48.*

Giraud, E., Vignard, E. 1946. Un rendez-vous de chasse mésolithique, les Rochers, commune d'Auffargis. *BSPF,* 43.

Girininkas, A. 1985. Narvos Kulturos raida. *Lietuvos Archeologija,* 4.

Gob, A. 1977. La notion de "style de débitage" peut-elle servir de repére chronologique dans Mésolithique? In: *Escalon de Fonton, M. (ed.) 1977.*

Gob, A. 1981. *Le Mésolithique dans le bassin de l'Ourthe.* In: *Sociètè Wallonne de Palethnologie, Memoire 3,* Liege.

Gob, A. 1981 a. Le Mésolithique final dans le bassin de l'Ourthe (Belgique). In: *Gramsch, B. (ed.) 1981.*

Gob, A. 1984. Les industries microlithiques dans la partie and de la Belgique. In: *Cahen, D., Haesters, P. (ed.) 1984.*

Gob, A. 1985. *Typologie des armatures et taxonomie des industries du Mésolithique au nord des Alpes. Cahiers de l'Institut Archéologique Liègeois,* 2.

Gob, A. 1990. *Chronologie du Mésolithique en Europe.* Universite de Liège, CIPL, Liège.

Gonzales Morales, M., Clark, G.A. (ed.) 2004. *The Mesolithic of the Atlantic Façade; Proceedings of the Santander Symposium.* In: *Arizona State University, Anthropological Research Papers* 55.

Gramsch, B. 1959/60. Der Stand der Mittelsteinzeitforschung in der Mark Brandenburg. *Wissenschaftliche Zeitschrift der Humboldt Uniwersität zu Berlin,* 9.

Gramsch, B. 1966. *Untersuchungen zum Mesolithikum im nördlichen und mittleren Tief – ladsraum zwischen Elbe und Oder* (typescript of the Ph. D. Theris). Potsdam.

Gramsch, B. 1973. *Das Mesolithikum im Flachland zwischen Elbe und Oder. VP,* 7.

Gramsch, B. 1976. Bemerkungen zur Palökologie und zur Besiedlung während des jüngeren Boreals und des älteren Atlamtikums im nördlichen Mitteleuropa, In: *Kozłowski, S.K. (ed.) 1976.*

Gramsch, B. (ed.) 1981. *Mesolithikum in Europa. VP,* 14/15.

Gramsch, B. 1981. Spätglaziale und frühholzäne Entwicklung des Paläolithikums in der Tschechoslowakei. In: *Gramsch, B. (ed.) 1981.*

Gramsch, B. 1987. Ausgrabungen auf dem mesolithischen Fundplatz bei Friesack, Bezik Potsdam. *VP,* 21.

Gramsch, B. 2000. Friesack: Letzte Jäger und Sammler in Brandenburg. *Jahrbuch des Römisch-Germanischen Zentralmuseums Mainz,* 47.

Gramsch, B., Kloss, K. 1988. Excavation near Friesack: an Early Mesolithic Marshland Site in the Northern Plain of Central Europe. In: *Bonsall, C. (ed.) 1988.*

Gross, H. 1940. Die Rennitierjäger-Kulturen Ostpreussens. *PZ,* 30–31.

Grøn, O. 1987. Dwellings organisation – a key to the understanding of social structure in Old Stone Age societies. An example from the Meglemose culture. In: *AI,* 8.

Grøn, O. 1988. General Spatial Behaviour in Small Dwellings: a Preliminary Study in Ethnoarchaeology and Social Psychology. In: *Bonsall, C. (ed.) 1988.*

Guerreschi, A. 1987. Hypothèse concernante la continuité

culturelle entre populations du Tardiglaciaire wurmien et de l'Holocene antique en Italie. In: *AI*, 8

Guilaine, J. (ed.) 1998. *Atlas de Néolithique europeen, Europe occidentale*. In: *ERAUL, 46.*

Gumpert, K. 1925. *Fränkisches Mesolithikum*. Leipzig.

Gumpert, K. 1933. Eine Paläolithische und mesolithische Abrisiedlung an der Steinbergwand bei Endsdorf In der Oberfplaz. *Mannus, 25.*

Gurina, N.N. 1956. Oleneostrovski mogilnik. *MIA, 47.*

Gurina, N.N. (ed.) 1966. *At the Sources of Early Cultures, the Mesolithic Age* (in Russian). In: *KSIA, 126.*

Hagen, A. 1956–57. Vassdragreguleringen og hoyfjellsarkeologi. *AUO.*

Hagen, A. 1960–61. Mesolitiske jedergrupper i norske høyfjell. *AUO.*

Hallam, J.S., Edwards, B.J.N., Barnes, B., Stuart, A.J., 1973. A Late Glacial elk with associated barbed points from High Furlong, Lancanshire. *PPS, 39.*

Khalikov, A.H. 1966. Mezolit srednego Povoizhia. *MIA, 126.*

Heesters, W. 1967. Mesolithicum te Nijnsel. *Brabants Heem.*

Heesters, W., Wouters, A. 1968. Een vroeg-mesolithische Kulturen te Nijnsek. *Brabants Heem.*

Higgs, E. 1959. Excavations at a Mesolithic Site at Downtown, near Salisbury, Wiltshire. *PPS, 25.*

Hinout, J. 1962. Un gisement Tardenoisien de Fère-en-Tardenois. *BSPF, 59.*

Hinout, J. 1964. Gisements tardenoisiens de l'Aisne. *Gallia-Préhistorie, 7.*

Hinout, J. 1976. Les civilisations de l'Epipaléolithique et du Mésolithique dans le Bassin Parisien. In: *Lumley, H. de (ed.) 1976.*

Hinout, J. 1984. Les outils et armatures – standards mésolithiques dans le Bassin Parisien par l'analyse des domés. *Revue Archeologique de Picardie.*

Hofman-Wyss, 1978. *Liesbergmühlich VI, eine Mittelstein-zeitliche Abristation im Birstal. Schriften des Seminars für Urgeschichte der Universität Bern, 2.*

Huntley, B., Birks, H.J.B. 1983. *An Atlas of Past and Present Pollen Maps for Europe: 0–13000 yers ago.* Cambridge University Press.

Indreko, R. 1948. *Die mittlere Steinzeit in Estland*. Stockholm.

Indrelid, S. 1978. Mesolithic economy and settlement patterns in Norway. In: *Mellars, P. (ed.) 1978.*

Jaanits, L. 1970. Mezoliticheskoe mestonahozhdenye v Pulli. In: *Archeolocheskie Otkrytia 1969 goda*. Moscow.

Jaanits, K. 1981. Die mesolithischen Siedlungsplätze mit Feuersteininventar in Estland. In: *Gramsch, B. (ed.) 1981.*

Jablonskyté-Rimantiené, R. 1960. Stoianka kamennego i bronzo-vogo vekov Samantonis. *SA.*

Jablonskyté-Rimantiené, R. 1963. Žemiaju Kaniukiu IV–I tukstantmečiu pr. m. e. stovyklos. In: *Lietuvos TSR, A, 14.*

Jablonskyté-Rimantiené, R. 1963 a. Velyvojo mezolito stovykla Lampédžiuose. In: *Lietuvos TSR, A, 15.*

Jablonskyté-Rimantiené, R. 1966. Maglenoziné ankstyvojo mezolito stovykla Maksimonys IV (Varenos Raj. Merkinés Apyl). In: *Lietuvos TSR, A, 22.*

Jablonskyté-Rimantiené, R. 1971. Paleolit i mezolit Litvy. Vilnius.

Jaccotey, L. 1999. Le Mésolithique récent et final franc-comtois. In: *Thévenin, A. (ed.) 1999.*

Jacobi, R. 1980. *The Early Holocene Settlement of Wales*. In: *BAR-BS, 76.*

Jacobi, R.M. 1973. Aspects of the "Mesolithic Age" in Britan. In: *Kozłowski, S.K. (ed.) 1973.*

Jacobi, R.M. 1978. Northern England in the eighth millenium bc: an essay. In: *Mellars, P. (ed.) 1978.*

Jarman, M.R., Higgs S. (ed.) 1972. European deer economies and the Advent of the Neolithic. In: Higgs, E. (ed.). *Papers in economic prehistory.* Cambridge University Press.

Jochim, M.A. 1976. *Hunter-Gatherer Subsistance and Settlement. A Predictive Model.* In: *Studies in Archaeology.* Academic Press, New York, San Francisco, London.

Jochim, M.A. 1977. Recherche des influences Mésolithiques. In: *Escalon de Fonton, M. (ed.) 1977.*

Jochim, M. 1990. The Late Mesolithic in Southwest Germany: Culture Change or Population Decline? In: *Vermeersch, P., Van Peer, P. (ed.) 1990.*

Jochim, M.A. 1998. *A Hunter-Gatherer Landscape Southwest Germany in the Late Palaeolithic and Mesolithic.* Plenum Press, New York, London.

Jørgensen, S. 1956. Kongemosen. En Aamose-boplads fra den aeldre Stenalder. *Kuml.*

Jussila, T., Matiskainen, H. 2003. Mesolithic settlement during the Preboreal period in Finland, In: *Larsson, L. et al. (ed.) 2003.*

Kaczanowska, M. 1985 *Neolithische Feuersteinindustrien im Nordteil des Flussgebiets der Mitteldonau.* PWN, Warsaw.

Kertesz, R. 1996. The Mesolithic in the Great Hungarian Plain. In: *Tálas, L. (ed.) At the Fringes of Three Worlds.* Szolnok.

Kindt, C.J. 2003. Das Mesolithikum in der Talaue des Neckars. In: *Landesenkmalamt Baden Würtemberg.* Konrad Tress Verlage, Stuttgart.

Kindt, C.J. 2006. Transport of raw materials in the Mesolithic of south-west Germany. *Journal of Anthropological Archaeology.*

Knutsson, K., Falkenström, P., Lindberg, K.F. 2003. Appropriation of the Past. Neolithisation in the Northen Scandinavian Perspective. In: *Larsson L. et al. (ed.) 2003.*

Koltsov, L.V. 1963. Stoianka u s. Kopirino na Verkhnei Volge. In: *Pamiatniki kamennogo i bronzovogo vekov Evrazii.* Moscow.

Koltsov, L.V. 1965. Mezolit Volgo-Okskogo mezhdurechia (typescript of the Ph.D. thesis). Moscow.

Koltsov, L.V. 1965a. Nekotorye itogi mezolita Volgo-Okskogo mezhdurechia. *SA.*

Koltsov, L.V. 1966. Nowye raskopki stoianki Yelin Bor. *MIA, 126.*

Koltsov, L.V. 1971. Mezoliticheskaia stoianka Butovo. *KSIA, 126.*

Koltsov, L.V. 1973. Nekotorie problemy mezolita Volgo-Okskogo mezhdurecia. In: *Kozłowski, S.K. (ed.) 1973.*

Koltsov, L.V. (ed.) 1989. *The Mesolithic, of the USSR* (in Russian). In: *Arkheologia SSSR.* Nauka, Moscow.

Koltsov, L.V., Zhilin, M.G. 1999. *Mesolithic of the territory between Volga and Oka rivers,* (in Russian). Nauka, Moscow.

Koltsov, L.V., Zhilin, M.G. 1999 a. Tanged points cultures in the upper Volga Basin. In: *Kozlowski, S.K. et al. (ed.) 1999.*

Kozłowski, J.K. 1973. The Problem of the So-Called Danubian Mesolithic. In: *Kozłowski, S.K. (ed.) 1973.*

Kozłowski, J.K. 1980. Technological and Typological Differentiation of Lithic Assemblages in the Upper Palaeolithic: An Interpretation Attempt. In: *Schild, R. (ed.) Unconventional Archaeology.* Ossolineum, Wrocław.

Kozłowski, J.K. (ed.) 1982. Orgin of the chipped stone industries of the Early Farming Cultures in Balkans. In: *Zeszyty Naukowe UJ, Prace Archeologiczne, 33.* Cracow.

Kozłowski, J.K. 1983. Le Bassin Danubien au VIII–VI millénaires B.C. In: *Kozłowski, S.K. (ed.) 1983.*

Kozłowski, J.K. (ed.) 1988. Chipped Stone Industries of the Early Farming Cultures in Europe, In: *AI*, 9.

Kozłowski, J.K. 2005. The Importance of the Aegean Basin for the Neolithisation of South-Eastern Europe. *Journal of the Israel Prehistoric Society*, 35.

Kozłowski, J., Kozłowski, S. (ed.) 1984. Advances in Palaeolithic and Mesolithic Archaeology. In: *AI*, 5.

Kozłowski, J., Kozłowski, S. (ed.) 1987. New in Stone Age Archaeology. In: *AI*, 8

Kozłowski, S.K. 1967. The Komornician, on the background of Central European Mesolithic (in Polish*) Światowit*, 28.

Kozłowski, S.K. 1971. The North-Eastern Mesolithic Complex (in Polish). In: W. Chmielewski (ed). *Z polskich badań nad epoką kamienia*. Wrocław, Ossolineum.

Kozłowski, S.K. 1972. *Prehistory of Polish teritories from 9th to 5th millenium BC.* (in Polish) PWN, Warsaw.

Kozłowski, S.K. 1972 a. The Kudlaevka type assemblages (in Polish). *Światowit*, 33.

Kozłowski, S.K. (ed.) 1973. *The Mesolithic in Europe. Papers read at the International Archaeological Symposium on the Mesolithic in Europe.* Warsaw University Press.

Kozłowski, S.K. 1973a. The introduction to the History of Europe in Early Holocene. In: *Kozłowski, S.K. (ed.) 1973.*

Kozłowski, S.K. 1975. *Cultural Differentiation of Europe from 10th to 5th Millenium BC.* Warsaw, University Press.

Kozłowski, S.K. (ed.) 1976. *Les civilisations du 8e au 5e millénaire avant notre ére en Europe.* UISPP 9th Congress, Nice, Gap.

Kozłowski, S.K. 1976 a. K-points. *Archaeologia Polona*, 18.

Kozłowski, S.K. 1976 b. Rectangles, Rhomboids and Trapezoids in Northwestern Europe. *Helinium*, 16.

Kozłowski, S.K. 1976 c. Les courants interculturels dans Mésolithique de l'Europe occidentale, In: *Kozłowski, S.K. (ed.) 1976.*

Kozłowski, S.K. 1977. Foreigin and local elements in the British Mesolithic. *Wiadomości Archeologiczne*, 42.

Kozłowski, S.K. 1977 a. Project d'une cartographie des éléments typologiques mésolithiques en Europe. In: *Escalon de Fonton, M. (ed.) 1977*

Kozłowski, S.K. 1979. Quelques rémarques sur l'art. Zoomorphique mésolithique de la region de la Mer Baltique. In: *Bandi, H.G., et al. (ed.) 1979.*

Kozłowski, S.K. 1980. *Atlas of the Mesolithic in Europe.* Warsaw University Press.

Kozłowski, S.K. 1981. Bemerkungen zum Mesolithikum in der Tschechoslowakei und in Österreich. In: *Gramsch, B. (ed.) 1981.*

Kozłowski, S.K. 1981 a. PE – Points. *Archeologia Polona*, 19.

Kozłowski, S.K. (ed.) 1983. *Les changements, leurs méchanismes, leurs causes dans la culture du 7e au 6e millénaire av. J-C. en Europe. AI* 2.

Kozłowski, S.K. 1983 a. Le material archéologique de la couche mésolithique de la Grotte du Coléoptere. In: *Société Wallonne de Palethnologie. Mémoires*, 5.

Kozłowski S.K. 1983 b. Les courants interculturels dans le Mésolithique de l'Europe occidentale. In: *Kozłowski, S.K., (ed.) 1983.*

Kozłowski, S.K. 1984. Carte de la culture de Beuron-Coincy (Beuronien). In: *Elements de Pré- et Protohistoire Européenne. Memorial Book of J. P. Millotte.* Paris.

Kozłowski, S.K. 1985. South-eastern elements in the Polish Mesolithic. In: *Memoires Archéologiques, Memorial Book of J. Gurba.* Lublin, University Press.

Kozłowski, S.K. 1988. The Pre-Neolithic base of the Early neolithic stone industries in Europe. *AI*, 9.

Kozłowski, S.K. 1988 a. A Survey of Early Holocene Cultures of the Western Part of the Russian Plain. In: *Bonsall, C. (ed.) 1988.*

Kozłowski, S.K. 1989. *Mesolithic in Poland, a New approach.* Warsaw. University Press,

Kozłowski, S.K. 1991. Le Desnenien. *Anthropologie*, 29.

Kozłowski, S.K. 1996. Early postglacial adaptation in Poland and Central Europe (Mesolithic/Epipalaeolithic). In: *Kozłowski, S.K., Tozzi, C. (ed.) 1996.*

Kozłowski, S.K. 1996 a. The Trialetian "Mesolithic" Industry of the Caucasus, Transcapia, Eastern Anatolia, and the Iranian Plateau. In: *Kozłowski, S.K., Gebel, H.G. (ed.) 1996. Neolithic Chipped Stone Industry of the Fertile Crescent, and Their Contemporaries in Adjacent Regions.* Ex Oriente. Berlin.

Kozłowski, S.K. 1999. The Eastern Wing of the Fertile Crescent. In: *BAR-IS*, 760.

Kozłowski, S.K. 2001. Eco-Cultural/Stylistic Zonation of the Mesolithic/Epipalaeolithic in Central Europe. In: *Makay, J., Kertesz, R. (ed.) 2001 From the Mesolithic to the Neolithic.* Archaeolingua Budapest.

Kozłowski, S.K. 2002. E pluribus unum? Regards sur l'Europe mésolithique. In: *Congres des sociétées Historiques.* Lille.

Kozłowski, S.K. 2003. The Mesolithic: What we know and what we believe? In: *Larsson, L. et al. (ed.) 2003.*

Kozłowski, S.K., Aurenche, O. 1999. *La naissance du Néolithique au Proche Orient.* Errance. Paris.

Kozłowski, S.K., Burdukiewicz, J.M. 1977. Les pointes PB et PC. *Acta Archaeologica*, 48.

Kozłowski, S.K., Dalmeri, G. 2002. Riparo Gaban: the Mesolithic layers. *PA*, 36.

Kozłowski, S.K., Desbrosse, R. 2000. Pyrenées, Alpes et Carpathes: Barrières culturelles pour les derniers chasseurs-predateurs. In: *Les Paleoalpins, Hommage a Pierre Binz.* Edtion Université Joseph Fourieré. Grenoble.

Kozłowski, S.K., Gebel, H.G. (ed.) 1996. *Neolithic Chipped Stone Industries of the Fertile Crescent and Their Contemporaries In the Adjacent Regions.* Ex Oriente. Berlin.

Kozłowski, S.K., Gurba, J., Zalizniak, L.L. (ed.) 1999. *Tanged Points Cultures in Europe.* Maria Curie-Skłodowska University Press, Lublin.

Kozłowski, S.K., Kozłowski, J.K. 1975. *Prehistory of Europe from 40th to 5th millennium. BC.* (in Polish). PWN, Warszawa.

Kozłowski, S.K., Kozłowski J.K. 1977. *Stone Age in Poland* (in Polish). PWN Warszawa.

Kozłowski, S.K., Kozłowski, J.K. 1978. Pointes, sagaies et harpons du Paléolithique et du Mesolithique en Europe centre-est. In: *IIIᵉ Colloque International sur l'os préhistorique, Sénanque.* Paris.

Kozłowski, S.K., Kozłowski, J.K. 1979. *Upper Palaeolithic and Mesolithic in Europe.* In: Ossolineum, Wrocław.

Kozłowski, S.K., Kozłowski, J.K., Dolukhanov, P.M. 1980. *Multivariate analysis of Upper Palaeolithic and Mesolithic stone assamblages. Prace Archeolo- giczne*, 30.

Kozłowski, S.K., Kozłowski, J.K. 1983. Lithic industries from the multi-layer Mesolithic site Vlasac in Yugoslavia. *Prace Archeologiczne*, 33.

Kozłowski, S.K., Kozłowski, J.K. 1984. Chipped stone industries from Lepenski Vir. Yugoslavia. *PA*, 19.

Kozłowski, S.K., Kozłowski J.K. 1984 a. Le Mésolithique a l'est des Alpes. *PA*, 19.

Kozłowski, S.K., Kozłowski, J.K. 1986. Foragers of Central

Europe and their acculturation. In: *Zvelebil M. (ed.) 1986. Hunters in Transition,* Cambridge. University Press.

Kozłowski, S.K., Kozłowski, J.K., Radovanović, J. 1994. *Meso- and Neolithic Sequence from the Odmut Cave (Montenegro).* Warsaw. University Press.

Kozłowski, S.K., Tozzi, C., Cremaschi, M., Dini, M. 2003. L'industria di Isola Santa in Toscana el a sua pozizione nel Sauveterriano italiano. *RSP,* 53.

Kozłowski, S.K., Dimi, M., Grifoni-Cremonesi, R., Molara, G., Tozzi, C., Molara, G., Tozzi, C., 2007/8. L'industria castelnoviana della Grotte di Latronico 3 (Potenza). *RSP.*

Kriiska, A. 2003. Colonisation of the west Estonian archipelago. In: *Larsson, L. et al. (ed.) 2003.*

Kruglikova, J.T. (ed.) 1977. *Monuments of the Mesolithic Age* (in Russian). In: *KSIA,* 149. Nauka Moscow.

Krüger, G., Taute, W. 1964. Eine mesolithische schlagstätte auf dem "Feuersteinacker" In Stumperten Rod im oberhessische Kreis Alsfeld. *Fundberichte aus Hessen,* 4.

Lacaille, A.D. 1954. *The Stone Age In Scotland.* Oxford.

Lacam, R., Niederlander, A. 1944. Le gisement mésolithique du Cuzoul-de-Gramat. In: *Archives IPH,* 21.

Lanfranchi (de), F., Weiss, M.C. 1997. *L'aventure humaine, Préhistoire en Corse.* Albiana. Ajaccio.

Larsson, L. 1983. *Ageröd V, an Atlantic Bog Site in Central Scania.* In: *AAL, Series in 8°,* 12.

Larsson, L. 1973. Some Problems of the Mesolithic Based Upon the Finds from the Raised Bog Ageröds Mosse. In: *Kozłowski, S.K. (ed.) 1973.*

Larsson, L. 1978, *Ageröd I:B–Ageröd I:D, a Study of Early Atlantic Settlement in Scania.* In: *AAL, Series in 4°* nr 12.

Larsson, L. 1982. Segebro, en tidigatlantsk boplads vid Sege ås Mynning. In: *Malmöfynd 4 Utgiven av Malmö museum.*

Larsson, L. 1988. Late Mesolithic Settlements and Cemeteries at Skateholm, Southern Sweden. In: *Bonsall, C. (ed.) 1988.*

Larsson, L. (ed.) 1996. *The Earliest Settlement of Scandinavia.* Almquist and Wiksell International. Stockholm.

Larsson, L. *et al.* (ed.) 2003. *Mesolithic on the Move.* Oxbow Books, Oxford.

Larsson, L. 2003. The Mesolithic of Sweden in retrospective and progressive perpectives. In: *Larsson L. et al. (ed.) 2003.*

Larsson, L., Larsson, U.K. 1977. Sur les pointes en os à tranchants de silex trouvées dans la Sud de la Suède. In: *Escalon de Fonton, M. (ed.) 1977.*

Leggee, A.J., Rowley-Conwy, P.A. 1988. Some Preliminary Results of a Re-Examination of the Star Carr Fauna. In: *Bonsall, C. (ed.) 1988.*

Leitner, W. 1983. Zum Stand der Mesolithforschung in Österreich. In: *Bagolini, B. (ed.) 1983.*

Lindgren, C. 2003. My way or your way. On the social dimension of technology as seen in the lithic strategies in eastern middle Sweden during the Mesolithic. In: *Larsson, L. et al. (ed.) 2003.*

Loze, I. 1973. Mesolithic Art of Eastern Baltic Region. In: *Kozłowski, S.K. (ed.) 1973.*

Loze, J.A. 1988. *Stone Age Settlements of the Lubana Lowland; Mesolithic, Early and Middle Neolithic* (in Russian). Zinatne, Riga.

Lozovski, V.M. 1999. Late mesolithic bone industries in the Central Russian Plain. In: *Kozłowski, S.K., Gurba, J., Zalizniak, L. (ed.) 1999.*

Lozovski, V. 1999. L'industrie en os du Mésolithique récent en Russie centrale. In: *Thèvenin, A. (ed.) 1999.*

Lødøen, T.K., 2003. Late Mesolithic Rock Art and Expressions of Ideology. In: *Larsson, L. et al. (ed.) 2003.*

Luho, V. 1956. *Die Askola-Kultur. SMYA,* 57.

Luho, V. 1967. *Die Suomusjärvi-Kultur. SMYA,* 66.

Lumley, H. de (ed.) 1976. *La préhistoire française.* Editions CNRS. Paris.

Malmer, M.P. 1981. *A chronological Study of North European Rock Art.* In: *Kungl Vitterhelts Histoire och Antiquitets Akademiens, Antikvarska serien* 32.

Manushina, T.N., Lozovski, V.M. *et al.* (ed.) 2001. *Stone Age of the European Plain. Materials of the international conference* (in Russian). Podkova, Sergeev Posad.

Marchand, G. 1999. Éléments pour la définition du Retzien. In: *Thèvenin, A. (ed.) 1999.*

Marchand, G. 2000. Facteurs de variabilité des systémes techniques lithiques au Mésolithique récent et final dans l'ouest de la France. In: *Crotti, P. (ed.) 2000.*

Marchand, G. 2000 a. La néolithisation de l'ouest de la France: aires culturelles et transferts techniques dans l'industrie lithique. *BSPF,* 97.

Marchand, G., Laporte, L. 2000. L'habitat Mésolithique et Néolithique de la Grange à Surgéres (Charente-Martime). In: *Thèvenin, A. (ed.) 2000.*

Markevich, V.J. 1974. *The Bug-Dniester Culture* (in Russian). Shtiintsa. Kishinev

Martens, J., Hagen, A. 1961. Arkeologiske undersøkelster langs elv og vann. *Norske Old-funn,* 10.

Martin, E. 1995. Early inhabitants and changing shoreline of Estonia. In: *Fischer A. (ed.) 1995.*

Martini, F., Tozzi, C. 1996. Il Mesolitico in Italia centro-meridonale. In: *Tozzi, C., Kozłowski, S. (ed.) 1996.*

Mathiassen, T. 1943. *Stenalder bopladsen i Aamosen.* In: *Nordiske Fortidsminden,* 3.

Mathiassen, T. 1948. *Danske oldsager.* København.

Matiskainen, H. 1988. The Chronology of the Finnish Mesolithic. In: *Bonsall, C. (ed.) 1988.*

Matiskainen, H. 1989. *Studies on the Chronology, Material Culture and Subsustance Economy of the Finnish Mesolithic 10.000–6.000 b.p. Ishos,* 9.

Matiskainen, H. 1990. Mesolithic Subsistence in Finland. In: *Vermeersch, P., Van Peer, P. (ed.) 1990.*

Matiskainen, H. 1995. Coastal adaptation in the East Baltic Countries. In: *Fischer, A. (ed.) 1995.*

Matiskainen, H. 1996. Discrepancies in Deglaciation Chronology and the Appearance of Man in Finland. In: *Larsson, L. (ed.) 1996.*

Matiskainen, H., Zhilin, M.G. 2003. A Recently Discovered Mesolithic Wet Site at Riihimäki, South Finland. In: *Larsson, L. et al. (ed.) 2003.*

Matiushin, G.N. 1964. Mezolit i neolit Bashkirii. Moscow. (typescript of the Ph. D. thesis).

Matiushin, G.N. 1964 a. Neoliticheskaia stoianka Yangelka na ozere Czebarkal. *KSIA,* 101.

Matiushin, G.H. 1976. *Mesolithic of Southern Ural* (in Russian). Nauka, Moscow.

Matskevoi, D.G. 1977. *Mesolithic and Neolithic of the Eastern Crimea* (in Russian). Naukova Dumka. Kiev.

Matskevoi, L.G. 1991. *Mesolithic of the Western Ukraine* (in Russian). Naukova Dumka, Kiev.

McCartan, S.B. 2003. Mesolithic hunter-gatherers in the Isle of Man: adaptations to an island environment? In: *Larsson, L. et al. (ed.) 2003.*

Mellars, P. 1976. The appearance of "Narrow blade" microlithic industries in Britain. The radiocarbon evidence, In: *Kozłowski, S.K. (ed.) 1976.*

Mellars, P. (ed.) 1978. *The Early Postglacial Settlement of Northern Europe.* Duckworth, London.

Mihailović, D. 1996. Upper Palaeolithic and Mesolithic chipped stone industries from the rock-shelter of Medena Strjena. In: *Srejović (ed.) Prehistoric Settlements in caves and rock-shelters of Serbia and Montenegro,* 1 Belgrade.

Milner, N., Woodman, P. (ed.) 2005. *Mesolithic Studies at the Beginning of the 21st century.* Oxbow Books, Oxford.

Moore, J.W. 1950. Mesolithic Sites in the Neighbourhood of Flixton, North-East Yorkshire. *PPS,* 16.

Morrison, A. 1980. *Early Man in Britain and Ireland.* Croom Helm, London.

Morrison, A., Bonsall, C. 1988. The Early Post-Glacial Settlement of Scotland: a Review. In: *Bonsall, C. (ed.) 1988.*

Naber, F.B. 1968. Die „Schräge Wand" in Bärental, eine altholozäne Abrifundstelle im nördlischen Frankenjura. *Quartär,* 19.

Naber, F.B. 1970. Untersuchungen an Industrien postglazialer Jägerkultturen. *Bayerische Vorgeschichts-Blätter,* 35.

Narr, K.J. 1968. *Studien zur alteren und mittleren Steinzeit der Niederen Lande. Antiquitas* 2/7.

Newell, R.R. 1970. *The Mesolithic Affinities and Typological Relations of the Dutch Bandkeramik Flint Industry.* (typescript of Ph.D.) London University.

Newell, R.R. 1973. The Post-Glacial Adaptations of the Indigenous Population of the Northwest European Plain. In: *Kozłowski, S.K. (ed.) 1973.*

Newell, R.R. 1981. Mesolithic Dwelling Structures: Fact and Fantasy. In: *Gramsch, B. (ed.) 1981.*

Newell, R.R., Constandse – Westermann, T.S., Meiklejohn, C. 1979. *The Skeletal Remains of Mesolithic Man in Western Europe. Journal of Human Evolution,* 8.

Newell, R.R., Kielman, D., Constandse-Westerman, T., van der Sanden, W., van Gijn, A., 1990. *An enquiry into the ethnic resolution of Mesolithic groups; The study of Heir decorative ornaments in time and space.* E.J. Brill, Leiden.

Nordquist, B. 2000. Coastal Adaptations in the Mesolithic. *Göteborg University, Departmant of Archaeology.* Göteborg.

Nummedal, A. 1929. Stone Age Finds In Finnmark. In: *Institutionen for Sammenlignende Kulturforskning,* B, 13.

Nuzhnyi, D.Y. 1992. *Development of the Microlithic technolohy during the Stone Age* (in Ukrainian). Naukova Dumka. Kiev.

Odell, G.H. 1977. L'analyse fonctionelle microscopique des pierres tailées, un nouveau système. In: *Escalon de Fonton, M. (ed.) 1977.*

Odner, K. 1966. *Komsakulturen i Nesseby og Sør-Varanger.* Trömsø-Oslo-Bergen.

Onoratini, G. 1977. Un faciès provençal du Sauveterrien: l'abri de Saint-Mitre, à Reillanne (Alpes de Haute-Provence). In: *Escalon de Fonton, M. (ed.) 1977.*

Oshibkina, S.V. 1983. *Mesolithic of the Sukhina river and the eastern Onega region* (in Russian). Nauka, Moscow.

Oshibkina, S.V. 1988. The Material Culture of the Veretye-type Sites in the Region to the East of Lake Onega. In: *Bonsall, C. (ed.) 1988.*

Oshibina, S.V. (ed.) 1996. *Neolithic of the Northern Eur-Asia* (in Russian). Nauka, Moscow.

Oshibkina, S.V. 1997. *Veretie I, site of the Mesolithic Age in Northen Europe* (in Russian). Nauka, Moscow.

Oshibkina, S.V. 1999. Tangend point industries in the North-West of Russia. In: *Kozłowski, S.K., Gurba, J., Zalizniak, L. (ed.) 1999.*

Ostrauskas, T. 2002. Kundos kulturos terinéjimų problematika. *Archeologija,* 23.

Ostrauskas, T. 2002. Mezolitine Kudlajewskos Kultura Lietuvoje. *Archeologija,* 23.

Otte, M. (ed.) 1988. *De la Loire á l`Oder.* In: *BAR – IS* 444.

Palma di Cesnola, A. (ed.) 1983. La position taxonomique et chronologique des industries à pointes à dos. *RSP*

Palmer, S. 1988. Mesolithic Sites of Portland and their Significance. In: *Bonsall C. (ed.) 1988.*

Perez, J.A. 1977. Le Mésolithique de la région de Valence (Espagne). In*: Escalon de Fonton, M. (ed.) 1977.*

Perez, J.F., Oliver, B.M., Cabanilles, J.J. 1987. L'industrie lithique du Néolithique ancien dans le versant méditerranéen de la Peninsule Iberique. In: *Kozłowski, J.K. (ed.) 1987.*

Perlès, C. 1984. Aperçu sur les industries mésolithiques de Franchthi, Argolide, Grèce. In: *AI,* 5.

Perlés, C. 1987. Les industries du Néolithique précéramique de Grèce: nouvelles ètudes, nouvelles interpretations. In: *Kozłowski, J.K. (ed.) 1987.*

Perlés, C. 1991. *Les industries lithriques taillées de Franchthi (Argolide, Grece), Les industries du Mésolithique et du Néolithique. In: Excavatias at Franchthi care cave,* 2.

Pequart, M. and S.J. 1934. La nécropole mésolitihique de l'île de Hoëdic, Morbihan. *L'Anthropologie,* 44.

Pequart, M. and S.J. 1954. *Hoëdic.* Antwerpen.

Pequart, M. and S.J., Boule, M., Valois, H.V. 1937. *Téviec, stadion nécropole mésolithique du Morbihan.* In: *Archives IPH,* 18.

Pericot-Garcia, L. 1945. *La Cueva de la Cocina (Dos Aguas).* In: *Archivi de prehistoria Levantina,* 2.

Peters, E. 1934. Das Mesolithikum der oberen Donau. *Germania,* 18.

Petersen, E.B. 1988. Vaenget Nord: Excavation, Documentation and Interpretation of the Mesolithic Site at Vedbaek. Denmark. In: *Bonsall, C. (ed.) 1988.*

Pion, G. 1989. Le gisement de la Fru, commune de Sain-Christophe-la-Grotte (Les Echelles département de Savoie). In: *Aimé, G., Thévenin, A. (ed.) 1989.*

Pion, G. (ed.) 1994. *Actes de la Table Ronde de Chambéry. Association Départamentale pour la Recherche Archéologique en Savoie.* Chambery.

Pion, G. 1994. La séquence mésolithique de l'aire III de l'abri de La Fru en Savoie. Situation chrono – industrielle et paléoenvironnementale. In: *Pion, G. (ed.)1994.*

Pion, G. 2000. Le Mésolithique ancien de l'abri de La Fru (Savoie), industrie et paléoenvironnement. In: *Crotti. P. (ed.) 2000.*

Pirazzoli, P.A. 1991. *World Atlas of Holocene Sea-Level Changes.* Elsevier, Amsterdam – London – New York – Tokyo.

Pirazzoli, P.A. 1996. *Sea-Level Changes. The Last 20.000 Years.* John Wiley and Sons, Chichester, New York.

Płonka, T. 2003. *The Portable Art of Mesolithic Europe.* Wrocław University Press. Wrocław.

Price, T.D. 1973. A Proposed Model for Procurement Systems in the Mesolithic of Northwestern Europe. In: *Kozłowski, S.K. (ed.) 1973.*

Price, T.D. (ed.) 1996. *Mesolithic Miscellany,* vols. 1–17.

Price, T.D. 1978. Mesolithic settlement systems in the Netherlands. In: *Mellars, P. (ed.) 1978.*

Prošek, F. 1959. Mesolitická obsidiánová industries ze stanice Barca I. *AR,* 11.

Radley, J., Mellars, P. 1964. A Mesolithic Structure at Deepcar, Yorkshire, England and the Affinities of its Associated Flint Industry. *PPS,* 30.

Radmilli, A., Cremonesi, G., Tozzi, C. 1976. A propos du Mésolitique en Italie. In: *Camps, G. (ed.) 1976.*

Radmilli, A.M. (ed.) 1984. *Il Mesolitico sul Carsto Triestino.* In:

Societá per la Preistorie e Protostorie della Regione Friuli-Venezia Giulie, 5. Editione Italo Svevo. Trieste.

Radovanovic, I. 1999. Mésolithique et Néolithique ancien dans la région des Portes de Fer – occupations, modes de subsistance et chronologie. In: *Thèvenin, A. (ed.) 1999.*

Rankama, T. 2003. The Colonisation of Northernmost Finnish Lapland and the Inland Areas of Finnmark. In: *Larsson, L. et al. (ed.) 2003.*

Rankine, W.F. 1952. A Mesolithic Chipping Floor at the Waren, Oakhanger, Selborne, Hants. *PPS,* 18.

Rankine, W.F. and W.M. Dimbleby, G.W. 1960. Further Excavations at a Mesolithic Site at Oakhanger. *PPS,* 26. *Regionalisation of Europe.* 1971. Federation Internationale de Documentation. La Haye.

Roche, J. 1960. *Le gisement Mésolithique de Moita do Sebastiao (Muge-Portugal).* Lisboa.

Roche, J. 1970. L'industrie de l'amas coquillier mésolithique de Cabeç da Amoreira, Muge (Portugal). In: *Actes du VIIᵉ Congrès International des Sciences Pré- et Protohistoriques.1,* Praha.

Roche, J. 1971–1972. Les amas coquilliers (concheiros) méso-lithiques de Muge (Portugal). In: *Schwabedissen, H. (ed.) 1971–1972.*

Roche, J. 1976. Les amas coquilliers de Muge. In: *Camps, G. (ed.) 1976.*

Roche, J. 1976. Les origines de l'industrie de l'amas coquillier de Moita do Sebastiao, In: *Kozłowski, S.K. (ed.) 1976.*

Roche, J. 1983. Les origines de l'industrie de l'amas coquillier de moita do Sebastião, In: *Kozłowski, S.K. (ed.) 1983.*

Roussot-Larroque, J. 1887. Le cycle Roucadourien et la mise en place des industries lithiques du Nèolitique ancien dans le Sud de la France. In: *Kozłowski, J.K. (ed.) 1987.*

Rozoy, J.G. 1968. Typologie de l'Epipaléolithique franco-belge. *BSPF,* 64 and 65.

Rozoy, J.G. 1971. Tardenoisien et Sauveterrien. *BSPF,* 68.

Rozoy, J.G. 1971–1972. La fin de l'Épipaléolithique ("Méso-lithique") dans le nord de la France et la Belgique. In: *Schwabedissen, H.(ed) 1971–1972.*

Rozoy, J.G. 1972. L'évolution du Tardenoisien dans le Bassin Parisien. *L'Anthropologie,* 76.

Rozoy, J.G. 1973. The Franco-Belgien Epipalaeolithic. Current Problems. In: Kozłowski, S.K. (ed.) 1973.

Rozoy, J.G. 1976. Evolution des groupes humains en France et en Belgique de 6500 à 5000 avant J.C. In: *Kozłowski, S.K. (ed.) 1976.*

Rozoy, J.G. 1976 a. Les cultures de l'Epipaléolithique-Méso-lithique dans le Bassin de la Somme, en Picardie et en Artois. In: *Lumley, H. de (ed.) 1976.*

Rozoy, J.G. 1976 b. Les cultures de l'Epipaléolithique-Méso-lithique dans la région Champagne-Ardennes. In: *Lumley, H. de (ed.) 1976.*

Rozoy, J.G. 1977. Chronologie de l'Epipaléolithique de la Meuse à la Méditerranée. In: *Escalon de Fonton, M. (ed.) 1977.*

Rozoy, J.G. 1978. *Les derniers chasseurs.* In: *Bulletin de la Société Archéologique Champanoise.* Rheims.

Rozoy, J.G. 1978 a. Typologie de l'Epipaleolithique. *BSPF.*

Rozoy, J.G. 1981. Les changement dans la continuité. Les débuts de l'Epipaléolithique dans l'Europe de l'Ouest. In: *Gramsch, B. (ed.) 1981.*

Rozoy, J.G. 1983. Evolution des groupes humains en France et en Belgique de 6500 à 5000 avant J.C. In: *Kozłowski, S.K. (ed.) 1983.*

Rozoy, J.G. 1988. The Revolution of the Bowmen in Europe. In: *Bonsall, C. (ed.) 1988.*

Rozoy, J.G. 1999. Le mode de vie au Mésolithique. In: *Thévenin, A. (ed.) 1999.*

Rust, A. 1936. Die Grabungen beim Stellmoor. *Offa,* 1.

Rust, A. 1943. *Die alt- und mittelsteinzeitlichen Funde von Stellmoor.* Neumünster.

Rust, A. 1958a. *Die Funde vom Pinnberg.* Neumünster.

Salomonsson, B. 1964–65. Linnebjär. A Mesolithic Site in South-West Scania. *Meddelanden fraan Lunds Universitets Historiska Museum.*

Sacchi, D. 1976. Les escargotières et niveaux archéologiquest a Hélicidés dans le Midi de la France pendant le Mésolithique. In: *Kozłowski, S.K. (ed.) 1976.*

Sarauw, G.F.L. 1911–14. Maglemose-Ein Steinzeitlicher Wohnplatz im Moor bei Mullerup auf Seeland verglichen mit verwandeten Funden. *PZ,* 3, 4.

Schild, R., Królik, H., Marczak, M. 1985. *Chocolate flint mine at Tomaszów* (in Polish). Ossolineum, Wrocław.

Schilling, H. 2003. Early Mesolithic settlement patterns in Holmegårds Bog on South Zealand, Denmark. A social perspective In: *Larsson, L. et al. (ed.) 2003.*

Schuldt, E. 1959. Die mittelsteinzeitliche Wohnplatz von Flessenow, Kreis Schwerin. *Jahrbuch für Bodendenkmalpflege in Mecklenburg.*

Schuldt, E. 1961. *Hohen Viecheln, ein mittelsteinzeitlicher Wohnplatz in Mecklenburg.* Berlin.

Schwabiedissen, H. 1944. Die mittlere Steinzeit im Westlischen Norddeutchland. Neumünster.

Schwabedissen, H. 1957–58. Die Ausgrabungen im Satruper Moor. *Offa,* 16.

Schwabedissen, H. 1964. *Die Federmesser Gruppen der nordwest-europäischen Flachlandes.* Neumünster.

Schwabedissen, H. (ed.) 1974–1972. *Die Anfänge des Neolithikums vom Orient bis Nordeuropa (Fundamenta).* Böhlan Verlag. Köln, Wien.

Schwantes, G. 1939. *Die Vorgeschichte.* In: *Geschichte Schleswig-Holsteins.* Neumünster.

Siiriainen, A. 1984. The Mesolithic of Finland. A Survey of Recent Investigations. In: *AI.* 5.

Smith, C., Openshaw, S. 1990. Mapping the Mesolithic. In: *Vermeersch, P., Van Peer, P., (ed.) 1990.*

Sonneville – Bordes (de), D. (ed.) 1979. *La fin des temps glaciaires en Europe.* Editions *CNRS,* Paris.

Sorokin, A.N. 1990. *Butovian Mesolithic Culture* (in Russian). Institute of Archaeology AN SSSR, Moscow.

Sorokin, A.N. 1999. Le problème de l'influence du Mèsolithique de la région de Volga-Oka Rivers sur l'origine de la culture de Kunda. In: *Thèvenin, A. (ed.) 1999.*

Sorokin, A.N. 1999. Neighbours of the Butovo Culture on the upper Volga and Oka Rivers. In: *Kozłowski, S.K., Gurba, J., Zalizniak, L. (ed.) 1999.*

Spier, F. 1989. Aperçu sur l'Epipaléolithique – Mésolithique du Grand-Duché de Luxembourg. Réparation – Caractéristiques – Essai de chronologie. In: *Aimé, G., Thévenin, A. (ed.) 1989.*

Spier, F. 1990. Les industries mésolithiques du Grand-Duché de Luxembourg et leur attribution chronoculturelle: Etat de la question. In: *Vermeersch, P., Van Peer, P., (ed.) 1990.*

Spier, F. 1991. Mésolithique récent et Néolithique ancien au Luxembourg: état des recherches. In: *Thévenin, A. (ed.) 1991.*

Spier, F. 1994. Bilan de la recherche sur l'Épipaléolithique et le Mésolithique du Grand-Duché de Luxembourg, approche territoriale. In: *Pion, G. (ed.) 1994.*

Spier, F. 1999. L'Épipaléolithique et le Mésolithique entre Ardennes et Vosges. In: *Thèvenin, A. (ed.) 1999.*

Spikins, P. 1996. Rivers, Boundaries and change. In: *Pollard, T., Morrison, A. (ed.), The Early Prehistory of Scotland.* Edinburgh University Press, Edinburgh.

Srejović, D. 1988. The Mesolithic of Serbia and Montenegro. In: *Bonsall, C. (ed.) 1988.*

Srejović, D., Letica, Z. 1978. Vlasac, mesolitiko naselia u Djerdapu. In: *Serbian Academy of Sciences and Arts, Monographs, 62.* Belgrade.

Stanko, V.N. 1967. *Mezolit Severo-Zapadnogo Prichernomoria* (Abstract of Ph.D, dissertation), Kiev.

Stanko, V.N. 1971. Mezolit Dniestro-Dunajskogo miezhdurechia. In: *Materialy po Arkheologii Severnogo Prichernomorya.* Odessa.

Stanko, V.P. 1972. Types of sites and local cultures in the Mesolithic of the northern Black Sea region (in Russian). In: *MIA, 183, Paleoliti i Neolit, 7.* Moscow.

Starnini, E. 1994. Typological and technological analysis of the Körös Culture stone assemblages of Méhteiek – Nádas and Tiszacsege. *Josef András Muzeum Erkönyve, 36.*

Stoczkowski, W. 1987. The Mesolithic Society In: *AI, 8.*

Stoczkowski, W. 1994. *Anthropologie naïve, anthropologie savante.* Editions CNRS, Paris.

Svoboda, J.A. 2003. Mesolith severnich Čech. *Dolnovestonické Studie, 9.*

Takala, H. 2003. Recent excavations at Preboreal site of Lahti, Ristola in southern Finland, In: *Larsson, L. et al. (ed.) 2003.*

Taute, W. 1963. Funde des spätpaläolithischen "Federmesser-Gruppen" aus dem Raum zwischen mittlerer Elbe und Weichsel. *Berliner Jahrbuch für Vor- und Frühgeschichte, 3.*

Taute, W. 1967. Grabungen zur mittleren Steizeit in Höhlen und unter Felsdächern der Schwabischen Alb, 1961, bis 1965. *Fundberichte aus Schwaben, 18.*

Taute, W. 1968. *Die Stielspitzen-Gruppenin in Nördlichen Mitteleuropa.* In: *Fundamenta.* Köln-Graz.

Taute, W. 1971. *Untersuchungen zum Mesolithicum und zum Spätpaläolithikum in Südlichen Mitteleuropa* (typescript of habilitation work). Tübingen.

Taute, W. 1973–74. Neolithische Microlithen und andere neolithische Silexartefakte in Süddeutschland und Österreich. *Archäologische Informationen,* 2 and 3.

Telegin, D. 1981. Fragen der Chronologie und der Periodisierung des Mesolithikums in der Ukraine. In: *Gramsch, B. (ed.) 1981.*

Telegin, D.Y. 1973. Pozdni mezolit Ukrainy. In: *Kozłowski, S.K. (ed.) 1973.*

Telegin, D.Y. 1982. *Mesolithic Monuments in Ukraina* (in Ukrainian). Naukova Dumka. Kiev.

Telegin, D.Y. 1985. *Mesolithic Monuments in the Ukrainian SSR* (in Russian). Naukova Dumka, Kiev.

Telegin, N.D. 1887. Stone tools of the Neolithic cultures of south-western regions of the USRR. In: *Kozłowski, J.K. (ed.) 1987.*

Terberger, T. 2003. Decorated objects of the older Mesolithic from northern lowlands. In: *Larsson, L. et al. (ed.) 2003.*

Thévenin, A., Sainty, J. 1972. *L'Abri de Rochedane à Villars sous Dampjoux (Doubs). Revue archéologique de l'Est et de Centre-Est, 23.*

Thévenin, A., Sainty, J. 1972a. Une nouvelle stratigraphie du postglaciaire: l'abri du Mann-lefelsen à Oberlarg (Haut-Rhin). *BSPF, 69.*

Thévenin, A. 1976. Les civilisations de l'Epipaléolithique dans le Jura et en Franche-Comté. In: *Lumley, H. de (ed.) 1976.*

Thévenin, A. 1976. Paléo-histoire de l'Est de la France du 7o au 6o millénaire avant J.C., In: *Kozłowski, S.K. (ed.) 1976.*

Thévenin, A. 1981. La fin de l'Epipaléolithique et les débuts du Mésolithique dans le Nord du Jura Français. In: *Gramsch, B. (ed.) 1981.*

Thévenin, A. 1982. *Rochèdane.* In: *Mèmoires de la Faculté des Sciences Sociales, Université des Sciences Humaines de Strasbourg,* Strasbourg.

Thévenin, A. 1983. Paléo-histoire de l'Est de la France de 7e au 6e millénaire avant J.C., In: *Kozłowski, S.K. (ed.) 1983.*

Thévenin, A. 1990. Le Mésolithique de l'Est de la France. In: *Vermeersch, P., Van Peer, P. (ed.) 1990.*

Thévenin, A. (ed.) 1991. Mésolithique et Néolitisation en France et dans les regions Limitrophes. In: *113 e Congrès National des Sociétés. Savantes.* Editions CTHS, Paris.

Thévenin, A. 1994. Le Mésolithique ancien de l'est de la France: nouvelle approche. In: *Pion, G. (ed.)1994.*

Thévenin, A. 1996. Le Mésolithique de la France dans le cadre du peuplement de l'Europe occidentale. In: *Tozzi, C., Kozłowski, S. (ed.) 1996.*

Thévenin, A. 1998. Les grandes lignes du Mesolithique en France et dans regions Limitroptes. *Urgeschitliche Materialhefte, 12.*

Thévenin, A. 1999. L'Epipaléolithique et le Mésolithique en France et régions voisines. In: *Thévenin, A. (ed.) 1999.*

Thévenin, A. (ed.) 1999. *L'Europe des derniers chasseurs.* Éditions CTHS, Paris.

Thévenin, A. 2000. Le Mésolithique du centre – est de la France. *Revue de l'Archéologie de l'Est, 49.*

Thévenin, A. 2000. Les premiéres manifestations du Mésolithique en France. In: *Thévenin, A. (ed.) 2000.*

Thévenin, A. 2000. Stabilité et changement dans les équipements des derniers chasseurs. llems: relation avec leur, environnement. In: *Richard, H., Vognot, A. (ed.), Equilibes et ruptures dans les ecosystèmes durant des derniers millénaires en Europe de l'Ouest.* Presse Universitaire France – Comtoise, Besançon.

Thévenin, A., Sainty, J. 1977. Géochronologie de l'Epipaléolithique de l'Est de la France. In: *Escalon de Fonton, M. (ed.) 1977.*

Tilley, C.Y. 1979. *Post-Glacial Communities in the Cambridge Region.* In: *BAR – BS 66.*

Tixier, J. 1963. *Typologie de l'Epipaléolithique du Maghreb.* Paris.

Toepfer, V. 1967. Die alt- und mittelsteinzeitliche Besiedlung der Altmark. *Jahresschrift für mitteldeutsche Vorgeschichte, 51.*

Tolan-Smith, C. 2004. Radiocarbon Chronology and the Colonization of the British Sector of the Atlantic Façade. In: *Gonzales Morales, M., Clark, G.A. (ed.) 2004.*

Thommessen, T. 1996. The Early Settlement of Northern Norway. In: *Larsson, L. (ed.) 1996.*

Tozzi, C., Kozłowski, S.K. (ed.) 1996. *The Mesolithic, Colloquium XIII–XIV, XIII International Congress of Prehistoric and Protohistoric Sciences, Forli – Italie.* Abaco, Forli.

Tozzi, C., Notini, P. 1999. L'Èpigravettien final et le Mésolithique de l'apennin tosco-émilien et de la vallée du Serchio (Toscane septentrionale). In: *Thévenin A. (ed.) 1999.*

Tozzi, C., Weiss, M.C. (ed.) 2000. *Les prèmiers peuplements Olocenes de l'Aire Corso Toscane.* Edizioni ETS.

Tringham, R., 1971. *Hunters, Fishers and Farmers of Eastern Europe, 6000–3000 BC.* Hutchison University Press. London.

Turk, J. 2004. *Viktorjev spodmol in/and Mala Triglarca.* In: *Instituti Archaeologici Slovenia.* Ljubljana.

Valdeyron, N. 1994. *Le Suveterrien.* Mémoire de doctorat, Université de Toulouse-le-Mirail, typescript.

Valoch, K. 1962–63. Ein mittelsteinzeitlicher Wohnplatz bei

Smolin in Südmähren. *Quartär,* 14.

Valoch, K. 1978. Die end-paläolithische Siedlung in Smolin. In: *Studie Archeologickeho Ustavu Československe Akademie Ved* v Brne. Brno.

Valoch, K. 1988. The Mesolithic Site of Smolin, South Moravia. In: *Bonsall C. (ed.) 1988.*

Vebaek, C.L. 1938. New Finds of Mesolithic Ornamented Bone and Antler Artifacts in Denmark. *Acta Archaeologica,* 9.

Vebaek, C.L. 1940. Bøllund, en boplads fra den aeldre i Vestjylland. In: *Fra Danmarks Ungtid.* København.

Verhart, L.B.M. 1990. Stone Age and Antler Points as Indicators for "social territories" in the European Mesolithic. In: *Vermeersch, P., Van Peer, P. (ed.) 1990.*

Verhart, L.B.M. 1995. Fishing for Mesolithic. The North Sea: a submerged Mesolithic landscape. In: *Fischer, A. (ed.) 1995.*

Vermeersch, P.M. 1977. La position lithostratigraphique et biostratigraphique des industries épipaléolithiques et mésolithiques en Basse Belgique. In: *Escalon de Fonton, M. (ed.) 1977.*

Vermeersch, P.M. (ed.) 1982. *Contributions to the Study of the Mesolithic of the Belgian Lowland.* In: *Studia Praehistorica Belgica,* 1. Kings Museum of the Central Africa. Tervuren.

Vermeersch, P. M. 1984. Du Paléolithique final an Mésolithique dans le nord de la Belgique. In: *Cahen, D., Haesters, P. (ed.) 1984.*

Vermeersch, P.M., Van Peer, P. (ed.) 1990. *Contributions to the Mesolithic in Europe.* Leuven University Press. Leuven.

Vermeersch, P.M. 1991. Y-a-t-il eu coexistence entre le Méso-lithique et le Néolithique en basse et Moyenne Belgique. In: *Thévenin, A. (ed.) 1991.*

Vermeersch, P.M. 1996. Mesolithic in the Benelux, south of Rhine. In: *Tozzi, C., Kozłowski, S. (ed.) 1996.*

Vermeersch, P.M. 1999. Processus post-dépositionnels sur des sites épipaléolithique et mésolithiques en région sableuses de l'Europe de l'Ouest. In: *Thévenin, A. (ed.) 1999.*

Vilain, R. 1966. *Le gisement Sous-Balme à Culoz (Ain) et ses industries microlithiques.* In: *Documents des Laboratoires de Géologie de la Faculté des Sciences de Lyon,* 13.

Villaverde Bonilla, V., Marti Oliver, B., 1984. *Paleolitic i Epipaleolitic.* F. Domenech, S.A. Valencia.

Wainwright, G.J. 1960. Three Microlithic Industries from South-West England and their Affinities. *PPS,* 36.

Welinder, S. 1971. *Tidigpostglacial mesoliticum i Skaane. AAL series in: 8°,* 1.

Welinder, S. 1973. The Chronology of the Mesolithic Stone Age on the Swedish West Coast. In: *Studies in North European Archeology,* 9.

Welinder, S. 1977. The Mesolithic Stone Age of Eastern Sweden. In: *Kungl. Vitterhets Historie och Antiquitets Akademien, Antiquarist archiv,* 65.

Więckowska, H., Marczak, M. 1965. The cultural subdivision of the Mesolithic in Mazovia (in Polish). In: *Chmielewski, W. (ed.) 1965. Materiały do prehistorii Polski w plejstocenie I wczesnym holocenie.* Ossolineum, Wrocław.

Woodman, P.C. 1978. The chronology and economy of the Irish Mesolithic: some working hypoteses. In: *Mellars P. (ed.) 1978.*

Woodman, P.C. 1978. The Mesolithic in Ireland. In: *BAR – BS 58.*

Woodman, P. 1985. *Excavations at Mount Sandel, 1973–77.* Department of Environment for northern Ireland. University Press, Belfast.

Woodman, P., Andersen, E. 1990. The Irish Later Mesolithic: A Partial Picture? In: *Vermeersch, P. Van Peer, P. (ed.) 1990.*

Woodman, P. 2004. The Exploitation of Ireland's Coastal Re-sources – a Marginal Resource Through Time?, In: *Gonzales Morales, M., Clark, G.A. (ed.) 2004.*

Woodman, P. *et al.* (ed.) 2005 *Meso. The international conference on the Mesolithic in Europe – Belfast. Abstracts.*

Woss, M. 2005. *Technology of Flint knapping of the Janislawcian* (in Polish). In: *Monografie Instytutu Archeologii Uniwersytetu Łódzkiego,* 3. Łódź.

Wymer, J.J. 1962. Excavations at the Maglemosian sites at Thatcham, Berkshire England. *PPS,* 28.

Wymer, J.J. (ed.) 1977. *Gazeteer of Mesolithic Sites in England and Wales* In: *CBA Research Raport* 20.

Wyss, R. 1957. Eine mesolithische Station bei Liesbergmühle. (Kt. Bern). *Zeitschrift für Schweizerische Archäologie und Kunstgeschichte,* 17.

Wyss, R. 1960. Zur Erforschung des schweizerschen Meso-lithikums. *Zeitschrift für Schweizerische Archäologie und Kunstgeschichte,* 20.

Wyss, R. 1968. *Das Mesolithikum.* In: *Ur- und Frühgeschichtliche Archäologie der Schweiz,* 1. Basel.

Wyss, R. 1973. Zum Problemkreis des schweizerischen Meso-lithikums. In: *Kozłowski, S.K. (ed.) 1973.*

Wyss, R. 1976. L'évolution écologique et culturelle du Méso-lithique en Europe Centrale, In: *Kozłowski, S.K. (ed.) 1976.*

Wyss, R. 1979. *Das Mittelsteinzeitliche Hirschjägerlager von Schötz 7 im Wauwiler Moos.* Zürich.

Wyss, R. 1983. L'évolution écologique et culturelle du Méso-lithique en Europe central. In: *Kozłowski, S.K. (ed.) 1983.*

Yven, E. 2003. The Deposits of Raw Materials and the Quarry-sites during Mesolithic in the Trégor in Brittany. In: *Larsson, L. et al. (ed.) 2003.*

Zagorska, J. 1974. Mesolithic Fishingspear in Latvia, *Arch-eologija un Etnografia,* 11.

Zagorska. I. 1981. Das Frühmesolithikum in Lettland. In: *Gramsch, B. (ed.) 1981.*

Zagorska, I., Zagorskis, F. 1988. The Bone and Antler Inventory from Zvejnieki II, Latavian SSR. In: *Bonsall, C. (ed.) 1988.*

Zagorskis, F. 1973. Das Spätmesolithikum in Lettland. In: *Kozłowski, S. K. (ed.) 1973.*

Zalizniak, L. 1997. *Mesolithic Forest Hunters in Ukranian Polessye.* In: *BAR – Tempus Reparatum – IS,* 659.

Zalizniak, L. 1998. *Prehistory of the Ukraine in 10th–5th millennium BC* (in Ukrainian). In: *Biblioteka Ukraincia.* Kiev.

Zalizniak, L. 2005. *Final Paleolithic and Mesolithic of the Continental Ukraine* (in Ukrainian). In: *Kamiana Doba Ukraini,* 8, Shiah, Kiev.

Zhilin, M. 2003. Early Mesolithic communication networks in the East European forest zone. In: *Larsson, L. et al. (ed.) 2003.*

Zhilin, M., Matiskainen, H. 2003. Deep in Russia, deep in the bog. Excavations at the Mesolithic Sites Stanovoje 4 and Sakhtysh 14, Upper Volga region. In: *Larsson, L. et al. (ed.) 2003.*

Ziesaire, P. 1989. Identification et cadre chrono-culturel du Mésolitique ancien: le gisement de plein air d'Altwies-Haed, Luxemburg. In: *Aimé, G., Thévenin, A. (ed.) 1989.*

Zubkov, W.I. 1950. Nowye sbory na borkowskoi mezoliticheskoi stoianke. *KSIA,* 32.

Zvelebil, M. (ed.) 1986. *Hunters in Transition.* Cambridge University Press. Cambridge.